WORKSHOPS IN COMPUTING
Series edited by C. J. van Rijsbergen

Also in this series

AI and Cognitive Science '89, Dublin City University, Eire,
14–15 September 1989
A. F. Smeaton and G. McDermott (Eds.)

Specification and Verification of Concurrent Systems, University of
Stirling, Scotland, 6–8 July 1988
C. Rattray (Ed.)

Semantics for Concurrency, Proceedings of the International
BCS-FACS Workshop, Sponsored by Logic for IT (S.E.R.C.), University
of Leicester, UK, 23–25 July 1990
M. Z. Kwiatkowska, M. W. Shields and R. M. Thomas (Eds.)

Functional Programming, Proceedings of the 1989 Glasgow
Workshop, Fraserburgh, Scotland, 21–23 August 1989
K. Davis and J. Hughes (Eds.)

Persistent Object Systems, Proceedings of the Third International
Workshop, Newcastle, Australia, 10–13 January 1989
J. Rosenberg and D. Koch (Eds.)

Z User Workshop, Proceedings of the Fourth Annual Z User Meeting,
Oxford, 15 December 1989
J. E. Nicholls (Ed.)

Formal Methods for Trustworthy Computer Systems (FM89), Halifax,
Canada, 23–27 July 1989
Dan Craigen (Editor) and Karen Summerskill (Assistant Editor)

John Rosenberg and J. Leslie Keedy (Eds.)

Security and Persistence

Proceedings of the International Workshop
on Computer Architectures to Support
Security and Persistence of Information

8–11 May 1990, Bremen, West Germany

Published in collaboration with the
British Computer Society

Springer-Verlag
London Berlin Heidelberg New York
Paris Tokyo Hong Kong

John Rosenberg, BSc, PhD
Department of Electrical Engineering and Computer Science,
University of Newcastle
NSW 2308, Australia

J. Leslie Keedy, BD, DPhil, PhD
Faculty of Mathematics and Computer Science,
University of Bremen,
Bibliothekstrasse, Postfach 330440,
D–2800 Bremen 33,
West Germany

ISBN-13:978-3-540-19646-4   e-ISBN-13:978-1-4471-3178-6
DOI: 10.1007/978-1-4471-3178-6

British Library Cataloguing in Publication Data
International Workshop on Computer Architecture to support Security and Persistence
of Information (1990; Bremen, Germany)
Security and persistence:proceedings of the International Workshop on Computer
Architecture to support Security and Persistence of information, 8–11 May 1990,
Bremen, West Germany.
    1. Computer systems. Design
    I. Title   II. Rosenberg, John 1953–   III. Keedy, J. Leslie (James Leslie) 1940–
IV. Series
004.21
ISBN-13:978-3-540-19646-4

Library of Congress Cataloging-in-Publication Data
International Workshop on Computer Architecture to Support Security and Persistence
of Information (1990:Bremen, Germany)
Security and persistence:proceedings of the International Workshop on Computer
Architecture to Support Security and Persistence of Information, 8–11 May 1990,
Bremen, West Germany/John Rosenberg and J. Leslie Keedy, eds.
    p.cm. – (Workshops in computing)
"Published in collaboration with the British Computer Society." Includes index.
ISBN-13:978-3-540-19646-4

    1. Computer security – Congresses.   2. Computer architecture – Congresses.
I. Rosenberg, John, 1953–   .   II. Keedy, J. Leslie (James Leslie), 1940–
III. British Computer Society.   IV. Title.   V. Series.
QA76.9.A25156 1990   90-10347
005.8–dc20   CIP

2128/3916–543210   Printed on acid-free paper

Preface

During a short visit to Bremen in December 1989 John Rosenberg had several discussions with me about computer architecture. Although we had previously worked together for more than a decade in Australia we had not seen each other for over a year, following my move to Bremen in 1988. Meanwhile John was spending a year on study leave at the University of St. Andrews in Scotland with Professor Ron Morrison and his persistent programming research group.

From our conversations it was quite clear that John was having a most fruitful time in St. Andrews and was gaining valuable new insights into the world of persistent programming. He was very keen to explore the significance of these insights for the MONADS Project, which we had been jointly directing since the early 1980s.

MONADS was not about persistent programming. In fact it had quite different origins, in the areas of software engineering and information protection. In an earlier stage of the project our ideas on these themes had led us into the world of computer architecture and even hardware design, in our attempts to provide an efficient base machine for our software ideas. The most important practical result of this phase of the project had been the development of the MONADS-PC, a mini-computer which would be better compared with say a VAX 11/750 than with a personal computer, despite its unfortunate name. Since our encounters with the persistent programming world we have begun to think that it would be better to understand the letters PC in our MONADS-PC as "persistent computer". It has an architecture with 60-bit virtual addresses which allows all objects in the system to be addressed directly and unambiguously, making a conventional file store superfluous. Objects such as programs and files simply persist in the persistent virtual memory and, subject to stringent capability based checking, can be directly invoked or addressed (from the appropriate type manager).

Although our reasons for producing such a design had been scarcely influenced by persistent programming considerations, it turned out that we had built a "persistent" computer which in principle provided an interesting and efficient way of supporting persistent programming. Yet it did not necessarily provide all the answers. The persistent programming world demanded much more rigorous standards than we had previously set ourselves regarding the stability of the virtual memory, both in a single computer environment and in a network environment. Over and above this was the issue of consistency as understood in transaction oriented database systems.

The MONADS approach was clearly not the only way. The persistent programming community had independently developed other approaches for implementing persistent stores, usually based on more conventional file store implementations. These raised quite different issues, especially in the area of information security. By and large the programming language designer's view, anchoring security issues in language techniques such as type checking, had tended to prevail. To John Rosenberg and myself, having interested ourselves in computer protection at the architectural level for several years, this seemed far from satisfactory.

As we discussed these things in December 1989 it seemed to us that the time was ripe to hold a workshop in which some of the outstanding issues should be tackled. We also felt that this would give us an opportunity to hear more about other work in these areas and perhaps encourage persistent programmers as well as researchers interested in security questions to work closer together in future.

The workshop was organised to take place in May 1990 in Bremen, to take advantage of the already existing travel plans of various participants from Europe and Australia. Despite the relatively short notice we were delighted with the interest shown by prominent researchers in the field.

We were able to attract Professor Roger Needham from Cambridge as a keynote speaker well experienced in issues concerning computer architecture and computer security. His talk was not quite what I had expected. But all the better for that. He presents a refreshing historical perspective on what capabilities are all about and shows how over the last two decades the wheel has turned full circle. In the second keynote talk, Professor Ron Morrison provides an equally refreshing view of the issues from the standpoint of persistent programming.

The remaining conference contributions present a wide spectrum of viewpoints on the issues, ranging from principles and models for approaching the issues to descriptions of specific security regimes, architectures and hardware. Then come papers on particular issues, including the questions of fault tolerance and stable stores, persistence and operating systems, and how consistency can be achieved for database applications.

When we first considered organising the workshop on such a short timescale, I had severe doubts about its chances of success. I am glad to say now that those doubts were quite unnecessary.

Finally I would like to thank all those who directly or indirectly contributed to the success of the workshop. In particular thanks are due to Renate Post-González and Peter Brössler for their invaluable assistance in organisational matters. Thanks are also due to the organisers of the International Workshops on Persistent Object

Systems who not only encouraged us to hold this workshop but also provided valuable support for it. Finally thanks are also due to the University of Bremen for their assistance with some of the costs.

August 1990   Leslie Keedy,
                                                      University of Bremen
                                                Federal Republic of Germany

Workshop Chairman

J. Leslie Keedy
Faculty of Mathematics and Computer Science
University of Bremen
West Germany

Organising Committee

Peter Brössler
Faculty of Mathematics and Computer Science
University of Bremen
West Germany

Renate Post-González Garcia
Faculty of Mathematics and Computer Science
University of Bremen
West Germany

J. Leslie Keedy
Faculty of Mathematics and Computer Science
University of Bremen
West Germany

John Rosenberg
Department of Electrical Engineering and Computer Science
University of Newcastle
Australia

Programme Committee

Mark Evered
Faculty of Mathematics and Computer Science
University of Bremen
West Germany

Berndt Freisleben
Faculty of Informatics
University of Darmstadt
West Germany

J. Leslie Keedy
Faculty of Mathematics and Computer Science
University of Bremen
West Germany

John Rosenberg
Department of Electrical Engineering and Computer Science
University of Newcastle
Australia

Contents

Contents   xi

List of Authors

Atkinson, M. P.
University of Glasgow, Department of Computing Science, Glasgow
G12 8QQ, Scotland.
mpa@cs.glasgow.ac.uk

Baumgarten, U.
University of Oldenburg, FB 10 (Computer Science), Postfach 2503,
D2900 Oldenburg, West Germany.
0011580@DOLUNI1.BITNET

Brössler, P.
Faculty of Mathematics and Computer Science, University of
Bremen, PO Box 330440, 2800 Bremen 33, West Germany.
pb@informatik.uni-Bremen.de

Brown, A. L.
Division of Mathematical and Computational Sciences, University of
St Andrews, North Haugh, St Andrews, Fife KY16 9SS, Scotland.
ab@uk.ac.st-and.cs

Brunnstein K.
University of Hamburg, Faculty for Informatics, Schlüterstr. 70,
2000 Hamburg 13, West Germany.
brunnstein@rz.informatik.uni-hamburg.dbp.de

Campbell, R. H.
Department of Computer Science, University of Illinois at
Urbana-Champaign, 1304 W. Springfield Avenue,
Urbana, IL 61801-2987, U.S.A.
roy@cs.uiuc.edu

Cockshott, W. P.
Department of Computer Science, University of Strathclyde,
Livingstone Tower, 26 Richmond Street, Glasgow G1 1XH, Scotland.
wpc@cs.strath.ac.uk

Connor, R. C. H.
Division of Mathematical and Computational Sciences, University of
St Andrews, North Haugh, St Andrews, Fife KY16 9SS, Scotland.
richard@cs.st-andrews.ac.uk

Cutts, Q. I.
Division of Mathematical and Computational Sciences, University of
St Andrews, North Haugh, St Andrews, Fife KY16 9SS, Scotland.
quintin@cs.st-andrews.ac.uk.

Davies, R. A. J.
Department of Computer Science, University of Essex, Colchester
C04 3SQ, U.K.
davbob@essex.ac.uk

Dearle, A.
Department of Computer Science, University of Adelaide, North
Terrace, Adelaide, S.A. 5000, Australia.
al@chook.ua.oz.au

Eckert, C.
Universität Oldenburg, FB Informatik 10, Postfach 2503, D2900
Oldenburg, West Germany.
eckert@uniol.uucp

England, A.
Perihelion Software Ltd., The Maltings, Charlton Road, Shepton
Mallet, Somerset BA4 5QE, England.
andy@perisl.uucp

Evered, M.
Faculty of Mathematics and Computer Science, University of
Bremen, PO Box 330440, 2800 Bremen 33, West Germany.
markev@informatik.uni-Bremen.de

Fischer-Hübner, S.
University of Hamburg, Faculty for Informatics, Schlüterstr. 70,
2000 Hamburg 13, West Germany.

Foulk, P. W.
Department of Electrical and Electronic Engineering, Heriot-Watt
University, 31/35 Grassmarket, Edinburgh EH1 2HT, Scotland.
pwf@ee.hw.ac.uk

Freisleben, B.
T. H. Darmstadt, Fachbereich 20, Alexanderstr. 10, D6100
Darmstadt, West Germany.
xib1bfre@addathd21.bitnet

Gehringer, E. F.
Department of Electrical & Computer Engineering & Computer
Science, North Carolina State University, Box 7911, Raleigh, NC
27695-7911, U.S.A.
efg@csl.csl.ncsu.edu

Hannaford, M. R.
Department of Electrical Engineering and Computer Science, The
University of Newcastle, New South Wales 2308, Australia.
mrh@nucs.cs.nu.oz.au

Härtig, H.
German National Research Centre for Computer Science, Postfach
1240, Schloß Birlinghoven, D5205 St. Augustin 1, West Germany.
haertig@gmdzi.gmd.de

Henskens, F. A.
Department of Electrical Engineering and Computer Science, The
University of Newcastle, New South Wales 2308, Australia.
henskens@nucs.cs.nu.oz.au

Kaiser, J.
German National Research Centre for Computer Science, Postfach
1240, Schloß Birlinghoven, 5205 St. Augustin 1, West Germany.
kaiser@gmdzi.gmd.de

Kammerer, P.
T. H. Darmstadt, Fachbereich 20, Alexanderstr. 10, D6100
Darmstadt, West Germany.
xib1bfre@ddathd21.bitnet

Keedy, J. L.
Faculty of Mathematics and Computer Science, University of
Bremen, PO Box 330440, 2800 Bremen 33, West Germany.
keedy@informatik.uni-Bremen.de

Kirby, G.
Division of Mathematical and Computational Sciences, University of
St Andrews, North Haugh, St Andrews, Fife KY16 9SS, Scotland.

graham@cs.st-andrews.ac.uk.

Koch, D. M.
Department of Electrical Engineering & Computer Science, The
University of Newcastle, New South Wales 2308, Australia.

dmk@nucs.cs.nu.oz.au

Kowalski, O. C.
German National Research Centre for Computer Science, Postfach
1240, Schloß Birlinghoven, D5205 St. Augustin 1, West Germany.

kow@gmdzi.gmd.de

Kroeger, R.
German National Research Centre for Computer Science, Postfach
1240, Schloß Birlinghoven, 5205 St. Augustin 1, West Germany.

kroeger@gmdzi.gmd.de

Kühnhauser, W. E.
German National Research Centre for Computer Science, Postfach
1240, Schloß Birlinghoven, D5205 St. Augustin 1, West Germany.

kuehnhsr@gmdzi.gmd.de

Lavington, S. H.
Department of Computer Science, University of Essex, Colchester
C04 3SQ, U.K.

lavington@essex.ac.uk.

Lux, W.
German National Research Centre for Computer Science, Postfach
1240, Schloß Birlinghoven, D5205 St. Augustin 1, West Germany.

lux@gmdzi.gmd.de

Madany, P. W.
Department of Computer Science, University of Illinois at
Urbana-Champaign, 1304 W. Springfield Avenue, Urbana, IL 61801-
2987, U.S.A.

madany@cs.uiuc.edu

Manke, S.
Institut fuer Informatik, Universität Karlsruhe, Postfach 6980, D-7500
Karlsruhe 1, West Germany.

manke@ira.uka.de

Mock, M.
German National Research Centre for Computer Science, Postfach 1240, Schloß Birlinghoven, 5205 St. Augustin 1, West Germany.

mock@gmdzi.gmd.de

Morrison, R.
Division of Mathematical and Computational Sciences, University of St Andrews, North Haugh, St Andrews, Fife KY16 9SS, Scotland.

ron@cs.st-and.ac.uk

Müller, W.
Faculty of Mathematics and Computer Science, University of Bremen, PO Box 330440, 2800 Bremen 33, West Germany.

muew@informatik.uni-Bremen.de

Munro, D. S.
Division of Mathematical and Computational Sciences, University of St Andrews, North Haugh, St Andrews, Fife KY16 9SS, Scotland.

dave@cs.st-and.ac.uk

Needham, R. M.
Computer Laboratory, New Museums Site, Pembroke Street, Cambridge CB2 3QG, U.K.

rmn@cl.cam.ac.uk

Newberry Paulisch, F.
Institut fuer Informatik, Universität Karlsruhe, Postfach 6980, D-7500 Karlsruhe 1, West Germany.

newberry@ira.uka.de

Pose, R. D.
Department of Computer Science, Monash University, Clayton, VIC. 3168, Australia.

rdp@bruce.cs.monash.oz.au

Reitenspieß, M.
Siemens AG, ZFE IS SOf 43, Otto-Hahn-Ring 6, D8000 Munich 83, West Germany.

rei@ztivax.UUCP

Rosenberg, J.
Department of Electrical Engineering and Computer Science, The University of Newcastle, New South Wales 2308, Australia.

johnr@nucs.cs.nu.oz.au

Sarkar, M.
Department of Computer Science, North Carolina State University,
Box 8206, Raleigh, NC 27695-8206, U.S.A.

sarkar@csl.csl.ncsu.edu

Schumann, R.
German National Research Centre for Computer Science, Postfach
1240, Schloß Birlinghoven, 5205 St. Augustin 1, West Germany.

schumann@gmdzi.gmd.de

Stemple, D.
Department of Computer and Information Science, University of
Massachusetts, Amherst, MA 01003, U.S.A.

stemple@cs.unmass.edu

Tichy, W. F.
Institut fuer Informatik, Universität Karlsruhe, Postfach 6980, D-7500
Karlsruhe 1, West Germany.

tichy@ira.uka.de

Vogt, C.
Forschunginstitut für Funk und Mathematik (FFM), Neuenahrer Str.
20, D-5307 Wachtberg-Werthhoven, West Germany.

vgt@rspstun5.ffm.fgan.de

Wallace, C. S.
Department of Computer Science, Monash University, Clayton, VIC.
3168, Australia.

csw@bruce.cs.monash.oz.au

Part I

Invited Presentations

Capabilities and Security

Roger M. Needham,

University of Cambridge, UK

ABSTRACT

The paper reviews some of the history of ideas to do with capabilities and of implementations based on them, and concludes with a discussion of some current manifestations of the same general outlook.

1. CAPABILITIES

Capabilities are representations of the results of early-bound access-control decisions.

This definition may not appeal to everyone but it is reasonable if one takes the view that there are precisely two problems in computer science - naming and binding. One of the most serious differences between systems is their attitude to binding, particularly to the time at which binding is done. It isn't an accident that the idea of capabilities was invented in 1966 by Dennis and van Horn [3] in reaction to and by contrast with the contemporaneous development of the Multics system. Multics made a virtue of binding names to values as late as possible, namely at the first attempted reference to the value, and indeed bound names to values as tenuously as it could. If a binding changed while your program was running then you would have a surprise. If the access controls on some thing changed to your disadvantage while your program was running then your program would stop running. The Multics motto might well have been "Never commit yourself until you must, and do it half-heartedly then". Capabilities were thought of, among other things, as a source of certainty. The ground would not shift under your feet; your package would continue to do what it used to; if you wanted to stay with version 2 of a library when the system management was peddling version 6 then nobody could stop you. Jerry Saltzer coined the term "administrative unreliability" for a disease that afflicts computer users. It means not being able to get on with your work because of actions of the management; one of the ideas of capabilities was to be a defence against administrative unreliability.

Some of the properties of capabilities follow from what I've already said. First, they've got to be unforgeable. If I can manufacture from whole cloth, as the Americans would say, the representation of a decision that I should have access to some particular thing, then the purpose of the operation is lost. Second, the existence of a capability for a thing should imply the existence of the thing. If a user has a capability for a file and when attempting to use it is told that it doesn't exist, he is entitled to feel ill-treated, contrary to one of the objectives. It's because of this aspect of capabilities that there's a general view that they can't be revoked. Over the years there has been a lot of work on revocation of capabilities - thought by many to be a contradiction in terms, for these reasons.

I haven't yet said anything about added security or protection - something that quickly became associated with capabilities. Again we go back to Multics and look for contrasts. Multics made a big deal of protection, but didn't do too well at protection within the operating system and didn't cope at all with mutually suspicious subsystems. This latter was because of the basically hierarchical nature of the protection offered. You couldn't have access to A without having access to B if A were at a higher level of privilege that B. People who wanted to design systems that didn't have this limitation were drawn to capability-based mechanisms as a means of doing so. A program would execute in an environment defined by the capabilities available to it, and all these capabilities would be independently assigned. It would never be a mechanical consequence of having one capability that you had to have another, and the principle of least privilege could be strictly adhered to.

By now we were well onto the slippery slope. In order to do least privilege properly it was necessary to manage access to data in a very detailed way. This meant handling, in particular, access to memory with care. If I call a program to do something to some data, I should give it access to that data and to nothing else. The data quite likely resided on a stack (most data do) so I would find myself constructing a separate capability for the miserable bit of stack I should pass. Constructing capabilities is of course a privileged operation, or at any rate the mechanics of it are. Anyone can take a capability for some thing (I am avoiding the word "object" because it unfortunately doesn't mean anything any more, even as a pronoun) and have an attenuated capability constructed for him. The actual construction needs to be done by the kernel or the microcode, or something that can conveniently be swept under the rug.

If we seriously pay attention to the idea of minimum privilege the environment in which a program executes becomes rather complicated. It has lots and lots of capabilities, and whenever a call is made to a procedure that requires to be executed in a slightly different environment that environment has to be set up for the occasion. For example, if the called procedure has need to know the identity of the caller, then it should be passed a capability which identifies the caller, and not otherwise. This leads to heavy costs of procedure calls, or at any rate of procedure calls that change protection environment. Vast amounts of engineering effort were spent in the 1970's planning representations of protection environments and smooth transition between them. It wasn't obviously a good idea, in retrospect. People in general aren't happy to pay a lot in performance for increased protection, and capability architectures seemed to have fairly fundamental limitations. No matter how we tried to optimise representations, build caches, and so on, the capability system would obtrude at those intimate places which affect performance most directly - memory access and procedure call. If you've constructed a a capability for a section of two or three words, it's going to be given effect to by an address translation which goes down to the bottom bit in the addressing. This costs. If we've got to bring into being a whole capability environment when doing a procedure call then this will take time on an action people are very sensitive about.

The engineering complexities were pretty formidable too. In the CAP [10] we optimised the representation of capabilities rather thoroughly for the operations of passing them between procedures within a process. This had the consequence that we couldn't pass them between processes at all. Andrew Herbert designed the CAP III in which you could only pass capabilities between processes. The Intel iAPX 432 processor [6], designed with much influence from Carnegie-Mellon University, was not a commercial success; people wondered what all those electrons could be doing for so long while domains changed. If someone had based a product on the CAP it could well have been better - but probably not much. Capability ideas went into some disrepute at about this time. It became the conventional wisdom that capabilities that were sufficiently context-independent and detailed to work well would be too inefficient to interpret.

This was a pity, because, as I've tried to make evident from what's already been said, the aspects of the ideas that led to inefficiency were not absolutely intrinsic to the capability principle. They resulted from trying to manage protection in very great detail and from having very frequent changes of protection environment. The CAP operating system changed protection environment at the drop of a hat - as for example when reading the next few characters from a file. Simple protection environment change was not too expensive, but they were not all simple. One reason for the relative cheapness was that there were limitations on what sorts of thing could be passed as arguments. Some kinds of complex structures would not work, though protected procedures could always be passed. It's reasonable to say that, in the CAP, procedural encapsulation was taken about as far as it could be. Yet it was very far from implementing the principle of least privilege. When a student (Douglas Cook [2]) set off to conduct an access audit of the CAP system he found vast degrees of over-privilege, almost all resulting from the optimisation adopted of having a so-called global capability segment per process. This had capabilities for the name of the user and various other things, and was available in all protection environments. Very usually not all the global capabilities were strictly necessary, and this led to over-privilege. Yet had the capabilities in question always been passed as arguments when needed, the performance cost would have been great.

What went wrong?

Looking back at it one can see that the system implemented on, say, the CAP, was very different from one which viewed capabilities as representations of the results of early-bound access-control decisions. Most of the things that one had capabilities for were not in the ordinary way topics for access control at all. It was all much more like the Plessey System 250 [4], which used capabilities for resilience reasons and was not originally conceived of as a general-purpose computer at all. That machine worked perfectly well, because the manipulations needed on its capabilities were less general and thus cheaper.

Another problem with capability systems of that time was related to security. Much emphasis was laid on protection of information from unauthorised access, without noticing or at any rate without taking properly into account the fact that people seriously interested in protection tended to have an interest in security too. This led to requirements for solutions of the confinement problem, and equivalently for security in the sense of Bell and LaPadula [1], and capability based systems of the then current sort are quite useless in that context. Being able easily to pass around prebound permissions to access, valid in any context, is the opposite of what secure systems need. P.A. Karger, in work done for his Ph.D. dissertation [5], made successful attempts to salvage some capability ideas in secure contexts. He treats capabilities as representations of necessary but not sufficient conditions for access, and shows how confinement problems can be solved. He also talks about the use of capabilities for rather more gross objects than was the case in, for example, the CAP. There would be fewer of them, used in less detail. One would not achieve the universal paranoia of the CAP, which didn't have a kernel and in which what are generally regarded as intimate parts of the operating system were regarded with total suspicion by the rest of it.

Garbage Collection

Recall that one of the properties of capabilities was that if you had a capability for an object, then it existed. An obvious corollary is that nothing can be destroyed while any capabilities for it exist. We evidently have a garbage collection problem, and its solution depends on being able to find all instances of a capability for something. This requirement was for some time regarded as a significant obstruction to capability-based filing systems, but is perhaps not much of a dragon really. The Cambridge File Server [9] showed that provided that capabilities are stored in known places, even concurrent garbage collection is not too hard.

2. CRYPTOGRAPHIC CAPABILITIES

This brief mention of capability-based file systems forms a natural transition to a discussion of capabilities of a quite different form from those used in machines such as CAP or the Plessey 250. In the Cambridge File Server capabilities were 64-bit quantities which derived their security from the difficulty of guessing them. If you came up with a particular 64-bit quantity, generated at random, the presumption was that you had been told it rather than that you had guessed it. Similar ideas have been employed in many systems. It seems to be the case now that more and more use is being made of capabilities which depend on being unforgeable for sparseness reasons, though the word "capability" is not so often used. They really do, however, go back to the definition given at the beginning, being very directly "representations of the results of early-bound access-control decisions". My first encounter with this sort of idea was given in a 1979 paper called "Adding Capability Access to Conventional File Servers" [8] (which, oddly enough appeared adjacent to a paper by our present host). In this note I suggested that a file server could, when accessed by a properly authenticated user, provide on request an encrypted statement of the form "user's name, directory name, file name, access status". That encrypted statement could be passed to anyone, and could be offered to the file server which would determine access on the basis of its contents. The encryption key was known only to the file server. As actually stated in the 1979 paper, what was being encapsulated was not really an access control decision but the data on the basis of which an access control decision could be taken. It might have been better to say that the encrypted message was "directory name, file name, access permitted", genuinely having bound the access decision at the time of creation of the capability.

It is no accident that the use of encrypted capabilities has grown alongside the use of distributed computer systems and local area networks. In capability-based computers one can take hardware measures to preserve capabilities from corruption or forgery; such measures aren't available over networks and cryptographic methods seem to be all that's available. It's worth spending a minute or two on properties of encryption and how it can be used in the present context.

Encryption is used to guarantee integrity of material, on the assumption that if material resulting from decryption is recognisable, then that material was what was encrypted, and the encryption was done with the appropriate key. If you decrypt a bag of bits and get the Ten Commandments, then the bag of bits was made by encrypting the Ten Commandments. This contrasts with encryption for secrecy, in which it is assumed that you could only turn the bag of bits into the Ten Commandments if you knew the appropriate key. Similar considerations apply to authenticity.

Using these properties we can see how capability ideas are put to work. In the example above the encryption is used to guarantee both integrity and authenticity;

it incidentally ensures secrecy too but this is more of a nuisance than anything else. The holder of the capability has no way of finding out directly what it's a capability for. Contrary to what I said in that paper, it is case where public-key encryption would be better, because what is actually wanted is signature, i.e. encryption with the server's public key. The same result could be achieved less elegantly by means of as cryptographic checksum or any other sort of message authentication code.

A different use of encryption in this context is is to help with the avoidance of copying. In an internal capability system capabilities can be copied and passed around between procedures or processes but, as it were, only voluntarily. Someone needs to have written the code that does the passing. In a distributed system it is typically the case that anything passed can be copied by all comers, and this may be undesirable. The answer here is to pass the capability via a secure channel, or even by an intermediary if central monitoring is needed.

3. NECESSARY BUT NOT SUFFICIENT CONDITIONS

Just as it has been suggested that internal capabilities should be treated as necessary but not sufficient conditions for access to something, similar effects are easy with cryptographic capabilities in distributed systems. The commonest additional condition to require is timeliness - or to put it another way, capabilities are often given expiry dates after which they will no longer work. Another requirement is user identity or group membership. One may issue a capability that gives access to something provided that the caller belongs to a certain group. The practical implementation of this is to require that additional evidence be presented in the shape of a certificate of group membership. We are now moving into a world where capability language is uncommon, and terms like "ticket" are much more usual [7]. The wheel comes full circle here, for had I been writing this in 1970 not 1990 I would have defined a capability as an unforgeable ticket of permission to do something or another, rather than as the representation of the results of an early-bound access-control decision. Perhaps the current way to look at things is to say that capabilities represent early-bound *partial* access control decisions, showing that access matrices should not be represented "by rows" or "by columns" but in mixed ways as appropriate in particular circumstances.

References

1.   Bell, D.E., and LaPadula, L.J. "Secure Computer Systems: Mathematical Foundations". Technical Report ESD-TR-73-278, MITRE Corp. Bedford, Ma 1973

2.   Cook, D.J. The "Evaluation of a Protection System", University of Cambridge Ph.D. dissertation, 1978

3.   Dennis, J.B. and van Horn, E.C "Programming Semantics for Multiprogrammed Computations", *CACM* 9,3 1966

4.   England, D.M. "Architectural Features of System 250", Operating Systems: Infotech State of the Art Report 14, 1972

5.   Karger, P.A. "Improving Security and Performance for Capability Systems", Cambridge Ph.D. dissertation, 1988

6.   iAPX 432 General Data Processor Reference Manual, Intel Corp. 1981

7.   Miller, S.P. et al "Kerberos Authentication and Authorization System", Project Athena Technixal Plan, MIT, 1987

8.   Needham, R.M. "Adding Capability Access to a conventional File Server", *Operating Systems Review* 13, 1, 1979

9.   Needham, R.M. and Herbert, A.J. "The Cambridge Distributed Computing System", Addison-Wesley 1982

10. Wilkes, M.V. and Needham, R.M. "The Cambridge CAP computer and its Operating System", Elsevier, 1979.

Persistent Languages and Architectures

R Morrison
University of St Andrews

M P Atkinson
University of Glasgow

ABSTRACT

Persistent programming is concerned with creating and manipulating data in a manner that is independent of its lifetime. The persistence abstraction yields a number of advantages in terms of orthogonal design and programmer productivity. One major advantage is that the abstraction integrates the database view of information with the programming language view. For this reason **persistent programming languages** are sometimes called *database programming languages*.

A number of design principles have been devised for persistent systems. Following these rules, languages may be designed that provide persistence as a basic abstraction. This in turns begs the question of how these languages should be implemented and what architectural support is required for persistence.

Here we will review the concepts of persistence and re-examine the design issues that appear in persistent languages and architectures.

1. INTRODUCTION

Our aim is to support the activity of applications construction. Currently the underlying technology relies on a number of disparate mechanisms and philosophical assumptions for support and efficient implementation. Among these are:

- a plethora of disparate mechanisms is used in constructing applications [6] - command languages, editors, file systems, compilers, interpreters, linkage editors, binders, debuggers, DBMS - DDLs and DMLs, query languages, graphics languages, transaction managers, concurrency models, machine types etc.

- a reliance on the computing system as a data store or a data processor and separating the models.

- a late 60s and early 70s models of computation based on small, volatile, fast main stores and large, non-volatile, slow rotating technologies.

The incoherence and complexity arising from utilising many different and diverse application and system building mechanisms increases the cost both intellectually and mechanically of building even the simplest of systems. The complexity distracts the application builders from the task in hand forcing them to concentrate on mastering the programming systems rather than the application being developed. Perversely the plethora of disparate mechanisms is also costly in machine terms in that the code for interfacing them causes overheads in both space and time to execute.

Most application support systems, such as the Ada APSE, rely on a model of computation that separates program and data. Programs are stored in program libraries and data is stored in the filing system or a database management system. More modern modelling techniques such as object-orientation rely on the fact that program and data are intimately bound. This mismatch between the language and the modelling technique adds complexity to the programming system.

Finally, the model of computation based on small, volatile, fast main stores and large, non-volatile, slow rotating stores, which was developed in the late 1960's has survived and still influences the manner in which applications are constructed.

The advent of new hardware technologies with different time, space and cost trade-offs together with the development of new application areas, such as office automation, CAD/CAM, CASE etc. has led to proposals for different models of computation both linguistically and architecturally. Persistent systems are one such proposal. The persistence abstraction allows some of the complexity to be removed thereby reducing the cost of designing, implementing and maintaining applications using long term data.

In the following sections we will review some of the tradition of persistence and look at the challenges for the future.

2. PERSISTENCE DEFINITION

We defined the persistence of data is the length of time for which the data exists and is usable [6]. A spectrum of persistence exists and is categorised by

- transient results in expression evaluation,

- local variables in procedure activations,

- own variables, global variables and heap items whose extent is different from their scope,

- data that exists between executions of a program,

- data that exists between various versions of a program, and

- data that outlives the program.

The first three categories are usually provided by a programming language whereas the last three are provided by a filing system or a database management system.

A persistent programming system accommodates all categories of longevity in data. We aspire to systems where the use of the data is independent of its persistence.

2.1. Principles of Orthogonal Persistence

We have also identified the following principles which define the persistent abstraction. They are:

- *The Principle of Persistence Independence*

  The persistence of data is independent of how the program manipulates the data. That is, the user does not have to, indeed cannot, program to control the movement of data between long term and short term store. This is performed automatically by the system.

- *The Principle of Data Type Orthogonality*

  All data objects should be allowed the full range of persistence irrespective of their type. That is, there are no special cases where objects of a specific type are not allowed to be persistent.

- *The Principle of Persistence Identification*

  The choice of how to identify and provide persistent objects is orthogonal to the universe of discourse of the system. That is, the mechanism for identifying persistent objects is not related to the type system.

The application of the three principles yields *Orthogonal Persistence.*

2.2. Loss of Orthogonality

Loss of orthogonality of persistence occurs by disregarding any of the three principles. Most serious is persistence independence since if it is broken it is hard to see how the persistence in the system is orthogonal in any way.

Some programming language designers have taken a very pragmatic approach to persistence and disregarded data type orthogonality for specific types. Pascal/R [41] and DBPL [29] are persistent programming languages where only first order relations are persistent and then only relations that do not contain pointer types. This models the relational world well but causes difficulty when other modelling techniques are used.

The identification of persistent objects is commonly performed by the system automatically computing the transitive closure of objects from some persistent root [4,5,13,14,18]. Where this is not the case languages often associate persistence with type. This breaks the third principle and as a side effect the second one as well. It also gives rise to dangling reference problems, or at least invalidated references, for persistent objects that point to non-persistent objects. The E programming language [37], nearly all the persistent extensions to C^{++} [43] and the PGraphite language [46] use this technique. Figures 1 and 2 illustrates the problem.

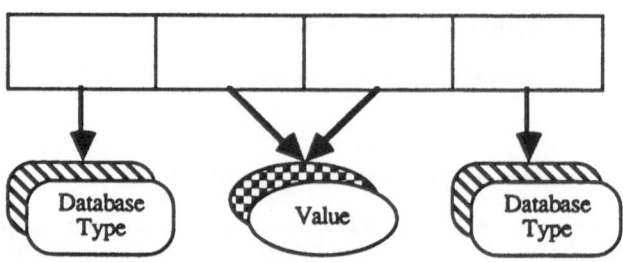

Figure 1: Persistent objects before being sent to the persistent store.

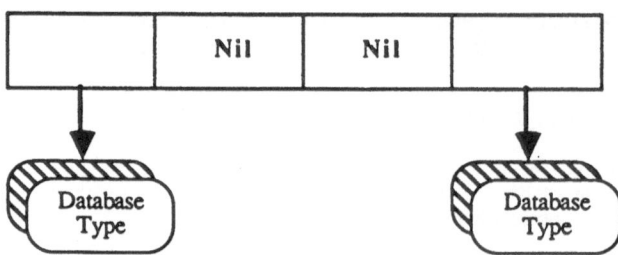

Figure 2: The same objects as in Figure 1 in the persistent store.

Figure 1 shows an object which points to two other objects of database types and a non-database value before being preserved in the persistent store. Figure 2 shows that in the persistent store only the database types are preserved and the non-database value is lost, being replaced by a nil value if such is available or a dangling reference. Here the persistent store model of data is not consistent with the main store model, a position we wish to avoid since this adds complexity to the system for the programmer to master.

2.3. Savings with Persistence

The advantages of persistence can be summarised as follows:

- Reduced complexity.

- Reduced code size and time to execute.

- Protection mechanisms that operate over the whole environment.

- Referential integrity preserved over the environment.

The first saving of persistent systems is in the reduced complexity for application builders. Traditionally the programmer has to maintain three mappings among the database model, the programming language model and the real world model of the application as can be seen in Figure 3.

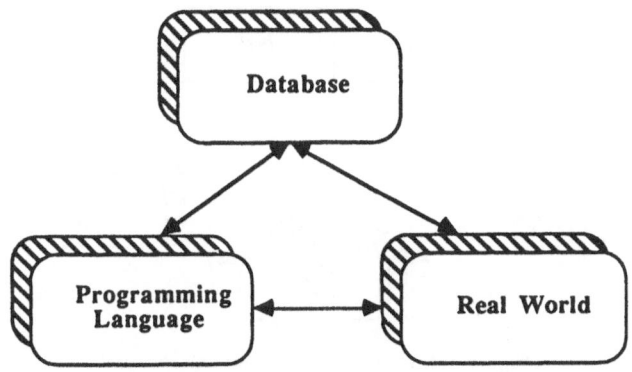

Figure 3: The mapping in traditional applications systems.

The intellectual effort in maintaining the mappings distracts the programmer from mastering the inherent complexity of the application to concentrate on overcoming the complexity of the support system. Figure 4 illustrates that in a persistent system the number of mappings is reduced from three to one thereby simplifying the application builders' task.

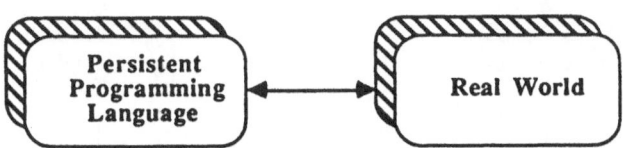

Figure 4: Mapping in a persistent system.

Corresponding to the intellectual savings of persistence there is also a saving in the amount of code required to maintain the mappings. This has been estimated at 30% of the total code for a typical database application [6]. The code that is unnecessary is concerned with the explicit movement of data between main and backing store and the code required to change the representation of the data for long term preservation and restoration. An example of the former is input and output code and of the latter is code to flatten and reconstruct a graph before and after, output and input respectively. Not only is the size of the application code reduced thereby producing savings throughout the software life cycle of the application but also the time to execute and store this code is saved in physical terms.

The third benefit of persistent systems is that a single model of protection may operate over the whole environment. In most programming languages the simplest way to break the type system is to output a value as one type and input it again as another. Thus the type security is lost over the persistent store. Using a single enforcable model of type reduces complexity while increasing the protection over many current systems [35].

The final advantage of persistence is that referential integrity is preserved over the environment. Figure 5 illustrates a data structure where one of the components is pointed at or shared by two others. This sharing should be preserved within the persistent store.

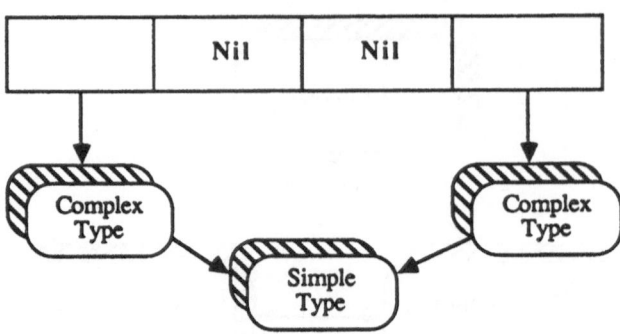

Figure 5: Sharing and referential integrity.

Figure 6 shows how referential integrity may be broken as in the persistent models of Amber [16] and a proposal for ML.

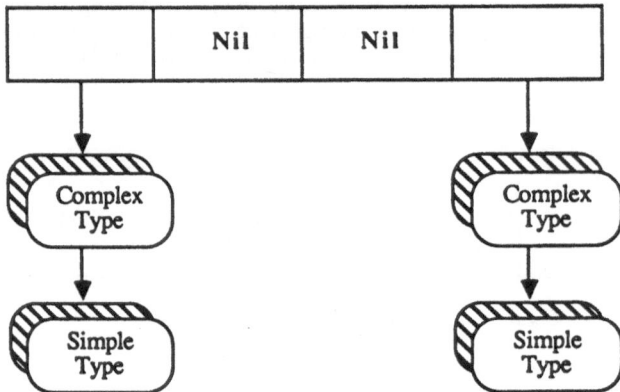

Figure 6: A lack of referential integrity.

2.4. Costs of Persistence

In common with all abstraction mechanisms there are costs in using and constructing persistent programming systems. The main costs over traditional systems are :

• The cost of constructing a stable object store.

• The loss of efficiency with some applications due to the abstraction.

• The cost of providing language independent binding mechanisms.

The cost of constructing a stable object store can vary according to the method used. Several schemes for extending the work of Lorie in using the virtual memory manager to identify and preserve modified data have been proposed [27,38,40,44,45]. Other techniques similar to software segmentation are also common [5,13,14,18]. The cost of constructing the stable stores is considerable regardless of the method used.

There is a loss of efficiency in implementing some algorithms within a persistent store. This is due to the fact that the user does not have full control of all the physical properties of the machine. Since these are deliberately abstracted over, they may not be used. The situation is similar to that of a virtual memory system that does not allow users to perform their own paging.

Finally, there is a cost to be paid for language independent bindings. These mechanisms usually have to integrate disparate type systems which can be very expensive [10,31].

2.5. Myths

There are two myths about persistent systems that were first thought to be true. We now feel that the claims were premature. They are :

- persistence can be added to any language, and

- persistence can model all our computational needs efficiently.

The integration of a programming language with a persistent store requires some basic facilities within the language for success. A good example of an unsuitable host is the language Ada [26] where there is a clear distinction between program and data. Programs are kept in libraries and data in the file system. Furthermore input and output on access types is undefined. Both of these problems make it impossible to add persistence without redefining the language which in this case is forbidden.

The second myth is that persistent languages can model all our computation needs efficiently. It should be obvious that some algorithms, such as a disk sort, cannot even be implemented in orthogonally persistent systems.

2.6. Orthogonal Persistence Systems Requirements

Orthogonal persistence requires the following for support :

- Programming languages in which computations may be expressed using orthogonal persistence, and

- System architectures, both software and hardware, to support the implementation of these languages.

We will now discuss both of these.

3. PERSISTENT PROGRAMMING LANGUAGES

The provision of persistence should be orthogonal to all other aspects of programming language design. Therefore it should be possible to have applicative, relational, logic, object, query and imperative persistent programming languages. Some known persistent programming languages are :

- Pascal/R [41] - relational,

- DBPL [29] - relational,

- PS-algol [36] - imperative,

- Leibniz [23] - object,

- E [37] - sort of object (C++),

- Galileo [2] - object with extentional classes,

- Poly [30] - applicative,

- Staple [28] - applicative,

- Amber [16] - applicative,

- Persistent Prolog [19,24] - logic,

- χ [25] - capability,

- Napier88 [33] - store and multiparadigm.

Plus many other claims, counter claims and proposals! The status of each implementation can be obtained by asking for a copy of the system.

3.1. Challenges for Persistent Languages

The provision of an environmental model of computation does have an influence upon certain language features to support its wholistic view of information. Most notably it must pay attention to the following aspects of language design :

- *Name Space Control* - to uniquely identify objects,

- *Scale* - to express computations on large bodies of data,

- *Data Evolution* - to control change including schema evolution,

- *Sharing* - to avoid re-invention of wheels,

- *Protection* - to ensure the integrity of valuable data,

- *Concurrency* - to allow parallel access,

- *Transactions* - to give a semantics to generalised update in a concurrent shared environment and provide a notion of stability, and

- *Complexity Control* - to avoid the failures of current technology and achieve simpler more cost effective solutions.

Thus nearly all aspects of language design have to be re-thought to accommodate the integrated view of data that persistence provides.

3.1.1. Name Space Control and Binding

For independently prepared programs and data to be correctly composed requires a binding mechanism [10,31]. We wish the following facilities :

- Re-useability and distribution of programs and data.

- The ability to combine data from many sources.

- Incremental program and data definition.

- The ability to identify data - how are names used?

The challenges in name space control and binding are :

- To find the balance between static and dynamic binding.

- To develop generic software architectures for applications' construction.

- To find language constructs to express flexible incremental binding (FIBS) to avoid forcing binding too early.

3.1.2. Scale

Persistent programming languages with their environmental view of data require the ability to manipulate large bodies of data. Large scale is a natural consequence of longevity but may also occur in automatic data collection. Scale is relative and becomes an issue when the size of the data approaches the limits of the technology. Today's large scale may be small by tomorrow's standards.

The challenges of scale are to invent :

- A method of describing large scale data and computations.

- Efficient storage and algorithms to manage access to the large scale data.

- Methods to ensure that data creep does not occur since that will eventually become unacceptable.

3.1.3. Data Evolution

Since the uses of the data cannot be predicted fully in advance a method of evolving existing data is required. It is unlikely that all data will change on every computation which means a method of incremental change is required. The changes to data have 3 categories :

- Changes in representation.

- Changes in organisation.

- Changes in the meta data.

The challenges of data evolution are :

- To find understandable semantics for change.

- Because of scale, change may require incremental algorithms for adequate performance.

- Limiting the propagation of change especially in the case of meta data evolution.

3.1.4. Sharing

A large body of data requires a community effort for its construction and maintenance. This requires the ability to share the data and gives rise to a number of other motivators. These are :

- Protection - to protect users from

    - the system

    - other users

    - themselves
- Concurrency - to allow parallel access
- Transactions - a model to provide

    - availability of data for access

    - a notion of stability

The challenge of sharing is to find and implement a *good* model of sharing

3.1.5.   Protection

Large bodies of data are inherently valuable. It is essential to protect them from accidental and deliberate misuse either by software or hardware [35]. Among the mechanisms commonly used for protection are :

- Integrity constraints - used in database systems to ensure that the data is kept mutually consistent.

- Type systems - used in programming languages to control the interaction of objects.

- Stable storage - used to ensure that when failure does occur that the system can limit its losses due to component failure.

- Capability architectures to control access.

The challenges of protection are :

- To perform as much eager checking as possible.

- To design an adequate model of type for persistent programming.

- To design mechanisms for ensuring integrity & security.

- To design and engineer stable stores sufficient for our applications.

3.1.6.   Concurrency and Transactions

Different models of both concurrency and transaction may have to be provided for persistent systems [32]. Long lived data has an impact on the choice of transactional model since serialisability may be too restrictive for the efficient sharing of data. We require at least the following :

- There should be mechanisms to permit and control shared and concurrent usage.

- It should be possible to encapsulate any sequence of operations on the store into a transaction and have it behave like a single operation.

The challenges of concurrency and transactions are :

- To implement concurrency and transaction models efficiently.

- To find models without serialisability.

3.1.7. Controlling complexity

Complexity in the development system causes the user to be distracted from the computational task to concentrate on mastering the implementation technology. Abstraction is a process that allows the general pattern to be observed while ignoring the inessential details. By supporting powerful abstraction facilities and keeping the development system simple, there is the possibility of concentrating on the complexity of the application. This allows more complex and more powerful systems to be developed.

The challenge of controlling complexity is to invent and implement appropriate abstractions for persistent programming

3.2. Type Systems for Persistent Programming

The long term goal of research into type systems is to develop an adequate model of type that meets the computational needs of persistent systems [3]. Ideally we would like a simple set of types, and a type algebra, so that by a succession of operations and the provision of parameters, any data model or conceptual data model can be defined [7].

Type systems provide two important facilities within both databases and programming languages, namely data modelling and data protection. Data modelling is performed in databases using data models and in programming languages by a classical type system. In the future the traditional database schema will be regarded as a type. Data protection is provided by integrity constraints in databases, type checking in programming languages and dynamic constraints such as capabilities in operating systems. All these mechanisms require integration into a coherent whole.

The issue of type checking is central to this activity. Static checking allows assertions to be made and even proved about a computation before it is executed. It therefore provides a level of safety within the system. Dynamic checking is however sometimes necessary for rebinding or merging of schema. The aim is to persue the limits of static checking.

There are two approaches currently used to provide static checking for database type systems. The first is constraint specification where constraints over the data for a particular computation are expressed in some language. The checking requires a powerful theorem prover beyond the limits of those currently available. Such systems are usually undecidable and an unsuccessful check may be caused by the limitations of the theorem prover rather than inconsistent constraints. The second approach is to extend classical type systems. These describe decidable types with a simpler syntax which allows the user to better understand type checking failures. Both these approaches need to be persued. Hopefully they will converge.

The major challenges for type systems for persistent programming are to provide the following:

- Polymorphism

  Polymorphism is essential to the expression of generic computations. Some known and well studied forms of polymorphism include parametric, inclusion, bounded quantification and subtyping [15,17,20,34]. Further forms and efficient implementations are required in the next generation of persistent systems.

- Bulk Types

Persistent systems express computations on large scale data. The data may be aggregated in bulk data types such as relations, sets, lists and arrays and is computed upon using query languages. One interesting innovation is the extentional notion of type that appears in OODBMS where a class is defined as the set of existing values of a particular type. Queries are made over the classes [9,12,47]. The theory of classes is not as yet well worked out and the semantics of update in queries over bulk types still not resolved. A further advance may also come from heterogeneous collections.

- View Mechanisms

  View mechanisms are used in database to allow users to concentrate on a subset of the data in a database. Such mechanisms are essential to the integrity of the database since a system administrator can use a view to restrict the access given one one or a class of users. At present views are constructed by ad hoc methods and no underlying theory of views exists. Recently abstract data type have been proposed as one possible solution to this in the form of existentially quantified types [20]. This work is however in its infancy and needs more research to be convincing for large scale applications.

- Performance of Type Checkers

  The type of a database schema can become very large. This raises performance issues of how to best represent the type within the database. Also of concern is the performance of the type checking algorithm since it is used when persistent systems as schema are merged. Very little work has been done in this area.

- Object Migration

  Can objects change their type?. For example, can a person become a student for a period of a computation? This is clearly desirable in modelling terms and has to be better understood in type checking terms.

- Schema Evolution

  A type system for a persistent programming language requires a mechanism to provide modularity, storage and reuse of type definitions for incremental schema evolution. Schema evolution may be provided by using the reflective facilities of the next section.

3.3. Reflection

Reflection is the ability of a system to support its own evolution. This may entail changes to the data, the programs that manipulate the data and the schema. Reflection is of great interest in persistent systems since they require the ability to evolve. It yields an extreme form of dynamic binding. Given that a language is Turing complete, reflection cuts out a level of interpretation that would be required to provide the extra layer of expressablity to support total evolution.

Reflection can be used to provide the following :

- genericity [42],
- browsing [22],

- schema evolution [22],

- querying,

- data models,

- adding types to the value space [22].

Work on reflection in persistent systems is as yet not well developed.

4. PERSISTENT ARCHITECTURES

Persistence poses the same set of problems for architectures as it does for languages [8,11,21]. However, whereas the persistent languages are concerned with the expression of computations using the persistence abstraction, the architectures are concerned with the efficient implementation of these languages. Given that the technologies for the efficient translation of languages is well understood we will concentrate on the technology for the implementation of the object store.

4.1. Intrinsic Properties of the Persistent Store

The properties of a persistent store can be divided into intrinsic and technological. The intrinsic properties are those that are desirable for the persistent store to possess whereas the technological properties arise in trying to implement the intrinsic properties.

The intrinsic properties are:

- a freedom in binding mechanisms that allows the reuse of components in the store to match the needs of the particular application,

- unbounded capacity to match the conceptually unbounded nature of the stores provided in some languages,

- infinite speed, and

- error free.

The above intrinsic properties of persistent stores are not realistic in terms of implementation with current technology. They therefore have to be approximated in such a manner that the persistence abstraction is not totally compromised. In particular, a gross violation would occur if the user is required to write code to support the movement of data.

4.1.1. Binding Mechanisms

The intrinsic problems of binding are indentifying persistent data and avoiding binding too early. Persistent data is normally identified by computing the transitive closure of data from some root. The technological problem is how to perform this efficiently. For example, it should be possible to compute the transitive closure without bringing all the data into the main store which is very expensive in terms of disk transfers.

For efficient implementation, current technology requires binding that is too early. The assumption in most current systems is that a persistent store will be populated with a large number of statically bound objects that can be dynamically bound into an application invocation. The fewer dynamic binds that are performed the more efficient the system. However, static binding restricts the flexibility of using the components of the statically bound objects.

The early binding problem occurs at two levels. In order to build an efficient persistent store some assumptions are made about the pattern of use of the store. This constitutes a binding at the system construction time. Two reasons for this are the efficient management of address bits and efficient garbage collection. However little is known about the use of persistent stores and the early assumptions may be invalid over a long period of time.

The second manifestation of early binding occurs at the data modelling level. For example the object-oriented model binds data within objects for the lifetime of the object. The problem is that static binding in a persistent store is forever and if it is subsequently discovered that the binding is inappropriate then the user is stuck.

We require binding that will allow the reuse of components appropriate to the applications needs - not the needs of the architecture. For example O_2 [12] queries look inside objects as do the views of Napier88 [33]. The group and ungroup options in MacDraw allows the freeing and rebinding of objects and is a hint as to how both static and dynamic binding may be accommodated together in persistent systems.

4.1.2. Unbounded Capacity

The intrinsic property of a store of unbounded capacity is how to name objects within it. A flat name space or a conceptual name space can be used. The technological properties are :

- Movement of data to the active store.

- Movement of data to the long term store.

- Management of very large values.

- Management of very large stores.

  - very large address space - Monads [1,39], System 38 [45].

  - extensible contextual addressing.

  - distribution and coherence of data.

  - copying, detaching and merging stores.

  - garbage collection.

  - store fragmentation.

  - very large physical stores

4.1.3. Infinite Speed

There are only technological properties of systems trying to simulate infinite speed. Concurrency mechanisms are used in both modelling data and for improving the performance of the overall system. At an architectural level this involves multiprocessors if real concurrency is to be achieved. In turn this poses the question of whether distribution is and appropriate language and architectural model. Both store and processor distribution are possible. Finally system wide locking has to be provided to ensure the integrity of data and allow transactions to be implemented.

4.1.4. Error Free Stores

A persistent store should be free from unexpected failures of hardware and software. The intrinsic problem is the semantics of failure. That is, how is failure explained to the user

The technological problems centre around the following

- Stability mechanisms
    - implicit stability - e.g. shadow paging ...
    - explicit stability - e.g. transaction logs ...
- Protection mechanisms.
    - integrity constraints.
    - type checking - static and dynamic.
    - capabilities - software and hardware.

4.1.4.1. Questions of Stability

There are some technological properties associated with stability alone. They are:

- What percentage of the data is required to automatically survive a failure of any or all of the equipment at a single site?
- Is some data more valuable than other data?
- What percentage of the data is required to be restorable?
- How frequently should data be written to stable store?
- What processing and equipment overhead is acceptable for stability?
- How quickly must data be restored?
- How are restorations performed? - interactively to avoid cascading?

• How is restoration explained to the user?

5. THE ULTIMATE CHALLENGE

To build a persistent system the high ideals should be adhered as closely as possible. The particular instance of the architecture yields an efficient implementation for a particular class of problems. It will almost certainly be general purpose but not the most efficient for all applications.

Most persistent programming systems are still small scale. The largest PS-algol system is about 200 megabytes (2.5 million objects) in a company that expects serious users to have between 1 to 10 databases of about 10 to 20 gigabytes.

We need a series of large experiments to refute or verify all the ideas and concepts.

ACKNOWLEDGEMENTS

The work was supported by ESPRIT II Basic Research Action 3070 - FIDE.

REFERENCES

1. Abramson, D.A. "Hardware Management of a Large Virtual Memory", *Proceedings 4th Australian Computer Science Conference*, Brisbane 1981, pp. 1-13.

2. Albano A., Cardelli L. & Orsini R. "Galilieo: A Strongly Typed, Interactive Conceptual Language." *ACM Transactions on Database Systems*, vol. 10, no. 2, 1985, pp. 230-260.

3. Albano, A., Dearle, A., Ghelli, G., Marlin, C., Morrison, R., Orsini, R & Stemple, D. "A Framework for Comparing Type Systems for Database Programming Languages". *2nd International Workshop on Database Programming Languages*, Oregon (1989), pp. 203-212.

4. Atkinson, M.P., Chisholm, K.J. and Cockshott, W.P. "PS-algol: An Algol with a Persistent Heap", *ACM SIGPLAN Notices*, 17, 7, July 1981, pp. 24-31.

5. Atkinson M.P., Chisholm K.J. & Cockshott W.P. "CMS - A Chunk Management System." *Software Practice and Experience*, vol. 13, no. 3, (1983), pp. 259-272.

6. Atkinson M.P. Bailey P.J., Chisholm K.J. Cockshott W.P. & Morrison R. "An Approach to Persistent Programming." *The Computer Journal*, vol. 26, no. 4, 1983, pp. 360-365.

7. Atkinson, M.P. & Morrison, R. "Integrated Persistent Programming Systems". *19th International Conference on System Sciences*, Hawaii, U.S.A., (January 1986), pp. 842-854.

8. Atkinson, M.P., Morrison, R. & Pratten, G.D. "Designing a persistent information space architecture". *10th IFIP World Congress*, Dublin (September 1986), pp. 115-120.

9.   Atkinson, M.P. & Morrison, R. "Polymorphic Names, Types, Constancy and Magic in a Type Secure Persistent Object Store". *2nd International Workshop on Persistent Object Systems*, Appin, (August 1987), pp. 1-12.

10.   Atkinson, M.P., Buneman, O.P. & Morrison, R. "Binding and Type Checking in Database Programming Languages". *The Computer Journal*. 31,2 (1988), pp. 99-109.

11.   Bancilhon F., Barbedette G., Benzaken V., Delobel C., Gamerman S., Lecluse C., Pfeffer P., Richard P. & Valez F. "The Design and Implementation of O₂, an Object Oriented Database System". Proc. 2nd International Workshop on Object-Oriented Database Systems, West Germany. In *Lecture Notes in Computer Science, 334.* Springer-Verlag (September 1988), pp. 1-22.

12.   Bancilhon, F., Cluet, S. & Delobel, C. "A Query Language for the O₂ Object-Oriented Database". *2nd International Workshop on Database Programming Languages*, Salishan, Oregon (1989).

13.   Brown A.L. & Cockshott W.P. "The CPOMS Persistent Object Management System." Universities of Glasgow and St.Andrews PPRR-13, Scotland, (1985).

14.   Brown A.L. (Ph.D. Thesis) "Persistent Object Stores." Universities of Glasgow and St.Andrews PPRR-71, Scotland, (1989).

15.   Cardelli, L. & Wegner, P. "On understanding types, data abstraction and polymorphism". ACM *Computing Surveys* 17, 4, (December 1985), pp. 471-523.

16.   Cardelli, L. *Amber*. Tech. Report AT7T. Bell Labs. Murray Hill, U.S.A. (1985).

17.   Cardelli, L. "Typeful Programming". *DEC SRC Report*, (May 1989).

18.   Cockshott, W.P., Atkinson, M.P., Bailey, P.J., Chisholm, K.J. and Morrison, R. "POMS: A Persistent Object Management System", *Software Practice and Experience*, 14, 1, (January 1984), pp. 49-71.

19.   Coloumb, R.M. "Issues in the Implementation of Persistent Prolog". *Proceeding of the 3rd International Workshop on Persistent Object Stores,* Newcastle, N.S.W. (Jan 1989), pp. 67-79.

20.   Connor, R.C.H., Dearle, A., Morrison, R. & Brown, A.L. "Existentially Quantified Types as a Database Viewing Mechanism". *Advances in Database Technology - EDBT90*, Venice. In **Lecture Notes in Computer Science**. 416. Springer-Verlag (1990), pp. 301-315.

21.   Connors T. & Lyngbaek P. "Providing Uniform Access to Heterogenous Information Bases". Proc. 2nd International Workshop on Object-Oriented Database Systems, West Germany. *In Lecture Notes in Computer Science, 334.* Springer-Verlag, (September 1988), pp. 162-173 .

22.   Dearle A. & Brown A.L. "Safe Browsing in a Strongly Typed Persistent Environment". *The Computer Journal* 31,6, (December 1988), pp. 540-545.

23   Evered, M. "Leibniz - A Language to Support Software Engineering". PhD thesis Technical University of Darmstadt (1985).

24. Gray, P.M.D., Moffat, D.S. & Du Boulay, J.B.H. "Persistent Prolog: A Searching Storage Manager for Prolog". *Proceedings of the 1st International Workshop on Persistent Objects Systems,* Appin, Scotland (August 1985), PPRR-16-85, Universities of Glasgow and St Andrews, pp. 353-368.

25. Hurst, A.J. & Sajeev, A.S.M. "A Capability Based Language for Persistent Programming: Implementation Issuse". *Proceeding of the 3rd International Workshop on Persistent Object Stores,* Newcastle, N.S.W. (Jan 1989), pp. 186-201

26. Ichbiah et al., The Programming Language Ada Reference Manual. ANSI/MIL-STD-1815A-1983. (1983).

27. Lorie A.L. "Physical Integrity in a Large Segmented Database." *ACM Transactions on Database Systems,* vol. 2, no. 1, 1977, pp. 91-104.

28. McNally, D.J. "Code Generating Functional Language Modules for a Persistent Object Store". University of St Andrews STAPLE/89/2 (1989).

29. Matthes, F. & Schmidt, J.W. "The Type System of DBPL". Proceeding of the 2nd International Workshop on Database Programming Languages, Salishan, Oregon (June 1989), pp. 219-225.

30. Matthews, D.C.J. "Poly Manual" Technical Report 65, University of Cambridge, U.K. (1985).

31. Morrison, R., Brown, A.L., Dearle, A. & Atkinson, M.P. "Flexible Incremental Binding in a Persistent Object Store". *ACM Sigplan Notices,* 23, 4 (April 1988), pp. 27-34.

32. Morrison, R., Brown, A.L., Carrick, R., Connor, R.C. & Dearle, A. "On the Integration of Object-Oriented and Process-Oriented Computation in Persistent Environments". Proc. 2nd International Workshop on Object-Oriented Database Systems, West Germany (1988). In **Lecture Notes in Computer Science**, 334. Springer-Verlag, (September 1988), pp. 334-339.

33. Morrison R., Brown A.L., Connor R. & Dearle A. "The Napier88 Reference Manual." Universities of Glasgow and St.Andrews PPRR-77, Scotland, (1989).

34. Morrison R., Dearle A, Connor R.C.H. & Brown A.L. "An ad hoc Approach to the Implementation of Polymorphism". University of St Andrews CS/90/1 (1990).

35. Morrison R., Brown A.L., Connor R.C.H., Cutts, Q.I., Dearle, A., Kirby, G., Rosenberg J.,& Stemple, D.., & Munro D.S. "Protection in Persistent Object Systems" *International Workshop on Computer Architectures to Support Security and Persistence,* Universität Bremen, West Germany, (May 1990).

36. "The PS-algol Reference Manual fifth edition." Universities of Glasgow and St.Andrews PPRR-12, Scotland, (1988).

37. Richardson, J.E. & Carey, M.J. "Implemeting Persistence in E".. *Proceeding of the 3rd International Workshop on Persistent Object Stores,* Newcastle, N.S.W. (Jan 1989), pp. 302-319.

38. Rosenberg J., Henskens F., Brown A.L., Morrison R. & Munro D.S. "Stability in a Persistent Store Based on a Large Virtual Memory." *International Workshop on Computer Architectures to Support Security and Persistence*, Universität Bremen, West Germany, (May 1990).

39. Rosenberg, J., Keedy, J.L. and Abramson, D.A. "Addressing Mechanisms for Large Virtual Memories", Research Report CS/90/2, University of St. Andrews, (1990).

40. Ross G.D.M. (Ph.D. Thesis) "Virtual Files: A Framework for Experimental Design." University of Edinburgh, (1983).

41. Schmidt, J.W. "Some high level language constructs for data of type relation". *ACM.TODS* 2, 3 (1977), pp. 247-261.

42. Stemple, D., Fegaras, L., Sheard, T. & Socorro, A. "Exceeding the Limits of Polymorphism in Database Programming Languages". *Advances in Database Technology - EDBT90*, Venice. In **Lecture Notes in Computer Science**. 416. Springer-Verlag (1990), pp. 269-285.

43. Stroustrup B. *The C++ Programming Language*, Addison Wesley (1986).

44. Thatte S.M. "Persistent Memory: A Storage Architecture for Object Oriented Database Systems." *Proc. ACM/IEEE 1986 International Workshop on Object Oriented Database Systems*, Pacific Grove, CA, (September 1986), pp. 148-159.

45. Traiger, I.L. "Virtual Memory Management for Database Systems", *Operating Systems Review*, 16, 4, (October 1982), pp. 26-48.

46. Wileden, J.C., Wolf, A.L., Fisher, C.D. & Tarr, P.T. "PGraphite: An experiment in Persistent Typed Object Management". *SIGSOFT88* (1988), pp. 130-142.

47. Zdonik, S.B. "Query Optimisation in Object-Oriented Databases". *22nd Hawaii International Conference on System Sciences* (Jan 1989), II, pp. 19-25.

Part II

Principles and Models

Dimensions of Addressing Schemes

Manojit Sarkar
Edward F. Gehringer
Department of Computer Science
North Carolina State University

ABSTRACT

This paper attempts to bring some order to the apparent disorder of numerous addressing schemes. Various addressing strategies are examined, and four orthogonal dimensions identified. These are: (i) number of address spaces per system, (ii) number of address-mapping tiers, (iii) when and how often mapping functions are performed and (iv) implementation of the access matrix (via capabilities or access-control lists). The number of address-mapping tiers in a system is directly related to the number of different forms of addresses present in the system. We discuss the functionality that can be achieved by the various options along the four dimensions. We focus on three important functionalities: sharing, protection and persistence. The functionality of dynamic linking is also discussed briefly. Twelve commercial and research computer systems have been selected and classified into three categories: (i) ordinary virtual-memory systems, (ii) non-persistent object systems and (iii) persistent object systems. The success of these systems in providing the above functionalities is traced back to their addressing schemes.

1. Introduction

The central purpose of an addressing scheme is to store information and make information available to any computation. In addition to performing this basic function, sophisticated addressing schemes must also facilitate sharing, protection and persistence of information. Needless to say, performance and cost are two other important issues.

Sharing. In multitasking systems, it is desirable that processes be able to share information with each other in a controlled manner. To share a piece of information, different processes must be able to address it. Or, in other words, processes sharing information in a controlled manner must share parts, but not all, of their address spaces. Addressing schemes designed in the past provide controlled sharing without compromising generality[1] through one of the following two means [8]:

- Through a single systemwide address space. All processes execute within the *same* address space. That is, if two processes use the same address, they refer to the same information. The MONADS system [14] is a typical example.

- Through an extra level of mapping. In systems where different processes have their own private address spaces, an additional level of mapping must be used to allow sharing. An example is Multics [17], with its linkage segments.

At first glance, it might seem that the single address space would be the more efficient of the two solutions in terms of execution-time overhead. But as we shall see in Section 2.1, a single address space imposes certain overheads, while the extra level of mapping can be performed by

---

[1]Fabry's paper identifies four schemes. The other two are (i) global assignment of segment numbers of shared segments, usually by the operating system (which makes it impossible to share segments that are not predefined as "shared segments"), and (ii) multiple segment tables per process (which make it difficult or impossible to pass segments as parameters).

following a pointer that has been preloaded into a register. Thus, it is not clear which scheme is faster.

Protection. Protection is closely related to sharing; in some sense it is the opposite goal. Early virtual-memory systems with one address space per process can protect one process's address space against others by making all address spaces disjoint. They can also provide coarse-grained protection by protecting individual segments (in segmentation systems) or pages (in paging systems). Finer-grained protection and multiple protection domains per process require a more sophisticated protection scheme.

Capabilities and access-control lists are two mechanisms employed to provide protection. Only some sort of capability (or "ticket oriented") approach will suffice to protect information *within* a process against unauthorized access by the process, since it is not efficient to check access-control lists on each reference. Again, there are two options:

- A process can obtain a ticket for an object by authenticating its access rights at the time it begins to use the object.

- Capabilities can be used uniformly throughout the system.

Persistence. If information is to persist after the process that created it has terminated, the system must support process-independent names or addresses that can be retained between program executions. Again, this can be achieved in two ways:

- Through a single systemwide address space, as in MONADS [15] or the IBM System/38 [4].

- Through a single systemwide name space, as in Multics [17] or name-based mapping [11].

Many addressing mechanisms have been designed to provide the above functionalities, as well as other requirements, such as providing virtual memory and facilitating dynamic linking. This paper will consider address-mapping tiers that can meet all of these goals, singly or in combination. In general, our descriptions will abstract away detail that is irrelevant to these goals. To limit the scope of the paper, discussion of related issues such as dynamic binding or concurrency will be omitted. Issues of space and time efficiency are also largely ignored except when they are directly related to the above functionalities.

2. Dimensions of Addressing Schemes

In this section we elaborate on the four dimensions of addressing schemes: (i) number of address spaces per system, (ii) number of different address-mapping tiers, (iii) address-mapping instants, and (iv) implementation of the access matrix.

In the discussion that follows, we use the term *address* to mean a location-dependent reference, and the term *name* to mean a location-independent reference. *Reference* will sometimes be used to mean either a name or an address.

Forms of reference. Address-mapping tiers translate between different *forms* of references. Sophisticated virtual-memory systems may represent references in several different forms at various times (Figure 1). A *program address* refers to the address appearing in the compiled code. This may or may not be the same as a *virtual address*, which we define to mean an address in a virtual address space. A virtual-address space is in turn defined as a linear sequence of addresses that is not permanently tied to any physical storage. A virtual address is at least one level above the *physical address*, which directly refers to the physical location of information. This implies that there needs to be at least one mapping tier to obtain a physical address from a virtual address. In ordinary VM systems, the program address may be a virtual address. In more sophisticated object-oriented systems, program addresses and virtual addresses may be different.

A *name* is another form of reference that is independent of either virtual or physical location. A name is valid within a locality called a *name space*. If the name space covers the entire system, the names in the name space identify objects uniquely

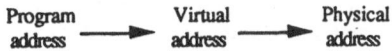

Program address → Virtual address → Physical address

Figure 1: Mapping from a program address to a physical address. In many systems, two or three of the forms of address shown here are identical, so no mapping is needed between them.

in the system. A name space can have different subspaces, which are name spaces in their own right. A file directory, for example, is a name space, as are its subdirectories.

There can be other forms of references in a system. Sometimes they are called "logical addresses," "effective addresses" or "absolute addresses." Their meaning varies from system to system.

2.1. Number of Address Spaces per System

Let us choose the number of potential address spaces in a system[2] as the first orthogonal dimension of addressing schemes. Either there is a single address space for the whole system, or each process has its own address space. In the latter case, a process may be composed of several threads that share address space (e.g. Carnegie Mellon's Mach [24], the University of Washington's Presto [2]), but different processes' address spaces are still disjoint. Most computer systems fall into the multiple-address-space category. Notable exceptions are IBM's S/38 and AS/400, the Intel 432, and MONADS.

Single address-space systems can provide persistence and sharing in a natural way. The address space is large enough that addresses never need be reused. Thus, an object can be identified uniquely and persistently by its systemwide address. Another advantage of a single address-space system is that it can provide fine-grained protection with the help of capability-based addressing, as in MONADS.

A single address space, though, is not without its costs. These costs depend on whether the address space is segmented or paged. A single *segmented* address space treats each object as a separate segment. It has a central *object table* that keeps track of the location of each object, and usually the number of outstanding references to it. Storage can be reclaimed when an object's reference count becomes zero. But reference counting is expensive, and may require hardware support. A bigger problem, however, is the size of the object table. The average object in a system may be small, not much larger than the average object-table entry. The object table itself may consume a substantial portion of the system's on-line storage. The Intel 432 is an example of a single segmented address-space system.

A single *paged* address space allows the representation of an object to begin anywhere within a page and to cross page boundaries. This form of a single address space requires that disjoint parts of the system's address space, as well as physical memory, be allocated to the executing processes. Reference counting cannot be used because there is no central table to hold the counts. It is hard to move or delete an object, because pointers to it, which may be scattered throughout the system, must be found and updated. Such an address space is usually very large and needs to be broken up into parts for the purpose of garbage collection. About four levels of virtual-to-physical address translation are required to map such a large address virtual address. The page table in main memory usually needs to be organized as a hash table, because a single process may use pages that are scattered throughout the virtual space (so a linear table might be

[2]Throughout this paper, unless otherwise stated we are concerned with the address spaces of the executing processes in the primary store and not the address space(s) in the secondary store or the persistent store.

very sparsely occupied). MONADS, and IBM's S/38 and AS/400 are examples of single paged address-space systems.

2.2. Address-Mapping Tiers

We define a *tier* of address mapping as a separate mapping that needs to be performed in order to translate one form of reference to another. Some tiers of mapping are one-way and some are two-way. For example, in some persistent object systems, it is necessary to map from a persistent name to a local address when the object is brought into a process's address space, and map from the local address to the persistent name when it is written out.[3] The mapping process begins with a program address and ends with a physical address. We use the term "tier" rather than "level," because each tier may consist of multiple levels of mapping. For example, the virtual-to-physical address mapping that is logically a single translation requires traversing multi-level tables if the address space is large.

2.2.1. Purposes of address-mapping tiers

Each mapping tier in an addressing scheme serves either to enhance efficiency or to provide one or more functionalities. Let us identify several functionalities.

(1) Providing virtual memory (VM). Virtual memory is usually incorporated in a computer system to increase the size of the address space size beyond the size of physical memory. But occasionally, the virtual address space is smaller than the amount physical address space (e.g., in several early microprocessors and at least one current system, the U. S. Navy's standard MTASS/M 16-bit computer [23]). In this case, the entire virtual address space can be mapped to different parts of physical memory at different times. Used in this way, virtual memory helps the hardware to address a larger physical memory. In any case, virtual memory provides flexibility of addressing by delinking the process's address space from the physical memory. Although virtual memory may require multilevel mapping tables, it still constitutes a single tier of mapping, because the translation takes place from one form of address to another, and there are no meaningful forms of addresses in between.

(2) Providing name-to-address mapping (NA). By mapping object names to object addresses, this tier provides *location independence* for object references. For example, the Smalltalk-80 bytecode interpreter [12] uses an object table to map object names (called "object pointers") to physical addresses. The location independence achieved through this tier can be used to relocate objects inexpensively, since the name-address mapping can be changed by simply rewriting an object-table entry, without the need to garbage-collect and modify pointers throughout the system. Some systems support persistence by giving unique systemwide names to objects. In such a system, this tier of mapping provides translation from systemwide names to some form of address.

(3) Linking address spaces to allow sharing (SH). As stated earlier, to share information, processes need to share parts of their address spaces. Hence a system with a single systemwide address space provides sharing naturally. But in systems where each process has its own address space, an additional tier of mapping is required to link disjoint address spaces to allow sharing. This is the function of mapping through linkage segments in Multics [17].

---

[3]The Persistent IDentifier to Local Address Map (PIDLAM) in CPOMS [Bro 89] is an example of a two-way map.

(4) Providing protection (PR). Capability-based systems that use tagged memory[4] inherently provide protection without a special tier of mapping, since a process can reference an object only if it holds a capability for the object. However, this is not true of access-list based protection mechanisms, which associate access-rights information with the objects themselves. Before an executing process can reference the object, its access rights must be checked. It would be impossibly inefficient to consult access-rights information in the object itself before every reference to the object (and it might also cause additional protection problems). Instead, the access-rights information must be prefetched and stored in some fast-access mapping table. Each reference to the object must be intercepted and checked against this mapping table to ensure protection. This is the function of the protection tier in access-list based protection systems such as Multics.

(5) Facilitating dynamic linking (DL). To link an object dynamically to an address space at execution time, information regarding the presence or absence of the object in the address space has to be available. Some sort of table is needed for this purpose. Entries are inserted in this table when an object (or segment) is linked dynamically during execution. Examples are Multics segment tables, the LOOM object table, and the PIDLAM in CPOMS. They will be discussed further in Section 3.

(6) Increasing efficiency (EF). Space and time efficiency concerns can motivate additional tiers of mapping. For efficiency's sake, systems like LOOM group small objects together into pages on secondary storage. When fetched, objects must be mapped into the virtual address space before being used. Different caching techniques such as loading addresses into registers to speed up computation also fall into this category. There is not room in this paper to explore the details of these schemes, but they are considered when directly related to functionality.

2.2.2.   Combining address-mapping tiers

Some mapping functions are performed early, before a program begins execution or a when another module is linked. Others may occur late, when a program refers to instructions or data.

No system that we are aware of performs more than two tiers of address mapping on each reference at execution time. However, they are not thereby limited to accomplishing two of the objectives on the list above, since some mapping can be done before execution time, and one tier of mapping can often perform more than one function from the list. A zero-tier system would be a system with no virtual memory and no distinction between name and address. It would be limited to the amount of physical memory and use absolute physical addresses for referencing objects. Single-tier systems can provide virtual memory as in SOAR, or they can provide name-address translation as in Smalltalk-80. Two-tiered mapping schemes that support object addressing usually use the first tier to map from an object name (often in a capability) to a virtual address, and the second tier to map from a virtual to a physical address. Both tiers need not be performed for each memory reference; virtual-address information can be cached, for example, in capability registers so that the object-to-virtual-address translation needs to be performed only rarely. Such caching is the key to building versatile and efficient systems.

2.2.3.   Implementation of tiers

The address mapping at each tier is in principle specified by some kind of mapping table, which may be monolithic or multilevel. Of course, it is not efficient to perform a table lookup before each memory reference, so some kind of optimization is always employed. These optimizations fall into two categories:

---

[4]Systems that protect capabilities from unauthorized modification by segregating them in special *capability segments* require an extra tier of mapping to get from a capability segment to its associated data segment. This can be considered an extra tier of mapping needed for protection.

- Programmable registers. The program is responsible for loading a mapping-table entry into a register. Each memory reference specifies a register to be used for mapping. When used in a VM tier, such a register is loaded with a segment-table entry, and is often called a *segment register*, as on the Intel 286 [16]. When used in an NA tier, such a register may hold a capability, in which case it is called a *capability register*, as in MONADS [10].

- Non-programmable caches. The program is written as if all references were translated via the mapping table, but a cache memory is provided to bypass the table for mappings that are in active use. A VM-tier cache is usually called a *translation lookaside buffer*, and is employed on many systems, including Multics, the VAX, and IBM's large systems. Such a cache can also be used in the NA tier, as is the Intel 432's *object-table cache* [6].

Programmable registers have certain advantages. Their hardware is less complex than a non-programmable cache, and they usually require less chip area. The compiler can take advantage of whatever knowledge it can glean about the program's future behavior to optimize register allocation. Ultimately, this optimization should be more successful than cache-replacement strategies, which can only rely upon the recent past as a predictor of the near future. However, optimization of register usage across procedure boundaries is still an active research area.

Non-programmable caches have their advantages too. They do not require the compiler to insert instructions to load the cache, nor must these extra instructions be executed at run time. Each cache entry can be tagged with the identity of the process that created it; this means that other processes can be prevented from using entries whose tags do not match without the need for explicit invalidation of cache entries at every context switch. Programmable registers, however, need to be explicitly saved and restored at a context switch. This increases the size of the process state and the time needed for a context switch. This cost could be circumvented if each process had its own private set of registers, but then the chip-area advantage of the register approach might no longer apply.

The number of mapping tiers does not depend on whether the system supports a single virtual address space or multiple virtual address spaces. Intuitively, this is true because the number of mapping functions an address is subjected to has nothing to do with whether other processes also use the same set of mapping tables. We have seen examples of sophisticated single virtual-address space schemes, and multiple address-space systems that are simple by comparison. However, the reverse can also be true: a primitive zero-tier system that has no protection and no base-register relocation supports a single address space, while a sophisticated virtual-memory system like Multics may support multiple address spaces. Thus, tiers of mapping are our second orthogonal dimension of address schemes.

2.3. Address-Mapping Instants

One form of address can be mapped to another form at various points in time. Apart from translation by the compiler or linker/loader, which we will not consider, there are at least three *instants* when mapping can occur: (i) at dynamic-link time, (ii) when loading a register for future use, and (iii) on each reference to memory. This paper is mainly concerned with mappings in category (iii), which have the largest performance impact.

The instant when an address mapping is performed is orthogonal to the number of address spaces in the system, and also to the number of mapping tiers in the system. In general, it is possible to perform any mapping at various instants. For example, consider the protection tier. If access to a directory hierarchy is required to check access rights, it is more efficient to check when a segment is first linked, and cache the information locally. Similarly, virtual-memory translation could in principle be performed at link time, if the linker could identify and translate all virtual addresses. For most systems,[5] this is not an attractive option because of the complexity and inefficiency it would entail. It is usually better to perform virtual-to-physical translation at the latest possible moment.

2.4. Implementation of the Access Matrix

There are two standard means of implementing an access matrix, capabilities and access-control lists [20]. With access-control lists, each object has an associated list of authorized users and their access rights. The access-control list keeps the access-rights information for the object in one place. This property of the access-control list renders it easier to alter or revoke access rights without raising integrity issues. A capability is a pair (*address*, *access-rights*), where the "address" is a special kind of pointer that can only be created by the system and that is needed to address an object. The validity of the access can be checked using the access-rights component of the pair. Capabilities, unlike access-control lists, reside with the accessing entities and may be scattered across the system, thus making it expensive to alter or revoke access rights.

Two important aspects of a protection scheme are (i) granularity of protected information, and (ii) number of protection domains per process. The goal of a fine-grained protection scheme should be to be able to protect each semantically distinct piece of information individually. In other words, each object should be given individual protection. Many computations need their access rights to change as the execution point passes from one module to another. The ability to have multiple domains within a process provides this flexibility. Capability-based systems provide fine-grained protection and multiple protection domains more elegantly than access-control-list-based systems, but capability systems require a more elaborate implementation.

Neither protection policy decisions nor their implementation is determined by the rest of the addressing scheme. The use of capabilities or access-control lists is quite independent of other aspects of address translation. Capabilities have been used on at least one system lacking virtual memory [21], and access-control lists have been used on sophisticated virtual-memory systems like Multics. Hence implementation of the access matrix is our final orthogonal dimension of addressing schemes.

3. Example Addressing Schemes

In this section we examine the addressing schemes of twelve systems. The systems are arranged into three categories: (i) early virtual-memory systems, (ii) non-persistent object systems and (iii) persistent object systems. The options chosen by each system's designers along the four orthogonal dimensions of addressing schemes are indicated. Different forms of references used by each system are identified. Functionalities provided by the systems are pointed out.

3.1. Early Virtual-Memory Systems

Three virtual-memory systems are discussed here. These are (i) the Burroughs B6700, (ii) BSD Unix, and (iii) Multics. The B6700 is a segmented virtual-memory system, BSD Unix is a paged virtual-memory system and Multics uses a combination of segmentation and paging.

B6700 Dimensions	
No. of Address Spaces	One per process
No. of Mapping Tiers	One (VM)
Mapping Instants	On each reference
Access-Matrix Impl.	Access-control lists for files; no protection in main memory.

B6700 Functionalities	
Virtual Memory	Yes, segmented
Sharing	Yes, restricted
Persistence	No
Protection	No, left to the compiler
Dynamic Linking	No

---

[5]Although this is what is done in LOOM (see Section 3.2).

The **B6700** system [18] has one address space per process.

It uses a segmented virtual memory. There are two forms of addresses in the B6700: (i) virtual addresses and (ii) physical addresses. Since a virtual address appears directly in executable code, program addresses are the same as virtual addresses. A single tier of mapping (VM) translates virtual addresses to physical addresses at execution time on each reference. A restricted form of sharing segments is permitted between children of the same parent process; descriptors for shared segments can be copied to different parts of the "cactus stack" shared by a tree of processes.

BSD Unix Dimensions	
No. of Address Spaces	One per process
No. of Mapping Tiers	Two (VM, SH)
Mapping Instants	• VM each reference,
	• SH while accessing shared segments
Access-Matrix Impl.	Access-control lists

BSD Unix Functionalities	
Virtual Memory	Yes, paged
Sharing	Yes
Persistence	No
Protection	Yes, Coarse-grained (pages), single domain per process
Dynamic Linking	No

Protection is entirely left to the compiler; there is no run-time mechanism to protect the address spaces of a process.

Persistence and dynamic linking are not supported by the B6700.

Each **BSD Unix** [1] process has its own address space.

On most platforms, BSD Unix provides paged virtual memory. There are three forms of addresses in BSD Unix: (i) virtual addresses, (ii) physical addresses, and (iii) names for shared global segments. One tier of mapping (VM) is used to translate virtual addresses to physical addresses. Sharing is supported by means of the named global segments. Accessing information in the global segments is obtained through system calls, which map segment names to the physical addresses of the segments (SH tier).

Each virtual address space is protected against others. Individual pages can be protected through the page table, but individual *objects* are not protected. Each process has a single domain of pro-

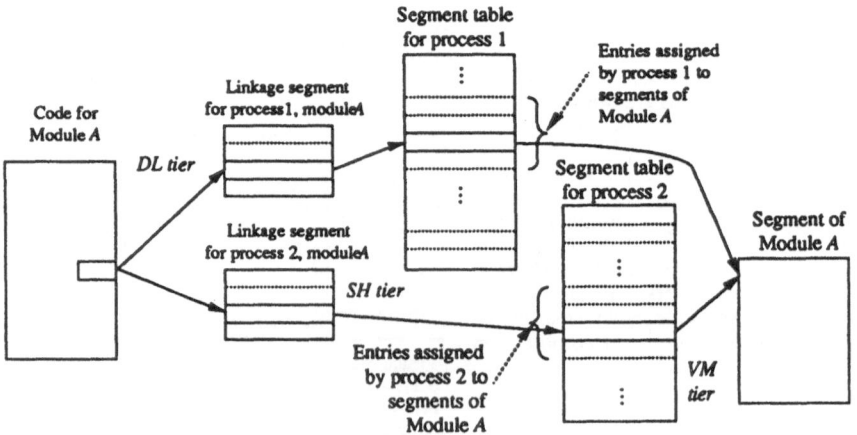

Figure 2: Address mapping in Multics

39

tection, except that a supervisor mode is used for system services.

BSD Unix does not provide persistence or dynamic linking.

In **Multics** [17] each process has its own address space.

A Multics process has a segmented virtual address space. This address space is described by the process's segment table. Multics segment tables facilitate dynamic linking (DL), hold access-rights (PR) for active segments, and also provide virtual memory (VM). Segments are paged, so the VM tier has two levels in Multics.

Since each process in Multics has its own virtual address space, a shared segment may occupy different virtual addresses in different processes. Linkage segments (SH) for each (*process, code segment*) combination are used to provide the necessary indirection for sharing, by allowing the same instruction to refer to different segment numbers in different processes (Figure 2). Multics, however, provides no linkage segments for data segments and hence sharing multi-segment data structures among different processes is impossible [8].

There are four forms of segment references in Multics: (i) segment names, (ii) linkage-segment indices, (iii) (process-dependent) segment numbers, and (iv) physical addresses (Figure 3). A (*segment number, offset*) pair functions as a virtual addresses. The mapping between segment names and linkage-segment indices (DL) is specified in the compiled code; these indices refer to linkage-segment entries that are created when dynamic linking takes place. The other two tiers of mapping—linkage-segment indices to segment numbers (SH), and segment numbers to physical addresses (VM, PR)—are performed at run time on each reference to a segment.

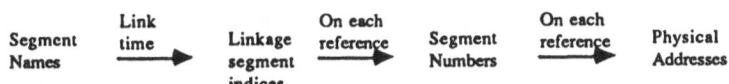

Figure 3: Multics mapping tiers and instants

The segment is the unit of protected information in Multics. Code and data units grouped in a Multics segment are semantically more closely related than those in a BSD Unix page. In this sense Multics (and also the B7600) provide finer-grained protection than BSD Unix, but not fine enough to protect each object[6] individually.

Multics also was the first system to provide multiple protection domains per process, which it did by implementing concentric rings of decreasing access privilege with a computation [19].

Multics also supports persistent segments through a single systemwide name space for segments. Persistent segments can be dynamically linked to a process's addresses space.

Multics Dimensions	
No. of Address Spaces	One per process
No. of Mapping Tiers	Three (DL, SH, VM-PR)
Mapping Instants	• DL performed at dynamic-linking time
	• SH and • VM-PR performed on each reference
Access-Matrix Impl.	Access-control list

Multics Functionalities	
Virtual Memory	Yes, segmented and paged
Sharing	Yes
Persistence	Yes
Protection	Yes, coarse-grained (segments), multiple domains per process
Dynamic Linking	Yes

---

[6]Segments are generally larger than objects. An object is semantically a single piece of information but a segment may consist of several weakly related data and code units.

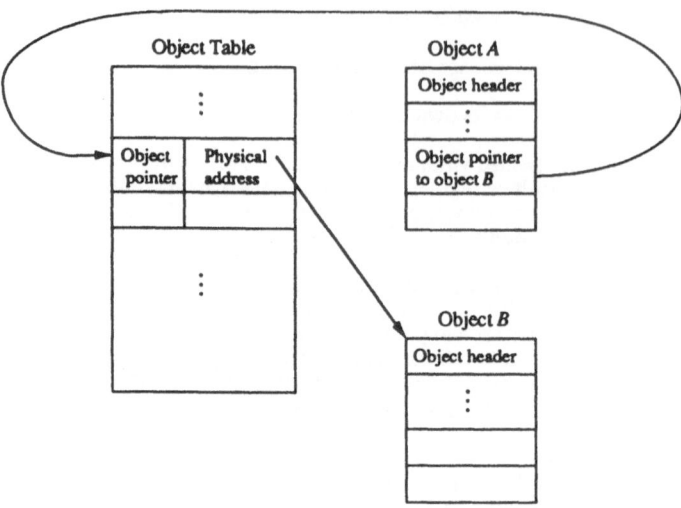

Figure 4: Object-pointer-to-physical-address translation in Smalltalk-80

3.2. Non-Persistent Object Systems

This section examines three non-persistent object systems: (i) Smalltalk-80, (ii) LOOM, and (iii) SOAR.

Smalltalk-80 is the best known object-oriented system [12]. It is a single-user, single-tasking system and does not attempt to provide sharing, persistence, or protection. The Smalltalk-80 bytecode interpreter uses two forms object references: (i) object pointers, which are basically names, and (ii) physical addresses. The tier of mapping between these two levels (Figure 4) provides name-address separation (NA) that helps in inexpensive relocation of objects and reference counting.

Smalltalk-80 uses 16-bit object pointers and supports only 2^{16} objects. LOOM was developed to extend the address space of Smalltalk-80 system to support 2^{32} objects on the same 16-bit narrow machine. To do this efficiently LOOM uses the same 16-bit object pointers to refer to the main memory resident objects, but uses 32-bit pointers to refer to objects in the secondary store. LOOM has three forms of object references: (i) 32-bit long object pointers, (ii) 16-bit short object pointers, and (iii) physical addresses (Figure 5). The tier of mapping from short pointers to physical addresses provides location independence (NA), and is performed at execution time on each reference. The tier of mapping from long pointers to short pointers provides both virtual memory (VM) and dynamic linking (DL). This tier of mapping is performed only when a leaf object (an object whose representation

Smalltalk-80 Dimensions	
No. of Address Spaces	Single address space (per active Smalltalk-80 system)
No. of Mapping Tiers	One (NA)
Mapping Instants	On each reference
Access-Matrix Impl.	Not implemented (a process can access all objects)

Smalltalk-80 Functionalities	
Virtual Memory	No
Sharing	Not applicable
Persistence	No
Protection	No
Dynamic Linking	No

41

is still in secondary store) is referenced. LOOM is a single-user system; it does not attempt to provide sharing, protection, or persistence. It does provide an extended address space, dynamic linking, and reference counting through location independence (the NA tier) in main memory.

SOAR (Smalltalk on a RISC) [22] is also a single-user single-tasking virtual-memory implementation of Smalltalk-80. SOAR has two forms of addresses, virtual addresses and physical addresses. Its single tier of mapping provides virtual memory. Since none of the reference forms are location independent, SOAR cannot use reference counting in an inexpensive way. Instead, SOAR uses garbage collection to reclaim free memory. SOAR does not attempt to provide sharing, protection, persistence, or dynamic linking.

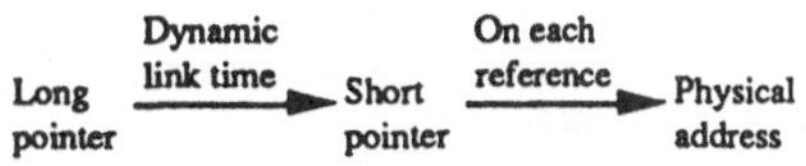

3.3. Persistent Object Systems

Six systems that support persistent objects are examined here. There is little difference between IBM's System/38 and AS/400 and hence these two systems are considered together.

IBM's **System/38** [7] and **AS/400** [9] are both single address-space, single name-space systems.

There are three forms of object references: (i) names, called *unresolved system pointers* , (ii) virtual addresses, called *resolved system pointers* and (iii) physical addresses. In the unresolved state, a system pointer specifies the name of an object and not its location. When the pointer is first referenced the machine determines the location of the object and the location, which is the virtual address, is stored in the pointer. The pointer is then said to be in the *resolved state* [4]. This process is function-

Figure 5: LOOM
address-mapping tiers and instants

LOOM Dimensions	
No. of Address Spaces	Not applicable
No. of Mapping Tiers	Two (NA, VM-DL)
Mapping Instants	• NA on each reference
	• VM-DL on object swapping
Access-Matrix Impl.	Not implemented

LOOM Functionalities	
Virtual Memory	Yes, contains variable-sized objects
Sharing	Not applicable
Persistence	No
Protection	No
Dynamic Linking	Yes

SOAR Dimensions	
No. of Address Spaces	Not applicable
No. of Mapping Tiers	One (VM)
Mapping Instants	On each reference
Access-Matrix Impl.	Not implemented

SOAR Functionalities	
Virtual Memory	Yes, paged
Sharing	Not applicable
Persistence	No
Protection	No
Dynamic Linking	No

ally equivalent to dynamic linking. In System/38, the virtual address is 48 bits long, while in the AS/400, it consists of 64 bits. The virtual address space is divided into segments which contain objects.

Virtual memory is implemented through paging. Resolved system pointers are mapped to physical addresses on each reference at execution time. Unresolved system pointers are converted to resolved system pointers through dynamic linking. Resolved system pointers function as capabilities and contain access-rights information. Both systems implement capability-based protection by tagging words of memory as capabilities or data.

Sharing and persistence are directly supported by both systems through their single address space and single name space, respectively.

The **Intel 432** (or iAPX 432) is a segmented single address-space system. It has three forms of references: (i) instruction data references (program addresses), (ii) access descriptors (or ADs, the Intel 432 word for "capabilities"), and (iii) physical addresses. There are three address-mapping tiers in the Intel 432.

The full addressing path of the Intel 432 is shown in Figure 6. In the Intel 432, a program address is called an *instruction data reference* [13]. An instruction data reference consists of two components, an *access descriptor* selector and a displacement. The AD selector refers to a capability in one of four *entry access segments* (EASs), which hold the ADs for all currently ad-

System/38, AS/400 Dimensions	
No. of Address Spaces	One per system
No. of Mapping Tiers	Two (VM-SH, NA-DL)
Mapping Instants	• VM-SH on each reference
	• NA-DL while resolving system pointers
Access-Matrix Impl.	Capabilities (protected by tagging)

System/38, AS/400 Functionalities	
Virtual Memory	Yes, paged
Sharing	Yes
Persistence	Yes
Protection	Yes, fine-grained (objects), multiple domains per process
Dynamic Linking	Yes

dressable objects. The object name in the capability is translated directly to a physical base address by a two-level *object table* (in the diagram, the first level is called the "object-table directory"). The displacement is then added to the base address.

Except for two complications, the preceding is a complete description of 432 addressing. The first complication is that an EAS is itself an object, and thus needs to be located via the two-level object table. The second is that an object must be made addressable before it can be accessed. This is done by making a segment that contains a capability for it be one of the EASs. The Enter Access Segment instruction accomplishes this by overwriting one of the four EAS pointers in the current procedure's activation record.

Altogether, there are three tiers of mapping, the first performed by the Enter Access Segment instruction, the second in mapping from an AD selector to a capability, and the third in mapping from a capability to a physical address. The first tier is an EF tier, since entry access segments could be eliminated altogether if each object reference named a particular slot in a capability list instead of an AD selector (but then each object reference would be much longer). The second tier permits an single instruction to refer to different objects at different times, since different ca-

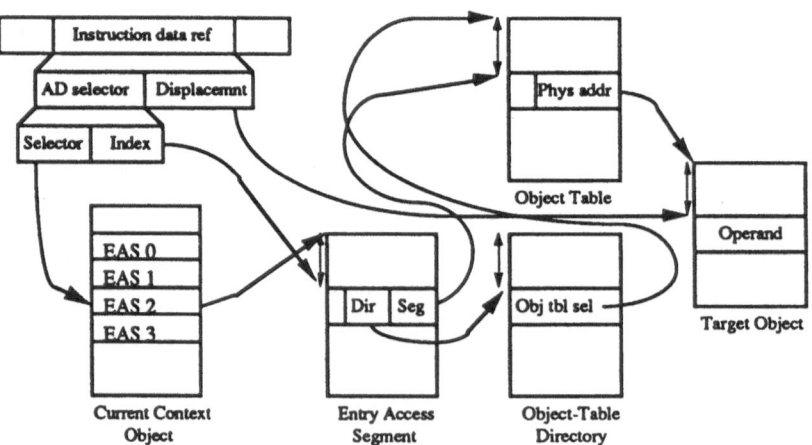

Figure 6: Intel 432 addressing path

pabilities can reside in the same capability slot at different times. This has much in common with dynamic linking, so let us call it a DL tier. The third tier clearly provides an NA mapping.

The access matrix is implemented through capabilities, which are protected by partitioning objects into two parts: one part contains the capabilities, and the other part holds ordinary data.

Sharing and persistence are naturally supported by the single systemwide address space of the Intel 432.

MONADS [14, 15] is a single-address space system. The MONADS virtual memory is paged. Each object, which is kept in a separate segment, is free to cross page boundaries.

MONADS has four forms of addresses (Figure 7). These are termed (i) program addresses, (ii) logical addresses, (iii) virtual addresses (called "effective addresses"), and (iv) physical addresses [10]. Virtual addresses and physical addresses refer to segments. Logical addresses refer to capabilities in the capability lists. Program addresses can refer to either. One type of program addresses refer to segments containing objects; they are (*capability register number*, *offset*) pairs. The other type of program addresses, which are basically the same as logical addresses, refer to the capabilities in the capability lists. These addresses appear in the operand fields of *Load Capability* instructions, which are used to load capabilities into capability registers from the capability lists. Capabilities, in turn, are basically virtual addresses of segments along with appropriate access rights.

Intel 432 Dimensions	
No. of Address Spaces	One per system
No. of Mapping Tiers	Three (EF, DL and NA)
Mapping Instants	• EF at run time, but not on each reference
	• DL and • NA on each reference.
Access-Matrix Impl.	Capabilities, kept in a protected part of each segment

Intel 432 Functionalities	
Virtual Memory	Yes, segmented object memory
Sharing	Yes
Persistence	Yes
Protection	Yes, fine-grained (objects), multiple domains per process
Dynamic Linking	Yes

The mapping from program addresses that reference segments to virtual addresses (PR), and the mapping from virtual addresses to physical addresses (VM, SH) are done at execution time on each reference. Capability registers are loaded with capabilities at run time, prior to referencing an object. This tier is used for reasons of efficiency (EF).

MONADS's single systemwide address space along with use of capability-based addressing provide persistence, sharing and protection.

CPOMS [3] is a persistent object management system that functions on top of an existing hardware. It has a single systemwide name space in its persistent store; the names are called Persistent IDentifiers (PIDs). CPOMS is used to enable the interpreter for the PS-algol language [5] to manipulate persistent objects. Each process has

MONADS Dimensions	
No. of Address Spaces	One per system
No. of Mapping Tiers	Three (EF, PR, VM-SH)
Mapping Instants	• EF while loading a capability register
	• PR and • VM-SH both on each reference
Access-Matrix Impl.	Capabilities, partitioned memory

MONADS Functionalities	
Virtual Memory	Yes, paged
Sharing	Yes
Persistence	Yes
Protection	Yes, fine-grained (objects), multiple domains per process
Dynamic Linking	Not necessary, everything is in the single large address space

program address → (On each reference) → virtual address → (On each reference) → physical address

Figure 7: MONADS mapping tiers and instants

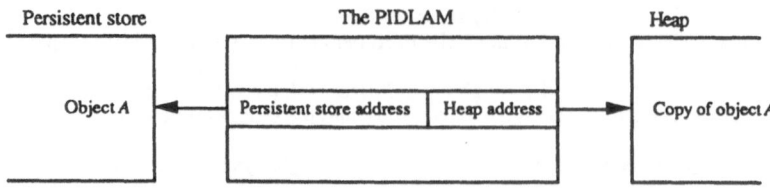

Figure 8: Function of the PIDLAM in CPOMS [3]

its own copy of the interpreter and CPOMS.

There are two separate address spaces in the system: (i) the persistent address space (for secondary store) and (ii) the heap address space (in the primary store). The PS-algol interpreter is responsible for translation between addresses in the persistent store and the addresses in the primary store. Mapping between persistent store addresses and heap addresses is performed through a map called the Persistent IDentifier to Local Address Map (PIDLAM), which is maintained by the interpreter (Figure 8). This mapping is performed on the first reference to an object's PID, at which time the object is swapped in to the heap in primary memory.

CPOMS provides persistence through its single name space (the PID space). Objects can be dynamically linked to a process's address space. Sharing in the primary store, protection, and virtual-memory functionality depend on the base system.

Name-Based Mapping (NBM) [11] is conceived of as a single-address space, single-name space system that provides sharing, protection, persistence and dynamic linking.

There are three forms of object references in the NBM scheme, (i) variable-size unique names (like segment names in Multics), (ii) fixed-size short names, and (iii) physical addresses. There are no virtual addresses. Systemwide unique names, also called long names, are directly mapped to short fixed-size names through hashing (VM-DL) on the first reference to a persistent object. An object table provides short-name-to-physical-address mapping (NA) as well as holding access rights for active objects (PR).

Short-name-to-physical-address mapping occurs on each reference. Long names are mapped to short names at dynamic-link time.

Protection is intended to be implemented through access-control lists. Each individ-

CPOMS Dimensions	
No. of Address Spaces	Depends on base machine. Persistent store has a single name-space
No. of Mapping Tiers	One for CPOMS (NA-DL) The rest depend on the base machine
Mapping Instants	On 1st reference to object
Access-Matrix Impl.	Depends on base machine

CPOMS Functionalities	
Virtual Memory	Depends on base machine
Sharing	Depends on base system
Persistence	Yes
Protection	Depends on base machine
Dynamic Linking	Yes

NBM Dimensions	
No. of Address Spaces	One per system
No. of Mapping Tiers	Two (NA-PR, VM-DL)
Mapping Instants	• NA-PR on each reference • VM-DL on dynamic linking
Access Matrix Impl.	Access-control lists

NBM Functionalities	
Virtual Memory	Yes, segmented object-memory
Sharing	Yes
Persistence	Yes
Protection	Yes, fine-grained (objects), multiple domains per process
Dynamic Linking	Yes

ual object is protected separately, and there are multiple domains per process.

NBM provides sharing and persistence through a single address space and single name space respectively.

4. Evaluation

The discussion of the previous section can be summarized by a table of where each example system falls into our classification scheme. This table can be seen below.

System	# of Addr. Spaces	Tiers	Functionalities
B6700	Multiple	1 VM	Virtual memory
BSD Unix	Multiple	2 SH, VM	Virtual memory Sharing Protection, coarse-grained
Multics	Multiple	3 DL, SH, VM-PR	Virtual memory Sharing Protection, coarse-grained Persistence Dynamic linking
Smalltalk-80	Not applicable	1 NA	None
LOOM	Not applicable	2 VM-DL, NA	Virtual memory Dynamic linking
SOAR	Not applicable	1 VM	Virtual memory
System/38 AS/400	Single	2 NA-DL, VM-SH	Virtual memory Sharing Persistence Protection, fine-grained Dynamic linking
Intel 432	Single	3 EF, DL, NA	Virtual memory Sharing Protection, fine-grained Persistence Dynamic linking
MONADS	Single	3 EF, PR, VM-SH	Virtual memory Sharing Protection, fine-grained Persistence (Dynamic linking not needed)
CPOMS	Depends on base system	1 DL	Persistence Dynamic linking
NBM	Single	2 VM-DL, NA-PR	Virtual memory Sharing Protection, fine-grained Persistence Dynamic linking

46

We have identified four orthogonal dimensions of addressing schemes: number of address spaces per system, address-mapping tiers, address-mapping instances, and implementation of the access matrix. All twelve addressing schemes that we have considered seem to fit easily into this framework. From the above table, it is clear that two tiers of execution-time mapping are sufficient to provide sharing, protection, and persistence.

A glance at the table reveals the benefits of having a single address space. Clearly, it facilitates sharing on an object-by-object basis (although an additional tier of mapping can serve the same function). A system that allows selective sharing can easily furnish protection for non-shared information. And a single address space is one of two mechanisms for supporting persistence (the other being a single systemwide name space). Further evaluation of existing single address-space systems is clearly warranted, as is research into their efficient implementation.

Acknowledgments

This research was supported by the Office of Naval Research under contract N00014-K-88-0037.

REFERENCES

1. Maurice J. Bach, *The Design of the Unix Operating System*, Prentice-Hall, 1986.
2. Brian N. Bershad, Edward T. Lazowska, and Henry M. Levy, "PRESTO: a system for object-oriented parallel programming," *Software—Practice and Experience*, 18:8, August 1988.
3. Alfred L. Brown, "Persistent Objet Stores," Persistent Programming Report 71, Universities of St. Andrews and Glasgow, Oct. 1989.
4. V. Berstis, C. D. Truxal, J. G. Ranweiler, "System/38 addressing and authorization," IBM System/38 Technical Developments, General Systems Div., International Business Machines Corporation, Pub. no. 0-933186-00-2, 1978, pp. 51–54.
5. W. P. Cockshott, M. P. Atkinson, K. J. Chisholm, P. J. Bailey, and R. Morrison, "Persistent object management system," *Software—Practice and Experience*, 14, 1983, pp. 49–71.
6. Robert P. Colwell, Edward F. Gehringer, E. Douglas, "Performance Effects of Architectural Complexity in the Intel 432," ACM Transactions on Computer Systems, Vol. 6, No. 3, August 1988, pp. 296-339.
7. R. E. French, R. W. Collins, L. W. Loen, "System/38 machine storage management," in *IBM System/38 Technical Developments*, General Systems Division, International Business Machines Corporation, Publication no. 0-933186-00-2, 1978, pp. 59–62.
8. R. S. Fabry, "Capability-based addressing," *Communications of the ACM*, 17:7, July 1974, pp. 403-412.
9. R. O. Fess, K. R. Reid, C. D. Truxal, R. J. Lindner, "AS/400 system overview," in *IBM Application System/400 Technology*, IBM Application Business Systems, Pub. no. SA21-9540-0, 1988, pp. 2–10.
10. Edward F. Gehringer, "MONADS: A Computer Architecture to Support Software Engineering," MONADS Report no. 13, Monash University, Clayton, Victoria, Australia, 1982.
11. Edward F. Gehringer, "Name-based Mapping: Addressing Support for Persistent Objects," *Proc. Third Workshop on Persistent Object Systems*, Newcastle, NSW, Australia, Jan. 10–13, 1989, pp. 139–157.
12. Adele Goldberg and David Robson, *Smalltalk-80: The Language and its Implementation*, Addison-Wesley, 1983.

13. Intel Corporation, "iAPX 432 General Data Processor Architecture Reference Manual, Preliminary Manual 171860-001, Intel Corporation, Santa Clara, CA, 1981.

14. J. Leslie Keedy, "An Implementation of Capabilities without a Central Mapping Table," *Proc. Seventeenth Annual Hawaii International Conference on Systems Sciences,* 1984.

15. J. Leslie Keedy, John Rosenberg, "Support for Objects in the MONADS Architecture," *Proc. Third Workshop on Persistent Object Systems*, Newcastle, NSW, Australia, January 10–13, 1989, pp. 202–213.

16. Borivoje Furht and Veljko Milutinovíc, "A survey of microprocessor architectures for memory management," *IEEE Computer*, 20:3, March 1987, pp. 48-67.

17. Elliott I. Organick, *The Multics Systems: An Examination of Its Structure*, MIT Press, Cambridge, Massachusetts, 1972.

18. Elliott I. Organick, *Computer System Organization: The B5700/B6700 Series*, Academic Press, 1973.

19. Jerome H. Saltzer, "Protection and the Control of Information Sharing in Multics," *Communications of the ACM*, 17:7, July 1974, pp. 388-402.

20. Jerome H. Saltzer and Michael D. Schroeder, "The protection of information in computer systems," *Proc. IEEE*, 63:9, September 1975, pp. 1278–1308.

21. Howard E. Sturgis, "A post-mortem for a time sharing system," Ph.D. thesis, U. of California, Berkeley, May 1973. Reprinted as CSL 74-1, Xerox Palo Alto Research Ctr.

22. A. Dain Samples, David Ungar, and Paul Hilfinger, "Soar: Smalltalk without Bytecodes," *OOPSLA '86 Proceedings* (ACM SIGPLAN Notices, 21:11, November 1986), pp. 107–118.

23. U. S. Navy, *User's Handbook for Navy Standard 16-Bit Computers, Support Software*, NAVSEA 0967-LP-598-2050, Volume V, Rev. B, Change 2, December 1984.

24. M. Young, A. Tevanian, R. Rashid, D. Golub, J. Eppinger, J. Chew, W. Bolosky, D. Black, R. Baron, "The duality of memory and communication in the implementation of a multiprocessor operating system," *Proc. Eleventh ACM Symposium on Operating Systems Principles(ACM Operating Systems Review*, 21:5), November 1987, pp. 63–76.

Protection in Persistent Object Systems

R. Morrison, A.L. Brown, R.C.H. Connor, Q.I. Cutts and G. Kirby
University of St Andrews

A. Dearle
University of Adelaide

J. Rosenberg
University of Newcastle

D. Stemple
University of Massachusetts

ABSTRACT

Persistent programming is concerned with the creation and manipulation of data with arbitrary lifetimes. This data is often valuable and therefore protected to ensure that it is free from misuse. The mechanisms used to protect the data vary with a tradeoff between static expression of the protection and the flexibility in modelling it. In this paper we explore the full range of protection mechanisms in persistent systems from static to dynamic checking and contrast it with the corresponding balance between safety and flexibility in the system. Protection by capabilities, dynamic universal union types, encapsulation, subtype inheritance, existential quantification and predicate defined invariants will be explored with reference to manipulating long lived data.

1. INTRODUCTION

Persistent object systems support large collections of data that have often been constructed incrementally by a community of users [3]. Such data is inherently valuable and requires protection from deliberate or accidental misuse. Protection is required to guard against system malfunction, such as hardware failure, to ensure that users do not misuse the common facilities such as the operating system and finally to protect users from other users and even themselves.

Before discussing methods of enforcement we will place protection in the context of the total system function. Protection mechanisms are concerned with conserving the integrity of data. There are two quite separate ways in which this integrity may be compromised. Firstly, some kinds of failure, which jeopardise this integrity, such as hardware malfunction, have little to do with protection and are best dealt with by other techniques such as incremental dumping or stability strategies [18, 26]. That is, periodically the data is copied to a secure device from which it may be retrieved if a failure occurs. Failures may, of course, occur in all the multiple copies of the data simultaneously leading to the conclusion that there is no absolute notion of data integrity. Protection mechanisms are built on the assumption that the underlying system does not fail. In the case of hardware error this assumption is incorrect. Fortunately an acceptable level of stability can usually be obtained for an acceptable price but the notion of absolute integrity no longer exists.

Given an acceptable level of stability, the integrity of the data can still be compromised by users. A number of mechanisms, such as capability systems, encryption methods, type systems and database integrity constraints have been used to add protection against data misuse in persistent systems. All of these mechanisms add security but at some cost and furthermore there is also a limit to the level of security that can be achieved. For example, once a program gains access to data it may alter it in a legal but undesirable manner. This can happen because the constraints placed on the user by the capability system, type system or integrity constraint system provide rather coarse grain control over the data. This coarse grain control trades expressiveness for security. The principle of minimum necessary privilege often causes the protection mechanism to be too fine grained to be enforced efficiently or even expressed succinctly. For example, the granularity of most type systems allows the user to restrict the use of a variable to a particular type such as integer. A finer grained system may allow the specification of types that only allow a subrange of the values such as 3..4 on Tuesday and Wednesday and 2..5 on other days. This is fine grained but neither succinct nor easily efficiently enforced.

Thus the second problem with integrity is that the checking system may allow the integrity of the data to be preserved but still contain information that is no longer of real use or is even erroneous. That is, even when enforced, the protection mechanism will not guarantee that programs produce desirable transformations on the data. For example, the age recorded for a particular person may be incorrect. The challenge is to find an acceptable level of security that can be obtained for a reasonable price in terms of efficient checking and succinct expression.

In protection mechanisms there is always a tension between the time of checking and the flexibility of the system. Checks that can be performed by static analysis allow the programmer to state or even prove some properties of the program before it runs. This increases confidence that the program is correct and explains the desire of most programming language designers to employ static type checking as one of the mechanisms for protection. The same desire has also led to capability systems that can be statically checked [19] and to proposals for the static checking of database integrity constraints [28] A second aspect of static checking is that programs so checked are usually more efficient. By performing the checking statically the need for dynamic checking is reduced making the program execute faster and in less space.

Taken to the extreme statically checked languages are not very interesting since they have a very limited ability to accommodate change. Flexibility is introduced by dynamic checking. Constraints placed on the data that depend on the evaluation of the program may only be checked in this manner. For example, the integrity constraints checked just prior to a transaction commit usually employ dynamic checks of this kind.

Another dimension of static versus dynamic checking is the ability of the system to support its own evolution safely. This property is sometimes called reflection [29] and on other occasions type magic [5]. In capability systems, which are usually the most dynamic, the type magic is the ability to issue and check the validity of capabilities. Capabilities are only issued by a trusted kernel and may not be manufactured by a user program. Compilers may generate representations of programs which when given a capability by the kernel become programs within the system. Since the security checking is always performed by the kernel, programs may be generated by many different compilers. Thus mixed language facilities are available up to the constraints imposed by the capability system. An example of such a system is given in [25].

As the checking is made more static the ability to mix languages is lessened. The magic in the system now lies with the type checkers which can only check languages with related type systems. The reflection in the system is also restricted by the type systems since only languages that adhere to the type system can be checked by the type checker. This is usually less general than a capability system. Example of systems displaying high level reflection at the type system level are [21, 24].

The semantics of failure is another dimension of protection that depends upon the time of checking. With dynamically checked systems an error such as an invalid capability or type error may be discovered at run time. An exception mechanism may be used to deal with such errors. In a statically checked system the errors are discovered at compile time and there is no notion of an exceptional event for these checks.

One final point is that the system security can be compromised if the type magic can be impersonated. This is often necessary for maintenance and repair of systems and again yields a weakness in the security system. It often depends on how difficult it is to break the password checking for initial access to the system.

We will now explore the full range of protection mechanisms in persistent systems from static to dynamic checking with the corresponding balance between safety and flexibility. Protection by capabilities, dynamic universal union types, encapsulation, subtype inheritance, existential quantification, and predicate defined invariants will be explored with reference to manipulating long-lived data.

2. CAPABILITIES AND TYPE SYSTEMS

Capabilities were first proposed by Dennis and Van Horn [13] as a technique for describing the semantics of controlled access to data. The idea was extended by Fabry who proposed a computer system based on capabilities [14]. There have been several attempts at constructing such a capability-based system. Some of these enlisted hardware support and others were purely software implementations. Although these systems differ greatly the fundamental principles of capability-based addressing are the same.

The basic idea is that access to objects is controlled by the ownership and presentation of capabilities. That is, in order for a program to access an object it must possess a capability for the object. In this sense capabilities may be viewed as keys which unlock the object to which they refer. Since the possession of a capability gives a right to access an object it is important that programs are not able to manufacture capabilities, since this would allow a program to access data which was not supposed to be available to it. Methods of protecting capabilities include segregation [30, 31], tagging [15, 23] and password schemes [2]. A capability for an object can thus only be obtained by creating a new object or by receiving a capability from another program.

Capabilities have three components. These are a unique name identifying the object, a set of access rights and some status information as shown in Figure 1. Capability systems use names for objects which are unique for the life of the system. The name given to an object will never be re-used, even if the object is deleted. This avoids aliasing problems and provides a means of trapping dangling references. Such unique names are not difficult to generate and addresses in the order of 64 bits are sufficient to ensure that the system will never exhaust all possible names.

Figure 1: A Capability Structure

Although the ownership of a capability guarantees the right to access the corresponding object, the access rights field may restrict the level of access allowed. The facilities provided by access rights vary greatly between different capability systems. They may be as simple as read, write and execute, or they may be based on the semantics of the different objects, for example a list of procedures for accessing an abstract data type. When a capability is presented in order to access an object, the system checks that the type of access does not exceed that specified in the capability. There is usually an operation which allows a new capability to be created from an existing one with a subset of the access rights allowing for the construction of restricted views.

The third field of a capability contains status information which indicate which operations can be performed on the capability itself. Again, these vary greatly. The minimum usually provided is a *no copy* bit which restricts the copying of the capability, perhaps on a user basis. This may be used to stop a user from passing a capability on to other users to limit propagation. Other status bits may include a *delete* bit which allows the holder of the capability to delete the object.

A final facility provided on some capability systems is the ability to revoke access. That is, after giving a program a capability it may be desirable at a later time to revoke this capability. Implementation of revocation may not be easy. The simplest technique is to change the unique name of the object which will effectively invalidate all existing capabilities. Selective revocation may be supported by using indirection through an owner controlled table of access rights or by providing multiple names for the object which can be individually invalidated.

Capabilities provide a uniform model for controlling access of data. However, entry to the system itself, by logging on, must in the end be based on some form of password. An advantage of capability-based systems is that, even if the password system is broken, there need not be any single password which provides access to all data of the system. That is, there need not be a superuser.

Capability systems employ dynamic checking and represent one end of our spectrum of checking times. Being dynamic they are expensive to implement since the check has to be performed every time the capability is used. For this reason hardware assistance is usually employed for efficient implementation. The expense of implementation partially explains why capabilities have commonly been used to control access to data via the addressing mechanism rather than to perform more elaborate dynamic type checking. Validating capabilities usually means comparing two addresses which is a cheap operation that may be implemented efficiently.

The dynamic nature of the checking means that a mechanism must be provided to allow recovery from checking failure. An exception handler is one such mechanism. This semantics of failure allows more flexibility in the system since capabilities can be revoked or altered dynamically without fear of violating the protection mechanism. Furthermore, a capability system is required to arbitrate among programs and data that mutually distrust one another. This distrust may change as the programs are evaluated and eventually wish to communicate. A capability system is able to deal with these changing needs.

Controlling access to objects in a capability system is achieved by limiting a program to a subset of the access rights of the object. Capabilities address objects with these access rights. An analogy has been made with abstract data types where the interface procedures define the access rights [19]. Limiting the interface procedures by a viewing mechanism or a subtyping mechanism allows the restrictions on access normally found in capability systems to be extended to type systems.

This analogy also allows an extension of more traditional capability systems. Checking for equality of capabilities depends upon the system being able to generate unique addresses for each different access type. This may require a large number of address bits. Alternatively the checker can employ a more elaborate check to decide the equality of two capabilities; this could be a full type check. The difference is similar to the difference between name and structural type equivalence in type systems.

Type systems themselves provide two facilities within programming systems. These are a modelling ability and a protection mechanism. Type systems may be dynamically checked but some systems employ static checking. In such systems there is no notion of type failure at run time and that the checking may be factored out at compile time.

It has long been realised that in supporting independently prepared program and data in a persistent store, some form of dynamic checking is required to perform the binding [4]. That is, where a program is to be bound to data expressed at run time, the system is required to support this dynamic bind. Part of this binding involves a check that the type is correct [22]. Thus some dynamic checking is performed and has many similarities to software capabilities.

It is interesting to speculate how and where dynamic checking of a capability system may be made static. It is also interesting to discover how and where statically typed persistent data requires dynamic binding. We explore both of these issues in the following sections.

3. DYNAMIC TYPE CHECKING

Capabilities may be implemented in software and even within type systems. The cost of software capability checking is high and therefore it is sensible to use it less often than where hardware checking would be used. Examples of software capabilities are dynamic integrity checks that occur just prior to a transaction commit and in the projections out of infinite union types found in some programming languages. In the first case the capability being checked is the capability to allow the transaction to proceed. This capability is very flexible and depends on the values within the database itself. In the second case, the system is checking that the user has the correct type with which to use an object.

The difficulty with capabilities described by dynamic types is that all computations in the system have to be couched in terms of the type algebra. This is usually where the ability for mixed languages is lost since the system can only describe computations in languages whose type systems are subsets of the overall one. Furthermore the type systems only provide controlled access to objects and not protection on how the capability is itself manipulated. There are usually no type system equivalent operations for *no copy*, *revoke* and *delete*. To implement such facilities another layer of abstraction must be placed on the capability leading to further inefficiency.

The difference between dynamically checked type systems and capabilities is in the algebra used to describe access in capability systems, and therefore the ability to manipulate the object, and the algebras over types. Capability descriptions are usually more flexible and extensible than type algebras although this need not be the case. As described above, the capability can be considered as the access route to an object and the view of the data accessible from that capability. To obtain two different types of access requires two different capabilities. This is also true in type systems with the difference being the mechanism used to construct the view.

Type **any** in the languages Amber [9] and Napier88 [21] is an infinite union type that can contain an object of any type. Type checking is performed on the type at the point of dynamic projection from the union. An object may be injected into type **any** where it is then compatible with any other object of type **any**. For specific use the object must be projected from type **any** onto its exact type. The following example shows how an integer with the operations read and write may have its access restricted to reading.

```
type intAccess is structure (read : proc (→ int) ; write : proc (int))
type intReadAccess is structure (read : proc (→ int))

let protectedInt := 0
let Read = proc (→ int) ; protectedInt
let Write = proc (x : int) ; protectedInt := x

let rwobject = intAccess (Read, Write)
let robject = intReadAccess (Read)

let readCapability = any (robject)
let readwriteCapability = any (rwobject)
```

Figure 2: Read and Read Write capabilities

In Figure 2, two structure types are declared. The first, *intAccess*, contains two fields containing the procedures, *read* and *write* and the second, *intReadAccess*, a procedure field called *read*. The declaration of *rwobject* initialises it to an instance of the type *intAccess* which contains the procedures *Read* and *Write*. These procedures manipulate the object *protectedInt* within their closures.

The object *robject* is initialised to a structure with the same read procedure as the other structure *rwobject*. The objects *robject* and *rwobject* have different types for static type checking. However, by injecting them into the infinite union **any** they now have the same universal type. Thus, *readCapability* and *readwriteCapability* can be passed around interchangeably. Just like proper capabilities they are not equal to one another. Notice that in the above example only the access mechanism is protected not the original data. This could be remedied by using a procedure with a password parameter to generate it as can be seen later. Figure 3 shows how the capabilities may be used.

```
let useobject =      proc (capability : any)
                project capability as X onto
                    intAccess           : ... ! code using read and write
                    intReadAccess       : ... ! code using read only
                default                 : ... ! code for some other activity

useobject (readCapability)
useobject (readwriteCapability)
```

Figure 3: Using Capabilities

In Figure 3, the procedure *useobject* takes an object called *capability* of type **any** as a parameter. The **project** clause allows the user to match the type against the real one. If a match is found then the original interface is exposed. No coercion or breaking of the type system is allowed, merely a dynamic check.

Such a type facility has many similarities to capabilities in that the objects of the universal union type can be used interchangeably, and expose only the correct interface to an object on projection. Original data can also be protected by password. More controversially the mechanism cannot be used directly to revoke an access right. The user of such a dynamic type must state statically the access they are to be allowed. If the dynamic test of these rights succeeds they are guaranteed for as long as the user expects to possess the object.

Infinite union types allow partial specification of the schema in persistent systems. That is, to use the persistent store the type must be described at least to the points where dynamic resolution will take place. Type **any** described above can be used for this and the facility allows incremental evolution of the system since the partial specification can always be extended by a new object of type **any** with a different real type. Where programs and data are prepared separately as in persistent systems there is a requirement to protect the dynamic binding of them. This involves dynamic protection of the kind described with type **any**.

One final variation on software capabilities is the module mechanism of the language Pebble [8] where the modules may be protected by a password. Access to a module depends upon calling it with the correct password which is similar to protection in most capability systems except that the passwords are explicit. Different access to the same object is achieved by using different passwords.

All of these methods of software capabilities simulate the access control aspects of capability systems. None of them controls the distribution of capabilities themselves. This has to be done by a separate mechanism.

Given the requirement for capabilities in persistent systems, even if implemented by software, we now turn our attention to what protection can be implemented statically.

4. STATICALLY CHECKED CAPABILITIES

Jones & Liskov [19] have proposed a system where the checking of access is performed statically. In this, each object has a type which determines the legal accesses to it. Variables are used to access objects and are declared to have a subset of the full access rights. Variables have qualified types which have two parts. A qualified type Q is written $T\{r_1,....r_n\}$, where T is some type name and $\{r_1,....r_n\}$ a subset of the access rights. The two parts of the qualified type are the base, where base (Q) = T and the access rights, where rights (Q) = $\{r_1,....r_n\}$.

The variables contain capabilities since each different variable potentially provides a different set of access rights. The problem now is to find a substitution rule where capabilities may be substituted for one another, that is assigned or passed as parameters, while conserving static checking.

The substitution,

$v \leftarrow e$

where v is a variable of type T_v and e is an expression of type T_e is valid if,

$Te \geq Tv$

Type T_e is greater than or equal to T_v if,

base (T_e) = base (T_v) and rights $(T_e) \geq (T_v)$

That is, a substitution is valid if the new access path provides at most a subset of the old rights. An example given by Liskov and Jones is the procedure heading,

procedure P (x : T1 {f,g}) **returns** T2 {k}

and the declarations,

a : T1 {f,g,h}
b : T2 {k}
c : T1 {f,h}

The statement b ← P(a) is legal and statically checkable since $T_x \leq T_a$ in the call and T_b is the same as the return type T2{k}. However b ← P(c) is not legal since $T_x \nleq T_c$. The reason for disallowing this is that the procedure may make use of the access right g specified in its interface and that it is not available from the calling parameter expression.

This notion of type is a simplified version of what has more recently become known as inclusion polymorphism [11] in that T_e is considered as a subtype of T_v for the binding to be valid. Apart from the inequality symbol being reversed the semantics are the same.

Jones and Liskov also found the semantic anomaly later described in [1, 10] for structured types containing references. Consider their example,

    procedure P (a : **array** [T {f}]{all} ; x : T {f})
    begin
        a [1] := x
    end ;

The array declaration specifies that the elements are restricted to T{f} and that all the operations on arrays are available. The procedure appears to be type correct since in the assignment the value x has the same type as the elements of the array, namely T{f}. However, consider the declarations,

    b : **array** [T{f,g}] {all}
    y : T {f}
    z : T {g}

and the call

    P (b,y)

This call also appears correct since $T_b \leq T_a$, since rights $(T_b) \geq$ rights (T_a), and $T_y \leq T_x$. The problem is with the assignment,

    z := b (1)

The value b (1) which is updated in the procedure to the value y has by this assignment the access right f only. The variable z has the access right g only. However the array has access rights f and g and the assignment should be legal since it would have been had it been performed before the procedure call. This anomaly is not statically checkable.

To overcome this anomaly and preserve static type checking Jones and Liskov propose *?types* which are now more commonly known as bounded universal quantifiers. The substitution rule for objects of this type is the same as proposed in Napier88 to overcome the same subtyping difficulty. That is, that two such types are only substitutable if they known to have exactly the same access rights. It should be noted that two types with different *?types* names but the same set of access rights cannot be guaranteed to have the exactly the same type.

For example the above would now be written as

```
procedure P [ t ≤ T {f}] (a : array [t] {all}; x : t)
begin
    a [1]:=(x)
end
```

The assignment is legal since the elements of a and x have the same type t. However the call

P (b,y)

is not legal since *t* would have to have rights {f,g} and {f} simultaneously. While either one is acceptable, both are not simultaneously. This rule also overcomes a simpler but similar semantic anomaly specified by Cardelli for inclusion polymorphism.

5.   INFORMATION HIDING

A higher level method of protecting data within software systems is the use of information hiding. This is defined as any programming method which limits the computation allowed by the type system upon data, by restricting either the access or type interface to it. It may also be possible to provide abstractions over the basic operations defined by the type system, including complex and dynamically evaluated constructs. Where such abstractions have type system support they are usually referred to as abstract data types. It is important to note that information hiding may only be relied on as a protection mechanism within the context of a strong type system, since if arbitrary address arithmetic is allowed data may always be accessed from outside the programmed interface.

Programming language type systems themselves operate by the use of information hiding over the operating system and hardware operations available to them. This abstraction is at a lower level, and is not necessarily available to the programmer. For example the integer type is defined in most type systems not as a mathematical integer but instead as a restricted interface over its hardware implementation. In strongly-typed languages the user is prevented from using operations such as rotate and xor on these values, and extra functionality such as conversion to and from equivalent character strings is also provided. Similarly, in a system which does not use hardware capabilities, it is only the use of information hiding which may prevent the use of arithmetic on address values.

There are three well-known mechanisms which allow the programming of information hiding within a strong type system. These are subtype inheritance, procedural encapsulation (1st-order information hiding) and existential data types (2nd-order information hiding). Subtype inheritance achieves protection by removing type information, causing the static failure of programs which may try to perform undesirable accesses. 1st-order information hiding prevents the protected data from being named by an untrusted program, allowing access only through a procedural interface. 2nd-order hiding is somewhere between these two, allowing access mainly through procedures, but also allowing the protected data to be named. This data is, however, viewed through a mechanism which causes type information loss, which allows only a limited set of operations to be performed on it. These mechanisms may also be used effectively in combination.

To avoid confusion, it should be mentioned that the terms first and second order information hiding are perhaps unfortunate. There is no implication that second order information hiding provides any greater protection than first order, but rather provides more controlled and flexible protection.

5.1 Subtype Inheritance

In general, systems which allow subtype inheritance allow any data object to be used in place of one with less functionality. One type is a subtype of another if it defines all, and perhaps some more, of its operations. In the most general form of subtyping, known as inclusion polymorphism, it is type correct for the use of any value to be replaced by the use of any of its subtypes.

Subtype inheritance is usually viewed as a general modelling technique. In particular it allows the declaration of procedures which operate over any type with at least a set of required properties. However, using an object as one of its supertypes is also equivalent to hiding some of the functionality which the object possesses. For example, the following introduces the names *employee* and *person* as record types:

type employee **is structure** (name,address : **string** ; salary : **int**)
type person **is structure** (name,address : **string**)

In the above, two structure types are declared. The first, called *employee*, has three fields called *name*, *address* and *salary* with types string, string and integer respectively. The second, called *person*, has two fields called *name* and *address* both of type string. Type *employee* is a subtype of type *person* using implicit structural equivalence and an object of type *employee* may be used in any context where an object of type *person* is expected. This would have the effect of hiding the salary field by the loss of type information. If another user is only to be allowed this restricted access to employee objects, this view of the object may be exported, for example by use of an explicit type coercion:

let joe = employee ("Joe Doe","1 Assignment Boulevard",100000)
let exportJoe : person = joe

In this *joe* is declared to be an object of type *employee* with the given field values. *exportJoe* is of type *person*, denoted by the type after the : symbol, but has the value *joe*. This means that a user of the value *exportJoe* will now have the value of the original record. However, it is not possible to express an operation to access the salary field of this value due to the restrictions of the static type system. That is, the *salary* field cannot be used with the object *exportJoe* since such a program would not type check, even although it would be able to execute without error.

This mechanism allows only simple information hiding compared with the other methods of 1st and 2nd order information hiding. Its advantages are that it is simple and elegant to use, and is easy to understand.

This inheritance is more flexible than the scheme described by Jones and Liskov, which defines essentially the same subtyping rule but allows it only for values of a particular type. In their scheme, an object is created with a finite set of operations of which restricted views may be passed around. In this scheme arbitrary types may be used, so long as they contain the common functionality.

5.2 1st-Order Information Hiding

Access to data can also be restricted by only allowing access to procedures which are defined over the data, and not allowing the data itself to be visible. This is a common model for abstract data types, and is known as 1st-order information hiding. It may be achieved in a number of ways but we will describe it in terms of a language which has first-class procedure values and block-style scoping. Access to the original data may then be removed simply by its name becoming unavailable. This allows a much more flexible interface to be constructed. For example, the following type defines a *Person* as a record containing procedures which define three operations:

type Person **is structure** (getName, getAddress : **proc** (→ **string**) ; putAddress : **proc** (**string**))

This allows a finer restriction than that above in that the name and address may be read, but only the address may be changed. Access to the data may be removed by placing its declaration in a block which is retracted immediately after the *Person* object has been constructed and exporting procedures with the data encapsulated within their closures, as shown in Figure 4. Again, this relies upon the static properties of the system to prevent the access since a program which attempts direct access to *joe* will fail statically.

```
let exportJoe =
begin
    let joe = employee ("Joe Doe","1 Assignment Boulevard",100000)
    Person (proc (→ string) ; joe (name),
            proc (→ string) ; joe (address),
            proc (new : string) ; joe (address) := new)
end
```

Figure 4: Hiding the Data Representation

In Figure 4, *exportJoe* is declared to have the value obtained by executing the block. This is a structure of type *Person* with three procedure fields. Each procedure uses the object *joe* which is inaccessible by any other means on exit from the block. Notice that a number of different interfaces may be programmed like this, and exported from the original data, rather than just a single one as here. This allows the construction of multiple views on the same data.

Further flexibility is possible using encapsulation in that dynamic properties may be specified, and access may be denied dynamically if required. For example, perhaps there exists an integrity constraint that an address may not be more than 100 characters long. This can be programmed in the procedural encapsulation, as shown in Figure 5. The only difference here is that the *putAddress* procedure checks the dynamic constraint, and raises an exception if it is not met.

```
let exportJoe =
begin
    let joe = employee ("Joe Doe","1 Assignment Boulevard",100000)
    Person (proc (→ string) ; joe (name),
            proc (→ string) ; joe (address),
            proc (new : string) ;
                if length (new) ≤ 100 then joe (address) := new
                                      else raise longAddress (new))
end
```

Figure 5: Refining the Interface

A particular example of a dynamic constraint allows access to the original data to be protected by password, or by a software capability. A procedure can be provided in the interface which will return the access to a user with sufficient privilege. To prevent unrequired noise in this example we will use subtyping as above for users who do not expect to require this privilege, allowing most users not to even be aware of its existence. Figure 6 shows the extended definition required, with an extra procedure in type *extraPerson* which returns the raw data only if it is supplied with a string equivalent to the password used to create it. Now whoever is responsible for the construction of the view will have enough information to extract the representation. Alternatively, it is possible to arrange system-wide capabilities which would decide whether access is allowed or not.

```
type extraPerson is structure (getEmployee          : proc (string → employee) ;
                                getName,
                                getAddress  : proc (→ string) ;
                                putAddress  : proc (string))

let exportJoe = proc (password : string → extraPerson)
begin
    let joe = employee ("Joe Doe","1 Assignment Boulevard",100000)
    extraPerson (proc (s : string → employee)
                        if s = password then joe else failValue,
             proc (→ string) ; joe (name),
             proc (→ string) ; joe (address),
             proc (new : string) ; joe (address) := new)
end
```

Figure 6: Protection by Password

Since *extraPerson* is a subtype of *Person* an object of this type may be used where an object of the supertype *Person* is specified.

5.3   2nd-order Information Hiding

2nd-order information hiding does not restrict access to the protected values, but instead abstracts over the type of the protected value to restrict operations allowed on it. Thus the protected values may be manipulated for some basic operations, such as assignment and perhaps equality, but their normal operations are not allowed due to the type view. This allows the representation objects themselves to be safely placed in the interface along with the procedures which manipulate them.

This power can almost be achieved using a combination of subtyping and 1st-order hiding. For example, Figure 7 shows how a reference to the representation may be safely placed in the interface by effectively removing all type information from it. The representation may be accessed as a value, but only a highly restrictive access is possible as there is very little type information available. It may be assigned and tested for equality, but none of its fields may be accessed due to the static typing restrictions.

```
type Person is structure (absPerson          : structure ();
                          getName,
                          getAddress : proc (→ string);
                          putAddress : proc ( string))

let exportJoe =
begin
    let joe = employee ("Joe Doe","1 Assignment Boulevard",100000)
    Person (joe,
            proc (→ string) ; joe (name),
            proc (→ string) ; joe (address),
            proc (new : string) ; joe (address) := new)
end
```

Figure 7: Removing the Type Information

In Figure 7, within the block *joe* is used to initialise one of the fields of type **structure** (). *joe* is of type *employee*, which is a subtype of **structure** () and the initialisation is legal. However, the fields of *joe* may not be accessed by this route.

Using this technique it is not possible to know that two such abstracted values are the same type, which may be desirable for some applications. For example, a *Person* may also have a father and mother in the interface, along with a field for a favourite parent which changes between them. This technique does not provide enough information to allow this. For example, if the definition is:

> **type** Person **is structure** (absPerson,mum,dad,favourite : **structure** () ;
> getName,getAddress : **proc** ($\rightarrow$ **string**) ;
> putAddress : **proc** (**string**))

then it is not in general allowable to write

> exportJoe (favourite) := exportJoe (mum)

as there is no way of telling that *mum* and *favourite* are indeed the same type.

A mechanism which allows 2nd-order information hiding is the existential data type described by Mitchell & Plotkin [20]. This allows the definition of interface types which are abstracted over. As names for these types are declared before the existential type definition, different parts of the definition may be bound to the same type. As before, only the basic operations defined on all types are allowed over these, but values which are abstracted by the same name are statically known to be compatible. *Person* as above may be redefined as:

> **type** Person **is existentialType** [absPersonType] (
> absPerson,mum,dad,favourite : absPersonType ;
> getName,getAddress : **proc** ($\rightarrow$ **string**) ;
> putAddress : **proc** (**string**))

The name in square brackets before the body of the type declaration declares a name for a type which is abstracted over. This allows a tighter definition of such types, as it can now be seen where the same type appears in the interface. For example,

> exportJoe (favourite) := exportJoe (mum)

may now be statically determined to be type correct, as the *favourite* and *mum* fields must be type compatible to allow the object to be created.

This static binding of equivalent types may also be used to allow the interface procedures to be defined over the type of the hidden representation. A more flexible definition which allows the name and address operations to be performed on any of the people in the interface would be:

> **type** Person **is existentialType** [absPersonType] (
> absPerson,mum,dad,favourite : absPersonType ;
> getName,getAddress : **proc** (absPersonType $\rightarrow$ **string**) ;
> putAddress : **proc** (absPersonType,**string**))

This allows the definition of n-ary operations over the hidden representation type. For example, a procedure may be placed in the interface which tests if two people have the same address:

```
type Person is existentialType [ absPersonType ] (
    absPerson,mum,dad,favourite   : absPersonType ;
    getName,getAddress            : proc (absPersonType → string) ;
    putAddress                    : proc (absPersonType,string) ;
    sameAddress                   : proc (absPersonType,absPersonType → bool))
```

This example illustrates a major difference in power between 1st-order and 2nd-order information hiding. With 2nd-order, a type is abstracted over, and procedures may be defined over this type. With 1st-order hiding, it is the object itself which is hidden within its procedural interface. Procedures which operate over more than one such object may not be defined sensibly within this interface. Therefore any operations defined over two instances must be written at a higher level, using the interface. At best this creates syntactic noise and is inefficient at execution time. It also means that such operations are defined in the module which uses the abstract objects, rather than the module which creates them. Some examples are not possible to write without changing the original interface. The power of such existential types is discussed fully in [12].

6. DATABASE CONSTRAINTS

Capabilities and type-oriented protection are mechanisms based on interfaces, signatures, or access rights to objects. Another approach to protection is based on predicates stating invariants that must hold over changes to persistent objects. The simplest example of this is probably the sub-range types from most programming languages, e.g. ADA's subtypes with range constraints. Such types lead to notoriously difficult type-checking problems, which are normally resolved by dynamic checking. In databases, such protection is the domain of integrity constraint maintenance and can involve both static and dynamic checking.

The basic idea is quite simple: any type can be refined by adding a predicate on values of the type; only values obeying the predicate are in the new subtype. In databases, functional dependencies and referential integrity can be expressed in this way. A functional dependency is a predicate added to a relational type. Referential integrity is captured as a predicate stating that a column of one relation (a "foreign key" column) is contained in a key column of another (or the same) relation. This predicate, like other interrelational constraints, must be added to the database type itself. The problem is that non-trivial theorem proving is now required as part of static type-checking in order to avoid very expensive dynamic checks, and for quite simple predicate and manipulation languages static type-checking is either computationally intractable or undecidable. One response to this difficulty is to limit the constraint and manipulation languages as well as raising their level of abstraction. With limited languages some effective theorems can be used to design procedures for checking computations and generating optimized run-time checks [6, 7, 16, 19, 28]. Redundant data and special run-time integrity subsystems can be used to speed up checking. Most approaches in the literature work independently of a type system.

It is possible to integrate a theorem prover into the type checker in order to maximize the amount of static type checking achievable in the presence of predicates. The setting in which this appears to be feasible consists of high level languages limited in expressiveness and with the same formal base for the predicate and update languages. It is also possible that static predicative type checking will only be effective with small programs such as typical teleprocessing database transactions.

One benefit of a theorem prover embedded in a type checker is that a broader range of conditions could be used in specifying bounded universal quantification. Normally the conditions on the instantiating types of bounded universally quantified types only specify the existence of operators. This is easy to check. If a theorem prover is available, further predicates on the operators can be added. These conditions need to be proved from the properties of any instantiating type. This can be expensive and even incomplete, though it typically needs to be done in response to a compile-time resolvable declaration, not a run-time action.

Significant effort has gone into building an efficient, though necessarily incomplete, type checker for the set-oriented database programming (or specification) language ADABTPL [28]. Efficient proofs of integrity constraint maintenance have been achieved in ADABTPL by limiting the set of constraints and update primitives and by building a set of generic theorems about the interaction of the primitives.

Many of the ADABTPL theorems are higher order theorems, and engineering effective ways to use them is crucial to achieving efficiency. It is quite difficult to characterize the limits of the current ADABTPL techniques. It is, in effect, an expert system with heuristics coded in Lisp and rules that are all proved theorems. It can be improved by adding to its heuristics or to its theorems. The incompleteness of the reasoning is one of the aspects that is most troubling about this approach. Failing to prove that predicates are not maintained is ambiguous in this setting. It means either that the program can produce invalid data or it is too difficult to prove that it obeys the predicates.

There are several responses to a failed proof. The first is to add the unproved residue of the theorem to the transaction as a precondition. In many cases this is the proper response, indicating that the designer forgot the precondition. In other cases, the residue indicates that certain updates were left out. A simple case illustrates this. Suppose a database includes employees and dependents, and each dependent is constrained to relate to an employee. If we attempt to prove that a transaction consisting solely of a delete of an employee preserves the constraint, then an unprovable residue will be left at the end of the unsuccessful try. The residue will be the predicate stating that there are no dependents related to the employee being deleted. This predicate could be added as a precondition of the transaction, indicating that the transaction was only intended for use in deleting employees with no dependents. However, it may be the case that the designer forgot to include the deletion of the dependents in the transaction. In this case, the transaction is rewritten to include the deletions and the proof is attempted on the new transaction.

Because of the incompleteness of non-trivial, efficient theorem proving, the residue may in fact be true in all valid databases, but unprovable by the static checker. There are three ways of handling this case open to a designer.

- Allow the check to be made anyway, since the informal proof that convinced the designer that the residue was a theorem may be faulty.

- Simplify the transaction or integrity constraints specification without changing their meaning or change the transaction or constraints if consideration of the precondition reveals that they did not have the intended semantics and retry the proof.

- Tell the system that the check need not be made, thus overriding the checking in this case.

A description of the kind of theorem proving that is needed in assuring the maintenance of predicate-based integrity will clarify some of its limits and costs. The following theorem is the kind that needs to be proved to show that a transaction T leaves a database in a consistent state if it was consistent before the transaction. IC is the single predicate collecting all the different predicates constituting the specification of database integrity. I stands for the input to the transaction. (The input needs to be checked to see that it obeys its type constraints. This is a dynamic check, of course.)

$$IC(DB) \rightarrow IC(T(DB,I))$$

A form of theorem that is quite useful in proving such theorems is the following:

$$CONSTR(UPDATE(D)) = SIMPLER(D) \ \& \ CONSTR(D)$$

The idea behind this form is that the integrity of an updated database will be expressed in terms of constraint predicates (CONSTR) on updated data elements (D), the lefthand side of the equation. The righthand side form, which will replace expressions like the lefthand side during a proof, is a good form since the latter part (CONSTR(D)) will occur in the antecedent of the theorem, expressing the assumption that the database is initially consistent. This allows CONSTR(D) to be removed immediately from the proof obligation. Thus we are left with SIMPLER(D) where CONSTR(UPDATE(D)) appears in the theorem. An example will make this clear.

A theorem (assuming i is not in R) that is useful in maintaining a key constraint on a relation is:

$$key(insert(i,R),K) = i.K \notin project(R,K) \ \& \ key(R,K)$$

This states that the condition of a column K being a key of a relation R after a new tuple i has been inserted is equal to the K component of the new tuple not being in the K projection of R and R being keyed on K. This is useful in proving that a particular insert does not violate the key constraint. Since the second term in the righthand side is assumed to be true, the proof of the key property in the updated relation has been reduced to a check for non-membership in a projection. Further proving may verify that the insert only occurs in a position in which the non-membership is assured, in which case this part of the overall theorem has been proven. If the non-membership cannot be proven, it can be added to the transaction as a dynamic check. This case is quite simple but indicates the basic approach to using theorem proving to assure that predicates are invariants of transactions.

There are two further points to be made. The first is that the SIMPLER predicate should be better than the constraint on the updated data in some sense, either by having less computational complexity or in facilitating further reduction, in order for this approach to be effective. The second point is that a uniform formal base and limitations on the integrity constraints and update functions are probably necessary in order to build a set of effective theorems (and heuristics) for this application of theorem proving. This approach embodies both static checking, in the form of the theorem proving, and dynamic checking, in the form of the reduced integrity constraints executed at run-time. Other than the cost of the theorem proving, which in ADABTPL currently runs to less than half a minute for six hundred term theorems on modern workstations, and the cost of the run-time checks, this approach requires building effective theorem bases for different styles of databases, limiting language expressiveness, and formalizing constraint and update languages in a uniform manner.

7. CONCLUSIONS

We have presented a number of mechanisms that are used to preserve the integrity of data in persistent systems. In statically checked systems, these mechanisms range from the integrity constraints of the language ADATPBL, through the statically enforced existentially quantified types of Napier88, encapsulation by scoping, subtype inheritance and the software capabilities of Jones & Liskov. In dynamically checked systems, the universal union type **any** of Amber and Napier88 may be used as software capabilities as may dynamically checked database integrity constraints.

A major goal in system design is the ability to describe the properties of a system without having to execute it. However, as we have seen, this ability conflicts with the flexibility of dynamic checking. At any level of abstraction, the requirement is for static checking that is commensurate with the expressiveness needed for a particular application.

Not all constraints on data may be captured statically. Employing a theorem prover allows more powerful static checking but it may not be possible to prove all the theorems. This could be because they are in error or because the theorem prover is not sophisticated enough computationally to prove them in a reasonable time. A solution is to provide a more dynamic check where this occurs in a system.

A strategy, similar to the ones found in the ADAPTBL and DIADA [27] projects, may be developed where all the constraints on data are specified in the one language. A theorem prover is then employed to capture as many of these constraints as it can statically. Where it cannot, a second, but less expensive in terms on technology, level of checking may be provided by a type system. Where the type system cannot enforce the constraint statically, a dynamic check is produced. This check may be enforced by hardware or software.

ACKNOWLEDGEMENTS

This work was undertaken at St.Andrews University during the study leave period of Prof. J. Rosenberg of the University of Newcastle, New South Wales. The work was supported by SERC Grant GR/F 28571, SERC Post-doctoral Fellowship B/ITF/199, ESPRIT II Basic Research Action 3070 - FIDE, a grant from the DTI and a visit to St Andrews by David Stemple.

REFERENCES

1.   Albano, A., Ghelli, G. & Orsini, R. "Types for Databases: The Galileo Experience." *Proc. 2nd International Workshop on Database Programming Languages*, Oregon, June 1989, pp 196-206.

2.   Anderson, M., Pose, R.D. & Wallace, C.S. "A Password-Capability System." *The Computer Journal*, 29, 1, 1986, pp. 1-8.

3.   Atkinson, M.P., Bailey, P.J., Chisholm, K.J., Cockshott, W.P. & Morrison, R. "An Approach to Persistent Programming." *The Computer Journal*, 26,4, November 1983, pp. 360-365.

4.   Atkinson, M.P., Buneman, O.P. & Morrison, R. "Binding and Type Checking in Database Programming Languages." *The Computer Journal*, 31,2, 1988, pp. 99-109.

5.   Atkinson, M.P. & Morrison, R. "Polymorphic Names, Types, Constancy and Magic in a Type Secure Persistent Object Store." *2nd International Workshop on Persistent Object Systems*, Appin, August 1987, pp. 1-12.

6.   Bernstein, P. A. & Blaustein, B. T. "A Simplification Algorithm for Integrity Assertions and Concrete Views." *Proc. of the Fifth International Computer Software and Applications Conference*, 1981, pp. 90-99.

7.   Bernstein, P. A., Blaustein, B. T, & Clarke, E. M. "Fast Maintenance of Semantic Assertions Using Redundant Aggregate Data." *Proc. of the Sixth International Conference on Very Large Databases*, 1980, pp. 126-136.

65

8. Burstall, R. & Lampson, B. "A Kernel Language for Abstract Data Types and Modules." *Proc. international symposium on the semantics of data types*, Sophia-Antipolis, France, 1984. In *Lecture Notes in Computer Science*, 173. Springer-Verlag, 1984.

9. Cardelli. L. "Amber." Tech. Report AT&T. Bell Labs. Murray Hill, U.S.A., 1985.

10. Cardelli, L. "Typeful Programming." *DEC SRC Report*, May 1989.

11. Cardelli, L. & Wegner, P. "On Understanding Types, Data Abstraction and Polymorphism." *ACM Computing Surveys*, 17,4, December 1985, pp. 471-523.

12. Connor, R.C.H., Dearle, A., Morrison, R. & Brown, A.L. "Existentially Quantified Types as a Database Viewing Mechanism." *Advances in Database Technology - EDBT90*, Venice. In *Lecture Notes in Computer Science*, 416. Springer-Verlag, 1990, pp. 301-315.

13. Dennis, J.B. & Van Horn, E.C. "Programming Semantics for Multiprogrammed Computations." *Comm. ACM*, 9, 3, 1966, pp 143-145.

14. Fabry, R.S. "Capability Based Addressing." *Comm.ACM*, 17,7, 1974, pp. 403-412.

15. Feustal, E.A. "On the Advantages of Tagged Architecture." *IEEE Transactions on Computers*, C-22, 7, July 1973, pp. 644-656.

16. Hsu, T. & Imielinski, T. "Integrity Checking for Multiple Updates." *Proc. of the ACM-SIGMOD International Conference on Management of Data*, 1985, pp. 152-168.

19. Jones, A.K. & Liskov, B. "A language extension for expressing constraints on data access." *Comm.ACM*, 21, 5, 1978, pp. 358-367.

18. Lorie, R.A. "Physical Integrity in a Large Segmented Database." *ACM Transactions on Database Systems*, 2, 1, March 1977, pp. 91-104.

19. McCune, W. & Henschen, L. "Maintaining State Constraints in Relational Databases." *Journal of the ACM*, 36, 1, January 1989, pp. 46-68.

20. Mitchell J.C. & Plotkin G.D. "Abstract Types have Existential type." *ACM Transactions on Programming Languages and Systems*, 10,3, July 1988, pp. 470-502.

21. Morrison, R., Brown, A.L., Connor, R.C.H. & Dearle, A. "Napier88 Reference Manual." Persistent Programming Research Report PPRR-77-89, Universities of Glasgow and St Andrews, 1989.

22. Morrison, R., Brown, A.L., Dearle, A. & Atkinson, M.P. "Flexible Incremental Binding in a Persistent Object Store." *ACM Sigplan Notices*, 23, 4, April 1988, pp. 27-34.

23. Myers, G.J. & Buckingham, B.R.S. "A Hardware Implementation of Capability-Based Addressing." *Operating Systems Review*, 14, 4, 1980.

24. "The PS-algol Reference Manual fourth edition." Persistent Programming Research Report PPRR-12-87, Universities of Glasgow and St.Andrews, 1987.

25. Rosenberg, J. & Abramson, D.A. "A Capability-Based Workstation to Support Software Engineering." *Proceedings of 18th Annual Hawaii International Conference on System Sciences*, 1985, pp. 222-230.

26. Rosneberg, J., Henskens, F.A., Brown, A.L. & Morrison, R. "Stabilitity in a Persistent Store based on Large Virtual Memory." *Proc of the International Workshop on Security and Persistence of Information*, Bremen, West Germany, May 1990.

27. Schmidt, J.W., Wetzel, I., Borgida, A. & Mylopoulos, J. "Database Programming by Formal Refinement of Conceptual Design." *IEEE - Data Engineering*, September 1989.

28. Sheard, T. & Stemple, D. "Automatic Verification of Database Transaction Safety." *ACM Transactions on Database Systems,* 12, 3, September, 1989, pp. 322-368.

29. Stemple, D., Fegaras, L., Sheard, T. & Socorro, A. "Exceeding the Limits of Polymorphism in Database Programming Languages." *Advances in Database Technology - EDBT90,* Venice. In *Lecture Notes in Computer Science*, 416. Springer-Verlag, 1990, pp. 269-285.

30. Wilkes, M.V. & Needham, R.M. *The Cambridge CAP Computer and its Operating System.* Elsevier North Holland, Inc., 1979.

31. Wulf, W.A., Levin, R. & Harbison, S.P. *HYDRA/C.mmp: An Experimental Computer System.* McGraw-Hill, New York, 1981.

A Model for Protection in Persistent Object-Oriented Systems

M. Evered and J.L.Keedy

University of Bremen

ABSTRACT

Lampson's protection matrix provides a simple model for defining how subjects can access objects in a system. In real systems protection requirements can often be expressed in terms not easily captured by this simple view of subjects and objects. The paper considers how a system can be viewed as a collection of objects of particular classes and types and with particular compositions. In order to express the variety of possible protection conditions relevant to such a system we propose a new general protection model based on access rules and show how this can be applied to object-oriented systems. We then propose two orthogonal ways of classifying protection requirements. Protection mechanisms are then classified into 3 levels (architectural, language and programmed) and related back to the classification of requirements. Finally we present the MONADS protection mechanisms as an example of an efficient implementation for access rules, showing how a security policy might in practice be implemented to fulfil protection requirements expressed in terms of the model.

1. INTRODUCTION

The protection of private information and of proprietary programs is an extremely important goal in the design of computer systems. Failure to achieve this goal adequately can have serious consequences, ranging for example from very severe threats to national security [17] to the financial downfall of a major software house. Yet in the great majority of computer systems this goal is rarely achieved adequately. By and large protection in computer systems consists of collections of ad hoc mechanisms which are individually incomplete and collectively inadequate.

The range of different protection mechanisms which often exists in a single computer system clearly indicates that system designers have not drawn upon a conceptually clear and simple abstract model of protection. Yet it is almost twenty years since Lampson proposed his simple and elegant matrix model [13], which provides a conceptually clear basis for understanding, for example, the relationship between capability lists and access control lists.

Despite its elegance Lampson's model leaves open some issues which can be fruitfully considered in the light of more recent trends in software and computer architecture design. In particular object-oriented programming techniques reinforce the idea that protection should be formulated in terms of interactions between objects (which was of course inherent in Lampson's model) and raise the question whether this can be a departure point for further insights about protection, for example with respect to the concept of inheritance. Similarly persistent programming, with the implicit tendency of many of its advocates to prefer monolingual systems, raises questions about the role of types as a protection mechanism.

Another important issue which is not addressed by Lampson's model is the ability to confine a called object in such a way that it cannot pass on information about another object to which it is given temporary access, e.g. in order to perform a service such as printing or editing, in an unauthorised way or retain an unauthorised copy of such an object or the access rights to it.

In this paper we explore such issues further, taking as our starting point the idea that a computer system can be viewed as a collection of interacting objects, and we assume that the goal of a protection system is to ensure that only acceptable interactions should be permitted to proceed. We start by explaining what we mean by the concepts of object and of interacting objects. We then consider what kinds of interactions between objects can be regarded as acceptable and propose a model general enough to express these requirements.

2. VIEWING A SYSTEM AS A COLLECTION OF OBJECTS

The object-oriented programming paradigm has emphasised, rightly in our view, the idea of viewing a system as a collection of interacting objects. However, there is no standard accepted definition of "objects". Therefore we consider this question further in the present section in order to avoid misunderstandings later in the paper.

2.1. Objects, Classes and Types

We assume that each object in a system belongs to a "class" of objects such that all the objects of a class can be characterised by the same abstract *user specification*, i.e. a specification defining its properties for potential users. We further assume, following the information-hiding principle and the notion of abstract data types, that such a user specification can be expressed entirely in operational terms, whereby we distinguish two main categories of operations: *procedures* and *enquiries*. A procedure changes the state of an object, whereas an enquiry simply returns information about the state without changing it. We consider enquiries to be confined, because they may not change the internal state of an object (and therefore cannot store unauthorised information in it) and may only call the enquiries of other objects. Procedures, on the other hand, can be defined as either unconfined or confined. A confined procedure, like an enquiry, may not change the internal state of an object; it may only call confined procedures and enquiries of other objects except the procedures of objects for which its confining caller has given authority for it to call unconfined procedures.

Individual objects which meet the same user specification are regarded as *instances* of the class defined by the specification.

There are usually many different ways of meeting a user specification. In engineering environments *product specifications* are therefore used as a means of defining the properties of particular implementations. We refer to different implementation techniques as "types" and to different objects which share the same implementation mechanism as *instances* of the type. The implementation mechanisms themselves we call *type managers*. If two type managers conform to the same user specification then the objects which they produce are instances of the same class but not necessarily of the same type.

To understand this difference we might think of the abstract class of integers, which may have different implementation possibilities (e.g. the type "ones complement" and the type "twos complement"). Similarly we may think of a file class with operations for opening, closing, reading, writing, etc. with alternative implementations (e.g. B-tree and indexed sequential). As a third example we may have a class "stack" defined in terms of push, pop and top operations but with alternative implementations as an array and as a linked list. It is clear from these examples that the instances of a class may be functionally equivalent, but only when used with the correct type manager, i.e. type managers are not interchangeable.

It should be noted that the above definitions of "class" and of "type" are not identical to those found elsewhere in programming terminology, where the two concepts are often used synonymously. One reason for this is that programming languages frequently assume that the same implementation will be used for all the instances of a class. This is usually reasonable for "small" objects (such as integers) but it is unrealistic in large systems, where major objects such as files, which need the same functional interface (e.g. to guarantee file independence in programs), may for efficiency reasons be implemented in different ways.

2.2. Inheritance of Properties and of Implementations

The concept of inheritance, which has been popularised through Smalltalk, has to be more closely defined when a distinction is drawn between classes as types, as in the previous subsection. Using the standard terminology *superclass* we refer to a class of objects with general properties which can be inherited by a *subclass*, characterised by the properties of its superclass(es) together with some more specific properties which distinguish it from instances of other subclasses of the same superclass(es).

3. COMPOSITE OBJECTS

So far we have considered objects as individual entities. Yet in computer systems, as in the real world which they model, objects may be composed from other, simpler, objects. In this section we shall consider how complex objects may be constructed from simpler objects.

3.1. Collections of Objects

In computer systems, as in real life, it is common to group together collections of objects (usually of the same kind) because of some feature(s) which they have in common, e.g. bank account objects for all the customers at a particular bank branch. One advantage of this is that the entire collection may be treated as a single entity with its own (additional) properties, e.g. its cardinality, its combined size or weight, etc. Another advantage is that the same operation or protection requirement can easily be defined for all its members.

Such collections may be represented in various programming languages, operating systems or database systems as arrays, files, relations, etc. Regardless of their various possible implementations we shall simply refer to all these generically as "collections". Individual objects in a collection will be termed "members" of the collection.

3.2. Component Hierarchies

Forming collections from individual objects of the same kind is a relatively straightforward way of producing complex objects. In the general case, however, it is usual to find much more subtle, hierarchically organised, constructions, with complex objects being built from a range of component objects of different kinds. For example, a variety of components are used to construct an internal combustion engine, and this in turn can be used as a component, along with other major components such as a body, a transmission system, an electrical system and a steering system, to make a complete motor car.

At the lowest level relevant to the car designer are the "primitive", mostly general purpose, components such as nuts and bolts, castings, sparking plugs, etc. (Of course to the sparking plug manufacturer or to the physicist these are by no means primitives.) Similarly, at the lowest level relevant for software, computer systems consist of collections of instructions and data types (such as integers, booleans and characters) supported directly by the computer. Modern programming languages allow programmers to use these as components for objects of more complex types (e.g. enumerated types, records, abstract data types). These in turn can be used to construct objects such as program modules, then programs and files, and complete software systems.

3.3. Independent Objects

We can of course pursue such thoughts about component hierarchies to much higher levels. For example, a motor car can be considered as a component of a traffic system. At this point, however, we notice a change. The component objects of a car are determined by the *type* of the car and the interactions between the components are relatively static. For example the engine is connected through the transmission to the wheels in a particular way which is not alterable for a particular type of car. The interactions between the components of a traffic system are much more flexible. It is conceivable that a car could at various times be driven by many different drivers and on many different roads. In fact we can recognise two fundamentally different kinds of components: "independent" major objects, such as motor cars (and other components of traffic systems such as motor cycles, drivers, roads, traffic lights, pedestrians, pedestrian crossings, and so on), which have an existence and a history of their own, and "dependent" components of these objects (such as car engines, wheels, eyes, arms and legs, posts, light bulbs, etc.), the fate of which is inseparable from that of the independent object in which they are embedded.

Although it is not fashionable to view them in this way, we consider that the same holds true in principle in software systems. For example it seems to us natural that we can recognise integrated dependent objects (individual program statements, procedures, integers, booleans, characters, records, arrays, etc.) as components of major independent objects such as programs and files. The main significance of this difference will become evident in the following sections, where we consider the nature of interactions between objects as a basis for our protection model. Before we do this, however, it will be fruitful to consider the nature of independent objects from a different viewpoint.

3.4. Semantic Interfaces

The model of reality which underlies conventional file system interfaces can be characterised as a "filing cabinet" mentality. The interface to persistent information typically found in this conventional approach is based on procedures to open and close files and to read and write the records which they contain. Consequently the semantic operations appropriate to the information held in these files is usually buried in application programs, often as internal subroutines [8].

However, object-oriented persistent programming opens new horizons, freeing us from this mental model and allowing us instead to associate semantically appropriate operations with persistent objects in the same way that the introduction of abstract data types in the past allowed programmers to define temporary objects in terms of suitable operations. Thus whereas in the past a (composite) bank accounts file object appeared simply as a collection of records, in a persistent, object-oriented environment it might be defined, much more appropriately, along the lines shown in Figure 1.

Such a class might of course be implemented as a composite object containing, for example, a file system-like object or a collection of record objects. Nevertheless such internal objects would

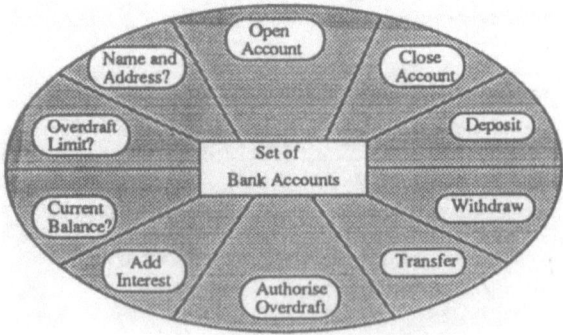

Figure 1: An Object-Oriented View of a Bank Accounts Module

normally[1] not be visible to users of the bank accounts "file".

Apart from its software engineering advantages this approach opens the way for a protection system which corresponds more closely to the semantics of user applications than conventional file protection mechanisms based on permissions to read or modify files, etc. Figure 2 illustrates how different subjects might be given appropriate permissions to access such a bank accounts file, assuming that protection is based on the right to invoke the operations of an object.

4. A GENERAL MODEL OF PROTECTION

Given the above definitions we are in a position to describe a general model for expressing which interactions in a persistent object-oriented system are to be considered *acceptable*. The protection matrix concept developed by Lampson is a simple and elegant model for describing the allowed kinds of access between individual subjects and objects in a system at a particular moment in time. For an object-oriented system it is a snapshot showing whether a particular object can currently make use of a particular operation of another object. The protection matrix may be seen as a set of triples each of which can be written as:

subject → object.operation

meaning that this subject may use this operation of this object.

Being a snapshot view of a system and being based on individual objects Lampson's model leaves open two very interesting questions:

1.   To what extent and in what way can *dynamic* access requirements be specified?

2.   How can more *general* access conditions be formulated?

In terms of the system concepts outlined above this leads to several more specific questions. How can we express access restrictions which are dependent on

	Teller	Branch Manager	H.O. Accountant	H.O. Auditor
Open Account	y	y	n	n
Close Account	y	y	n	n
Deposit	y	y	n	n
Withdraw	y	y	n	n
Transfer	y	y	y	n
Add Interest	n	n	y	n
Authorise Overdraft	n	y	n	n
Name and Address?	y	y	n	y
Overdraft Limit?	y	y	y	y
Current Balance?	y	y	y	y

Figure 2: Access Rights to Bank Accounts based on the Right
to Invoke Operations

---

[1] In Section 4.2.2 we shall consider an exception to this rule.

(a) the classes and superclasses of the objects involved?

(b) the types and component hierarchies of the objects involved?

(c) the state and history of the objects involved?

(d) the collections of objects in the system?

4.1. The Access Rule Model

To deal with these questions we introduce a more general model of protection based on the idea of *access rules*. An access rule is a logical statement of implication specifying the condition which must be fulfilled for an access to be considered acceptable. Each access rule may be written as:

condition: x → y.p

meaning that a subject x can invoke the operation p of the object y if the condition is fulfilled. The condition is a logical expression which may contain predicates concerning any aspect of the system. This endows the model with great generality. By allowing quantifiers to be used in the conditions the model can also express access rules which concern more than a single subject, object or operation.

A protection matrix is of course a special case of our model consisting of a set of access rules of the form:

true: subject → object.access_right

By using the access rule model arbitrarily complex combinations of conditions can be specified to ensure that an operation is being performed in an acceptable way. For example:

∀ x: x → my_object.operation

i.e. anyone may use this operation of my_object.

has_driving_licence(john) ∧
¬ out_of_fuel(my_car) ∧
¬ ∃ x driving(x,my_car):   john → my_car.drive

i.e. john may drive my car as long as he has a driving licence, it is not out of fuel and it is not already being driven.

∀ x
is_instance_of(x,bank_teller) ∧
works_at(x,branch_123) ∧
is_instance_of(my_account,bank_account) ∧
held_at(my_account,branch_123) ∧
¬ overdrawn(my_account) :   x → my_account.withdraw

i.e. the tellers at branch_123 may withdraw from my_account if it is not overdrawn

4.2. Applications to Object-Oriented Systems

Using this very general model we can formulate and consider conditions of interest for a particular kind of system. In this section we show how the model can express the kinds of access restriction important in persistent object-oriented systems as described above. This is done by defining appropriate predicates for use in the conditions.

4.2.1. Classes and Inheritance

Given the predicate 'is_instance_of' which expresses the class of an object access rules can be formulated which grant access only to certain classes of subjects. For example:

∀ x is_instance_of(x,adult): x → my_car.drive

i.e. only adults are allowed to drive my car.

Furthermore given a definition of inheritance such as:

(is_subclass_of(c,c2) ∧ inherits_class(c2,c1)) ∨ (c = c1) ⇒ inherits_class(c,c1)

we can also express rules in which access rights are inherited. For example the rule:

∀ x ∀ c
is_instance_of(x,c) ∧ inherits_class(c,adult): x → my_car.drive

where

is_subclass_of(man,adult) and is_subclass_of(woman,adult)

would allow both men and women to drive my car by virtue of being adults.

4.2.2. Types and Components

In order to guarantee information hiding within objects their type (as opposed to their class) should not be externally visible. In particular the components of an object should in general only be accessed via the semantic operations of the containing object. For example the 'insert' operation of a B-tree may only be reached by the 'open_account' operation of a bank account object. An exception to this restriction may be allowed for a special 'repairman' subject who is responsible for directly accessing the component object to make repairs if this should become necessary. Given a predicate 'is_component_of' access rules expressing this kind of condition can be written as follows:

is_component_of(B_tree,x) ∨ is_repairman_for(x,B_tree): x → B_tree.insert

i.e. the B-tree object may only be accessed via (the semantic operations of) the bank account object or by a repairman.

4.2.3. Collections of Objects

A further interesting type of access restriction in object-oriented systems is one in which access rights are dependent on membership in a certain collection or set. These conditions are very difficult to implement with the usual general protection mechanisms. An example of this kind of restriction is:

∀ x ∈ billiard_club: x → billiard_table.use

i.e. only members of the billiard club can use this billiard table.

Similarly a subject may be granted access to all the objects in a set. For example:

∀ a ∈ accounts_at_branch_123: manager_of_123 → a.authorise_overdraft

i.e. the manager of branch 123 can authorise overdrafts for all accounts held at that branch.

4.2.4. The History and State of Objects

In general it is useful to formulate access restrictions dependent on arbitrary aspects of the state or the history of the subject and object. Special cases of this are concerned with synchronisation and the order in which operations of an object may be used.[2] Some simple examples are:

∀ x ¬ empty(stack): x → stack.pop

i.e. a pop operation on an empty stack is not acceptable.

∀ x has_opened(x,file) ∧ ¬ being_read(file) ∧ ¬ being_written(file) : x → file.write

i.e. a file must be opened before being used and should not be changed when being read or already being changed.

---

[2] In this case the conditions are often of the kind that are expressed in specification languages or (in the case of synchronisation) *path expressions*[3].

4.2.5. Confined Operations

For security reasons we may wish to insist that a certain subject only call confined procedures of certain objects as described above. In the case of a spooler, for example, the purpose of the call may be to pass information through the spooler into another object (e.g. a printer) without the spooler retaining a copy of the information. Given a predicate 'confined' for expressing that a procedure is confined and a predicate 'confined_to' for expressing the confinement associated with an invocation of an object we can then formulate access rules expressing this kind of security consideration. For example:

confined(pass_print_job) $\wedge$ confined_to(spooler,printer):
subject $\rightarrow$ spooler.pass_print_job

i.e. the subject can only invoke the spooler if it is restricted to writing to the printer.

5. A CLASSIFICATION OF PROTECTION CONDITIONS

Just as there is a straightforward implementation of the protection matrix model as a large central sparse matrix, there is also a straightforward and general implementation for access rules. Each time an operation is used within the system the access rules could be used to perform a logical inference based on the current state of the system to determine whether the access can be allowed to proceed. And just as a large sparse matrix is an unacceptable implementation in a real system neither do we propose that a protection mechanism be implemented in this naive rule-based way. Rather, now that we have defined a simple and general model our aim is to find a *sufficient set of efficient mechanisms* which guarantee the protection conditions expressed in the access rules for a particular system. In this section we distinguish several different kinds of condition for controlling interactions between objects in systems. This then forms the basis for the subsequent investigation of appropriate protection mechanisms.

We identify two orthogonal ways of categorising the conditions which occur in access rules.

(a) **semantic vs policy conditions:** Semantic conditions are those which prevent access which does not make sense, would not work or would give rise to an inconsistency. Policy conditions are those which make sense and would work but which as a matter of policy in the design of the system are to be forbidden. A special case of policy conditions are the security constraints used in database systems to restrict access to tables. The integrity constraints of database systems are a special case of semantic conditions. It should be noted that while policy rules are those which are usually associated with protection, violations of semantic rules (by giving rise to unexpected system states) can intentionally or unintentionally lead to violations of policy.

(b) **static vs dynamic conditions:** It is readily seen from the examples given above that some of the conditions can be tested statically since they never change during the lifetime of the system while others must be tested dynamically. This still does not necessarily mean that the rule must be reevaluated at every access, simply that some mechanism must ensure that the rule is never violated. Note that the categorisation of a condition as either static or dynamic depends on the specification of the system. In a banking system for example it may be assumed that the employees belong to a fixed class such as 'teller' and 'manager' or it may be assumed that a particular employee can act as a teller on one day but not on the next.

Examples:

Static semantic conditions

is_instance_of(my_account,bank_account) $\wedge$ ... :   x $\rightarrow$ my_account.withdraw

i.e. an object may only be used via the operations it actually possesses.

Static policy conditions

is_instance_of(x,bank_teller) $\wedge$ ... :   x $\rightarrow$ my_account.withdraw

i.e. the access is restricted according to the type of the subject (assuming now that the membership of an object in the class 'teller' is static).

is_component_of(B_tree,bank_account):   bank_account → B_tree.insert

i.e. the low-level operations of the B-tree should only be used via the semantic operations of the bank-account.

Dynamic semantic conditions

¬ empty(stack) : x → stack.pop
¬ out_of_fuel(my_car) : x → my_car.drive
has_opened(x,file) ∧ ¬ being_used(file) : x → file.change

Dynamic policy conditions

works_at(x,branch_123) ∧ held_at(my_account,branch_123) : x → my_account.inspect
aged_at_least(x,18) : x → my_car.drive
¬ overdrawn(my_account) : x → my_account.withdraw

6. A CLASSIFICATION OF PROTECTION MECHANISMS

We now turn to the question of what kinds of mechanisms a system may include in order to ensure compliance with this wide range of possible protection conditions. In doing so we distinguish three levels of protection mechanism:

(a) **Architectural Mechanisms:** Every secure system must be based on a *trusted abstract machine* which implements fundamental architectural protection mechanisms. The abstract machine offers an interface defining a particular language which forms the basis of higher levels in the system. At one extreme the machine may be kept to an absolute minimum in order to avoid implementation errors. In this case it may only check for those semantic violations which could lead to violations of policy decisions (e.g. treating a capability as an integer). At the other extreme it may be designed to prevent as many kinds of unacceptable access as possible. In this case the interface may already define a high level language or intermediate code. In the following section we give an example of what we consider to be a minimal sufficient set of fundamental mechanisms.

(b) **Language Mechanisms:** At this level a system may offer various programming languages each of which is compiled into the basis language of the trusted abstract machine. Each language can offer additional mechanisms for detecting and preventing certain kinds of unacceptable access to objects. These mechanisms may be compile-time checks or code generated to do run-time checks. Compile-time checks are naturally preferable if possible since they must only be performed once. In a monolingual system in which the compiler is trusted the language level is of course indistinguishable from the architectural level. If a system is multilingual the mechanisms at this level may check for kinds of access which are not desirable but are non-critical (e.g. treating a real as an integer) or indeed for kinds of access which are permissible for some applications but should be prevented for others (e.g. a debugging language which can by-pass the semantic operations defined for an object).

(c) **Programmed Mechanisms:** At the third level are mechanisms written into new type managers using the programming languages of the second level. These can check for the kinds of access which are allowed from the architectural and language viewpoints but which are nevertheless inappropriate (e.g. bad parameters, wrong time or context of use).

Based on these three levels we can investigate the protection mechanisms of a system for supporting the kinds of protection condition described above.

Mechanisms for Static Semantic Conditions: These conditions are primarily concerned with the classes and types of objects in the system and in particular with ensuring that an object is accessed only via the operations of its class and the implementations of its type manager. For independent components of the system this demands an architecture which supports the concepts of object, class and type. For dependent components language mechanisms may suffice but this can give rise to problems in passing parameters between objects (especially if these have been written in different languages).

Mechanisms for Static Policy Conditions: These conditions enforce static decisions about which objects or classes of objects can access which other objects and in what ways. This demands an architecture which allows some kind of static linking. Again for dependent components the internal linking within a module can be handled at the language level. In one language proposal [6] each variable is associated with a set of access rights as well as an underlying type so that certain static access checks are possible. Conditions involving classes or types demand an architecture in which information (in this case an access right) can be shared by all objects of a particular class or type.

Mechanisms for Dynamic Semantic Conditions: This is the vast set of conditions for specifying exactly when a particular operation of a particular object can meaningfully be used. Clearly these can in general only be specified at the third level by the programmer of a new type manager. Special cases are the types known to the architecture or predefined in a language (e.g. bounds checks for arrays). While the checks themselves must be individually programmed, the lower two levels can of course offer useful general mechanisms to support these checks. Such general mechanisms may include a synchronisation mechanism, an exception mechanism, a mechanism for opening and closing persistent objects, etc.

Mechanisms for Dynamic Policy Conditions: This category is potentially as vast as the previous category given that an arbitrarily complex condition may be specified for when an access to an object can be allowed to proceed. In such complex cases the only solution as above is to program the appropriate mechanism individually. General architectural mechanisms which can be useful here are the identification of the calling object as well as its type and class and the identification of the current process (assuming an in-process system). For the simple condition that access should be restricted to some particular set of subjects an architectural protection mechanism such as capabilities (with revocation) or access control lists can be used.

7. AN EXAMPLE: THE MONADS-PC SYSTEM

Just as a conceptually simple implementation of Lampson' matrix model (as a two dimensional array) is impractical in most systems, so a conceptually straightforward implementation of the model presented above is also impractical. Nevertheless we consider that the proposed model can be implemented in a wide variety of practical ways. In this section we demonstrate one such implementation, that found in the MONADS-PC system, first describing the mechanisms involved and then illustrating how they can be used to implement a particular security policy.

7.1. The MONADS-PC Protection Mechanisms

The MONADS-PC hardware, microcode and software kernel represent the trusted abstract machine[3] mentioned above. Its main characteristics include support for:

(a) a very large uniform, persistent virtual memory which eliminates the need for a conventional file store (and thus reduces the number and simplifies the nature of protection mechanisms in the system),

(b) a two-level capability scheme, which distinguishes between the mechanisms for protecting access to virtual memory segments and to higher level objects (thus providing a basis for an efficient implementation of capabilities as well as simplifying the implementation of user-determined security policies relating to the protection of major objects, i.e. objects comparable to files and programs in conventional systems);

---

[3] In its present implementation the kernel software is not minimal, it has not been proved correct and it almost certainly contains unknown errors. These problems are currently receiving attention.

(c) a fully procedure-oriented [15] persistent process model in which each registered user typically owns one or more processes which persist between login sessions (so that all the services used by a user, including "operating system" services, are carried out by software executing on his own stack),

(d) uniquely identified major objects structured according to the information hiding principle, whose interface routines (procedures and enquiries) can only be invoked (on the stack of the calling process) by presenting a module capability with appropriate access rights for the routine to be called. Only the type manager routines of an object may access its internal structure;

(e) mechanisms to create new objects (process stacks, type managers/code modules, instances of major objects) in a form which can guarantee their subsequent protection;

(f) mechanisms to assist synchronisation and communication between processes [7,11,12];

(g) encryption of information stored on disc or being transmitted in a network of MONADS-PC systems[4] [4].

Details of the implementation of this architecture have been published elsewhere [9,10] and need not be repeated here. In this context we can also avoid detailed discussion of most of the basic mechanisms described above and concentrate on the implementation of module capabilities and the modules to which they provide access, together with some further mechanisms needed to complement them.

7.1.1. Module Capabilities

Module capabilities contain four fields of interest in this context: a unique module name which is never re-used (identifying the address space in the virtual memory containing the identified module); a set of access rights (indirectly identifying the routines of the module which may be called using this capability); some status bits (e.g. defining whether the capability can be copied); and a password field (used to confine procedures).

A capability for a code module (e.g. a compiler or library of routines) identifies the address space containing the (entrypoint information about the) code, thus allowing the microcode to execute inter-module calls. A capability for an object (an instance of some type) identifies the address space containing the (segment capabilities for the) instance data. Information hiding is enforced on objects in that the instance address space also contains a pointer to the code address space containing the type manager, the appropriate entrypoint of which is invoked when an instance capability is used to make an inter-module call. A module capability cannot be used to gain direct access to data.

Module capabilities can be held in segments of any module. They are protected from unauthorised modification or forgery by the access rights of the segment, which allow only appropriate operations such as copying to another module capability segment (subject to the copy rules and the copy bit being set in the status field) or reducing the access rights.

When a code module is created its individual routines are marked as normal procedures, enquiries or confined procedures and the appropriate rules are automatically applied when they are executed. The kernel can also be requested to refine a module capability in such a way that it can only be used to call the enquiries or confined procedures of the module to which it refers.

There are basically three ways of revoking capabilities. First, the kernel allows a module to be re-named, thus rendering all existing capabilities with the old name invalid. Second, the meaning of the access rights field (which is interpreted indirectly) can be changed (thus allowing rights to be reduced or increased). Third, no-copy capabilities can be deposited in a directory to which some users have normal access and the revoking user has delete access.

---

[4] This aspect of security is currently in the planning stage and has not yet been implemented.

7.1.2. Confinement and Module Capabilities

The confinement mechanism used in MONADS is similar to that described by Anderson et al.[1]. Passwords are used to confine called modules in such a way that they may not change their own internal state and may only call those capabilities containing password fields enhanced by the appropriate password in an unconfined manner. Modules called using capabilities with inappropriate passwords may be called only in a confined mode. The scheme relies on the password field in a capability being wide enough to ensure that confined modules cannot systematically break passwords in reasonable compute time.

This confinement technique would for example allow a user to create a new (empty) text module and pass a capability for it to a confined editor. The latter could then use the unconfined routines of the text type manager to store text in the module without being able to make a further copy in its own state information or in, for example, another text module which it has itself created.

7.1.3. Fulfilling Other Access Requirements

Module capabilities demonstrate a subject's right to access defined operations of an object, but must be complemented by further guaranteed information if some of the kinds of access restrictions defined earlier are to be met. The approach adopted is for the kernel to provide guaranteed information about objects and processes on request, thus allowing programmers to build secure programmed mechanisms at the third level described above.

An unprivileged instruction identifies the process number of the process in which it is executed. Since the process model is fully in-process (procedure oriented) and since process numbers uniquely identify persistent processes, this instruction can be used, for example, to allow a service module (such as an editor, a spooler or a proprietary software module) to identify its customer and charge him accordingly[5]. It can also be used by a user-written mailbox called in the sender's process to identify in a secure manner the sender of each message.

A similar instruction exists to identify the unique module number of both the calling module instance and of its type manager[6]. Thus a called module can ascertain both the identity of the object which calls it and the type manager for the object. Using these instructions a printer driver could for example check that its caller is a spooler and if necessary which particular spooler. A module can similarly also determine its own identity and type.

The same information (object and type manager) can be acquired about an arbitrary capability presented to the kernel. This allows such possibilities as dynamic type checking of major objects passed as parameters, and allows a directory module to determine whether a capability in a directory refers to a further directory object. The ability to identify object instances also allows directory software to check for cycles and the danger of losing objects.

7.1.4. Directories

Directories have no special status in the MONADS architecture. They are simply modules which map names onto capabilities. Consequently, users can develop their own type managers for directories. In fact, since module capabilities can be stored in segments of any module[7], a security policy can be implemented such that capabilities for important documents, for example, are not stored in directories, making them extremely difficult to find by unauthorised persons who may have penetrated the system.

---

[5] Higher level software can of course be built to map process numbers onto usernames. Such software then becomes an extension to the trusted abstract machine.

[6] It is planned to extend the architecture to have a minimal knowledge of classes.

[7] e.g. a capability for a B-tree instance module could be held in a semantic bank accounts module.

It is also possible to organise directories such that a separate directory structure exists for each user, rooted in his own persistent process(es). As mentioned above a user can achieve capability revocation by the use of directories. As we shall briefly illustrate in the following section, they can also be effectively used to implement particular security policies.

7.2. Implementing a Security Policy above the Kernel

To illustrate the flexibility of the above techniques, we outline a solution for a conventional (mandatory access control) security policy in which we have a set of objects, each with a defined security level (e.g. top secret, secret, confidential, unclassified) and a set of users with corresponding clearance levels. Informally, the security rules are that a user may not access documents at a higher security level than his clearance, and may not copy information from a document at a particular security level to a lower security level (the *-property in the Bell-LaPadula model[14])[8]. We further assume that for each security level there is an authorised declassifier, who can reduce the security level of a document, and that there is also a superclassifier, who can increase the classification of a document.

7.2.1. Specifying the Security Requirements using the Access Rule Model

In an object-oriented system the simple security condition and *-property can be expressed in terms of four kinds of operations on objects. Firstly there are the usual enquiry operations and procedures as described above. The enquiry operations by definition can not change the state of the object, that is, they can not write to any sharable data in the object. Furthermore they can only invoke enquiry operations of other objects in the system.

In addition to these there are also special procedures for declassifying an object and for reclassifying an object (to a higher level). These are to be invoked only by specially privileged subjects in the system.

We can define predicates for distinguishing enquiries from procedures and functions for determining the classification of an object and the clearance of a subject. Using these together with the additional predicates 'declassification' and 'reclassification' to determine how an operation changes the classification of an object and 'is_authorised_to_declassify' and 'is_authorised_to_reclassify' with the obvious meanings we can formulate the MAC security policy as follows:

$\forall$ x $\forall$ y $\forall$ p
(clearance(x) $\geq$ classification(y) $\wedge$ enquiry(p)) $\vee$
(clearance(x) = classification(y) $\wedge$ procedure(p) $\wedge$ $\neg$ reclassification(p)
$\wedge$ $\neg$ declassification(p)) $\vee$
(is_authorised_to_declassify(x,y) $\wedge$ declassification(p)) $\vee$
(is_authorised_to_reclassify(x,y) $\wedge$ reclassification(p)):   x $\rightarrow$ y.p

7.2.2. Implementing the Security Requirements using the MONADS Mechanisms

Each document is accessed via a module capability, which can be retrieved from a directory. For each security level there is a directory which serves as a root for the documents at that level. For simplicity we assume that capabilities for documents are stored in these directories with full access rights. Each of these root directories uses the same type manager, which offers *inter alia* the following routines:

---

[8] For a recent discussion of models of this kind see [16]. In this context we ignore the issue of covert channels.

```
class security_directory
proc insert_document(document_name: string; m: modcap)
proc remove_document(document_name: string)
enq give_read_access(document_name: string): modcap
enq give_write_access(document_name: string): modcap
proc declassify_document(document_name: string; level: modcap)
proc reclassify_document(document_name: string; level: modcap)
end security_directory
```

We assume that appropriate exceptions are defined for errors detected by each routine.

Each user in the system has a capability for the root directory for his clearance level, with access rights for "give_read_access" and "give_write_access". Using this he can retrieve capabilities with appropriate access rights for all documents at his clearance level; in addition he can retrieve capabilities with "give_read_access" only to documents at lower security levels (thus guaranteeing the *-property). To achieve this the root directory at each security level includes a capability, with "give_read_access" access to each lower security level root directory.

The "insert_document" and "remove_document" routines only insert/remove documents at the level of the root directory called. It then becomes a policy decision whether all users at a clearance level have capabilities with these rights or not.

Each level's declassifier has access to the "declassify_document" routine, which removes the module capability corresponding to the document name from the current level and places it in the appropriate lower level directory, using the "insert_document" routine of that directory via the module capability passed as the parameter "level". This module capability passed by the declassifier serves as the evidence that he has the right to declassify, distinguishing him from ordinary users who will at most have the right to work at their own clearance level. In principle "reclassify_document", which allows a superclassifier to increase the security level of a document, might have been identical to "declassify_document", since the "level" capability provides evidence of the right to insert at a specified level. However, this would potentially allow declassifiers also to reclassify up to their own level. To avoid this the declassify and reclassify routines could check that the new classification is in the appropriate direction. This could be achieved by checking against a list of the names of directory roots which direction the new classification would involve. This in turn can be securely achieved by the type manager using the basic instructions to determine his own identity and that of the level parameter. It would then be sensible to have a further module in which the ordering of the security levels were stored, accessible only to the root directories.

Such a system could (redundantly) be made more secure by maintaining lists of users (persistent process numbers) and their classification level, thus allowing the directory type manager to check against the process number of the caller. The types of parameters passed as module capabilities would of course also be checked to ensure that they are for directories where appropriate. As presently defined, the model appears not to need the confinement mechanisms but these would of course be available, should it be necessary to confine, for example, a spooler for the printing of documents.

8. CONCLUSION

We have presented a view of software systems as collections of information hiding objects each of which is used by other objects via semantically appropriate operations. Protection is defined in terms of whether a particular invocation of an operation can be considered acceptable. We have identified various aspects of persistent object-oriented systems which are of importance in specifying protection requirements.

The class of an object together with the subclass hierarchy define which operations an object possesses without specifying how they are implemented. The type of an object defines its components and the algorithms used for implementing its operations. Independent objects whose

bindings with each other are loose and dynamic are distinguished from dependent objects which
are relatively tightly and statically bound. Enquiry operations which do not change the state of an
object are distinguished from procedures which do and procedures are further classified as
confined and non-confined.

The access rule model presented in this paper provides a simple and powerful way of expressing
protection requirements based on these important aspects of object-oriented systems. Lampson's
protection matrix model which does not address such issues is included as a special case as are the
security constraints and integrity constraints of database systems. The generality of the model allows a very wide range of protection conditions to be formulated. This has in turn allowed a
categorisation of the conditions and an evaluation of the mechanisms offered by a system.

In the scope of this paper the mechanisms used in an implementation have only been informally
related back to the conditions expressed in access rules. An interesting area of further research is
to investigate how the access rule model can be used as a more formal specification of the protection requirements of a software system. Indeed since the rules are general enough to specify both
semantic and policy conditions they can be used to generalise object-oriented specification
languages and some aspects of synchronisation specifications as well as security specifications in
a uniform way. They could then form the basis of an independent evaluation of the functionality
and security of a particular implementation without forcing an artificial classification of the system in one of the "orange book" security classes.

Another area of interest is the possibility of a step-wise transformation of the access rules of a
specification in terms of implementation mechanisms which are gradually introduced. Thus the
initial access rules may be expressed entirely in terms of abstract predicates whereas at a later
stage of the transformation some access rules may be expressed in terms of capabilities, process
numbers, interface routines, etc.

The three level description of protection mechanisms as trusted architectural mechanisms,
language mechanisms and programmed mechanisms enables a clearer analysis of which kinds of
mechanisms are appropriate and necessary for the different categories of protection condition. In
particular the kernel mechanisms of the capability based MONADS-PC have been shown to fulfil
the requirements of an important security policy expressible in the model.

Generally speaking capability systems have difficulties in implementing MAC-oriented systems
which aim to enforce the *-property [2,5]. The extensions which have made this a fairly straightforward activity in the MONADS system include the ability to identify in a secure manner the
identity and type of a module from its capability, the ability to restrict inter-module communication to a form which ensures information hiding, the ability to restrict access rights to enquiries,
as well as the ability to revoke capabilities and to ensure that they cannot be passed between users
in an unauthorised way. These are all mechanisms which our consideration of protection requirements for general object-oriented systems led us to include in the architecture.

REFERENCES

1. Anderson, M., Pose, R.D. and Wallace, C.S. (1986) "A Password-Capability System", *The Computer Journal*, 29, 1, February 1986, pp.1-8.

2. Boebert, W.E. "On the Inability of an Unmodified Capability Machine to Enforce the *-Property", *Proceedings of the 7th DoD/NBS Computer Security Conference, September 1984*.

3. Campbell, R.H. and Habermann, A.N. (1974) "The Specification of Process Synchronisation by Path Expressions", *Lecture Notes in Computer Science*, vol. 16, Springer, Heidelberg, pp. 89-102.

4. Freisleben, B. and Kammerer, P. (1990) "Capabilities and Encryption: The Ultimate Defense against Security Attacks?", *Proceedings of the International Workshop on Computer*

82

Architectures to Support Security and Persistence of Information, Bremen, 1990.

5. Gong, L. "On Security in Capability-Based Systems", *ACM Operating Systems Review*, 23, 2, 1989, pp.56-60.

6. Jones, A.K. and Liskov, B.H. (1978) "A Language Extension for Expressing Constraints on Data Access", *Communications of the ACM, 21, 5, pp. 358-367.*

7. Keedy, J.L. and Freisleben, B. (1989) "Priority Semaphores", *The Computer Journal*, 32, 1, 1989, pp. 24-28.

8. Keedy, J.L. and Richards, I. (1982) "A Software Engineering View of Files", *Australian Computer Journal*, 14, 2, May 1982, pp.56-61.

9. Keedy, J.L. and Rosenberg J. (1987) "Object Management and Addressing in the MONADS Architecture", *Proceedings of the International Workshop on Persistent Object Systems*, Appin, Scotland, 1987.

10. Keedy, J.L. and Rosenberg J. (1989) "Support for Objects in the MONADS Architecture", *Proceedings of the International Workshop on Persistent Object Systems*, Newcastle, Australia, January 1989, pp. 202-213.

11. Keedy, J.L., Rosenberg J. and Ramamohanarao, K. (1979) "On Implementing Semaphores with Sets", *The Computer Journal*, 22, 2, May, 1979, pp. 146-150.

12. Keedy, J.L., Rosenberg J. and Ramamohanarao, K. (1982) "On Synchronising Readers and Writers with Semaphores", *The Computer Journal*, 25, 1, February 1982, pp. 121-125.

13. Lampson, B.W. (1971) "Protection", *Proc. 5th Princeton Symposium on Information Sciences and Systems*, Princeton University, reprinted in *ACM Operating Systems Review*, 8, 1, 1974, pp.18-24.

14. Landwehr, C.E. "Formal Models for Computer Security", *ACM Computing Surveys*, 13, 3, September 1981.

15. Lauer, H.C. and Needham, R.M. (1979) "On the Duality of Operating System Structures", *ACM Operating Systems Review*, 13, 2, pp. 3-19.

16. McLean, J. (1990) "The Specification and Modeling of Computer Security", *IEEE Computer*, 23, 1, 1990, pp.9-16.

17. Stoll, C. "Stalking the Wiley Hacker", *Communications of the ACM*, 31, 5, 1988, pp.484-497.

Part III

Security

CHARGING IN A SECURE ENVIRONMENT

C.S. Wallace and R.D. Pose
Department of Computer Science
Monash University

ABSTRACT

The Monash Multiprocessor Architecture incorporates a monetary system at the lowest kernel level, integrated with a password capability scheme. Although the capability scheme is quite flexible, providing support for non-hierarchic security and access policies, abstract type management and information confinement, we show that it is possible for service providers to command use-based fees for service. The fee charging protocols must be designed with some care to avoid breaching required information confinement constraints when user and provider are mutually suspicious, but need not be very complicated.

1. INTRODUCTION

Most current multi-user operating systems do not support a satisfactory means for the providers of software and other services to charge for their services. The provider of, for example, a compiler may reasonably wish to be paid for use of this compiler. In most current systems, the only options for the provider are outright sale or some form of licence arrangement. In either case, the price charged must be calculated on the expected level of use and availability of the software rather than actual use, which is not normally readily discovered. Thus, a multi-user site hosting one or two users with an occasional need for the compiler may have to pay as much as a site having many frequent users. The problem is even more marked in large networked systems where cost factors force the network managers to purchase a licence for only one or two computers in the network, so that users elsewhere have to send jobs to a remote site for execution rather than having the necessary software available locally.

A sufficiently secure system can at least allow the provided software to make a tamper-proof record of its use for later billing. However, a suspicious client, perhaps wishing to use the compiler to compile a program of high commercial value, has then no guarantee that the billing records accumulated by the compiler do not capture sensitive information about the client's program. Further, it is not unreasonable for a client to object to the loss of anonymity consequent on the creation of a billing record which must at least serve to identify the client to the provider, and to indicate the scale and frequency of the client's activity. While it is no doubt possible to invent protocols for use-based charging without risk of unauthorised disclosure of clients' information and activity, and without risk of unauthorised copying or alteration of provided software, the protocols will almost certainly be rather elaborate. In this paper, we show how relatively simple but effective charging mechanisms can be built into a secure operating system. The system described is capability-based [1, 2]. Only the aspects of relevance to charging will be described here.

2. PASSWORD CAPABILITIES

2.1 Objects

Data, programs, processes and I/O resources are all treated as "objects" in this system. Broadly, different kinds of object are distinguished only on the basis of the different kinds of access permitted to them. Thus, the access right "send message to" can exist only for an object which is a process, and the access right "execute" would exist only for objects comprising executable code. The distinction is not absolute: in some circumstances read and write accesses may be permitted on an object normally treated as a process.

The distinction between processes and other objects is the one of most significance, since the system expects and enforces a certain format on process objects, whereas other objects are, at the lowest level, treated simply as a consecutively numbered set of words.

All objects can also act as stores for money.

2.2 Capabilities

A capability is a datum, knowledge of which permits a process or other agent to exercise one or more defined rights of access to a specific object.

There may be several capabilities for the same object. One of these, the *master*, is created when the object is created, and confers whatever rights the creator specifies. The others are known as derivatives. The set of capabilities for the object forms a rooted tree, the derivative tree, with the master at the root. Every capability save the master has a parent, namely the immediately adjacent capability in the direction of the root. An agent knowing a capability may call the system to create a derivative, which becomes a child of the original, and which may have any specified subset of the rights of the original.

The format of a capability is a 64-bit unique *object name* and a 64-bit randomly-chosen *password*, sometimes considered as comprising two 32-bit password fields P1 and P2. Such a capability is depicted in figure 1. The various capabilities for an object share the same name, but have different passwords. Note that a capability is not tagged or physically segregated from other data. It is simply a 128-bit datum which may be represented in any data structure, copied, printed, written on a piece of paper etc. The security of the capability system relies on the infeasibility of guessing a valid password.

Figure 1: A Password Capability

The capabilities do not explicitly encode the size or exact location of the objects they name, nor the rights they confer. This and other information relating to a capability is held in a *catalogue*, which is a system data structure outside the world of objects, and for which there is no capability. The catalogue entry for a capability records its rights and its parent (if a derivative) or size, status, and location information (if a master).

When a new capability is created, its password is generated by a special hardware unit [3] guaranteed to produce an unpredictable sequence of words, and the password checked to ensure it is unique among all the capabilities for the same object.

2.3 Rights

Broadly, rights can be grouped into three classes: those applicable to processes, those applicable to passive data, and those applicable to objects of any kind.

Process rights: These include rights to send a message, to suspend or resume execution, and to *lock* (a security-oriented operation described later.)

Data object rights: These include read, write and execute rights, and the right to extend or contract the object size. Read, write and execute rights can be limited in extent, allowing access only to a consecutive subset of the words in the object, called a "window".

General rights: General rights for the most part relate to the capability conferring these rights rather than to the object itself. They include rights to derive another capability for the object of equal or lesser rights, the derivative becoming a child of the original; the right to destroy the capability, and implicitly all its derivatives; the right to rename the capability, in effect destroying it and all other capabilities for the object but replacing it with one of equal rights, which becomes the new master; the right to deposit money and the right to withdraw money. It is these last rights which will be of most concern in this paper.

Money rights: As has been mentioned, every object, besides its role as a process or body of data, is a store of money. The record of the amount held by the object resides in the catalogue entry of its master capability, in a *moneyword*. Derived capabilities also have money words, but these do not represent funds additional to those in the master money word. Rather, the money words of a derivative bounds the amount of the object's money which is accessible via the derivative. When a sum S is withdrawn from an object using a derived capability C, the money words of C, the master capability, and every capability in the derivation tree on the path from C to the master are decreased by S, and must remain non-negative. Each of these capabilities must, of course, have the "withdraw" right.

Conversely, when a sum S is deposited using a derived capability C, the money words of all capabilities from C to the master are increased by S, and each capability must have the "deposit" right. There is no requirement that the money word of a capability be less than that of its parent, nor that it have any relation to the money words of its derivatives, or their sum.

3. OBJECT RENTAL

Periodically, the system deducts rent from the money of each object in proportion to its size. If its money is thereby exhausted, the object is archived and eventually destroyed. It was for this purpose, of removing "garbage" from the system, that the money mechanism was originally introduced. The system has no concept of object ownership or user account numbers, so no user can be identified as responsible for the continued presence of an object. Further, the fact that valid capabilities may be recorded outside the computer system, and later legitimately presented for use, makes it impossible for the system to detect when an object has become inaccessible by any agent. The rent scheme ensures that objects will survive only so long as some agent is willing to pay its rent, and that any system memory occupied by objects is paid for.

4. SYSTEM CHARGES AND PROCESS CASH

A process object essentially comprises a processor state image, a mailbox for the receipt of messages, a set of capabilities defining the current context of the process (i.e. the code, stack, data and other objects visible in the process logical address space), a *lockword*, and a *cashword*. None of this information is normally directly readable or alterable by any process. The cashword represents a sum of money additional to the sum stored in the process object itself, and is immediately accessible to the process during execution, without requiring reference to the catalogue.

The process is charged for processor time, and for services invoked by system calls, with payment being deducted from the cashword. Money deposited by the process into objects (including itself) is taken from its cash, and withdrawals add to its cash. One may consider object moneywords as bank accounts, and process cash as spending money. A process which exhausts its cash is suspended, even if the process object contains money.

The inter-process message system, which basically allows a process to send a small message to another process and wake it up, also allows money to be sent. Money in a message is added to the cash of the receiving process immediately, and the size of the sum may be discovered by the process by a "receive message" call. Messages may be sent anonymously, or may include the name of the sending process. The receiving process may also discover the capability for itself used to send the message. Thus, if a process distributes various derived capabilities for itself to other agents, it may discover to which "hat" an incoming message (and perhaps payment) has been directed.

5. CREATION OF MONEY

Money is consumed by the system in two ways. Rent is collected from objects hence depleting their funds and processes are charged for their processor time and other system services. Unless more money is injected into the system the total money supply could eventually become exhausted.

There is a trusted system administrator who is able to create objects containing money. He would normally only do this in return for some form of legal currency. When a user first wants to use the system he pays the system administrator an amount of real money. The system administrator creates an object containing the equivalent amount of system funds at the current exchange rate and gives the user a capability with withdrawal rights for the object. The user can immediately rename the object in order to prevent anyone else having a capability through which these funds may be withdrawn.

The system administrator will also convert system funds into real money. Given a capability with withdrawal rights he will destroy the specified system funds and give the person an equivalent amount of real money. In this way surplus funds may be withdrawn from the system.

One of the aims of the system administrator is to have the computer system run at a profit or at the very least break even. The exchange rate between real money and system funds is thus set so that the rent charged for objects reflects the actual costs incurred in operating the hardware on which the objects are located and allowing for eventual replacement at the end of its service life. Similarly the charging for processor time and system services should reflect the actual costs of providing the services and may also include a profit component. It is expected that market forces will prevent the system administrator setting the exchange rate at unrealistic levels. If he charges too much people will not use his system and if he charges too little he will not recover his costs.

6. SIMPLE CHARGING

Many useful services may take the form of simply providing some code which the client may execute. The provider of such software may extract a fee for service very easily. The provider (or a process acting as her agent) installs the software as an object of executable code, and makes publicly available a derived capability for the object having only the execute right. A client process wishing to use the service may call the code by using this capability, and execute the code in-process. The code extracts payment from the client by depositing in itself a sum which it calculates on the basis of the scale of service. The money of course is taken from the client user's process cash. This scheme is depicted in Figure 2.

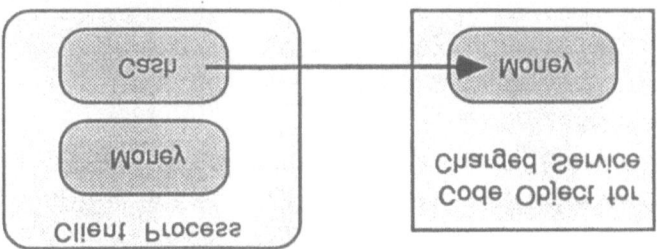

Figure 2: Simple Charging.

Funds accumulating in the code object may be withdrawn from time to time by the provider's agent, and by no-one else, since only the provider has a capability for the code giving withdrawal right.

This simple scheme places all the direct costs for processor time, temporary data storage etc. on the client, since it is the client's process cash which must be used to pay for these system services. The money deposited by the provided software in itself is wholly income for the provider save for rental cost incurred by the software object.

The above scheme is not limited to services provided by in-process execution. The provided code may create new objects, including new processes, and may itself call other service providers in the same way. Ultimately, all funds passed to other providers, or used in paying the system costs for new objects and processes, is drawn from the original client process cash. While simple and efficient, the scheme should be an adequate charging mechanism whenever the provider is not suspected of misusing client information, and where the entire fee for the service can be computed and captured while the client process is under the control of provided code.

7. TYPE-MANAGED SERVICES

Some services cannot be provided by a single call on server code. An example is a service for creating, updating and querying a database. In such case, the client will expect to make many calls on the service interspersed with execution of his own code. Further, one or more data objects may have to be made by the server, which must survive between calls on the server, whose rental is the client's responsibility, but whose internal structure should not be visible to the client. Such services are often called *abstract type managers*, and the data objects they create on behalf of a client *instances* of the type.

Our system provides a mechanism useful for such servers, allowing them to be provided as pure code objects just as in the simple case of section 5, without requiring the provider to assume responsibility for the rental or identification of instances.

When a type manager routine creates an object on behalf of a client process which has called it, the manager may *seal* the capability for the object by XOR-ing the P2 field of the capability with a key pattern K embedded in the manager code object. The sealed capability is returned to the client, who must pass it back to the manager whenever requesting a further action on the instance. The manager can of course recover the original instance capability by XOR-ing the P2 field of the sealed capability with K. The client, however, cannot access the instance. Figure 3 shows a process calling a type manager to create an instance of a type.

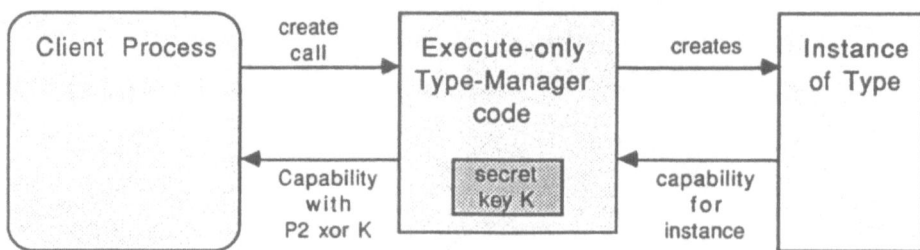

Figure 3: Creating a Typed Object.

Many systems can support type managers of this general sort. However, it is usually necessary for the client to call on the type manager for even the most routine management of the instance. In our case, it would seem that the client would have to call the type manager whenever the client wished to deposit funds in the instance, or to derive a child capability for the instance, or to copy the instance. In fact, our system allows the client to use the sealed capability directly for these purposes.

If a client presents a sealed capability to the system, its original unsealed version can be found in the catalogue by matching the object name and P1 fields alone. The system can then discover the seal key K as the XOR of the true and sealed P2 fields. The system will accept the sealed capability as sufficient authority for any action within the rights of the true capability, except actions which could reveal or alter the data in the instance. If the requested action is *derive, copy* or *rename*, involving the creation of a new capability, the system will seal the new capability with K before returning it to the client. Thus, a client may pay rent for, share use of or copy an instance without reference to the type manager, but any new capability created can be fully exercised only by the manager.

A type-managed service routine can charge for its use whenever called, and has available all instance information relevant to the fee calculation. However, it need carry no cost for the maintenance of the instances between calls, and need not even maintain itself any list or identification of extant instances.

8.   VULNERABILITY OF PASSWORDS

The 64-bit password field of a capability provides quite good security against malicious forgery. It might be considered that, given that some objects may have many valid capabilities, even this password size would be vulnerable to a systematic search. However, the charging mechanism is used to make such an attack infeasible. Whenever an invalid password is presented to the system, a small fine is levied on the offending process. The fine, of order a cent, is small enough to be tolerable for occasional innocent mistakes by user processes, e.g. an attempt to access an object previously destroyed, but large enough to make the cost of a serious attack prohibitive.

It may seem that the willingness of the system to accept for some purposes capabilities with invalid P2 fields opens a much cheaper line of attack. It seems that an attacker could exhaustively try different P1 values, say for a *derive* operation, until one succeeds, then try all P2 values together with the successful P1 value, say for a *read* operation, until a fully valid capability is discovered. The number of fines to be paid would then be of order 2^{32} rather than 2^{64}, and perhaps tolerable if the stakes are high enough. However, the system defeats this line of attack by returning an apparently successful result on any operation where only a valid P1 is required, even if the presented P1 is invalid. For instance, a *derive* operation, when given an invalid P1, will happily return a derivative. The nature of the operations permitted using sealed capabilities is such that their success can be determined only by the later success or failure of an operation requiring a fully-valid capability. If this fails, the attacker cannot know whether the failure was due to an invalid P1, an invalid P2 or both, and is so left with a search space of 2^{64}.

Note that sealing is transitive. If client U uses manager M1 (key K1) which in turn uses manager M2 (Key K2), the instance capabilities returned to U for objects created by M2 will be sealed by both K1 and K2, and can be unsealed and used by M2 only if passed back through M1.

9. LOCKING

The above simple charging schemes are inadequate if the client suspects that the server may misuse the client's data. The capability system has a mechanism called *locking* which can prevent such disclosure. It is available both in-process (i.e. when the server is called as a procedure) and out-of-process (when the server is a separate process.) The former will be assumed here: there is little difference in the two cases.

A process may make a *protected procedure call* which differs from a normal procedure call in that

(a) capabilities immediately available to the caller (i.e. objects which are visible to the caller because it has previously presented capabilities for them) may be hidden. The capabilities are placed in a stack in the process object which is not directly accessible to the process, and the objects will reappear only on return from the protected procedure (the server).

(b) the caller specifies an arbitrary 64-bit *lock* L.

(c) a set of capabilities may be passed to the procedure by the caller. However, the password (both P1 and P2 fields) of each is XOR-ed with L and only the modified form is visible to the called routine.

(d) 64-bit *lockword* W in the process object is replaced by W XOR L.

During execution of the server procedure, all capabilities presented by the procedure to obtain access to an object are automatically XOR-ed with the new W before the catalogue is consulted. If W was originally zero, and the original capabilities passed in to the procedure were valid, the catalogue search will succeed. Further, if the server procedure creates any new capabilities, the form returned to the server by the system will have its password XOR-ed with W. The effect is that the locked procedure can freely access those objects passed to it by the caller, can freely create and use new objects, but cannot access any other preexisting object. Any object which the procedure creates may survive return from the procedure, and the procedure may return to the client (as an ordinary datum value) a capability for the object which the caller, knowing L, can unlock. However, even if the procedure, through some covert channel, can succeed in conveying to a third party a capability for some client or new object, the capability will not be valid, and cannot be unlocked without knowledge of L. Thus, disclosure by the server of any client data is infeasible. Figure 4 shows a process locking itself.

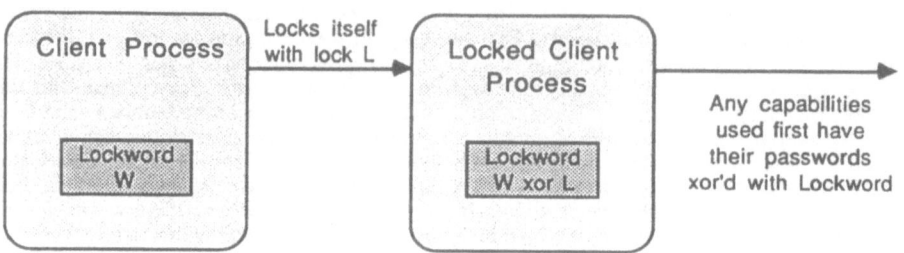

Figure 4: Locking a Process.

Note that locking is transitive. If a process with W=0 (i.e. unlocked) calls server S1 with lock L1, S1 will run under lockword W1=L1. If S1 calls server S2 with lock L2, S2 will run under lockword W2=L1 XOR L2. If S2 creates a result object and returns to S1 its capability, the capability will be locked by W2. Knowing L2, S1 can remove the lock L2, giving a form locked by L1, and hence usable by S1. In fact, there is no real distinction between locked and unlocked states; a process cannot discover whether or not it is locked, let alone what its lockword might be.

When a locked process creates a new process, the new process normally inherits the lockword of its creator, and so has no more or less freedom than its creator. However, the creating process may if it wishes apply a further lock to the new process, in effect achieving an out-of-process form of the protected procedure call.

There is one exception to the automatic application of lockwords. A capability whose rights do not allow any change of state of the object or any capability for it is called a *non-alter* capability, and a reserved digit of the capability format is used to mark it as such. Non-alter capabilities are not locked on being passed in a protected procedure call, nor XOR-ed with the lockword on presentation, since they cannot be used to convey information to third parties. This exception allows a server procedure to exercise read-only or execute-only capabilities embedded in its code, for instance to call other procedures or to read tables of constants.

A cautionary note: No user of a locked service should pass to the locked server routine or process any capability which the user has received from a third party. If the user does so, it is possible that the third party has conspired with the service provider to place a copy of the capability somewhere where the locked server can read it using a non-alter capability. The server, by comparing the true copy with the locked version passed to it, could then discover the lock under which it is running, and hence disclose any information it liked. To prevent this possibility, a user should always rename or derive an equivalent of any capability received from third parties before passing it to a locked server.

10. CHARGING FOR LOCKED SERVICES

Charging for a locked service is rather more complex than for a trusted service. First, a locked routine cannot deposit fees in itself. To permit it to do so, while allowing the provider or her agent to withdraw the deposited funds, would open a covert channel through which the locked routine could, by the timing and/or value of its deposits, convey client information to the provider. Indeed, if the covert transmission is to be entirely blocked, the total fee recovered by the provider cannot be allowed to be a function of client information, and so must be fixed before the provider gains access to the client's data. Thus, the client must inform the provider's agent about the scale of service requested, and the agent must fix a price for the service, before the service commences.

Second, while it is necessary to lock the server procedure to prevent it from disclosing client data, it must still be possible for the procedure to alter the state of some object external to the procedure, but inaccessible to the client, so as to record the fact that service has been provided. Otherwise, once the client had paid for a service, there would be no memory outside the client's reach as to whether the service had been performed, and the client could re-use the service without further payment. We require that provision of the service alter some state information which is:

(a) presettable by the provider, so as to fix the amount of service to be performed;

(b) invisible to the provider, lest the alterations caused by the service procedure disclose information;

(c) inaccessible to the client, lest the client reset the state to erase memory of service performed and hence steal additional service.

Our system allows these requirements to be met. Assume the service will be provided in-process by a locked procedure. The client describes the task to the provider. The provider quotes a price to the client. The client sends the provider the stated fee. Now the provider creates a data object containing a description of the amount (and perhaps nature) of the service to be done. The provider derives a capability C for this object, having only read, write, deposit and rename rights, then seals C with key K, and sends the sealed form to the client.

The client cannot read or alter the data object. However, he can deposit in it enough money to ensure its survival for the duration of the service (any excess will be lost). He then *renames* the capability, in effect destroying it and receiving a replacement with the same rights, a different password, and still sealed with K. The client cannot, of course, read or write using the new capability, but now the provider can no longer reach the object at all, since any capability for the object she may have retained is no longer valid. The client now calls the service procedure (the capability for which can be publicly known) via a protected procedure call with some lock L, and passing in a capability for his data, and the sealed, renamed capability C.

The service procedure has constant K in its code body, and so can unseal C. Note that the unsealed version will still be locked, but sealing and locking commute. The service procedure can now read and write the "amount of service" object, and decrement the amount as it proceeds. It will, of course, cease work if the amount decreases to zero.

This change of state in the "amount of service" record is invisible to the provider because of renaming, and inaccessible to the client because of sealing.

Note that if the service is a type manager, it can when first called copy the "amount of service" record into a type instance object, so it can accumulate the total amount of service provided over a succession of calls. The type instance is also inaccessible to the client (because sealed) and to the provider (through ignorance of its name). Such charging is depicted in Figure 5.

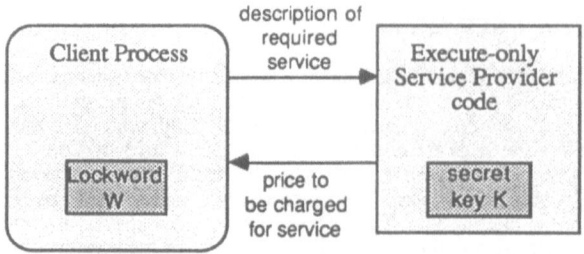

Step 1. Getting a quotation for the service.

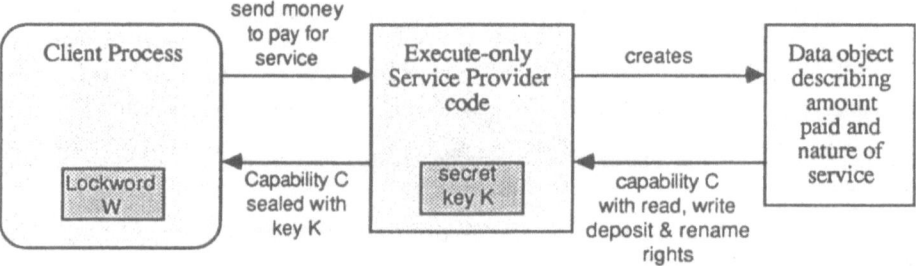

Step 2. Paying for the service.

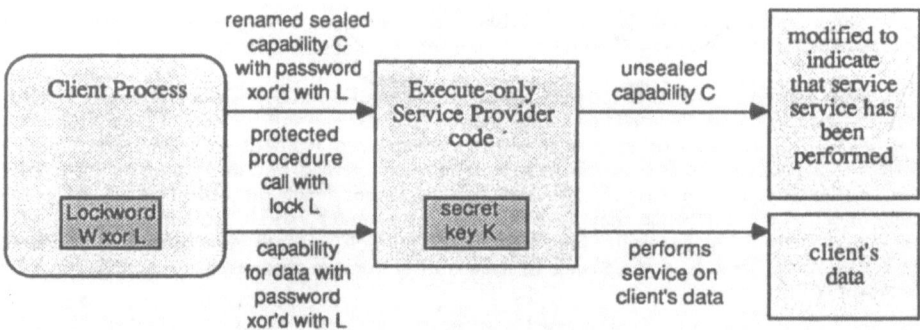

Step 3. Performing the service.

Figure 5: Charging for Locked Services.

The above scheme for charging for locked services is easily modified for out-of-process services. In this case, the provider when paid may construct a process to perform the service and give the client a capability for the process which does not allow the deposit or the sending of funds to the process. The initial cash placed in the process by the provider can be calculated to limit the amount of service provided by the process. It is still necessary for the client to rename and lock the server process, to block any information channel between server and provider. Note that, as the mailbox in which a process receives messages is finite, a process receiving messages can convey information to the process sending them by the timing of its reading and clearing the mailbox. By renaming the server process, we prevent the provider from sending it messages.

This is not the only scheme which may be devised for charging for locked services.

The service provider can make available a capability with execute-only rights for an object containing procedures which can provide quotations for service and which can charge for requested services. The charging procedure deposits the funds and records details of the type of service for which payment has been received and a randomly chosen password in an object whose capability is embedded in the execute-only code. A server process is created by the charging procedure. Its program code will perform the required service. A read-only capability for the object containing the record of payment and password and the password itself is placed in the server process. A capability for the server process with rights to deposit and withdraw funds, to lock the process and to send and receive messages but not to alter other aspects of the process is returned to the client. These procedures are run unlocked. The client should immediately rename the process to ensure that no-one else can make use of it as an information channel or just to steal services for which the client has paid. Note that when an existing process is locked, all loaded capabilities are revalidated to ensure that they are allowed to be used in the locked environment. This is required to prevent alter capabilities being used for information channels.

When the client wishes to have the service performed he may lock the server process and send it a message containing capabilities for objects defining the work to be performed. The process can verify the password and the service for which the client has paid by examining the object in which the charging record is stored using the read-only capability. It cannot however alter the charging record to indicate that the service has been performed since its capability only provides read access.

This scheme for charging for locked services uses a different mechanism for ensuring that the client does not use the service more than once without being charged for subsequent use. Instead of having the service adjust the "amount of service" data to reflect the actual use of the service, the use of the service is reflected in the changing of the program counter of the server process from its initial state. Because the client has no capability allowing for the program counter to be reset to the start of the service program, there is no way for the service to be used again without going through the charging procedure. The password allows for many charging records to be stored in the one object. If there is only one charging record in the object the password is not necessary.

11. CONCLUSION

The use of password capabilities makes a money system attractive if only as a means for garbage collection. However, the money system can then be used to allow rational used-based charging for services, even when those services are not trustworthy. The capability sealing and locking mechanisms, although introduced to facilitate type managers and information confinement, prove useful in implementing some versions of charging.

ACKNOWLEDGEMENT

We acknowledge the significant contribution of Mark Anderson in devising and implementing the Password Capability System and data confinement mechanism on which these charging mechanisms are based.

REFERENCES

1. Anderson, M., Pose R.D. and Wallace, C.S., "A Password-Capability System", *The Computer Journal,* Vol. 29, No. 1, 1986, pp. 1-8.

2. Anderson, M. and Wallace, C.S., "Some Comments on the Implementation of Capabilities", *The Australian Computer Journal*, Vol. 20, No. 3, 1988, pp. 122-130.

3. Wallace, C.S., "A Physically Random Generator", *Computer Systems Science and Engineering,* Vol. 5, No. 2, 1990, pp. 82-88.

Algorithms for Data Encryption

Wilhelm Müller
Universität Bremen

ABSTRACT

An overview of well known and not so well known data encryption systems is given. Some suggestions for their use in capability based computer systems are made and problems are pointed out.

1. ENCRYPTION AND A CAPABILITY SYSTEM

It is widely accepted that computer systems which use capabilities to control access to resources provide a high level of security. So what may encryption be necessary for in such a system, one may ask.

One use of it is, of course, its "standard application"—the protection of data transmitted across conventional links. But we shall see that in a system with capabilities and a large linear virtual address space other applications of data encryption are needed, too.

1.1. Capabilities in a computer network

If advantage is to be taken of all the abilities of a capability based computer in a transparent (and homogeneous) distributed system—especially the fact that knowledge about the actual storage location of objects shall usually not be necessary for almost all of the systems operation, even not during everyday administrative activities—capabilities have to be transmitted across the network to the storage location of an object. In the process of this transmission and during the checking if the presented capability permits the desired operation, it has to be ensured that no forgery can be committed.

1.2. Capabilities and removable storage media

There is another problem occurring with data generated in a capability system: when they are stored on a medium like a floppy disk, it may or may not be desirable that they be accessible when this medium is to be read by a machine which has no or other protection mechanism.

2. DIFFERENT ENCRYPTION SYSTEMS

Several different encryption systems have been described during the last years. They can be classified—quite superficially, though—as either "conventional" ones, that is, by knowing the algorithm and the key used for encryption, it is possible to decipher a message, or "public key systems," that is, though the encryption key and the algorithm are known to everybody (who wants to know them), deciphering is only possible for the intended recipient of a message.

2.1. DES

Of the conventional encryption systems, only DES (and enigma) are used in larger applications. The main reason is probably that DES was specifically designed to be an ANSI standard. One of the points that are usually used in arguments against DES is that some of the mathematics which were needed to built the S-boxes are confidential, thus prohibiting a real examination of its security...[13]

DES uses a essentially conventional enciphering matrices, together with some amount of non-linearity introduced by the permutations given by the S-boxes.

With DES, it is not possible to check that the communication partners are the ones they pretend to be (the signature problem).

2.2. Superincreasing knapsack

One of the first public key systems was based on the NP completeness of the knapsack problem [8].

2.2.1. How knapsack encryption works

If A wants to receive encoded messages, chooses—randomly—two integers a and m so that $\gcd(a, m) = 1$ and a vector v_i with n elements,

$$\sum_{j=0}^{k} v_j < v_{k+1} \qquad \text{for all } k < n - 1$$

(that is, the vector is *superincreasing*), and $v_{n-1} < m$.

A then publishes the vector $w_i = a v_i \bmod m$ and keeps the v_i, a, and m secret. An n-bit message consisting of the bits e_i is encrypted as

$$C = \sum_{j=0}^{n-1} e_i w_i.$$

Let b be the multiplicative inverse of a $\pmod{m}$. Decoding is done by computing bC which is equal to

$$\sum_{j=0}^{n-1} e_i v_i.$$

Recovering the v_i from bC means in fact to solve the knapsack problem. But because of the special properties of the v_i, the ones present in that sum can be recovered quite simply—which means that the e_i can be recovered.

Since it is based on a quite special variant of knapsack, Shamir could show that this variant of knapsack encryption could be broken in polynomial time [15]. But there are modifications to encryption scheme to which Shamir's solution does not apply [9].

The other problem with knapsack encryption is the same as with DES: signatures cannot be transmitted easily.

2.3. RSA

The public key encryption system which is best known to the public, is the one published by Rivest, Shamir, and Adleman (thus the name) at about the same time as the knapsack algorithm [1]. It makes use of the fact that the problem of factoring a large integer is still quite difficult, while there are efficient methods for testing if a number is prime or composite without revealing a factor in the latter case (though actually these algorithms are probabilistic—the result is either "the number is composite" or "the probability that it is composite is less than 0.5 (or 0.25 for some algorithms)").

2.3.1. The RSA algorithm

RSA makes use of Euler's generalization of Fermat's Little Theorem in a slitely modified form:

Theorem 1 (Euler) *If $\varphi(n)$ denotes the positive integers less than n and prime to n (Euler's φ-function), then*

$$a^{\varphi(n)+1} = a \pmod{n},$$

if n is not divisible by a square besides 1.

The algorithm works as follows: A user selects two (large) primes p and q and computes $n = pq$ and $\varphi(n) = (p-1)(q-1)$. She then selects an integer d prime to $\varphi(n)$, that is, $\gcd(d, \varphi(n)) = 1$, and computes e so that $de = 1 \pmod{\varphi(n)}$. d and n are published and used for encryption in the following form: if P is (the coded form of) a plaintext message less than n, $C = P^d \bmod n$ is the encrypted message. According to the above theorem, $C^e = P \pmod{n}$. (Because of the commutativity of the multiplication, it is actually of no importance if e or d is published, as long as only one of them is known to everybody.)

2.3.2. Signatures with RSA

The last two sentences show one important difference between the knapsack algorithm and this one: the encrypting and the decoding function are the same. With this in mind, it is simple to imagine a signature system: if someone wants to ensure that a message may be recognized to have been origined from her, she publishes the encrypted message $D = P^e \bmod n$. Everybody may read the message by computing $D^d \pmod{n}$, but, since e is not known to anybody, no-one else can generate the encrypted message D.

Combining these two encryption processes—that is, encrypting with the private key e_S of the sender and the public key d_R of the recipient—ensures that a message stays secret and has provably been sent by S.

2.3.3.   A word about the breakability of RSA

The RSA algorithm relies on two facts: that $\varphi(n)$ cannot be simply computed without knowing the prime factors of n, and that factorization as such is difficult. While less is known about the first fact, factorization has been a large research area for centuries.

The best algorithm for factoring large integers n has a time complexity of

$$e^{\sqrt{(1+\varepsilon)\log n \log\log n}}.$$

Though this currently seems to be the definite limit (with $\varepsilon \to 0$), this is still to be proved. The work of Lenstra [10] gave a hint that better algorithms for factorization may use quite unexpected means. But if this limit were proved, RSA would be highly recommendable public key algorithm, the only requirement being that the size of n be increased with increasing computer power. (Of course, there will be several restrictions imposed on the primes p and q, unless the factorization of n is to become too simple.)

2.4.   Algorithms based on logarithms in finite fields ("discrete logs")

Of the different discrete log systems, only one will be described here, the one published by El Gamal. The main reason is that the two best known other ones have either another intention—Diffie-Hellman [4] is a system which lets two users agree on a key they will use for another encryption system—or require several transmissions of differently encrypted versions of the same message (Massey-Omura, [11]).

2.4.1.   What are discrete logs?

In a finite field F_q, q power of a prime, it is simple to compute the k-th power of an element g, that is, multiplying g k times with itself—essentially by the same method used with real numbers. But, quite different from these, finding an exponent k for a given b and g so that $b = g^k$, is very difficult (for most gs).

2.5.   The El Gamal system

Every user uses the same field F_q and element g of this field. She then selects a secret field element a and published g^a. If someone wants to send her a message P, she actually receives the pair $Pg^{a_R a_S}$. If it holds that deriving $g^{a_R a_S}$ from g^{a_R} and g^{a_S} in a more efficient way than solving the discrete log problem is not possible, only the one who knows a_R will be able to quickly decipher this message by computing $(g^{a_S})^{a_R}$ and dividing the second element by it (or $(g^{a_S})^{q-1-a_R}$ and multiplying the second element with it, cf. theorem 1) [6].

2.5.1.   How secure are discrete logs?

In the general case, the discrete log problem seems to be as difficult to solve as the factorization of numbers, which is suggested, too, by similarities of some algorithms for these two tasks.

However, in the very convenient case of q being a power of 2, say, 2^n, which means that g, a, k, and P are simply bit strings, special algorithms apply, so that n should be chosen to be at least 1000—which makes all the computations rather slow again [3].

2.6. Elliptic curves

Elliptic curves have been analyzed by algebraic geometry for quite a while. Since it is possible do define finite groups (not fields—there are no other finite fields besides those with p^n elements, p prime, $n > 0$ integral) by means of these, cryptosystems using them have been developed over the last years [16, 9].

A reason for the interest in other groups besides the multiplicative ones of finite fields is that the structure of the latter ones is well understood and not very complicated. If groups with a more complex structure were used, it might be possible to find "one way functions" which are more difficult to break than the examples given above for finite fields.

2.6.1. What is an elliptic curve?

In general, an elliptic curve is the set of all points (x, y) fulfilling the equation

$$y^2 + a_1 xy + a_3 y = x^3 + a_2 x^2 + a_4 x + a_6$$

with the a_i, x, and y being elements of some field. This general formula can be transformed into simpler ones, depending on the characteristic of the field. For the our purposes, the forms

$$y^2 = x^3 + ax^2 + bx + c$$

for characteristic 3,

$$y^2 + y = x^3 + ax + b$$

for characteristic 2 (which is actually not general enough, but will do here), and

$$y^2 = x^3 + ax + b$$

for other characteristics will be used. (The right side of the equation must not have multiple roots. The reason for different formulas in different fields is that $2 = 0$ if the characteristic is 2, and $3 = 0$ if the characteristic is 3.)

2.6.2. Defining a group over an elliptic curve

Let's for a moment assume that our field is the one of the real numbers. If you plot an elliptic curve in a cartesian coordinate system, you will obtain a small closed curve and one branch which approaches $\pm\infty$ with $x \to +\infty$. We will include the point at infinity, designated by E, in the set given by our equation, that is, we will use a projective plane and include the projective point $(0, 1, 0)$.

We define the operation $P_1 * P_2$ for two elements of our elliptic curve geometrically. If either element is E, the result will be the other operand, thus E is the neutral element. Otherwise, we draw the line through P_1 and P_2. (If $P_1 = P_2$, we will use the tangent.) This line intersects the elliptic curve at exactly one more point (possibly at E). The point symmetric to the intersection point with respect to the x axis is the result of $P_1 * P_2$. This implies that P_1^{-1} is the point symmetric to P_1 with respect to the x axis.

Some computations show that the elliptic curve together with this operations really has the structure of an Abelian group (but is, obviously, not finite). The operations may formally be defined in the same manner for elliptic curves over finite fields, thus giving a means to generate a huge amount of finite Abelian groups. It can be shown that these groups are cyclic or the product of two cyclic groups. The number N of elements of such a group can be computed in polynomial time, but an even simpler estimate is given by

Theorem 2 (Hasse)

$$|N - (q + 1)| \leq 2\sqrt{q}$$

which suffices for most purposes.

2.6.3. How to use these groups for enciphering

Theorem 2 shows that finite groups over elliptic curves of every desired size will exist, thus allowing for an embedding of any desired messages in such a group.

Every cryptographic algorithm based on discrete logs may as well be used with the finite groups generated by elliptic curves. Instead of raising some element g to some power n, one applies the operation $*$ to the point itself n times, for which we still write g^n. There seems to be no simple way to recover n when knowing g and g^n, whereas computing g^n from n and g is a simple and repeated application of some elementary operations.

Especially, the system of El Gamal will take the following form: a finite field F_q, an elliptic curve C and some point on it, B, are fixed and publicly known. Each user selects a (secret) integer a and publishes B^a. If a message P is to be send to her, the sender transmits the pair $P * B^{a_S a_R}$, which can be deciphered only if a_R is known. (Of course, care has to be taken when choosing the C and B.)

2.7. "Zero knowledge systems"

Zero knowledge systems are no cryptosystems by themselves, but provide means to communicate the message "I know the information $\mathcal{I}$" without revealing the message itself. Here, I'll present only one algorithm which relies on the intractability of the discrete log problem [5].

2.7.1. The algorithm by Guillou and Quisquater

Everyone who may have to prove its identity I (the "claimee" **C**) obtains a value B such that $B^p * I = 1 \pmod{N}$ for publicly known N and p. (The factorization of N must, of course, not be known to anybody besides the organization issuing the identification values B.)

If the claimee has to prove its identity to a verifier **V**, it proceeds as follows:

1. C sends I—that is, the identity it claims to be—to V.

2. C selects a random r, $1 < r < N - 1$, and transmits r^p mod N to V.

3. V selects a random element D, $0 < D < p - 1$, and transmits it to C.

4. C computes
$$t = rB^D \bmod N$$
and transmits it to V.

5. V computes
$$t^p I^D \bmod N,$$
which will be the same value as r^p mod N if the claimee is who it pretends to be.

This is a called a zero knowledge prove since it will not be possible for the verifier to find out the authentication value B (if N and p are correctly chosen) [7].

3. PRACTICAL APPLICATIONS OF AND PROBLEMS WITH CRYPTO-GRAPHIC ALGORITHMS IN CAPABILITY SYSTEMS

This section will only give some hints to the subject, since there will be more said about it later by Mr. Freisleben.

While there are not many problems (algorithmic ones, that is) when an encryption system is applied to conventional data on a storage medium or in telecommunication links, in a system like the MONADS/PC special requirements have to be considered.

3.1. Why public key at all?

In a network of capability based computers, at least one type of information transmitted on possibly insecure channels has to be verified for its validity: the capabilities. Public key encryption offers itself since it provides algorithms for exchanging and verifying signatures electronically.

3.2. Size of plaintext and ciphertext

All public key systems, as described here, make use of some finite field F_{p^n}. Unless p happens to be 2—which is a bad choice for the El Gamal algorithm—, the encrypted data will need more storage capacity than the plaintext.

Now, in the MONADS/PC [14], like in other persistent storage systems, data are transferred from secondary storage to main memory in a manner which is of no interest to the application program, in this concrete case by paging. (This is, of course, even true if the data reside on another machine.) If we wanted to solve the security problem for removable storage media by storing only encrypted data, this would result in a quite complex paging algorithm: the paging routine would not only have to decipher the data, but it would need an additional buffer for storing the encrypted page since this wouldn't fit into the destination frame.

3.3. Computation time

Many uses of public key systems either take place in an environment where time is not (very) important–whether checking the validity of a autoteller card takes $2\mu s$ or 2s doesn't matter—, are simple exchanges of one time keys for faster—but possibly less secure—encryption algorithms, or ensure the identity of the communication partners, that is the (long) message is not encoded, but only unforgeably signed. ([2] says that RSA is about 1000 times slower than DES!)

On the other hand, using such algorithms for data on a secondary storage device, accessed by paging (or segmentation), requires fast (and simple) algorithms, imposing quite strong restrictions on the used system. This means that RSA will be a quite obvious, though maybe not the best, choice, since hardware supporting RSA encryption is readily available.

3.4. Capabilities

These problems do not necessarily apply to capabilities. Using some encryption mechanism would allow to spread capabilities which may be used only be the designated recipient, though she doesn't know the actual value of it. She would receive an encoded copy which must be presented instead of the capability itself when an access is to be made. If one wants to ensure that this copy cannot be transferred to other users, the encoded form would contain the identification of the intended one in some coded form, as well, and a zero knowledge system would provide the means for validation:

Each user R (or computer in the network, or whatsoever) gets its private identification I together with the authentication value B, when it is established in the system (or network, or ...). When R is to receive a capability C, the identity of R is validated using the algorithm given above (or a similar one). Then some value D is computed by a one-way function from C and I, that is $D = f(C, I)$, and C and D is sent to R. If this D is established similarly to B, it will not be necessary for R to send D itself if it wants to use C, but it can prove that it has a valid copy and thus may access the data protected by it.

REFERENCES

1. Adleman, Rivest, Shamir "A method for obtaining digital signatures and public-key cryptosystems." *Comunications of the ACM,* 1978

2. Brassard Modern Cryptology. New York, Berlin, 1988.

3. Coppersmith "Fast evaluation of logarithms in fields of characteristic two." *IEEE Transactions in Information Theory IT-30,* 1984.

4. Diffie, Hellman "New directions in cryptography." *IEEE Transactions in Information Theory IT-22,* 1976.

5. Fiat, Shamir How To Prove Yourself: Practical Solutions to the Identification and Signature Problems. Weizmann Institute of Science, Rehovot, 1986.

6. El Gamal "A public key cryptosystem and a signature scheme based on discrete logarithms." *IEEE Transactions in Information Theory.*

7. Guillou, Quisquater A practical zero-knowledge protocol fitted to security microprocessor minimizing both transmission and memory. In *Eurocrypt,* 1988.

8. Hellman, Merkle "Hiding information and signatures in trapdoor knapsacks." *IEEE Transactions in Information Theory IT-24*, 1978.

9. Koblitz A Course in Number Theory and Cryptography. New York, Berlin, 1987.

10. Lenstra "Factoring integers with elliptic curves." *Report 86-18*, Universiteit van Amstgerdam, 1986.

11. Massey "Logarithms in finite cyclic groups—cryptographic issues." *Proceedings of the 4th Benelux Symposium on Information Theory*, 1983.

12. Meyer, C. Cryptography: a guide for the design and implementation of cryptographic systems. John Wiley & Sons, Inc. 1982

13. National Bureau of Standards Data Encryption Standard. Washington, DC, 1977.

14. Rosenberg MONADS-PC System Management Instructions. Newcastle, N.S.W., 1987.

15. Shamir "A polynomial time algorithm for breaking the basic Merkle–Helman cryptosystem." *Proceedings of the 23rd Annual Symposium on the Foundations of Computer Science*, 1982.

16. Silverman The Arithmetic of Elliptic Curves. New York, Berlin, 1986.

Capabilities and Encryption:
The Ultimate Defense Against Security Attacks ?

B. Freisleben and P. Kammerer
University of Darmstadt

J.L. Keedy
University of Bremen

ABSTRACT

Capability–based addressing is an attractive mechanism to control access to information in an object–oriented system. Several capability–based systems have been built in the past, but most of them proved to be unsatisfactory because they suffered from severe performance penalties due to a number of implementation problems. In the *MONADS-PC* these problems have been solved by providing dedicated architectural support for a two–level capability scheme which is used to efficiently address and protect segments in its large uniform virtual memory and to control access to the semantic operations of major objects. Although this organization has many advantages for protecting information within a *MONADS PC* system, it is not sufficient to cope with the security attacks outside its sphere of control, such as physically copying software from removable storage devices or intercepting insecure communication lines in a network of computers. One way to avoid such security violations is to use encryption techniques. The focus of our research is to investigate the suitability of different encryption techniques in a *MONADS* environment. We discuss the issues involved in using encryption in conjunction with capabilities and postulate that both methods are necessary to provide a high degree of system security.

1. INTRODUCTION

The general aim of protection mechanisms in computing environments is to prevent unauthorized users from accessing the system resources illegitimately. Several such mechanisms have been proposed, at the hardware level, in the operating system and in the file and/or database system to ensure the secrecy, privacy, authenticity and integrity of information. But no one of these or combination thereof is sufficient to guard against all possible security attacks, because there is no way to provide protection without relying on some fundamental assumptions about the trustworthiness of certain components, services, or people involved in the development of a computer system. Since trust is an essential ingredient of all protection endeavours, intruders prepared to invest in breaching the security will always find possibilities to be successful. Protection mechanisms are needed to make this as hard as possible.

In this paper we present the approaches taken to provide protection within a centralized and distributed *MONADS-PC* environment [1, 13, 19]. The *MONADS-PC* computer system has been built to provide architectural support for the features of object–oriented software development [10]. It is rigorously based on a few but powerful design principles, most notably the notion of a large uniform persistent virtual memory with an efficient implementation of capability–based addressing [3, 12].

This paper proposes enhancements to the existing capability mechanisms to provide stronger protection via a three–fold cooperative effort. First, the capability–based protection mechanism is used to control access to objects. Second, since the *MONADS* capability scheme is based on dedicated hardware and operating system kernel support, the trustworthiness of these components is ensured by using encryption techniques. Third, encryption is also employed to securely transfer information across a network of *MONADS-PCs* and between each processor and its secondary storage devices.

The *MONADS* capability scheme is discussed in section 2. Our solution to the problem of authenticating the hardware and the kernel is presented in section 3. The focus of section 4 is the use of encryption techniques in a distributed *MONADS-PC* system. Conclusions and future research topics are discussed in section 5.

2. PROTECTION IN THE MONADS–PC

This section presents the protection mechanisms provided by a stand–alone *MONADS-PC*. The capability scheme is described first.

2.1. Capabilities in MONADS

The most natural and attractive protection mechanism for object-oriented systems is *capability-based addressing* [5]. A capability is informally equivalent to a ticket in the sense that possession of the ticket allows the holder access to the object described in the capability, provided that the access mode is compatible with the access rights stored within the capability. Several systems using the capability concept have been built in the past [8, 9, 16], but most of them were unsuccesful as a result of inefficient implementations. In the *MONADS-PC* these problems have been solved by providing dedicated architectural support for a capability scheme used to efficiently address and protect objects in its large uniform virtual memory. Capabilities in the *MONADS-PC* system have the following properties:

- Each capability contains a virtual address used to identify the object to which it provides access.

- Identifiers (virtual addresses) are unique and are never re-used to refer to a different object.

- Each capability also contains a list of operations which its holder may invoke on the object.

- There may be several capabilities for an object, possibly with different access rights, allowing several users to have shared access to an object.

- There is no way of forging a capability or changing its contents in an unauthorized way.

A unique characteristic of the *MONADS-PC* design, included for reasons of efficiency and organisational simplicity, is the implementation of two forms of capabilitiy corresponding to two quite separate levels of system implementation. The first of these, the *segment capability*, implemented with hardware support, is used to address individual segments of memory. It contains access rights which permit read and write operations as well as some special operations on certain segments. It also contains an indication of the segment's length, so that the hardware can check that a segment capability is not used to attempt to gain access to a contiguous segment (figure 1).

| Start Address | Length | Access Rights |

Figure 1: A Segment Capability

Segment capabilities are not visible to programmers or end users. They are collected in lists which define the segments from which a module is composed.

Access to a major object can only be gained by presenting a *module capability* which is fully supported in microcode and cannot be arbitrarily modified. A module capability uniquely identifies the object by the appropriate address space number and contains access rights indicating the interface procedures of the object which may be called by the presenter of the capability (figure 2).

| Address Space No. | Status Bits | Access Rights |

Figure 2: A Module Capability

Module capabilities are protected by being held in separate segments which may appear in any user object. Thus user objects may contain their own module capabilities and thus define their own calling environment. What prevents them being modified are the access rights in the segment capabilities by which they can be addressed. These define the content as module capabilities and specify what operations can be carried out on them.

Directory objects, which are used to map an object's name, represented as a string of characters, onto a module capability, can be supported as normal objects in the *MONADS-PC* system. Module capabilities can be stored in user accessible segments and manipulated with a defined set of (safe) operations, including transfer between segments, duplication etc. The standard *MONADS* directory object is actually a type manager which can be used to generate many individual directory objects. Since a directory is itself an object a capability for it may be inserted into another directory. It follows that directory objects may be individually programmed and used to construct arbitrary tree and graph structures. An example of the directory mechanism is presented in section 4. Furthermore, any object, not only those specially designed to serve as directories, can contain module capabilities.

The two-level capability organization is both very efficient and flexible, because forgery of capabilities is effectively prevented by dedicated hardware support and fine–grained protection of objects can be achieved under user control by allowing capability segments to appear in any user object.

The *MONADS* implementation of capabilities is a powerful and general conceptual basis for effectively providing security in a centralized environment. Because of the simplicity and uniformity of the capability approach, the *MONADS-PC* does not offer intruders the opportunity to exploit the complexity of the ad hoc schemes found in many other computer systems.

There are no arbitrary restrictions on the policy to be adopted for authorising access to objects, but since the default approach is no access without a capability, the protection of information becomes a straightforward matter. If there are strict controls over the distribution of capabilities, it is virtually impossible to violate the secrecy, privacy and integrity of information, because an intruder cannot present or generate an appropriate capability to invoke any operation in the system.

2.2. User Authentication

In conventional systems the operating system is responsible for checking the authenticity of users when they log in and this is usually carried out by checking the user's *password* against a file of passwords. The disadvantages of this organization are fairly obvious. First, since all users are subjected to the same system–defined method of checking, an intruder already knows what kind of test he or she has to pass. Second, since very sensitive information is stored in a central file which is usually owned by a special user, the *superuser*, an intruder easily knows the target of his or her attacks to breach the security of all users in the system.

Since the virtual memory organization of the *MONADS-PC* guarantees that all sorts of information, including state information about user processes, will persistent between closedowns unless deliberately deleted, the weaknesses of system password checking are easy to avoid. This is achieved as follows. When a user logs out he or she invokes a user–defined security module as part of the logout command after the usual deallocation procedures have been carried out. Instead of deleting the user process, the security module advises the system to deactivate it. When the user logs in again, his or her process is reactivated without any authenticity checks being carried out by the system. The process resumes at the point where it previously left off, i.e. in the user's security module. This can now carry out any type of check or sequence of checks the user has programmed, such as asking several questions with totally unrelated answers or requiring different passwords for each day of the week and/or dependent on the system clock. Thus appropriate protection is guaranteed for each user individually and intruders have a hard time to gain access to a user's working environment.

2.2. Subject Authentication

The standard presumption in capability systems, that possession of a capability is sufficient to permit access to an object, is often too weak in real situations. There are several cases where an invoked object may need to verify the identity of the invoking subject, such that the interpretation of "subject" can have different meanings.

In the first case it may be desirable to identify the *user* on whose behalf the object has been invoked (e.g. to ensure that the cost of the invoked service is charged to the correct user). Since in *MONADS* a user process can persist between terminal sessions (see section 2.2. above), its identifier (an address space number which is never reused) can serve as a unique user identifier. Any object which has been invoked can call the unprivileged machine instruction

$$< get\_process\_\# >$$

to ascertain this identifier.

Sometimes it is desirable to ascertain the identity of the (software) module invoking another module, for example to record the identifier of the module by which a security breach was attempted. This is supported in the *MONADS-PC* by the unprivileged machine instruction

$$< get\_calling\_module\_\# > .$$

Finally it may be useful to ascertain which type manager invoked the current object. For example, a printer driver might want to ensure that it is only invoked from accredited spooler type managers. For this purpose the unprivileged machine operation

$$< get\_calling\_type\_manager\_\# >$$

is available.

Effectively these instructions permit the introduction of checks which allow a "mandatory access control" policy to be applied over and above the "discretionary access controls" typically presupposed in conventional capability systems [4].

3. HARDWARE AND KERNEL AUTHENTICATION

All the mechanisms presented indicate that protection in a centralized MONADS-PC largely relies on trusting the hardware and the kernel, but as already mentioned there is no way that one can avoid trusting certain components in a computer system. However, there are means to increase the trustworthiness of these components. We discuss these in the following.

In general, users working with a computer system are practically unable to make sure that their system has the correct functionality and does not contain security flaws. The only thing they can do is to rely on the operating system producer. But on the other hand the operating system producer cannot take any responsibility if there is no guarantee that a system once delivered is not faked or changed in some way (e.g. to include secret trap-doors copying sensitive information) before installation. What is here needed is an installation procedure which allows the user (or a system manager) to ascertain the integrity and authenticity of the operating system currently running on the machine. The same arguments hold in an analoguous way for the underlying hardware. Both parties, the user and the operating system producer, have to rely on the correct functioning of the CPU. None of them can test the whole functionality of the CPU, in order to make sure that there are no security leaks. The only instance able to guarantee the correct functioning of a CPU is the hardware producer. But again a manufacturer can only take the responsibility if there are methods to ensure the authenticity and integrity of the CPU.

The above problems can be solved by the use of encryption techniques [14, 15]. A detailed description of the design and analysis of encryption methods is beyond the scope of this paper, but instead we merely summarize some characteristics which are essential to understanding the use of encryption in a *MONADS* environment.

3.1. Encryption Methods

There are two main classes of encryption methods:

- conventional or symmetrical encryption which is based on using the same key for encrypting and decrypting information (e.g. the DES method [11])

- public–key or asymmetrical encryption which is based on using separate keys, a public and a private one, for encrypting and decrypting information (e.g. the RSA method [18])

The most attractive features of the RSA method are its ease of use in distributing the keys among the communication partners and the simplicity of authenticating the sender of a message. In the DES method a separate logical channel, independent of the one established for communication, must be used to transfer the key to a communication partner. This clearly is a major security flaw. It is the great advantage of the RSA method that the secret decryption key does not need to be transfered and public keys can be distributed even without any encryption, making a separate channel obsolete. On the other hand, the DES method can be more efficiently implemented than RSA or other public-key crypto-systems. Recent hardware implementations of the DES method allow encryption rates of several Mbits/sec in contrast to 68 Kbits/sec for RSA chips [20], which clearly favours the DES method if large amounts of data must be encrypted.

3.2. Secure Booting

Due to its advantages for authentication, the RSA method is more attractive to the problem at hand and in fact has been used to verify the authenticity of software products within the software distribution process [7]. The following discussion is mainly based on a proposal which uses encryption techniques to securely boot the kernel of an operating system [6] and therefore provides the trust necessary to implement protection mechanisms for the rest of the system.

The usual way of achieving authentication using public–key methods is to arrange for the sender to encrypt a message with its own private key and with the receiver's public key. The receiver subsequently decrypts them with the complementary keys and can therefore easily verify the digital signature of the sender [2]. There is one problem with this ar-rangement: the sender cannot decide if the receiver's public key is the right one once an intruder masquerades as the desired receiver and claims its public key correct. A solution to this problem, known as the *key distribution problem*, requires a trusted third party as a *certification instance*. It is used to authenticate public keys with the help of signatures which we then call certificates.

We now describe a secure booting procedure which relies on the existence of two such trusted entities, the hardware manufacturer (HWM) and the operating system manufac-turer (OSM), each equipped with a pair of keys. The protocol is divided into three parts, the preparation phase, the boot process and the authentication phase. In the preparation phase the CPU generates, after it has been manufactured, a secret and a public key and makes the public key available to the HWM. The HWM creates a so called CPU certificate by applying its secret key to the unique identity of the CPU and the CPU's public key (figure 3). This certificate is assumed to be stored in the CPU key storage, a special hardware extension which also holds the secret key of the CPU. In this way the CPU can obtain a certified pair of keys without showing its secret key to anyone.

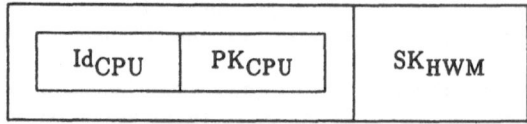

Figure 3: A CPU Certificate

The last action of the preparation phase is the creation of a secure boot module, consisting of the required code and the unique identity of the operating system, by the OSM. The boot module (or just a one–way checksum function applied to it for efficiency reasons) is then signed with the OSM's secret key (figure 4). We additionally assume that is possible to make the public keys of the HWM and the OSM securely available to the CPU. This can for example be achieved by using an EPROM containing the keys.

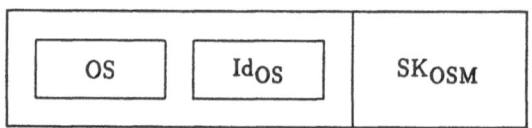

Figure 4: A Secure Boot Module

In the boot process, the second part of the protocol, the boot module is loaded into memory and the signature of the OSM is verified with the public key of the OSM. If this proves to be succesful, the CPU assigns a pair of keys to the operating system and stores it in the operating system key storage, a dedicated part of the main memory. The CPU then creates a boot certificate which contains the identity of the loaded operating system, the public key of the assigned pair of keys and the public key of the OSM (figure 5). At the end of the boot process, the operating system controls the CPU. It is the only entity which has access to the information contained in the CPU key storage, which is easily achieved by making it unaccessible until the next hardware reset.

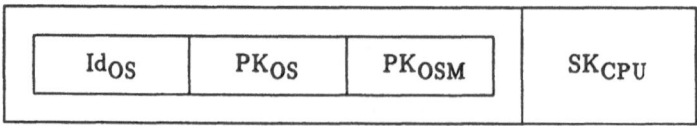

Figure 5: A Boot Certificate

The third part of the protocol, the authentication phase, serves to identify the trustworthiness of a running system to a user working with it or to another system willing to cooperate with it once it has been installed in a network. In order to achieve this, a random number is sent to the operating system in question. The operating system in turn signs it with its secret key and sends it back along with the CPU certificate and the boot certificate (figure 6).

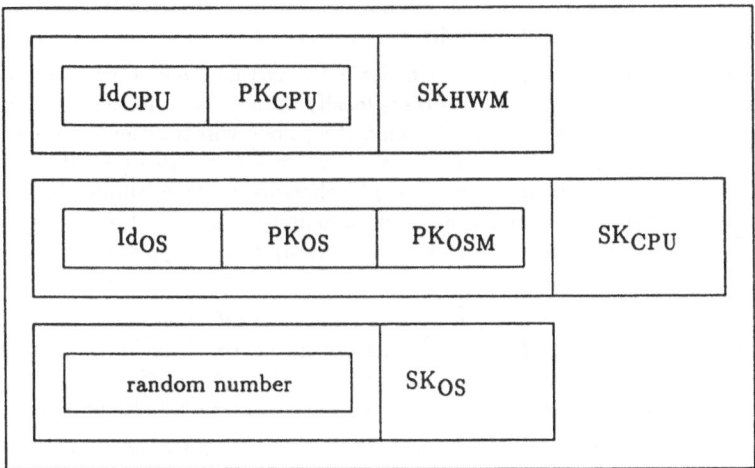

Figure 6: Operating System Authentication

The signature of the HWM in the CPU certificate can be verified by applying the HWM's known public key to it. The authentic public key of the CPU is then extracted and used to prove the signature of the CPU in the boot certificate. This enables the testing entity to obtain the authentic public keys of the operating system and the OSM used during the boot process. A comparison of the public key of the OSM and already known authentic public keys of trustworthy OSMs shows the authenticity of the OSM. Finally, the signature of the operating system on the random number is verified, which indicates that the operating system is still active and no replayed messages have been send by it. The same protocol may then be employed by the tested system in a network of computers in order to check the trustworthiness of the testing system. This is a straightforward solution for achieving mutual authentication in a distributed environment.

The presentation of this secure booting procedure has been kept general, because it is not only applicable to a *MONADS* environment. However, in combination with the capability scheme described in the previous section, it effectively provides a high degree of security within a centralized *MONADS* system. Security attacks outside its sphere of control, such as physically copying data from removable storage devices or intercepting insecure communication lines in a network of computers require additional protection efforts. We present these in the next section.

4. PROTECTION IN A NETWORK OF MONADS–PCs

The *MONADS* networking philosophy is based on the concept of a uniform distributed virtual memory which has previously been described in more detail [1]. We will briefly summarize the results.

4.1. Network Organization

The entire network shares a common virtual memory with a single range of unique addresses. Each node will have its own main memory and its own address translation unit. A node may, but need not, have its own disks.

The normal unit of transfer between the nodes is the virtual page. Each node detects its own page faults, and if possible resolves them locally. Otherwise it places a request for the missing page on the network. Eventually some other node will transfer the required page, which will then be noted in the address translation unit and the process which caused the page fault will be allowed to proceed. A page coherence scheme, similar in principle to cache coherence schemes to manage shared data, is implemented automatically [1]. Thus from the viewpoint of any node, the rest of the network simply appears to be a collection of remote disks.

In this way the user need not be aware of the location of information he wants to access, because symbolic names (which will be translated into capabilities using directories) are used to refer to it. No special mechanisms are needed to pass directories or capabilities between workstations, because they too are contained in normal pages of memory.

It is therefore easy to extend the idea of capabilities to a network of computers by allowing one computer to hold a capability for something inside another. These capabilities must still be unforgable, both within the machines and in transit across the network.

4.2. Capabilities and Encryption

In general, security violations in a distributed environment pose a more serious threat than those which exist on stand-alone machines since they permit an intruder access to multiple machines.

The only way to avoid such security violations is again to use encryption techniques in order to render the information useless for an attacker and to authenticate the parties willing to communicate with each other. It should, however, be mentioned that encryption methods cannot replace other protection mechanisms, such as capabilities. There are two reasons for this. First, some form of protection is needed anyway to protect the keys and the encryption algorithms. Second, fine-grained protection of object usage as provided by capabilities is not possible with encryption methods. From this it is fairly obvious that both techniques must be used in conjunction in order to enjoy their individual benefits for providing a high degree of system security. In the sequel we discuss the use of both mechanisms in a distributed *MONADS* environment.

4.2.1. Secure Paging

As already mentioned, the protection mechanisms in a stand–alone *MONADS*–system ensure that all information is secure as long as it is inside the hosts main memory. The two main areas for potential attacks which cannot be protected by capabilities are the transfer of information over the network and the transfer of information from and to the disks. Since each node in a distributed *MONADS* system treats the rest of the network as if it were a large disk, we in principle need only devise one solution to take care of both problem areas.

In the following we describe a straightforward protocol for resolving remote page faults in a secure manner. The protocol makes use of both the RSA and DES encryption methods and it is based on the fact that the kernel of each node is already equipped with an authenticated public key and a private key as a result of the secure booting mechanism described in the previous section. The public key of each node is made available to all machines as part of the authentication phase of the booting procedure.

When the virtual memory manager of a node has detected a remote page fault, it generates a DES key, appends it to the request message demanding the missing page, encrypts it with the public key of the node where the required page is located and sends it to the remote virtual memory manager to service the page fault. It in turn decrypts the message with the private key of the node it belongs to and transfers the required page, encrypted with the submitted DES key, over the network. Upon arrival at the node initiating the request, the page is decrypted with the DES key and the process which caused the page fault is allowed to proceed (figure 7).

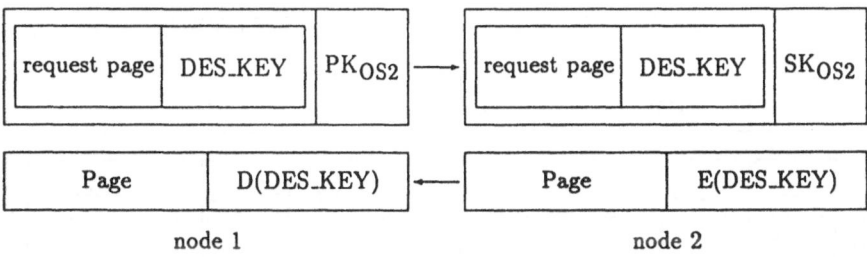

Figure 7: Secure Paging

The DES method may not only be used for sending pages over the network, but also to encrypt them when they are written back to a node's local disks and decrypt them when they are transfered to main memory as a result of servicing a local page fault. This ensures that all information in a *MONADS* system is securely stored and propagated among its components.

There might be some concern about the complexity of the above procedure, especially about whether it is necessary to operate with two different encryption methods. Although in our proposal public–key encryption is only used to set up the initial contact between two nodes and to securely exchange DES keys, the whole protocol would equally work with the RSA method alone. However, there are two important reasons why we decided to use the DES method for transfering virtual memory pages across the network. First, the encryption rates of the RSA implementations available today (see section 3) are by no means sufficient to avoid serious performance deteriorations which would render remote disk I/O, the basis of the *MONADS* distributed system organization, practically infeasible. Second, the RSA method cannot guarantee to maintain the length of information encrypted with it, because the ciphered text may become longer than the plaintext [17]. This property is particularly unsuitable for the disk based paging environment on which the *MONADS* system is based.

In order to realize our approach efficiently, a hardwired implementation of both the RSA and DES method is required. Since several encryption chips are already available, it will be a relatively straightforward task to extend the *MONADS* memory management hardware to provide the desired functionality.

4.2.2. Accessing Remote Objects

In order to gain access to remote objects, the kernel of each node maintains a table with entries for each node containing pairs of unique node numbers and their public keys. Since at least one capability is needed to initiate the use of objects stored on other nodes in the network, each entry in this table is additionally supplied with a capability for a special directory object on the associated node. A user willing to offer some of his or her objects for network–wide access deposits capabilities in this directory (or in a directory reachable from this directory) and likewise any system service intended for globally shared use is represented by its capability. Thus the directory serves as the principal point of contact for making objects available to users on remote machines (figure 8).

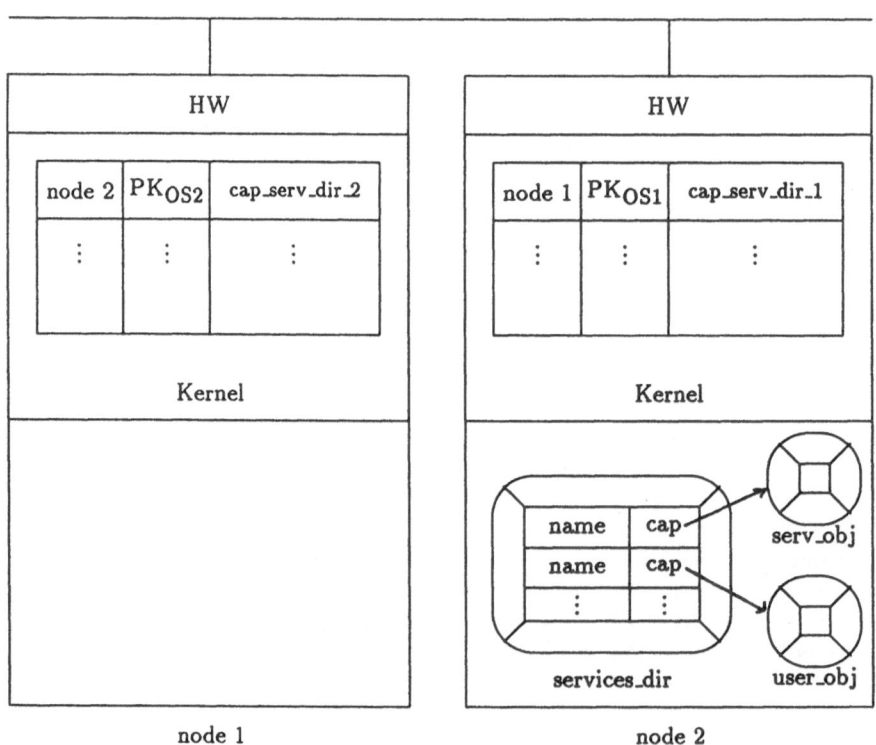

Figure 8: Capabilities for Remote Directories

4.3. Mailbox Example

We now present an example to illustrate how the *MONADS* facilities may be used to set up a simple but secure distributed mail service, using the existing default directory class of the *MONADS-PC* operating system. A directory entry includes the following items: a user-supplied name for the entry, the username of the user creating the entry, the process number of the process which made the entry, a module capability for the module to which the directory entry refers, a user-supplied text (normally used to describe the object described by the entry) and the date and time the entry was made. The interface operations supported by the class are the usual ones for inserting, removing, retrieving and listing entries, etc. The process number of the process which made the entry is guaranteed to be correct in that it is obtained not from a user parameter but rather by the directory module calling the kernel operation $<$ *get_process_#* $>$ (see 2.3). Similarly the username of the user creating the entry is guaranteed by the directory module calling the "user manager" module, which, as the module which creates new user processes, can guarantee the mapping from username to process number.

We first describe how such directories can be used to establish a simple local mailing system, allowing users registered at the same node to communicate with each other. Then we extend this model to allow communication between users registered at different nodes.

In a single node system there is a central directory (the "mailbox list"), for which all users inherit, when their user process is created, a module capability with access rights which allow (a) retrieval of the capabilities held in all entries and (b) the creation of a new entry. If a user is willing to receive mail from other users he or she creates a new entry by depositing a module capability for a private directory module (i.e. for his "mailbox") in the mailbox list directory. It should be noted that the mechanisms described above guarantee that entries in the mailbox list are for users for whom they purport to be; in other words, a user cannot masquerade as (and therefore receive mail intended for) another user. Any user can send mail to a user registered in the mailbox list by (a) retrieving from the mailbox list the capability chosen for the user's mailbox module and (b) calling this module to insert a mail entry. This entry can use the user-supplied name to describe the subject of the mail. Similarly the user-supplied text can be used as a short message. If a longer message is required, this can be passed as a capability for a text module. Alternatively the module capability field can be used to pass a module capability for any purpose. The date and time fields of the entry can as usual guarantee when the message (mail) was sent. Significantly, the username of the user creating the entry and the process number of the process which made the entry are guaranteed by the system so that authentication of the sender of mail is automatically guaranteed. Users can of course examine their mail with the standard directory listing facilities.

This simple model can be implemented with existing software which was originally designed to support directories rather than a mail system. With relatively trivial extensions it becomes possible to support a much more sophisticated mail system, e.g. with checks to accept mail only from a list of selected users, or with direction of mail to different mailboxes according to the sender's status, etc.

Extension of the mail system to a distributed environment based on the mechanisms described in earlier sections is remarkably simple. As indicated in section 4.2, the kernel of each node maintains a table with entries containing the node numbers and public keys of other nodes in the network, together with a capability for a directory at each other node. If this capability is the capability for the mailbox list at the remote node, and it is made accessible to users either directly or via the local mailbox list module, for example, then remote mail can function in exactly the same manner as local mail, with the same guarantees about authenticity of sender and receiver (with encryption in the background to ensure that physical tampering cannot take place).

5. CONCLUSIONS

In this paper we have presented the approaches taken to provide security within a centralized and distributed *MONADS-PC* environment. The two primary protection mechanisms used are capability-based addressing and encryption methods. Capabilities allow fine-grained access control to objects, whereas encryption is employed to both authenticate the hardware and kernel on which capabilities rely and to enable secure transfer of information in a network of *MONADS-PCs* and between each node's main memory and secondary storage devices. Further research is needed to practically demonstrate the feasibility of our approach by integrating the proposed encryption mechanisms in the *MONADS* architecture.

REFERENCES

1. D.A. Abramson and J.L. Keedy.
   Implementing a Large Virtual Memory in a Distributed Computing System.
   In *Proc. of the 18th Hawaii Int. Conference on System Sciences*, pages 515–522, 1985.

2. S.G. Akl.
   Digital Signatures: A Tutorial Survey.
   IEEE Computer, 2:15–24, 1983.

3. P. Brössler, F.A. Henskens, J.L. Keedy, and J. Rosenberg.
   Addressing Objects in a Very Large Distributed Virtual Memory.
   In *Proc. of the IFIP Conference on Distributed Processing*, pages 105–116, Amsterdam, 1987. North Holland.

4. M. Evered and J.L. Keedy.
   A Model for Protection in Persistent Object–Oriented Systems.
   In *Proc. of the Int. Workshop on Computer Architectures to Support Security and Persistence*, pages 5(1)–5(15), Bremen, West Germany, 1990.

5. R.S. Fabry.
   Capability Based Addressing.
   Communications of the ACM, 17(7), 1974.

6. M. Groß.
   How to Achieve Trustworthy Basis Systems With Secure Booting.
   Technical Report, GMD Darmstadt, 1989.

7. A. Herzberg and S. Pinter.
   Public Protection of Software.
   ACM Transactions on Computer Systems, 5(11):371–393, 1987.

8. IBM.
   IBM System/38 Technical Developments.

IBM General Systems Division, 1980.

9. INTEL.
Introduction to the iAPX432 Architecture.
INTEL Corporation, no. 17821-001 edition, 1981.

10. A.K. Jones.
The Object Model, a Conceptual Tool for Structuring Software, volume 60 of *Lecture Notes in Computer Science*, pages 7–16.
Springer–Verlag, 1978.

11. A. Kalinski, R. Rivest, and S. Sherman.
Is DES a Pure Cipher, volume 218 of *Lecture Notes in Computer Science*, pages 212–221.
Springer–Verlag, 1985.

12. J.L. Keedy.
An Implementation of Capabilities without a Central Mapping Table.
In *Proc. of the 17th Hawaii Int. Conference on System Sciences*, pages 180–185, 1984.

13. J.L. Keedy.
The MONADS–PC System: A Programmer's Overview.
Technical Report 8–89, University of Bremen, 1989.

14. E. Kranakis.
Primality and Cryptography.
Teubner–Verlag, Stuttgart, 1986.

15. C. Meyers and S. Matyas.
Cryptography.
Wiley & Sons, 1982.

16. R.M. Needham.
The CAP Project – an Interim Evaluation.
In *Proc. of the ACM Symposium on Operating System Principles*, pages 17–22, 1977.

17. H. Paetzold.
Encryption Methods for Distributed Systems (in German).
Master's thesis, University of Darmstadt, Dept. of Computer Science, 1989.

18. R. Rivest, A. Shamir, and A. Adleman.
A Method for Obtaining Digital Signatures and Public Key Cryptosystems.
Communications of the ACM, 21(2):120–126, 1978.

19. J. Rosenberg and D.A. Abramson.
MONADS-PC: A Capability Based Workstation to Support Software Engineering.
In *Proc. of the 18th Hawaii Int. Conference on System Sciences*, 1985.

20. H. Sedlack and U. Golze.
A Public Key Code Cryptography Processor.
Informationstechnik, 281(3):157–161, 1986.

Part IV

Architectures

Implementing 128 Bit Persistent Addresses on 80x86 Processors

W.P.Cockshott
University of Strathclyde

P.W.Foulk
Heriot-Watt University

ABSTRACT

The Intel architecture for the 80x86 series machines lends itself well to the implementation of persistent object oriented languages. They are also by a wide margin the most commonly used CPUs in the world. Mass production has driven down the costs of machines using these processors and they thus make an appealing platform for experimentation.They have a model of store which corresponds well to the 7 layer model of persistent memory proposed by the authors: with physical, paged and segmented memory interfaces. One could map persistent objects directly onto Intel segments, but this would suffer from the small size of the segment identifier which only permits 16K of objects. For a distributed object oriented system one needs a much larger number of objects. The paper examines software and hardware techniques that can be used to map dynamically from network wide object identifiers to hardware supported segments. Four techniques are presented, two software and two hardware assisted techniques. The two software methods and one of the hardware methods have been implemented.

1. INTRODUCTION

The computing world today is divided into communities using different computer architectures. The two most popular architectures are those produced by Intel and Motorola with the 80x86 series from Intel and the 680x0 series from Motorola. To an extent the division into these two architectures is seen as corresponding to the IBM world on the one hand and the Mackintosh and Sun world on the other. The development of standardised processor architectures is a relatively recent phenomenon brought about by VLSI technology. These standard families of CPUs offer performance superior to conventional mini-computers and their cheapness enables a wide variety of computer manufacturers to produce machines that are software compatible with each other. The relevance of industry standard CPU chips to research into wide address space and persistent computers is that they make it relatively less economic to develop non-standard processor architectures like Monads [4]. There is such a large base of software for the standard architectures that the overhead costs of establishing a new architecture become prohibitive. The growing scale and complexity of the new CPUs argues against any attempt to develop fundamentally new CPU designs unless one has a very large scale of funding available. The 68040 and 80486 processors all incorporate more than one million transistors, an order of magnitude increase in complexity compared to the 68000.

We believe that instead of designing entirely new processors it is more practical to investigate means by which these standard architecture machines can have their architecture extended to support wide address space persistence. We have already reported on an extension that we designed for the 68000 series machines to support persistence [2]. The Intel architecture for the 286,386 ... series machines lends itself well to the implementation of persistent object oriented languages. They are also by a wide margin the most commonly used CPUs in the world. Mass production has driven down the costs of machines using these processors well below those of competitors. They thus make an appealing platform for experimentation.

2. ARCHITECTURE

There is a number of ways in which the Intel architecture is better suited to supporting persistent programming than is the Motorola architecture. Motorola adopt the convention of a uniform flat address space whereas Intel use a segmented address space which corresponds more closely to the idea of an object store. On the 386 and 486 processors, this segmented memory is built on top of a paged virtual memory [3]. This division corresponds closely to the division between layers 2 and 3 in the layered model of persistent store proposed by the authors [1]. We will give a short description of the Intel architecture, presented in evolutionary sequence of origin of the features.

2.1. 8086

The 8086 type of processor with its variants and subtypes was the mainstay of the personal computer industry until recently. All subsequent 80x86 machines preserve binary compatibility with the 8086, so that the standard 8086 operating system MSDOS continues to be used on more recent machines. Most of our experimental work has been carried out on machines operating in 8086 compatibility mode.

Addresses on the 8086 have one of two forms, the so called **short** and **far** forms. A short address is simply a 16 bit byte address, and in its simplest mode of use, the 8086 is rather like a PDP11 configured with a separate codespace and dataspace each of 64k bytes. This is the operating mode of the Minix operating system by Tannenbaum under which our object manager was first developed [5]. In the long form, addresses are 32 bits long and are interpreted as a 16 bit segment number and a 16 bit offset. This allows a total of 64K segments each of a maximum of 64k bytes. There is a restriction in the use of the long addresses stemming from the fact that the CPU has a physical address space of only one megabyte. The 64k segments have to be mapped down onto this limited space. The hardware mechanism for this is very simple: $physaddr(s,o) = (s \times 16) + o$. Most memory access operations come in two forms, either the short or the far address types.

2.1.1. Drawbacks

The main drawback of the 8086 segmentation scheme is that it lacks any form of protection or virtual memory support. Although it allows a large virtual address space, there are no hardware checks on the use of virtual memory. This has not prevented the implementation of virtual memory based operating systems on the 8086: the Windows system provides support for segmented virtual memory on the 8086, but it relies upon programmers using a strict discipline in their use of addresses. In the absence of software checks, one can address beyond one segment and into another, possibly corrupting data.

2.2. 80286

The 80286 remedied the most obvious limits of the 8086 segmentation system in a manner that allowed binary compatibility of 'well written' programs. The 16 bit segment numbers used in far addresses were redefined to be what were called segment **selectors**. A segment selector is an index into a segment table. The segment table is made up of segment **descriptors**. These descriptors are 8 byte records that specify:

> the base address of a segment
> its size
> access rights to it
> a flag indicating if the segment is resident in memory

The segment table itself is accessible only to the operating system, all other code must access data via this segment table. In fact there are two tables: the global segment table, and a local segment table. The global table is shared by all processes whereas the local table is process specific. The new mechanism allows for persistent objects if appropriate software is provided to swap objects into memory. Any attempt to access a non resident object results in a trap which allows the object to be brought in by the operating system.

2.2.1. Drawbacks

There are two remaining problems with the 80286 for implementing persistent systems:

> the segment selectors are too small.
> the segments are too small.

The selectors are still only 16 bits, limiting us to 64k objects. This is not really enough for anything but a small single user system. The objects are themselves limited to 64k bytes by the maximum size of the offset. Whilst this should be enough for the great bulk of objects, a few things, such as bitmapped images, need more space.

2.3. 80386

One of the restrictions of the 80286 has been lifted on the 80386 and 80486 machines. The size of the offset field of an address has gone up to 32 bits, giving a far address space of 2^{48} bytes. Individual objects can now hold 2^{32} bytes of data. It would be impractical to bring objects containing several megabytes in from disk in one transfer, so an additional layer of virtual memory has been added.

The segment table now holds the base addresses of segments within a paged virtual memory. Address translation takes the form: **selector -> virtual address -> physical address**. This two stage process allows large objects to be brought into memory a page at a time as required.

2.3.1. Drawbacks

The other drawback of the 80286, the small number of available segments remains. There are some indications in the Intel documentation that the next machine in the series (80586) may increase the size of the segment selectors to 32 bits. This would go a long way towards meeting the objections to the current model, but would probably still be too small for networked environment. Our research has been directed at providing prototypes for an addressing system that increases the number of addressable segments to 2^{128}.

3. SOFTWARE TECHNIQUES

In the first software technique, network wide Persistent IDentifiers or PIDs are dynamically translated into segmented addresses each time they are used, by means of a hash table. This is done within a run time library so that user programs never have direct access to object addresses. In the second software technique, the active objects are accessed via PID handles which provide a compact, process specific identification of an object . The run time library provides two way translation between the handles and the PIDs. This technique gives gains in speed over the previous one, but is potentially less secure.

In [1] we proposed a layered interface to persistent stores. This was loosely based on the ISO 7 layer model. We proposed a 7 layer model of persistent store in which each layer was characterised by a set of abstract types exported to the superincumbent layers. These types had a defined set of operations on them which were used to construct the types of the next higher layer. It was envisaged that different programming languages would interface to the object store on different layers:

Layer 7 :	Applications
Layer 6 :	Abstract Types
Layer 5 :	Aggregates :- arrays, structures
Layer 4 :	Base Types
Layer 3 :	Untyped Object Store
Layer 2 :	Persistent Linear Store
Layer 1 :	Physical memory

We will ignore the first two layers which are concerned with physical store and concentrate on the higher levels. Layer 3 provides a simple object store in which persistent objects are identified by PIDs and accessed via Get and Set operators. Internally the objects are simple arrays of bytes. Layer 4 introduces types for the fields of objects: REAL, INTEGER, CHAR. Layer 4 provides essentially the lowest level of useful access to the store. It corresponds loosely to what one might call 'persistent programming in C'. In fact the layers 3 and 4 are defined as a C subroutine library. Layer 5 provides things like arrays, lists and structures in persistent store. Layer 5 provides a suitable interface to languages such as PS-algol, and our experimental PS-algol systems basically make calls on layer 5.

All of the layers above 3 use the definition of the type PID that layer 3 provides and they build up their more complex types in terms of PIDs. In our first implementation, the PIDs were defined to be 128 bits long. The system relies for security on the difficulty of synthesising members of such a sparse set.

PS-algol represents all pointers, vectors and strings as PIDs. Accesses of vector elements are implemented as calls on layer 5, which checks for bounds violations before passing the action on to layer 3, which performs the fetch. There are two major inefficiencies in this:

> the PIDs take up a lot of space on the stack. In consequence, assignment of PIDs must be implemented as block move instructions These are slower than simple integer assignment and take more instructions to set up.

> the PIDs must be translated into valid store addresses by layer 3. This requires a hash and a compare operation. A hash is easy, one just selects an appropriate set of bits from the PID. The compare, defined as 4-long-integer comparisons, is slow.

With this architecture the only area in which performance could be improved is to speed up the hashing process. By replacing the key **PID -> address** translate functions with hand coded assembler equivalents, we did in fact find a marked improvement on one of our standard benchmarks. This involves constructing a binary tree from 1000 random numbers between 1 and 999, saving it to the database, bringing it back in and looking up the 1000 numbers again.

	Tree Insertion seconds	Commit seconds	Fetch and Scan seconds
Long Pids	11	15	16
Long Pids and assembler hashing	8	27	12
16 bit PID handles	9	46	14

Table 1: Binary Tree Benchmark

4. SHORT PID HANDLES

In an attempt to overcome the second bottleneck arising from use of 16 byte PIDs, an implementation was built that retained the full length PIDs for pointers within data objects, but which provided a different implementation for pointer variables on the stack. Since all access to the persistent store is via a small collection of interface procedures, it is possible to change the external view of what a PID is without altering the internal implementation. In particular, the interface to Layer 3 provides 2 primitive operations for extracting a pointer from or inserting a pointer into an object.

```
GetPid(int offset,PID *obj, PID *field);
SetPid(int offset,PID *obj, PID *field);
```

Provided that this is the only technique used for accessing PIDs within objects, one can alter the implementation of PIDs seen above layer 3 without altering the stored format of a PID. Suppose we introduce a new representation of PIDs, denoted by *PID* to be used above layer 3.

This representation can differ from that used below the layer 3 to layer 4 interface. We then redefine all of the operations supported by layer 3 to use these *PIDs*:

> *GetPid*(int, *PID* *, *PID* *);
> *SetPid*(int, *PID* *, *PID* *);
> *SetBytes*(int,int, *PID* *, char *);
> *GetBytes*(int, int, *PID**, char *);

etc,....

Layer 3 can effect an invertible pair of one to one mappings between PIDs and *PIDs*:

> ToIntern(PID -> *PID*)
> ToExtern(PID -> *PID*)

so that whenever it is asked to access a field of *PID* it applies the appropriate mappings. Thus:

> *SetBytes*(off,len,obj,buf) $\equiv$ SetBytes(off,len,ToIntern(obj),buf)
> and
> *SetPid*(ofs,obj,fld) $\equiv$ SetPid(ofs,ToIntern(obj),ToIntern(fld))

Similarly, ToExtern can be applied by *GetPid* to obtain the appropriate *PID* from a PID field.

4.1 Mapping onto a smaller address space

We would like to make the external *PID* format smaller than the internal format of a PID within an object. Ideally we would like *PIDs* to fit into a single machine word. The constraint is that this has to be done whilst preserving a bijection

> *PID* -> PID

It is not immediately obvious that this is possible since a machine word will code for $W=2^{16}$ objects whereas a full PID can code for 2^{128} entities. It would seem that each *PID* would end up standing for up to 2^{102} PIDs.

However, we can take advantage of the fact that we intend to use the *PIDs* as values for variables in a high level language. What we must ensure is that a given pointer variable implemented as a *PID* produces the same effect as would a variable implemented as a full PID. If we have the program fragment:

```
let total=proc(*int m->int)
            begin
                let t:=0
                for i=lwb(m) to upb(m) do t:=m(i)+t
            end
```

The lexical symbol **m** will be mapped by the compiler to a particular location in the dynamic environment of the procedure **total**. That location on stack can either hold a *PID* or a PID which in turn refers to a persistent object, but that reference must be consistent. That is to say that for the duration of the procedure the PID or *PID* at location **addr(m)** must refer to the same object. Given what we know about the maximum size of a stack segment on a 80286 and given that a *PID* is to occupy 16 bits, we can calculate the maximum number of variables V like **m** that can be in scope at any one time to be 2^{15}. Since each such variable can refer to only one persistent object, and since some of the objects may be referred to by more than one variable we can deduce the following about O the number of objects in scope at any one time: $O \leq V \leq 2^{15} < W$

It is only the subset of objects currently in scope for which a consistent one to one mapping between *PIDs* and PIDs is required and since the cardinality of this subset $O < W$ the cardinality of the set of possible *PIDs*, there is no difficulty constructing the mapping. *PIDs* as well as objects now become a garbage collectable resource. The garbage collector can determine which *PIDs* are not currently in use and make these available for remapping to PIDs.

4.2 Implementation details

We actually implemented the *PID* type as a segment selector that referred to an object access segment. The object access segment has the format:

```
struct { FULLPID objid;
            char * baseaddr;
            unsigned length;
            ....
        }
```

By using this representation we not only make the *PIDs* small and easy to copy, we also make the process of translating PIDs to addresses efficient. The code to extract an integer field from an object can be accomplished in 3 instructions:

```
subsi  macro
; assume that pid handle on top of stack
; field offset as parameter #1 to macro
        pop es      ; es points at pid descriptor
        les si,dword ptr es:baseaddr ; es:si points at object
        push es:[si+#1]
        #em
```

Access to pointer fields of object must still go through a subroutine interface which slows it down, but access to scalar fields is markedly improved. This is shown by comparative speeds, on an Erastostenes benchmark program, that uses a vector of booleans on the heap.

Implementation	Time in Seconds	
Sun 3/160 PS-algol	28.5	
Linn Rekursiv S-algol	13	
386/20Mhz Long Pids S-algol		87
386/20Mhz 16 bit PID handles	16	

Table 2: Erastostenes 20 times up to 5000}

The marked improvement in access to scalar fields is to be contrasted to the more modest improvement in access to pointer fields shown in the binary tree benchmark.

5. HARDWARE TECHNIQUES

5.1. PID Translation Cache

The first hardware technique is an associative cache interfaced to the IBM PC/AT bus. This translates PIDs to Intel segment selectors. It is comparatively simple to implement in both hardware and software terms, and can be accommodated by existing operating systems.

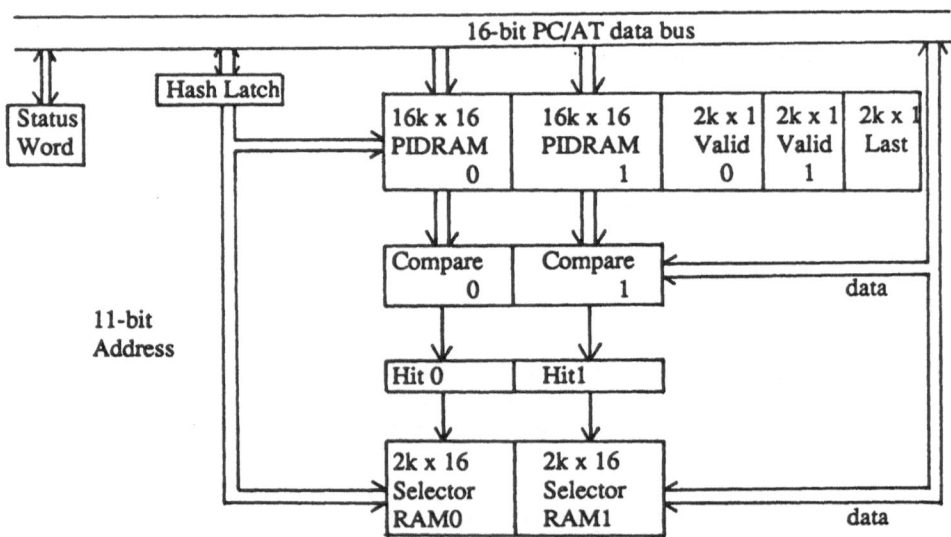

Figure 1: PID translation cache, 16 bit data

The PC/AT bus is a 16-bit data bus operating at 8 MHz. Hence data must be transferred in 16-bit words, a 128-bit PID being 8 words, and therefore needing 8 bus transfers. The maximum stack size is 4096, so this is the maximum number of objects allowed. Figure 1 gives a block diagram of the hardware. The PID store is 2-way associative, and uses high-speed static RAM. Such RAMs are conveniently available in 16k x 4 bit chips. Using 4 chips per store, 2 stores of 2048 x 8 words are provided. Each set needs a valid bit for each PID (2048 x 1 bit, valid0 and valid1) to indicate whether the contents are valid or not. Each set needs a single bit to implement a least-recently-written algorithm (2048 x 1, last) by toggling the bit every time a set in the cache is written into, and using this bit to determine which member of the set to write into. 11 bits of the first word of the PID are used to hash to a value to provide the address of one of the sets in the PID store, the PID being stored in one of the pair of locations in this set. The associated selector is stored in the equivalently addressed word in the appropriate 2k x 16 bit selector store.

Initially all the valid bits are set to 0. When a process runs, its PIDs and selectors are stored on the board as the objects are brought into memory, and the appropriate valid bits are updated. When the process requires a translation, it presents the PID to the board as 8 words. The board hashes on the first word of the PID to get the address of the appropriate set, and compares the contents to see if the set is holding valid translation information for this PID. If it is (a hit) the selector is retrieved from the corresponding selector store and returned to the process. If a miss occurs, an invalid selector is returned. The process then scans its tables to find the translation information, updates the cache ready for the next time a translation on this PID is required, and accesses the object.

The board is designed to handle four persistent processes. The current process may be swapped out during a translation without loss of information if a process swap is initiated by the operating system during this time. All that needs to be saved is in the status word and hash latch, so these have to be saved on process swapping. For safety, the operation can be easily rolled back by the operating system in case the relevant cache location is modified between the PID compare and the selector retrieval, or the translation can be invalidated in such a rare case, without a significant performance penalty. The board resides in the I/O space of the computer for ease of implementation, and appears as three I/O registers to the software. One of the unfortunate aspects of the PC/AT bus is that it requires several 8MHz bus cycles for a transfer, and so the speed-up offered by the cache is only a few times the speed of a software translation, even though the cache can easily run much faster. It would be preferable to implement the board in the memory address space of 80386/80486 processors to take advantage of their 32-bit transfers, and also the faster memory bus transfers on the MCA or EISA busses. Such an arrangement is shown in figure 2. Two cycle writes and reads are practicable, and hence would allow a translation to be made easily within one microsecond, or even half a microsecond with a fast CPU. This would give a further considerable speed-up even with the current memory chips, at the expense of more complex hardware.

5.1.1. Drawbacks

The main drawback of this technique is the additional cost of the board, although a VLSI version of the control hardware would reduce costs to a few pounds over the cost of the memory chips. This method does not provide any additional security since any process can read the PID information if it knows it is there. All the other drawbacks of the 16-bit selectors apply. The board can be extended easily to handle selectors of 32-bits if this becomes desirable for newer CPUs.

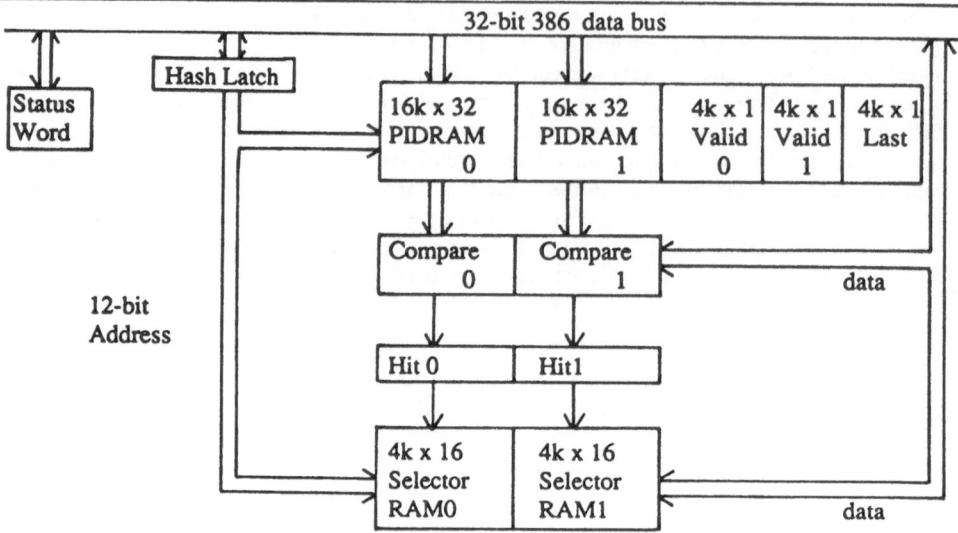

Figure 2: PID translation cache, 32 bit data

5.2. Protected PID Cache

An alternative scheme makes full PIDs the only means of accessing data. In some PS-Algol implementations, the abstract machine involves the use of two stacks. The main stack holds integers and reals whilst the P-stack holds pointers to persistent data items. The P-stack of PS-Algol can be implemented using a segment on the 80386: for instance the segment selected by the FS register. The P-stack in the F-segment would be made up entirely of 16-byte persistent identifiers. A particular register, say the EDX register (the extended DX register) would act as a pointer to the top of the P-stack.

Consider the following fraction of PS-Algol code:

        structure M(string name)
        let p1 = M("John")
        let v1 = vector 1..3 of p1

This might result in the following data on the P-stack:

        Contents of EDX   32
        Address 0   Pointer to class M
        Address 16   pntr p1
        Address 32   vector v1

Suppose we now want to access the **name** field of **p1** we would plant the following code:

lea eax	[edx-16]	Load the offset of p1 into eax
mov es	eax	Extra segment now points at structure p1
add edx	16	Advance pointer stack pointer
mov fs:[edx}	es:name	Push first word of name PID
mov fs:[edx+4]	es:name+4	Push next word of name PID
mov fs:[edx+8]	es:name+8	Push 3rd word of name PID
mov fs:[edx+12]	es:name+12	Push last word of name PID

The unusual point about this is that we have used the offset of the pointer **p1** in the F-segment as a segment selector to be loaded into the ES register. This implicitly assumes that there is a one-to-one translation between offsets on the P-stack and the segment numbers of the objects the P-stack points at. Although one could not normally assume this to be the case, the addition of relatively simple hardware would enable it to be the case.

We want a block of hardware to implement the function:

F(PIDAddress-> Descriptor)

such that when the address of a PID on the P-stack is sent out by the CPU, the hardware returns the appropriate descriptor (the descriptor contains the base address, limit and attributes of the segment, and is used to by the CPU in accessing the segment, i.e. the persistent object in this case). When we load the ES register with the offset of **p1** (=16), we cause the CPU to fetch the segment descriptor located at offset 16 in the segment table. According to the value in the Segment Table Base Register (STBR) this fetch may be anywhere in the address space. If we know the base address of the segment table, we can implement the following function:

$$MemRead(a\text{->}datum) = if\ a\ is\ in\ SegTable$$
$$then\ F(a\text{-}STBR)$$
$$else\ Mem(a)$$

We can implement the function *F* provided we have an associative lookup function:

PIDlam(PID->Descriptor)

Thus *F* becomes:

$$F(a) = PIDlam(Pstack(a))$$

By functional decomposition we obtain a new definition for memory read:

$$MemRead(a\text{->}datum) = if\ a\ is\ in\ SegTable$$
$$then\ PIDlam(Pstack(a\text{-}STBR))$$
$$else\ Mem(a)$$

Suppose we place the segment table so that it coincides in physical address with a special memory board on the expansion bus. Let us assume for simplicity that this board occupies 128k of address space. The lower 64k holds a 'virtual' segment table and the upper 64k holds the P-stack.

We call it a virtual segment table because it is not really there. It just fools the CPU into thinking it is. When the memory board is asked for the word at offset 16 in the virtual segment table, it actually does the following:

Step	Action
1	Board is sent address of segment descriptor in virtual segment table
2	Board adds 64k to this and obtains PID corresponding to this descriptor
3	Board presents the PID to an associative cache memory
4	Cache memory produces descriptor for this PID
5	Board returns to CPU the descriptor associated with **p1**
6	CPU reads and validates descriptor, and accesses **p1**

Step 2 corresponds to the function application $x <- Pstack(a-STBR)$. Step 3 corresponds to application $PIDlam(x)$.

This approach would entail the PID cache board having two types of memory on it. One bank would be used to hold the P-stack and the other would be a set associative cache similar to that described earlier. We will assume that some special I/O ports exist for initialising and loading the cache. Otherwise the board would appear as two logical blocks of addresses:

1. The virtual segment table. An access to this causes the corresponding PID in the P-stack area to be translated to a descriptor and returned.
2. The P-stack. This is treated as normal read/write memory.

Figure 3 illustrates the procedure, showing the various memory blocks, and the steps numbered above being applied to a translation as the CPU attempts to access the virtual segment table for a persistent object descriptor. The CPU sends out the address in the segment table (1) which is intercepted by the board and remapped into the P-stack (2). The contents of this location, the PID, are accessed and presented to the associative cache (3). The cache does an associative compare, and returns the descriptor corresponding to the PID (4). The control of the board then sends this descriptor back to the CPU as if a normal segment table access had taken place (5). Finally, using the descriptor information, the CPU makes its normal access to the persistent object (6).

The blocks need not be 64k in size. They could be made of an arbitrary number of 4k pages and the 80386 paging system could be used to make them look like one or more sets of P-stacks mapped onto the 64k segment table. Using the paging hardware, multiple accesses could use the board provided that all P-stack pages resident in memory were loaded onto the cache memory board.

5.2.1 Supporting Software

This model of cache would have to run in fully protected mode with support from the paging kernel of an operating system. With the segment table implemented as a virtual segment table, the machine would essentially be operating as a 128 bit addressed processor, which would make existing virtual memory operating systems for the 80386 unusable This implies that a new operating system would be needed. Developing this is obviously a much greater expense than developing the hardware. As a way of reducing costs it might prove possible to implement the Monads operating system on 80386 machines fitted with this sort of hardware extension.

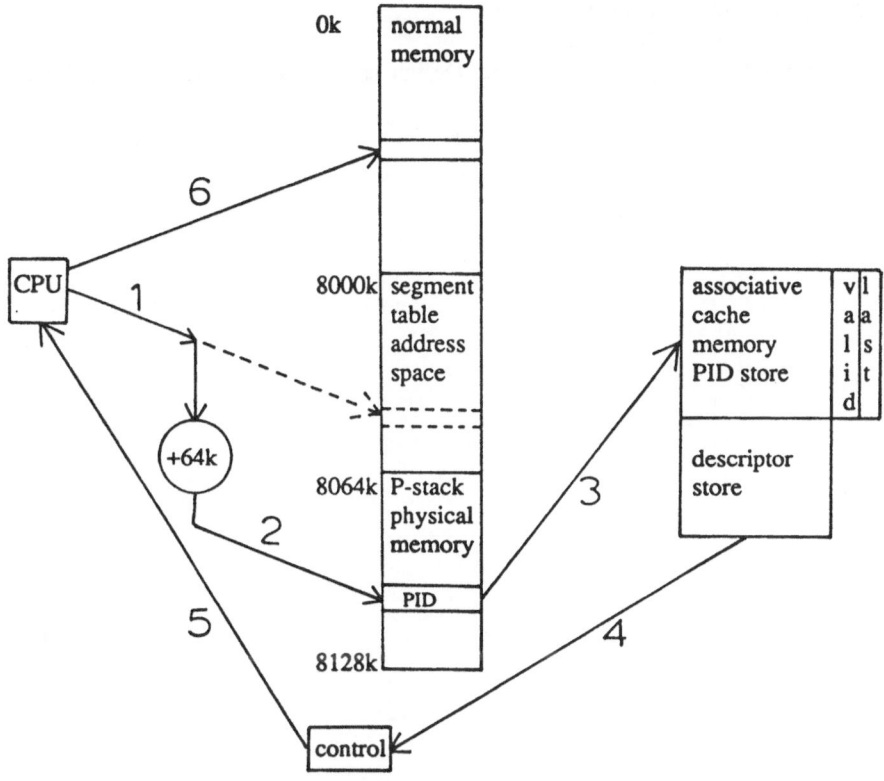

Figure 3: Protected PID cache

6. CONCLUSIONS

Four methods of accessing persistent data with 128 bit addresses have been presented,two software ones and two hardware assisted ones. They are particularly suited to segmented memory systems such as that on the Intel 80x86 series of processors.

REFERENCES

1   Balch, P., Cockshott, W. P. and Foulk, P. W. "Layered implementations of persistent object stores". *Software Engineering Journal,* March, 1989.

2   Cockshott, W. P., "Design of POMP - Persistent Object Management CoProcessor" *Research report ARCH-1-88,* University of Strathclyde Dept of Computer Science.

3   "i486 MICROPROCESSOR", Intel, April 1989.

4   Keedy, J. L., "The MONADS-PC System: A Programmers Overview" *Bericht Nr. 8/89* , Universitat Bremen Informatik

5   Tanenbaum, A., "Operating Systems, Design and Implementation" Prentice Hall, 1987

Active Memory for Managing Persistent Objects

S H Lavington and R A J Davies
University of Essex

ABSTRACT

The useful notion of abstract data types has, almost by definition, seldom been seen to produce requirements for the functionality of underlying hardware. When these types take the form of persistent objects, there is a real need for hardware support for memory management functions. We describe an **active memory** which provides such support, whilst at the same time allowing inherent parallelism to be exploited for certain well-used data structures such as sets, relations and graphs. We outline the performance of the active memory, and give an example of its use via persistent-object enhancements to C++.

1. INTRODUCTION

The development of error-free software is made easier if the programmer is allowed to define a rich variety of data types at the applications-program level. These types can reflect the abstract objects of the problem domain, thereby helping to isolate problem-solving activity from the implementation details of run-time software. If the problem is data-intensive, the abstract data types or objects will naturally require to exhibit the operational characteristics of databases or knowledge bases. In conventional programming terms, such types need to exhibit persistence. In this paper, we emphasise the requirements of data types which are persistent.

In a conventional programming environment, abstract data types such as sets, relations and graphs are created by a user out of the primitive types provided in a high-level language. These primitive types, such as **cardinal** or **pointer**, are themselves implemented at the machine level by fine-grain bit/byte/word manipulations carried out by general-purpose hardware. Exceptionally, a particular primitive type such as **real** may use dedicated (type-specific) hardware such as a floating-point unit. However, the general picture is of a data hierachy consisting of three levels: abstract types; language primitives; semantics-free hardware. The permitted types are seldom persistent.

If we are to permit a rich variety of persistent types at the abstract level, the primitive level will also require enrichment. This is liable to lead to significant run-time inefficiencies, as for example in the case of SETL [ref 1], unless a means can also be found for supporting persistent types at the hardware level. The problem, then, is as follows. Can we choose an appropriate repertoire of primitive persistent types at the language level, which are automatically supported by (special-purpose) hardware? It need hardly be said that the new primitives should be integrated within a well-respected programming language and that any new hardware should be easily integrated within a conventional computing system and its virtual memory.

In Section 2 of this paper we expand on the notion of persistent types and objects. The emphasis is on providing a mechanism whereby the type system of a programming language may become enforceable on all relevant data structures, irrespective of where these data structures are physically held. This implies a uniformity of naming schemes and memory management, independent of physical storage characteristics - (e.g. whether semiconductor or spinning memory). The requirements for managing persistent types suggest the concept of **active memory** which also has practical implications for the exploitation of inherent parallelism, especially in the case of structures based on the super-type **relation**. These architectural aspects are discussed in Section 3.

It is generally agreed that types are the major organising principle in object-based programming. In Section 4 we give examples of how our active memory can be used to support persistent objects from within a C++ framework. Practical OOP issues such as inheritance are discussed.

Finally, in Section 5 we outline a hardware realisation of our active memory. We give performance figures for various generic operations on structured data to show that the conceptual requirements of managing persistent objects need not conflict with the call for better run-time performance via better exploitation of parallelism.

2. FUNCTIONAL REQUIREMENTS: A TOP - DOWN VIEW

Object based persistent languages, for example PS-algol [ref. 2] and Arjuna [ref. 3] allow data structures and types created in RAM to survive longer than the programs which created them. Persistent languages declare the data to be persistent, or else they define data to be persistent if it is reachable from a distinguished object (or objects) called the root. As identified in [4], persistence is independent of type, and access to data is independent of persistence. Persistent objects can cross-reference one another. Persistent languages are distinguished from traditional languages by having a persistent object manager that handles the transfer of objects from RAM to secondary storage. A good example is CPOMS for PS-algol [ref. 5]. One of the main requirements for hardware would be to take over most of the tasks undertaken by the persistent object manager.

From an architectural viewpoint, the most important attribute of a persistent object store would appear to be the ability to access objects of various sizes without requiring a priori knowledge of their physical location, In addition, a persistent object store should allow:

> maintenance of structural relationships between objects
> protection of (logical sets of) objects
> ability to modify large structures in place.

From a programming viewpoint, persistence is made easier if the names used for objects at the applications programming level are used to access objects at the storage level, independent of memory technology. This implies some form of universal identifier, or uid. Such a truly global naming convention necessarily decouples the programmer and run-time code from all forms of physical location information. The usual decoupling, achieved via a virtual to real address mapping, can of course be used with very large addresses to support persistence [ref. 6]. Alternatively, the concept of a name could be taken through to the memory units themselves, which then become associative (i.e. content addressable). We examine this notion further in Section 3.

Pure associative memory may violate the principle of data encapsulation. It may thus be necessary to restrict associative access using certain forms of interrogand. However, the extent to which data encapsulation should be strictly enforced is a matter of some debate. Extensions to the object oriented paradigm that support object equality as well as identity [ref. 7] and relational semantics [refs.8,9] can easily be supported by an associative memory. This is illustrated in Section 4, by the use of the **find** and **relation** extensions to C++.

Encapsulating both executable code and data, as method and state, in a reusable object is a helpful concept in software engineering. Attempts to implement this concept in a pure way at the hardware level may prove more difficult - especially if efficient run times are important. On conventional architectures, inefficiencies arise because the device which executes code (i.e. the CPU) is physically separate from the device that holds data (i.e. RAM). In Section 3 we explore the possibility of allowing memory to take autonomous data-manipulation action, thus 'moving the operation to the data'.

The normal model of persistence seems to impose different priorities to those associated with conventional information systems. Thus, PS-algol supports persistence primarily for process continuity, the aim being that any data structure built by an application should survive to be used again when the application dies. This approach is good for transparency and flexibility but lacks the fine grained control needed for sharing data among concurrent applications. It also seems to be somewhat inadequate for querying and query optimization. This contrasts with the ideal requirements for hardware support, which should add to traditional object oriented programming languages persistence, secure concurrent transactions and fast direct access and manipulation of data structures, including relational algebraic operations (discussed in Section 3).

The active memory which we describe in the next Section seeks to satisfy all of the above requirements. It supports information models from semantic nets to abstract data types and can potentially store persistent objects for both persistent and non-persistent languages (e.g. C++). The data objects stored by the active memory are also transferable between different languages. This contrasts with several persistent object systems (i.e. a persistent object in Napier is not transferable to Arjuna). The active memory will support primitive, composite and complex objects by storing the static data view of objects. Its processing ability allows it to manipulate such objects in situ.

3. AN ACTIVE MEMORY ARCHITECTURE

3.1 MOVING THE OPERATION TO THE DATA

The availability of cheap hardware has caused certain frequently-used tasks to be removed from the software domain. For cases where the set of values of an object is closely defined, together with the permitted operations on those values, it has become economic to employ special-purpose hardware units to carry out specific tasks autonomously. Examples are add-on graphics boards and laser printers. We now extend this principle to memory units.

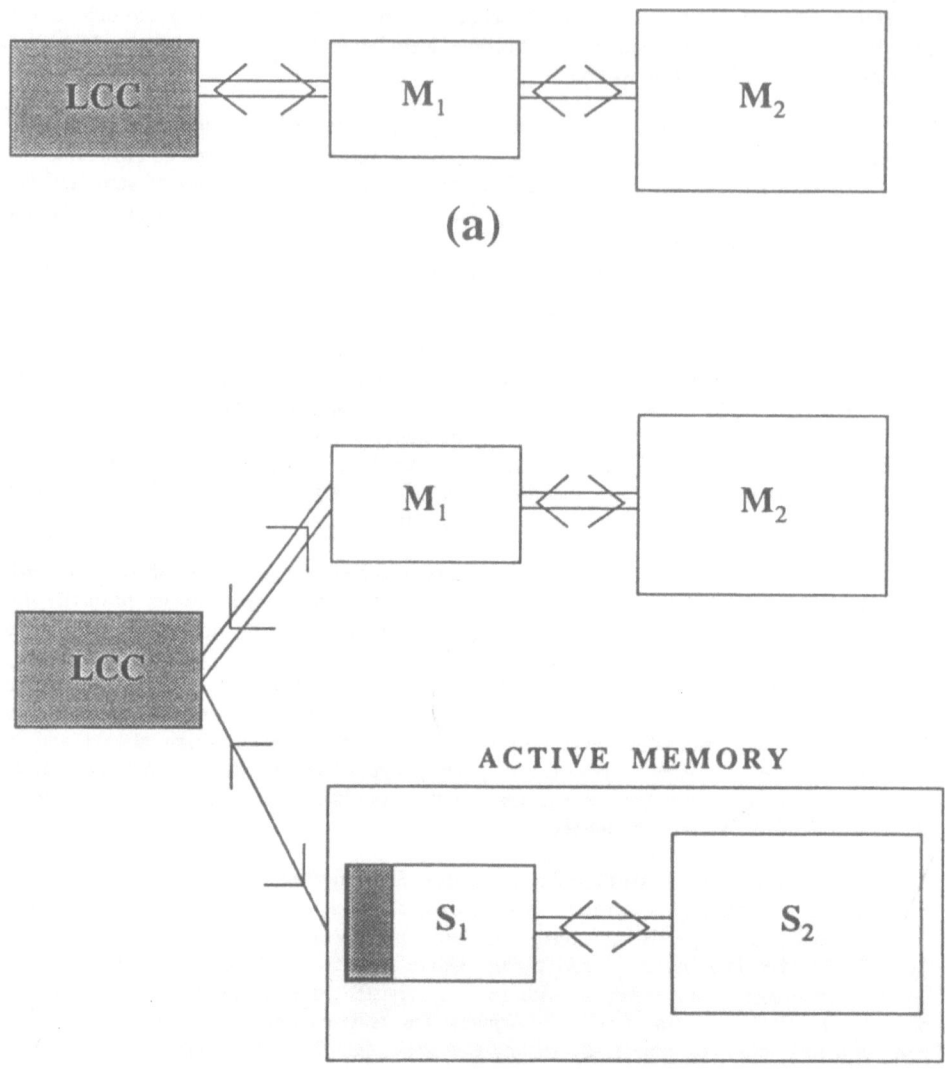

Figure 1: adding active memory to a conventional computer

Figure 1(a) shows a conventional hierarchy of memory devices, M_1 (faster, volatile) and M_2 (slower, non volatile). For present purposes it is not necessary to know whether this hierarchy is connected to one CPU or to several CPUs. Accordingly, we show the memory hierarchy controlled by a single box labelled Locus of Computational Control (LCC). In Figure 1(a) data processing can only proceed if the data to be processed is within the LCC's addressing range (here M_1). Thus, persistent data structures are in general moved from M_2 to M_1, whereupon the LCC takes (reads) fine-grain elements of the data structure in order to operate upon them. There are three points to note about the conventional computing environment represented by Figure 1(a):

   i)   A physical address-mapping is necessary between M_1 and M_2; this physical mapping does not normally reflect the logical structure of the data. Hence memory management ('paging and protection') is carried out with reference to coarse physical address boundaries.

   ii) The bandwidths of both interconnecting highways has to be high, if high overall performance is to be maintained.

   iii) All responsibility for the exploitation of parallelism resides within the LCC. Assuming LCC to be based on a general-purpose von Neumann computational model, responsibility for exploiting parallelism is actually moved into software (at the compiler and/or source program level) for most programming languages.

In Figure 1(b) the system has been augmented by the addition of an autonomous unit labelled Active Memory. This may also contain a hierarchy of devices, S_1 (fastest, volatile) and S_2 (slowest, non-volatile), but this internal arrangement is invisible to LCC. Both S_1 and S_2 have limited (i.e. special-purpose) computational ability in addition to their ability to store information. Apart from explicit **insert** and **delete** commands, data is persistent within the Active Memory. This property of persistence is extended to any new data structures created as a result of operations involving existing data structures. Such action has implications for data consistency, naming conventions and version control. These are issues which are the subject of current research.

The Active Memory has a number of other unusual properties, as follows. The Active Memory is associative, i.e. content-addressable. That is to say, LCC can only refer to a data object held within the Active Memory by a unique name. The term 'name' is taken to include 'descriptor', 'interrogand', or 'pattern', so that variables and wild cards are accommodated. A consequence of this is that named objects can have varying granularity. The hidden memory management within the Active Memory is also of variable granularity, being based on logical descriptors rather than on physical addresses. The data-manipulation commands built into the Active Memory reflect the common operations on frequently-used data structures such as relations, sets and graphs. Such operations exhibit much scope for parallelism. The repertoire of commands is discussed in Section 3.3; their hardware implementation is discussed in Section 5. Note that the Active Memory is primarily intended for structured data arising from a finite, but useful, sub-set of users' abstract data type declarations. Other (possibly un-structured) data may be held as usual in M_1 and M_2 in Figure 1(b). Since the Active Memory's commar.∷ are memory-mapped, it is open to the LCC's system software to integrate $(M_1 + M_2)$ and $(S_1 + S_2)$ into a one-level virtual store. It is, of course, not so easy to offer persistence within the $(M_1 + M_2)$ section of this integrated virtual memory.

In summary, Figure 1(b) differs from Figure 1(a) in that, for certain named data structures:

i)   There is automatic hardware memory management of certain well-used persistent objects, according to their logical structure.

ii)   Since operations on named objects are carried out autonomously in situ, the highway between the LCC and the object store need not have a high bandwidth.

iii) Responsibility for the exploitation of parallelism during certain structure manipulation now resides with a hardware unit which has been tailored to the characteristics of the structures. The LCC, and hence software, does not have to take any special action in this respect.

3.2   LOW - LEVEL INFORMATION REPRESENTATION

The active memory of Figure 1(b) must be semantics-free, in the sense of being able to support a variety of applications, programming languages and information models. As mentioned above, the active memory is associative. For convenience we refer to each entry, or line, of this memory as a tuple. The requirement to be semantics-free means that tuples may take a variety of formats. If we regard the principal section of each tuple as a well-formed formula, then the general format for an active memory entry might be expressed as:

$$<L><T1><T2> ... <Tm><M1><M2> ... <Mn> \qquad ... eqn.(1).$$

where: $<L>$ is an optional label (eg gödelisation, etc.)

$<T1><T2>...$ are terms in a wff

$<M1><M2>...$ are optional modifiers for the $<L>$ and $<T>$ fields.

The <terms> may be lexemes (eg character strings), integers, labels (eg gödel numbers), structure tokens, abstract nodes, existentially-quantified variables, etc. Since the active memory is associative, some mechanism is required for distinguishing between identical internal bit-patterns which happen to be used to encode different external <terms>. Two schemes suggest themselves. In the first scheme, all <terms> are mapped into a common internal identifier (ID) space, with some of the ID bits being used to segment this space into a number of different primitive 'types' such as lexeme, integer, label, etc. The format for an ID would thus be:

$$<unique\ encryption\ within\ segment> \qquad ...eqn.(2).$$

Following the scheme used in the first version of the Intelligent File Store (IFS/1) [ref.10], the ID could be up to 64 bits in length, of which the top four bits are reserved for the segment (or tag) bits.

The disadvantage of the above scheme is that it sets a practical limit on the number of segment-types known to the system. An alternative scheme is to precede each active memory tuple with a tuple-descriptor, D. This is a simple integer which identifies not only the number of fields in a tuple but also the <type> of each field. In other words, the tuples in the active memory are variant records and D gives the variant number for each stored record. The format for each active memory entry now becomes:

$$\langle D \rangle \langle L \rangle \langle T1 \rangle \langle T2 \rangle ... \langle Tm \rangle \langle M1 \rangle \langle M2 \rangle ... \langle Mn \rangle \qquad ...eqn.(3).$$

where $\langle L \rangle, \langle T \rangle$ and $\langle M \rangle$ are as before and $\langle D \rangle$ can either be omitted for very simple fixed-format information models, or else $\langle D \rangle$ can be a system-configuration constant in the range one byte to four bytes. This gives up to 2^{32} possible tuple formats - enough to accommodate the low-level storage requirements of a very rich variety of abstract data types and knowledge representation formalisms. In this scheme IDs are now simpler, being straightforward encryptions within the field $\langle type \rangle$ defined by $\langle D \rangle$. The number of bits used for the $\langle T \rangle$ and $\langle L \rangle$ IDs can be a system-configuration constant in the range 2 - 8 bytes. The longer options give such a large ID space that any particular encryption can safely be regarded as persistent.

As with the IFS/1 implementation, a special subsidiary associative memory called the Lexical Token Converter (LTC) is used as a hardware symbol table to give rapid mapping between character strings and IDs and vice versa [ref.11]. The LTC also enforces uniqueness of encryption for lexemes. Hardware support for $\langle labels \rangle$ is also given, in respect of enforcing uniqueness and speeding the dereference operation.

3.3. LOW - LEVEL PROCEDURAL INTERFACE

The active memory is to be used both for the storage and manipulation of persistent objects. The primitive storage commands are simply **insert, delete** and **search**. For the **search** command, the interrogand takes the form of equation (1) or (3) above, with none, one, or several of the $\langle L \rangle$ and $\langle T \rangle$ fields being unspecified (ie wild cards). Thus a **search** command may yield a set of responders. The system tasks concerned with one-level memory management are in general invisible to software, so a discussion of these is left to Section 5.

With regard to the manipulation of persistent objects, we have studied many database, knowledge base, and AI applications in an endeavour to extract a repertoire of generic operations on structured data. It is clear that pattern- directed search, set intersection, transitive closure, relational join, and path-navigation in graphs, are amongst the most useful operations. Fahlman et al. [ref. 12] also promotes the first three as generic tasks; we have not come across any other convincing analysis of generic operations in the literature.

Since sets and graphs can be represented by relations, the super-type for all the above operations seems to be the type **relation**. The operations themselves are not, of course, limited to classical relational algebra - especially in the case of support for linear recursive query evaluation in deductive databases. For convenience we present the complete repertoire of active memory hardware operations, including storage commands, under five headings as follows:

> **Relational algebraic primitives**: insert, delete, member, select, project, intersect, difference, union, join, unique.

> **Set aggregate primitives**: cardinality, maximum, minimum, average.

> **Recursive query primitives**: transitive closure of a relation, reachable node set, nth wave of tuples, is there a path between two specified nodes? return the path

between two specified nodes, composition of relations.

Graph aggregate primitives: shortest path, longest path, arc average, node average.

Special primitives: (to be decided, but possibly including sort,modify, Euclidean distance, Hamming distance, range search, fuzzy search).

The first two groups of commands need no comment. The justification for the primitives which support linear recursive query evaluation will be found in ref.13. There are naturally other graph operations such as sub-graph isomorphism, but it is felt that these more complex actions should be decomposed into the simpler primitives on the grounds of wishing to keep the hardware cost- effective. With regard to fuzzy searching, the LTC already gives fuzzy and range searching on lexemes. Since the active memory will normally use IDs for the low-level representation of symbolic data, straightforward equivalence matching is the major activity in most of the above primitive operations.

The active memory hardware primitives are presented to users via various levels of software, at the lowest level of which is an applications-independent and model-independent C procedural interface. There are procedures at this lowest level for all of the hardware actions listed above. For example, there are two main versions of the search (or select) command, the general forms of which are as follows:

    p-search(patt, A)
    r-search(patt, resp)

Both commands assume that the required C declarations have been made, and that 'patt' has been initialised to a desired interrogand pattern, including wild cards where desired. 'A' is the name by which the responder set will be known. 'resp' is an area in the user's memory to which responders may be returned. The first command, p-search, automatically inserts any responders back into the active memory, creating a persistent structure   named A.   There are, of course, some consequential issues concerning version-number to be resolved in practical database systems. Hardware support within the active memory for automatic versioning of structures is under consideration at the time of writing. The second command, r-search, is a variation which returns responders to the host processor into a buffer pointed to by resp.

Above this lowest level, various software strategies are possible. We may, for example, wish to enrich the primitive types of the applications programming language by adding types which reflect the structure of the tuples we wish to store in the active memory. An example of this is given in the next Section.

4. SOFTWARE INTEGRATION

To the programmer, the active memory described in the previous Section gives the ability to build abstract data types as if in RAM, which then become persistent without further programmer action. In this Section we show how the applications programmer can remain unaware that special-purpose hardware may be invoked on his or her behalf, during the management of persistent objects. C++, the object oriented super-set of C, is used in the following examples because it represents a language that can benefit from the data persistence facilities offered by our active memory. Furthermore, C++ has found favour for real industrial applications where efficiency and maintainability of code is important. However, the primitives of our procedural interface could clearly be built into other object oriented programming languages besides C++.

Access to the active memory is through the procedural interface described previously, which is written in C. The procedural interface uses a number of well defined primitives to insert, search and delete tuples in situ in the active memory. These primitives have been used, as shown below, to build extensions to the C++ language that will allow programs to access and manipulate data in the active memory in the same way as transient objects. In this way the active memory and RAM may be seen by the programmer as a unified memory system. Furthermore, when persistent objects are required, the active memory can manage these objects - thus freeing the programmer from directly transferring data between RAM and disc or interfacing to a query language such as SQL. Storage of objects in the active memory takes place in terms of tuples. All (persistent) data objects are stored in the form:

<object id><instance reference><attribute_name><attribute>

This is a tuple with four <terms>, as defined by eqns (1) and (3) of section 3.2. The attribute field could be another object id, allowing complex objects to be stored. Examples of how tuples store the data for an instance of a class are shown later in this Section.

To use the active memory, we extend the C++ language by adding five new functions to the C++ language to support the persistence of static objects. These are:-

> create;
> destroy;
> get;
> find;
> relation;

The functions **create** and **destroy** are used for directly inserting and deleting data in the active memory, while the **get** function returns instances of a class.(Of course, the **destroy** function would not be used for persistent information). The **find** function is much more flexible than the simple **get** function, being able to take wild cards and then return all responders found. In other words, the **find** function is a pattern directed search which does not depend on classical indexing techniques or pointer following. The **relation** function can be used for multiple inheritance, instance inheritance or for support of a relational object oriented model within the active memory. Note that our functions are declared in an external header file.

To show how the active memory can be used to support the C++ language, throughout the rest of this Section examples will be taken from the following artificial application.

An imaginary nationwide automobile breakdown repair and recovery service needs an intelligent scheduling tool to find the best responses to customer calls for assistance. The response is based on the type of service the customer has paid for, and the location and fault with the vehicle. The data types stored in active memory and the relation constructs that can exist between the data types is shown in figure 2 . The scheduling tool that uses

146

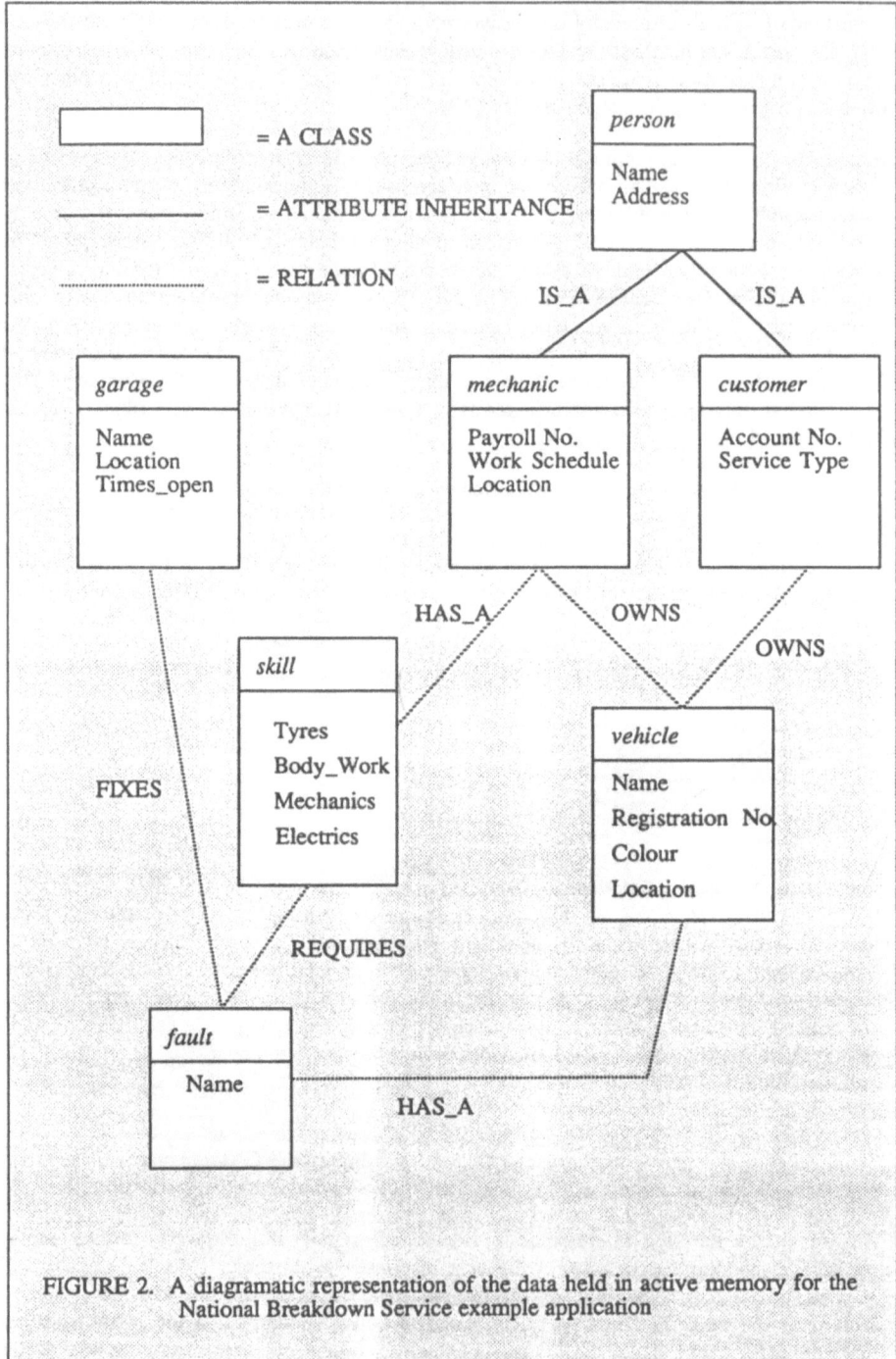

FIGURE 2. A diagramatic representation of the data held in active memory for the National Breakdown Service example application

this data resides in RAM where it manipulates the data stored in the active memory.

As an example of how to use the persistent extensions to the C++ language, the class mechanic with its constructor and destructor which uses the **create** and **destroy** functions is shown in figure 3. Figure 3 takes a somewhat unconventional view of the class mechanic, in order to illustrate the notion that some of the tedious (pointer - following) operations familiar to C++ programmers can actually be regarded as search operations supported by the active memory. The **create** function as used in the constructor of the class mechanic, will insert the following tuples into active memory for an arbitrary instance:

```
<person><#165><name><Smith>
<person><#165><addr><Wivenhoe_Village>
<mechanic><#165><payroll_no><10344555>
<mechanic><#165><work_schedule><4am-2pm>
<mechanic><#165><location><Hertfordshire>
```

The number #165 is just an arbitrary value for the instance reference; in terms of section 3.2 it is an abstract node.

The **find** function is used generally over all the data in the active memory, irrespective of class, so it does not have to be declared first. The **find** function implies an interpretation of a class as a set of instances, whereas a conventional C++ programmer might be more concerned with structuring the class in terms of sub - lists in order to avoid large searches. However, it is a property of the active memory that, for a given number of wild cards in the interrogand, search times are independent of set cardinality. An example of how to use the **find** function to retrieve the set of all the instances of the class person is as follows:

```
find("person","name","address")
```

Note that a **find** operation may translate into more than one of the search primitives described in section 3.3. The **destroy** and **find** functions can use wild cards and this is where the power of using the active memory is seen to advantage. Data does not have to be shipped to the main processor for manipulation. The wild card "?" will return all the responders matching the query when used in conjunction with the **find** function. For example,

```
find("mechanic","?","?","Oxfordshire")
```

will return all the mechanics who are located in Oxfordshire. To give an indication of timing, the active memory could identify the responders to this query in about 500 microseconds. The responders would normally remain in the active memory. If it is required to transfer them back to the host processor, e.g. for printing, then the transfer - time may add a few additional milliseconds if large numbers of responders are involved.

Another wild card, "ALL", can be used to return all the instances of a class. For example:

```
find("mechanic","ALL")
```

will return the set of all the instances of the class mechanic. This wild card should of course be used with caution when used with the **destroy** function (see the destructor for the class mechanic). Using these functions in this way encapsulates the data description within the

```
class mechanic : person {

/* the following will be persistent for this class - see the constructor

                int     payroll_no;
                char *work_schedule,
                     *location;                              */

public:

        mechanic(char*,char*,int, char*,char*); // constructor
        ~mechanic();                           // destructor
        is_available();   // calculates if mechanic can respond to call out

    };

mechanic::mechanic(char * n, char *addr, int pay, char *wk,char *loc)
{
create( "mechanic","payroll_no,"pay, "work_schedule",wk,"location",loc);
    }

mechanic::~mechanic()
{
destroy(ALL);
}
```

Figure 3 The declaration, constructor and destructor for the class mechanic

```
class garage {

/* the following will be persistent for this class - see the constructor

        char *name,
                *location,
                *times_open;
        relation(fixes,fault);                              */

public:
        garage(char*,char*,char*,char*);
        show_garage();
};

garage::garage(char* n,char* loc,char* times,char*flt)
{
relation("garage","fixes","faults",flt);

create("garage","name",n, "location",loc,"times_open",times,"fixes",flt);
    }
```

Figure 4   The declaration, constructor and destructor for the class garage, showing the use of the relation function

class. Access to the data is achieved only via the defined interfaces to the class. Manipulation of data using these basic functions can be defined separately for each class and not generally, therefore simplifying the operations. This means that complex rules for types and value encoding are not necessary. In addition, the functionality of the active memory means that the object oriented paradigm as supported by C++ can be extended so that its persistent data structures enjoy support for the following :-

i)   generic types
ii)   set inclusion semantics for inheritance
iii) instance and default inheritance, as well as attribute inheritance
iv)   multiple inheritance (not supported by pre 1989 AT&T C++)
v)   identification of objects either by identity or value
vi)   semantic relations between objects.

In order to support relations between instances of persistent data types in the store the function **relation** can be included in a class description. How the relation is used can be seen by the declaration and constructor for the class garage in figure 4. To support the **relation** function, the tuple format is extended, and takes the following form:

<object id><instance ref.><relation><object id><instance ref.>

For example, the **relation** function as used in the constructor for the class garage could result in the following tuple being inserted in active memory:

<garage><x223><fixes><fault><#344>

So using find("garage","quickfix","Oxfordshire","?","fixes","?")

(see the constructor for the class garage, fig.4) would return all the fault types fixed by that garage.

It can be seen that if the relation was an IS_A (attribute inheritance) then multiple inheritance can also be supported. In our example application the is_a (instance inheritance) is not used. An example from a CAD application of how tuples using the is_a relationship could be stored in active memory is as follows:

<square><q234><side1><is_a><side><w234>

Within the active memory, objects can be identified either by their identity or value using the **find** function. We take the view that this can be a useful tool for the application programmer. An objection to the identifying of objects by value (i.e. content-addressability), and also to the semantic relations between objects, is that these features compromise data encapsulation. For example, updating a joint relation by one class will affect the other. However, this can be seen to be a virtue [ref. 8]. A relation abstractly represents a constraint between two or more classes, but this need not compromise true information hiding because the relation is declared only within the affected classes.

5. HARDWARE REALISATION

The underlying structure of the active memory follows that of the IFS/1 [ref.10] and the IFS/1's relational algebraic processor [ref.14]. Both these units employ SIMD-parallel search engines and hardware-hashed RAM to give very rapid search rates. This permits associative matching tasks to be carried out over large volumes of information in a more cost-effective manner than would be possible with CAM chips. In the active memory the storage functionality and the relational processing activity are combined within the same hardware unit. The main difference between the former IFS/1 implementation and our active memory now under construction is that the latter uses transputers in place of PAL-based finite state machines for control purposes. Using several transputers for distributed control gives greater functional flexibility, better modular extensibility, and very much shorter development times. Since the data-intensive work is still carried out by special SIMD search engines, there is little degradation of overall performance compared with the IFS/1's MSI control hardware.

Figure 5 shows a section of the active memory now being built at Essex. The boxes T_{bc}, T_{bf}, T_n and T_r are TRAMS - (transputer-plus-RAM modules). The subscripts bc, bf,n and r respectively stand for: branch control, branch fan- out, node and root. The box labelled H alongside each node transputer is a memory-mapped hardware hasher. The search modules SM each consist of 1Mbyte of 80nsec. DRAM, a 32-bit wide search engine, and a small amount of organisational logic for masking, etc. The search modules are mapped into T_n's address space for control purposes. In the prototype there are four search modules per node, giving 12Mbytes of associative (ie content-addressable) memory in Figure 5. The memory per module, and the nodes in the tree, can easily be extended in future. Overflow is to disc(s), which are organised into logical hashing bins compatible with the organisation of the search modules.

Based on the existing IFS/1 performance [refs. 10,, 14] and upon Occam simulations of Figure 5, we expect the active memory to yield the following approximate timings when operands are held in the RAM-based search modules. (Note that these are times measured at the nodes; they do not include any transfers to/from the host).

> **Insert a tuple**: 60 microseconds.
> **Member operation**: 40 microseconds (fixed time, independent of relation cardinality).
> **Search with one wild card**: 400 microseconds (independent of relation cardinality; varies with number of responders, but assumes these responders are kept within the active memory and not returned to the host).
> **Join operation**: join of two 1000-tuple relations in about 5 milliseconds.
> **Transitive closure**: up to 600 microseconds for a 1000-node graph, depending on bushyness.

The relation format for the above operations is very general, no assumptions being made about position of key fields, presence of sorted values, etc. Hand-coded software, running on a uniprocessor of compatible technology, only offers competitive speeds for very small data structures of cardinality typically less than 20.

The associatively-accessed disc in Figure 5 is naturally the non-volatile part of the active memory, for which the search modules appear as a cache. Data is moved between the disc(s) and cache in logical sets, according to a scheme known as semantic caching [ref. 15]. Cached sets, for example 'all people living in Ipswich', also have their set-descriptor (corresponding to <?><lives.in><Ipswich>) placed in the cache. As discussed

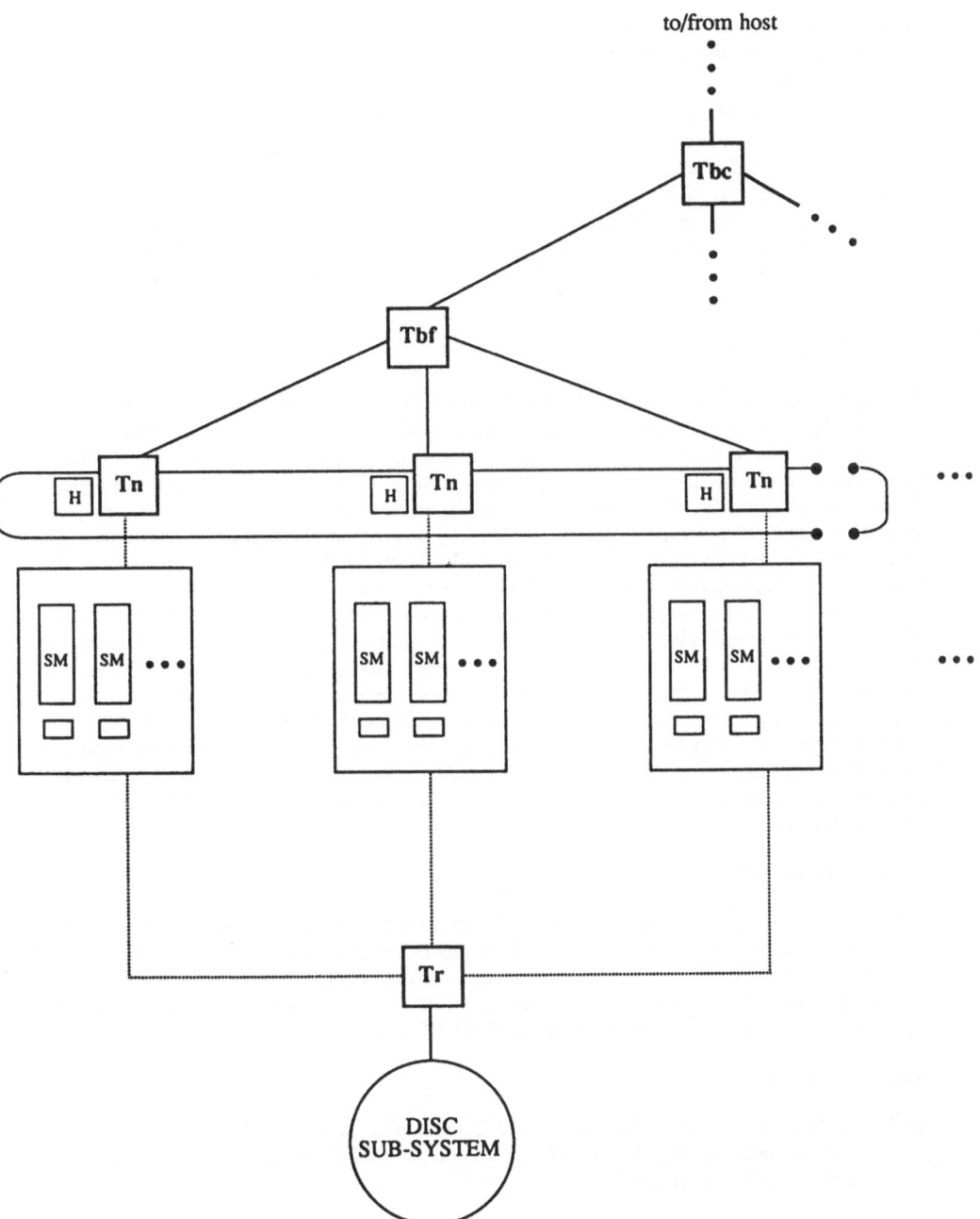

Figure 5: One unit of active memory, consisting of three leaves. Each leaf, or node, is under the control of a node transputer, Tn.

in ref. 15, testing cached set-descriptors is sufficient to determine whether a requested set is totally, partly, or not at all contained within the cache. It is shown that the overheads of carrying out these tests is small provided that $R \gg 2^t$, where R is the performance ratio of RAM to disc (typically $> 10^4$) and t is the number of <terms> in the interrogand which are not wild cards. Initial studies of a binary relational database gave reasonable results, indicating that an average hit-rate of 89 percent was achieved with a cache size in the range 5 to 10 percent of the total database size. However, we have not yet used semantic caching in earnest on very large databases. A strategy for concurrent-user control based on the same variable-granularity set-descriptors for lock specifiers has also been proposed [ref. 15]. A combination of pre-conflict locking and post-conflict (optimistic) locking is envisaged.

6. CONCLUSIONS

We have introduced the idea of 'moving the operation to the data', and hence of constructing a hardware unit which both stores and manipulates structured information. The resulting **active memory** seems to have the potential for solving many of the memory-management problems associated with persistent objects. In particular, the active memory is a one-level store, in which long- term data is manipulated in exactly the same way as short-term data. Any <type> system enforced by a programming language on short-term data in the active memory is also enforced automatically on long-term data. The large ID space in our associatively-accessed active memory gives a very large persistent name space; this is in some ways equivalent to having an extremely large conventional virtual address space which gives direct random-access addressing to all levels of physical memory - but without the need to agonise over addressing mechanisms. The active memory's functionality reduces the amount of structure-manipulation code that has to be written at the applications level. It also eliminates the need to write system code which is concerned with the translation and movement of data. Although we have not pursued the topic in this paper, the active memory's extensible SIMD architecture allows the inherent parallelism in certain well-used data structures to be exploited 'in situ', without any effort on the part of the user.

7. ACKNOWLEDGMENTS

It is a pleasure to acknowledge the helpful discussions with other members of the IFS team at Essex. Martin Waite, in particular, has greatly added to our understanding of the architectural implications of types. We also thank John Rosenberg (University of Newcastle, Australia) for his comments on a draft of this paper. The work described in this paper has been supported by SERC grants GR/E/05018 and GR/F/06319.

REFERENCES

[1.]   R B K Dewar ,E Schonberg and J T Schwartz "High-Level Programming - An Introduction to the Programming Language SETL" *Courant Institue of Math Sciences*, New York 1983.

[2]   Persistent Programming Research Group "PS_algol Reference Manual", *Fourth Edition,Persistent Programming Research Report 12*. Department of Computing Science, University of Glasgow and Department of Computational Science, University of St. Andrews 1987.

[3]   G N Dixon, G D Parrington et.al "The Treatment of Persistent objects in Arjuna", *The Computer Journal, Vol.32, No.4* August 1989 pages 323 - 332.

[4]   P Balch, W P Cockshott and P W Foulk "Layered Implementations of Persistent Object Stores", *Software Enginnering Journal Vol.4, No.2* March 1989 pages 123 - 131.

[5]   A L Brown, and W P Cockshott. "CPOMS - A revised version of the Persistent Object Management system in C" *Persistent Programming Research Report 13.* Universities of Glasgow and St. Andrews, 1985.

[6]   J Rosenberg and J L Keedy "Software Management of a Large Virtual Memory". Proceedings of the 4th. Australian Computer Science Conference, Brisbane, February 1981, pages 171 - 183.

[7]   S L Osborn, "Identity, Equality and Query Optimization" *2nd International Workshop on Object-Oriented Database Systems,* Bad Munster am Stein-Ebernburg, FRG, September 1988, pages 346 - 351.Printed by Springer-Verlag as Lecture Notes in Computer Science no. 334.

[8]   J Rumbaugh "Relations as Semantic Constructs in an Object-Oriented Language" *Conference on Object-Oriented Programming Systems, Languages and Applications,* Orlando, Florida, October 1987 pages 466 - 481. (Published by acm press, Special Issue of SIGPLAN Notices, Vol.22, No.12).

[9]   A J Berre "SOOM and Tornado - Experience with Database-support for Object-Oriented Applications" *2nd International Workshop on Object-Oriented Database Systems,* Bad Munster am Stein-Ebernburg, FRG, September 1988, pages 104 - 109. Printed by Springer-Verlag as Lecture Notes in Computer Science no. 334.

[10]   S H Lavington, "Technical Overview of the Intelligent File Store". *Knowledge-Based Systems, Vol.1,No.3,* June 1988, pages 166 - 172.

[11]   C J Wang and S H Lavington "The Lexical Token Converter - A High Performance Associative Dictionary for Large Knowledge Bases" Department of Computer Science, University of Essex, *Internal Report CSM-133,* August 1989.(Submitted to Knowledge and Data Engineering).

[12]   S E Falman, G E Hinton and T J Sejnowski "Massively Parallel Architectures for AI:NETL,THISTLE and Boltzman machines" *Proceedings of the National Conference on Artificial Intelligence,* Washington, USA (1983) pages 109 - 113.

[13]   J Robinson and S H Lavington "A Transitive Closure and Magic Functions Machine" *To be presented at the Second International Symposium on Databases in Parallel and Distributed Systems,* July 1990, Dublin.

[14]   S H Lavington, J Robinson and K Y Mok, "A High Performance Relational Algebraic Processor for Large Knowledge Bases". *Presented at the International Workshop on VLSI for Artificial Intelligence, Oxford,* July 1988. Published in: VLSI for Artificial Intelligence, eds. Delgado-Frias and Moore, Kluwer Academic Press, 1989, pages 133 - 143.

[15]   S H Lavington, M Standring, Y J Jiang, C J Wang and M E Waite, "Hardware Memory Management for Large Knowledge Bases". *Proceedings of PARLE, the conference on Parallel Architectures and Languages Europe,* Eindhoven, June 1987, pages 226 - 241. (Published by Springer-Verlag as Lecture Notes in Computer Science, Nos. 258 & 259).

A Layered Persistent Architecture for Napier88

A.L. Brown, R. Morrison, D.S. Munro
University of St.Andrews

A. Dearle
University of Adelaide

J. Rosenberg
University of Newcastle

ABSTRACT

In recent years a range of single programming language systems have been developed that are supported by a persistent store. Examples of such systems include Argus, Galileo, PS-algol and Smalltalk. Although each of these systems is based on a subtly different concept of persistence a common approach is to utilise a layered architecture. This paper presents the design of one such layered architecture that can be used to support a persistent object store where the protection is enforced by a high level type system. The architecture has been used to construct the persistent programming system for Napier88 and is powerful enough to support languages with similar type systems.

1. INTRODUCTION

In recent years a range of single programming language systems have been developed that are supported by a persistent store [2, 4, 6, 8, 28, 29]. Examples of such systems include Argus [17], Galileo [1], PS-algol [25] and Smalltalk [13]. Although each of these systems is based on a subtly different concept of persistence a common approach is to utilise a layered architecture. This paper presents the design of one such layered architecture that can be used to support a persistent object store where the protection is enforced by a high level type system. The architecture has been used to construct the persistent programming system for Napier88 [22] and is powerful enough to support languages with similar type systems, for example Galileo, Hope+ [24] and Staple [20].

The architecture is able to support programming languages that utilise the concept of orthogonal persistence. Orthogonal persistence requires the persistence abstraction to be applicable to all data types without regard to their lifetimes or patterns of use. That is, all data in a system may be manipulated independently of its physical location, size, storage format, storage media or any other physical property it may exhibit [3].

A persistent store that supports orthogonal persistence has certain perceived properties. For example, since the storage format of data is hidden, a persistent store may be viewed as a uniform store. Its size is also conceptually unbounded since the physical properties of the storage media are hidden. Furthermore, failures are hidden with the result that the store must appear failure free.

In practice it is not possible to build a store of unbounded size or one that is failure free. However, a wide range of techniques is available that may be used to simulate the properties of unbounded size and absolute stability. In section 2 we will discuss some of these techniques and distinguish the architectural mechanisms required, namely an addressing mechanism, a storage management mechanism and a stability mechanism. The composition of a persistent store will then be described in terms of architectural layers that provide the required architectural mechanisms.

An important feature of a persistent system is that all data within the system is subject to the protection mechanisms required by the programming languages that manipulate it. Consequently, the design of the system architecture must accommodate any interactions between the different protection mechanisms that may be applied to shared data. In section 3 we discuss some possible protection mechanisms.

Finally, we describe a layered architecture for a persistent system composed from an appropriate selection of the protection and storage mechanisms. The resultant architecture, that for Napier88, has been implemented on conventional hardware and makes use of a high level protection mechanism.

The strength of the layered architecture is that it is flexible and allows a high degree of reuse without compromising efficiency. The architecture is generic in that layers may be replaced to expedite experimentation. Thus, many versions of the layers may exist as a set of tools and these may be composed, subject to the constraints of the layer interfaces, to yield an instance of the persistent architecture. This genericity, based on plug-in tool sets, allows a version of the architecture to be appropriately specialised to a particular implementation of a language.

It is also intended that each of the layers, or groups of layers, may be reused as tools in other systems. Indeed, this is exactly what has happened in the implementation of the persistent store for the language Staple.

Finally, in any implementation the layers may be virtual layers. The compiler may, for efficiency reasons, wish to avoid mapping through the interfaces. This may be achieved for any combination of the layers. Alternatively, as in the case of the Rekursiv [5], hardware can be used to implement a layer.

2. PERSISTENT STORES OF UNBOUNDED SIZE

As described above, a store that supports orthogonal persistence has certain perceived attributes including uniformity, unbounded size and absolute stability. We shall now describe a number of techniques that may be used to simulate a uniform stable store of unbounded size. As part of the discussion we shall consider the issues of addressing the object store, managing the object store and making the object store stable.

2.1. Addressing the Object Store

The first issue we will consider is how the store may be addressed. There are several levels of addressing that may be present in a computer system ranging from the symbolic addresses used by a programmer, to the logical addresses used by an instruction set, to the physical addresses that must be used by the hardware.

Since a persistent store appears uniform, a single addressing mechanism is required at the external interface in order to provide an appropriate level of abstraction over the entire store. Although the store is addressed by this single mechanism, there may be several more primitive addressing mechanisms that support it as well as several higher level mechanisms that are mapped onto the store interface. For example, the store may be viewed as an object space supported by one or more mapping tables that record the physical location of each object. In this case access to an object is achieved using a lower level addressing mechanism that may be different for each kind of physical storage in which an object may reside.

In the following sections we show three different levels of addressing abstraction that may be used to provide a uniform store. In practice a system may support multiple levels of addressing where each level corresponds to one or more of these three abstractions, in any combination.

2.1.1. Symbolic Addressing

A persistent store may be addressed purely in terms of symbolic addresses. At this level of abstraction the name of an object would be mapped onto a lower level address and a second mapping table would map a field name onto a location within the object. The result of the two mappings can then be combined to form the address of the desired data within the underlying storage. This is illustrated in Figure 1.

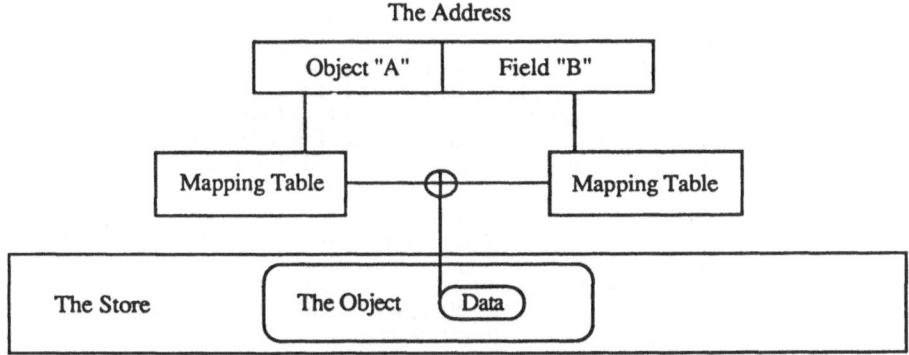

Figure 1: Addressing a Field "B" of an Object "A"

The main advantage of this uniform addressing mechanism is that it may abstract over many different physical storage mediums or lower level addressing mechanisms and it imposes no limits on the amount of storage that can be addressed. Furthermore, the dynamic name resolution allows a program to operate over any objects that contain data with the required field names.

One disadvantage of this abstraction is that the dynamic resolution of names may be inefficient, particularly if no restrictions are placed on the length of symbolic names. This disadvantage may be alleviated by only performing the address mapping once and thereafter using the lower level address. The optimisation may not always be appropriate since it implies the preservation of a binding from the symbolic name to the lower level address. An example of a system that utilises dynamic name resolution with this optimisation is the Multics system [12].

2.1.2. Object Numbers

An alternative to symbolic addressing is to view the object store as an object space where each object is identified by a number and each field of an object is identified by an offset into the object. Thus, an address consists of two components, an object number and an offset. These may be provided as a single partitioned integer or as separate integers depending on the implementation [5, 12]. This abstraction relies on a mapping table that maps object numbers to lower level storage addresses and is illustrated in Figure 2.

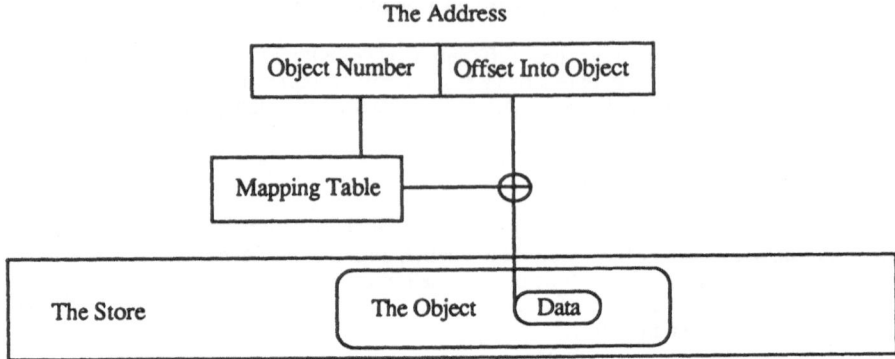

Figure 2: Addressing Data Within an Object Using a Partitioned Address

A major advantage of this addressing abstraction is that the decoding of the object address and the offset within the object may be efficiently performed in hardware. The partitioning of the address space also supports the dynamic growth and shrinkage of objects, up to the maximum length that can be addressed via an offset. Thus stack and file objects may be conveniently modelled using this approach. However, there are two potential disadvantages.

Firstly, the fixed partitioning of the address space imposes a fixed relationship between the maximum number of objects that can be created and maximum size of objects that may be created. Depending on the chosen partitioning, this ranges from a few large objects to a large number of small objects. In the absence of an additional mechanism to concatenate objects [6, 9] or the use of large addresses, the abstraction may be unable to cope with a combination of a few large objects with large numbers of small objects.

The second disadvantage is that the choice of partition size may result in object numbers being exhausted before the store is filled. This problem may be overcome by using larger addresses with any increased overheads in storage or address translation being minimised by the appropriate use of contextual addressing.

An example of a system that uses this approach is the Rekursiv. The hardware of the Rekursiv supports the efficient mapping of object numbers to physical addresses and the automatic caching of the first word of an addressed object. The Burroughs B5700/6700 series [23] is another example.

2.1.3. Virtual Addresses

The addressing of an object store may also be performed by viewing the entire system storage, in all its physical forms, as a flat virtual store and providing a higher level architecture to support an object view of this virtual store. This level of abstraction is illustrated in Figure 3. There is only one address space at this level of abstraction and it may be supported by any one of a number of well known techniques. For example, a paged virtual memory mechanism could be used based on conventional hardware.

The advantages of this scheme are that no mapping table is necessary to locate an object within the storage, locations within an object can be directly addressed, conventional hardware can be employed, alternative storage organisations can be implemented without affecting the addressing mechanism and the address space need not be larger than the available physical storage.

The Address

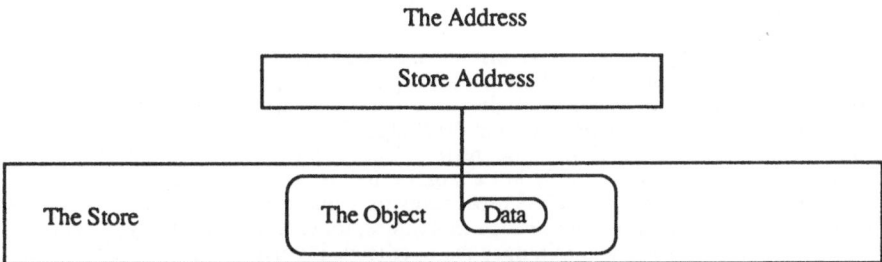

Figure 3: Addressing Data Within an Object Using a Direct Address

A disadvantage of this level of abstraction is that objects may be required to change address if the higher level architecture reorganises the mapping of objects onto virtual storage. Although a similar problem may arise in higher level addressing mechanisms, the higher level mechanisms abstract over the mapping of objects to storage thereby allowing an object to be relocated without altering its logical address.

The MONADS-PC [26] is an example of a system that utilises this level of address abstraction within its hierarchy of addressing mechanisms. MONADS supports a very large virtual address space the organisation of which is the responsibility of a higher level architecture.

2.2. Managing the Object Store

Each of the above addressing abstractions require a mechanism to organise the available storage into objects. Addressing abstractions based on symbolic names or object numbers view the organisation of the store into objects as a function of a lower level architecture whereas, the virtual addressing abstraction assumes that objects are provided by a higher level architecture. In each case the addressing and organisation of the object store may be viewed as distinct architectural layers.

There is a wide variety of techniques that may be employed to organise a store into objects. Many of these techniques have been developed for use with programming languages that support objects whose lifetimes may be independent of the procedure activations that create them. Thus, each technique has had to address the problems of dynamic storage allocation, storage reclamation and any associated fragmentation.

A store organisation can be designed to suit a particular application. However, the effectiveness of a particular choice of store organisation is dependent on both the scale of the store and the manner in which it is used. This may not be known at the design stage of a general purpose system.

2.2.1. Simulating Unbounded Size

The simulation of unbounded size involves managing an object store in such a way that, conceptually, it is always possible to create more objects. However, since a physical store is of finite size it is necessary to reuse the storage allocated to objects that are no longer required. This may be achieved either by explicitly deleting objects or performing some form of automatic garbage collection. A further consideration is whether or not the addresses of deleted objects may be reused.

The explicit deletion of objects is employed by systems that can statically determine the lifetime of data. For example, if first class procedures are not supported, the storage allocated to an activation record can be recovered when a procedure call returns. Explicit deletion of objects is also used by programming languages such as C [15] and Pascal [31].

A wide range of garbage collection algorithms has been developed and integrated with the storage allocation mechanisms of different store organisations [11]. Each of these algorithms and their host stores are designed to support a particular pattern of use or scale of data. For example, the garbage collector employed in the S-algol [21] heap storage uses a single list of free storage [19]. Since S-algol does not create objects at a very high rate the cost of object creation and garbage collection only has a small effect on overall system performance. In contrast, systems supporting first class procedures may make intensive use of a heap. Such systems require the support of sophisticated techniques, for example the buddy system [16] or generation scavenging [30], that minimise the overheads involved in storage allocation and garbage collection.

The deletion of an object requires that all references to an object are invalidated. This can be achieved by searching the store for all references to the object and removing them. Alternatively, indirect addressing could be used and the address mapping for the object invalidated. This option requires that addresses not be reused so that the mappings remain invalid. In turn, this requires the number of available object addresses to be so large that they can never be exhausted. Examples of systems that support this technique include Hydra [10] and MONADS.

2.3. Simulating Stability

The persistence abstraction attempts to hide all the physical attributes of data. Consequently, the components of a persistent store are also hidden, requiring any failures in the components to be hidden. Therefore the persistent store is conceptually failure free, that is, it is stable.

The potential failures that may occur within a store can be categorised as either being hard failures or soft failures. A hard failure is a failure that results in physical damage to the store, such as a head crash on a disk. A hard failure destroys data. In contrast, a soft failure is a failure that may cause a system to halt, possibly resulting in some minor corruption of data. In general, it will not result in the wholesale destruction of data.

The provision of a stable store must address the issues of protecting data from the potential side effects of both hard and soft failures. The techniques for recovering from hard failures range from taking complete dumps on removable media to maintaining multiple on-line copies. These techniques are out with the scope of this paper and are discussed elsewhere [8]. For the purposes of this paper we shall only consider techniques that allow the simulation of stability with respect to soft failures.

2.3.1. Soft failures

A soft failure may occur during a series of updates thereby preventing a logical operation from completing. As a result, the data held in the store may not be self-consistent. To ensure that a store remains self-consistent, it is necessary to perform all updates to the store as some form of atomic transaction. That is, a modification either completes or it is totally undone. One mechanism for achieving a transaction is to maintain a record of which data has been changed, together with either its original value or its intended value. To ensure that the appropriate action can be taken on a failure, the record must be placed in stable storage before the update takes place.

The complexity of transaction mechanisms provided by a system may be extremely varied. For example, consider a traditional database system such as IBM's System R [14]. System R supports several complex transactions operating concurrently, implemented by a combination of logging and checkpointing. Logging takes the form of recording all operations on stable storage before the operation is performed. In addition to the normal operations, a record is kept of any checkpoints. Thus, when a failure occurs, System R can determine from the log how to restore its database to a self-consistent state.

To complement the logging mechanism, System R also provides a simple checkpointing mechanism that places the entire stable storage in a self-consistent state. The implementation of the checkpointing mechanism is based on shadow paging [18]. In normal operation, System R accesses its database via a paging mechanism. When a virtual page is modified, a copy of it is written to a new physical page and a mapping created between the two versions of the page. The effect of the checkpoint is to update the page mappings so that the modified version of each page is treated as the original version. The paging mechanism as described is continually forming a record of the changes to the system by preserving the original versions of each page.

In contrast to the complexities of a traditional database system, a persistent object store can adopt a much simpler transaction mechanism. Since stability is an orthogonal property of the data within a persistent store, a simple checkpointing mechanism is sufficient to ensure that the object store remains self-consistent with respect to failures. The checkpointing mechanism records incremental changes to the persistent store and may operate on individual objects or the storage in which the objects reside.

Shadow paging is used by the PS-algol/ Shrines system implemented under VAX/VMS [28]. Shrines operates by mapping a file holding the persistent store onto the virtual address space of a running program. This is achieved by directly manipulating the VMS page tables using a special purpose paging algorithm. The purpose of the paging algorithm is to ensure that when a page is to be modified, it is first copied and then the copy is modified. In this way, the original version of the persistent store is preserved while a new version is incrementally constructed. The checkpointing mechanism supported by Shrines allows the new version of the persistent store to become the original in a single atomic action. A similar scheme is proposed to support stability in the MONADS machine [27].

The alternative approach, adopted by systems such as the PS-algol/ CPOMS system [6], is to record different versions of an object rather than different versions of a page. In these object based systems, the record of changed objects may be in one of two forms. Either it is a record of the original versions of the objects, known as a *before look*, or it is the new versions of the objects, known as an *after look*. A before look may be used to restore the store to a previous consistent state, whereas an after look may be used to complete the recorded updates and establish a new consistent state. In both cases, an update to the store is not performed until the entire before or after look is complete. Hence, the size of a before or after look is dependent on the number of updates performed between each checkpoint.

The choice between a before or after look will depend on the particular use made of a store. For example, the design of the CPOMS anticipated that updates to the persistent store would contain a large proportion of new objects. Thus, a before look was chosen since it would have to record less data than an after look. The act of forming a before look may be expensive if additional accesses to a disk are necessary to retrieve the original value. Hence, the configuration of a system's buffering mechanisms may determine that an after look is more efficient. Ideally, a system using a before look or after look strategy should be able to switch between the two depending on the current use of the system.

2.4. Composing a Persistent Object Store

A persistent object store may be implemented by composing a suitable selection of the techniques described above. For example, any combination of the three levels of addressing abstraction can be adopted to provide a uniform store. The selected addressing abstractions can then be combined with a storage management scheme that is able to simulate unbounded size. This composition will result in a uniform store of unbounded size. Finally, a stability mechanism may be integrated with the store that operates in terms of objects or the storage in which the objects reside. In either case stability is an orthogonal property of the store and as such it may be viewed as a distinct architectural layer. The result of the composing the three architectural layers namely, the addressing abstraction, the storage management and the stability mechanism, is the simulation of a uniform, stable, object store of unbounded size.

Although the result of a particular implementation strategy may be to merge or otherwise integrate the three architectural layers, the functionality of the layers can still be distinguished. In the architecture to be described these distinctions are preserved by forcing the separate implementation of the architectural layers. The resulting architecture is flexible enough to allow each layer to be reimplemented independently of the others. An instance of the layered architecture may be composed from an arbitrary choice of layer implementations even if some of the layers make use of special purpose hardware. This permits cost effective experimentation with implementation techniques and the manner in which these techniques interact within the context of the architecture.

3. TYPE SECURITY

All data within a persistent object store may be manipulated without regard to its physical attributes. Hence, the data may be manipulated by any programming language supported by the system architecture. This requires the data to be subject to the protection mechanisms required by those programming languages that manipulate it. Furthermore, the protection mechanisms applied to shared data must not be able to compromise each other.

3.1. Store Level Protection

The protection mechanisms provided by a persistent system are dependent on the kinds of programming language that are supported. For example, if programming languages such as C or assembly language are supported then the protection mechanism must be applied at the storage level. These languages may arbitrarily manipulate addresses and thereby access the implementation of an object. Thus, every operation on the store must be dynamically checked to ensure that it is safe. That is, an attempted store operation must conform to a predefined set of type rules and it must not allow a program to gain unauthorised access to data. A store may be described as type secure if all the permitted operations are safe.

At the store level type security must be enforced in two ways. Firstly, since programming languages such as C may exhibit arbitrary behaviour, a mechanism is required to prevent programs manufacturing or capturing addresses that could be used to gain unauthorised access to data. Secondly, the interpretation of the accessible data must also be controlled so that programs only apply appropriate operations to the data. Systems that provide this form of store level protection are known as capability systems and require some level of hardware support.

One technique that is used to prevent addresses being manufactured is to segregate address from non-address data and to only permit certain operations on the addresses. The operations may be limited to the creation of new objects and to copying an address between address only storage areas. An alternative technique is to tag locations containing addresses and to automatically reset the tags if the locations are updated. In this way an address is invalidated if it is illegally altered. The address manipulation facilities provided by the system preserve the tags.

To complement the controlled creation of addresses capability systems may provide mechanisms to limit the propagation of addresses. For example, a limited copy access right might be used to copy an address but the copy of the address may not be copied. Another technique is to associate a key with an address. The address may be freely passed around between programs but it may only be used in conjunction with the original key. This limits the context in which an address may be used.

In addition to controlled address propagation a capability system may support the revocation of addresses. That is, an address may be invalidated and all access to the object to which it refers can be removed. This may be expensive to implement since it may require the support of indirect addressing or the ability to find all references to an object.

The control of address creation and propagation is just a special case of the controlled interpretation of data. In the non-address case this is usually of a very limited nature. For example, access to an object may be restricted to read, write or execute, without any additional constraints on how the data should be interpreted. Thus, an object containing a floating point number may be erroneously viewed as an integer without an error being detected.

A less primitive approach is to tag individual locations within an object and thereby specify the type of data each location contains. This allows simple data types such as integers and floating point numbers to be differentiated. Other supported data types may include pixels, addresses, character strings, arrays, structures and procedure closures.

The main advantages of store level protection are that it can support programming languages such as assembly language and C, it can allow arbitrary combinations of programming languages and segregate them if necessary, it can dynamically alter access to and interpretation of data, and for simple data types it can be efficiently implemented in hardware. However, on their own, store level protection mechanisms may not be able to efficiently support recursively typed data structures since the necessary run time checks can prove extremely expensive. Furthermore, once a particular mechanism has been implemented in hardware it may be very costly to alter.

Finally, in isolation, this approach to protection limits the programmer's confidence that a program is correct. That is, certain programming errors may not be detected until runtime and any programming language data types not supported by the protection mechanism may be misinterpreted resulting in erroneous program behaviour.

3.2. High Level Protection

Type security may be enforced at a higher level of abstraction by a programming language hiding the implementation of objects. In this case, a compiler may check the operations to be performed by a program to see if they conform to the type rules. This allows a program to run without the overheads of dynamic checking and may permit optimisations to be performed. For example, accessing a structured object may involve checking that the object exists, checking that the object contains the required data and finally indexing the object. If the result of the two checks can be determined by a compiler then the data may be directly addressed.

A further advantage of high level protection is that very sophisticated type systems may be used. These type systems may require expensive type checks to be performed but, the type checking need only be performed once at compile time and not each time a program accesses data of a particular type.

Not all operations may be fully checked at compile time. For example, a vector indexing operation may require a run time check to ensure that a legal index is used. In cases such as this, the compiler is able to generate additional code to dynamically check the operation. However, the dynamic checking may be simplified by removing from it any component checking that may be statically determined.

Statically determining the type correctness of a program reduces the range of potential errors that may occur at runtime. For example, any attempt to misinterpret a programming language data type will be detected at compile time. In comparison with purely dynamic checking, this increases the programmer's confidence in the correctness of a program.

Although high level protection mechanisms can provide sophisticated control over the interpretation of data they are not well suited to controlling access. One reason for this is the assumption that once access to an object has been established it is permanently available. This problem may be alleviated by extending the type rules to include data types that must be dynamically checked for availability. However, this may reduce a programmer's confidence in a program being correct in that it introduces a potential source of programming errors.

The combination of programming languages requires any shared data to have an equivalent interpretation under both type systems. If this is not possible the programming languages must be totally segregated from each other. The segregation need only be a logical structuring of an object store if high level protection is sufficient for each programming language, otherwise the segregation must be enforced by a store level protection mechanism.

High level protection may allow a type secure store to be efficiently implemented without the need for special purpose hardware. If this is the case, the protection mechanism may be altered relatively cheaply since no hardware need be modified. However, dynamic checking may be delegated to a store level protection mechanism if one is available. Finally, a high level protection mechanism enables a program's view of data to be an abstraction over the physical storage of the data.

To summarise, high level protection provides the following benefits:

- There are no unnecessary dynamic checks.
- Optimisations may be possible as a result of static checking.
- Sophisticated type systems may be supported.
- The range of potential runtime errors is reduced.
- Special purpose hardware is not required to support an efficient implementation.
- An abstract view may be imposed over the physical storage of data.

4. DEVELOPING THE LAYERS

In the preceding discussions the distinct architectural mechanisms required to support a persistent object store have been identified. They include, a uniform addressing mechanism, a storage management mechanism, a stability mechanism and a protection mechanism. We shall now present the design of a layered architecture that provides the above mechanisms as a set of distinct architectural layers. The architecture to be described supports orthogonal persistence and has been used to implement the persistent programming language Napier88 and the functional programming language Staple.

4.1. The Basic Layers

The layered architecture has been designed with the aim of supporting cost effective experimentation with the implementation of persistence. The key to achieving this aim is the separation of the distinct architectural mechanisms into well defined layers. Thus, each architectural mechanism is provided by a distinct architectural layer that must conform to a particular specification. In this way, individual layers may be independently reimplemented without reference to the implementation of the other layers. It is also possible to merge adjacent layers provided that the interface to the top-most layer is preserved.

The architectural layering has been chosen to take advantage of the persistence abstraction by ensuring that programs are not able to discover details of how objects are stored. This divides the architecture between the architectural layers that provide the persistent object store and the those facilities that may be programmed by a supported programming language. The architectural layering is shown in Figure 4.

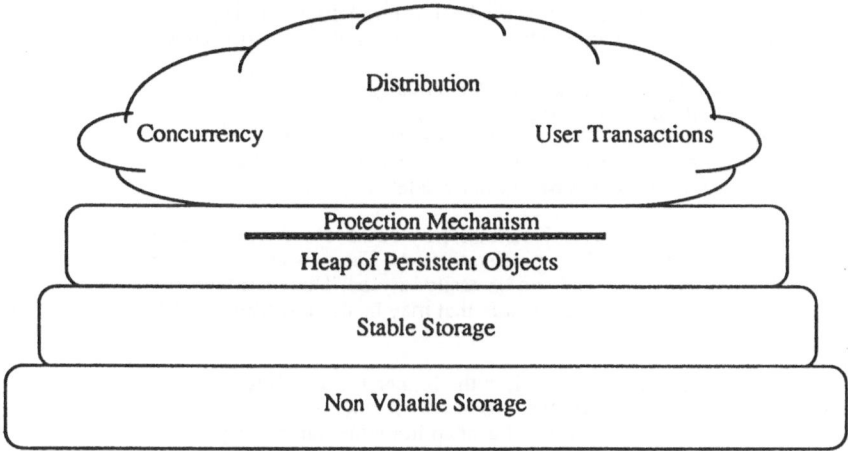

Figure 4: The Basic Architectural Layers

The division has an important consequence for the provision of concurrency, transactions and distribution. Since each of these three mechanisms are essentially modelling techniques they may be implemented by the programming language level and need not be primitive facilities provided by the persistent store. This allows experimental implementations to be constructed without the need to redesign the entire architecture. However, once a particular implementation technique has been identified as essential one or more layers of the persistent store may be reimplemented to incorporate the mechanism. If a layer interface is changed the change is only visible to the layer immediately above thereby limiting the required reimplementation.

4.2. The Persistent Object Store

The layer of the persistent object store which is visible to the programming language level, is the heap of persistent objects shown in Figure 4. The heap layer provides a view of the persistent store that appears stable, is conceptually unbounded in size and may be uniformly addressed. All objects in the heap are reachable from a single distinguished root object and conform to a single object format that distinguishes object addresses from non-address data. The interpretation of an object is responsibility of the higher level architecture. The persistent object store does not support object formats specific to any particular programming language, thereby allowing the persistent object store to operate independently of the supported programming languages.

Within the persistent store, stability is simulated by a simple checkpointing mechanism. This mechanism is provided as part of the heap interface for two reasons. Firstly, it may be made available to the programming language level to support user level transactions. For example, a transaction may maintain a log of operations to be performed and may wish to ensure that the log is preserved in stable storage prior to performing the actual operations. Another reason for making the checkpoint explicit is that it allows the higher level architecture to cache data outwith the persistent store. When a checkpoint is required any data held in registers or other special purpose hardware is copied back to the persistent store. Thus specialised code generation techniques can be used without impacting on the implementation of the persistent store.

The heap is implemented as a set of object management procedures that organise a single contiguous stable store. To ensure that the heap is correctly used, its interface includes a set of five conventions to which the higher level architecture must conform. They are:

- objects will only be created by the heap management procedures,
- addresses will not be manufactured,
- all addresses will be held in the address fields of an object,
- all addressing is performed by indexing object addresses and
- a reachable object will not be explicitly deleted.

These conventions ensure that objects can only be accessed by following object addresses starting from the root object of the persistent store. They also ensure that all object addresses are held in the persistent store and can be easily located. This facilitates the implementation of storage utilities such as garbage collectors that may be used to simulate the perceived property of unbounded size.

Adherence to the heap interface requires the higher level architecture to address the store in terms of indexing object addresses. However, it does not define the level of addressing abstraction employed. Thus, a particular heap implementation may treat object addresses as object numbers and perform all addressing via table lookups to determine an object's address in the stable storage. Alternatively, object addresses may be in the form of stable storage addresses and not require mapping by the heap implementation. In either case the higher level architecture is constrained to address objects using an object address and a separate index. This corresponds to the addressing abstraction described in section 2.1.2.

The heap layer forces the higher level architecture to view the persistent object store as a uniform stable store of unbounded size. To extend this view to that of a type secure persistent object store a protection mechanism is required to ensure that the higher level architecture conforms to the specified conventions and correctly interprets the data held in the store. The architectural layering can support both high level and low level protection mechanisms.

Low level protection may be supported by encoding the appropriate checking mechanisms into the heap implementation. This may be further complemented by tagged memory locations. For example, the implementation of the architecture on the Rekursiv enforces the interface definition using a hardware address translator that only accepts object number, index pairs and by tagging addresses to prevent their unauthorised manufacture. Similar approaches to store level protection may be employed by alternative implementations of the heap layer.

High level protection may be provided by compiling all supported programming languages against a compatible type system with suitable dynamic checks being planted to accommodate those situations that cannot be statically checked. This approach allows the persistent object store to assume that all attempted operations are type correct. However, to achieve an efficient implementation without hardware support an instance of the architecture is constrained to use programming languages that make exclusive use of high level protection. Otherwise, some hardware support may be necessary to efficiently implement the dynamic checking.

The provision of a low level protection mechanism must be specified as part of the heap interface. For example, if a heap implementation does not provide a low level protection mechanism then it can only support programming languages that rely on high level protection. Thus, the heap interface must specify the supported protection mechanism to ensure that an instance of the architecture is composed from compatible layer implementations.

The architecture implementation for Napier88 relies on high level protection and requires all programs to be compiled by the one compilation system.

4.3. The Stable Store

The heap layer is directly supported by a single contiguous stable store, see Figure 4. The stable storage layer provides the required stable storage mechanism described in section 2.3. It also supports a uniform addressing mechanism over the stable storage that corresponds to the virtual addressing abstraction described in section 2.1.3. In practice the virtual addressing is supported by lower level addressing mechanisms that give access to the non-volatile storage, the main memory and any other physical storage devices provided by the underlying hardware.

The interface to the stable storage has been designed to provide a contiguous range of virtual addresses that is always in a self consistent state. This is achieved by implementing a checkpointing mechanism that preserves the current state of the store on non volatile storage. At any point in time the non volatile storage contains a self consistent version of the store. The act of performing a checkpoint replaces the previous recorded state in a single atomic action. When a failure occurs the store is automatically restored to the state recorded by the most recent checkpoint. This simple checkpointing mechanism is sufficient to simulate a stable store.

Although the semantics of the required checkpointing mechanism are simple, the actual implementation may be quite sophisticated. To accommodate as much flexibility as possible the interface includes a set of procedures that allow the use of the virtual address space to be dynamically configured. For example, the implementation of the heap layer may use some temporary data structures that are reconstructed each time the system is restarted. In this case, changes to the storage containing these data structures need not be recorded between checkpoints and the data itself need not be recorded by a checkpoint. In contrast, any changes to user data must be recorded between checkpoints to support the reconstruction of the previous consistent state and the new values of the data must be recorded by a checkpoint.

The range of storage uses that are supported include:

- Read-only   This is the default state for all user data.

- Save-only   This describes an area of store that must be saved at the next checkpoint but it does not form part of the previous checkpoint.

- Shadow   All changes to the specified area of storage must be recorded. It contains data that is part of the previous checkpoint and must be part of the next checkpoint. This requires the allocation of non volatile storage to record any changes.

- Scratch   The specified area of storage is for use by temporary data. The data is not part of the previous checkpoint and need not be protected from store failures.

- Reserve   The specified area of storage may be required following the next checkpoint operation. It must be allocated non volatile storage but the storage may be used for other purposes prior to the next checkpoint.

• Not-required   The area of storage is no longer required to contain data. The non volatile storage allocated to the area may be reallocated for other purposes.

Given this detailed information on the desired use of the virtual address space the layer implementation may be able to optimise its checkpointing and storage allocation strategies. Thus it may be possible to use the available physical resources to their full effect.

4.4.   Napier88

To conclude we shall now briefly describe the persistent programming language Napier88 and how it has been implemented using the layered architecture.

Napier88 is a persistent programming language with a sophisticated type system that permits the recursive definition of data structures including abstract data types and polymorphic first class procedures. As far as possible the Napier88 compilation system performs static type checking. That is, the compiler will determine whether or not an attempted operation is type correct. However, there are certain situations where this is not possible.

Firstly, dynamic checks are generated by the compiler for vector indexing operations and field updates to dynamically created data structures. The first check is to ensure that a vector index is legal and the second check ensures that constant locations are not updated. Neither of these checks may be statically determined from the type system.

The second situation that cannot be statically checked is the use of a value from an infinite union. Napier88 provides a type **any** that is the infinite union of all data types. A value obtained from a variable of type **any** must be projected onto its actual type before it can be used. The projection must be performed dynamically since, in general, it is not possible to statically determine the actual type of the value.

To aid the separate preparation of programs and data the type checking is based on structural equivalence. This allows the Napier88 system to perform dynamic type checking without the use of a centralised type dictionary. However, if available, a centralised dictionary can be used to optimise the dynamic checking.

Napier88 supports first class procedures via a block retention mechanism. The block retention mechanism implements a program stack with a separate object for each activation record. A garbage collector is relied on to automatically determine which activation records are not part of a procedure closure and can be discarded. Consequently, the block retention mechanism can be directly supported by a persistent object store without the need to provide large extensible objects to model a stack.

Polymorphism and abstract data types are supported by a combination of compilation abstraction and a set of adhoc primitive operations. The adhoc primitives use an integer key to identify the size of stack elements to manipulate and the rules for performing equality. The integer keys are made available to polymorphic code as part of the static environment provided by the block retention.

The Napier88 compilation system maps programs onto an abstract machine [7]. The abstract machine is based on block retention and is responsible for implementing those primitives necessary to support the polymorphism and abstract data types. In turn, the abstract machine views the persistent object store as a single heap of persistent objects that is assumed to be a stable store of unbounded size. Since the abstract machine does not allow direct access to the persistent store it ensures that the compilation system is unaware of the implementation of the object storage thus separating the use of an object from the way it is stored.

4.5. The Napier88 Implementation

The implementation of Napier88 on the layered architecture is a simple matter of interfacing the abstract machine to the persistent object store. The resulting architectural layers are shown in Figure 5.

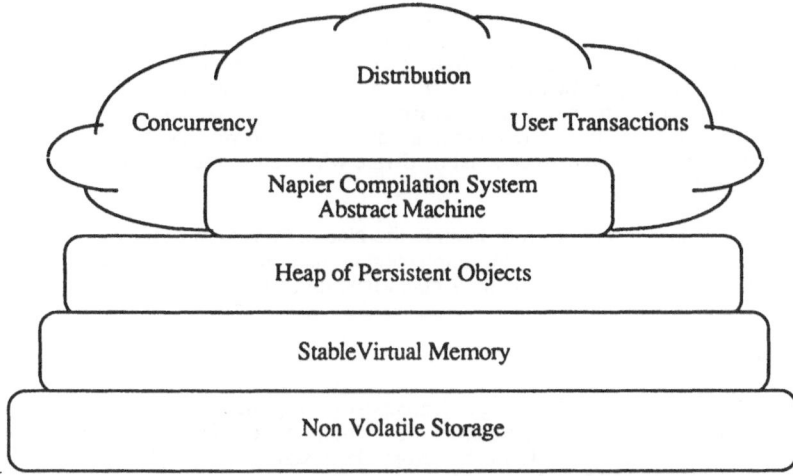

Figure 5: The Architectural Layers Used to Implement Napier88

The Napier88 compilation system ensures that all operations attempted by a program are type correct. The operations that perform the dynamic checking are also type correct and are implemented by language level operations. Thus, the Napier88 compilation system performs the task of a high level protection mechanism.

The abstract machine to which Napier88 is compiled operates against the heap layer of the architecture and adheres to the conventions specified by the heap interface. For efficiency reasons it maintains some data and object addresses in special purpose registers. However, in keeping with the interface specification it copies all the cached data back to heap objects prior to requesting garbage collection or checkpoint operations.

Since the compilation system provides a high level protection mechanism the heap layer of the architecture does not attempt to enforce any form of protection. Thus, it is able to perform the task of organising the stable storage without the support of special purpose hardware. It is also possible to optimise the addressing of objects since the attempted operations may be assumed to be type correct.

There are currently two functionally equivalent implementations of the stable storage layer that support the heap layer. One implementation performs its own address translation and input/output buffering. The resulting performance is poor but is acceptable if the abstract machine maintains an object cache in main memory. An alternative implementation is available on Sun workstations using memory mapped files. This implementation performs all addressing using the Sun memory management hardware to provide efficient access to the stable storage.

The efficiency of the second implementation has been greatly enhanced through the effective use of the dynamic configuration procedures provided by the stable storage interface described in section 4.3. In future implementations increased control over the paging algorithms will further improve the system performance. Thus, it is possible to construct an efficient implementation of a persistent object store on conventional hardware.

5. CONCLUSIONS

We have briefly described the architectural mechanisms required to support a type secure persistent object store and shown how they may be modelled as separate architectural layers. A layered architecture has also been described that provides the architectural mechanisms as separate architectural layers that must conform to a specified interface. The benefits of the layered architecture include the ability to easily construct experimental systems based on new implementation techniques for one or more of the architectural layers and the ability to construct efficient implementations on conventional hardware where a high level protection mechanism may be employed.

Examples of the layered architecture include the Napier88 system described above and the Staple functional programming system. Implementations of the stable storage and heap layers are available on Sun workstations and the Apple Macintosh for experimental use.

ACKNOWLEDGEMENTS

This work was undertaken at St.Andrews University during the study leave period of Prof. J. Rosenberg of the University of Newcastle, New South Wales. The work was supported by SERC Grant GR/F 28571, SERC Post-doctoral Fellowship B/ITF/199, ESPRIT II Basic Research Action 3070 - FIDE and a grant from the DTI.

REFERENCES

1. Albano A., Cardelli L. & Orsini R. "Galilieo: A Strongly Typed, Interactive Conceptual Language." *ACM Transactions on Database Systems*, vol. 10, no. 2, 1985, pp230-260.

2. Atkinson M.P., Chisholm K.J. & Cockshott W.P. "CMS - A Chunk Management System." *Software Practice and Experience*, vol. 13, no. 3, 1983, pp259-272.

3. Atkinson M.P. Bailey P.J., Chisholm K.J. Cockshott W.P. & Morrison R. "An Approach to Persistent Programming." *The Computer Journal*, vol. 26; no. 4, 1983, pp360-365.

4. Atkinson M.P., Bailey P.J., Cockshott W.P., Chisholm K.J. & Morrison R. "The Persistent Object Management System." Universities of Glasgow and St Andrews PPRR-1, Scotland, 1983.

5. Beloff B., McIntyre D. & Drummond B. "Rekursiv Hardware." Linn Smart Computing Ltd, 1988.

6. Brown A.L. & Cockshott W.P. "The CPOMS Persistent Object Management System." Universities of Glasgow and St.Andrews PPRR-13, Scotland, 1985.

7. Brown A.L., Carrick R., Connor R.C.H., Dearle A. & Morrison R. "The Persistent Abstract Machine." Universities of Glasgow and St.Andrews PPRR-59, Scotland, 1988.

8. Brown A.L. (Ph.D. Thesis) "Persistent Object Stores." Universities of Glasgow and St.Andrews PPRR-71, Scotland, 1989.

9.   Buckle J.K. *The ICL 2900 Series*, Macmillan Computer Science Series, Macmillan, 1978.

10.   Cohen E., Corwin B., Jefferson D., Lane T., Levin R., Newcomer J., Pollack F. & Wulf B. "Hydra: Basic Kernel Reference Manual." Department of Computer Science, Carnegie-Mellon University, November 1976.

11.   Cohen J. "Garbage Collection of Linked Data Structures." *ACM Computing Surveys*, vol. 13, no. 3, 1981, pp341-367.

12.   Daley R.C. & Dennis B.D. "Virtual Memory, Processes and Sharing in MULTICS." *Comm. ACM* vol. 11, no. 5, 1968, pp306-312.

13.   Goldberg A. & Robson D. Smalltalk-80: The language and its Implementation. Addison Wesley, 1983.

14.   Gray J., McJones P., Blasgen M., Lindsay B., Lorie R., Price T., Putzolu F. & Traiger I. "The Recovery Manager of the System R Database Manager." *ACM Computing Surveys*, vol. 13, no. 2, June 1981, pp223-242.

15.   Kernighan B.W. & Ritchie D.M. *The C programming language*. Prentice-Hall, 1978.

16.   Knowlton K. "A Fast Storage Allocator." *Comm. ACM*, vol 8, 1965, pp623-625.

17.   Liskov B.H. "Refinement - From Specification to Implementation, The Argus Language and System." *Lecture Notes for the Advanced Course on Distributed Systems - Methods and Tools for Specification*, Institute for Informatics, Technical University of Munich, 1984.

18.   Lorie A.L. "Physical Integrity in a Large Segmented Database." *ACM Transactions on Database Systems*, vol. 2, no. 1, 1977, pp91-104.

19.   McCarthy J. "Recursive Functions of Symbolic Expressions and their Computation by Machine." *Comm. ACM*, vol. 3, no. 4, 1960, pp184-195.

20.   McNally D.J. "Code Generating Functional Language Modules for a Persistent Object Store." Staple Project Research Report, Staple/StA/89/2, University of St.Andrews, Scotland, 1989.

21.   Morrison R. "S-algol: A Simple Algol." *BCS Computer Bulletin Series II*, no. 31, March 1982, pp17,20.

22.   Morrison R., Brown A.L., Connor R. & Dearle A. "The Napier88 Reference Manual." Universities of Glasgow and St.Andrews PPRR-77, Scotland, 1989.

23.   Organick E.I., *Computer System Organisation: The B5700/B6700 Series*, Academic Press, New York, 1973.

24.   Perry N. "Hope+." Imperial College Internal Report IC/FPR/LANG/2.5.1/7, 1987.

25.   "The PS-algol Reference Manual fifth edition." Universities of Glasgow and St.Andrews PPRR-12, Scotland, 1988.

26.   Rosenberg J. & Abramson D.A. "MONADS-PC: A Capability Based Workstation to Support Software Engineering." *Proc. Eighteenth Annual Conference on System Sciences*, Honolulu, Hawaii, 1985.

27. Rosenberg J., Henskens F., Brown A.L., Morrison R. & Munro D.S. "Stability in a Persistent Store Based on a Large Virtual Memory." *International Workshop on Computer Architectures to Support Security and Persistence*, Universität Bremen, West Germany, May 1990.

28. Ross G.D.M. (Ph.D. Thesis) "Virtual Files: A Framework for Experimental Design." University of Edinburgh, 1983.

29. Thatte S.M. "Persistent Memory: A Storage Architecture for Object Oriented Database Systems." *Proc. ACM/IEEE 1986 International Workshop on Object Oriented Database Systems,* Pacific Grove, CA, September 1986, pp148-159.

30. Unger D. "Generation Scavenging: A Non-Disruptive High Performance Storage Reclamation Algorithm." *ACM SIGSOFT/SIGPLAN Software Engineering Symposium on Practical Software Development Environments*, Pittsburgh, April 1984.

31. Wirth N. "The programming language Pascal." *Acta Informatica*, vol. 1, no. 1, 1973, pp35-63.

AN OBJECT-ORIENTED APPROACH TO SUPPORT SYSTEM RELIABILITY AND SECURITY

Jörg Kaiser

German National Research Center for Computer Science

1. INTRODUCTION

MUTABOR (Mapping Unit for The Access By Object References) is an object-oriented architecture which provides a set of mechanisms for supporting secure and reliable computing. The architecture was designed to achieve the local functionality needed to construct reliable distributed applications based on objects and atomic actions.

The level of security in a computer system can be measured by the amount of difficulty a user will have to access system information or resources in a way unauthorized by the system administrator. This widely accepted definition of security only considers malicious, planned intrusion. However, if we justifiably want to place reliance on a delivered system service, we have to extend the model and additionally consider the impact of failures introduced by physical events or by human errors. These factors may also impair integrity and consistency of data and lead to a denial of service. Therefore, we aim at a dependable secure system architecture which, in addition to a powerful access control concept, provides system level error detection, damage confinement and error processing.

In a strict sense, security is explicitely included in the definition of dependability [19] in terms of avoidance or tolerance of intentional faults. But conventionally, the mechanisms to deal with intentional faults generally are not appropriate to increase system dependability in respect to reliability, availability, or at least safety. On the other hand, most work on dependability considering accidental faults is not aimed at the provision of system security. Only the exploitation of the full scope of dependabilty will lead to trustworthyness of computation.

An object-oriented architecture contributes in many ways to this goal. In general, a couple of well defined constraints regulate the access to objects. Since any constraint implies some form of checking, these mechanism are most suitable for system level error detection. The interface specification of an object serves as an appropriate assertion to validate each access to an object. Fine-grain access control to objects is realized by a capability based protection mechansm which exploits the type information available for objects and thus, going beyond the read/write/execute semantics of traditional access control. Since any access to an object is strictly evaluated at the object interface and because of the hardware enforced encapsulation property of an object in our system, we assume that damage will not easily propagate beyond object boundaries. In addition to these mechanisms, data consistency is further protected by efficient object related error recovery.

Because of dependability reasons and improved performance we migrated critical, trusted operations into the hardware/firmware of the system. A coprocessor performs these operations related to protection and basic system resource management. Moreover, it provides the basic mechanisms for object recovery by the so called save/restore management of recovery points. The coprocessor extends the instruction set of the CPU (MC 68020). Functions of the coprocessor can only be executed via the standard coprocessor protocol and cannot be modified by a user or a system administrator, thus, providing the same level of trustworthiness as operations of a (hardwired or microprogrammed) proprietary instruction set processor.

One major impact on performance in object-oriented systems results from the inherent addressing overhead, the need to traverse complex addressing information with every object access. We reduce the address translation time by providing a very large address tranlation cache which stores the address translation together with object related constraints. These constraints, including type, access rights, and base/bound of an object are checked on-the-fly with every object access.

The coprocessor and a first version of the address translation cache are implemented and oparable. They are currently integrated and tested in a Unix workstation.

The following section will introduce the basic security terms and requirements and their relation to dependability means. The third chapter presents the architecture of MUTABOR and relates its features to the requirements discussed in chapter 2. Chapter 4 discusses the hardware support and the performance improvements of our approach are sketched in chapter 5. Related work and concluding remarks, addressing future research are outlined in chapter 6 and 7, respectively.

2. SECURITY REQUIREMENTS

The Framework of "DOD Trusted Computer Evaluation Criteria" [10], also known as *Orange Book* identifies three fundamental computer security requirements : *Policy, accountability*, and *assurance*. All necessary mechanisms to meet these requirements are usually embedded in a so called *trusted computing base (TCB)*. A substantial part of the TCB is the *security kernel*. In terms of the Orange Book, the security kernel is the implementation of an abstract machine, the *reference monitor,* which mediates all accesses from subjects to objects. The general rules to determine which objects may be accessed by a subject are defined by the *security policy*.

The policy formulates the organisational aspect of computer security in the sense that it reflects to a certain degree the structure of an organisation in which the sensitive information is used and processed. According to the policy, *mandatory access* control is defined which is imposed to all users of the system. Mandatory access control requires the association of certain sensitivity labels to data objects and security clearance attributes to individuals (subjects) which will be allowed to access the information accordingly. A set of formally defined rules regulate the access between subjects as acting parts and objects and thus, specify the information flow in the system. Within the constraints of mandatory access control, a finer granularity of control is required based on the principle of *least privilege* or *need to know*. This so called *discretionary access control* gives an individual user the possibility to decide which kind of access to his/her private information other users of the same classification may exercise.

Accountability should assure that individual subjects are properly identified and that their actions on sensitive information are recorded in an audit trail. This allows to trace security-relevant events to the responsible party.

Assurance is the requirement which refers to system architecture. Mechanisms have to be provided which guarantee that the requirements of the security policy and accountability can be enforced by the computer system. These mechanisms constitute the basis on which all higher level security functions rely. Therefore, exceptional care should be devoted to their specification, design, and implementation.

Particularly, these mechanisms should have the following properties :
- they must be conceptually clear and simple
- they must support the modular construction of secure systems
- they must be tamperproof in the sense that they cannot be bypassed by any user or process in any state of the system. Even a system administrator, operating in supervisor mode should not have access to the basic security mechanisms. This also implies that there must not be an unprotected *boot phase* of the system.

The contribution to security of our system architecture is in the area of *operational assurance*. Our goal was to provide tamperproof mechanisms which allow the efficient and flexible construction of a dependable secure system. Although we formally specified parts of the system in a methodology similar to HDM [25], we did not aim at a completely formally verified architecture, the ultimate class in the Orange Book. But except these formal correctness proofs the architecture should meet the highest possible security standard regarding the requirements of operational assurance. Fig. 1 sketches the most important requirements for system architecture of the security class B3 of the Orange Book.

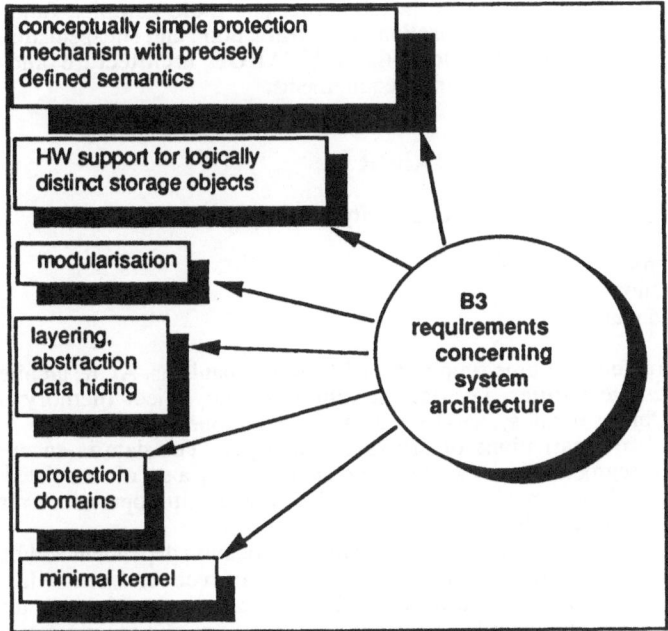

Fig. 1 Security requirements for system architecture

In many respects, these requirements support dependability in a broader sense than just security. According to the terminology in [19] the first five requirements in Fig.1 can be viewed as contribution to dependablity procurements: *fault-avoidance* and *fault-tolerance*. Fault-avoidance covers the constructive means to master the complexity of a system and thus, avoid design faults. Decomposition of the system into well-defined modules and the structuring capabilites of layering, abstraction, and data hiding are assumed to prevent a substantial portion of design faults. Moreover, design errors can be detected by a clear description of functions and interfaces of the individual modules. This corresponds to the state-of-the-art software engineering concepts. In respect to hardware, modularisation is supported by logically distinct storage objects such as segments with individual size, type, and protection attributes. Hardware provides these attributes at run time and thus, contributes to fault-tolerance by checking the constraints imposed to accesses.

The protection mechanism is the basis to enforce the internal modularisation of the system. This mechanism should implement the principle of *least privilege* or *need to know* which defines a fine grain access control giving an accessing entity only those rights to an object which are absolutely neccessary. Combined with the hardware supported storage objects it provides the basis of secure *data encapsulation*. The protection mechanism should be embedded in the lowest levels of the system which are inaccessible and immutable for the user. All higher level security functions and policies can then be constructed on this trusted protection mechanism.

The *protection domain* is the set of objects which can be accessed by a process. Processes shall be isolated by the provision of distinct address spaces. Beside the security aspect,

this supports damage confinement in case of a failure. Address space separation between processes can easily be achieved even with conventional memory management hardware.

The problem is the controlled sharing of objects between processes.

A *minimal kernel* is demanded to facilitate the validation of kernel functions. The construction of the secure system according to the concepts discussed above, largely supports the minimization of kernel complexity in the sense that only basic protection critical functions have to be sealed in the kernel and more complex functions can be securely constructed using modularisation, data abstraction , and encapsulation.

The following section introduces the MUTABOR architecture and relates its characteristics to the presented security requirements.

3. THE ARCHITECTURE OF MUTABOR

The basic mechanisms which enforce security in our system are:
- capability based addressing
- object encapsulation
- data abstraction
- protection domains

MUTABOR provides run-time support for all these mechanisms. At the architectural level, objects are passive entities, i.e. data structures in our object memory provided by MUTABOR. Objects in our system have the following properties:
-   Objects are incarnations of *abstract data types*. The data is encapsulated in a protected segment which can only be manipulated by a set of associated procedures, the so called *type specific operations*. The type specific operations realize a well-defined interface to the encapsulated data.
-   Objects are referenced by *name* rather than by location dependent address.
-   Objects are the entities which individually can recover from failures. Because special support is provided for individual object recovery they are termed *robust objects*. Since the detailled description of recovery and atomic action support is beyond the scope of this paper the interested reader is refered to [17].

Fig.2 shows the basic structure of an object and the main addressing path. Every process which wants to access an object must have an appropriate capability. A capability comprises a type field together with a so called *object short name* and the individual rights of the process.

The type field identifies the specific capability type e.g. whether it is a capability defining basic read/write/execute-rights or a vector of higher level type-specific rights.

The object short name is defined in the virtual address space directlyto addresses the object descriptor via a hierarchy of page tables. For simplicity reasons these tables are ommitted in Fig.2. (A detailed description of addressind structure is found in [14]). To identify persistent, shared objects on disk or at a remote site, a systemwide unique identifier (UID) is additionally assigned to these objects and kept as part of the capability. All objects which are never moved to disk for long term storage only need an object short name. Experiments from the object-oriented operating systems StarOS and Hydra have shown that only 5% of all objects in the running system are persistent and hence, have to be equipped with a UID [2].

The capability selects an object descriptor which contains the object base address. Moreover, the descriptor comprises the basic information to check the compatibility of an operation on the object according to a basic system type (type field) and the proper addressing range (length field) at runtime. The status field in the object header contains a valid and a modified bit, the lock status of the object, one bit which identifies persistent shared objects, and information preserved for recovery purposes.

As shown in Fig.2, objects are represented in one segment consisting of a capability and a data part. All references, i.e. capabilities, are contained in the capability part. For security reasons, it is especially important to protect capabilities from arbitrary inadvertent or malicious accesses and modifications. Therefore, various schemes have been proposed to segragate capabilities from other data. Early versions of the iAPX 432 and the capability machines like CAP [22] and Plessey 250 [7] totally separated capabilities in extra objects

177

or capability segments respectively.

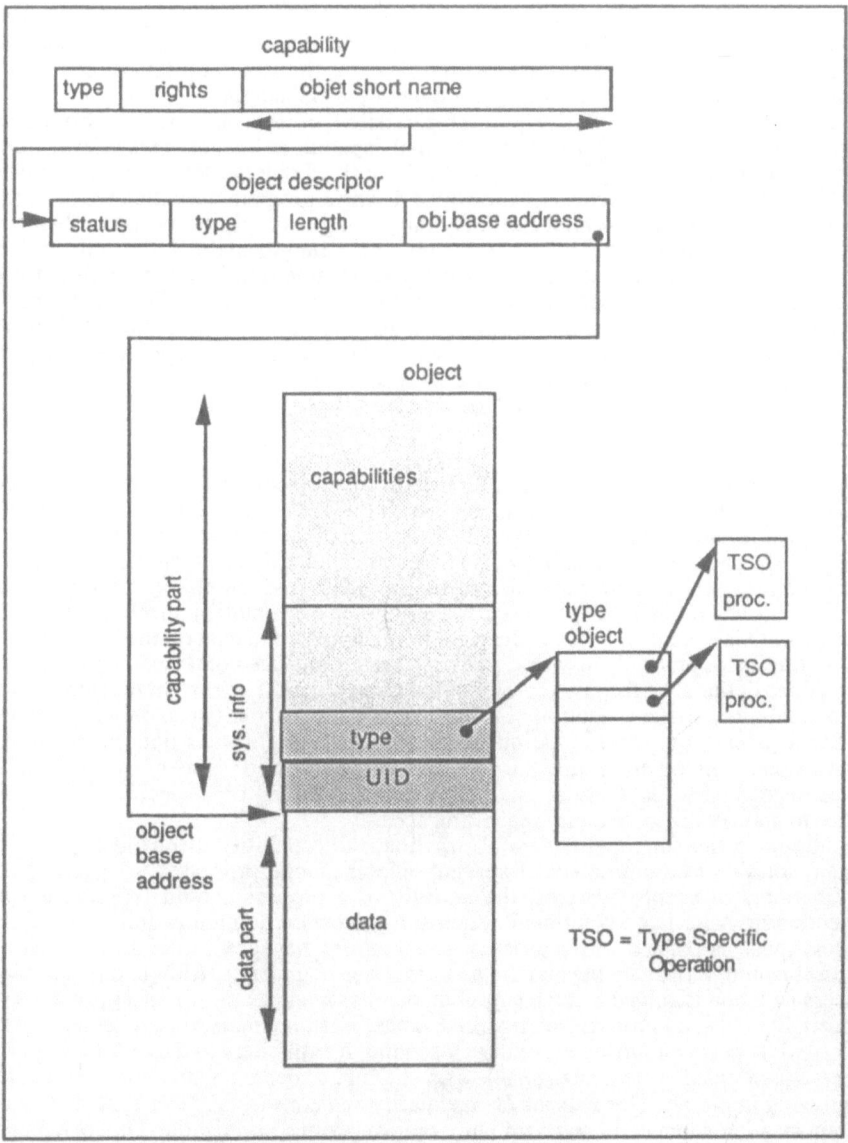

Fig.2 Basic object structure

The current version of iAPX432 [21], Hydra [29], and StarOS [12] implemented different styles of the 'fenced segment' approach which partitions a single segment into two parts. We adopted a method similar to the StarOS addressing scheme in which data can only be referenced with positive offset and capabilities with negative offset. Therefore, the object base address points to the first word of the data part in the object. In order to increase security and the convenience of capability handling, capabilities in our system are accessed via special capability instructions performed by the coprocessor. It is impossible for the

CPU to generate a negative offset and hence, to directly access and modify a capability. Capabilities can only be accessed by well-defined capability functions executed by the MUTABOR coprocessor. If a capability is copied to the data part of an object which can be manipulated by the CPU, it cannot be included into the capability part any more and hence, used to address an object. This prevents a capability from being forged. The secure encapsulation of an object is further improved by the run time length check which guarantees that an access never propagates over object boundaries.

The first slots in the capability part of persistent objects are used to store system information which is distinguished from normal capabilities by tags. This information can be viewed as part of the object descriptor for long-lived objects. Because it is not needed for objects dynamically created and destroyed during a program execution we decided not to store it in the object descriptor itself. By this, a single descriptor format is obtained for all objects. As shown in Fig.2, the system part includes the UID and additional information which is dedicated to support data abstraction. The mechanism for data abstracton assures that objects are only accessible via their well defined interface. This interface is specified by a set of procedures, called *type-specific operations (TSO)* which are accessed via the type object . The type object is linked with the object via the type field in the capability part. An invocation of a TSO specifies :

-    the object by an abstract capability
-    a TSO-index into the type object
-    parameters

An abstract capability comprises a reference to the object and a vector of type-specific rights which can immediately be compared with the TSO-index to see whether the rights granted by the abstract capability allow the execution of the desired TSO.

To guarantee that the data of an object is always manipulated via the procedural interface, a mechanism to seal this structure has to be provided. We adopted a sealing/unsealing mechanism which has been proposed for a number of capability machines [12,13,30]. When a TSO is executed, it needs the right to manipulate the data on the basis of reading and writing bytes or words in memory. These basic rights are contained in so called basic capabilities defined for the raw representation of an object. The system restricts the use of basic capabilities to the execution of TSOs, i.e. a basic capability can only be used inside a TSO to access the representation of an object. This enforces data abstraction and information hiding by preventing the data from being accessed via memory level reads and writes instead of TSOs. Only abstract capabilities, defining type-specific rights, can be copied to another object or entity requesting access.

In addition to the support for data abstraction, the capability mechanism provides an elegant solution to the problem of sharing objects among processes. According to the requirements of secure systems, the activity of a process should be confined to its protection domain. In conventional systems, a protection domain is defined by a virtual address space associated with a process. The memory management hardware assures that accesses cannot propagate beyond the address space boundaries. Although the problem of process isolation is solved in such a system, the disadvantage of this scheme occurs when cooperation between processes is required. Then, it is inevitable to provide a mechanism to share data between processes, either by sending it explicitly to a requesting process in a message-oriented system or to enable data sharing. Process cooperation is essential and of growing importance for reasons of modularity and concurrency in a system. Operating system standards like early standard Unix only supported cooperation between processes by sharing *files*. This is rather inefficient. Data is explicitly copied to the address space of another process via a file. The constructs of *pipes* and more recently, the *sockets* in Berkely Unix also rely on the concept of a (intermediate, memory resident) file. To provide a more efficient inter-process communication via shared data, the constructs of *shared segments* (AT&T, System V) or the *mmap* system call (BSD Unix) have been introduced. They basically allow to map portions of real memory into the virtual address space of multiple processes. However, these mechanisms are not appropriate for data sharing in secure systems. Recently, an idea introduced by mainframe operating systems like Multics [24] has been adopted for the design of modern operating system concepts like Chorus [3] or Mach [26]. They allow parts of files to be shared by mapping them into so called regions of the virtual address spaces of different processes. In current implementations access rights (read/write/exec) can be associated to the regions for every process on the basis of Unix style access control lists.

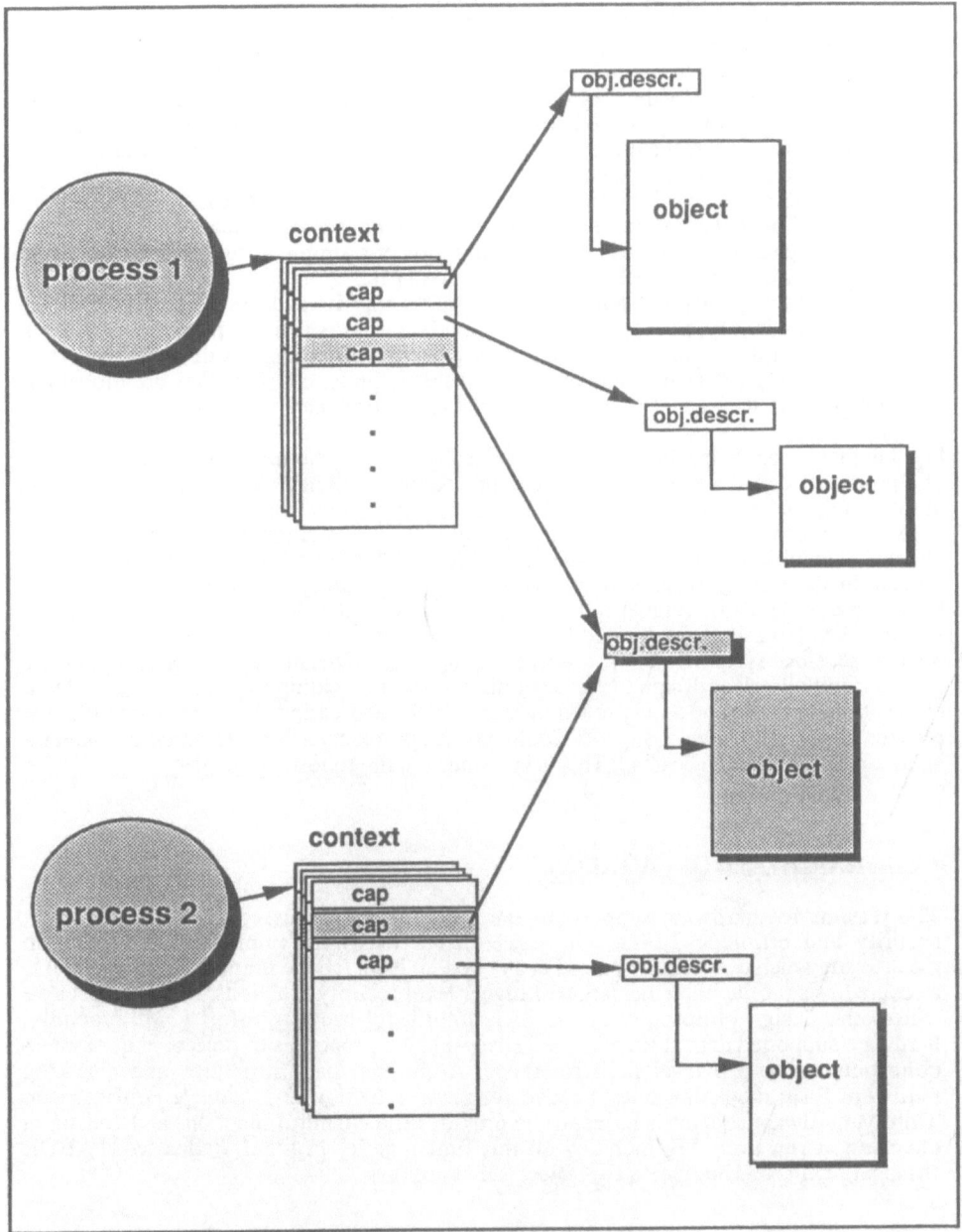

Fig.3 Process isolation and object sharing

Basically, these systems treat files as lineary addressable parts of the virtual memory and are an important step towards a flexible structure of persistent data. Particularly, persistent object management systems can be built on top of such operating systems exploiting the

uniform treatment of virtual memory and file storage [16].
There are, however, some problems which are not yet solved adaquately in these systems, partly because they intentionally avoid any hardware assumptions.

- the treatment of objects smaller than a single page; this is important because it is desirable to define data structures independently from constraints like page sizes. Particularly, encapsulation and protection are still unsolved issues.

- security issues; protection relevant information like e.g. address map entries in Mach [26] is held and maintained by the kernel. This implies that this information can only be accessed by an expensive kernel call. The implementation of sophisticated fine grain protection mechanisms without the support of dedicated hardware seems difficult to be implemented efficiently.

- references are only valid inside a virtual address space of a process. When an object is shared between processes, this object cannot have a reference to another object inside the same process address space in terms of a simple virtual address but must use a UID or an additional level of indirection [16].

- a process may map multiple different objects into its address space. There is no means to identify, at execution time, individual objects inside a process and protect them from unintended modification by a program running inside a process. It is possible to set page or segment related protection bits, but since they are global for the process, they are of little use in respect to this problem.

Fig.3 depicts process isolation and object sharing in our system. The protection domain of a process is called a context and comprises a set of capabilities. Accesses are restricted to those objects for which the process holds a capability in its context. There is no way to bypass this mechanism and access an object or even a portion of plain memory via an illicit channel. The object short name in the capability (refer to Fig.2) is a global reference for objects in the virtual address space. This, straightforwardly, enables object sharing . Every process holds individual rights to an object, realising fine grain protection on the semantic level of user defined objects.

Of course, since system design is to some extent the art of balancing tradeoffs, we pay for this conceptually clear design the price of more effort in creating a context compared to a conventional system and an increased overhead in the addressing structure. Therefore, we provide hardware/firmware support for the protection mechanisms presented to maintain an acceptable performance level. This is introduced in the following chapter.

4. THE HARDWARE OF MUTABOR

The reasons for hardware support for the mechanisms discussed above are twofold, security and efficiency. First, we argue that a hardware implemented protection mechanism which cannot be bypassed at any system level (above immutable microcode) is a secure basis for the implementation of higher level security functions. In this respect we follow the design philosophy of the SRI multilevel security effort [23]. Secondly, hardware supported data abstraction and encapsulation properties of objects in our system contribute to system level fault tolerance. Additional data structures and checking hardware form the redundancy needed for error detection and damage confinement. Thirdly, hardware support is necessary to provide all the control functions and constraint checking at run time. We included all this functionality in a unit called MUTABOR (Mapping Unit for The Access By Object References).

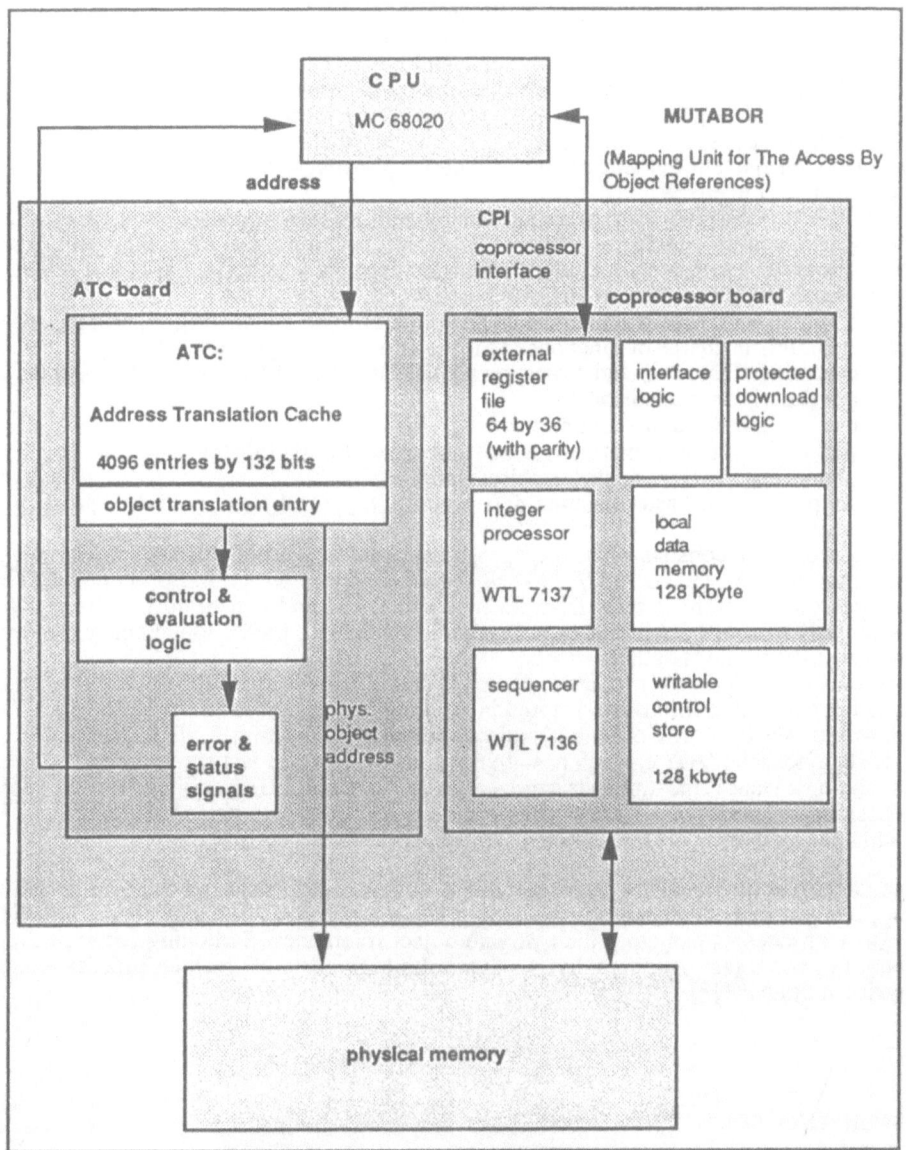

Fig.4 System Architecture

MUTABOR is placed between CPU and main memory and thus, controls every memory access. It comprises an ATC (Address Translation Cache) and a coprocessor for the 680x0 family. The entire architecture is implemented on two VME-bus boards. They are integrated into a Unix workstation and work in a Unix environment. The overall schematic is sketched in Fig.4. We preferred the processor/coprocessor approach opposed to a single microcoded special purpose processor mainly because of two reasons, one concerning the implementation of our system, the other concerning performance. First, the general purpose 68020 processor gives us access to a wide range of conventional software, which can coexist with object-oriented applications. This is emphasized by our ATC which supports two modes of addressing, the object-oriented mode and a conventional paging mode (currently for UNIX). The entire 4 Gbyte address space is divided into an object space and a UNIX space by the most significant bit of the virtual address. Thus, Unix addresses and object references can freely be mixed in the ATC even within the address space of one process. So, it is possible to work in a protected object-oriented environment but still use e.g. the desktop manager of your UNIX system as a convenient user interface.

Secondly, concurrency can be exploited by having two separate processors. The coprocessor may perform garbage collection, memory clearing, or other maintenance/housekeeping operations which are especially important in object-oriented systems concurrently with the CPU.

The coprocessor was designed to give us great flexibility in conducting experiments with the system. It is in charge of functions of the lower operating system level, e.g:

- executing all security and protection related functions like e.g. capability operations and descriptor manipulations
- creating and updating cache entries
- performing memory management and garbage collection functions
- performing activities related to object recovery
- supporting the basic machine data types like data objects, modules, processes, mailboxes, etc.

The coprocessor consists of a microprogrammable Weitek 32 bit sequencer/integer processor chip set (WTL 7137/7136 [28]) and cooperates with a Motorola 68020. The writable control store is built from 35 ns static RAM and can be loaded from main memory. However, even in our experimental environment, protection circuitry prevents arbitrary modifications of the microcode.

One intrinisic overhead in object-oriented systems derives from the need to maintain complex addressing information stored in multilevel tables which must be traversed for address translation. We cope with this problem by providing a very large Address Translation Cache (ATC) which has 4096 entries to store the last recently used address translations. Hence, most objects can be accessed in a single memory cycle. All checks necessary to guarantee the constraints of an object access are performed concurrently within this memory cycle by dedicated hardware.

Simulation results show that the hit rate of the ATC is over 98% [14]. Moreover, the ATC supports fast process switches by providing 16 sections with 256 entries each, in which up to 16 processes can store their private object references. Switching between these sections can be fast. Additionally, we avoid the high costs of flushing process related entries in the ATC [8].

5. PERFORMANCE

The MUATBOR coprocessor and a restricted version of the ATC are running and have been evaluated. However, we have not yet a complete secure system implemented on our hardware. The raw performance of the coprocessor is according to basic benchmark tests like search, sieve, and drystone about 3 times the performance of a 68020 running at 16 MHz. The ATC performs address translation without causing an additional waitstate. In the final version, translation of object references and complete checking of object related constraints will need one additional waitstate. This is as fast as standard VLSI-implementations of off-the-chip MMUs but exhibits a much richer functionality. The performance improvement over our software simulation is about two orders of magnitude.

183

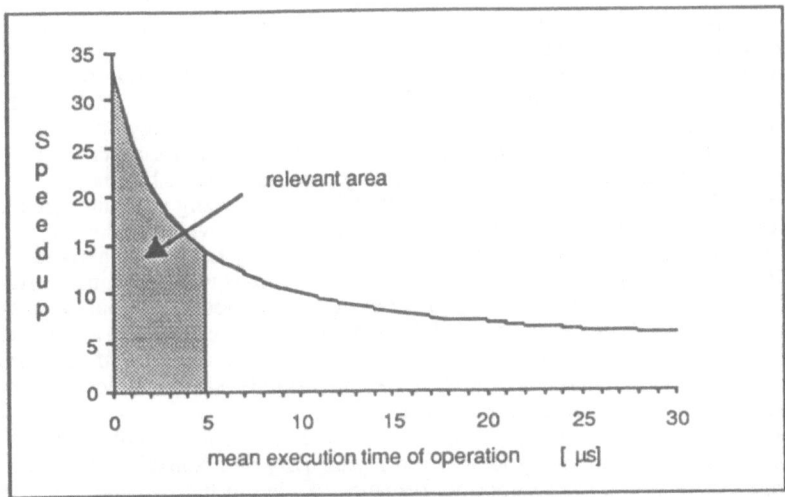

Fig.5 Speedup of coprocessor operations vs. system call implementation

We also expect a dramatic performance improvement from a conceptional advantage of the coprocessor approach over conventional implementations of system security. In conventional systems, all security relevant operations have to be implemented via kernel calls because of poor hardware protection facilities. This may take a substantial portion of the overall execution time in secure applications. In our system, such operations can be implemented as coprocessor functions without protection compromise. The speedup of this realisation is shown in Fig.5

The raw time for a system call without parameter transfer was measured to be 100 μsec in a SUN-like workstation running 4.3 BSD Unix. The coprocessor protocol of the 68020 needs only 3μsec for a coprocessor function. Hence, for short operations, the speedup factor is more than 30 as shown in Fig.5. Obviously, the performance advantage is lower if execution time of a function is large in relation to the setup time. According to our software simulation we estimated that the relevant range for performance improvement is in the shaded area.

6. RELATED WORK

Although it is very desirable, so far only few systems provide extensive hardware support for objects. Many conceptual features have been inherited from these systems and tailored to our specific reqirements.The early capability machines Plessey 250 [7] and CAP [22] provide a capability-based protection mechanism for segments in order to improve error detection and damage confinement. In these systems, capabilities are basically segment descriptors specifying individual access rights for a process. To protect the capabilities against unauthorized accesses they are stored in dedicated registers (Plessey) or in special segments (CAP). The Plessey 250 has only 8 capability registers, which are not enough to deal with an object-oriented system. In the CAP computer capabilities only specify process local names and therefore, cannot be used for object sharing between processes required in our system. The IBM SYSTEM/38 [4] aimed at conventional applications in COBOL and RPG, provides objects in a single level store. Objects are stored in "one or more" 16 Mbyte so-called segment groups, each equipped with a single header describing the object attributes. The hardware assistance consists of a microprogrammable engine and tagged memory to protect pointers (capabilities) from arbitrary modification. The basic machine architecture, especially the memory management hardware is not tailored to efficiently support small objects for which our system is designed.

On the conceptual level, our system also exhibits similarities with the MONADS-PC [15]. There are, however, some major differences concerning the architecture. MONADS uses very long addresses (60 bits) and thus, addresses all available memory space including real memory and disk in a uniform manner. This is an ideal basis for a persistent single level store. However, this implies that a proprietary processor has to be designed. Due to our coprocessor concept, we rely on the (32 bits) 68020 addressing structure. Hence, we implement single level store on the basis of special managers which make the memory hierarchy transparent to a program. Since these managers only have to be activated when an object is not in the virtual address space, the overhead seems to be acceptable. Another major difference of MONADS compared to our system is the notion of small objects. For efficiency reasons, small objects in MONADS are contained as segments in a larger entity, called module. In contrast to our approach, these segments are not viewed as individual objects with a type associated to each, but as a collection of similar objects which are accessed via the procedural interface of the module.

The approach coming closest to our design with its basic concept of an object is the Intel iAPX 432 [13] that derived many ideas from Hydra [29] and StarOS [12]. The major disadvantage of iAPX 432 was its poor performance [6]. In our hardware architecture we took care to avoid some of the major performance bottlenecks.

A unique feature which distinguishes our architecture from the systems mentioned above is the basic support of error recovery on the hardware/firmware level. Objects in our system are comparable to the robust data types proposed by Liskov and Weihl [20].

7. OPEN PROBLEMS AND FUTURE WORK

Our design decisions when developing the MUTABOR system were motivated by the goal to construct a dependable secure system. In addition, to prevent intented security attacks, this system should provide mechanisms for system level fault-tolerance, particularly detection of unanticipated errors and damage confinement, at an acceptable performance level. The chosen concepts of data abstraction, object encapsulation, fine grain capability based protection, and process protection domains are justifiably considered to contribute to this goal. There are excellent papers by Colwell,Gehringer, and Jensen [6] elaborating the intrinsic overhead of such complex architectures. However, little information is available to quantify the benefits of these mechanisms. Therefore, we plan to extensively evaluate our prototype in three directions:

- robustness against security attacks like virus, trojan horse, and protection violations. This will be done by planned attacks with all information about the system available to the intruder.
- detection of and robustness against (unintended) software faults. We plan to apply *mutation testing* techniques [5,9] to systematically evaluate which failure modes will be covered by our architecture.
- detection of certain hardware faults and behaviour of the system in the presence of such faults. As statet in [12], general mechanisms which precisely define interfaces to data can be exploited as *last moment checks* of complex hardware faults. Beside the error detection facility, these mechanisms may also make possible a *fail soft* behaviour of the system. This means that the system does not crash uncontrolled but is orderly stopped. In this respect, the availability of two largely independent processing units, the CPU and the coprocessor will support mutual tests and and will aid to maintain a controlled system behaviour. Fault insertion techniques as proposed by [1] will be applied.

It is often argued (e.g. [11]) that capability systems are not appropriate to support an open system design. In his paper C. Landau [18] invalidates many of the arguments and stresses the benefits of capabilities and object-orientation in an open system. Security in a network is mainly determined by the following parameters :

- the security and trustability of the participating sites

-    the security of the data transfers including the security of the physical medium
An open network includes heterogenous systems which may have different levels of trustworthiness. In our opinion capabilities are a suitable mechanism to support an open system design where sensitive information has to be protected from arbitrary access by untrusted sites. The benefits of capabilities in the local system has been presented in this paper. Security in the local system is the primary requirement for security in the network. If a capability is send over an untrusted network to an untrusted site, cryptographic mechanisms have to be applied to protect a capability from arbitrary modification as it is proposed in [27]. Since capabilities precisely define the access rights, attacks by virus or trojan horses can be defeated more easily. A problem is the revocation of rights once granted by a capability. Ad hoc solutions are an additional level of indirection or the renaming of the respective object. We will investigate these problems.

REFERENCES

1.   J.Arlat, M.Aguera, L.Amat, Y.Crouzet, J.-C.Fabre, J.-C.Laprie, E.Martins, D.Powell
Fault Injection For Dependability Validation:
A Methodology and some Applications
LAAS Research Report No.89-124, Toulouse, 1989

2.   G.T.Almes
Garbage Collection in an Object-Oriented System
PhD thesis, CMU,1980

3.   V.Abrassimov, M.Rozier, M.Shapiro
Generic Virtual Memory Management for Operating System Kernels
Proc. 12th SOSP, Litchfield Park, Arizona, 1989

4.   Berstis:
Security and Protection of Data in the IBM System/38
Proc. of the 7th Int. Symp. on Computer Architecture, 1980

5.   T.A.Budd
Mutation Analysis: Ideas, Examples, Problems and Prospects
in: B.Chandrasekaran, S.Radicci (eds.)
Computer Program Testing
North-Holland, Sogesta, 1981

6.   R.P.Colwell, E.F.Gehringer, E.D.Jensen
Performance effects of Architectural Complexity in the Intel 432
ACM Trans.on Comp.Systems, Vol.6,No.3, 1988

7.   C.Cosserat
A Capability Oriented Multiprocessor Operating System for Real-Time Aplications
Proc. First Int. Conf. Comp. Comm., 1972

8.   C.Czaja
Entwurf eines Translation Lookaside Buffers für objektorientierte Architekturen
GMD-Studie Nr.117, Birlinghoven, 1987

9.   R.A.DeMillo, D.S.Guindi, K.N. King
An Extended Overview of the Mothra Software Testing Environment
2nd Workshop on Software Testing, Verification, and Analysis, Banff,Cananda, 1988

10. Dept. of Defense : Trusted Computer Evaluation Criteria
    DOD 5200.28-STD, Dept. of Defense, 1985

11. L.Gong
    On Security in Capability Based Systems
    Operating Systems Review, Vol.23, No.2, 1989

12. A.K.Jones, R.J.Chansler, I.Durham, K.Schwans, S.R.Vegdahl
    StarOS, a Multiprocessor Operating System for the Support of Task Forces
    Proc. 7th Symp. Operating system Principles, 1979

13. iAPX 432 General Data Processor Architecture Ref. Manual
    Intel Corp., Aloha, Oregon, 1981

14. J. Kaiser
    MUTABOR, A Coprocessor Supporting Memory Management
    in an Object-Oriented Architecture
    IEEE Micro, Vol. 8, No. 5, October 1988

15. J.L.Keedy
    The MONADS-PC System: A Programmer's Overview
    Tech.Report No. 8/89, Bremen, 1989

16. R.Kröger, M.Mock, R.Schumann
    The RelaX Transactional Object Management System
    Int. Workshop on Comp. Arch. to Support Security and Persistence, Bremen, 1990

17. J.Kaiser, E.Nett, R.Kröger
    MUTABOR: A Coprocessor supporting Object-Oriented Memory Management and
    Error Recovery
    Proc. HICSS-21, Vol.1,1988

18. C.R.Landau
    Security in a Secure Capability-Based System
    Operating System Review, 1989

19. J.-C. Laprie
    Dependable Computing and Fault-Tolerance:
    Concepts and Terminolody
    Proc. FTCS-15, Ann Arbor, Michigan, June 1985
    pp. 2-11

20. Liskov, Scheifler
    Guardians and Actions: Linguistic Support For Robust Distributed Programs
    Proc. 9th ACM Symp. on OS Principles, Bretton Woods, 1983

21. G.J.Myers
    Advances in Computer Architecture
    2nd Ed., John Wiley&Sons,1982

22. R.M. Needham, R.D.H. Walker
    The Cambrigde CAP Computer and Its Protection System
    Proc. 6th Symp. OS Principles, 1977

23. P.G. Neumann
    On the PSOS Design Concept
    In: P.G.Neumann, J.A.Goguen, K.N.Levitt, P.M.Melliar-Smith, J.Meseguer,
    R.L.Schwartz, R.E.Shostak

Technology for provable Secure Systems
Final Report: PSOS Implementation Study, SRI,1983

24. E.I. Organick
The Multics System: An examination of its structure
MIT Press, Cambridge, MA,1972

25. L. Robinson
The HDM Handbook
SRI Project 4828, June 1979

26. R.Rashid, A.Tevanian, M.Young, D.Young, R.Baron, D.Black, W.Boloski,
J.Chew
Machine-independent virtual memory management for paged uniprocessor and
multiprocessor architectures
IEEE Transactions on Computers,37(8),pp 896-908,1988

27. A.S.Tanenbaum, S.J.Mullender, R.van Renesse
Using Sparse Capabilities in a distributed operating system
Proc. 6th IEEE Int. Conf. on Distrib. Comp.Systems,
Cambridge ,MA, 1986

28. Weitek WTL7138 System Designer's Note
Weitek Corp., Sunnyvale CA, 1986

29. W.A.Wulf, R.Levin,S.P.Harbison
HYDRA/C.mmp: An Experimental System
McGraw-Hill,1981

30. M.Wilkes, R.Needham
The Cambridge CAP Computer and its Operating System
North Holland 1979

A Secure RISC-based Architecture Supporting Data Persistence

David Koch and John Rosenberg
Department of Electrical Engineering & Computer Science
University of Newcastle
Australia

ABSTRACT

The MONADS project has as its principle aim the investigation of techniques for the development of secure and reliable computer systems. However, unlike many other comparable projects we have not limited our investigations to software, but have sought solutions in terms of an integrated architecture involving both hardware and software. We begin by describing the MONADS architecture and show how it supports protected information-hiding modules and persistence in an in-process environment. From this discussion we derive four requirements of a physical implementation of the architecture. We then describe the MONADS-MM implementation and demonstrate how a conventional RISC processor can be used as the basic processing element of a system meeting these requirements. The resulting system provides fine-grain control over access to data and inherent support for persistence. An additional feature of the MONADS-MM design is support for a main memory of up to 64 gigabytes.

1. INTRODUCTION

The MONADS project has as its principle aim the investigation of techniques for the development of secure and reliable computer systems. However, unlike many other comparable projects we have not limited our investigations to software, but have sought solutions in terms of an integrated architecture involving both hardware and software. This research has resulted in the design of the MONADS architecture [18] of which there are two current implementations known as MONADS-PC and MONADS-MM. The MONADS-PC system was developed in 1985 [17] and is based on a purpose-built microcoded processor. The MONADS-MM system, which is the topic of this paper, is currently being designed and is based on the SUN SPARC processor [20].

The MONADS architecture has been strongly influenced by our philosophy for the construction of systems, particularly with regard to objects, protection and concurrency. In the MONADS system all major software entities are represented as information-hiding modules with purely procedural interfaces and, optionally, some encapsulated state information [15]. Thus, for example, a program is considered to be a module with a single interface. This approach is extended to include files which are viewed as modules which provide appropriate interfaces to access the encapsulated file data. In order to support this, modules are allowed to persist for an arbitrary length of time not related to the program which created them.

Given such a system, protection is achieved by controlling which interfaces of which modules are accessible to the currently executing process. The MONADS protection mechanism is based on capabilities [5] which are supported at the architectural level. In order to call an interface, a process must present an appropriate capability. Capabilities are themselves protected by the architecture so that it is not possible to forge or modify them.

The MONADS system adopts an "in-process" approach to concurrency wherein requests for service are achieved by procedure calls to modules within the current process [9]. As a result of this, processes and modules are orthogonal and many processes may be concurrently executing in one module. Synchronisation is the responsibility of the module, but may of course be automated by a programming language.

In order to implement information-hiding and security in an in-process system it is essential that a change of protection domain takes place on an inter-module call. This allows a module's addressing environment to be restricted to that data which it is authorised to access The architecture provides explicit support for multiple protection domains.

The MONADS-PC system is a prototype implementation of the architecture. The key feature of the MONADS-PC is support for a very large persistent virtual address space of 2^{60} bytes in which all objects reside [19]. Although this address space is considerably larger than that on conventional machines, it is not large enough for a realistic implementation of our ideas regarding the organisation of the store, particularly with regard to networks [2, 7]. In addition it is constructed out of quite old technology resulting in only fair performance in current terms. For these reasons we have embarked on a new implementation of the MONADS architecture, known as MONADS-MM, which amongst other features has a 2^{128} byte address space.

There is another motive for the development of the new machine. Given large virtual addresses it becomes possible to also have very large physical addresses and thus a very large main memory. It has been argued in the literature [6, 20] that a large main memory (in the order of gigabytes) can be used to achieve supercomputer speed for certain applications on a relatively modest speed processor. The MONADS-MM machine is being designed to support up to 64 gigabytes (GB) of main memory to allow experimentation in this area.

In this paper we begin by describing the MONADS architecture and show how it supports protected information-hiding modules and persistence in an in-process environment. From this discussion we derive four requirements of a physical implementation of the architecture. We then proceed to describe the MONADS-MM implementation and demonstrate how a conventional RISC processor can be used as the basic processing element of a system meeting these requirements. The resulting system provides fine-grain control over access to data and inherent support for persistence. Diagnostic and performance analysis facilities are an integral part of the design.

2. THE MONADS ARCHITECTURE

The MONADS architecture provides support for objects [11]. A distinction is made between large objects, called *modules*, and small objects, called *segments*. Modules are used to represent major software resources such as programs, files and operating system entities. They consist of encapsulated data and procedures for accessing that data. Modules are protected by *module capabilities* which define the access allowed to the module in terms of semantic operations appropriate to that object. Segments are used to represent small objects such as integers and records. They are protected by a lower level mechanism based on *segment capabilities*, which still guarantees security and protection.

The reason for the distinction is that the frequency and style of access varies between large and small objects and this separation allows an efficient implementation for small objects without compromising flexibility for large objects. The architecture does not enforce any minimum size rules and any object may be modelled as a module or segment.

Both module and segment capabilities are protected by the architecture so that it is not possible for a program to manufacture or modify a capability. A capability is provided by the system when a new object is created. The only other way to gain access to an object is to be given a capability by another program. A module's internal data, called its database, consists of segments containing data which may include module and segment capabilities.

2.1 Processes

Each process in the MONADS system is represented by a stack which is used for linkage on procedure calls, storage of local data which will be deleted on exit from the procedure and for expression evaluation. All data on the stack is held in segments which are addressed using segment capabilities. It is thus possible to enforce scope rules and to guarantee that a procedure does not access data which belongs to a procedure of another module.

A special segment called the *computational area* is automatically maintained at the top of the stack. This is the only segment which can change size dynamically. Data may be pushed onto and popped off the computational area and the architecture detects an underflow situation. The computational area may only contain simple data, i.e. segment and module capabilities cannot be held in the computational area.

Process stacks are held in the virtual memory. The process state information is held in a red-tape area of the stack so that processes may persist between login sessions. This has several advantages from a user management point of view [18].

2.2 Segmentation and Addressing

All data in the MONADS system is held in arbitrary sized segments, each of which has the same basic format, with three sections as illustrated in figure 1. The control section defines the size of the segment and details about the contents of the information section. Segments may contain module capabilities, one of a small number of system defined types or arbitrary data. The architecture restricts access to the information section appropriately for the type it contains. For example, arbitrary modifications may be performed on ordinary data, whereas module capabilities may only be assigned and used to call another module. The capability section contains references to other segments so that arbitrarily complex graph structures of segments may be produced.

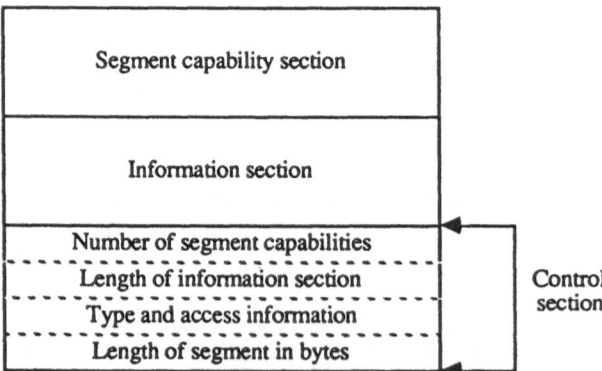

Figure 1: Segment format

Segments may only be addressed by segment capabilities. A segment capability need only contain the address of the identified segment since segments are self describing. For efficiency, the architecture provides a set of addressing registers, called *capability registers*, of the format shown in figure 2.

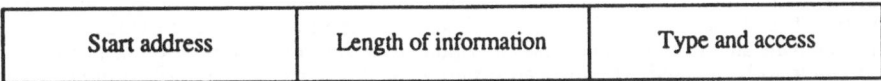

Start address	Length of information	Type and access

Figure 2: Capability register format

In order to address a segment the segment capability is loaded into a capability register, with the information length and type and access being obtained from the segment itself. Machine instructions therefore address data using addresses of the form <capability register number> <offset within segment>. The architecture guarantees that any attempt to access beyond the end of the information section will cause a run-time exception. This provides implicit support for array bounds checking.

Loading of capability registers is obviously critical to system security. A special machine instruction is provided for this purpose. This instruction will only load a capability register with a segment capability contained in a segment currently pointed to by another capability register. Using this facility it is possible to traverse arbitrary data structures in a secure fashion. Similarly a machine instruction is provided to store segment capabilities in the segment capability section of a segment. This instruction enforces certain rules which limit the propagation of segment capabilities in the system. These rules simplify the problem of garbage collection and allow most segment capabilities to be maintained in an abbreviated form [18].

The root of all addressing is defined by a special segment, of which there is one per process, called the *base table*. An additional machine instruction is provided to load a capability register to point at the base table. By changing the contents of the base table the current addressing environment may be modified. This is the key to the module protection scheme as will be described in the next section.

2.3 Procedures and Modules

The code of procedures is also held in segments. However, these are usually not directly addressable from the base table. Rather there is a dedicated capability register which holds a segment capability for the current procedure. This is automatically changed on a procedure call. The architecture ensures that a procedure can only exit via a return instruction. A jump to outside of the code of the current procedure will cause an exception.

When a module is compiled, the compiler produces the procedure segments and two additional segments. The first, called the *interface entry-point list*, contains a segment capability for each interface procedure of the module (i.e. procedures which can be called by other modules). The second, called the *internal entry-point list*, contains an equivalent set of segment capabilities for procedures internal to the module. The locations of these entry-point lists for the current module are always available to the architecture via some red-tape information associated with each module. There are two procedure call instructions, one for internal calls and one for inter-module calls. The call instructions specify the procedure to be called as an index into the appropriate entry-point list. Thus the call instruction may retrieve the segment capability for the called procedure.

On each procedure call a new segment is created. Parameters are passed by either copying the value into this segment (pass by value) or by copying a segment capability into the segment (pass by reference). The call mechanism adds a segment capability for this new segment into the base table to make it addressable in the called routine and removes it on the return. A similar mechanism is used to create and delete local data for the called routine.

In order to call a procedure of another module the program must present a valid module capability. These have the format shown in figure 3. The module name provides sufficient information to the architecture to allow the entry-point lists and a root segment for the private data of the module to be located. The mechanism used for this purpose is described in [18]. The access rights define which of the procedures of the identified module may be called using this module capability. The status bits define which operations may be performed on the capability itself, e.g. whether it can be copied.

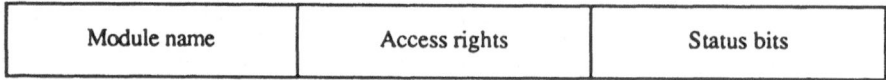

| Module name | Access rights | Status bits |

Figure 3: A module capability

The inter-module call instruction checks the supplied module capability to ensure that the procedure to be called is included within the access rights. It then transfers control to the procedure, obtaining a segment capability for the procedure from the interface entry-point list. The call mechanism modifies the base table to include a capability for the root segment of the private data for the called module and to remove and save the segment capability for the root segment of the private data of the calling module. That is, the call mechanism causes a change of protection domain.

The above description has provided a logical view of the module mechanisms. There are several optimisations that can be performed to minimise the effort required on procedure calls. These are described in [18].

2.4 Space Management and Persistence

In this section we discuss the issue of how segments are organised within the large virtual store. The virtual address space is partitioned into regions called *address spaces*. Similarly addresses are partitioned so that the high order bits indicate an address space number and the low order bits indicate an offset within that address space. Ideally, each address space is large enough to contain all the segments of a module and the address space numbers are large enough to allow a new number to be allocated whenever a new address space is created. In the MONADS-PC implementation the address space number is 32 bits and the offset 28 bits. The address space number is too small to guarantee uniqueness and the offset field is limiting for some applications. This is one of the motivations behind the MONADS-MM which has 96 bit address space numbers and 32 bit offsets.

Each address space is paged. However, it is not a traditional paged segments scheme. Instead segments are mapped onto the paged address spaces by segment capabilities and appear as windows into the address space. Thus segments may be smaller than a page or may overlap several page boundaries [10]. Such a scheme allows both small and large segments to be handled efficiently in terms of space by minimising fragmentation.

Each address space is used to hold a related group of segments. For example, all procedures for a module are located in a single address space and the private database of a module is located in an address space. Indeed, the name of a module is simply the name of the address space in which its private data resides. The grouping of segments into address spaces, combined with the rules regarding propagation of pointers greatly simplifies garbage collection of segments.

The use of unique names for address spaces considerably simplifies the management of modules. When a module is deleted it is not necessary to locate all of the module capabilities since the name in these capabilities will be invalid for evermore.

Persistence is completely orthogonal in the sense that all data resides within the virtual store which is persistent. Thus any data structure which can be created and manipulated by the architecture can persist.

2.5 Summary of Architectural Requirements

In summary we list the architectural features required to support security and persistence as derived from the above discussion.

- *A mechanism for addressing segments in a protected manner* - so as to constrain processes to operate only on those segments which they are authorised to access.

- *Support for very large addresses* - to avoid ambiguity and provide a uniform naming structure.

- *A mechanism for implementing a virtual memory beneath these addresses* - so that objects can persist in a virtual store.

- *A mechanism to add new instructions that manipulate capabilities in a controlled manner* - to support the implementation of the higher level architecture.

In the next section we describe how these requirements are met in the MONADS-MM system.

3. IMPLEMENTATION

The MONADS-MM is an implementation of the architecture described in the previous sections. It is based on a commercially available RISC processor, and meets all of the requirements listed above in section 2.5.

- Protected addressing of segments is achieved by an addressing unit external to the RISC processor.

- This addressing unit supports 128 bit addresses which are large enough to guarantee uniqueness forever.

- An address translation unit based on a hardware supported inverted page table provides efficient translation of large virtual addresses to physical addresses.

- Dedicated high speed memory is provided on the processor boards for capability management routines which are executed in supervisor mode and have privileged access to the addressing hardware.

In addition, the MONADS-MM provides limited support for multiprocessing by allowing up to 8 system processor units to operate on a common high performance bus. The centralised address translator supports multiple page sizes. The memory system provides high bandwidth access to physical memory of up to 64GB. Integral support is included for diagnostics and performance evaluation.

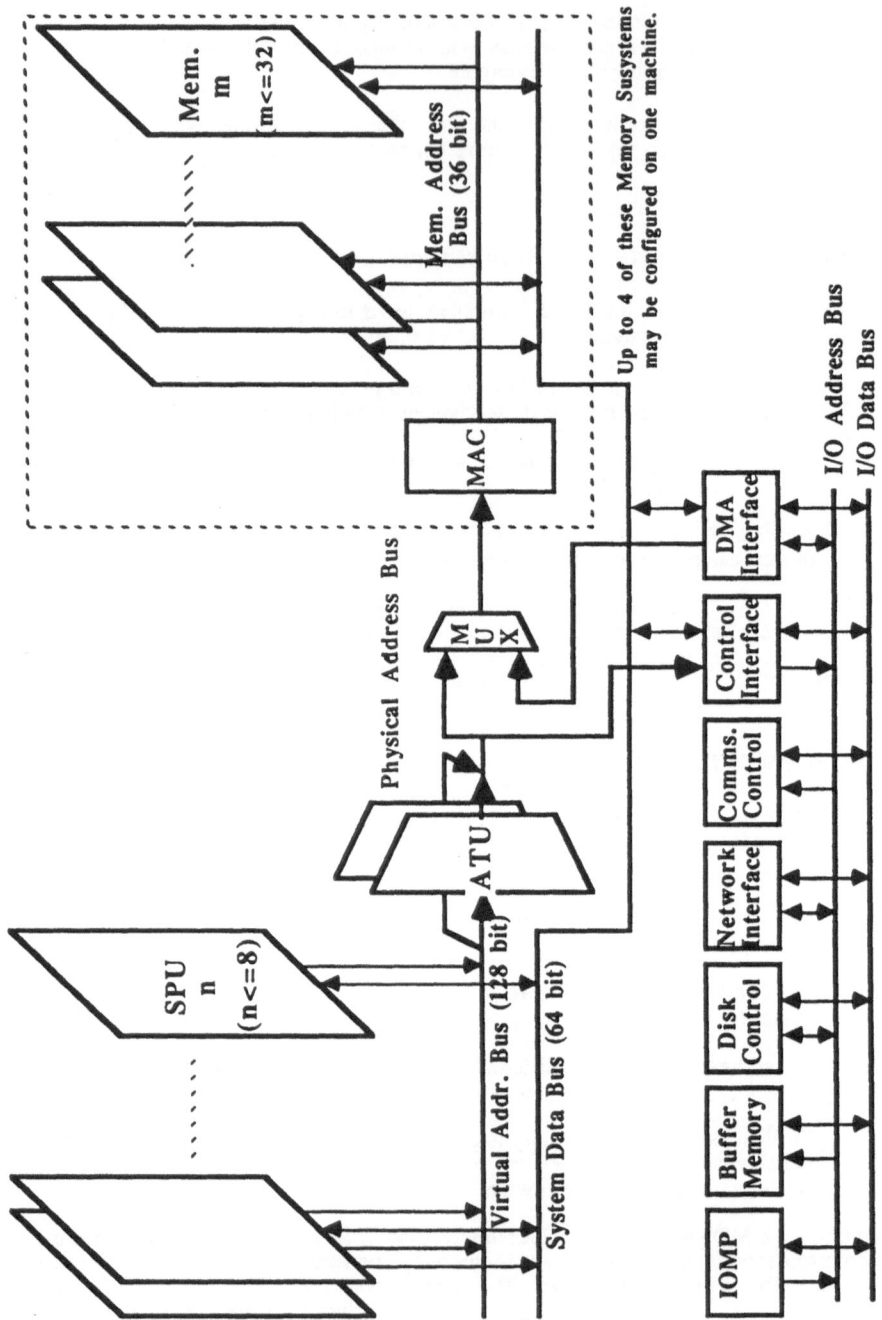

Figure 4: Block diagram of MONADS-MM

The following sections detail the implementation and functional aspects of each component. Figure 4 shows the basic structure of the machine.

3.1 The System Processor

The heart of the System Processor Unit (SPU) is a SUN SPARC processor [21]. SPARC implementations are offered by a number of silicon implementors. In particular both the CY7C601 from Cypress Semiconductor and the L64811 from LSI Logic provide a 32 bit unmanaged linear address space [4, 13]. In addition the architecture provides an Address Space Index (ASI) Register of 8 bits which can notionally be considered as a logical address extension from 32 to 40 bits. The provision of 4GB (2^{32} byte) address spaces is considered satisfactory for the purposes of this experimental machine. The SPARC architectural specification heavily constrains the use of the ASI to the point where it is of little value to our situation for assisting in the access and management of multiple user address spaces, but remains useful for the demarcation between user and supervisor (kernel) memory requests. The fact that it exists at all provides some hope for the future as the architectural definition is further refined. Four ASI values are currently defined by SUN [21]. These are user data, user instruction, supervisor data and supervisor instruction. A further 252 combinations are available, though only in supervisor mode and only using a restrictive addressing mode. Some of these have been allocated for the control of MMU and cache external to the SPARC core by various vendors [12], but considerably more than half have no specific purpose.

Ideally we would like to implement a machine having separate address and data ALUs so that address space size could be dictated by design rather than constrained by commercial devices. We recognise that for certain applications an address space upper limit of 4GB will be inadequate, though such a limit can generally be circumvented through the careful partitioning of data sets into multiple address spaces which can all be concurrently visible to the one process. A purpose-built processor could have been designed that would have fully met the project's aims. However the resources required for such a project would be beyond those available to us. Furthermore there is some advantage in adopting a widely used and well documented architecture, as a performance comparison may be made between machines of comparable technology, but differing operational regimes.

The prime adjunct to the features provided by the basic SPARC device is the addition of an external address processor. This provides for the inclusion of multiple overlapped sets of capability address registers which remain in lock step with the internal register sets of the SPARC chip itself. On each logical memory reference both a capability register number and an offset must be specified. Since user modification of the ASI is not possible under current SPARC architectural specifications and implementations, an alternate technique has been introduced to explicitly specify the register number. The scheme is dependent on compiler support . Two memory reference instructions are generated for each required memory access. The first instruction is always a load and contains as its address a capability register number. The second instruction is a load or store as required, and contains as its address the offset within the addressed segment. While this initial access appears to be a significant overhead on every user access, the impact is minimised by ensuring that it completes in minimum time. Its completion is immediately acknowledged as the transfer is to an external register rather than to memory. In addition part of the address computation can be overlapped with the execution of the subsequent user access. Low level kernel code and data, and user code memory references are sufficiently identifiable from the processor status (including the ASI) that this technique does not apply to such accesses. In future it should be possible to modify the basic VLSI core of SPARC to allow for user level specification of a range of ASI values providing directly for address generation of the form *<CR#>, offset* within one instruction. This aspect will be further investigated as the project develops.

An alternate strategy in using a commercial microprocessor for providing large address extensions would be to use high order address bits to select capability registers at the expense of address space size [16]. However, this scheme would require the compiler to generate extra code in order to avoid undetected run-time errors. For example, code would be required to check array bounds, since an index error could still result in the generation of a valid address.

Both the Cypress CY7C601 and LSI Logic L64811 provide 136 registers divided into 8 global registers and 8 sets of 24 partially overlapped user registers. We complement this with an identical arrangement of user capability registers which operate in lock step with these internal registers. In addition there are dedicated capability registers for accessing kernel code, kernel data, the computational area of the stack and the code of the current user procedure. All registers consist of an *address space number* (96 bits), an *offset within address space* (32 bits), a *segment length* (32 bits) and *type and access information* (32 bits). The first instruction of a memory reference pair (or the processor status in the case of code or kernel data) provides the index to the capability register. The logical address from the second memory reference instruction is added to the offset within address space and concatenated with the address space number to form the 128 bit virtual address. The segment length is then compared with the generated offset in parallel with checking the access rights.

There is a virtually addressed data and code cache on each SPU. Cache access commences on completion of the formation of the virtual address and operates in parallel with the length and access right checks. The majority of kernel code is not cached but is held in dedicated high speed static RAM. Cache coherence is simplified through caching on unique virtual addresses. Various multiprocessor cache coherence protocols are currently being investigated.

When the SPARC processor internal register set underflows or overflows, as detected in *save* or *restore* operations, an underflow or overflow trap occurs. The trap handlers, in addition to satisfying the detected condition, attend to the capability register set in the same manner. A dedicated hardware state machine provides an efficient method of manipulating the capability register sets. This same hardware assists in the copying of capabilities from one register to another to efficiently support the *call* and *return* operations.

Capability register manipulation instructions are provided through trap handlers for unimplemented SPARC instructions. These traps automatically and efficiently invoke supervisor mode to allow for execution of kernel procedures which handle the capabilities in a secure manner.

3.2 The Address Translation Unit

The Address Translator Unit (ATU) maps the very large virtual addresses onto physical addresses. It uses a hardware supported hash table using techniques similar to that used in the MONADS-PC system [3, 19]. However, the proposed vast size of main memory would normally introduce considerable difficulties in this or any other traditional approach to time and space efficient translation because of the very large number of pages [20].

A number of approaches to this problem have been contemplated. The solution adopted in the initial implementation is to support 2 pages sizes, 4 kilobyte (KB) and 4 megabyte (MB). These page sizes will be statically reconfigurable. In particular, large page sizes from 1 MB to 64MB seem worthy of empirical analysis. Main memory will be divided into large pages, with a selected number of these pages being further subdivided into the smaller 4KB pages. In a full 64GB system the number of large page entries could vary from 2^{10} page entires (based on 64MB pages) up to 2^{16} page entries (based on 1MB pages). A maximum physical memory allocation of 64MB to be split into the small page size would yield 2^{14} page entries. Both of these requirements are easily realised using a chained linear hash table simulating an inverted page table [19]. In particular the number of entries required for each page size is approximately the same.

It can be argued[1] that modules (and thus address spaces) in a system such as MONADS can be broadly classified as being either *small* or *large*. Small modules correspond to many of the entities supported in conventional systems, such as directories, operating system tables, process stacks and source and object programs. Large modules that a programmer would reasonably expect to grow to a considerable size are especially appropriate to a massive memory. Examples of these include database files, sparse matrices, functions implemented as lookup tables, heaps as produced by functional languages or languages supporting first class procedures to name a few. In many cases, these large modules only exist during the course of a single process invocation, and therefore require no backing storage.

All pages within an address space are of the same size and this is encoded in the address space number. Therefore it would be possible for one ATU module to handle both page sizes, varying the number of bits to be matched depending on the page size dictated for that address space. However for the sake of simplicity, multiple ATUs are supported, each ATU managing one page size. This allows the ATU modules to be essentially the same, though with differing strappings for the key comparison and data fields. Due to the modular design other promising translation regimes may be accommodated through alternate ATU structures, providing considerable scope for future work in this area.

The ATU is pipelined, allowing multiple concurrent translations to occur. This is essential for the case where the centralised ATU may be shared by several processors. It should be noted that virtual addresses are unique system wide and hence the ATU does not require flushing between process switches.

3.3 The Memory Subsystem

The memory subsystem consists of a Memory Access Controller (MAC) coupled with up to 32 memory array cards. The interconnecting bus is 64 data bits wide and operates in pipelined 50ns cycles. Up to 4 such subsystems can be configured into one MONADS-MM machine. Each subsystem provides a maximum of 16GB (using 4 megabit DRAM technology), resulting in a system total of 64GB, this limit being an implementation decision rather than an architectural limit.

The minimum read transaction is 64 bits with additional support for multiple word accesses on presentation of a single starting address. Data is transferred from memory modules after a 100ns latency, either in every cycle or every fourth cycle with provision for an additional 3 concurrent accesses in the intervening cycles, though not to the same array card. Thus the peak data transfer rate is 160MB/s or 40MB/s per active channel. The maximum block mode transfer is 4KB (512 64 bit accesses).

The minimum write transaction is a byte. Multiple word-aligned 64 bit accesses are possible in the same manner as for read operations.

The memory array cards are physically addressed, and support 4 way interleaving to make consecutive 50ns accesses possible. Each array card contains a T400 transputer [8] which acts through a dual port as a diagnostic processor. Linkage to a central diagnostic processor is via one of the 2.4MB/s serial links of the T400. The second 2.4MB/s serial link is reserved for potential use as an alternate link to the secondary storage system.

Memory data integrity is maintained through on card byte parity error detection. Byte parity error detection is provided on the SPU-Memory Bus.

---

[1] The case for this is not important here, but forms part of the overall justification for the project [20].

3.4 The Input/Output Subsystem

The Input Output Subsystem (IOS) provides the path to disk, tape, terminal and networking interfaces. This is accomplished by coupling commercial interface cards on an industry standard bus through a custom built bus interface channel. Initially Multibus I is being used, but the use of higher performance buses such as VMEbus, Multibus II or Futurebus+ is also feasible. Multiple IOS units can be configured on the system to support higher performance storage or communications requirements.

Processes request IO service through the Control Interface. The Input Output Management Processor (IOMP) orders, queues and manages requests for logical device services. A substantial portion of the kernel page fault handler and network manager is capable of being off loaded to the IOMP. Communication between the system processors and the IOMP occurs through shared memory buffers and an interrupt mechanism.

Data transfers to and from main memory occur through the buffered DMA interface, which attempts to minimise access impact on both the system data bus and the IO data bus. The DMA link to the system memory bus operates at the 40MB/s block mode rate through the buffered data interface.

3.5 Auxiliary Features

The MONADS-MM incorporates a number of other features to assist in its operational maintenance. The first of these is the ability to cater for live insertion and withdrawal of any card in the system. This was considered a necessary feature due to the very considerable time required to cold start a machine having up to 64GB of main memory and the requisite issues of confidence testing and memory transfers to and from secondary storage.

Implicit in the live insertion facility is the issue of reconfiguration to cope with the addition or subtraction of SPUs and memory cards and memory subsystems. Initially this will take place in a static manner, but it is planned that such resources will be able to be dynamically enabled or disabled, both to service the requirements of maintenance and testing, and also to assist in performance evaluation. Software tools will be provided to adjust ATU entries and to relocate active memory from a memory module requested for removal to memory on other available modules or to secondary storage. Likewise a request for the removal of an SPU will result in that unit saving current process state and being withdrawn from the pool of available processors. Removal of ATU or MAC modules will only be supported on a replacement basis.

Diagnostic access is provided directly to all SPUs and memory array cards, via high speed serial links from these cards. Other system cards (ATUs memory controllers, and I/O adapters) require SPU access via the bus. In all cases some level of diagnostic access is available to all active modules. However more detailed diagnostic analysis will be possible on modules that are off-line, in particular memory arrays cards. Currently a PC/AT is the diagnostic processor, but in the long term a custom built S-Bus[2] card for a SPARCstation will be used.

Support for performance evaluation will be provided in SPUs and ATUs. This will allow for a wide variety system parameters to be measured, particularly in relation to page sizes and management, and both object and data caching strategies.

System power is derived from an uninterruptable power source which buffers the system from mains power failure and glitches. The backup time provided is sufficient to allow the machine state to be saved in the event of a prolonged interruption. Recent advances in non-volatile

---

[2] SUN's high performance expansion bus for SPARCstations

FRAM[3] technology may dramatically reduce the backup time requirement by removing the need to write modified main memory to secondary storage.

3.6 Code Generation

The two instructions required to initiate the generation of the large addresses would seem a considerable complication. However it is not difficult to modify existing compiler and/or assembler output to provide these instructions. Existing SPARC compilers available in source form can be modified to automatically generate the additional instructions. Alternatively, it is possible to modify existing SPARC object code which includes no system or library calls, without reference to the source code, to run on this machine. This would allow new applications to be developed using existing SPARC compilers. Under this regime, the full range of SPARC compilers can be used although confinement can only be achieved by constraining a program to operate within a single, potentially large segment. Such programs are still able to communicate with the rest of the system via inter-module calls.

We are also intending to develop our own compilers which make full use of the architectural support for persistence and security.

4. CONCLUSION

In this paper we have described an architecture which provides explicit support for security and persistence. The MONADS-MM is an implementation of this architecture, not too dissimilar to an industry accepted architecture. The use of a commercial SPARC processor with attendant modifications demonstrates that security and persistence are achievable goals with current implementation technology, and without great performance penalty.

Four necessary system requirements have been identified as basic to the hardware support of the MONADS architecture. These are protected segment addressing for process confinement, very large addresses to support unique naming, underlying virtual memory support for large addresses, and the ability to define new protected system management instructions. All of these features are provided by the MONADS-MM system. In addition the system has integrated facilities for diagnostics and performance evaluation, as well as dynamic re-configuration.

An interesting and unusual feature of the MONADS-MM system is its support for a main memory of up to 64GB in the current implementation. The persistent programming paradigm provides an appropriate mechanism for harnessing the power of such a massive memory.

The MONADS-MM system is currently being designed and it is expected that a prototype will be operational by the end of 1991.

A custom VLSI implementation of the MONADS-MM architecture could provide equivalent performance to that provided in a conventional SPARC UNIX environment. The real hardware challenge is to encourage computer architects to decouple address manipulation from data manipulation and to provide appropriate support for the implementation of efficient persistent object stores. From a software standpoint, a new breed of languages is needed to harness the simplicity that data persistence offers and to make efficient use of very large main memories. Such languages are beginning to appear [1, 14].

---

[3] Ferro-magnetic Random Access Memories developed by Ramtron Inc USA/Aust. and currently available in 4Mx1 bit 60ns versions.

ACKNOWLEDGEMENTS

We wish to acknowledge the support provided by the Australian Research Council (grant number A48716316) and the University of Newcastle Senate Research Committee. Some of this work was undertaken during a period of study leave by John Rosenberg at the University of St Andrews which was supported by SERC grant GR/F 28571.

We are grateful for the comments and suggestions made by Prof. R. Morrison, Dr. A.L. Brown and Mr. D. Munro who reviewed earlier versions of this paper.

REFERENCES

1. Atkinson, M.P., Bailey, P.J., Cockshott, W.P. and Morrison, R. "PS-Algol Reference Manual", Universities of Glasgow and St Andrews, PPRR-12-88, 1988.

2. Abramson, D.A. and Keedy, J.L. "Implementing a Large Virtual Memory in a Distributed Computing System", *Proceedings of 18th Annual Hawaii International Conference on System Sciences*, 1985, pp. 515-522.

3. Abramson, D.A. "Hardware Management of a Large Virtual Memory", Proceedings 4th Australia Computer Conference, Brisbane 1981, pp. 1-13

4. SPARC RISC User's Guide, Cypress Semiconductor Corporation - Ross Technology Subsidiary, February 1990.

5. Fabry, R.S. "Capability-Based Addressing", *Comm. ACM*, 17, 7, 1974, pp. 403-412.

6. Garcia-Molina, H., Park, A. and Rogers, L.R. "Performance Through Memory", *Proc. ACM SIGMETRICS Conference*, May 1987, pp. 122-131.

7. Henskens, F.A., Rosenberg, J. and Keedy, J.L. "A Capability-Based Fully Transparent Network", Technical Report 89/7, Department of Electrical Engineering and Computer Science, University of Newcastle, Australia, 1989.

8. IMS T400 Transputer - Advanced Data, Pub. No. 42145200, INMOS, November 1989.

9. Keedy, J.L. "A Comparison of Two Process Structuring Models", MONADS Report 4, Monash University, Australia, 1980.

10. Keedy, J.L. "Paging and Small Segments: A Memory Management Model", *Proceedings 8th World Computer Congress (IFIP-80)*, Melbourne 1980, pp. 337-342.

11. Keedy, J.L. and Rosenberg, J. "Support for Objects in the MONADS Architecture", *Proc. 3rd International Workshop on Persistent Object Systems*, Newcastle, Australia, 1989, to be published by Springer-Verlag.

12. The L64815 Memory Management, Cache Control, and Cache Tags Unit Technical Manual, Part No. MD70-000101-99-A-Preliminary, LSI Logic Corporation, 1990.

13. The L64811 IU Technical Manual, Part No. MD70-000102-99-05-Preliminary, LSI Logic Corporation, 1990.

14. Morrison, R., Brown, A.L., Connor, R.C.H. and Dearle, A. "The Napier88 Reference Manual", Universities of Glasgow and St Andrews, PPRR-77-89, 1989.

15. Parnas, D.L. "On the Criteria to be Used in Decomposing Systems into Modules", *Comm. ACM*, 15, 12, 1971, pp. 1053-1058.

16. Pose, R.D. "Capability Based, Tightly Coupled Multiprocessor Hardware to Support a Persistent Global Virtual Memory", *Proceedings of 22nd Annual Hawaii International Conference on System Sciences*, 1989, pp. 36-45.

17. Rosenberg, J. and Abramson, D.A. "A Capability-Based Workstation to Support Software Engineering", *Proceedings of 18th Annual Hawaii International Conference on System Sciences*, 1985, pp. 222-230.

18. Rosenberg, J.L. and Keedy, J.L. "Object Management and Addressing in the MONADS Architecture", *Proceedings 2nd International Workshop on Persistent Object Systems*, Appin Scotland, 1987, available as PPRR-44, Universities of Glasgow and St. Andrews.

19. Rosenberg, J., Keedy, J.L. and Abramson, D.A. "Addressing Mechanisms for Large Virtual Memories", Research Report CS/90/2, University of St. Andrews, 1990.

20. Rosenberg, J., Koch, D.M. and Keedy, J.L. "A Massive Memory Supercomputer", *Proceedings of 22nd Annual Hawaii International Conference on System Sciences*, 1989, pp. 338-345.

21. The SPARC Architecture Manual - Version 7, Part No. 800-1399-08 Rev A 22/Oct/87, SUN Microsystems Inc., 1989.

An Architecture Supporting Security and Persistent Object Storage

M. Reitenspieß
Siemens AG, München

Abstract

Providing security features is essential for future computer architectures (in hardware and software). Persistent storage concepts provide an abstraction from the conventional main memory (also virtual memory) - external memory separation. Both requirements have been fulfilled in the BiiN^{TM} architecture. On-chip support for permanent checking of object type and rights is based upon a capability implementation. Also, capabilities are used for object addressing. Taking advantage of the hardware support, the operating system has been efficiently implemented. In addition, these features have been made available to application programmers for improved security of application programs. The support for persistent storage relieves programmers from the mapping between internal and external memory and facilitates the implementation of object-oriented systems.

Keywords: security architecture, capabilities, persistent objects, object-orientation, transaction support, fault tolerance support, Ada

1. BACKGROUND

It has long been argued ([5, 11]) that existing computer architectures do not adequately support security or fault tolerance requirements. Neither find programming language concepts like data abstraction ([1, 12, 14]) or object-oriented programming concepts ([19]) counterparts in commercially available computer architectures. The transaction concept is not generally available to application programmers, although it is a widely accepted feature in database and transaction systems to control the concistency of data sets ([10, 15]).

Some Terms: Security and Persistence

The term security is used in many contexts in different ways. In this paper a system is called secure, if it provides

- integrity: data or programs are not changed accidentally or on purpose without the necessary authority,
- confidentiality: data are not made available inappropriately or without the necessary permissions,
- dependability: to rightful users the system functions are available as specified.

Persistence is a property of objects. An object is called persistent, if its lifetime is independent of the lifetime of the creating program. Files or database records are typical examples of persistent objects.

Overview

The architecture, as discussed in this paper, has been developed with security and fault tolerance in mind. We start in chapter 2 by describing the capability based addressing mechanism as provided by the CPU and the operating system, because of its importance to security and persistent object storage.

The following chapters explain the system's security architecture, which is based upon the following building blocks:

- Protection mechanisms support the implementation of security policies to provide integrity and confidentiality of all available objects. They are described in chapter 3.
- Fault tolerance and transaction features improve system dependability and integrity and are described in chapter 4.
- Persistent object storage provides a homogeneous object concept to application programmers. The concept is described in chapter 5.

Finally, chapter 6 contains a summary with some important experiences drawn from the system's development and its performance.

2. ADDRESSING MECHANISMS

The implemented addressing mechanism is crucial for the system's security and for understanding the implementation of persistent objects. We therefore start with the virtual memory architecture based upon a capability mechanism. After that, the mapping of capabilities to external storage is discussed.

2.1. Virtual Memory

Capabilities/Access Descriptors

The system's addressing is centered around a capability mechanism ([8]) and a tagged memory architecture. Each memory word is 33 bits long, with the 33rd bit being the tag bit. A tag bit "on" identifies a capability, also called access descriptor (AD). Each AD is 32 bits long (plus one tag bit) and consists of the following components (see figure 1):

- Object index: identifies an entry in the object table. The object table entry contains an AD to the type identifier of the object and the base address of the page table, where the object's memory pages are administered.
- Type rights: the object comes with three generic type rights (use, modify, control). The meaning of these generic rights is dependent upon the type of the object. For example, for the hardware defined type process the meaning would be: use=execute, modify=schedule, control=delete/stop.
- Representation rights: the representation rights (read, write) are checked at each access to a page of the object the AD points to. Their meaning is selfexplanatory.

For accessing an object in main memory, a virtual address consisting of an AD and a 32 bit offset must be provided. The offset is interpreted as follows:

- Page table index: points to an entry in the page table, which uniquely identifies the page (4 KB) to be used for accessing the object.
- Page offset: points to the actual byte in the page identified by the page table index.
- 2nd paging level: for objects requiring more than 1024 pages, a second paging level may be introduced.

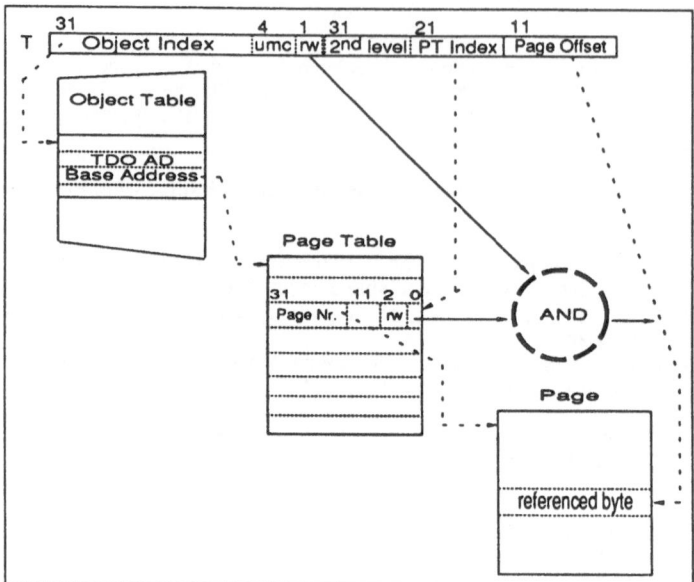

Figure 1: Addressing Scheme

Addressing Mechanism

Each page access consists of the following steps (see again figure 1):

1. Based upon the AD, the corresponding entry in the object table is found to get the associated page table.
2. The page table index identifies the page table entry, which contains the number of the required page.
3. Before accessing the page, the representation rights of the provided AD and the representation rights of the page table entry are combined in an **AND** operation. Write access is only allowed, if the result contains the write right. Read access is only allowed, if the result contains the read right.
4. Finally, the page offset in the offset part of the virtaul address is used to get the actual byte in the referenced page.

For performance reasons, caching is used to avoid repeated address translations of the same address. A working set strategy is used in the paging algorithm of memory management.

2.2. Secondary Storage

The operating system extends the object oriented addressing scheme to external storage media. This requires AD translation in two ways:

1. ADs must be preserved on external storage for later recognition,
2. ADs must be mapped from a system dependent form (entry in object table) to a unique external form independent of any system parameters.

AD Storage in Virtual Memory

The tagged architecture as implemented in main memory is mapped to external storage transparently by volume set management. Disk space is allocated in such a way that for each byte the existence of a tag bit is represented in a special block associated with each 8 blocks of raw data. In this way, ADs can be preserved when being stored to disk as part of virtual memory. When being read back again, the ADs are reconstructed from the 8 data blocks and their associated tag block.

AD Mapping on External Storage Media

A different approach is taken in case of transportable storage media (disks, floppy disks, streamer tapes). The operating system implements the concept of volume sets. Volume sets are the basic structure which can be exchanged between different systems or between different nodes in a distributed system. As can be seen from figure 1, an AD is dependent upon the object table, which is system (node) specific. To provide AD uniqueness between systems and nodes, an external AD format is used with the following components:

- unique name depending on time, volume set, and node identification (the node identification is unique for all systems through hardware manufacturing),
- type referring to associated type manager or predefined type,
- type rights depending upon object type.

All objects in virtual memory are called active objects. Their ADs are represented in the system (node) specific object table. The object table entry is mapped to its external representation (passive form) as soon as the AD is moved to external memory. This mapping is transparent to users, because it is implemented within a basic operating system module called passive store management.

3. PROTECTION MECHANISMS

The available protection mechanisms are supported in hardware and software. Since it was a requirement to continuously perform checking of access rights, the checking mechanisms had to be implemented on chip. Type checking is done in cooperation between hardware and operating system. The unforgability of ADs is completely hardware supported. Finally, the operating system provides protection on the type manager and object administration level.

The functioning of the protection mechanisms will be explained by means of an example. Assume a program has been created, which writes the string *hello world* to a window on the screen. The program is running as job termmgr of user rei. The program shall do two things. First, it must retrieve the AD of the terminal terminal_name, which is stored in the directory Terminal_Directory. terminal_name is where we want to write to:

AD = retrieve("/Terminal_Directory/terminal_name");

In the second step, we write the string *hello world* to the terminal terminal_name:

write(AD,"hello world");

The security checks M1 to M5 performed when running this program are shown in figure 2.

Identification Check (M1)

With each job, an ID list is associated, which contains a list of user names (IDs) the job may use. (rei, um) is part of this list meaning, the user rei with generic type rights use and modify. With each object, an authority list is associated, which identifies the users and the generic type rights they have on this object. (rei,umc) is part of the authority list of Terminal_Directory. In check M1, the running job's ID list is compared with the object's authority list. Since both lists

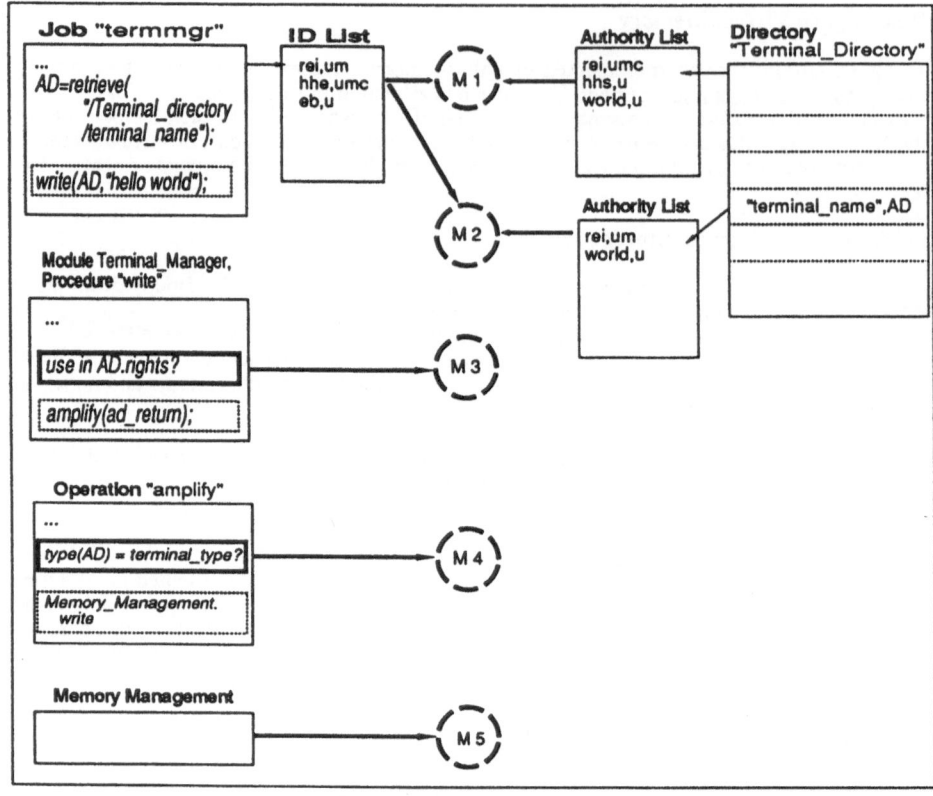

Figure 2: Security Checks

contain a common entry with at least the type right use (rei,u), the job may read directory Terminal_Directory.

Authority Check (M2)

When reading the entry ("terminal_name",AD) from the directory, it is checked that a common entry exists in the job's ID list and the authority list of the terminal (M2). The retrieved AD's type rights are constructed by conjunction of the type rights of the ID list entry and of the authority list entry. In our example, the retrieved AD has type rights use and modify (rei,um).

Type Manager Check (M3)

Using the retrieved AD, the program calls the operation write of the module Terminal_ Manager. Terminal_Manager is the type manager for terminals, i. e. it contains the code for accessing and managing terminals. The type manager is responsible for checking (M3) that the rights provided by the caller are sufficient to execute the required operation. To use the write function, the type right use must be presented to Terminal_Manager. This requirement is fulfilled in the example, since use is in (rei,um).

Type Checking (M4)

Only the module Terminal_Manager shall be allowed to access the representation of terminal objects. For accessing the representation of an object, the AD's representation rights must be added to the AD (this is called amplification). For this purpose, the type manager presents a type manager AD together with the given AD from the caller to the chip for adding representation rights. During this operation, the chip checks (M4), that the object's type (which is represented in the AD) and the type manager type (which is represented in the type manager AD) are identical. The type manager AD is only known to the type manager and must not be revealed.

Access Check M5

Finally, as has been shown in chapter 2, during each memory access, the representation rights of the AD which is part of the virtual address are checked against the requested rights as set in the page table (M5). Only if this check succeeds, the *hello world* string will be written to terminal terminal_name.

4. FAULT TOLERANCE SUPPORT

Secure systems require fault tolerance support for several reasons. First of all, the dependability of a system and its components is one corner stone of secure systems. Secondly, the enforcement of security policies is dependent upon the correct operation of protection mechanisms. We therefore describe the basic fault tolerance features which improve system dependability.

Fault Tolerance Levels

The system can be configured in three levels of fault tolerance: standard, fault checking, and continuous operation.

In the standard level, the memory access controller allows for the detection of double-bit errors and the correction of single bit errors in memory. It also allows scanning through memory to correct single bit errors. The system bus provides two parity bits, one for even bits, one for odd bits, so 2-bit errors in two neighbouring signals can be detected. A part of the memory is battery backed to provide memory availability in case of power failures. This memory area is primarily used as cache between internal and external memory to avoid inconsistency of external data.

In the fault checking level, two CPU/memory modules can be combined to form master/checker pairs (see figure 3). They operate in lock step and in case a hardware failure is detected, the faulty pair stops and is excluded from operation in a future reconfiguration of the system. Fault checking also implies the duplication of the system bus.

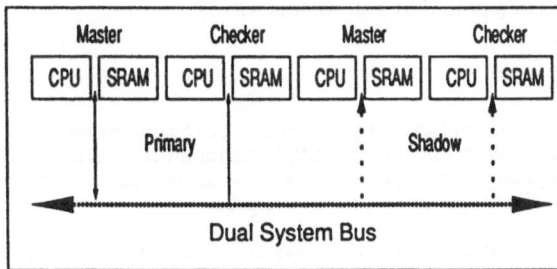

Figure 3: Fault Tolerance Levels

In the continuous operation mode, two master/checker pairs are combined to a primary/ shadow pair (see figure 3). In case of a permanent fault, the faulty master/checker pair is stopped and the remaining pair steps in on a reduced level of fault tolerance. This switch is invisible to software.

Operating system support is necessary for configuring the required

208

fault tolerance level. One system or node may contain up to 8 processors, providing for 2 primary/shadow pairs, for 4 master/checker pairs, or for 8 CPUs running in standard mode.

Confinement Areas

Confinement areas are an important concept in fault tolerance and are mainly used for isolating errors. Confinement areas are provided on hardware and on software level. Hardware confinement areas are formed by processor modules, by I/O modules, by memory modules and by the system bus. Software confinement areas are based on domains. A domain consists of all objects, which can be reached by a program at a certain point in time. Each program is built from one or more domains. Domain changes are effectuated by procedure calls. Calling a different domain means exchanging the address space and the code object of the program. If required, the stack object can be changed in addition (mutually suspicious subsystems, [13]).

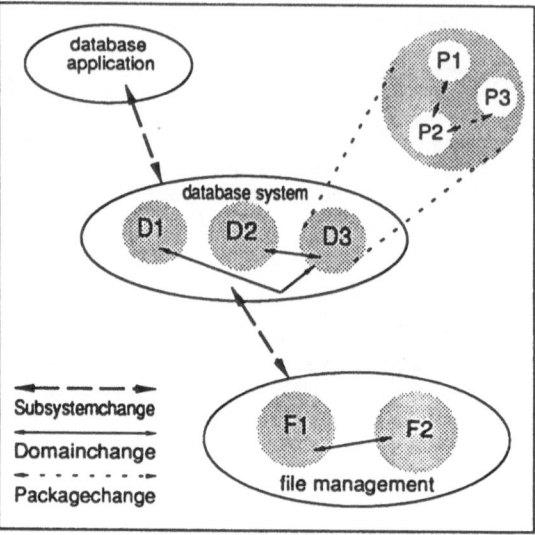

Figure 4: Domain Structure

Figure 4 shows a typical usage scenario based upon domains and subsystems. The database application calls the database system for data retrieval or updates. Since the database system cannot trust the application, the database system is implemented as a separate subsystem. I. e. during each call to the database system, the code object, the address object, and the stack object are changed. Within the database implementation code, several domains are used to implement the database functions (D1, D2, D3). E.g. D1 may contain backup/recovery modules and D2 may contain the query modules. The database modules do trust each other, but for error confinement and recovery reasons, they are implemented as separate domains. (Note: Figure 4 also indicates that a domain may be constructed from several Ada packages, e. g. P1, P2, P3.) Going one step further, the database system needs to call the operating system for file management support. Again, the operating system cannot trust the callers (file management may be called by several database systems and application programs). File management is therefore implemented as a separate subsystem with domains F1 and F2.

Confinement areas are important for several reasons. Firstly, errors can be confined and are more easily handled. Secondly, security violations can be restricted to the actual domains of a program. For example, the possible access to stack data (a typical protection hole) can be restricted by exchanging the stack object during procedure call and return.

Backup/Recovery and Transaction Support

The operating system provides interfaces to application programs (e.g. to support database system programmers or transaction system programmers) for implementing backup/recovery and transaction functionality. In this way, application oriented services can be integrated with the corresponding system features. Two advantages come with this approach:

1.   Power failures are detected and handled by the operating system. After a power outage, the system notifies each attached application service (a type manager) for recovery

actions.

2. Backups can be taken in one step from all attached type managers and only application specific actions need to be performed by the application programmer. The same is true, if after a roll-back recovery actions need to be taken. All attached type managers are notified by the system and can take appropriate action.

5. PERSISTENT STORAGE AND ITS VISIBILITY

The support for persistent storage has affected the system design in several ways. Firstly, the concept will be described as such and then the view of an Ada programmer will be shown.

5.1. Active/Passive Space

As has already been described in chapter 2 (addressing mechanism), the system distinguishes between active and passive objects. Active space consists of all active objects, i. e. all objects in virtual memory. Passive space is comprised of all passivated objects, i. e. all non-active objects on external storage. Persistent storage support means transparently mapping the active space representation of objects to their passive representation and vice versa. This mapping is described in the following sections.

Creating and Storing Objects

The creation of active objects is done by calls to memory management (allocate). The operating system allocates space in memory and returns an AD to the newly created object. After the object has been worked with as specified in the program, the object needs to be passivated for long-term availability. First, the AD must be stored on external memory. This is typically done by storing the AD in a directory (Directory_Management.Store). Then the contents of the object need to be moved to external memory by calling the update-operation of Passive_ Store_Management. Only after both actions have been performed, the object is permanently stored and available for later retrievals by the same or other programs. ADs can be used to build networks of objects. Such a network can be permanently stored within one update-operation. The operating system will make sure that the closure of all referenced objects gets stored

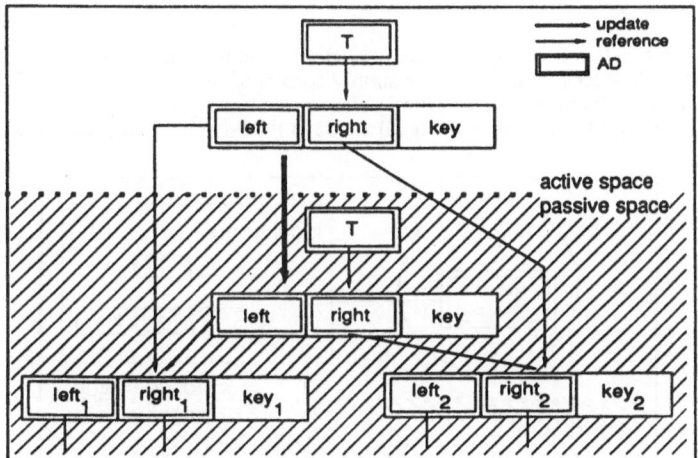

Figure 5: Active/Passive Space

permanently. Also, the passivation of objects is controlled by transactions to assure the consistency of passivated objects.

Figure 5 shows the relationship between the active and passive representation of a tree object. Through the update-operation, the tree T from active space has been transformed to its representation in passive space.

Using Stored Objects

Using a passive object means showing an AD of the object and accessing its contents. Before this can happen, the object must be moved to active space (activation). This is done by the operating system transparently to the using program as soon as the corresponding AD is presented. If the object contains references to other objects (i. e. if it forms a network of objects), the referenced objects are activated when needed. This is called activate on reference, which is also shown in figure 5. The branches left and right of T are pointing to other node objects. During activation, only the currently referenced object T is transferred. Indirectly referenced objects will only be transferred when needed.

5.2. Programming Language Support

The operating system support for persistent objects is directly available to Ada programmers. The Ada pointer concept is used for this purpose ([2, 9]). Ada pointer types can be used as shown in the insert. This declaration list says that the type tree is a reference to objects of type node. As defined in [1], new objects are created by allocators as follows:

```
type node;
type tree is access node;
type node is
  record
    key: integer;
    left, right: tree;
  end record;
T: tree;
```

```
T := new node;
        -- allocates space for new object of type node and
        assigns its reference to T.
```

The Ada concept of allocators has been extended to include objects allocated by the operating system, i. e. persistent objects. For this purpose the **pragma** access_kind has been defined, which influences the semantics of the **new** operation. The modes linear, heap, and object are supported.

Linear mode: Objects created by **new** are allocated in the local heap of a program. This is the default. References to these objects simply consist of the offset of a virtual address, since the AD to the local heap is implicitly allocated during program creation. This is represented in figure 6 with tree T being allocated in the local heap of program P.

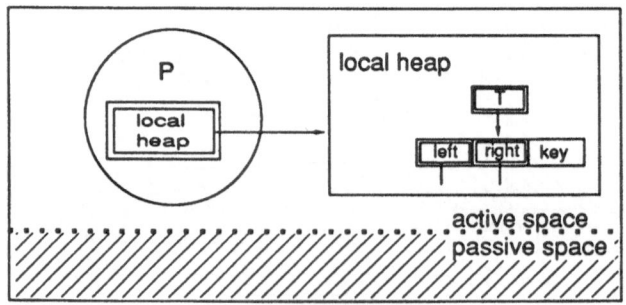

Figure 6: Linear Mode

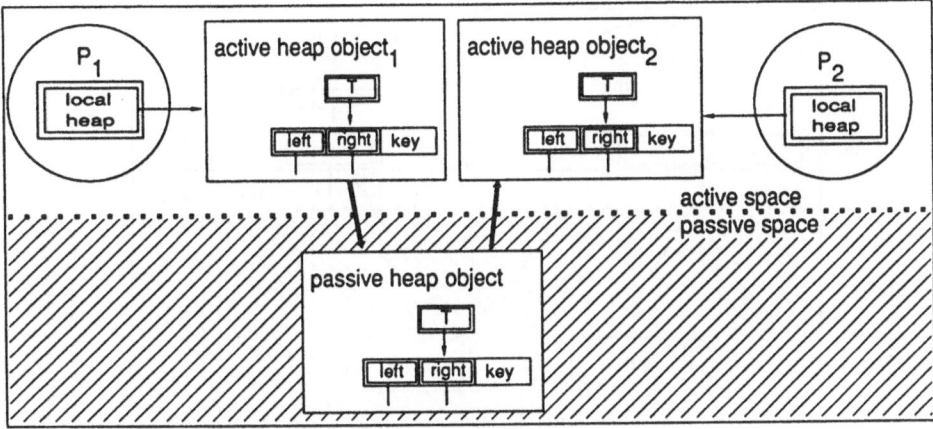

Figure 7: Heap Mode

Heap mode: Objects created by **new** are allocated in a predefined heap object. This heap object must be created, updated, and deleted by the application programmer using the available operating system interface for passive space objects. A heap object therefore can be preserved beyond the lifetime of a program. Addresses to heap objects consist of (heap AD, offset). heapAD is provided by the application programmer. offset is computed during compilation in the same way as for the local heap. The compiler run-time system is responsible for managing the heap space. Of course, it is assumed that heap objects are always accessed using the same memory management algorithms.

Figure 7 shows a passive heap object with tree T as element. It is created and passivated by program P_1 and actived and used by program P_2. The figure also shows that the passive object exists in two active versions (active heap object$_1$, active heap object$_2$), one in each activating program. Synchronization mechanisms have to be applied to assure the consistency and correctness of passive object representations with multiple parallel activations.

Object mode: **new** creates a new object using the available operating system interfaces for passive space management. The object structure is defined by the corresponding data type. Using this mode, a network of objects (e.g. tree) can be constructed with standard Ada language features. The objects (e.g. the tree) can be preserved in passive space and later be reused by other (or the same) Ada programs using the same type definition. It is this feature, which extends the file type as the only persistent object type in conventional systems to an unlimited set of data types as available in Ada.

Figure 8 represents the support for object mode allocation by showing a passive object T of type tree with two active representations (T_1 in program P_1, T_2 in program P_2). As discussed before, synchronization mechanisms must be used to assure consistency and correctness of passive objects with multiple parallel active representations.

5.3. System Integration

The above described features have been extensively used during the specification and implementation of system services like form generators or report generators. During the specification phase, the Ada type construction support has been used for specifying the operating system interfaces. During the implementation phase, the object implementation support could be used to facilitate the implementation and management of persistent objects as required for system

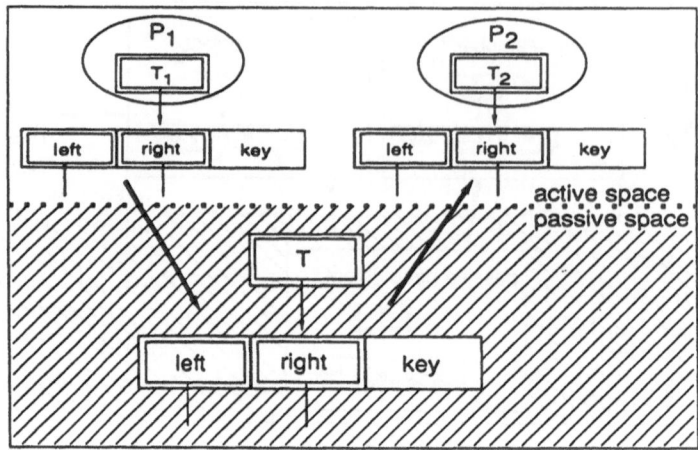

Figure 8: Object Mode

services. Of course, this can only be true for system modules <u>outside</u> of memory management. However, the system has been implemented in Ada **completely**.

6. EXPERIENCES

In this paper, we have addressed several important aspects of a new architecture supporting security, fault tolerance and persistent object storage. The system has been commercially available (BiiN^{TM}). Benchmark and simulation results showed that the capability based implementation does not adversely affect performance. Typical techniques for improving the addressing speed like large cache space can be used for tuning.

Security

The implemented security mechanisms are applicable to a wide variety of protection models. For highly secure systems, the implementation process must be carefully controlled to assure correct and complete application of the mechanisms. Ada can help in achieving these goals.

Fault Tolerance

Fault tolerance is a prerequisite for implementing secure systems. Not only is it necessary to assure system availability and dependability. Also the correct operation of the security mechanisms requires fault tolerance features. Persistence of objects can only be sufficiently assured with fault tolerance support in place. However, the required features must be carefully selected for reasonable price/performance ratios.

Persistent Objects

Persistent objects relieve the programmer from mapping internal data structures to data structures as available on external media (typically files). Objects can be directly moved in and out between internal memory (active space) and external memory (passive space). However, experience shows that these features are only slowly accepted in the commercial world. Reasons seem to be insufficient knowledge and unavailability of other comparable systems. Despite the

213

advantage of persistent objects, only through standardization and wider support their acceptance will be increased. The current drive for object-oriented systems seems to be one step in this direction.

REFERENCES

1. "Ada Programming Language". ANSI/MIL-STD-1815A, American National Standards Institute, 1983

2. Barnes, J.G.P. "Programming in Ada". Addison-Wesley, London, 1982

3. Booch, G. "Software Engineering with Ada". 2nd Edition, Benjamin/Cummings, Menlo Park, CA, 1987

4. Czerniakiewicz, A. "BiiN™ Solutions to Ada Development Issues". Proc. *Ada Expo '88*, 1988

5. Denning, P. "Why not Innovations in Computer Architecture?". *Computer Architecture News*, 8, 1980

6. Denning, P. "Fault Tolerant Operating Systems". *ACM Computing Surveys*, 8, 4, December 1976

7. "DoD Trusted Computer System Evaluation Criteria". DOD 5200.28-STD, USA Department of Defense, December 1985

8. Fabry, R.S. "Capability Based Addressing". *Communications ACM*, 17, 7, July 1974

9. Goos, G., Persch, G. and Uhl, J. "Programmiermethodik mit Ada". Springer-Verlag, Berlin, 1987

10. Gray, J. "Notes on Database Operating Systems". In *Operating Systems: An advanced course* (Eds Bayer, Graham, Seegmüller), Springer, New York, 1978

11. Jones, A. "The Narrowing Gap Between Language Systems and Operating Systems". IFIP *Information Processing 77*, (Edt B.Gilchrist), North-Holland Publishing Company, 1977

12. Lampson, B., Horning, J., London, R., Mitchell, J. and Popek, G. "Report on the Programming Language Euclid". CSL-81-12; XEROX PARC, CA, 1981

13. Linden, T.A. "Operating System Structures to Support Security and Reliable Software". *ACM Computing Surveys*, 8, 4, December 1976

14. Liskov, B., Snyder, A., Atkinson, R. and Schaffert, C. "Abstraction Mechanisms in CLU". *Communications ACM* 20, 8, August 1977

15. Mayer-Wegener, K. "Functional and implementational aspects of transaction-processing monitors". Internal Report 121/85, FB Informatik, Univ. Kaiserslautern, January 1985

16. Pollack, F. and Kahn, K. "The BiiN Mission Critical Computer Architecture". 1989 Workshop on *Operating Systems for Mission Critical Computing*, September 19-21, 1989

17. Shaw, M. and Wulf, W. "Toward Relaxing Assumptions in Languages and Their Implementations". CMU-CS-80-100, Carnegie Mellon University, Pittsburgh, PA, 1980

18. Strom, R. "A Comparison of the Object-Oriented and Process Paradigms". *Object -Oriented Programming Workshop*. In: *ACM SIGPLAN Notices*, 21, 10, 1986

19. Stroustrup, B. "The C++ Programming Language". Addison-Wesley, Reading, MA, 1986

20. "IT-Sicherheitskriterien". Zentralstelle für Sicherheit in der Informationstechnik (ZSI), Bundesanzeiger, 1989

Part V

Fault Tolerant Systems

PUMA - A Capability-Based Architecture to Support Security and Fault Tolerance

Carsten Vogt

Forschungsinstitut für Funk und Mathematik (FFM)

ABSTRACT

In this paper, we give an overview of the PUMA system, a fault-sensitive, object-based computer architecture. The primary goal in designing PUMA was to
build up a system in which hard- and software errors are either avoided before-
hand or definitely detected and corrected. Additionally, PUMA is intended to
overcome some drawbacks of the von Neumann approach and to provide a basis
for the efficient implementation of high-level languages.

We describe PUMA's object and process concept and sketch the architectural
design of the processor. Moreover, the implementation of object-oriented languages and the structure of the storage hierarchy are discussed.

1. INTRODUCTION

As the power of computer hardware is continuously growing, one aim of computer design is to
migrate basic functions from software to hardware, thus achieving safer and more efficient systems. Among other things, this approach can be employed to implement an object system directly in hardware, as e.g. in the REKURSIV [6], the PROFEMO [9] or the iAPX 432 [1]
systems. One architecture of this type is PUMA [4, 7], which was designed with the following
goals:

- Avoidance, detection and correction of a large class of hard- and software faults

- Overcoming of some weaknesses of conventional computers

- Support of the implementation of high-level languages

- Acceptable performance

These goals are reached by the following approach: PUMA has a *fault-sensitive hardware*,
which is able to detect all 1-bit-errors and to correct most of them. This is achieved by the comprehensive use of parity checking, circuitry duplication and hamming codes. A *service processor* can read all relevant system data, analyze the faults and restart the system after fault
correction.

The PUMA architecture is based on an *object concept* enforcing data and code modularity and
security by hardware: The processor abstracts from the linear, homogeneous storage of conventional computers and works on a set of typed objects instead that can only be accessed via pro-

INDEX or RINDEX 20 Bits	FIXIND	free	D	U	ETYPE	OTYPE	PROT	S	free	UID	INCR or WINDEX	OBJL	BASE
20 Bits	1	1	1	1	4	4	3	1	4	20	20	20	20

Figure 1: The structure of an object descriptor

tected *object descriptors*. Among the object types implemented, especially buffers (PUMA = Puffermaschine = buffer machine) play an important role in various applications.

Objects can be supplied with *exception handlers*: These procedures, which are automatically called when an error is raised during an object access, are a flexible means for reacting upon software faults. Besides error handling, this concept supports an efficient style of programming on the assembler level (e.g. an event-driven control) and the implementation of high-level languages.

Moreover, a *multiprocessing concept* is realized on PUMA's hardware level by a simple task attraction mechanism: Descriptors for all active processes are stored in a *process descriptor buffer*. The processor sweeps this buffer cyclically, on each turn executing a single instruction per process.

In this article, we give a survey of PUMA's fundamental operation principles and then discuss some fields of special interest within the PUMA project: We will sketch the processor's hardware structure and then describe its storage hierarchy and a scheme for the implementation of object-oriented languages.

2. THE OBJECT CONCEPT

All data and code in the PUMA system are contained in typed *objects*, which can be dynamically created and deleted. Objects are represented by sequences of 80-bit words of *main memory*. An object consists of a *header* storing the descriptions of its exception handlers plus some other information and a *body* with its entries. Object descriptors in a special 120-bit wide *descriptor storage*, which is implemented separately from main memory, are used to identify and access the objects. Their general form is shown by Fig. 1.

2.1. Object types

Object descriptors are extended capabilities [3]: A descriptor contains address and protection information of an object and additionally determines its type, which is composed of *object type* (OTYPE) and *element type* (ETYPE). OTYPE specifies the structure of the object and its access operations: There are scalar, linear (= array) and cyclic objects and, moreover, buffers and stacks. ETYPE characterizes the contents of the object, which can be integers and reals of different degrees of precision, booleans, code, object descriptors and process descriptors.

As in capabilities, the three protection bits PROT identify the operations that can be performed on the object with this descriptor.

2.2. Addressing mechanisms

The remaining descriptor entries are used by PUMA's addressing mechanism, which is implemented by the hardware functions of the *address generator* (see also Fig. 4): UID uniquely identifies the object the descriptor points to. The S-bit tells whether the object is currently on secondary storage; if not, BASE gives its base address in main memory and OBJL its length.

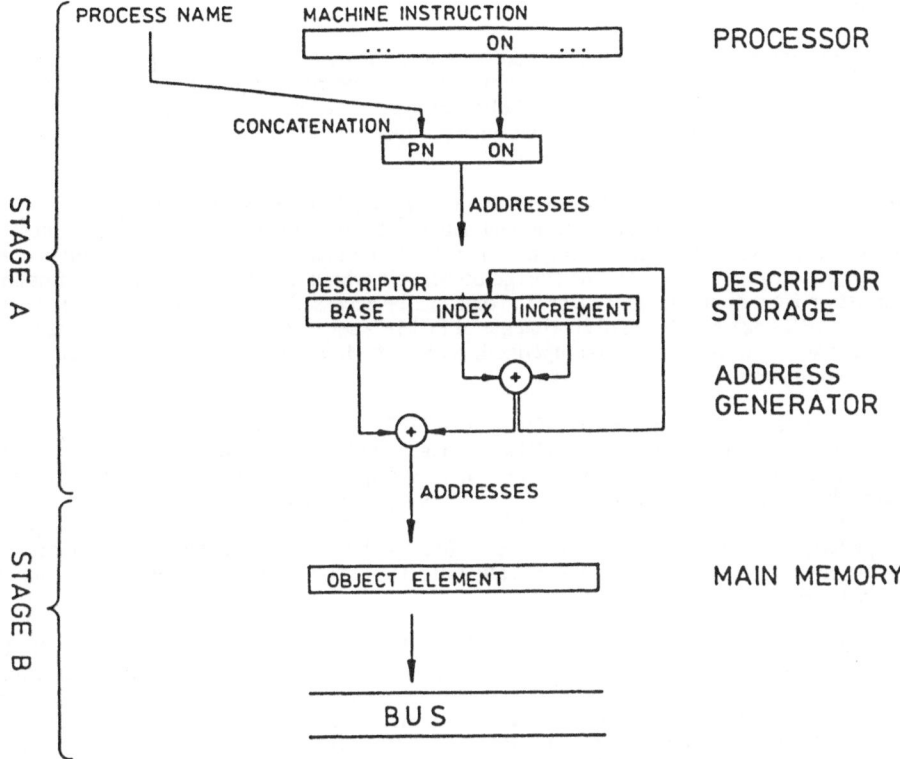

Figure 2: The scheme for object addressing

Additionally, there are dirty and use bits D and U employed by storage management.

BASE, INDEX and INCR are input parameters to the *address computation* procedure executed in the first step (stage A) of every access to main memory (see the centre of Fig. 2): INDEX is an offset into the object that determines the element to be read or written next. Prior to each access, INDEX is automatically incremented by INCR; the result is written back to the descriptor's INDEX component and simultaneously added to BASE yielding the address of a memory cell. This address is used in stage B to read or write the requested object entry.

This addressing mechanism has the following advantages:

• All addressing information is directly attached to the objects - it need not be collected from registers or main memory tables, as e.g. in the iAPX 432.

• INDEX, which stores the offset of the last access, is automatically recalled when the object is used for the next time. Together with the autoincrement technique, this allows stepping through linear data and code objects without explicitly computing and saving array indices. Especially, INDEX serves as an implicit instruction counter, as will be explained in section 3.

• The correct use of stacks and buffers is guaranteed: For a stack, INDEX always points to its top because its value is automatically incremented by 1 in read and decremented by 1 in write operations. Buffers are analogously realized with a pair of read and write indices, which are cyclically incremented.

Besides the address computations, the address generator performs *access control operations*: First of all, it checks whether the access is permitted as specified by the protection bits PROT and whether ETYPE conforms with the element type expected by the machine instruction. Moreover, it tests whether INDEX lies within its proper bounds. If not, an exception is raised - see below.

Hence, PUMA implements its object and element types directly in hardware: Primitive object types need not be simulated by software and data and code structures are efficiently protected from violation. As all information required for checks and address generation is contained in descriptor storage, PUMA eases the storage bottleneck, which results from reading addressing information from main memory before the data can be accessed (this is, for example, the case with the iAPX 432). Finally, as the two stages of PUMA's addressing scheme use separate hardware, the access to storage can be pipelined, such that addressing and control operations are performed in parallel to data operations.

Machine instructions address objects not by their UIDs (as e.g. in REKURSIV) but by *object names*. As Fig. 2 shows, these names ON are concatenated with the name of the executing process PN, thus yielding the address of a descriptor storage cell containing a descriptor for the object. Hence, the descriptors owned by the various processes are effectively separated from each others - the same object name used by different processes results in different descriptor storage locations. As descriptors can be copied (except those for buffers and stacks) and freely distributed among processes (i.e. dynamically bound to different object names), the sharing of objects is easy.

Because the capacity of descriptor storage is limited (currently 64 K), descriptors can also be stored in objects with element type "object descriptor". However, only descriptors in descriptor storage can be used to access objects as only these are bound to names. There are machine instructions to move descriptors between descriptor storage and main memory, i.e. to alter dynamically the binding between objects and names. Among other things, this mechanism can be employed to implement the principles of object-oriented programming - see section 5.

2.3. Exception handling

Headers of structured objects contain descriptors of *exception handlers* - code objects that are called when an exception condition is raised by the address generator. After a successful completion of the fault handling, execution can be continued by repeating the faulting instruction. The handlers are freely programmed and individually attached to the objects. This assignment can be dynamically modified such that an object may have different handlers in different applications.

The exception mechanism supports a scheme for *event-driven control* that is applicable far beyond plain fault-handling: Sequential code, for example, is stored in linear objects that are traversed with INDEX serving as an implicit program counter. Here, the exception "upper bound exceeded" triggers the return to the calling object. Cyclic objects, whose INDEX is reset to 1 when reaching the upper bound, are used to implement loops, whose exit conditions are determined by associated data objects: For example, a loop might have to read data from a buffer until the buffer is empty. Here, the handler for the exception "buffer empty" can jump back to the code object that called the loop - no explicit check of an exit condition is required.

A further example program illustrating the advantages of this approach is given in [7]: Here, the inner product of two vectors is computed by a loop that consists only of the two arithmetic instructions MULT and SUM - all address and control operations are implicitly performed by the address generator.

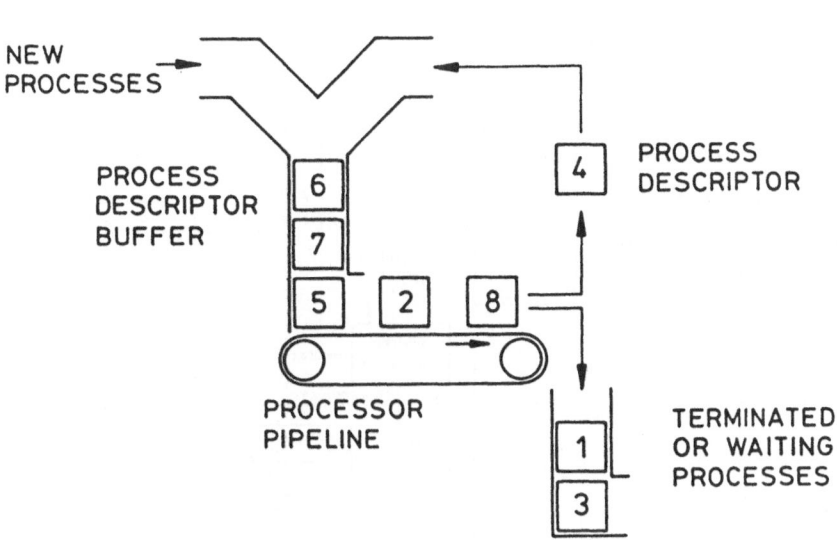

Figure 3: Execution of processes by means of task attraction

3. THE PROCESS CONCEPT

Processes are the active components on PUMA's machine level - programs executed in environments consisting of objects. They are - in analogy to objects - defined by *process descriptors* PD.

First of all, a PD contains a unique process identifier, PNAME, selecting the descriptor storage section where the object descriptors of this process are stored (remember Fig. 2) and thus defining the current environment of the process. Furthermore, the PD holds the name of the code object, ONAME, the process is currently executing. Instructions are read from this object in exactly the same way as data from a data object (Fig. 2). Hence, no hardware program counter register is required - the counter is always stored in the INDEX of the code object and automatically incremented by the address generator. Subprograms are called by stacking ONAME and replacing it with the name of the called code object.

The remaining entries of the PD serve accounting and exception handling purposes, e.g. recording the fault condition and the name of the faulting object.

Hence, a process is completely characterized by its descriptor. It does not need any registers with permanent contents, because all PUMA instructions are memory-to-memory operations and the program counter is stored in an object descriptor. Moreover, descriptor storage is divided into partitions simultaneously holding object descriptors for all processes. Therefore, a process switch requires only an exchange of two PDs which can be done very fast. This is the basis for PUMA's task attraction mechanism (see Fig. 3):

PDs of the currently active processes are contained in a special *Process Descriptor Buffer* (PDB) that is represented in main memory as all objects. To execute a machine operation, the PUMA processor firstly reads a PD from PDB, thus obtaining all information necessary to fetch the next instruction of this process. After its execution, the updated PD is written back to PDB. As there are no register contents to be saved, the processor is immediately ready to fetch the next instruction of the next process in the queue.

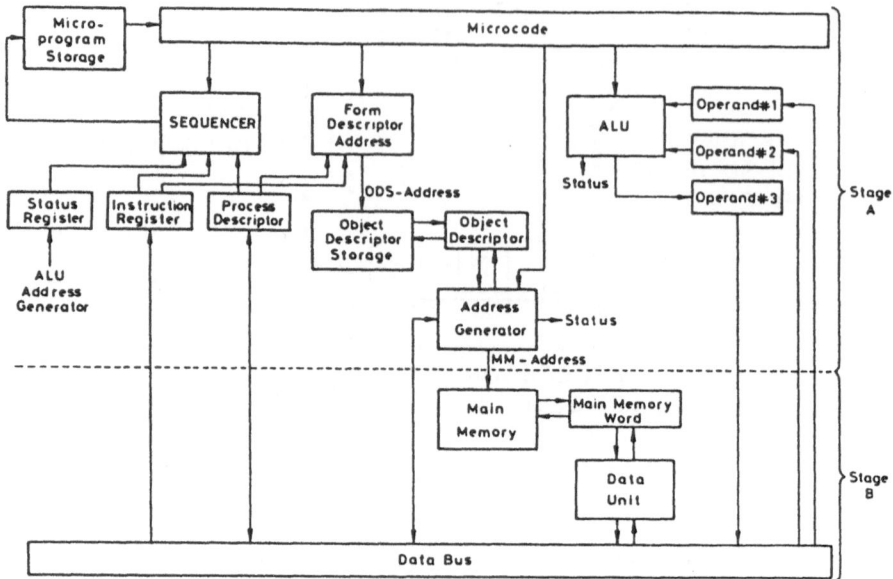

Figure 4: The structure of the PUMA architecture

This approach implements a fine-grained *multiprogramming scheme* directly on machine level, facilitates process switching and scheduling and makes fault analysis and recovery easier. Of course, these advantages are faced by the overhead of the two PDB accesses with each instruction. However, it is possible to pipeline the execution of instructions keeping the throughput of the machine high.

As can be seen, the support of buffers by hardware is essential for the implementation of PUMA's process concept. Other applications of buffers in this field lie for example in the buffered communication of data between processes or in the realization of process queues required by semaphores or other synchronization mechanisms. In all these cases, the scheme for handling "buffer full" and "buffer empty" exceptions can be efficiently used.

4. PUMA'S OVERALL STRUCTURE AND CURRENT ASPECTS OF INTEREST

The basic concepts described in the preceding sections can be realized by the architecture illustrated by Fig. 4. This microprogrammed structure is divided into three parts:

- *Sequencer* and *Micro Program Storage* control the execution of machine instructions. They depend on three registers, containing the current process descriptor, the instruction to be executed and the status, where errors detected by ALU or address generator are recorded.

- The path for memory accesses is made up of *Object Descriptor Storage*, *Address Generator*, *Main Memory* and *Data Unit*. The Data Unit packs and unpacks 80-bit memory words, which can contain one or more object elements, and transfers them from or to the 80-bit wide *Data Bus*. The other units implement PUMA's object concept, as explained in section 2.

• The ALU with its two input and one output register performs all data operations.

As mentioned above, the processor has only registers with temporary contents to cache the information necessary to execute an instruction. These registers do not hold any valid data between the instructions - this is solely done by main memory whose 7-bit hamming code allows error correction in case of a transient fault and the subsequent restart of the system. An external *service processor* can read and write all registers and memory cells and can control critical clock cycles.

All registers are implemented twice in order to realize the two-staged process pipeline proposed in section 2: They can hold information about the two processes that are alternatingly active in the system components corresponding to stages A and B in Figs. 2 and 4.

On hardware level, all units are designed to detect all possible 1-bit errors in any 8-bit data group: For example, each group of 8-bit lines is extended by a parity bit that is automatically computed and checked, and each memory word has a hamming code extension that allows the correction of 1-bit faults. As a faulty control signal must not affect more than one bit within an 8-bit byte (in order to prevent 1-bit errors from spreading to all eight bits, which cannot be recognized by a single parity bit), signals for the individual bits of this byte are generated separately, resulting in nine signals for the eight slices plus the parity bit.

One of the current topics of the PUMA project is to realize these concepts in a *VLSI circuitry*. Other topics of interest are:

• The design of a software *simulation and programming system* running on a window-based SUN workstation. This package, which is operating by now, is intended for the syntax-directed writing of PUMA programs and the subsequent testing, debugging and interpretive execution.

• The implementation of *high-level languages*. By now, we have a PASCAL compiler generating optimized PUMA code [5]. In order to exploit specific PUMA characteristics, the language concepts of PASCAL have been extended by several new constructs. One example for this is a modified FOR-statement that uses implicitly an array index as a loop counter.
Another approach is concerned with dataflow languages: The actions of a dataflow program are modelled by separate processes that communicate via buffers. The buffer exceptions can be used for process synchronization - an action stops firing (i.e. the corresponding process is deactivated) when its input buffer is empty. The single-assignment rule is implemented by the dynamic creation and deletion of data objects that are written only once.
Object-oriented programming will be treated below in greater detail.

• The design and implementation of the operating system. This includes concepts for process scheduling, I/O and storage management. Of these points, the storage hierarchy is outlined in section 6.

5. COMPOSITE OBJECTS AND OBJECT-ORIENTED PROGRAMMING

PUMA's object and type system is implemented entirely in the hardware of the address generator. Because this generator is not programmable, new object types can be introduced only by software simulation. In the following, an appropriate scheme is sketched for realizing and protecting complex object and type structures and thus implementing the basic concepts of OOP.

The term *object-oriented programming (OOP)* is commonly understood to include the principles of data abstraction, abstract data types and type inheritance [11, 14]: The contents of an object must be "hidden", i.e. must be only accessible by operations explicitly defined for this object. Moreover, objects are typed and the collection of types is structured by the method of

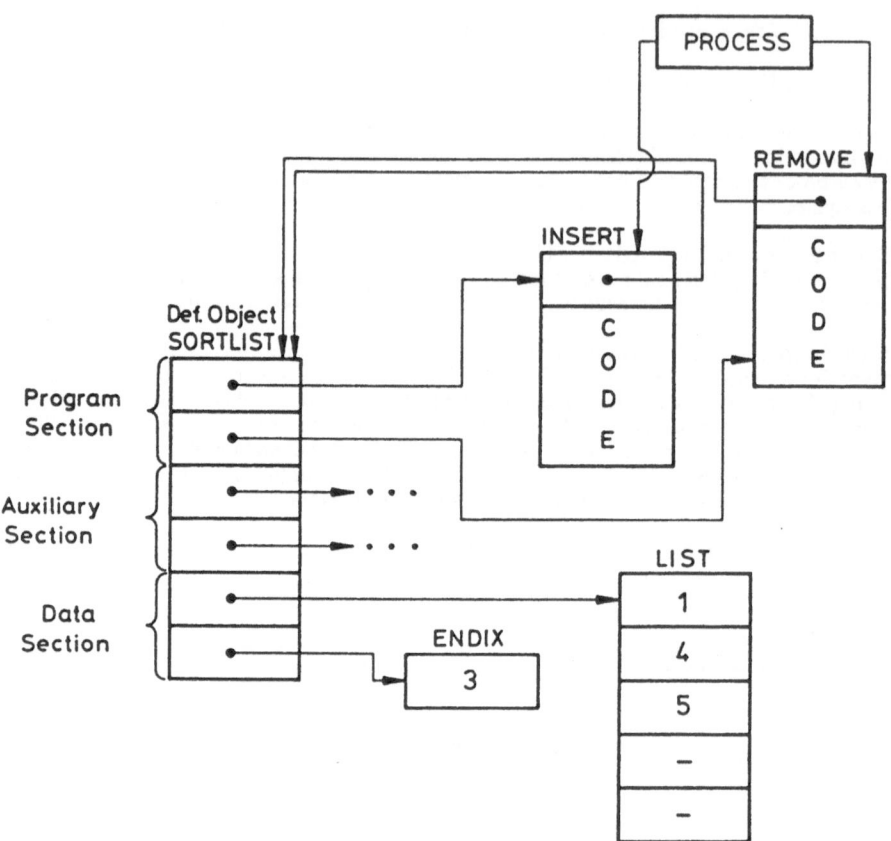

Figure 5: A composite object representing an ordered list

inheritance.

Hence, first of all a scheme is needed to construct *composite objects* (CO's) consisting of data and operations of arbitrary complexity and to protect them from illegal use. This has to be based on PUMA's primitive object and type system. As the PUMA hardware supports capabilities and array types, a solution similar to the classical segment table schemes [3] is applicable:

CO's are realized as collections of *primitive objects* - objects whose types are implemented in the address generator. Primitive *data objects* store the data of the CO and *code objects* contain the code for its access functions. The set of code objects is subdivided into *program objects* and *auxiliary objects*: Program objects describe the access functions that can be called from outside the CO whereas auxiliary objects can only be called within program or other auxiliary objects.

Descriptors for all these component objects are collected in a linear object of element type "object descriptor", called the *defining object* (DO) of the CO. Corresponding to the three classes of primitive objects, the DO is divided into a *program*, an *auxiliary* and a *data section*.

The example in Fig. 5 shows the representation of an ordered list, whose INSERT operation writes an element to the list with respect to the linear order and whose REMOVE operation reads the first entry. The list elements themselves are contained in the linear object LIST and

ENDIX holds the index of the last valid LIST entry.

Using this scheme, it has to be ensured that the data of a CO can be manipulated only by execution of one of its access functions. Hence, a process must not be able to move descriptors from the DO's auxiliary or data sections to descriptor storage when it is active outside the CO, for otherwise it could access these objects in a prohibited way. On the other hand, inside an access function the process must be able to make these moves in order to make the data accessible.

To solve this problem, an *object manager process* is introduced, which creates CO's, keeps the descriptors for their DO's and passes only descriptors for some or all of their program objects to user processes (see Fig. 5). The processes can use these descriptors only to call the code, as their protection bits are accordingly set. In order to make the auxiliary and data sections of the DO accessible, a program object stores a descriptor for the DO in its header. There exists a special machine instruction that reads this descriptor from the header of the code object currently being executed (other accesses to this position are not possible) and brings it to some descriptor storage location. From there, it can be employed to read the DO and thus to bind descriptors of data and auxiliary objects to object names.

This mechanism secures the required inaccessibility of the DO entries by hardware. However, before returning to the caller the access functions themselves must destroy all descriptors that have been moved out of the DO such that no further accesses are possible.

The generalization of this scheme to the definition of types is straightforward: Here, a composite *type-defining object* (TDO) contains templates for the components of a structured object. From this description, the function "Create Instantiation" (which is the only access function of the TDO) creates a composite object of this type. The concept of *inheritance* can be realized by the logical concatenation of several TDO's.

6. STORAGE MANAGEMENT

Designing PUMA's storage hierarchy, we had to take account of the fact that PUMA is an inherently segmented system with many relatively small objects and a high frequency of object generation and deletion operations.

Free storage management: Because of this high fluctuation, storage must be allocated and deallocated quickly, possibly by a single machine instruction - a demand not satisfied by any of the classical algorithms. Therefore, PUMA's free storage management uses a newly developed method [13], which is based on a set of *free storage buffers* $P_0, P_1,..., P_n$. P_i contains the descriptors for all free storage areas of length 2^i; descriptors are read and written from and to the buffers in the same way as in the buddy system [8], but normally no free areas are recombined when storage is deallocated. As the object type "buffer" is realized in hardware, storage can hence be (de)allocated in a single machine cycle - at least in the normal case. Processes access the buffers themselves - thus, the (de)allocation of storage normally does not require the call of system services.

However, there are the exception conditions "buffer full/empty" that trigger the execution of an exception handler. This handler splits and merges free areas and relocates objects in order to adjust the set of storage descriptors to the current demands. It is controlled by a set of *lower* and *upper buffer bounds* l_i and u_i bounding the resulting number of descriptors in each P_i from below and above. By this, after the execution of the handler there is not only one free position or one new descriptor in the faulting buffer P_i, respectively, but additional room for the subsequent (de)allocations - thus the next exception does not happen too soon afterwards.

Storage hierarchy: As PUMA is a markedly segmented system and, moreover, there is no spatial locality in programs (because of the unordered contents of the free storage buffers), a plain paging approach is of no great use. On the other hand, a purely segmented scheme runs into

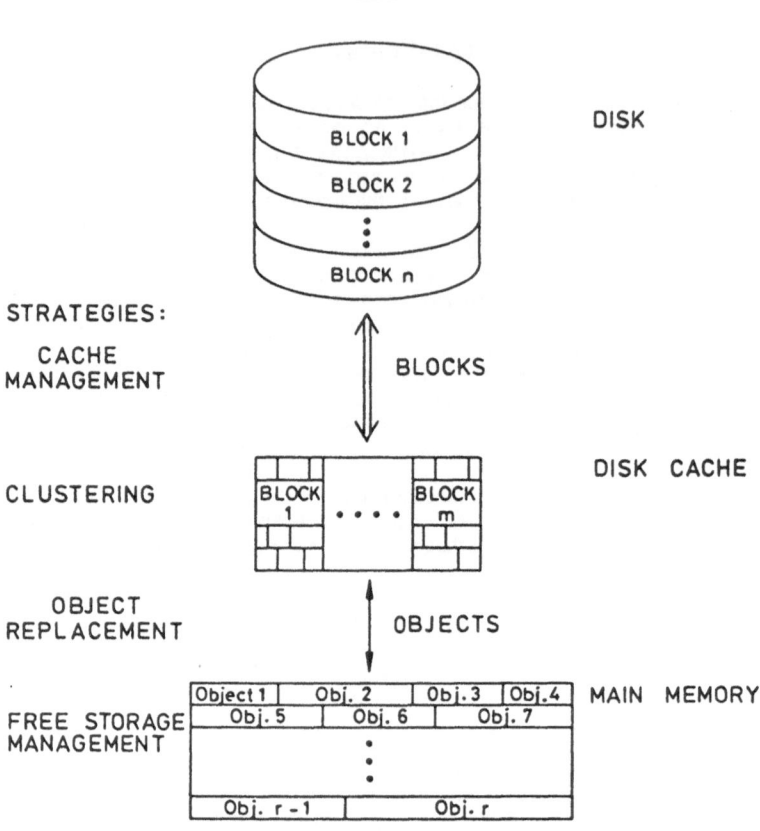

Figure 6: The storage hierarchy of PUMA

difficulties with a block-oriented secondary storage. Therefore, PUMA's storage hierarchy consists of the three stages (see Fig. 6) already suggested by Denning [2]:

Between *main memory* and *disk*, we put a so-called *disk cache* cooperating with main memory by transporting objects of various sizes and with the disk by moving disk blocks of a constant length. Hence, the disk cache is sort of an adapter having a memory of its own to store a number of blocks and working in parallel to the PUMA processor. On the one hand, its tasks are to cluster objects to blocks and to move them to the disk, and on the other hand to fetch blocks from the disk and to extract the objects demanded by the processor. Doing this, the cache should always hold the blocks that are currently mostly needed in order to reduce the access time gap between main memory and secondary storage.

Strategies: Several strategies are required for the management of such a configuration: Objects must be loaded into and removed from main memory, they must be clustered to blocks and blocks must be moved between cache and disk. Here, one could refer to classical algorithms (e.g. LRU, Working Set), but they alone will probably not suit the needs of this highly segmented system. Therefore, we supplemented these strategies by exploiting information about the current inter-object relationships, expressed by the positions of the object descriptors. For example, it is useful to cluster those objects that contain descriptors for each others (remember section 5.). Moreover, the relocation decision can be based on a collection of reference counters that specify the number of descriptors for each object in descriptor storage, main memory and secondary storage - these counters carry information about the "distance" of an object to descriptor storage and thus allow to estimate the time that will pass until the object is used next.

To evaluate the performance of these concepts, one can employ *optimal strategies* - e.g. VMIN [10] - whose performance values serve as lower bounds (and thus as a standard of comparison) to the values monitored in the real system. For this, we developed a scheme that helps to extend well-known optimal strategies for two-staged hierarchies to storage configurations with multiple stages [12].

7. SUMMARY

The principal aim of the PUMA project was to design a computer with comprehensive fault tolerance features. This resulted in a system that is able to detect and analyze all one-bit-errors and to correct most of them. PUMA's architecture, which is based on this secure hardware, is organized around an object concept implemented by hardware functions and enforcing data and code security and modularity. As most of the basic addressing and control operations are done by fast hardware and, moreover, can be performed in parallel to data operations, PUMA can be programmed efficiently. These characteristics and, additionally, the flexible exception handling scheme and the multiprocessing concept on PUMA's machine level support the implementation of high-level languages.

The PUMA system is currently being realized in hardware by a VLSI structure and in software by a simulation and programming system. Studies on some special topics are going on - besides programming languages they predominantly concern the implementation and evaluation of the operating system.

ACKNOWLEDGEMENTS

The fundamental work on the PUMA architecture was done by K. von der Heide, University of Hamburg. It is now being continued and extended together with a working group at FFM consisting of R. Ackermann, W.J. Grünewald, W. Jansen, C. Kirchner (from whom Fig. 3 was adopted), L. Rössing, U. Skupin and the author.

REFERENCES

1. Colwell, R. P., Gehringer, E. J. and Jensen, E. D. "Performance Aspects of Architectural Complexity in the Intel 432". *ACM Transactions on Computer Systems*, 6, 3, August 1988, pp. 297-339

2. Denning, P. J. "Working sets past and present". *IEEE Transactions on Software Engineering*, 6, 1, January 1980, pp. 64-84

3. Fabry, R. S. "Capability-based Addressing". *CACM*, 17, 7, July 1974, pp. 403-411

4. v. d. Heide, K., Kirchner, C., Skupin, U. and Vogt, C. "Die Puffermaschine: Entwurf und Realisierung einer fehlertoleranten, objektorientierten Rechnerarchitektur". Research Reports Nos. 387 / 391, Forschungsinstitut für Funk und Mathematik (FFM), D-5307 Wachtberg-Werthhoven, West Germany, December 1988/ May 1989

5. Grünewald, W. "PASCAL für die Puffermaschine". Research Report No. 397, Forschungsinstitut für Funk und Mathematik (FFM), D-5307 Wachtberg-Werthhoven, West Germany, March 1990

6. Harland, D. M. and Beloff, B. "OBJEKT - A Persistent Object Store With An Integrated Garbage Collector". *ACM SIGPLAN Notices*, 22, 4, April 1987, pp. 70-79

7. v. d. Heide, K. "A General Purpose Pipelined Ring Architecture". In *Proc. CONPAR 86, Lecture Notes in Computer Science*, 237, Springer-Verlag, 1986, pp.198-205

8. Knuth, D. E. "The Art Of Computer Programming, Vol. 1: Fundamental Algorithms". Addison-Wesley, Reading (Mass.), 1968

9. Nett, E., Großpietsch, K., Jungblut, A., Kaiser, J., Kröger, R., Lux, W., Speicher, M. and Winnebeck, H. "PROFEMO - Design and Implementation of a Fault Tolerant Distributed System Architecture". *GMD-Studien* Nr. 100, GMD, D-5205 St. Augustin, June 1985

10. Prieve, B. G. and Fabry, R. S. "VMIN - An Optimal Variable Space Page Replacement Algorithm". *CACM*, 19, 5, May 1976, pp. 295-297

11. Stroustrup, B. "What is 'Object-oriented Programming'?". In *Proc. ECOOP'87*, BIGRE + GLOBULE, 54, Rennes, France, June 1987, pp. 57-76

12. Vogt, C. "A new approach to optimal cache scheduling". *Information Processing Letters*, 30, 6, March 1989, pp. 303-310

13. Vogt, C. "A buffer-based method for storage allocation in an object-oriented system". *IEEE Transactions on Computers*, 39, 3, March 1990, pp. 375-383

14. Wegner, P. "Classification in object-oriented systems". *ACM SIGPLAN Notices*, 21, 10, October 1986, pp. 173-182

Stability in a Persistent Store Based on a Large Virtual Memory

John Rosenberg and Frans Henskens
University of Newcastle

Fred Brown, Ron Morrison and David Munro
University of St Andrews

ABSTRACT

Persistent systems support mechanisms which allow programs to create and manipulate arbitrary data structures which outlive the execution of the program which created them. A persistent store supports mechanisms for the storage and retrieval of objects in a uniform manner regardless of their lifetime. Since all data of the system is in this repository it is important that it always be in a consistent state. This property is called integrity. The integrity of the persistent store depends in part on the store being resilient to failures. That is, when an error occurs the store can recover to a previously recorded consistent state. The mechanism for recording this state and performing recovery is called stability. This paper considers an implementation of a persistent store based on a large virtual memory and shows how stability is achieved.

1. INTRODUCTION

Persistent systems support mechanisms which allow programs to create and manipulate arbitrary data structures which outlive the execution of the program which created them [6]. This has many advantages from both a software engineering and an efficiency viewpoint. In particular it removes the necessity for the programmer to *flatten* data structures in order to store them permanently. Such code for the conversion of data between an internal and external format has been claimed to typically constitute approximately thirty percent of most application systems [6]. In this sense a persistent system provides an alternative to a conventional file system for the storage of permanent data. This alternative is far more flexible in that both the data and its interrelationships can be stored in its original form. In order to achieve this a uniform storage abstraction is required. Such an abstraction is often called a *persistent store*. A persistent store supports mechanisms for the storage and retrieval of objects and their interrelationships in a uniform manner regardless of their lifetime.

Since all data of the system resides in the persistent store it is important that the integrity of the store be guaranteed, particularly after a system crash or hardware failure. The system must guarantee that, following a failure, the persistent store always returns to a consistent state as at some previous checkpoint. A store with this property is said to exhibit stability. We exclude here the question of total media failure which is a separate issue best handled by a backup or dumping strategy. This requirement for a recovery mechanism is not peculiar to persistent systems. The same problem occurs with conventional file systems. For example UNIX provides limited recovery features. However, the problem is perhaps more acute with persistent systems. In a conventional file system each file is essentially an independent object. A loss of a single file following a crash is usually not a major problem. In a persistent system there may be arbitrary cross references between objects and thus a loss of an object can result in dangling references to the lost object. This may well compromise the integrity of the store. In this sense the problem of recovery within a persistent store is much more closely related to recovery in database systems [3].

A number of proposals for stable persistent stores have already appeared in the literature. The earliest of these [17] was oriented towards recovery in database systems and developed a new technique known as *shadow paging*. Many of the later systems are based on this technique [10, 23, 24, 25]. Several of these designs envisaged the use of hardware support which simplifies the implementation of shadow paging and results in a more efficient system [24, 25]. Ross [23] also implements shadow paging but utilises the facilities of VAX/VMS memory mapped files. Similarly, a system based on memory mapped files under SunOS 4 has been developed by Brown [10]. A different method of enquiry which is based on non-paged object mapping has been developed in other systems [5, 7, 9, 14].

In this paper we describe a stable persistent store based on a very large virtual memory. The implementation of this store is based on the MONADS-PC computer system [19], which has hardware support for large virtual address translation. We begin by describing the general principles of shadow paging as a technique for implementing stability. We then describe a previous implementation of the MONADS store without the recovery features. This is followed by a description of the implementation of shadow paging for MONADS-PC. It is shown that, given appropriate hardware, it is possible to implement a recovery scheme which minimises disk space overhead and allows considerable flexibility in maintaining consistency between multiple stores.

2. SHADOW PAGING - THE BASIC MECHANISM

Stability requires that the persistent store evolves from one consistent state to another atomically. That is, in the event of a system failure, all the changes are either recorded or the system recovers to the previous stable state. A number of techniques have been developed for achieving stability, particularly in the context of database management systems [5, 7, 9, 10, 14, 17, 23, 24, 25]. The techniques differ in their efficiency with regard to the particular application area. However, there are two basic requirements. They are:

(a)   the ability to perform an atomic update operation, and

(b)   the ability to identify the old data and new data prior to the stabilise operation.

2.1 Atomic Update - Challis' Algorithm

In order to explain how atomic update may be implemented we will assume the following:

(a)   There exists a mapping table from virtual persistent store addresses to physical disk addresses. Such an address map is required in systems where the virtual address space is not mapped in 1-to-1 correspondence with the physical address space. All the data in the system can be found using this mapping table.

(b)   On system start up and after each stabilise operation a new copy of the mapping table and the data is made. Updates are made to these copies. That is, the old data is never overwritten. Such a system is unrealistic since the copy operation is too expensive but it

231

will serve as a model for explaining atomic update. We will return to an efficient implementation later.

Prior to a stabilise operation there are two sets of mapping tables and data - the new updated one and the one representing the state of the system at the previous checkpoint.

Challis' algorithm [11] uses two fixed blocks with known disk addresses that usually record the two previous stabilised states of the system. These are known as the root blocks. The root blocks contain information that allows the system to find the mapping table for a stabilised state. Figure 1 illustrates the state of the system prior to the n+1th stabilise operation. The root blocks record the two previous stabilised states n-1 and n.

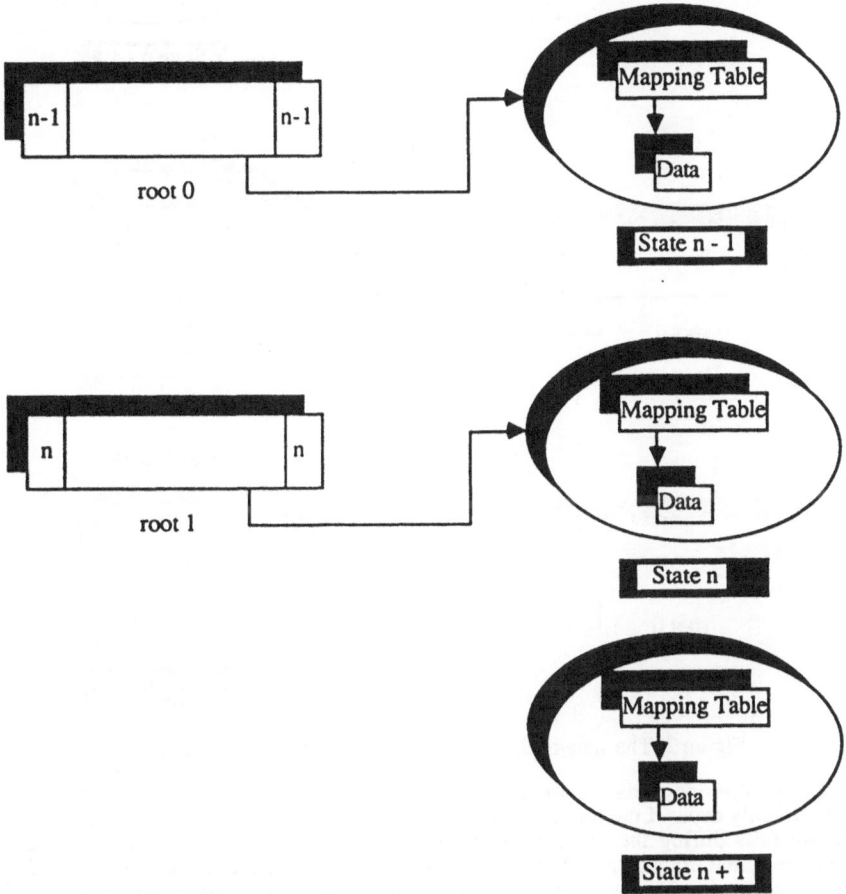

Figure 1: The state of the system prior to the n+1th stabilise operation

Each root block also contains a version number that enables the system to determine which contains the most recent state. This version number is written twice as the first and last word of the block.

The atomic update operation entails overwriting the root with oldest version number, in this case n-1, with a new version number, n+1, and a pointer to the new updated mapping table. The space occupied by the old stabilised state n-1 may now be reused. This is illustrated in Figure 2.

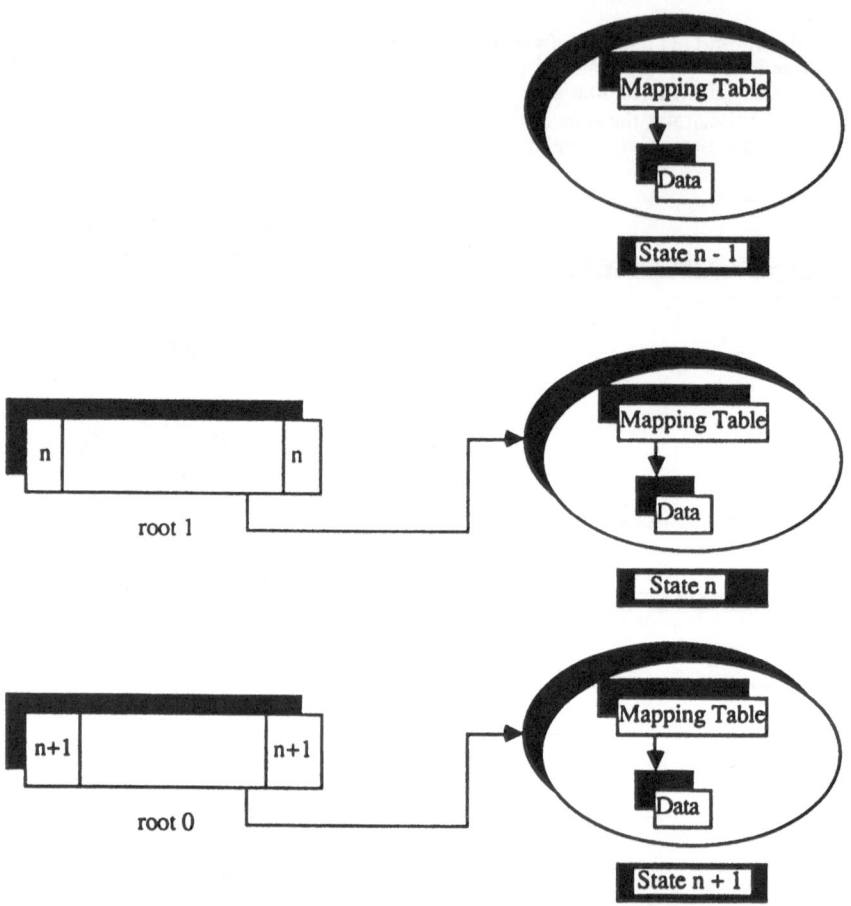

Figure 2: The state of the system after the n+1th stabilise operation

Challis' algorithm depends upon two critical points for safety. Firstly an error in an atomic update can only occur if the root block is written incorrectly. It is expected that if a disk write operation fails during the atomic update it will inform the system which can then take appropriate action immediately. If, however, the failure is more serious, the technique depends upon the version numbers at the start and end of the root block being different in order to detect failure.

On system startup the root blocks are inspected. If the version numbers are consistent within the root blocks, the most up-to-date version of the system can be found. If not, only one root block may have different version numbers at any one time unless a catastrophic failure has occurred, which in any case would have other implications for the integrity of the data. Thus, subject to the above proviso, the correct stable data can be identified.

Assuming that an atomic update can be performed by this mechanism we return to the question of making efficient copies of the data.

2.2 A Paged Persistent Store With Shadowing

In a paged persistent store, the virtual address space is split up into pages of a fixed size which may be stored in disk blocks and main memory page frames of the same size. Where the virtual address space is not mapped in 1-to-1 correspondence with the physical disk, a table is required to perform the mapping. We call this table the disk page table.

The system operates as a paged virtual store using a page replacement algorithm for moving pages in and out of main store. The essence of the shadow paging technique is to ensure that when a modified page is written back to disk from main store that it is never written to the place it was read from. Instead a copy of the page, called the shadow page, is used to store the contents of the page between stabilise operations. By this means, only pages that have been modified have shadow copies and the system evolves incrementally.

The mechanism works as follows. On system startup the disk page table is copied into main store. From this all the pages of the persistent store may be found. We will refer to the stable version of the disk page table as the stable disk page table and to the copy in main store as the transient disk page table. All disk mapping is now performed using the transient disk page table. When a modified page is written back to disk, a shadow page is created, if it does not already exist, and the transient disk page table is altered to record the virtual address to shadow address mapping. On subsequent use of this page, the shadow address, which is found in the transient disk page table, is used.

A stabilise operation involves ensuring that all modified data is written back to disk, writing of the transient page table to disk and then performing an atomic update of the root block as described above. System startup and restore after a failure can also be performed as described above.

In reality, the operation of shadow paging is more complicated since the system must keep track of the free space on disk, detect a write operation on a page in main store and determine when a shadow page has already been created to avoid a shadow being created on every modified page discard.

In the above system, there are two copies of the disk page table. One on disk in a stable state and one in main store. The disk page table may, however, be too large to be keep in main store and would in that case be stored in a transient area of disk. This causes difficulties in the disk mapping as there is now a transient disk area which has to be mapped in some manner and the disk area mapped by the disk page table.

A solution to the above is to incorporate the disk page table in the virtual address space itself. This means that the page table is paged and that updates to it create shadow copies. The advantage of this is that there is only one paging mechanism and that changes to all data, including the page table, is incremental. The only requirement for such an organisation to work is that the address of the first page of the disk page table must be held at a fixed location within the virtual address space.

Finally, since the free space list must also undergo atomic update it can also be kept in the virtual address space.

The advantage of shadow paging is that only the pages that are altered require shadow copies and that the shadow copies are created incrementally on demand. This should be much cheaper than copying the whole page table or database. The disadvantage is that the paging system has to be augmented. This is relatively cheap if performed at the design stage but may be quite difficult to retrofit to an existing system.

2.3   A More Detailed Account

We will now give a more detailed account of shadow paging by describing the total operation of the system.

As described in the previous section, the page table may be multi-level and is itself paged. The start address of the page table can always be found from the fixed position root block. In addition, the data contains a free space list for the disk. This must also be at an address known to the system within the logical address space. A shadow list is required to indicate that a shadow page has been created on disk and is being used. This list is not part of the virtual address space and is always considered transient. The final addition to the system is that each page frame requires a modified bit to indicate whether the corresponding page has been written on.

On system startup the information in the root block is brought into the main store. From this data all pages can be found on the disk. To evolve the system from one stable state to another efficiently, the technique makes changes incrementally, never overwriting the original data. Pages are only changed in main store and if they have been modified they are written out to a new disk block. Thus, updated pages, which may contain data, page tables or the free space list are duplicated incrementally, with the main store containing the volatile root of the updates. This volatile root will be different from the stable roots if any updates have been made.

There are six operations of the shadow paged store that concern us. They are:

(a)   Create a new page.

To create a new page on disk the free space list is used to find a suitable disk block. The free space list is updated. The new page table is then altered to record the disk address given from the free space list and that the virtual address now has a valid mapping. The shadow list is updated to indicate that further copies do not need to be made if this page is subsequently written on. This operation may be recursive as the extending of the page table or the free space list may also require other create operations.

(b)   Modify a page in main store.

The modify bit for the page frame is set when a page in main store is changed.

(c)   Page fault.

On a page fault the system uses the new page table to find the address of the page on disk. This will be the shadow address if the page has already been modified.

(d)   Page discard.

To discard a page from main store, the modify bit for the page frame is inspected. If it is clear the page frame can be overwritten without further action since a copy of the page exists on the disk. If not the shadow list is inspected. If a shadow exists the page can be written back to the address in the new page table which will be the shadow address. Otherwise a shadow page must be created. This involves finding a new disk block by using and updating the free space list and updating the page table to overwrite the entry for this virtual address. Again this may be recursive. The shadow list records the fact that a shadow has been created for this page to avoid further shadowing on subsequent replacement. The page may now be written back using the new page table. Finally the main store modify bit is cleared for this page frame which is now available for reuse.

(e)   Stabilise the persistent store.

To stabilise the persistent store, the system must first find all the pages in store that have been modified, since they have been altered but not yet written back to disk. If a shadow exists for these pages then they are written back immediately. Otherwise the system must create the shadow page as described above and write the page back to the shadow address given in the updated page table. An atomic update is then used to write the pointer to the new page table using the next system generated version number to the oldest root block. Finally, all modify bits in the main store and the shadow list are cleared. The system may now continue operation using the new version of the root.

The space occupied by the previous stable state can now be reused. This can be found by comparing the old and new page tables, performing a garbage collection to find the occupied disk blocks or by using a list of disk blocks which now have shadows that was constructed as the pages were altered.

(f)   Restore the persistent store.

To restart the persistent store the action is as described in atomic update above.

3. THE MONADS VIRTUAL MEMORY

The MONADS persistent store is based on a paged uniform virtual memory. The virtual memory utilises large addresses which, in the current implementation are 60 bits. All storage, both temporary, i.e. RAM, and permanent, i.e. disk, is accessed via this virtual memory. The large virtual memory is divided into regions, called *address spaces*, each of which is up to 2^{28} bytes in size. Thus a virtual address has two components, a 32 bit address space number and a 28 bit offset within address space[1]. The address spaces are paged, using a four kilobyte page size.

3.1 Higher Level Architecture

Since all data of the system resides within the virtual store it is necessary to restrict the manner in which programs may construct a virtual address, in order to be able to implement a security policy. There seem to be two possibilities for implementing such a system. The first is to restrict code generation to certain trusted programs such as compilers. This is the approach taken in systems such as Napier88 [18]. An alternative scheme, adopted in MONADS, is to support a higher level architecture which provides mechanisms which can be used by compilers to implement various protection protocols, but which themselves guarantee that the ability to generate code cannot violate the security of the system. The higher level architecture supports arbitrary sized segments. Segment boundaries are orthogonal to page boundaries and thus segments may be as small as a few bytes or as large as an address space [15]. Segments are addressed by *segment capabilities* which contain the start address and length of the segment, as well as some access information, e.g. read-only. Segments may themselves contain segment capabilities, so that it is possible to build arbitrary data structures.

---

[1] A new implementation of the MONADS architecture known as MONADS-MM [21] has a 32 bit offset within address space and a 96 bit address space number. The main reason for the increase in address space number size is related to support for a local area network [2] and is not relevant to this paper.

In order to control access to the virtual store, segment capabilities are protected in such a way that they cannot be constructed or modified by programs. A suite of system management instructions is provided for creating and manipulating segments, and thus segment capabilities, in a controlled manner. A normal program cannot generate an arbitrary virtual address, but is constrained to address only those segments for which it has a segment capability. The kernel, which amongst other things is responsible for managing the virtual store, is provided with mechanisms to allow it to manufacture an arbitrary segment capability when required.

Segments are grouped together into *modules*. Each module resides in a separate address space and has a purely procedural interface. Access to a module is controlled by a *module capability*, which identifies the address space containing the data of a module and the type of access allowed in the form of a list of procedures. Module capabilities are protected by the architecture so that it is not possible to manufacture or modify them. If a module is deleted, then the subsequent use of a module capability referring to it will cause an exception to be raised. The full details of the higher level architecture are described elsewhere [20] and are beyond the scope of this paper.

3.2 Management of the Store

The disk store is divided into areas called *volumes*. A volume may be an entire physical disk or a logical partition of a disk. Each volume has a unique number. All pages of a given address space are held on the same volume and the corresponding volume number is encoded as part of the address space number. The most significant 6 bits are used in the current implementation[2] as shown in figure 3. Each time a new address space is created on a volume it is given a new unique within volume address space number. The numbers of deleted address spaces are never re-used. This means that it is not necessary to garbage collect across the entire store in order to reclaim unused addresses. The size of the address space number ensures that the system will never run out of addresses. In addition there is no need to remove references to deleted address spaces, since the use of such a reference will cause an exception to be raised.

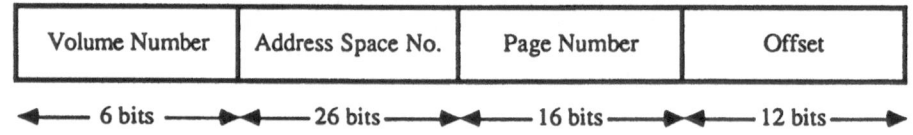

Figure 3: A MONADS virtual address

Access to a segment ultimately results in the generation of a virtual address. The data corresponding to that address may either be in memory or on disk, unless the address is invalid[3]. In conventional systems the page number portion of the address is used to index a page table which indicates whether the page is in memory or on disk and, in either case, indicates the address of the page as a disk block number or page frame address. This process is usually aided by an address translation buffer which caches recently used entries. The MONADS system uses a quite different technique which separates the task of translating virtual addresses for pages in memory from those for pages on disk. This is, in a sense, a return to the approach taken on the Atlas [16] and has many advantages in terms of efficiency and flexibility. These are discussed in [22].

---

[2] This is increased to 32 bits in MONADS-MM.
[3] At any point in time only some fraction of the virtual address space will be mapped to real store (either memory or disk). It is thus possible for an address to be generated which is invalid. This is most likely to happen if a deleted object is accessed since addresses are never re-used.

Translation of addresses for pages in main memory is achieved by the *address translation unit* (ATU). The ATU effectively simulates a very large associative memory and is implemented in dedicated fast memory as a hash table with imbedded overflow [1]. Similar schemes are described in [8, 13]. The hash table is large enough to hold an entry for every page frame of main memory. In fact it is several times larger to reduce the number of clashes. Thus the ATU, when given a virtual address, can either translate the address into a main memory address or indicate a page fault. The technique for maintaining the location of pages on disk is independent of the hardware and may even be different for separate address spaces. The ATU also supports read-only pages. An attempted write to such a page causes a write fault exception.

In the current implementation all address spaces are managed in the same manner. Each address space has associated with it a page table which holds the within volume disk addresses of each of its pages. This is called the *primary page table*. The maximum size of this page table is 2^{16} (2^{28-12}) entries or 2^{17} bytes, each entry being 16 bits. The primary page table is located at the highest addresses within the address space which it describes. A full size page table will occupy the last 32 pages. Note however that there may be gaps in the address space and pages of the page table are only created when required. That is, a page of the page table is created the first time one of the pages it references is created[4].

The key factor of this mechanism is that the page table is at a well defined address within the virtual address space and thus may be addressed using normal instructions. This considerably simplifies page fault resolution because no special mechanism need be used to access the page tables. On a page fault, the page fault handler is provided with the faulting virtual address. It then attempts to read the required page table entry, the address of which is easily generated since the address space number, the address of the page table within it and the faulting page number are known. If no page fault occurs when accessing the page table, then the disk address has been retrieved and the page fault is resolved. Otherwise the required page of the page table must be obtained. A separate *secondary page table*, or page table for the page table, is maintained for this purpose. It need only have 32 entries, one for each page of the page table, and it is held at a well defined address in page zero of each address space, along with some other red-tape information used by the higher level architecture. This is illustrated in figure 4. Thus, if a page fault occurs on the page table the address of the required secondary page table entry may be generated and the contents accessed.

The final problem to resolve is a page fault on page zero of an address space. Address space zero of each volume is used for this purpose and is called the *volume directory*. The volume directory has the same structure as other address spaces, with a primary and secondary page table. The data portion of the volume directory contains several data structures used by the system to manage the disk space. The two most important of these are the *hash table* and the *free space bit map*.

The hash table is a table containing the disk address of page zero of each valid address space on this volume. Given an address space number the hash table will either return the disk address of page zero or will fail. The latter indicates that the address space is invalid, either because it never existed or it has been deleted. Such an occurrence would cause an exception in the program causing the access. It is possible that a page fault occurs while accessing the hash table. However, this can be handled using exactly the same scheme as a normal page fault. Page zero of each volume directory, which contains the secondary page table for address space zero, is locked into main memory and so the process is always guaranteed to terminate. Page zero is called the *root page* and is located in a well known block of the disk. It is loaded into memory at system boot time, or whenever a new disk comes on-line.

---

[4]As an optimisation for small address spaces, the primary page table for the first one megabyte of an address space is actually held in the first page of the address space along with other red-tape information. The main primary page table is only created when the size of an address space exceeds one megabyte. This optimisation is ignored in the following discussion for simplicity.

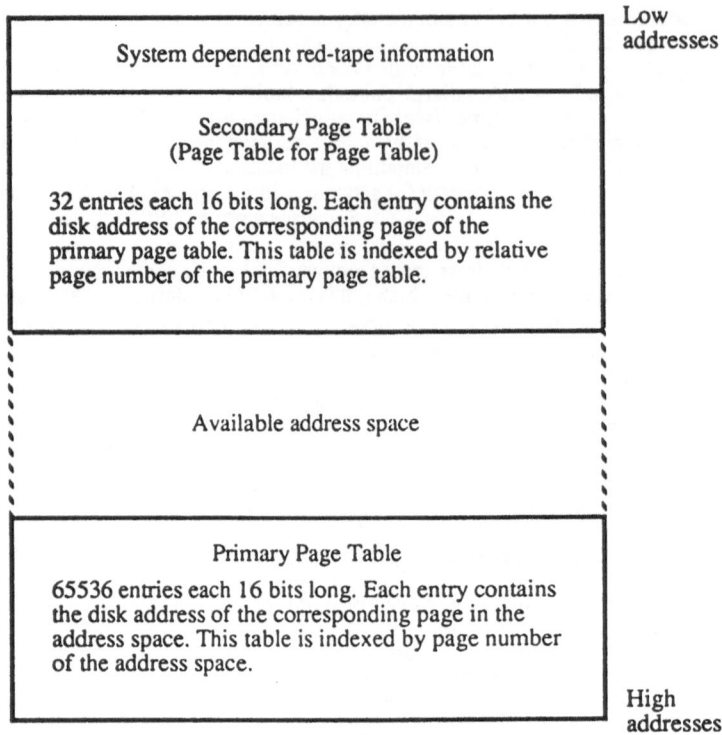

Figure 4: Address space structure

The free space bit map is a bit map indicating those disk blocks which are currently unallocated. In the current implementation the free space bit map is locked into main memory for each volume in order to simplify the page fault resolution process. This is not considered to be a serious deficiency since it is quite small, just over 8 Kbytes for a 256 Mbyte volume, and could be paged if necessary.

The final data structure worth mentioning is the *main memory table (MMT)*. The MMT is maintained on a global basis by the kernel and is locked into main memory. It contains one entry for each page frame of main memory. The MMT is used, amongst other things, for the allocation of page frames. Each entry indicates the corresponding virtual page number and the disk address of that virtual page, or that the page frame is currently unallocated. This is illustrated in figure 5. The disk address is used when a modified page is discarded in order to avoid accessing the page table again, since such an access may cause a page fault.

Page free	Virtual page number	Disk address of virtual page

Figure 5: A *main memory table* entry

4. STABILITY IN MONADS

During the normal course of operation of the MONADS system integrity can be achieved by ensuring that all modified pages within the main memory are copied to the secondary storage medium before shutdown. However, this will not handle unexpected situations such as a system crash or a hardware failure. In these cases it is essential that, on restart, the system returns to a well defined state. In particular, it is essential that the data stored be in a consistent state. That is, all updates up to a given point in time are valid and none after that time.

In this section we describe an extension to the MONADS virtual memory scheme which achieves stability. The MONADS implementation is based heavily on Lorie's original shadow paging scheme and has many similarities at the address space level with that of Ross [23]. However, it is greatly simplified by the fact that all page tables, the hash table and the free space bit map themselves reside within the virtual store.

A major difference between the MONADS environment and other systems is that MONADS has its store partitioned into volumes, each of which is self-contained, in terms of space management. At this stage we will consider the stabilise operation to be based on individual volumes. This is an over-simplification since there are cross references between volumes and it is essential that they be kept consistent. We will also initially ignore the question of processes which are represented by process stacks held in the store. On a stabilise operation the state of such processes should be preserved so that they can be restarted following a crash. We will return to these issues later.

4.1 Single Volume Stabilise

In order to implement stability in MONADS an additional data structure is required. We will call this the *shadowed pages table (SPT)* and it will contain an entry for each page which has been modified since the last stabilise operation. This is required since it is necessary to detect the first modification to a page so that a shadow copy may be created. Although the ATU can detect an attempted write and does indicate modified pages, it only contains entries for pages currently in main memory. Consider a page which is modified and then discarded to disk. In this case a shadow page will be allocated. At a later stage the same page may be brought back into memory and again modified. The SPT will indicate in this case that a shadow page has already been allocated. We will see later that the SPT is also required to manage the release of disk space used by pages which are part of the previous checkpoint. At this stage we will consider the SPT to be a linear table, but will later look at alternative implementations. There is one SPT for each volume. The SPT contains two values for each entry. These are the disk address at the last checkpoint for the corresponding page, called the *old disk address*, and the disk address to which the page will be written at the next checkpoint, called the *new disk address*.

The other feature which we will employ is the ability of the ATU to support pages marked as read-only. On a write access to such a page an exception, called a *write-fault*, occurs. This is used to detect the first occasion on which a page is modified. This should not be confused with the *modify* bit in each entry of the ATU which indicates whether the corresponding page has been modified since it was brought into memory. The distinction is important for a situation where a page is marked as read/write immediately on being brought into the store, in which case the modify bit indicates if the page has been changed. This is used by the page fault handler to determine whether a discarded page needs to be copied to disk.

As described in section 3, the root page of a volume is effectively the root of a tree of disk addresses of pages on the volume. From the root page the disk address of any given page on that volume can be located. Following a checkpoint every page on the volume will either be in that tree or in the free space bit map, which itself is in a page described by that tree. The key to implementing stability is to leave that tree undisturbed and to incrementally construct a new tree. This new tree can be pointed to by the in-memory copy of the root page, leaving the disk copy of the page pointing at the checkpoint version. Provided that none of the checkpoint pages is modified then, following a system crash, the system will return to the last checkpointed state without any processing being required. The new state described by the in-memory root page can be made the checkpointed state by a single disk write of the root page. In order to ensure that this write is atomic two root pages are maintained and Challis' algorithm, described earlier, is employed. Both of the root pages are placed at well known disk addresses so that they may be located at system start-up.

We now proceed to describe the rules for managing the shadow store, referring to the six operations described earlier. Note that some of these operations may result in subsequent faults. For example, a page fault may result in further page faults to retrieve a page table. These are handled recursively and each follows the procedure given below.

(a)   To create a new page a new disk block is allocated using the free space bit map. If there are no free blocks then a stabilise must be initiated as described later. An entry for this page, containing a null old disk address and the new disk address, is added to the SPT. The new disk address is inserted into the MMT entry and the page table entry for the page is updated. If this is page zero of an address space then an entry is added to the volume hash table.

(b)   The effect of modifying a page in main store depends on the read-only bit for the corresponding entry in the ATU. If the page is marked as read-write then the modify bit in the ATU is set and the access proceeds, otherwise a write fault exception occurs. In this case the original disk address of the faulting page is obtained from the MMT. A new disk block is allocated using the free space bit map. If there are no free blocks then a stabilise must be initiated as described later. An entry for this page containing the original disk address and the new disk address is added to the SPT. The MMT is updated with the new disk address and the page table entry for the page is updated. If this is page zero of an address space the hash table is updated with the new disk address.

(c)   On a page fault the disk address of the required page is obtained and the page is read into a free page frame. This may involve resolving further page faults The disk address is looked up in the new address column of the SPT. If it is found then the page is mapped into the ATU as read-write, otherwise it is mapped in as read-only. In either case an entry containing the disk address of the page is added to the MMT.

(d)   On a page discard, that is when a page is removed from memory, if the modify bit for the corresponding entry in the ATU is set then the page is written to the disk address indicated in the MMT. Note that if the page has been modified rules (a), (b) and (c) will guarantee that a new disk block has already been allocated.

(e)   A *stabilise* operation for a volume may either be automatically generated or explicitly requested by a user/program. In either case the following must be performed. For each entry in the SPT the old disk address is extracted and the corresponding bit in the free space bit map is set. We will assume that the free space bit map is locked into main memory and therefore cannot cause a page fault. All pages for this volume in memory which have been modified are copied back to disk. These can be easily located using the MMT and the ATU. Note that the order in which these are written to disk is not important since if there was to be a system crash, the old state described by the old root page on disk would be restored and thus all of the blocks allocated as part of the new state would be in the free space bit map. These pages should then be marked as read-only in the ATU so that, if they are subsequently modified, a new disk block may be allocated. Finally the root page for the volume is written back to disk. This final step makes the new state the stable state. At this point the SPT is cleared and the checkpoint is complete.

(f) A *restore* operation takes place following a crash of a volume. Since the entire state as at the last checkpoint still exists on secondary storage, and all disk blocks used since that checkpoint will still be in the free list of that checkpoint state, no modification to the secondary store needs to be performed in order to restore to the last checkpoint. The SPT for the volume is cleared and any pages from that volume in main memory must be removed from the ATU. The root page from the last checkpoint is then retrieved and system operation may continue.

Notice that in this scheme a new disk block is allocated *before* a page is modified. This guarantees that it is always possible to stabilise, that is there is always sufficient disk space. Given the page table structure it is possible for the page fault handler to statically calculate the maximum number of pages which may be modified as a result of processing a write fault and to ensure that there is sufficient disk space for each of these pages before granting write access to the page. This number of pages never exceeds five in the MONADS scheme.

We now return to the question of implementation of the SPT. There are three operations which must be performed on the SPT. These are insert a new entry, check if an entry with a particular new disk address is in the table and cycle through each entry in the table. We can suggest two alternative implementations. The first is a hash table, using selected bits of the new disk address as the hash key. This would provide good performance on all of the required operations. However, the size of the table is a potential problem since, in theory, it can grow quite large, with entries for half the number of disk blocks on the volume. However, in practice this is not likely to be a problem since it is sensible to checkpoint frequently. In any case, if the table became full a checkpoint could be forced. Since a checkpoint can be performed at any time it is possible for the system to enforce a policy on checkpoints to avoid this situation, e.g. checkpoint after n pages have been modified.

An alternative implementation of the SPT is to use two bit lists, both of which have one bit for each disk block on the volume. For the maximum size MONADS volume, 256 megabytes, this is only 8 kilobytes each, which it is feasible to lock into main memory. The bit lists effectively correspond to the two columns of the SPT, the first indicating the old disk addresses of modified pages and the second indicating the new disk addresses of modified pages. This allows the three required operations to be performed efficiently and in a fixed amount of store. In fact these bit lists operate in a similar manner to Lorie's MAP and shadow bits, but have the advantage that, since they are not in the page tables, they may easily be cleared following a stabilise operation.

4.2 Multi-volume Consistency and Processes

We indicated earlier that, in the MONADS system, it is possible to have cross references between address spaces on different volumes. Independent volume checkpointing in this circumstance could result in inconsistencies following a crash. A solution to this is to implement a multi-volume stabilise using a two-phase commit. This would rely on making one of the volumes, presumably on a fixed disk, a master volume. The master volume would record which root block to use on each dependent volume. Two copies of each root page are maintained as before. Each volume would be stabilised as above, but only the older of the two root pages is updated with the new timestamp. The master volume is updated last, with both root pages being written to guarantee that the write is successful. Following a crash the timestamps can be inspected to determine the most recent consistent state.

Processes can be included in such a scheme by saving the current state of each process, including the contents of screen buffers, etc., before commencing the checkpoint operation. At restart this state information can be retrieved and the processes continued. The process state information could either be saved on the individual process stacks or in a central object pointed to by the master volume.

A potential disadvantage of this scheme is that the entire store must stabilised at one time. For a large configuration with many volumes this could become quite expensive since all processes must be stopped during the stabilise. However, the situation is not be as bad as it at first seems. Much of the work takes place in parallel with the normal operation of the system as part of the page discard task and at most the entire memory of the machine, but usually much less, must be copied to disk at a checkpoint.

This scheme can be generalised to allow for a very flexible stable store in which volumes are stabilised in groups in such a way that the groupings may be changed as required. For example, it may be that a particular volume supports a self-contained related group of users and their data. In such a case that volume could be stabilised by itself. Given an appropriate mechanism it would then be possible to group that volume with another so that the two are stabilised together. As another example consider bringing a volume from another site and mounting it on a machine. It may be desirable for it to be stabilised with other volumes on that machine. This can easily be achieved by the proposed scheme.

5. DISCUSSION

We will now consider the effects of the above scheme on the placement of pages on the disk. After some period of time the pages of an address space may be randomly distributed across the disk. This is acceptable if the pages are to be randomly accessed. However, for sequential access it would be better if the pages were physically sequential. This was achieved in Brown's scheme [10] by creating a pre-copy of pages on disk and overwriting the original page in place, maintaining the original physical structure of the store. This has two disadvantages. First, each modified page must be physically copied and second, the store must be partitioned into two areas, store and shadow pages, potentially reducing the disk space utilisation. However, it is desirable to support efficient sequential access.

Lorie [17] has suggested a solution to this problem. The disk, or volume in our case, is organised into physical clusters. Each cluster consists of a set of disk blocks such that the head movement time between blocks in the same cluster is much smaller than the head movement time between blocks in different clusters. Each address space is associated with a cluster and when a new disk page is required for an address space it is allocated in this cluster, if possible. By careful choice of the cluster size it should be possible to achieve good locality for sequential access. Clustering need not be implemented globally, but can be an option on an address space basis.

In several of the schemes described in the literature [10, 24] there is a disk space overhead, even following a checkpoint operation. In the proposed scheme disk space is allocated fully dynamically. There is no static division of store into shadow and main store and once a stabilise has taken place all shadow store is immediately released. By implementing a clustering scheme as described above, this improvement can be achieved without serious performance degradation for sequential access.

There is an overhead in terms of both disk space and execution time in performing the shadow paging algorithm. It is quite likely that for certain address spaces containing temporary objects stability is of no importance. In these cases it is desirable to disable the shadowing. The MONADS scheme can be enhanced to support this option. Each address space can be flagged as either shadowed or non-shadowed. In the latter case the page table and red-tape information would still be shadowed, but not the data. This is required in order to ensure the integrity of store management data.

6. CONCLUSION

Persistent systems have the potential to provide a powerful and flexible software development environment. However, if they are to achieve that goal they must be both efficient and robust. We have addressed the former issue by providing purpose-built hardware specifically designed to support a large virtual store. In this paper we have suggested a scheme to make this virtual store stable.

The scheme is based on shadow paging but has the advantage that disk space allocation is fully dynamic. A minimum of disk space is used. At any time there are at most two copies of any page on disk, the last checkpoint version and the current version if the page has been modified. Following a checkpoint, there is only one copy of each page. At no time do pages have to be copied, either in memory or on disk. Following a system crash the system automatically returns to the last consistent state with no post-processing of the disks. The checkpoint process can be expensive but much of the work may be overlapped with the normal operation of the system.

The scheme gains simplicity through two techniques. The first is the maintenance of all of the virtual memory tables, free space bit maps, etc. within the store. This allows the shadowing technique to be used recursively on the page tables themselves, considerably simplifying the implementation. The second technique is the use of very large addresses. This allows the virtual address space to be partitioned to support multiple volumes, without fragmenting the primary or secondary store.

An interesting area for further research is the use of an *uninterruptable power supply (UPS)*. Technology in this area has improved considerably and it is now quite possible to provide battery backup to ensure maintenance of power to disks and memory for an extended time, at least in the order of hours [12]. Given this sort of technology the question of coping with power failure is no longer an issue. Following a power failure all data can simply be copied to disk. However, this does not cope with the situation of a system software failure or, even more seriously a hardware failure (e.g. processor error) where the power to processor and memory must be removed in order to rectify the fault. These situations will still require another mechanism such as stability. However, we are investigating possible simplifications and improvements to the proposed mechanism based on the use of a UPS. In particular it should be possible to considerably reduce the I/O overheads by shadowing within main memory.

ACKNOWLEDGEMENTS

The authors wish to thank Peter Broessler for reading several earlier drafts of this paper and making many helpful suggestions. This work was undertaken during John Rosenberg's study leave period at the University of St Andrews and was supported by SERC grant GR/F 28571.

REFERENCES

1. Abramson, D.A. "Hardware Management of a Large Virtual Memory", *Proceedings 4th Australian Computer Science Conference*, Brisbane 1981, pp. 1-13.

2. Abramson, D.A. and Keedy, J.L. "Implementing a Large Virtual Memory in a Distributed Computing System", *Proceedings of 18th Annual Hawaii International Conference on System Sciences*, 1985, pp. 515-522.

3.   Astrahan, M.M. et al "System R: Relational Approach to Database Management", *ACM Transactions on Database Systems*, 1, 2, June 1976, pp. 97-137.

4.   Atkinson, M.P., Chisholm, K.J. and Cockshott, W.P. "PS-algol: An Algol with a Persistent Heap", *ACM SIGPLAN Notices*, 17, 7, July 1981, pp. 24-31.

5.   Atkinson, M.P., Chisholm, K.J. and Cockshott, W.P. "CMS - A Chunk Management System", *Software Practice and Experience*, 13, 3, 1983, pp. 259-272.

6.   Atkinson, M.P., Bailey, P., Chisholm, K.J., Cockshott, W.P. and Morrison, R. "An Approach to Persistent Programming", *The Computer Journal*, 26, 4, Nov. 1983, pp 360-365.

7.   Atkinson, M.P., Bailey, P.J., Cockshott, W.P., Chisholm, K.J. and Morrison, R. "POMS: A Persistent Object Management System", Software Practice and Experience, 14, 1, January 1984, pp. 49-71.

8.   Berstis, V., Truxal, C.D. and Ranweiler, J.G. "System/38 Addressing and Authorization", IBM System/38 Technical Developments, 1978, pp. 51-54.

9.   Brown, A.L. and Cockshott, W.P. "The CPOMS Persistent Object Management System", Universities of Glasgow and St Andrews PPRR-13, Scotland 1985.

10.   Brown, A.L. "Persistent Object Stores", Ph.D. thesis, available as Persistent Programming Report 71, 1989, Universities of St. Andrews and Glasgow.

11.   Challis, M.F. "Database Consistency and Integrity in a Multi-user Environment", in *Databases: Improving Usability and Responsiveness*, B. Schneiderman (editor), Academic Press 1978, pp. 245-270.

12.   Copeland, G., Keller, T., Krishnamurthy, R. and Smith. M. "The Case for Safe RAM", *Proceedings of the 15th International Conference on Very Large Databases*, Amsterdam 1989, pp. 327-335.

13.   Edwards, D.B.E., Knowles, A.E. and Woods, J.V. "MU6-G: A New Design to Achieve Mainframe Performance from a Mini-sized Computer", *Proceedings of the 7th Annual Symposium on Computer Architecture*, Computer Architecture News, 8, 3, May 1980, pp. 161-167.

14.   Harland, D.M. "REKURSIV: Object-oriented Computer Architecture", Ellis-Horwood Limited, 1988.

15.   Keedy, J.L. "Paging and Small Segments: A Memory Management Model", *Proceedings 8th World Computer Congress (IFIP-80)*, Melbourne 1980, pp. 337-342.

16.   Kilburn, T., Edwards, D., Lanigan, M. and Sumner, F. "One Level Storage System", *IEEE Transactions*, EC-11, 2, 1962.

17.   Lorie, R.A. "Physical Integrity in a Large Segmented Database", *ACM Transactions on Database Systems*, 2, 1, March 1977, pp. 91-104.

18.   Morrison, R., Brown, A.L., Carrick, R., Connor, R., Dearle, A. and Atkinson, M.P. "The Napier Type System", Proceedings of the 3rd International Workshop on Persistent Object Systems, Newcastle, 1989.

19. Rosenberg, J. and Abramson, D.A. "A Capability-Based Workstation to Support Software Engineering", *Proceedings of 18th Annual Hawaii International Conference on System Sciences*, 1985, pp. 222-230.

20. Rosenberg, J.L. and Keedy, J.L. "Object Management and Addressing in the MONADS Architecture", *Proceedings 2nd International Workshop on Persistent Object Systems*, Appin Scotland, 1987, available as PPRR-44, Universities of Glasgow and St. Andrews.

21. Rosenberg, J., Koch, D.M. and Keedy, J.L. "A Massive Memory Supercomputer", *Proceedings of 22nd Annual Hawaii International Conference on System Sciences*, 1989, pp. 338-345.

22. Rosenberg, J., Keedy, J.L. and Abramson, D.A. "Addressing Mechanisms for Large Virtual Memories", Research Report CS/90/2, University of St. Andrews, 1990.

23. Ross, D.M. "Virtual Files: A Framework for Experimental Design", Department of Computer Science, University of Edinburgh, CST-26-83, October 1983.

24. Thatte, S.M. "Persistent Memory", *Proceedings of IEEE Workshop on Object-Oriented DBMS*, 1986, pp. 148-159.

25. Traiger, I.L. "Virtual Memory Management for Database Systems", *Operating Systems Review*, 16, 4, October 1982, pp. 26-48.

Stability in a Network of MONADS-PC Computers

Frans A. Henskens, John Rosenberg, and Michael R. Hannaford

Department of Electrical Engineering and Computer Science
University of Newcastle
N.S.W. 2308
Australia

ABSTRACT

The MONADS-PC computer system implements an architecture supporting a very large persistent store based on a uniform virtual memory. We have previously shown how this virtual memory scheme can be extended to encompass a local area network of MONADS-PC computers. In this paper we examine the question of the integrity of the store in such a network. A modification to the MONADS architecture to implement stability is reviewed and extended to guarantee stability of a network-wide persistent store. The stability scheme allows for temporary interruption to the physical network without affecting the validity of exported pages owned by a node.

1. INTRODUCTION

The MONADS project at the University of Newcastle, Australia and the University of Bremen, West Germany, has designed and implemented an unconventional and novel computer architecture [8, 9, 10, 16] known as the MONADS-PC [14].

A feature of the architecture is its very large persistent store, supported by a paged virtual address space. The store is single-level in that it has no conventional file system; rather disk storage is seen as an extension of physical memory. The system state at any time is described by a combination of the contents of physical memory and the disk store. The system would be left in an inconsistent state if the physical memory contents were lost because of, for instance, a power failure or system crash.

File-based systems use utilities such as fsck [19] to restore file system integrity after an unexpected system shut down. The possible resultant loss of files, whilst potentially annoying to the user, is usually not critical to the system because such files are independent entities. The MONADS persistent store, on the other hand, contains all data including system management information and references between objects. Inconsistencies in such data are critical to system integrity and security, and can lead to problems such as incorrect volume page tables and dangling references.

A network of MONADS-PC computers has been implemented [6]. This network distributes the large persistent store across the networked machines. The system is based on a network paging protocol which guarantees full coherency of shared objects as well as both naming and location transparency. The distribution of the store across a network increases the potential area of impact of an unexpected shutdown of a node.

We have previously described a scheme based on shadow paging which will guarantee the integrity of the store in a single node following a failure [15]. The presence of multiple nodes with cross references between them adds complexity to the problem because of the possibility of partial failure of the network.

In this paper we examine the question of the integrity of the store in such a network. The modification to the MONADS architecture to implement stability [15] is reviewed and extended to guarantee stability of a network-wide persistent store. The stability scheme allows for temporary interruption to the physical network without affecting the validity of exported pages owned by a node.

2. DESCRIPTION OF THE MONADS NETWORK

In this section we describe the basic operation of a network of MONADS-PC computers. Although the physical implementation of the network is not of importance to this discussion, we do make assumptions. First, it is assumed that we are dealing with a network of homogeneous machines. Second, it is assumed that any two nodes that need to communicate can do so, and that the network communication mechanism is either reliable or fails entirely. Issues related to achieving this service, such as the handling of duplicate packets, will not be considered in this paper.

All data in the MONADS network exists in a single virtual address space which is partitioned in such a way that each node is allocated an individual range of addresses. These addresses are guaranteed to be unique across the network by including the owning node number in the high order bits of each address. The range of addresses owned by a node is further divided into volumes. Each volume corresponds to a physical disk, or partition of a disk, located at that node. Finally volumes are divided into regions called address spaces. The full structure of a virtual address is illustrated in figure 1.

Node No.	Volume Number	Within Volume Address Space Number	Offset Within AS

Figure 1: Full Structure of a Virtual Address

Address spaces are used to hold a related set of data such as a program, an information hiding module, the equivalent of a file or a process stack. Address spaces are further divided into variable length segments, which are accessed by non-manufactureable and non-forgeable segment capabilities. For memory management purposes, the kernel sees each address space as a sequence of pages of fixed length, whilst the programmer or compiler sees each address space as a collection of its segments. Segments are mapped onto address spaces in such a way that page and segment boundaries are decoupled [7], thus avoiding the internal fragmentation problems associated with most combined paging and segmentation schemes [12, 13].

Segments may themselves contain segment capabilities, so that it is possible to build arbitrarily complex data structures. However the MONADS architecture enforces certain rules to limit the propagation of segment capabilities. These rules ensure that, with the exception of those held in process stacks, segment capabilities always point to a segment within the same address space. Process stacks may contain segment capabilities pointing into any address space. The structure of the higher level architecture makes it possible to determine and control which address spaces may be referenced from any given process stack. The mechanisms used to implement these controls are described in [10].

A practical implementation of this addressing scheme requires that the node number, volume number and within-volume address space number fields are large enough to ensure that a supply of unique values will never be exhausted. Virtual addresses in the prototype MONADS-PC network are 60 bits long. The maximum size of an address space in the prototype is 256 megabytes made up of pages of size 4 kilobytes. A new implementation of the MONADS architecture, the MONADS-MM, which is currently being designed, will allow for 128 bit virtual addresses, with 32 bits for each field [17].

Each MONADS node has an Address Translation Unit (ATU) [1] which maps virtual addresses into physical memory addresses. The ATU is an inverted page table implemented in hardware, and its size is proportional to the size of the physical memory of the node. The design of the ATU is such that the size of the virtual address space does not greatly affect the speed of translation.

Each individual address space is wholly stored on a single volume, and a volume will typically contain many address spaces. A disk page table is maintained for each address space, and this is held in a protected region of the address space which it describes. In addition a volume directory is maintained for each volume indicating the location of the page table for each address space on that volume. A root page for each volume effectively contains a page table for the volume directory. Thus a volume may be viewed as a tree of pages, with the volume root page pointing to the volume directory, which points to the page table for each address space. In this paper we will refer to these data structures as the volume and address space red-tape.

When a virtual address is presented to the ATU for translation, it either returns the appropriate physical memory address, or generates a page-fault. In addition the ATU can support read-only pages and a write fault is generated if an attempt is made to modify such a page.

If a page-fault is generated, the node number field of the faulting address is examined to determine if the volume containing the required page is stored on the local node. If it is, the page fault is resolved by copying the faulting page into physical memory, and the waiting process is reactivated. If the page is stored on another node, the kernel transmits a message to the remote node requesting a copy of the page. The system supports mechanisms that allow for movement of objects between volumes, and of volumes between nodes. These are described in [3]. In this paper, for simplicity, we assume that each object resides at the node on which it was first created, that is the node whose number appears in the addresses of data within the object. Moved objects and moved volumes may be stabilised using the techniques described in this paper in conjunction with the mechanisms described in [3].

Each node in the network maintains an Exported Pages Table (XPT) and an Imported Pages Table (IPT). These tables have the same structure as illustrated in figure 2. The XPT and the IPT maintain information on exported and imported pages respectively, and are used to implement the memory coherence algorithm described in [2, 6]. This algorithm implements a single writer/multiple reader protocol. Before an owner node brings a page off disk to resolve a page-fault, it must ensure that no read-write copy of the page exists at another node. This check is done by reference to the XPT. If a read-write copy does exist at another node, it must mark the page as read-only in its ATU and send a copy of the page back to the owner node. The page-fault at the owner node is, in this case, resolved using the copy of the page returned by the importing node rather than by disk access.

Pages are always exported with read-only access rights, and an importing node must request promotion to read-write access rights, if necessary, as a separate operation. It is allowable for multiple read-only copies of a page to exist in the physical memories of nodes in the network. If a read-write copy exists in the physical memory of a node, then it must be the only instance of the page in physical memory network wide. When an owner node receives a request for promotion of a page to read-write access, it must use the XPT to ensure that any other copies of the page are removed from the ATUs of all but the requesting node before granting the promotion request.

Node Number	Volume Number and Address Space Number	Within AS Page Number	Access Rights

One entry per exported page

Figure 2: Exported Pages Table

3. SINGLE NODE STABILITY

When a node is closed down in a controlled manner, all modified pages in physical memory are copied to secondary (disk) storage prior to completion of the shutdown. The disk locations of the contents of the pages of physical memory may be obtained from a data structure called the Main Memory Table (MMT) which is shown in figure 3. The ATU indicates whether the page has been modified. This controlled shutdown ensures that, on restart, all system management data and inter-object references are consistent.

In the case of unexpected shutdown caused by, for example, system software or hardware failure, copying of in-memory modified pages to disk cannot occur. So that the system has consistent stored data for restart, it is necessary that, when running, it systematically moves the stored data between consistent states. Achieving this goal is not easy, because the usual paging mechanisms associated with virtual memory management necessarily result in the essentially random flushing of modified pages to disk to free up physical memory. The act of permanently storing a stable state to which it is possible to revert is called checkpointing, and a system that can always be restarted from a consistent state is said to be stable.

AS#	Page#	Disk Address

One entry per page frame of physical memory

Figure 3: Main Memory Table (irrelevant fields omitted)

The stability scheme described in [15] is based on shadow paging as initially proposed by Lorie [11], and extended by others [4, 18, 20]. In this paper we initially consider this scheme for a single volume only. It can be extended to stabilise multiple volumes, which is required if there are cross references between volumes, by using a two phase commit as shown in [15]. This extension will be discussed later.

A Shadowed Pages Table (SPT) is maintained for each volume mounted on a node (see figure 4). The SPT is used to detect pages that have been shadowed since the last checkpoint to avoid multiple shadows being created, and to release disk space following a checkpoint operation. Only modified pages are shadowed, and at most two copies of a page exist on disk at any time, the latest version and the version at the last checkpoint. Disk space is dynamically allocated for pages, and at each checkpoint the disk space used for the previous checkpoint version of the page is returned to the free disk space pool. Following a checkpoint, the new stable version of pages forms the basis for further system operation.

Old Disk Address	New Disk Address

One entry per page in volume

Figure 4: Shadowed Pages Table

Checkpoint operations are regularly performed as part of normal running of the system, but can be instigated by user software if required. The latter is essential to allow synchronisation with higher level transaction mechanisms.

The SPT can be efficiently implemented as two bit lists of disk pages on the corresponding volume, one each for old and new disk pages. When a write fault occurs on a page the current (or old) disk page is marked in the first bit list and becomes the shadow page. In addition, a new disk page is obtained from the free list and is marked in the second bit list. When the modified page is written back to disk, it is written to the new disk page. A read-write page, of course, may be written back to disk at an arbitrary time as part of virtual memory management, and may subsequently need to be paged back in. This scenario presents the possibility of multiple write-faults on the same page between checkpoints, so the new disk page bit list is checked every time a page is brought into memory, and if the disk page is found, indicating that it has previously been shadowed, the virtual memory page is mapped into the ATU as read-write, thus ensuring that at most one shadow page exists for any virtual memory page.

A checkpoint operation returns all pages in the old disk page list (ie the previous checkpoint versions of pages that have since been modified) to the volume free page list, and copies to disk, marking as read-only in the ATU, all modified pages in main memory, thus creating a new checkpoint version of the volume. Changing the access rights of read-write pages to read-only ensures that the next attempt to write to any page will cause a write-fault on that page, meaning that it will be entered in the SPT ready for the next checkpoint operation. Since the data structures describing the allocation of disk pages are themselves stored in virtual memory, the final stage of the checkpoint operation involves the writing to disk of the root page of the data structures. To enable recovery from a system failure during this last stage the root page is written as an atomic operation using Challis' algorithm [5]. There are two root pages for each volume, with the most recent correct page pointing to the last stable state. Correctness is ensured by insertion of timestamps at the beginning and end of the root pages as they are written.

4. NETWORK-WIDE STABILITY

Exported read-only pages pose no threat to the stability of the volume on which they are stored. Stability for exported read-write pages is not ensured by the single node stability scheme described above because such pages will not reside in the physical memory of the owner node at the time of initiation of a checkpoint operation.

The first stage in ensuring network-wide stability is the sending by the owner node of 'please return up-to-date copy' messages to remote nodes with read-write access to pages from the volume about to be checkpointed. As each page is returned it is marked as read-only in the remote node's ATU. When the page arrives at the owner node, it is stored in one of a pool of physical memory pages allocated by the kernel for receipt of incoming messages. Once the transfer of the virtual page into physical memory is complete, an entry must be made for the page in the MMT. Part of the MMT entry is the disk page to which the virtual page will be written on checkpoint, so a new disk page must be available for completion of the entry.

As described in [15], the lack of free disk space on a volume is one of the reasons for initiation of a checkpoint. It is, then, clearly unsatisfactory to assume that free disk space will be available for storage of pages returned by remote nodes. The solution is to allocate the new disk page to an exported read-write page prior to the granting of read-write access. At the same time an entry is added to the SPT. Finally, the new disk page address is entered in the address space page table as the storage location for the virtual page, guaranteeing that space exists on the disk to save the virtual page during the next checkpoint.

The single node stability scheme [15] resolves page-faults by bringing pages off disk into memory with read-write access if an entry for the page appears in the SPT. This is not appropriate if the node is networked and a copy of the page exists in the physical memory of another node, because the page coherence algorithm does not allow a read-write page to appear in the physical memory of multiple nodes simultaneously. As described in section 2, the XPT is checked when page-faults occur as part of the page coherence algorithm. If an exported read-write copy of the page exists, the page will be returned by the importer, thus making disk access unnecessary. If an exported read-only copy exists, the page is brought into memory off disk. In both of these cases the page is mapped into the ATU of the owner node as read-only. If no entry for the page exists in the XPT, the page is not in the memory of any node in the network, and so it can be safely brought in off disk and mapped into the ATU of the owner node with read-only or read-write access depending on the SPT.

The page coherence algorithm [2, 6] does not allow a read-write page to appear in the physical memory of multiple nodes simultaneously, and thus no MMT entry can exist at the owner node for an exported read-write page. When an exported page is returned to its owner node, the page must be entered into the MMT, which involves knowledge of the corresponding disk page number. The disk page number could be obtained from the address space page table. However such access could cause page faults [15]. We have adopted an alternative approach, which avoids this possibility. This involves storing the new disk page information in the XPT, which is held in locked-down memory in the kernel of the system.

5. RECOVERY FROM NODE FAILURE

The above system will allow correct operation of checkpointing across the network with little change to the single node scheme, provided that modified versions of pages are always available at the time of a checkpoint operation. Unfortunately this may not be the case because of either the failure of a node or of the interconnecting media. There are two separate cases of a failing node. These are the failure of the importer of a page and the failure of the exporter of a page. We examine each of these cases separately.

5.1. Failure of an Importing Node

As described in section 4, the volume checkpoint operation results in the owner node requesting the return of all exported read-write pages. If an importing node fails, it obviously cannot respond to such a request. It is clear that any modifications to pages stored in the physical memory of a node are lost if the node fails, so examination of importing node failure reduces to analysis of the behaviour of the exporting node. In our analysis we presume, for simplicity, that a single page has been imported by the failed node. If multiple pages are affected, the described single-page scheme may be applied to each page individually.

After several attempts to retrieve the page the exporting node concludes that the importing node has failed, and that modifications to the exported page are lost. It is tempting to simply remove the SPT entry for the page, appropriately modify the volume and address-space red-tape information, and then continue the checkpoint operation as if the lost page had never been exported. This proposition is unsatisfactory if the following sequence of events relating to virtual pages 'X' and 'Y' occurs after the most recent checkpoint operation.

1. Pages X and Y are transferred to a remote node with read-write access.

2. A segment is created in page Y, and pointed to by a segment capability in page X.

3. As part of the normal page discard process on the importing node, page X is returned to the owner node.

4   The importing node fails, and subsequent to that the owner node attempts to stabilise the volume containing pages X and Y.

If the above sequence of events were to occur, and the stabilise proceeded without the inclusion of the modified version of page Y, then page X would continue to contain a reference to the now non-existent segment that had been created in page Y. The problem is potentially extremely serious from a security point of view because a new segment may subsequently be created in the same location in page Y as that pointed to by the segment capability in page X. This would allow access to a segment in violation of the capability protection scheme that is designed to protect it.

In order to maintain full consistency and security it is essential that only a consistent set of pages be saved at the time of a checkpoint. If this is not possible because a node containing a page from the volume does not respond, then the volume cannot be stabilised at that time. The four available options are to:

1   stabilise without including the unavailable page

2   not stabilise at this time

3   delay the stabilise until the non responding node returns the necessary page, or

4   revert to the previous checkpoint state.

Option 1 can only be allowed if it can be determined that excluding the missing page would not result in a dangling reference, i.e. the missing page contains no reachable segments. Such a determination can only be made by computing the transitive closure for the volume being stabilised. In general, this would be prohibitively expensive, and may not even be possible if the page containing the root of addressing is itself missing.

Option 2 may not always be possible because the stabilise may be essential before system operation can proceed. This may be necessary if the stabilise operation was instigated because of a lack of disk space, or that the stabilise was required as part of the implementation of a higher level transaction mechanism.

Option 3 must be subject to time-out since operation of the owner node on the volume cannot proceed until the stabilise operation has completed, and the remote node may be unavailable for an extended period.

We propose that option 3 be implemented with a parameterised time-out period. If the time-out is reached, then the system concludes that the stabilise cannot take place and the volume reverts to its last checkpoint state. Reverting to the last checkpoint state involves instructing all contactable nodes with pages from the volume to invalidate these pages. The importing nodes can be easily identified by reference to the XPT. In addition, pages from the volume in the memory of the owner node must also be invalidated, these pages being identified via the MMT.

The reversion to the last checkpoint state may not be as serious as it at first seems. It is expected that there will be a higher level transaction mechanism for controlling concurrency and serialisability. Such a mechanism could well provide a transaction log to allow a roll forward from the reverted state, thus recovering at least some of the lost modifications to the volume.

5.2. Failure of an Exporting Node

If an exporting node fails, it will restart at its last stable state, with any local modifications performed since that checkpoint being lost. It is interesting to consider the fate of a read-write page, 'X', exported by the failed node since the last checkpoint. Attempts by the importing node to page out X are unsuccessful, and X is effectively trapped in the physical memory of the importing node. Such a situation would be detrimental to performance at the importing node because its available physical memory would be reduced by the page size for each trapped page, this situation being potentially critical for a diskless node.

A solution is to use up/down protocol messages to periodically monitor the status of the owner of imported pages. If the owner of page X is found to be non-responding, page X is immediately marked as read-only, thus preventing further modifications, and an attempt is made to return a copy of the page to its owner. If the attempted return fails, the page is invalidated, thus losing any modifications to the page in exactly the same way that post-checkpoint modifications at the owner node are lost following a crash. In a similar fashion, on the detected failure of an exporting node, all read-only pages from that node are invalidated.

There is a further problem with this scheme. If an exporting node suffers a system failure, it will subsequently be restarted at its last checkpoint state. It is possible that other nodes have pages from volumes on the restarted node in their memory. Regardless of whether these pages are read-only or read-write, they may not be consistent with the checkpoint state to which the owner node has reverted. It is therefore imperative that any pages previously exported by the restarted node be invalidated at remote nodes. As described in the previous paragraph this will happen automatically if an importing node detects the exporting node's failure. However a short-term crash may not be detected.

When a node restarts, it broadcasts a message informing all other nodes that it is back on-line and that all pages previously imported from it are to be marked as invalid. Once any such pages have been invalidated, nodes return a message informing their existence, and the node names are stored by the restarted node. Any request for provision of a page to a remote node is refused if that node does not appear in this table and the requesting node is again instructed to invalidate all pages imported from the node. A successful acknowledgement to this instruction results in the requesting node being inserted into the table. We can thus guarantee that all inconsistent versions of pages will eventually be invalidated. As part of the up/down protocol, any newly on-line node is added to the table.

5.3. Failure of the Interconnecting Media

Failure of the interconnecting media appears the same as the failure of an exporting or importing node in that pages cannot be transferred between the nodes. The timeouts described in sections 5.1 and 5.2 will handle the situation of a media interruption of duration less than the time-out period. A longer term media problem is equivalent to a node failure, and is handled using the techniques described above.

There must be flexibility in the setting of the time-out periods to allow for different physical network implementations and for fluctuations in network traffic. It would also be sensible to provide a breakout facility to force a restart before the end of a time-out.

6. MULTIPLE VOLUME STABILISE ACROSS NODES

As was described in section 2, it is possible to have cross references between volumes. These are always held in the form of segment capabilities stored in stack address spaces. In order to ensure consistency it is essential that volumes containing cross references are stabilised together. In a network, these volumes can exist on different nodes. As part of the control of between-object references, a dependency graph must be maintained at each node to describe volume inter-relationships. Various protocols for constructing and maintaining the dependency graph are being investigated. The problem is considerably simplified in the MONADS architecture because of the clear distinction between within-address-space references and references to other address spaces, potentially on other volumes.

When a volume is stabilised, the dependency graph is consulted, and if cross references exist, what is essentially a two phase commit is used to cause all the related volumes to be stabilised together. The stabilise may involve volumes stored on more than one node. Appropriate protocols for implementing the two phase commit across the network are still under development.

7. CONCLUSION

Stability can be achieved for a single node persistent store by the use of shadow paging. The large virtual memory store can be extended to encompass a network of nodes, with the physical location of objects within the network being totally transparent to the user.

By extending the mechanisms used to achieve single node stability, we can ensure network-wide stability. Such stability is achieved with a minimum of network traffic overhead, and uses existing memory coherency protocol messages. In achieving stability, the service offered to the remote user is equivalent to that offered to local users, in that, at worst, modifications made since the last checkpoint for a volume on a failed node are lost.

The proposed scheme guarantees the security of data within the system. Via the use of time-out periods, temporary interruptions to the physical network media can occur without loss of data.

Where cross references exist between volumes, the volumes may be stabilised together utilising a two phase commit protocol over the network. When combined with an appropriate higher level transaction mechanism, it should be possible to roll forward to recover most modifications made to a volume between the last checkpoint on the volume and a system failure.

ACKNOWLEDGEMENTS

The MONADS project is supported by grants from the Australian Research Council and the University of Newcastle Senate Research Committee. Thanks are also due to Mr. P. Brössler, Dr. A. Brown, Prof. R. Morrison and Mr. D. Munro for their contributions and suggestions.

REFERENCES

1. Abramson, D. A. "Hardware Management of a Large Virtual Memory", *Proc. 4th Australian Computer Science Conference*, Brisbane, pp. 1-13, 1981.

2. Abramson, D. A. and Keedy, J. L. "Implementing a Large Virtual Memory in a Distributed Computing System", *Proc. 18th Hawaii Conference on System Sciences*, pp. 515-522, 1985.

3. Brössler, P., Henskens, F. A., Keedy, J. L. and Rosenberg, J. "Addressing Objects in a Very Large Distributed System", *Proc. IFIP Conference on Distributed Systems*, Amsterdam, pp. 105-116, 1987.

4. Brown, A. L. "Persistent Object Stores", Universities of St. Andrews and Glasgow, Report 71, 1989.

5. Challis, M. F. "Database Consistency and Integrity in a Multi-user Environment", in *Databases: Improving Usability and Responsiveness*, ed B. Scheiderman, Academic Press, pp. 245-270, 1978.

6. Henskens, F. A., Rosenberg, J. and Keedy, J. L. "A Capability-based Fully Transparent Network", University of Newcastle, N.S.W. 2308, Australia, Report 89/7, 1989.

7. Keedy, J. L. "Paging and Small Segments: A Memory Management Model", *Proc. IFIP-80, 8th World Computer Congress*, Melbourne, Australia, pp. 337-342, 1980.

8. Keedy, J. L. "A Memory Architecture for Object-Oriented Systems", in *Objekt-orientierte Software und Hardwarearchitekturen*, ed H. Stoyan and H. Wedekind, Teubner-Verlag, Stuttgard, pp. 238-250, 1983.

9. Keedy, J. L. "An Implementation of Capabilities without a Central Mapping Table", *Proc. 17th Hawaii International Conference on System Sciences*, pp. 180-185, 1984.

10. Keedy, J. L. and Rosenberg, J. "Support for Objects in the MONADS Architecture", *Proceedings of the International Workshop on Persistent Object Systems*, Newcastle, Australia, pp. 202-213, 1989.

11. Lorie, R. A. "Physical Integrity in a Large Segmented Database", in *ACM Transactions on Database Systems*, 2,1, pp. 91-104, 1977.

12. Organick, E. I. "The Multics System: An Examination of its Structure", MIT Press, Cambridge, Mass., 1972.

13. Randell, B. "A Note on Storage Fragmentation and Program Segmentation", in *Communications of the ACM*, 12, 7, pp. 365-369, 1969.

14. Rosenberg, J. and Abramson, D. A. "MONADS-PC: A Capability Based Workstation to Support Software Engineering", *Proc, 18th Hawaii International Conference on System Sciences*, pp. 515-522, 1985.

15. Rosenberg, J., Henskens, F. A., Brown, F., Morrison, R. and Munro, D. "Stability in a Persistent Store Based on a Large Virtual Memory", *Proceedings of the International Workshop on Architectural Support for Security and Persistence of Information*, Bremen, West Germany, 1990.

16. Rosenberg, J. and Keedy, J. L. "Object Management and Addressing in the MONADS Architecture", *Proceedings of the International Workshop on Persistent Object Systems*, Appin, Scotland, 1987.

17. Rosenberg, J., Koch, D. M. and Keedy, J. L. "A Massive Memory Supercomputer", *Proc. 22nd Hawaii International Conference on System Sciences*, vol 1, pp. 338-345, 1989.

18. Ross, D. M. "Virtual Files: A Framework for Experimental Design", University of Edinburgh, Report CST-26-83, 1983.

19. SUN Microsystems Inc. "Systems and Networks Administration", Report 800-1733-10, Revision A, 1988.

20. Thatte, S. M. "Persistent Memory", *Proc. IEEE Workshop on Object-Oriented DBMS*, pp. 148-159, 1986.

Part VI

Operating Systems

Veritos Distributed Operating System Project
– An Overview –

Uwe Baumgarten

University of Oldenburg
FB 10 (Computer Science)

ABSTRACT:

In this paper first of all the basic objectives of the *Veritos* project are presented. The view of distributed systems together with definitions of many terms from this area are shown. The concepts of the model will be shown including classes, active, and passive components, and communication concepts. These concepts are embedded in an experimental language called OlDiLa, which serves both as programming and specification language for distributed systems respectively.

The approach of stepwise refinement of concepts is presented and illustrated based upon a brief example for the levels of a distributed operating system ranking from abstractly distributed systems to a physically distributed computing system. The connection between adjacent levels is described by mappings. These mappings can be realized by sets of services. A few interesting attributes of distributed systems are shown including persistence of components.

A survey is given over current activities in research and development in the *Veritos* project.

1. INTRODUCTION

This paper gives a survey over the *Veritos* distributed operating system project, which is in progress at the university of Oldenburg [11]. The main objectives will be presented, the actual activities will be shown, and the state of the art will be sketched shortly.

The **main objectives** of the *Veritos* project can be described by the following statements.

The elaboration and definition of concepts and methods for developing, constructing, and implementing distributed operating systems with respect to a set of important attributes are the main objectives. Among the attributes *of interest are <u>functional attributes</u>, <u>structural attributes</u>, which are responsible for many different structures, and further <u>quality attributes</u> like performance, dependability, persistency, security, abstraction from physical distribution (transparency), and hiding of heterogeneity of the hardware configuration.*

Referring to [9] *distributed operating system* (DOS) can be characterized in contrast to local operating systems (LOS) and network operating systems (NOS). A distributed operating system is a system, which is divided into many functional components. These functional components are distributed over a network of computing sites (computational nodes), which are interconnected by a communication network. Based upon the communication network the functional components cooperate in order to do their work. The existence of a local operating system is reduced to a (mostly) common kernel, implementing the base primitives for resource management (processor and storage), and communication between sites. The existence of an operating system (local or part of the DOS) working *autonomous* on every site is not necessary.

Whereas distributed operating systems are mentioned as subject of construction, the concepts can easily be modified for construction of *distributed systems* in general.

Because the list of attributes which should be fulfilled in order to reach *high quality* distributed operating systems is very long, at a first step only some of them will be dealt with in the *Veritos* project in order to structure and to reduce the amount of work. In this sense the quality attributes of performance, dependability, and hiding of heterogeneity are put in the background being nevertheless always in mind. The reduction leads to a kernel of principles, its integration into a language, and four main directions of research and development in the *Veritos* project. The situation is presented in figure 1.

The principles for constructing distributed operating systems in the center of work, the language built around them, and the general approach will be explained in the next chapters together with the set of relevant quality attributes. Detailed explanations about the four areas of research and development will follow. These areas consist of *(i)* the kernel of a software engineering environment (*MoDiS* [1]), *(ii)* distributed applications with a file server as an example, *(iii)* experiments with parallelism and distribution in a concrete experimentation system, and *(iv)* the approach for a distributed operating system itself. Finally the special features and highlights of the *Veritos* approach will be shown together with statements about the state of art and concluding remarks.

2. GENERAL APPROACH

The approach in general can be characterized by a set of attributes. The development, construction, and implementation of distributed operating systems is **model-oriented**, and **top-down-driven** with **stepwise refinement of concepts**. These attributes will be explained in detail referring to the contents of figure 1.

---

[1]<u>Mo</u>del-oriented engineering environment for <u>D</u>istributed <u>S</u>ystems

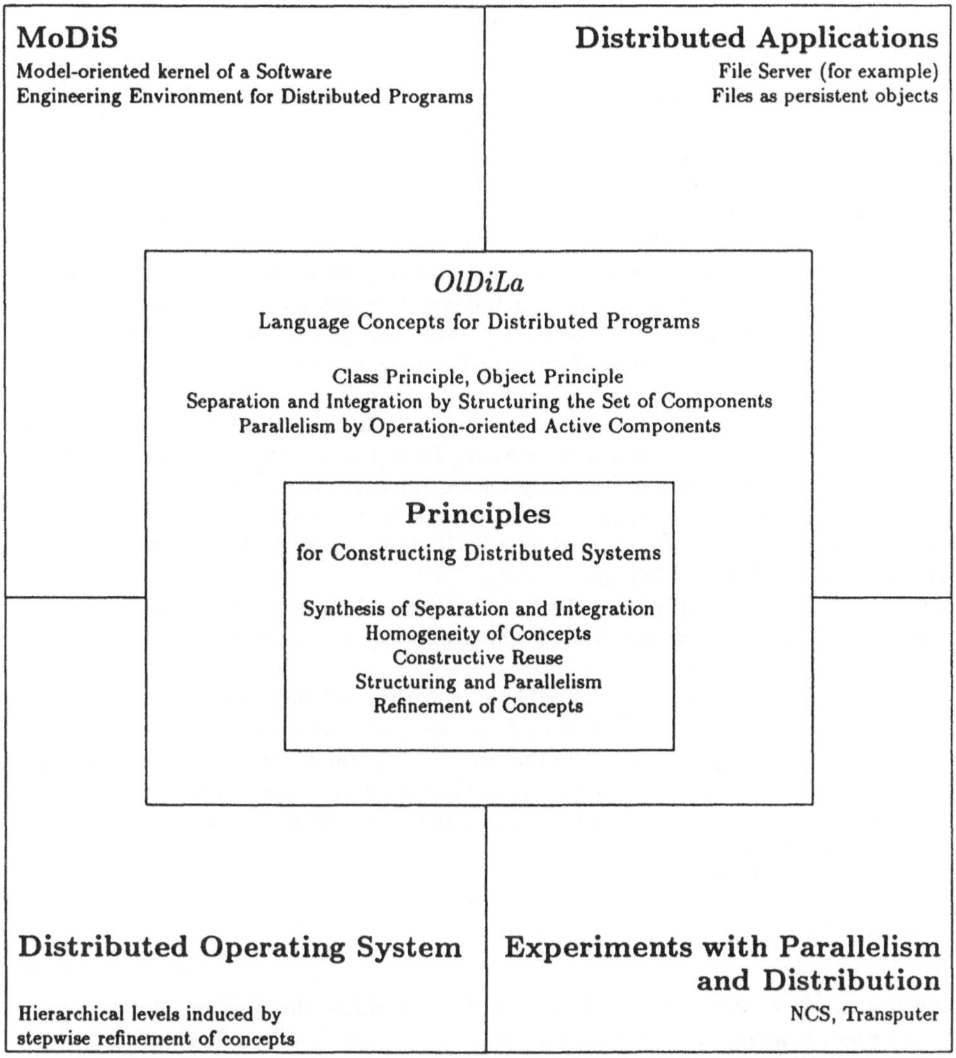

MoDiS

Model-oriented kernel of a Software
Engineering Environment for Distributed Programs

Distributed Applications

File Server (for example)
Files as persistent objects

OlDiLa

Language Concepts for Distributed Programs

Class Principle, Object Principle
Separation and Integration by Structuring the Set of Components
Parallelism by Operation-oriented Active Components

Principles

for Constructing Distributed Systems

Synthesis of Separation and Integration
Homogeneity of Concepts
Constructive Reuse
Structuring and Parallelism
Refinement of Concepts

Distributed Operating System

Hierarchical levels induced by
stepwise refinement of concepts

**Experiments with Parallelism
and Distribution**

NCS, Transputer

Figure 1: Directions of research and development in the *Veritos* project

2.1. Model-orientation in General at the Top Level

In the *Veritos* project distributed operating system[2] are regarded at a minimum of two levels of abstraction, namely an <u>abstract level</u> at the top and a concrete or <u>real level</u> at the bottom.

At the abstract level the whole system is defined using a homogeneous repertoire of concepts (*homogeneity of concepts*) as a wellstructured set of components with a wide spectrum of dependencies. Therefore every system has unique system images and interfaces independent from the underlying (different and perhaps heterogeneous) hardware configuration at the real level. Included in the repertoire are special concepts to <u>structure</u> the whole system and its set of components and concepts for <u>parallel</u> activities. The composition follows the principle of *constructive reuse*; components being constructed in earlier stages can be reused in order to define new ones. The structuring concepts enable the designer on the one side to *separate* and on the other side to *integrate* decisions, attributes, and details of the distributed system. By separation the system is divided into a set of components, which have closely related internal properties and operations and which are loosely coupled externally. By integration components with common properties or dependencies are brought in relation to each other in a way, that their interferences are reduced to a desired minimum.

At the top level parallelism forms the base for *abstractly distributed systems*.

All concepts together form the *model* for distributed systems, which explains the *model-orientation* of the approach.

With a view to components the repertoire of concepts and therefore the model can further be characterized by the *class concept*, its *object orientation, integration of persistent objects*, and *nesting of components* in the sense of definitional, executional, and life-span nesting (dependencies). This will be explained in detail in the next chapter.

Altogether the concepts constitute an appropriate base for many security policies and protection mechanisms (cf. [4]).

2.2. Language-orientation with *OlDiLa*

An overview over the model is given. In order to validate the concepts, to make experiences by examples, and to follow the steps to concrete distributed operating systems, the concepts and principles as described in the model are embedded in an experimental language, called *OlDiLa* (<u>Ol</u>denburg <u>D</u>istributed <u>La</u>nguage) [3], which serves both as programming and specification language for distributed systems.

OlDiLa is an experimental language and is subject of modifications and extensions. In many aspects similarities to Ada [1] exist. Nevertheless many differences in concepts belonging to the semantical area – e. g., rigorous usage of the class principle for all kinds of components, pure operation-oriented rendezvous concept; both will be explained below – are introduced. Less work in the *Veritos* project has been done in the syntactical area; therefore *OlDiLa* programs look like Ada programs in many aspects.

---

[2]In the following *distributed operating systems* and *distributed systems* are regarded as synonyms.

All concepts and principles founded on the model are transferred to the experimental language *OlDiLa*. They will be shortly explained without their concrete semantical and syntactical representation, but with addition of details to the description in the chapter above. The model-orientation goes through a detailed review.

In general distributed systems, as specified by distributed *OlDiLa* programs, are *well-structured sets of active and passive components*. Both kinds of components are *objects* referring to the principle of object-orientation [8] and offering a set of operations. Simple objects like constants or variables of elementary types (e. g., integers) or structured types (e. g., arrays or records) are not handled as separate self-reliant components; they exist only local to components. The components are *functional components* as mentioned in the definition of DOS in the introduction. They define a clear distinction between inner and outer properties and are able to hide information (and especially their implementation), which is local, following the information hiding principle. Their outer properties define an explicit interface with the possibility for fine grained import export restrictions. General attributes of components are their storing and computing facilities. Passive components have only storing facilities whereas active components may have both of them. Components are used (by other components) according to the principle of operation-orientation. The usage of passive objects is similar to *procedure calls*. The set of active components is divided into two sorts depending on their capability of communication. Two forms of active components exist depending on the degree of operations offered. In the first case active components can be influenced from their environment by communication; they offer operations for communication following the operation-oriented rendezvous concept. This synchronous rendezvous concept is the only communication concept for direct communication between active components. The other form of active components is not capable of communication from the outside environment. Their purpose is the separation of parallel (sometimes independent) parts of a computation. They have a clear interface in form of initial and final synchronization to those components they are depending on.
In addition to direct communication the synchronized usage of shared components (cp. the integration feature) for indirect communication is possible. Only passive components are useful for this purpose (cf. the monitor concept [6]).
All components are specified following the class principle using generators as type definition objects to specify those properties, which are common to all instances of a specific generator. They may be parametrized in different ways.

The set of components constituting a distributed system is structured in different ways. These structures belong to the most important parts of systems, of the development method, and of the development process itself. Therefore they will be introduced shortly.
The general concept behind all structures is the concept of nesting. Components may be nested in conformity with their definitional dependencies, executional dependencies in sequential and parallel manners, locality, and life-span.
In agreement with the class principle components are defined using generators. Generators define those properties common to all instances of that class represented by this generator. Generators themselves must be defined locally to components. This constitutes a dependency between any component instantiated referring to the generator and

that component defining this generator. In this way the definitional dependencies form the <u>definitional structure</u> of components (δ-structure). This structure is the base for visibility, usability, and further dynamical development. The definitional structure reflects the main aspects of separation and integration introduced above.

By calling operations of passive components or of active components with communication capability executional dependencies are established. The same dependencies result from instantiating active components irrespective of their communication capability. These dependencies form the <u>executional structure</u> (α-structure) with its sequential (σ), its parallel (π), and its communicational (κ) parts. A further aspect in this area is synchronization of active components, mentioned earlier for example in the context of parameter passing for components without communication capability.

Not only generators but also components may be <u>local</u> to other components. This kind of dependency forms the <u>locality structure</u> (λ-structure) of components. Local components may be private or public. Private components are hidden from the outside environment. Public components are exported and can be used from the outside; they form the <u>export structure</u> (λ_E-structure).

The stage between instantiation (start) and deletion (termination is a necessary precondition) is the life-span of components. The life-span of many components may depend on each other controlled by the principle of nesting. In this way the <u>life-span structure</u> (ε-structure) is formed.

The concepts of life-span of components are the points of contact for <u>persistence</u> [2]. Because distributed systems as a whole are modelled as *one set* of components (based upon homogeneity of concepts) – all applications and extensions over the time are included – the life-span of the whole system is determined by the life-span of its outermost component in the corresponding structure. Nothing can exist outside a system. In this sense activations of programs and activations of *"sub"*systems are local extensions of the whole system.

On the abstract level the outermost component defines by its life-span the frame for any dynamic development of components and *"sub"*systems. Therefore any degree of persistence is possible inside of the system. It is the task of the implementation (cf. the chapter about the operating system approach) to show that and how this is done.

The above mentioned concepts are closely related to the model. Besides, concepts from other areas, like software engineering in general or system quality, are of interest. In the current state of the *Veritos* project they are in consideration, but, are not yet integrated in the language *OlDiLa*. These concepts will be sketched now.

Because in general software systems evolve dynamically in time the problem of <u>incompleteness</u> at the stages of specification, compilation, and run time has to be solved. Work in this area is in progress based on concepts of object-oriented programming.

The same holds for an <u>inheritance concept</u> as known in object oriented programming.

Focal points in the area of quality attributes are dependability, protection, and verification. Concepts for <u>dependability</u> are not explicitly integrated in the language. The set of defined concepts provides a profound base for many mechanisms and strategies like shadowing both of active and passive components and general redundancy. The file server as mentioned in the chapter about distributed applications is an example in this field. Verification must be based on formal specifications with assertions and predicates. Solutions in this direction may be possible, but are not in progress. In the area of protection many concepts and principles, like the least previledge principle , are in consideration, ranking from restrictions enforced by the definitional structure (δ-structure) over import-export-limitations and capabilities [5] to cryptographic methods (cf. [4] and e. g., others activities in the area of protection models at the abstract level and cryptographic methods with key distribution algorithms).

Until now the abstract level of distributed systems with its concepts and principles and their integration into the experimental language *OlDiLa* has been shown. The boxes in the center of figure 1 have been explained.

2.3. Top-Down-Driven Stepwise Refinement of Concepts

As mentioned above distributed systems are modelled on two levels of abstraction. The gap between both has to be closed. This is done by top-down-driven stepwise refinement of concepts.

On the abstract level systems are *abstractly distributed*. Several components may be executed in parallel or may be active simultaneously. In addition systems are called *physically distributed* at the concrete level if they are implemented on base of a distributed hardware configuration, for example a local area network with multiprocessor nodes. Both abstractly and physically distributed systems are subjects of research in the *Veritos* project.

The approach of closing the gap uses a kind of *stepwise implementation* of abstractly distributed systems in a top-down-driven manner. The top level is a high level specification of those systems (*OlDiLa*). From the top level the implementation starts with a system, which is designed and structured corresponding to the above mentioned model. The result of the implementation is an executable system based upon physically distributed computing sites, which are interconnected by a communication network. The transition from one step of implementation to another is guided by the principle of stepwise refinement of concepts.

A sequence of steps and the resulting levels are defined in the *Veritos* project. Only a few of the most important features are mentioned here including *(i)* a uniform representation of components in an abstract system-wide storage, *(ii)* the management and distribution of storage in a life-span-oriented manner (cf. [4]), *(iii)* the clustering and distribution of components in a way favouring functional dependencies including migration and redistribution of components (cf. in this context [7]), and *(iv)* the integration of the concept of persistent components. But first of all the abstract properties of these components as defined by the model will be preserved. The abstract properties are like invariants for each level. No information is lost between levels in top-down direction.

In this *top-down-driven* approach the abstract properties are of primary interest. Therefore this approach is called model-oriented. This is in contrast to the *bottom-up approach* for constructing distributed systems, where the nodes of the systems, their communication systems, and their operating systems, if they exist, play the most important part.

Especially with respect to security, memory management and addressing the top-down-driven approach avoids many deficiencies of the bottom-up approach.

Figure 2 illustrates the approach. Abstractly distributed systems are specified as distributed *OlDiLa* programs.

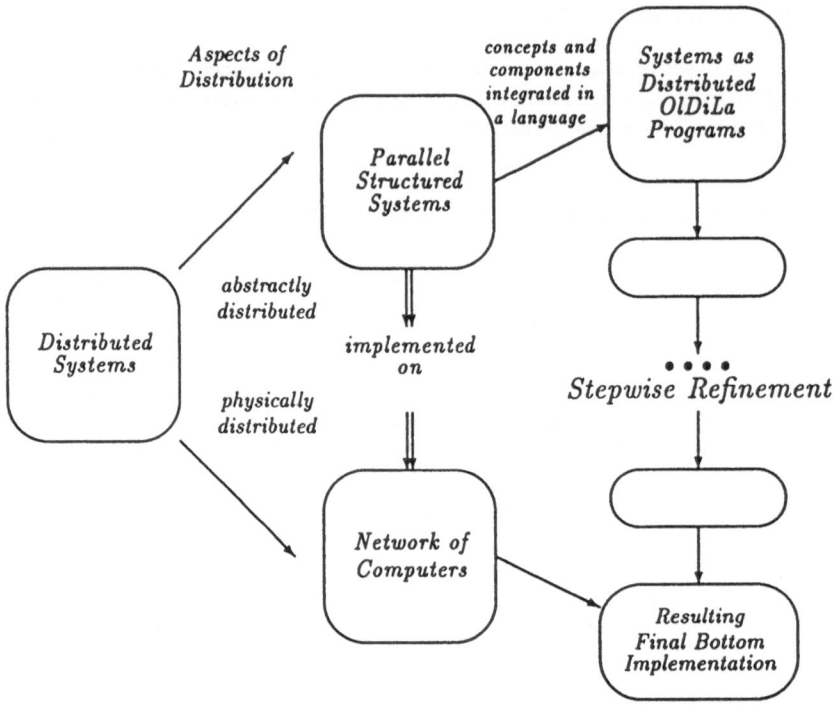

Figure 2: Top-down-driven stepwise refinement of concepts

The approach of *stepwise refinement of concepts* is presented and illustrated based upon an example ranking from abstractly distributed systems to a physically distributed computing system in the chapter about research in the area of distributed operating systems.

3. AREAS OF RESEARCH AND DEVELOPMENT

As shown in figure 1 four areas of research and development are in progress in the *Veritos* project.

3.1. MoDiS: a Kernel of a Software Enginering Environment

The development and construction of distributed systems using the experimental language *OlDiLa* must be guided by a method and must be aided by an integrated software engeneering environment. The objectives of *MoDiS* are to provide a kernel for a software engineering environment for distributed *OlDiLa* programs with a set of appropriate tools. At the moment a tool for *analyzing structures* is of primary interest. In the context of developing, extending, and completing *OlDiLa* specified systems this tool enables the developer to analyze system structures – like definitional and executional structures as defined above – and to prove many system attributes in any state of the development process. In addition prototypical experiments representing dynamic system evolutions can be made.

A prototype of the analyzer is implemented. *OlDiLa* programs can be processed including syntactical and semantical analysis and a transformation into a database. The implementation uses software tools from UNIX[3] for language processing (lex and yacc), Prolog for all kinds of analysis, and Open Dialog and X Windows for the user interface with graphical presentations of structures and attributes.

3.2. Applications

In general many distributed applications are possible. In the area of distributed operating systems an attractive example is a distributed file server. A file server has been designed using the concepts of *OlDiLa* including concepts for fault tolerance like atomic actions and protocols for their enforcement. The whole file server with its files and actions is realized using active and passive components and is integrated in a system according to the defined structures. The life-span of files and actions is defined by concepts; files are persistent components.

3.3. Approach to Distributed Operating Systems

The approach of stepwise refinement of concepts is introduced in general. Its benefits and usage can be primarily seen in the area of distributed operating systems as done in the *Veritos* project. Therefore the stepwise refinement of concepts will be presented and illustrated based upon a small example ranking from abstractly distributed systems to a physically distributed computing system.

The most important features of every component – and this holds especially for functional components as parts of distributed operating systems – are their *storing facilities* and their *computing facilities*.

In figure 3 typical examples for the approach in the *Veritos* project are shown. Stepwise

---

[3]UNIX is a registered trademark of AT&T in the USA and other countries, Open Dialogue of Apollo Computer Inc., X Window System of MIT, Quintus Prolog of Quintus Computer Systems Inc.

Level	Alternatives			
	experimental	*standard*	*advanced*	*innovative*
Functional	Still open, semantic required			
Operational	*OlDiLa* [C] Active Components [S] Active and Passive Components			
Structured	∅	[C] S-PR [S] Typed Segments		⇒ Requirements
Homogeneous	∅	[C] H-PR [S] Homogeneous Storage	[C] H-PR [S] Object Storage	⇒ Requirements
Real	C programs, processes, NCS	[C] R-PR [S] Virtual Storage, Main Memory, Backing Store	[C] R-PR [S] Main Memory, Backing Store	⇒ Requirements
Hardware (abstract)	Multiprocessor Nodes with LAN			
Hardware (concrete)	Apollo Domain with LAN	Mircoprocessor system with LAN	Advanced processing system with object storage	*to be built !*

[C] = computing facility, [S] = storing facility
S-PR, H-PR, R-PR are abstract processors prefixed by the name of the level.

Figure 3: Stepwise refinement of concepts with four alternative approaches

refinement leads to a set of five ordered levels as detailed levels of abstraction. These five levels are called *functional, operational* – hitherto the abstract level with its representation as *OlDiLa* programs –, *structured and homogeneous, real* and *concrete hardware* respectively.

Four alternative approaches are sketched. They are called *experimental*, experiments based upon given hardware, operating system and communication software are made, *standard*, this is the main line of development in the *Veritos* project (cf. [4]), *advanced*, based upon existing advanced hardware configurations (cf. e. g., [10]), and *innovative*, propagating requirements for the computer architecture derived in the *Veritos* approach.

The *operational level* was called abstract level above in the chapter about the general approach. This level is defined using the experimental language *OlDiLa*. It is a common base for every (of the four) approach. The active components define the computational facilities and both active and passive components have storing facilities.

The *functional level* is the result of a further step of abstraction. It is still open now. Its objectives are formal specifications of functionality especially with respect to verification.

On the remaining levels the <u>standard</u> approach gives the most understanding for the application of the principle of stepwise refinement. Only the aspects of storing and computing facilities are examined. The *structured and homogeneous level* defines a unique systemwide view of the whole systems. Physical distribution is transparent at this level. At the *structured 'sub'level* every component is realized as a set of specialized (typed) segments. A standard scheme is used for representation especially preserving all kinds of structural information. The segments have to be managed as memory resources. This is done at the *homogeneous 'sub'level* using a homogeneous storage, which can be seen as a one dimensional array of memory words. The design decisions, representations, and the concepts and mechanisms for their management at the structured homogeneous level will be detailed in [4].

With respect to the storing facilities the homogeneous storage has to be realized at the *real level* using e. g., virtual storage management, main memory, and a backing store.

All other approaches deviate form the standard way mainly with respect to the hardware level. The <u>advanced</u> approach is based upon existing processors integrating advanced processor and operating system technologies, whereas in the <u>innovative</u> approach only the requirements for the underlying computer (hardware) architecture are formulated. Both the concepts used for modelling distributed systems and the approach of stepwise refinement for implementing distributed systems produce lots of requirements – especially in the areas of protection, memory management, and dispatching – for computer architectures. They are part of the innovative approach.

In the <u>experimental</u> approach an existing pool of workstations interconnected by a local area network is used for experimental purposes. More details about this approach can be found in the next chapter about experiments with parallelism and distribution.

Using the standard approach with stepwise conceptual refinement a distributed operating system can be divided into four major parts. Each part represents a class of services (functional components) specific for a level. Among others they realize the mappings between adjacent levels. The resulting structure can be seen in figure 4.

270

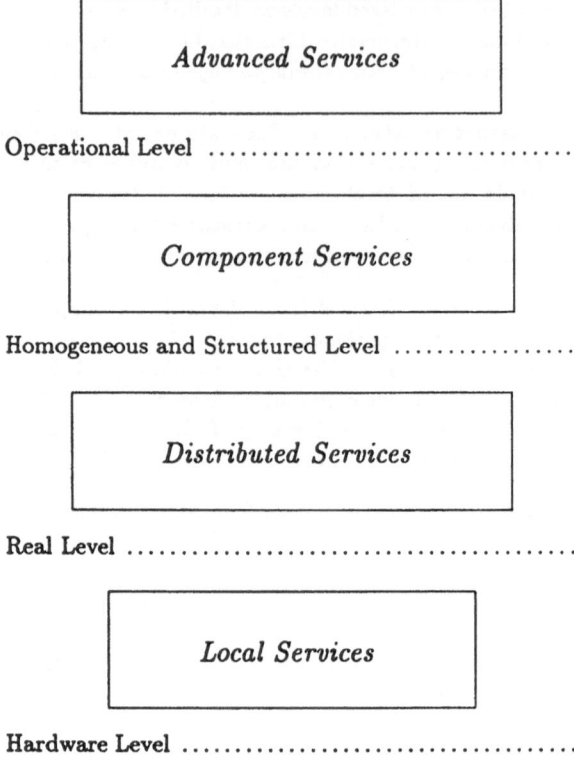

Figure 4: Integration of services and levels

Only a few examples for each group of services will be given here to sketch their functionality.

The *Local Services* must include `BasicActeurCommunication` to form a base for cooperation between active components, `BasicSynchronization`, `BasicScheduling Dispatching`, and `BasicMemoryManagement`. In sense of the DOS definition mentioned in the introduction the *Local Services* form the kernel common to all computing sites together with primitives for resource management.

The *Distributed Services* at the next level have to hide all kinds of distribution and any computing site dependent information. They may contain a `HomogeneousActeurMana ger`, a `HomogeneousMemoryManager`, and a `SystemWideDispatcher`.

The *Component Services* realize the specific representations of each component by `ComponentRepresentation`, which is not differentiated here.

At the top level *Advanced Services* may include a file system `FileSystem` – with files as persistent components –, an electronic mail system `EMail`, and many other services.

3.4. Experiments with Parallelism and Distribution

Based upon a local area network of workstations (HP / Apollo Domain) experiments with NCS[4] are in progress in order to get experience with parallel and distributed executions of programs. Active and passive components, as defined in the model, are implemented using processes, lightweight processes, and remote procedure calls. In the near future these experiments will be extended by the integration of transputers. Therewith the computing sites (workstations) become multiprocessor systems.

4. CONCLUDING REMARKS

The approach for developing, constructing, and implementing distributed operating systems in the *Veritos* project has been shown. In relation and delimitation to other approaches in the area of distributed (operating) systems some features have to be mentioned.

First of all every component concept supports the definition of clear functional (operation-oriented) interfaces. Dependencies on hardware concepts and facilities are intentionally excluded. Classical hardware-driven and hardware-oriented concepts, as known from the area of traditional operating systems, will be overcome by problem-oriented concepts for system structuring and component cooperation yielding high quality distributed systems. Examples are operation-oriented synchronous communication concepts and nesting of components with respect to many different relations. After all by means of stepwise refinement of concepts without loss of information migration of components between different computing sites and other dynamic decisions, protection at any level and dynamic development of systems, and its components are possible.

---

[4]NCS – Network Computing System – is a registered trademark of Apollo Domain.

The major areas of research and development in the *Veritos* project are briefly described. Nevertheless lots of work has to be done especially in the area of an experimental distributed operating system.

Acknowledgements

Work in the *Veritos* project in done – under the leadership of professor P.P. Spies – in a group including many advanced students.

REFERENCES

[1] The Programming Language ADA - Reference Manual, *American National Standards Institute, Inc., ANSI/MIL-STD- 1815A- 1983, LNCS, 155, Springer-Verlag, 1983*

[2] Atkinson, M.P., Bailey, P.J., Chisholm, K.J., Cockshott, P.W., Morrision, R., An Approach to Persistent Programming, *The Computer Journal, Vol. 26, No. 4, 1983*

[3] U. Baumgarten, R. Kewitz, D. König, P.P. Spies, Werkzeuge zur Entwicklung Verteilter Systeme, *GI - 18. Jahrestagung II, Hamburg, Oktober 1988, Informatik-Fachberichte, 188, Springer-Verlag, 1988*
(in german, title: "Tools for the Development of Distributed Systems")

[4] Eckert, C., Homogeneous Memory-Management in the Context of the *Veritos -* Project, *Proceedings of the Workshop on Computer Architectures to Support Security and Persistence of Information, Bremen, May 1990, in this issue*

[5] Fabry, R.S., Capability-Based Addressing, *CACM, Vol. 17, No. 7, July 1974, pp.403-412*

[6] Hoare, C.A.R., Monitors: An Operating System Structuring Concept, *CACM, Vol. 17, No. 10, October 1974*

[7] Jul, E., Levy, H., Hutchinson, N., Black, A., Fine-Grained Mobility in the Emerald System, *ACM TOCS, VOl.6, No.1, February 1988, pp.109-133*

[8] Meyer, Bertrand, Object-oriented Software Construction, *Prentice Hall, New York, 1988*

[9] Nehmer, J., Schmutz, H., Steinmetz, R., Netz-Betriebssystem/verteiltes Betriebssystem, *Informatik-Spektrum, Vol. 13, No. 1, 1990, pp. 38-39*

[10] Organick, E.I., A Programmer's View of the Intel 432 System, *McGraw-Hill Book Company, New York, 1983*

273

[11] Spies, P.P., Sprachkonzepte für die Konstruktion Verteilter Systeme, *Interne Berichte, Fachbereich Informatik, Universität Oldenburg, Bericht SA/88/2, August 1988*
(in german, title: "Language Concepts for the Construction of Distributed Systems ")

[12] Spies, P.P., Verteilte Systeme – Eine noch zu nutzende Chance –, *11. ITG/GI Fachtagung, Architektur von Rechensystemen, P. Müller-Stoy (Hrsg.), München, März 1990, pp. 415-428*

Homogeneous Memory Management in the Context of the VERITOS-Project

Claudia Eckert
University of Oldenburg

ABSTRACT

In this paper the design of a homogeneous memory management is presented. The homogeneous memory is currently developed within the VERITOS distributed operating system project. The project's aim is to elaborate concepts and principles to build distributed systems in a top-down approach starting at an operational level and reaching an ultimate hardware dependent realization level by stepwise refinement of concepts. The homogeneous storage is part of the intermediate hardware independent level. The concepts introduced for the design of the homogeneous memory management provide a separation of software management from hardware support, a uniform representation of the objects of the operational level, a lifetime oriented memory management maintaining structural relationships, and a protection basis to enforce security requirements.

The homogeneous memory management is based on a special segment concept, which will be discussed in detail.

1. INTRODUCTION

The design of a homogeneous memory management presented is part of the VERITOS distributed operating system project. The project's main objective is the elaboration of concepts and principles for constructing distributed systems, especially distributed operating systems. Such systems are developed in a model-oriented top-down manner guided by three main principles, which are the class principle, the object principle, and the principle of nesting of objects.

The key issue of the top-down approach pursued in the VERITOS project is to define a set of abstract concepts and methods, which are used in connection with software engineering techniques [3] to construct distributed system. The separation of abstract problem solving concepts from hardware support allows to construct systems with high performance and high quality.

Systems developed according to the abstract concepts are abstractly distributed. The implementation has to enforce a physical distribution of the abstract objects on the basis of a distributed hardware configuration.

In contrast to top-down approaches bottom-up approaches, like [5], are based on existing hardware architectures connected by a communication network. The main problem, which has to be solved within this approach, is the integration of the network in order to allow a transparent usage of services of the different nodes of the system. For this purpose new implementations of parts of the operating systems located on the nodes are necessary. The problem bottom-up versus top-down approach is discussed in [4].

The top-down approach of constructing distributed systems leads to a stepwise implementation starting with a system, which is designed and structured according to the above mentioned abstract concepts. The level, which defines the abstract properties of the system, is called the *operational level*. The operational level is mapped onto the next level called *hardware independent level*. By stepwise refinement of concepts the implementation results in an executable system on the *hardware dependent level* with physically distributed nodes connected by a communication network.

First, this paper will give a brief survey of the most important features of the operational level. A detailed description of the language concepts can be found in [1]. A survey of the approach pursued in the VERITOS project is given in [2].

The hardware independent level, which yields an abstract realization of the system, is of primary interest in this paper. The system on the hardware independent level can be viewed as an abstract machine with a homogeneous memory and with abstract processors. In order to implement the concepts of the operational level new concepts have to be introduced. In the following we will focus on the concepts needed to implement the abstract, homogeneous memory management. These concepts will be presented and the mapping between the operational and the hardware independent level will be outlined.

The integration of the hardware dependent mechanisms, which map the homogeneous storage to the physically distributed backing store and to the main memory of the nodes, is the task of the bottom level of the realization. Presuming a paged memory system as physical basis it seems appropriate to treat the main memory as a page cache for the homogeneous memory. Special hardware dependent mapping functions [6,7] are needed. The hardware dependent level will not be presented here.

2. SURVEY OF THE ABSTRACT CONCEPTS

The abstract concepts to specify distributed systems are embedded in a high level experimental programming language called *OlDiLa*, which serves both as programming and specification language.

A system on the operational level is defined as a set of active and passive objects. Objects are instances of classes called *generators*. The functionality of an object is defined by the set of operations. These operations, which may be used (invoked) by other objects, are called the *external properties* of the object. They are the interface to other objects. The *internal properties* of an object are defined by the abstract implementation, which enforces the information hiding principle. Invoking an external operation on an object causes a controlled change of the execution environment.

The properties of the objects are defined by the *generators*. Generators are themselves objects. Each generator defines the class properties, which all objects of this class have in common[1].

Passive objects only have storing facilities. Two kinds of passive objects called *depot* and *order*, respectively, exist. Depots may be long term storage objects. For that reason they especially can be used to implement files. The order concept is comparable with subprograms in high level programming languages, where the subprogram declaration is comparable with specification of an order generator and a subprogram invocation is comparable with the creation of an order object.

Active objects named *actors* possess computing facilities besides their storing facilities. Active objects are, therefore, the basis for parallel computations, whereas the execution of orders and depots is sequentially inserted into the computation of an actor. The communication between active objects is based on the operation-oriented rendezvous concept, but interaction using shared objects is allowed, too.

The set of active and passive objects is ordered by four interesting structures[2]. The most important one is the *definition* (δ) structure which essentially specifies the object's visibility and usability. The *execution* (α) structure represents the sequential and parallel computations and the communication between active objects. According to the nesting principle objects are declared local to other objects. This relationship is described by the *locality* (λ) structure. As the set of objects varies dynamically the lifetime of objects is of great importance. The *lifetime* (ε) structure guarantees the existence of objects as long as these objects are usable according to the concepts.

A more detailed description of the abstract concepts can be found in [1,2].

3. HOMOGENEOUS STORAGE DESIGN

As mentioned above the homogeneous storage is part of the intermediate hardware independent level. The homogeneous memory is a one-dimensional array of memory words representing the total amount of memory available on the hardware independent level. The following six requirements have influenced the design of the homogeneous memory management:

1. Management of a systemwide homogeneous memory. The abstract concept of active objects does not rely on hardware dependent features like, for instance, independent address spaces for each active object. Rather, the objects of the operational level may use common global objects according to the structures of the system. This motivates the demand for a systemwide homogeneous memory.

2. A uniform memory representation of the abstract objects. The hardware independent level has to abstractly implement the active and passive objects and their generators in a uniform way to present a simple interface to the hardware dependent level.

3. Separation of software management from hardware support. On the hardware independent level physical properties of memory such as memory capacity, number of

---

[1]In simple cases this is comparable with the type concept in high level programming languages.

[2]As generators are always locally nested in active or passive objects, there is no structural relationship defined on generator objects.

disks, modes of access, etc., which depend on the real hardware basis, are ignored to gain a general memory management scheme.

4. Preserving the structural relationships. As the system structures contain special information, one main objective of the hardware independent level is to preserve the abstract properties of the system of the operational level. Consider, for instance, a data object which is only accessible inside an order, because it is defined locally inside the order, and it is not visible outside the order. This is a structural information to be preserved by an appropriate hardware independent representation of the order object.

5. Management of storage in a lifetime oriented manner. The memory management according to the development facilities of the system is one key issue of the homogeneous memory management.

6. Establishment of a protection basis to enforce different security requirements.

In the following the hardware independent concepts, which are introduced to meet these, requirements are presented. With the requirements in mind we can separate two problems we heave to solve. The first problem concerns with the abstract implementation of the concepts in a uniform manner maintaining the structural relationships. The second problem refers to the lifetime oriented, systemwide memory management.

The first problem is solved by introducing special objects called *typed segments*. The segment concept is described in the next subsection.

3.1. Uniform representation

In order to gain a uniform representation of the objects of the operational level typed segments are introduced. The segment concept was influenced by the architecture of the Intel iAPX 432 [8] and by the BiiN architecture [9].

Segments are one-dimensional arrays of words indexed by bytes [3]. Segments represent a continuous set of words of the homogeneous memory.

Each kind of abstract object is represented by a well-defined set of typed segments. Important types of segments are the *access* segment, the *code* segment, the *data* segment, and the *process control block* segment[4]. Each segment type defines a set of operations, which is executable on instances of the type according to the object principle.

Each segment is described by a *segment descriptor*, which contains the segment's unique identifier, the segment's basis address in the homogeneous memory, the segment length, etc. The management of segments and their segment descriptors will be explained in the next subsection.

Segments are accessed via access pointers. These access pointers are comparable with

---

[3]With a hardware basis in mind which offers a distributed paging service, it seems appropriate to require that the segment basis address starts at a page boundary.

[4]Besides these segments, there are other special types of segments which will not be explained here.

capabilities [10] found, for instance, in [11]. An access pointer contains addressing information and access rights. These access pointers are not visible on the operational level and, therefore, it is not possible to forge or otherwise corrupt access pointers on the operational level.

Segments with type specific operations and the access pointers are the basic concepts to enforce a fine grained distribution of access rights.

With the introducing remarks we are able to explain the different segment types in greater detail.

Access segment:
The access segment is the most important segment in the context of this paper. Access segments only store access pointers and are, due to this feature, comparable with capability segments found, for instance, in the Hydra system [11]. The access segment of the representation of any abstract object contains all statical representation information, i.e., access pointers for all segments which are needed to represent the object itself. In addition the access segment is the root for the execution environment of the object, because the structural relationship between abstract objects is represented by access pointers, too. Whenever an abstract object X is in relation r to an abstract object Y, the access segment of the representation of X contains an access pointer to the access segment of the representation of Y.

One can imagine the access segment organized as a large array. Then, every access pointer is stored in a fixed array slot. To address a pointer the specification of the index of the array slot is needed. The general addressing schema is discussed in a subsequent section.

Invoking an external operation on an abstract object requires, on the abstract implementation level, the ownership of an access pointer for the access segment of the generator object of the specific operation. By partitioning the access segment into a private and a public part different access modes to the segment can be implemented. Access pointers stored in the public part are visible to other objects whereas the access pointers stored in the private part are invisible outside. This forms the basis to realize the information hiding principle and the controlled change of the execution environment on the hardware independent level.

The set of operations defined on access segments are *read_private_entry, write_private_entry, read_public_entry, write_public_entry*. The general structure of an access segment is outlined in figure 1.

Code segment
The code segment contains the instructions which define the functional behaviour of the represented object. The processors of the abstract machine, which realizes the hardware independent level, are able to execute these instructions. The operation defined on a code segment is *execute*.

Data segment
The data segment contains the local data objects (e.g. scalar variables) of the abstract object represented. A data segment has a (possible empty) public part and a private part. Only data objects stored in the public part are usable for objects being defined outside.

public part	data segment pointer	(pointer to the public part)
	generator pointers	(pointers to locally defined generator objects that are visible outside)
	...	
	λ_E pointers	(pointers to locally defined objects that are visible outside)
	...	
private part	δ pointer	(pointer to the object defining the generator)
	data segment pointer	(pointer to the private part)
	code segment pointer	
	process control block pointer	
	λ pointers	(pointers to locally defined objects not visible outside)
	α pointer	(pointer to a called object)
	σ pointer	(pointer to the caller object)
	κ pointers	(for communication activities)
	ε pointers	(for existence dependencies)
	...	

Figure 1: General structure of an access segment

On data segments *read_public*, *read_private*, *write_public* and *write_private* operations are predefined.

Process control block segment
Process control block segments are necessary for the representation of active objects. They provide information needed by the processors of the abstract machine (e.g., instruction counter, registers of the abstract processors, etc.). Operations defined on process control block segments are *read* and *write*.

The different segment types are used to implement abstract objects. Several kinds of special manager objects exist on the hardware independent level in order to perform the mapping between the operational level and the hardware independent level. The task of, for instance, an order manager is to create the uniform segment representation of an order object. Furthermore, manager objects are responsible for the distribution of access pointers according to the structural relationships of the system. In figure 2, there is an example of a segment representation of an order given.

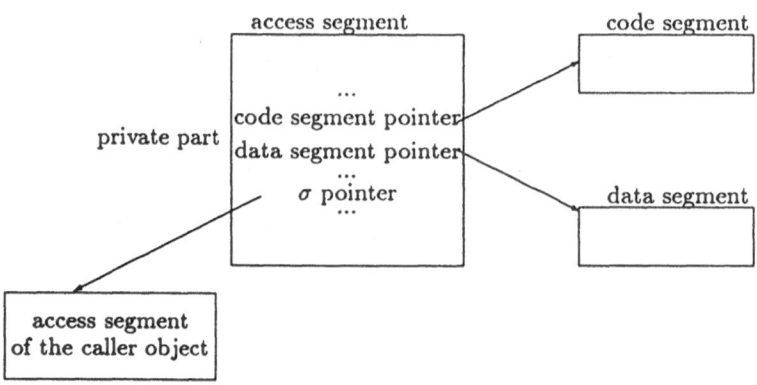

Figure 2: Segment representation of an order object

With the concepts introduced for the uniform representation of the abstract objects, two views of the homogeneous memory are possible. Looking top-down from the operational level the homogeneous memory provides a two dimensional segment space. Starting from the bottom hardware dependent level the homogeneous memory presents a one dimensional homogeneous interface. So the segment representation bridges the gap between abstract specification and real hardware.

After having discussed the uniform representation of abstract objects by typed segments the next subsection explains the concepts used on the hardware independent level to solve the problem of managing a systemwide homogeneous storage in a lifetime oriented manner.

3.2. Memory management concepts

The task of a systemwide homogeneous memory management is to satisfy requests for memory resources raised during the execution of the system. The objects in the system which are responsible for the dynamic development of the system, are the actors. During the execution of the operation defining the actor's functionality an actor creates other objects and, therefore, requires memory space for their representation. That means, that all actors compete for the systemwide memory. Except for synchronization events caused, for instance, by communication, the executions of actors are independent from each other on the operational level. Nevertheless, the implementation on the linear systemwide memory leads to artificial dependencies caused by synchronized memory accesses. A reasonable solution for the problem is to enable actors to manage on their own the memory representation of all objects that depend in lifetime from them. For this purpose special memory objects called *m-segments* (memory segments) are introduced and attached to actors. The m-segments are part of an actor representation on the hardware independent level.

3.2.1. The memory segment concept

The task of a m-segment is the local management of a part of the homogeneous memory. Every memory segment consists of a *local descriptor table* structured as an array with indexed access to the stored descriptors and of a *memory resource*. The memory resource has not to be a continuous part of the homogeneous storage. The m-segment's external properties are defined by the operations needed to manage the local memory resource. Every m-segment offers at least two operations named *allocate* and *deallocate*. Like a typed segment every m-segment is described by a segment descriptor. The access to a m-segment requires the possession of an appropriate access pointer.

The execution of an *allocate* operation results in the creation of a segment (e.g., access segment) and the creation of the segment descriptor for the new segment. The descriptor is stored in the local descriptor table of the m-segment, and an access pointer is created containing the addressing information for the new segment.

Executing the *deallocate* operation destroys a segment and removes the associated descriptor table entry. Access pointers are not explicitly revoked.

In contrast to the concept of single addressing spaces for every active object, the concept of m-segments allows the sharing of objects by distributing the access pointers in a controlled way.

The lifetime oriented memory management is based on the m-segment concept. As mentioned above the lifetime of every object on the operational level is determined according to the abstract system structures in VERITOS. That means, that the lifetime of objects is determined by the concept. This is in contrast to other object-oriented approaches [12], where the lifetime of objects depends on the existence of a pointer to the object. Sophisticated garbage collection mechanisms are needed in such approaches [13].

To take into account the different lifetime dependencies defined by the concepts of the operational level two kinds of m-segments – *stacks* and *heaps* – are necessary. The local memory resource of a stack segment is divided into two parts. One part is managed in a stack like manner (i.e., push and pop semantic of the management operations), whereas the other part is itself a heap segment. The stack part manages the segment representation of those abstract objects, whose lifetime express the linear ordering of the nesting structure of objects on the operational level. Order objects (i.e., subprogram invocations) are examples for objects represented on stack parts of stack segments.

Heap memory segments have to manage all other objects. Examples of objects, which are represented in heap segments are the actors themselves. More precisely, the stack segment of the actor is represented on a heap segment, whereas the uniform segment representation of the actor itself is stored in the stack part of its stack segment. So, the nesting of active objects leads to a nested m-segment structure.

Objects, which have a lifetime that lasts much longer than the lifetime of the creating object, are other examples for heap allocated objects.

Example 1:

The two-dimensional representation of an active object A1 managing in parallel a local order call O1 and an actor call A2 is shown in figure 3. The stack segment of the actor A1 itself is represented in a heap segment A0. During the execution of the actor A1 an order O1 is created. To allocate the segment representation of this order the local stack part of the actor A1 is used. To create, for example, an active object A2 a heap segment is needed, because the new actor may have a longer lifetime than the creating object. In simple cases the heap segment of the actor executing the actor call can be used to allocate the desired memory space. The stack segment of the created actor A2 is represented in the heap segment of actor A1.

The nesting of m-segments leads to a m-segment *tree* structure. The root m-segment of this tree is a stack segment S_0, which manages the whole homogeneous memory space. As explained above, the stack resource is divided into a stack part and a heap segment (H_0) part. Creating a new active object A_1 results in the creation of a new stack segment $S_1(A_1)$ for the representation of A_1. The memory request for $S_1(A_1)$ is satisfied by the heap segment H_0. The stack segment $S_1(A_1)$ again consists of a stack and a heap part. The tree structure of the m-segments of example 1 is shown in figure 4.

Consider, for instance, the stack segment A2. According to the tree structure of the m-segments we know, that the immediate predecessor of stack segment A2 in the tree, (i.e. the heap segment A1), had created stack A2 and had equipped stack A2 with a memory resource, which is afterwards locally managed by stack A2. In addition, in case of a memory overflow during the lifetime of stack A2, the immediate predecessor is responsible for handling this memory fault.

Objects represented in the stack parts of m-segments are popped from the stack (i.e., the deallocate operation is executed) as soon as they have terminated and their representation has reached the top of stack position. Deallocating the access segment of such objects results in the deallocation of all dependent objects (ε pointer), which are represented in the associated heap part of the stack segment.

The termination of an active object results in the deallocation of the stack segment re-

283

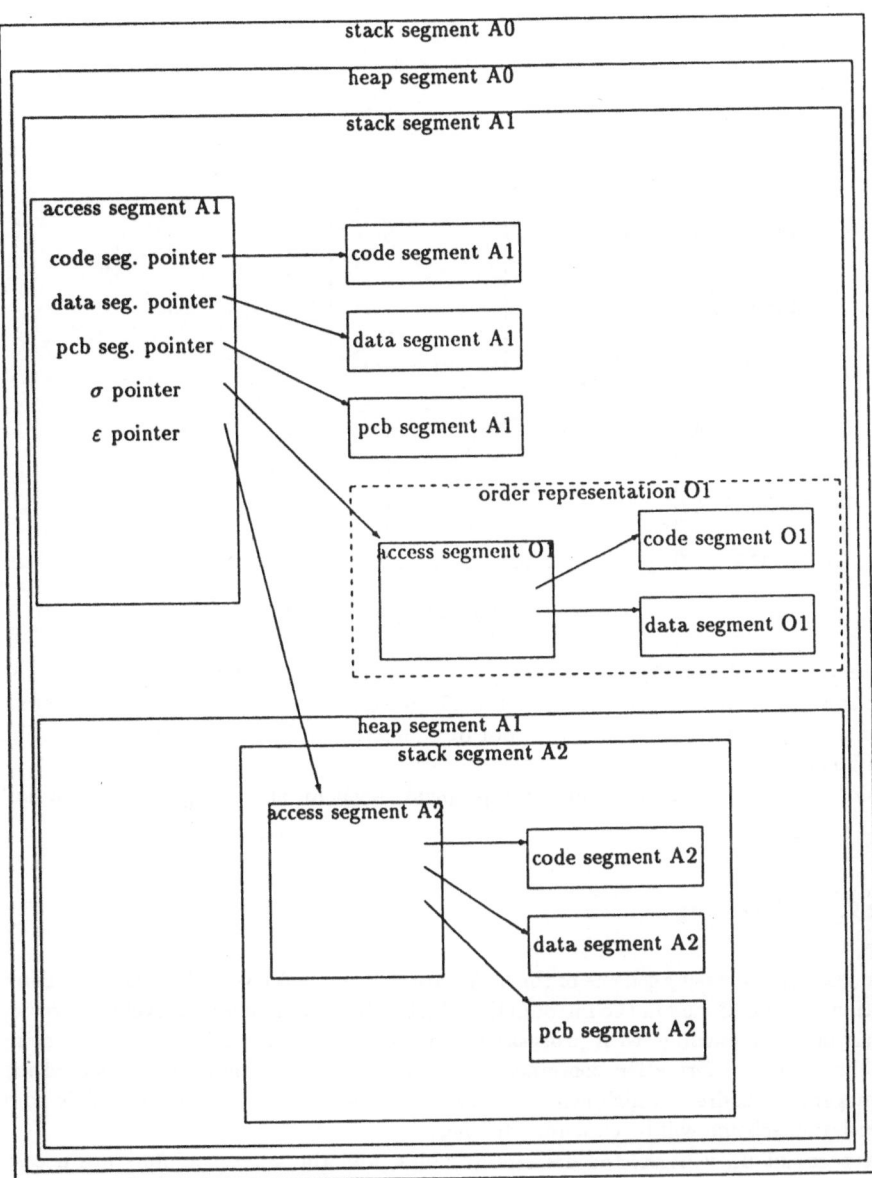

Figure 3: Nesting of segments

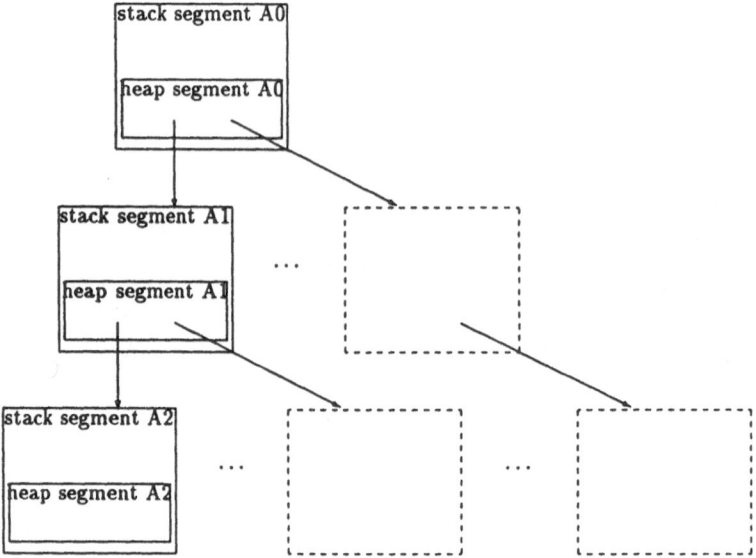

Figure 4: m-segment tree of example 1

presenting the object. The associated heap segment is automatically deallocated, too. The m-segment tree structure reflects the lifetime dependencies between m-segments. As soon as a m-segment, which is the root of a subtree, is deallocated, the whole subtree will be deallocated, too.

Besides, the tree structure yields an appropriate basis for specifying distribution units.

3.2.2. Addressing

The general addressing scheme of the hardware independent level will be described in this section. As mentioned in the introduction the hardware independent level can be viewed as an abstract machine with processors and a one dimensional homogeneous memory. So the address information contained in the access pointers must be translated into a homogeneous address, which can be processed by the abstract processors. This address translation scheme will be explained further.

The segment descriptors, the descriptor tables, and the access pointers are necessary objects for addressing segments and components of segments. Whenever a segment is created a new segment descriptor is produced. The allocation of the memory space for the new segment leads to an entry in the associated segment descriptor, which holds the base address of the segment and the segment's unique identifier (c.f. figure 5).

As mentioned above the descriptor of a typed segment is stored in the local descriptor table of the m-segment, which had allocated the segment on its local memory resource.

uid	segment length	type	...	homogeneous memory address (base address)

Figure 5: Segment descriptor

For the segment addressing scheme the index i of the descriptor table entry of the descriptor is used as part of the addressing information.

Because every segment is managed by a m-segment, the address of this segment especially of its local descriptor table is needed. The base address of the local table is contained in the m-segment's descriptor. Taking into account the nesting structure of m-segments, the address translation scheme needs the complete access path to address the desired m-segment-table.

Let M_n be the m-segment managing the typed segment which should be accessed. Let j_n be the index of the descriptor of M_n in the local table of the m-segment M_{n-1}. Then j_n is part of the address path. The same holds for M_{n-1}, unless it is the root of the path. The address scheme results in extremely long access paths and very large access pointers (c.f. figure 6).

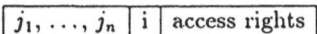

$j_1, \ldots, j_n$	i	access rights

Figure 6: General structure of an access pointer

Concepts and mechanisms are needed to reduce the length of the access paths considerably (e.g., a hierarchy of m-segment tables). Work in this area is still in progress. Presently, hashing is used to address the m-segments directly. The m-segment's uids are the keys of the hashing function. This approach results in a modified access pointer shown in figure 7.

m-segment uid	i	access rights

Figure 7: Modified access pointer

A logical address is defined by a pair (access pointer, offset). The base address of the segment being accessed is computed by hashing the m-segment uid in order to obtain the m-segment table base address. With the entry i the segment descriptor is selected, which yields the base address of the desired segment. With the specified offset the segment component is finally addressed.

During the address translation rights checks are performed.

4. PROTECTION

With regard to security requirements the abstract concepts of VERITOS supply an appropriate basis.

The concepts support a modular programming style. Data encapsulation and information hiding is achieved. The elaborated system structures are enriched with the capability to explicitly specify export and import restrictions for objects. This allows to restrict the access facilities of objects.

With the concept's features the *need to know principle* [16] based on a protection domain concept [15] is enforced.

Presently, a protection model is elaborated, based on an extended access matrix model. The operation orientation of the overall concepts allows to dispose access rights on a very high abstraction level.

The segment and access pointer concept of the hardware independent level provides an appropriate basis to enforce different security policies.

With the uniform segment representation scheme introduced in section 3.1. every abstract object as well as every single operation of an abstract object is separately represented.

Combined with the concept of typed segments this allows to confer fine grained access rights to single objects and even single operations. The controlled distribution of access pointers is the duty of the special manager objects mentioned above.

The uniform segment representation scheme supports in a direct manner the implementation of small protection domains and the *need to know* principle is easily realized.

In order to enforce a discretionary security policy specified by the protection model abstract capabilities or access lists may be introduced on the operational level. On the hardware independent level the access pointer concept is an appropriate mechanism to abstractly implement those abstract capabilities.

5. CONCLUSION AND FUTURE WORK

The design of the homogeneous memory management was presented. It was shown that the concepts introduced are appropriate to offer a uniform and simple interface to the hardware dependent level as well as to meet the requirements for a lifetime oriented memory management maintaining the structural relationships between abstractly specified objects. In addition, the integration of security issues was outlined

One objective of the concept of nested m-segments is to reduce the amount of undesired correlation between active objects. The nesting of m-segments raises strategical problems that have to be solved to meet this goal. The general problem can be stated as follows: what has to be done if the local memory resource of a m-segment has expired but there are still memory allocation requests pending?

The tree structure of the m-segments (see figure 4) is the basis for answering the question. The simplest policy is to request a new piece of homogeneous memory from the direct predecessor in the tree. A more elaborated policy is pursued in our present work. In this approach two thresholds will be defined to determine a lower and upper boundary. With the creation of a m-segment this two threshold are determined. If the amount of allocated memory falls short of the lower threshold during a time interval, then the memory resource of the m-segment will be reduced and the memory space will be made available to the immediate predecessor in the m-segment tree. If, on the other side, the amount of allocated memory goes beyond the upper threshold, then the m-segment claims for additional memory space to enlarge its resource. This request may be satisfied by the immediate predecessor in the m-segment tree. The work on this area is still in progress. In order to obtain quantitative results a simulation of the homogeneous memory design is being elaborated.

In addition, the m-segment concept may serve as the basis for specifying distribution units. As mentioned above the stepwise implementation requires the mapping of the hardware independent level on a real distributed hardware basis. Consider a set of nodes equipped with a given amount of backing store and connected with a communication network. The task of the hardware dependent level is to physically distribute programs written in OlDiLa. For this purpose the units of distribution or migration must be determined. The m-segment structure seems to be an appropriate basis to distribute the active objects. In current work the problems of mapping the m-segment structure onto the backing store, the memory coherence problem [14], etc., are dealt with.

The integration of security concepts is another area we are still working in. A protection model based on an extended access-matrix model is being developed.
The integration of security into a distributed system requires the integration of mechanisms for network security. In order to guarantee information security, the messages sent across the network have to be encrypted. Based on cryptographic methods, key distribution protocols, key renewal protocols, etc., are being elaborated.

REFERENCES

1. Spies, P.P. "Sprachkonzepte für die Konstruktion Verteilter Systeme ", *Technical report (Interner Bericht des Fachbereichs Informatik der Universität Oldenburg,)* SA/88/2, Oldenburg 1988

2. Baumgarten, U. "VERITOS Distributed Operating System Project –An Overview–", *in this issue*

3. Baumgarten, U., Kewitz, R., König, D., Spies, P.P. " Werkzeuge zur Entwicklung Verteilter Systeme", *Informatik-Fachberichte* 1988, Springer-Verlag, Berlin, 1988, p. 589 – 602

4.   Spies, P.P. "Verteilte Systeme – Eine noch zu nutzende Chance –", P. Müller-Stoy (Hrsg), *Architektur von Rechensystemen*, 11. ITG/GI Fachtagung, München, März 1990, p. 415 – 428

5.   Popek,G., Walker, B.J. "The LOCUS Distributed System Architecture", *The MIT Press*, Cambridge (Mass.), 1985

6.   Rashid, R., Tevanian, A., Young, M. Baron, R., Black, D. Boloski, W., Chew, J. "Machine-Independent Virtual Memory Management for Paged Uniprocessor and Multiprocessor Architectures", *ACM Proceedings of the Second International Conference on Architectural Support for Programming Languages and Operating Systems*, October 5-8 1987, Palo Alto, pages 31 –39

7.   Russo, V.F. and Campell, R.H. "Virtual Memory and Backing Storage Management in Multiprocessor Operating Systems Using Object-Oriented Design Techniques", *ACM Proceedings OOPSLA '89*, October 1-6, 1989, pages 267 – 278

8.   Organick, E. I. "A Programmer's View of the Intel 432 System", *McGraw-Hill Book Company*, 1983

9.   BiiN "BiiN Systems Overview", *BiiN*, Hillsboro, Oregon, 6AN9000-1AJ00-0BA2

10.   Dennis, J.B. and van Horn, E.C. "Programming Semantics for Multiprogrammed Computations", *Communications of the ACM*, vol 9(3), 1966, p 143

11.   Cohen, E. and Jefferson, D. : "Protection in the Hydra Operating System", *Proceedings of the 5-th Symposium on Operating System Principles*, 1975, p 141

12.   Meyer, B. : "Object-oriented Software Construction", *Prentice Hall International Series in Computer Science*, 1988

13.   Ungar, D. and Jackson, F. : "Tenuring Policies for Generation-Based Storage Reclamation", *ACM Proceedings OOPSLA '88*, September 25–30, 1988, pp 1 – 17

14.   Li, K. and Hudak, P. "Memory Coherence in Shared Virtual Memory Systems", *ACM Transactions on Computer Systems*, vol 7(4), November 1989, p 321

15.   Lampson, B.W. "Dynamic Protection Structures", *AFIPS Proc. Fall Jt. Computer Conference*, vol. 35, 1969, pp 27 – 38

16.   Saltzer, J.H. and Schroeder, M.D. "The Protection of Information in Computer Systems", *IEEE Proceedings*, vol 63(9), pp 1278 – 1308, Sept. 1975

Considerations of Persistence and Security in Choices, an Object-Oriented Operating System

Roy H. Campbell and Peter W. Madany
University of Illinois at Urbana-Champaign

ABSTRACT

Choices is an object-oriented operating system written in an object-oriented language and runs on bare hardware. It supports distributed, parallel applications on a network of multiprocessors. The kernel is implemented as a dynamic collection of objects that have been instantiated from classes. The classes are represented as objects at run-time. *Choices* has a paged virtual memory organized around memory objects. Each memory object can have its own separate backing store, page placement, and page replacement algorithms. It can be shared, both within a shared memory multiprocessor and between networked computers using a distributed virtual memory protocol.

Choices supports an object-oriented file system model in which files may be mapped into virtual memory. Together, the kernel and an object file store specialization of the file system model provide persistent objects. Applications are permitted controlled access to the methods of persistent objects. Security and protection are provided by a combination of object proxies, access lists, and name servers. This paper discusses the persistence and security design issues that are being studied in the *Choices* implementation.

1. INTRODUCTION

Choices is an object-oriented operating system written in an object-oriented language (C++). The system runs on bare hardware: the NS32332, the MC86030, and the Intel 386. It supports distributed, parallel applications on a network of Encore Multimax multiprocessors.

Choices has, as its kernel, a dynamic collection of objects. System resources, mechanisms, and policies are represented as objects that belong to a class hierarchy.[1] For programming convenience, the root of the hierarchy is an *Object* and the classes of the hierarchy are represented as *Class* Objects. A Class supports several methods including:

- isMemberOf, which takes a Class as its argument and returns whether the Object is an instance of the given Class,

- isKindOf, which takes a Class as its argument and returns whether the Object is an instance of the given Class or any of its subclasses, and

- isASubclassOf, which takes a Class as its argument and returns whether the Class is a subclass of the given Class.

---

[1] By convention, we use an initial capital letter to designate the class of such objects. Where we unambiguously refer to an instance of a class, we will use the name of the class of the object.

All entities in the operating system are modeled as objects and include system processes, user processes, files, regions of memory, and hardware devices like CPU's and disk controllers. The application/kernel interface is defined by method invocations from objects in user mode to objects in kernel mode. In user mode, a kernel object is represented by an *ObjectProxy*. An ObjectProxy may be static or created dynamically on demand if the protection policy of the kernel object is not violated. Kernel objects are mapped into ObjectProxies by special kernel objects called *NameServers*. The performance of the ObjectProxy approach is described in Section 7.

A *Choices* Process executes in a Domain, which maps a collection of logical data segments or MemoryObjects into a virtual memory. Each MemoryObject can be paged to its own backing store using independent paging algorithms. Distributed virtual memory[6] allows the dynamic addition or removal of a MemoryObject to or from the different virtual memories of a network of computers.

Persistent storage is based on an object-oriented file system model. MemoryObject subclasses support access to data stored on disks, files, or physical memory in a variety of formats. The formats include interface and data representations for UNIX 4.3 BSD file systems, MS-DOS file systems, and UNIX System V file systems [9, 8]. Files may be mapped into virtual memory and this allows transparent access to persistent data. Distributed virtual memory will allow files to be accessed remotely.

An object store is a specialized application of the file system. PersistentObjects reside in the store as MemoryObjects and are mapped into virtual memory on request. Method invocations on PersistentObjects are identical to method invocations on normal Objects. Distributed virtual memory will allow remote method invocations on PersistentObjects.

Security is provided by a combination of access rights maintained by the file system, individual objects, and a user/system protection mechanism. Kernel objects are protected by supervisor state and by the virtual memory hardware. Method calls to kernel objects from user applications cannot be performed unless the user has been granted permission to access the object. That permission is provided in the form of an ObjectProxy. Once provided, all method calls to the ObjectProxy are trapped and converted to method calls to the kernel object. During the trap, they are checked for validity by a kernel protection mechanism. Non-kernel objects are mapped into the virtual memory space of the application. Their data segments may be shared between applications using shared virtual memory or distributed virtual memory. Once access is established, method calls can be made directly from the application to the object.

This paper discusses the persistence and security design issues that are being studied by the Choices implementation.

2. VIRTUAL MEMORY SUPPORT FOR MEMORYOBJECTS

A *Choices* process executes in a Domain, which is a mapping between a virtual memory space and MemoryObjects[14]. Each memory-mapped MemoryObject has a single MemoryObjectCache that maintains physical memory management information associated with virtual memory. The information is kept in a machine independent and virtual memory address independent form. This allows a Domain to map a particular MemoryObject into several regions of its virtual address space. It also allows several Domains to share both a MemoryObject and its MemoryObjectCache and common physical memory management information.

The Domain resolves the virtual memory address of a page fault into a MemoryObject and offset pair. The Domain requests the MemoryObject to map the offset. In turn, the MemoryObject requests its MemoryObjectCache to repair the fault. The paging strategy is encapsulated entirely within the MemoryObjectCache. If required, a page frame is requested from the frame Store. The Store returns a descriptor that identifies the physical memory into which data will be paged. The MemoryObject fetches the data from backing store and returns the descriptor to the Domain. In turn, the Domain passes the descriptor to an AddressTranslation method that updates the hardware virtual memory mapping. Then the process that generated the page fault is resumed.

Distributed virtual memory is implemented by a subclass of MemoryObjectCache[6]. Page coherency is maintained through DVMPageRecords. Each DVMPageRecord defines the state of a page. The coherency protocol is defined by a state machine and state transitions. The current protocol used allows one computer to own a page at a time and ownership is driven by a demand to write. The owner responds to remote read requests for the page by changing its page to read-only access and copying the page to the requesting computer with read-only access. Before a write, all remote read-only copies of the page are invalidated.

Since distributed virtual memory is associated with the MemoryObject, the scheme is flexible and permits a Domain to share many distributed MemoryObjects, each of which may use a different coherency protocol and be shared by a disjoint set of remote computers. Distributed virtual memory is established by mapping a remote MemoryObject into virtual memory. A remote MemoryObject can be obtained in many ways including through method invocation on PersistentObjects and through the distributed file system interface.

3. AN OBJECT-ORIENTED FILE SYSTEM MODEL

The object-oriented file system model[7] structures the data of MemoryObjects with *StoredObjects*. The two main subclasses of StoredObject that organize storage are ObjectContainer and ObjectDictionary. FileStream and PersistentObject are two further subclasses of StoredObject that provide useful programming abstractions of a MemoryObject.

A MemoryObject provides read and write methods to access the logical collection of persistent data that it manages. The read and write methods transfer *blocks* of data. Additional methods are used to support memory-mapping and protection. MemoryObject subclasses are specialized by the storage mechanism used to store the data and include Disks that read and write sectors, Partitions that read and write clusters of disk sectors within a contiguous region of a Disk, and various logical "disks", or files, like UNIX inodes. Along with its data, the MemoryObject also records a specific subclass of StoredObject, and this determines how its data may be used. Each StoredObject is *based on* a single MemoryObject, which is called its *underlying* MemoryObject.

An ObjectContainer organizes a MemoryObject into an indexed collection of MemoryObjects. Compared with the original MemoryObject, the MemoryObjects of a Container correspond to a more abstract storage mechanism or higher level within the file system. The Container may impose a dynamic or static organization on the MemoryObject depending on the abstraction being implemented. By definition, MemoryObjects must belong to exactly one ObjectContainer and can be subdivided into at most one ObjectContainer. ObjectContainers can be nested to an arbitrary depth. A MemoryObject descriptor called an *IdNumber* includes a list of indices that uniquely identify the location of a MemoryObject stored in nested ObjectContainers.

All StoredObjects and their underlying MemoryObjects are persistent objects that can be activated and deactivated as well as created and deleted. Except for PersistentObjects (see Section 5), the activation and deactivation of StoredObjects is explicitly programmed within the methods of the Objects. ObjectContainers provide the methods open, close, and create to activate, deactivate, and create MemoryObjects, respectively. MemoryObjects are deleted if, after they have been closed, they are no longer referenced by any other objects in the file system. The open method takes an index as argument and returns the corresponding MemoryObject. Internally, the ObjectContainer associates a descriptor with each index that includes a reference to the MemoryObject once it has been opened. Successive opens return the reference obtained by the first open. An *activation* ReferenceCount is maintained by opens and closes and when this count returns to zero, the MemoryObject is deactivated.

ObjectContainer subclasses are specialized by the scheme used to provide an indexed collection of MemoryObjects and include DiskContainers, which divide the storage of a Disk into an collection of Partitions, and various stream-oriented file system containers, which divide the storage of a Partition into a collection of files and free blocks.

An ObjectDictionary, also called a directory, uses its underlying MemoryObject to store a mapping from convenient symbolic keys for MemoryObjects to the indices used by an ObjectContainer. Within any ObjectDictionary, the keys must be unique, but several keys may map to the same index. MemoryObjects can belong to one or more ObjectDictionaries. The open method takes a key as an argument and, if the key is found, returns the appropriate MemoryObject. It obtains this reference by invoking the open method on the ObjectContainer using the appropriate index. ObjectDictionaries also have methods to add and remove mapping entries. When a MemoryObject is added to an ObjectDictionary, the MemoryObject's *link* count is incremented. When a MemoryObject is removed from an ObjectDictionary, the MemoryObject's link count is decremented. ObjectContainers can use this link count to determine when MemoryObjects are no longer needed and therefore need to be deleted. ObjectDictionary subclasses are specialized by various file system standards for describing the storage layout of mappings.

The StoredObject subclass, FileStream, provides applications with a stream-oriented interface to MemoryObjects. FileStreams provide byte-addressability and the concept of a "current file position". Applications may use read and write methods to read and write multiple bytes of sequential data. These methods change the current file position. The seek method also changes the current file position. A FileStream either buffers individual application reads and writes and invokes block reads and writes on its associated MemoryObject, or it directly exploits the memory-mapping of MemoryObjects into an application's Domain.

Specializations of the file system model provide stream-oriented file systems that conform to operating system standards such as 4.3 BSD UNIX, System V UNIX, and MS-DOS[9, 8]. Preliminary performance data has been gathered for the 4.3 BSD UNIX specialization, see Section 7. The file system class hierarchy also supports the construction of customized and experimental file systems. Various instances of file systems can coexist and interoperate in a running *Choices* system.

The experimental file systems that have been built include a log-structured file system described in [11]. Log-structured file systems are designed to increase I/O throughput by reducing disk head movement. We have two working prototypes of log-structured file systems and we plan to measure and analyze their performance. Another experimental file system provides the UNIX stream-oriented interface to formatted files of various kinds including libraries and archives. The *Choices* stream-oriented file system tools can then be used on these formatted files without modification. A file system for the UNIX "ar" format has been finished and "tar", "cpio", "a.out", and "Mail" formats are in progress.

4. AN OBJECT-ORIENTED KERNEL INTERFACE

The *Choices* kernel is a dynamic collection of objects that is structured by a class hierarchy. Applications access kernel facilities by invoking methods on kernel objects. Abstract classes provide interfaces for generic services within the kernel, for example I/O services. New objects can be installed within the kernel and their methods can be invoked both by application programs and by other system objects using the abstract interfaces.

The ObjectProxy class provides a transparent capability to invoke the methods of kernel objects. An ObjectProxy is a protected object that delegates method calls to a specified object. The use of ObjectProxies requires no compiler modifications. They are syntactically and semantically identical to the objects they represent and may be used interchangeably with them. Kernel objects may be used instead of application objects in a user program with no change to the program. Kernel objects may also use ObjectProxies to access other kernel objects.

Without an appropriate ObjectProxy, application program access to kernel objects is prevented by the virtual memory mapping and supervisor mode protection of the hardware. An ObjectProxy is allocated in read-only memory so that it may be modified only by trusted system code. ObjectProxies are obtained from a NameServer that resolves requests involving symbolic names into ObjectProxy references.

An application invoking a method call[2] on an ObjectProxy follows the standard C++ conventions for method lookup by jumping indirectly through an indexed address in the virtual function table (vtable) associated with the object. The first word of a C++ object contains the address of its vtable. The second word of an ObjectProxy contains the address of the actual object to be accessed. All ObjectProxies share a common vtable and the resulting code that is executed records the method index and reinvokes the method on the actual object. When an application is making the method call, the code traps into kernel code before completing the method call reinvocation. Care is taken in the code to check that an ObjectProxy is not located in application memory.

5. PERSISTENT OBJECTS

In *Choices*, the concept of a *persistent object* provides a unification and simplification of several subsystems. Essentially, a persistent object is a member of a subclass of PersistentObject, which has methods, local data, and a lifetime comparable to a file in a file system. Its lifetime is "global"; that is, it does not depend on the lifetime of application or system processes and can survive reboots of the system. However, its lifetime does depend on maintaining the integrity of the *Choices* file system. To simplify programming, PersistentObjects may store references to other PersistentObjects in their local data. To avoid making a distinction between a PersistentObject and a conventional object, activating and deactivating a PersistentObject is performed transparently. This is in direct contrast with the way that persistent data is accessed in the file system, where files must be opened and closed explicitly.

5.1. Persistence

The mechanisms to support PersistentObjects are built as a specialization of existing mechanisms: the *Choices* object-oriented file system model and memory-mapped files. Except for the following minor restrictions, a PersistentObject has transparent usage:

1. A pointer cannot be used to store the virtual memory address of a PersistentObject within the local data of a PersistentObject because that address may be invalid or inappropriate in one of the many different virtual memory spaces into which the object may be mapped during its lifetime. Instead, PersistentObjects must use a *Reference* to store a descriptor for another PersistentObject. A Reference is a lightweight object that has the same operational syntax as a pointer.

2. The creation of a PersistentObject uses a method call rather than the standard C++ new operator.

These restrictions arise because *Choices* currently runs on 32-bit address virtual memory architectures. To maximize the virtual memory space available to a process, no virtual address range is used by deactivated PersistentObjects. PersistentObjects may be mapped at different addresses within different Domains during their lifetime. The virtual memory address of a PersistentObject within a particular Domain is always the same during an activation although

---

[2]For an object to be *proxiable*, its public methods must be *virtual* functions.

it might change after a period of deactivation. The Reference mechanism allows the operating system to avoid potential address conflicts.[3]

References contain a "pointer" that locates a PersistentObject within a persistent *object store*. When a Reference is first assigned the location of a PersistentObject, the corresponding MemoryObject may not be memory-mapped into the Domain containing the Reference. Before the Reference can be dereferenced to invoke a method on the PersistentObject, the PersistentObject must be "active" and *bound* to an address within the virtual memory. The initial dereference binds the Reference to an address and stores the address for future use. Subsequent method calls dereferencing the Reference use the stored address. The following steps are performed each time a Reference is used:

1. Check if the PersistentObject has been bound to a virtual memory address. If it has, proceed to step 10.

2. Request the retrieval of the underlying MemoryObject of the PersistentObject from the file system.

3. If the MemoryObject has not already been opened, the file system opens it.

4. Check the class of the MemoryObject against the class of the Reference.

5. If the code for the methods of the PersistentObject has not already been loaded, load the code from the file system.

6. If the MemoryObject has not already been mapped into any Domain, create a cache for it.

7. If the MemoryObject has not already been mapped into the current Domain, map the MemoryObjectCache into the current Domain.

8. Set the vtable pointer for the PersistentObject to the correct value.

9. Store the virtual memory address of the mapped MemoryObject for future use.

10. Proceed with the method call using the virtual memory address.

If the PersistentObject is a kernel object and the Reference is stored in the virtual memory of an application, the Reference will, if permitted by the NameServer, bind the address to an ObjectProxy representing the object. Having introduced the PersistentObject scheme, several Reference mechanism design considerations require further explanation.

5.2. References

References, which are used instead of pointers in the local data of PersistentObjects and applications, allow semi-permanent storage of complex data structures. References are only used to refer to PersistentObjects, thus the PersistentObject implementation imposes neither a time nor a space overhead on the use of memory-only C++ objects. They provide the following features: compile-time type checking, a syntax identical to pointers, transparent object activation and deactivation, and automatic garbage collection.

---

[3] A port of *Choices* to a machine with a 64- or 128-bit virtual memory address space would allow a single large virtual memory address space for all Domains. PersistentObjects could be assigned an address for the duration of their lifetime. This would allow us to remove the restrictions but would not require a change to applications or PersistentObject code.

Type Checking. To help ensure the correct usage of PersistentObjects, References are typed by a Reference class hierarchy that mirrors the PersistentObject class hierarchy. Typed References allow almost all uses of PersistentObjects to be type-checked at compile-time. (C++ compilers usually perform most type-checking for C++ programs.) Run-time type checks are needed only when the file system interface retrieves a PersistentObject from the file system's object store.

Pointer-like Syntax. A Reference encapsulates storage for the IdNumber of a Persistent-Object's underlying MemoryObject. The IdNumber is sufficient information to activate the PersistentObject. A Reference overloads the C++ assignment operator "=" with an assignment method. The IdNumber in a Reference may be changed by assignment using another Reference as an argument. For example, file system interface enquiry methods use assignment to return a Reference. The assignment method maintains a reference count of how many References contain IdNumbers for a particular PersistentObject.

The C++ dereferencing operator "->" is overloaded so that References may be used as pointers without any syntactic changes to the code. The first time a method on a Referenced PersistentObject is invoked within a Domain, its underlying MemoryObject must be mapped into virtual memory and it may need to be activated. These steps are performed by the dereferencing method.

The implementation maintains a read-only persistent object hash table of IdNumbers in the virtual memory of each Domain. The hash table associates a pointer with the IdNumber. The dereferencing method hashes the IdNumber into the table. The first time this happens, the IdNumber will not be found in the table. The dereferencing method uses the IdNumber to map the PersistentObject representation into virtual memory using the file system interface. During this update, the pointer associated with the IdNumber in the hash table is assigned the virtual address used by the Domain to map the MemoryObject into virtual memory. Subsequent dereferences hash into the table and use the virtual memory address that is stored in the pointer.

Activation and Deactivation. The number of References "pointing" to a Persistent-Object per Domain is recorded in an *activation* ReferenceCount. This ReferenceCount is increased whenever a Reference "pointing" to the PersistentObject is copied by assignment into another Reference.

PersistentObjects are retrieved from the object store, activated, and mapped into the virtual memory of a Domain by an initial Reference dereference. Further dereferences may map a PersistentObject into other Domains. The PersistentObject's MemoryObject maintains a *domain* ReferenceCount that contains the number of Domains into which it has been mapped. It is incremented when the MemoryObject is mapped into a new Domain.

Whenever a Reference is deactivated, reassigned, or destroyed, the ReferenceCount of the PersistentObject to which it "pointed" is decremented. If it reaches zero, the PersistentObject is removed from the virtual memory of the Domain, the persistent object hash table entry is removed, and the domain ReferenceCount is decremented. If the domain ReferenceCount reaches zero, the PersistentObject is deactivated and its data stored in the file system.

Garbage Collection. To conserve file space in a persistent environment, References help support "automatic" garbage collection of PersistentObjects that are no longer needed. This garbage collection is based on the concept of *unreachable* objects. The persistent object store specialization of the model file system contains a PersistentObject "forest" directory that is, by definition, reachable. The directory contains References to reachable PersistentObjects. In turn, these PersistentObjects may have References to other PersistentObjects and so on, forming a chain of References. A reachable PersistentObject must be in a chain of References from the forest. All other PersistentObjects are considered unreachable and their storage will be automatically reclaimed. A PersistentObject can be added to or removed from the forest using the methods persist and desist.

To simplify the current implementation, *link* counts are used to find unreachable Persistent-Objects. The management of link counts is transparent to programs that use PersistentObjects, and is similar to the reference counting mechanism used for activation and deactivation. When a Reference is assigned a PersistentObject's IdNumber, the PersistentObject's link count is incremented. If the Reference is destroyed or has another IdNumber assigned to it, the previous PersistentObject's link count is decremented. When a link count reaches zero, the PersistentObject is considered unreachable, and it is deleted.

The current object store supports garbage collection for frameworks of PersistentObjects that are modeled as directed acyclic graphs (DAG's). Garbage collection of cyclical data structures is planned but not currently supported.

Because one of the first applications of the *Choices* object store, an object-oriented software configuration management system[12], requires a framework modeled as a DAG with back-edges, two classes of References are supported in the current experimental implementation of the object store: References and TransientReferences.

References model forward-links, also called "strong" pointers. The ReferenceCounts control activation and deactivation. File system link counts control garbage collection and keep needed PersistentObjects from being deleted. TransientReferences model backward-links, also called "weak" pointers. They use ReferenceCounts only. Thus, they do not keep Persistent-Objects from being deleted.

TransientReferences are used to point from component objects back to aggregate objects that Reference them. Reference cycles would occur if the component objects also used References, preventing our simple garbage collection scheme from working. Implementation of improved garbage collection methods will eventually make these subclasses of Reference unnecessary.

Distributed and Shared Persistent Objects. A PersistentObject may be shared between Domains. A MemoryObjectCache, together with any mutual-exclusion policy implemented by subclasses of the PersistentObject class, will keep the data representation of the PersistentObject coherent. When the PersistentObject is no longer needed in virtual memory, any dirty pages are paged back to the file system and its MemoryObject is closed.

The concept of a PersistentObject extends to a distributed system using distributed virtual memory. The IdNumber used in a Reference to activate a PersistentObject is designed to locate a MemoryObject in a "distributed" file system. Thus, remote References may be assigned to local References and dereferenced to invoke methods on possibly remote PersistentObjects.

6. ISSUES OF SECURITY

Our goal is to recast operating system security and protection issues into an object-oriented framework. Security and protection policies and mechanisms should be encapsulated within objects. Related policies and mechanisms should be organized within a class hierarchy that allows the reuse of code. In this paper, we use security in the context of user concerns and protection in the context of the operating system.

In *Choices*, protection is physically implemented by the virtual memory hardware and user/-supervisor state and these are under the control of the kernel. Applications can only access kernel objects if the kernel NameServer builds an ObjectProxy to allow that access. Two important objects that the NameServer provides the application are the persistent object store and file system. The object store controls access to PersistentObjects. The file system controls access to persistent data. More complex security and protection mechanisms and policies are built from these primitives.

Naming. In *Choices*, we have tried to separate the issues of naming from protection. There are several different kinds of names that designate objects including:

1. a virtual memory address,

2. a MemoryObject IdNumber, or

3. a symbolic "path name" of keys that identify a file or PersistentObject through a sequence of directory searches.

A program may have access to a name but may not be able to invoke a method on the object that it designates. In general, permission to access the methods of a named object must be granted by an object implementing a protection or security policy before the named object can be used. Protection and security mechanisms ensure that an object cannot be used until this has been granted by a policy. In our study of protection and security so far, we believe that we can restrict the acquisition of names in "need to know" protection policies by protecting NameServers from general access.

ObjectProxies. ObjectProxies are like capabilities in the sense that they are associated with a group of Processes executing in a Domain and once they have been granted they may be exercised without any further checks. A limited form of revocation is possible by removing the ObjectProxy from service but this would normally result in the failure of the application using the ObjectProxy.

So far, the mechanism permits access to all the methods of an object or none at all. The rationale behind this behavior is that access to ObjectProxies is type-checked at compile time. An abstract class can be used to declare the appropriate application interface at compile time without requiring potentially inefficient checks at run-time.

The NameServer is a kernel object that provides the user interface to the ObjectProxy mechanism. It maintains a set of keys and the bindings of the keys to kernel objects. New kernel objects can be registered with the NameServer by other kernel objects.

The ObjectProxy mechanism is managed by a simple security policy that is associated with the NameServer. The policy responds to any request to access a kernel object by forwarding the request to the kernel object concerned, along with the class of the ObjectProxy expected and the Domain in which the request was made. The kernel object responds to the request by either not granting permission or by returning the address of an object. The object may be the kernel object itself or it may be an object to which it has delegated responsibility for user communication. In this way, the delegate may filter user method calls.

If the request is granted, the policy instructs the ObjectProxy mechanism to construct an ObjectProxy, and this is returned to the NameServer. The NameServer binds the ObjectProxy to the key within its internal data structures and returns a pointer to the ObjectProxy to the application. Subsequent requests from the same Domain to access the same kernel object use the new key binding.

File System. The security and protection mechanisms employed in the file system depend upon the specialization of the file system model that is in use. In general, only memory-mapped files are directly available to an application. Access to FileStreams, ObjectContainers, ObjectDictionaries, MemoryObjects, and Domains are all provided through ObjectProxies.

The methods of file system objects augment the functionality of the NameServer at the application interface. The file system interface updates a Domain's ObjectProxy table by creating ObjectProxies directly, if the request does not violate the file system's security policy. For UNIX-like file systems, the security policy is based on the user and group identifications of the file's owner, the user and group identifications of the Domain that is requesting access to the file, and the set of access rights associated with the file. In current implementations, the address of an ObjectProxy for a MemoryObject cannot be passed from one Domain to another through shared memory and used because the ObjectProxy protection mechanism prevents one Domain from using another Domain's ObjectProxies. In future file system specializations, access lists will be used to replace the access right mechanism.

Persistent Object Store. Since PersistentObjects can store References, they provide a very flexible mechanism to build protection and security schemes for accessing other PersistentObjects.

A kernel PersistentObject may use its own policy to update a Domain's ObjectProxy table using a similar scheme to that of the file system scheme described above. That policy can be based on access lists or rights of Domains stored with particular PersistentObjects or access rights that are stored in "capability-list" like PersistentObjects associated with the Domains of a user.

PersistentObjects can also be mapped into the user virtual memory of applications. In such cases, References can be used to pass "pointers" to PersistentObjects from one Domain to another through a shared PersistentObject. In such cases, the object store security policy still controls whether a Persistent Object passed by a Reference can be accessed in the new Domain.

7. PERFORMANCE ISSUES

Choices has grown from over 30,000 to over 75,000 lines of C++ code in the current "stable" version. Systems integration of the various *Choices* designs has allowed us to perform preliminary performance measurements[15]. These were measured on a NS32332, 10MHZ processor.

The performance of the object proxy approach compares favorably with the Encore Computer Corporation's UMAX (4.2 BSD UNIX) system call. The better performance of the object proxy call is a result of exploiting knowledge of the C++ virtual function calling convention. The implementation of the object proxy call avoids saving unnecessary context during the transfer from non-privileged to privileged execution.

The performance of the object-oriented file system model has been measured for the BSD 4.3 specialization of the *Choices* file system. We calibrated our measurements by repeating the same measurements on the UMAX operating system. In general, *Choices* takes slightly more time than UMAX to open or create a file but a little less time to close a file. *Choices* takes longer because its file system is memory-mapped and has additional associated data structures. Clearly, the most important operations on open files are read and write. The performance of these operations depends on whether the data is cached in main memory or written out to disk. For cached reads or writes of 8192-byte *aligned* blocks, *Choices* is faster than UMAX because it uses memory-mapped files and virtual memory support instead of a buffer cache. For uncached read and write operations, *Choices* and UMAX perform similarly because both systems are limited by the speed of the disk. *Choices* performs the lseek positioning of the file location pointer faster than UMAX, primarily because it provides a more efficient system call mechanism.

Times were also measured to copy large files from disk-to-disk and from cache-to-cache. For disk-to-disk copies, *Choices* performs slightly faster than standard UMAX, largely because of the efficiency of the *Choices* caching mechanism. For cache-to-cache copies, *Choices* completed the copy in less than half the time required by UMAX, again because of the efficiency of the *Choices* caching mechanism. *Choices* also provides a single operation, copy, to copy an entire file. By avoiding the overhead of making many system calls (2 per block copied), *Choices* provides a substantially faster file copy mechanism.

Future effort will be devoted to a more extensive analysis of the behavior of the file system and PersistentObjects under different loads.

8. DISCUSSION

Persistent objects are the subject of much investigation[3]. The persistent objects of *Choices* are influenced considerably by the C++ implementation and have similarities to persistence in a number of systems including E/EXODUS[13, 5], O++/ODE[2, 1], PS-algol[4], SOS[16], and Comandos[10]. Because of the diversity of different schemes, the comparison of our system with other systems is an ongoing project.

Both E and O++ are based on extended versions of C++ and include object storage managers. Their primary advantages are the smooth integration of persistence within the C++ language. Our design goal has been to provide this integration without compiler modifications or extensions. E and O++ also provide many other useful features for organizing and manipulating persistent objects; for example, they both provide functions to iterate over groups of objects. They do not, however, provide security or garbage collection.

PS-algol provides distributed persistent objects, multi-user support using transactions, and garbage collection based on reachability from one or more root objects. To use persistent objects in PS-algol, a programmer must adapt his programming style to use persistent primitives.

SOS and Comandos integrate persistent object support with customized operating systems. SOS uses an extended C++ compiler and Comandos currently uses an enhanced C compiler. They both support distributed persistent objects, but these objects are not implemented within a general file system model.

9. SUMMARY

In this paper, we have summarized the current design of the *Choices* persistent object implementation and outlined the research in progress. *Choices* is implemented as an object-oriented system and persistent objects appear to simplify and unify many functions of the system. Our research has demonstrated that persistent data can be accessed through an object-oriented file system model as efficiently as an existing optimized commercial file system. The object-oriented file system can be specialized to provide an object store for persistent objects. Several problems arise in building an efficient persistent object scheme in a small, 32-bit virtual address space that only uses paging. Our current PersistentObject/Reference solution does have limitations, but allows quite large numbers of objects to be active simultaneously, permits sharing, and allows efficient method calls.

ACKNOWLEDGMENTS

This paper was written while Professor Campbell was on sabbatical at the University of Edinburgh. The work was supported in part by NSF grant CISE-1-5-30035 and by NASA grants NSG1471 and NAG 1-163.

REFERENCES

1. Agrawal, R., and Gehani, N. H. "ODE (Object Database and Environment): The Language and the Data Model". *ACM*, 23, 1, January 1989, pp. 36–45.

2. Agrawal, R., and Gehani, N. H. "Rationale for the Design of Persistence and Query Processing Facilities in the Database Programming Language O++". In *Second International Workshop on Database Programming Languages*, Oregon Coast, June 1989.

3. Atkinson, M. P., and Buneman, O. P. "Types and Persistence in Database Programming Languages". *ACM Computing Surveys*, 19, 2, June 1987, pp. 105–190.

4. Brown, A. L. "Persistent Object Stores", Tech. Rep. Persistent Programming Report 71, Universities of St Andrews and Glasgow, October 1989.

5. Carey, M. J., DeWitt, D. J., Richardson, J. E., and Shekita, E. J. "Storage Management for Objects in EXODUS". In *Object-Oriented Concepts, Databases, and Applications* (Eds Kim, W., and Lochovsky, F. H.), Addison Wesley, Reading, Massachusetts, 1989, pp. 341–370.

6. Johnston, G., and Campbell, R. H. "An Object-Oriented Implementation of Distributed Virtual Memory". In *Proceedings of the USENIX Workshop on Distributed and Multiprocessor Systems*, Ft. Lauderdale, Florida, September 1989, pp. 39–58.

7. Madany, P. W. "An Object-Oriented Approach towards A General Model of File Systems", Tech. Rep. UIUCDCS-R-90-1607, University of Illinois at Urbana-Champaign, June 1990.

8. Madany, P. W., Campbell, R. H., Russo, V. F., and Leyens, D. E. "A Class Hierarchy for Building Stream-Oriented File Systems". In *Proceedings of the 1989 European Conference on Object-Oriented Programming*, Nottingham, UK, July 1989 (Ed Cook, S.), Cambridge University Press, pp. 311–328.

9. Madany, P. W., Leyens, D. E., Russo, V. F., and Campbell, R. H. "A C++ Class Hierarchy for Building UNIX-Like File Systems". In *Proceedings of the USENIX C++ Conference*, Denver, Colorado, October 1988, pp. 65–79.

10. Marques, J. A., and Guedes, P. "Extending the Operating System to Support an Object-Oriented Environment". In *Proceedings of OOPSLA '89*, New Orleans, Louisiana, September 1989, pp. 113–122.

11. Ousterhout; J., and Douglis, F. "Beating the I/O Bottleneck: A Case for Log-Structured File Systems". *Operating Systems Review*, 23, 1, January 1989, pp. 11–28.

12. Render, H. S., Jr., R. N. S., and Campbell, R. H. "an Object-Oriented Approach to Integrated Configuration Management and Project Management", Tech. Rep. UIUCDCS-R-89-1553, Dept. of Computer Science, University of Illinois at Urbana-Champaign, Nov. 1989.

13. Richardson, J. E., Carey, M. J., and Schuh, D. T. "the Design of the E Programming Language", Tech. Rep. Computer Sciences 824, University of Wisconsin, Madison, February 1989.

14. Russo, V., and Campbell, R. H. "Virtual Memory and Backing Storage Management in Multiprocessor Operating Systems using Class Hierarchical Design". In *Proceedings of OOPSLA '89*, New Orleans, Louisiana, September 1989, pp. 267–278.

15. Russo, V. F., Madany, P. W., and Campbell, R. H. "C++ and Operating Systems Performance: A Case Study". In *Proceedings of the USENIX C++ Conference*, San Francisco, California, April 1990.

16. Shapiro, M., Gautron, P., and Mossieri, L. "Persistence and Migration for C++ Objects". In *Proceedings of the 1989 European Conference on Object-Oriented Programming*, Nottingham, UK, July 1989 (Ed Cook, S.), Cambridge University Press, pp. 191–204.

Combining Verified and Adaptive System Components Towards More Secure Computer Architectures

Simone Fischer-Hübner, Klaus Brunnstein
University of Hamburg

ABSTRACT

Even so-called 'secure verified systems' proven to fulfill a certain security policy cannot guarantee security in its semantic sense of protection against all kinds of illegal misuses. A combination of formal and heuristically learning system components might help.
In this paper, we describe the concept of an Intrusion Detection and Avoidance System (IDA-System), that is a combination of a formal security kernel realizing the reference monitor concept with an adaptively learning intrusion detection component. This IDA-system is capable of detecting and avoiding intrusion, also such kinds of attack-strategies that are unknown so far or are spread over a large period of time. Thus it can significantly improve system security. Its deficiencies such as dangers to privacy and how to control them are also discussed.

1. INTRODUCTION

Several recent attacks on computer security, e.g. the NASA- as well as the KGB-hacks, and computer anomalies such as viruses, worms and trojan horses, have threatened computer scientists, users and the public and have demonstrated that more secure system architectures are needed.

Unfortunately security often is costly and often accompanied by unattractive restrictions, such as restrictions on command-usage or performance degradation. The consequence is that implemented higher security levels are often not used, e.g. very few users take advantage of the possibility to use access control lists for further protection.

Besides, in systems that are supposed to be secure, misuses by high privileged insiders are still possible.

Many security researchers believe, that the usage of a formal security model and formal design and verification techniques can overcome these deficiencies. This also the underlying idea of the Orange Book [4] and the German IT-Security Criteria [7]. Unfortunately, even today's so called "secure verified computer systems" (systems rated B2/ B3 or even A1 in the Orange book classification) can't guarantee total security.

Verification techniques can only prove the fulfillment of a certain security policy, but they cannot guarantee security in its general meaning, as verified systems are only capable of protecting against known kinds of intrusions, but are not suitable to prevent other types of attack-strategies, that are unknown so far, or that are spread over a large period of time.

302

Besides, state of the art specification and verification methods are still very complex and not fully automatically supported. Yet no practical tools exist for proofing a complete code correspondence without a huge manual effort, which can lead to new mistakes.

Moreover the instant of system conception differs greatly from the instant of system usage, so that the underlying formal models may not fit to the final system environment any longer [2].

Consequently heuristically learning system components are needed that are adaptable to new system environments and can detect and avoid new kinds of intrusions.

2. CONCEPT OF AN INTRUSION DETECTION AND AVOIDANCE SYSTEM

In our research group we are working on a concept and an implementation of an Intrusion Detection and Avoidance System (IDA-System): the security kernel of an operating system shall be combined with an intrusion detection expert system (see figure 2) [2]. The IDA-concept decribes the combination of a formal and a heuristic model. IDA's Intrusion Detection component is a heuristically learning component. In contrast to traditional intrusion detection expert systems commands, likely to be intrusive, are not only detected by IDA's expert system in real-time, but can also be aborted (avoided) in cooperation with the security kernel in time.

We have written a prototype of the Intrusion Detection component in OPS5 on a VAX/VMS-sytem, that has shown capable of detecting some simulated attacks. In a further step this system shall be rewritten in OPS83 and be combined with the security kernel of an operating system with an UNIX-surface, that is being developed in parallel.

The security kernel approach introduced by Shell is an often used method for building highly secure operating systems [1]. In our IDA-system approach the security kernel is the hardware and the software of the lowest operating system layer, that realize the reference monitor concept.

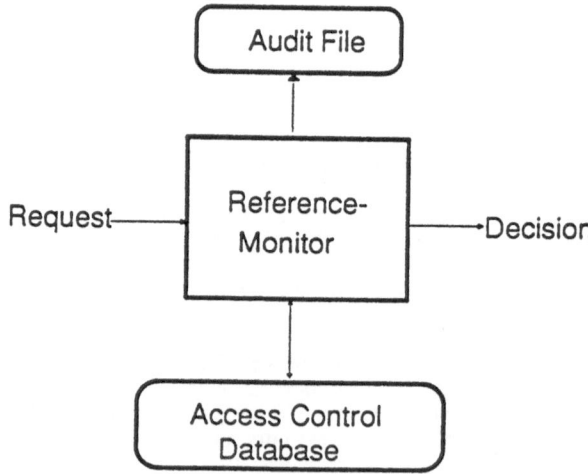

Figure 1: The Reference Monitor

The Reference Monitor validates every access of a subject (e.g. user, process) to an object (file, programm, terminal, etc.) whether it is conform with the underlying security model for discretionary and mandatory access control. In our approach we use the Bell LaPadula model despite that its suitability for non-military applications seem questionable to us. In a further step we also consider to integrate an integrity model in the reference monitor, so that besides confidentiality, integrity, that is more important for commercial applications, can be realized.

If a subject tries to reference an object, the reference monitor will receive an access request of the form
[KERNEL FUNCTION; SUBJECT; OBJECT; PARAMETER].

Following the Bell LaPadula model, the set of possible kernel functions include: get access, rescind access, give access, create object, delete object, change object security level, change subject current security level. Parameters indicate the kind of access requested. Using access control information such as access rights and security levels it will decide whether it causes this request to be executed or to send a negative respond to the requesting subject. All events are recorded in an audit file (see figure 1).

To successfully implement the reference monitor concept, the kernel should be complete, in that it mediates all accesses, isolated, in that it must be protected from tampering, and verified, in that the correspondence of the implementation and the security policy must be shown [1]. To fulfill these requirements, we need the support of specific hardware and software mechanisms, e.g. the completeness principle can be realized by memory protection through segmented virtual memory and segment descriptors, that support distinct access modes, and the isolation principle can only effectively be achieved through at least three different execution modes (kernel, supervisor, user). Despite the shortcomings and limits of verification, the correctness of the kernel should be demonstrated using state of the art formal methods. The kernel code should therefore be kept as small as possible.

To overcome the deficiencies of today's so called "secure verified systems" as described above, the reference monitor as a formal component shall be combined with an adaptively learning intrusion detection expert system component.

IDA's intrusion detection component is a rule-based expert system. It functionally follows Dorothy Denning's Intrusion Detection-model [3], which IDA develops towards a real time avoidance system.

Denning's IDES-model assumes that security violations can be detected by monitoring the system usage for abnormal behavior. The model includes rules to acquire statistical profiles from audit data describing the statistical behavior of subjects with respect to objects, and rules, that use these profiles and new audit records to detect statistical abnormal behavior likely to be intrusive. As the model is independent of any particular system, system vulnerability or type of intrusion, the system is capable of detecting unknown kinds of intrusions, which might otherwise go undetected by traditional security policies.

Meanwhile several Inrusion Detection Expert Systems have been developed, e.g. SRI International's IDES (Intrusion Detection Expert System [8]) and the US National Computer Security Centers MIDAS (Multics Intrusion Detection and Alerting System, [10]). (A good survey of Intrusion Detection activities is given in [9]).

Apart from analysis of anomalies these systems use so called a priori-rules, that encode information about hacker techniques and vulnerabilities of the system under observation. Running on separate machines, these intrusion detection systems are system independent, as is the underlying model. This separation results in the intrusion being detected only after the attack has occured, as the command's audit record is analyzed during and after command execution.

The Intrusion Detection component of the IDA-System is functionally dependent on the system under control, but it is capable of detecting and stopping attacks in time.

According to the IDES-model it is a rule based pattern matching system including a forward chaining inference engine and a knowledge base with the following kinds of facts and rules:

Facts:

audit records   (passed over by the reference monitor,
                            recording a request by a subject to reference an object)

profile_templates   (used to create profiles when a subject first uses an object)

profiles   (characterizing the statistical behavior of a subject using
                            the operational or the mean and standard deviation
                            model)

anomaly_records   (recording abnormal behavior)

Periodical statistical update rules
that are triggered by the change of a time period. They update statistical values for the next time period and the statistics (mean and standard deviation, if this model is used).

Rules to create profiles
that are triggered by the arrival of a new audit record. If this audit record matches a profile-template and no corresponding profile exist (a subject uses an object as described in the template for the first time), a new appropriate profile is created

Rules to analyse behavior and update statistics
that are triggered by the arrival of a new audit record. If the audit record matches a profile, the profile's statistic is updated and the event described by the audit record is analyzed whether it is normal or abnormal with respect to the profile's statistic. If abnormal behavior is detected an anomaly record will be created.

Alarm rules
that are triggered by a combination of anomaly records. They cause the request to be rejected or the whole process to be stopped.

IDA contains profiles and rules for a preprocessing checker as well as for a run-time checker [figure 2], that try to detect anomalous system usage likely to be intrusive.

Before a request is executed, the reference monitor first checks any attempt by a subject to reference an object and then passes the command's audit record containing information on access rights to IDA's preprocessing checker, that finally decides, whether the request shall be granted, be rejected or the whole process be stopped to avoid intrusion.

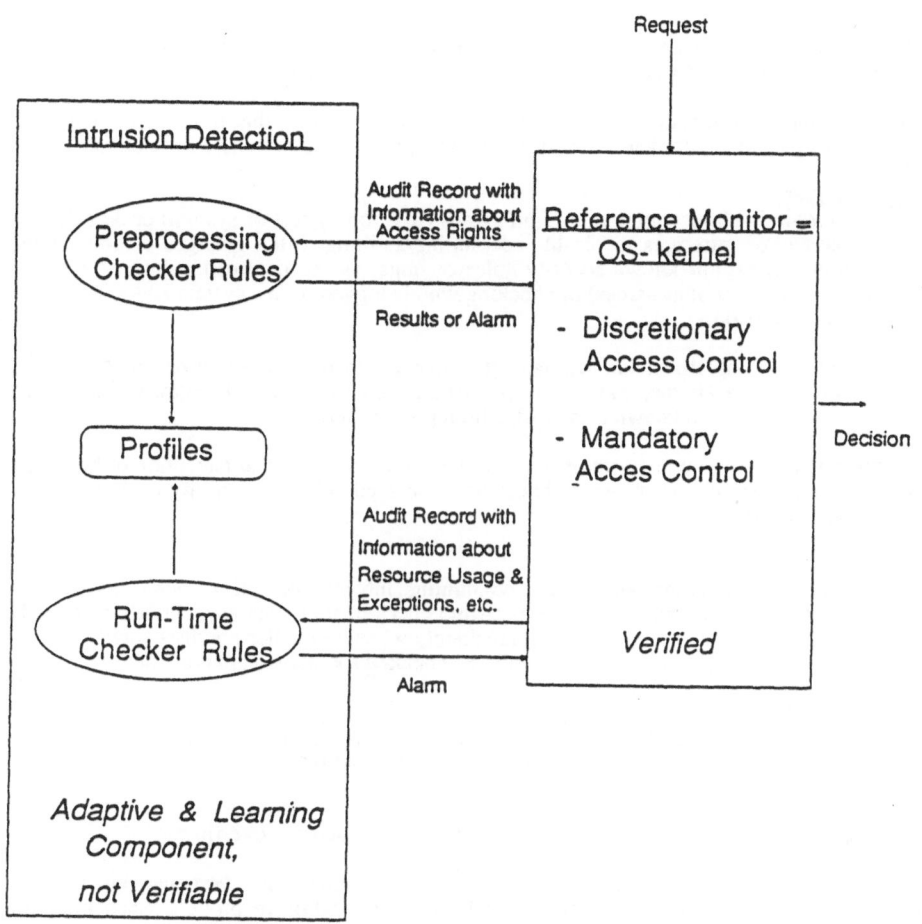

Figure 2: Intrusion Detection and Avoidance System

The preprocessing checker can, for example, check the following activities for statistical anomalies (these checks are already realized in our prototype implementation):

Login:
login-frequency, login-frequency/rate of login-attempts using false passwords, login-time, login-location, connection, time intervall since last login.

Program- / Command - Execution (of high risk):
execution frequencies of programs/program-types or commands/command-types, execution denial frequency.

Access to data:
read- / write- /create- / delete- frequencies, name checking (validation of object types accessed by programms of a special type), frequency of access-denial.

Furthermore the preprocessing checker can contain a priori- rules, that use a combination of suspicious usage patterns to detect security violations. Following activities for example could indicate
hacker-activities:
Attempts to login in using common account names (like root, guest or system) or default and common passwords, attempts to disable accounting/auditing, often changes of connection paths, attempts to exploit known security-holes or bugs, use of commands such as who or finger (to find valid account-names) or checking who is logged onto a system and to log out if a system-manager is on.

For our prototype implementaion we have just started to construct a priori rules that use entries of the virus catalogue, that we are publishing, to detect not only known viruses, but also unknown viruses of a known class with a high probability.

As a minimal function, an analysis of the access to sensitive data and execution of high risk commands and of some a priori rules should be performed before an activity is permitted by the reference monitor.

After command completion audit data containing information on resource usage and exception- condition are checked by the run-time checker, that runs asynchronly and sends alarm messages to the reference monitor immediately when anomalies are discovered.
Especially the following characteristics should be checked for statistical anomalies:

Resource Usage:
storage- /memory- usage, programm CPU-time usage, programm I/O, session CPU-time usage, session I/O, connect-time, amount of read- and written records.

Exception Condition:
file resource exhaustions, programm resource exhaustions, memory overflow.

Detection of anomalous resource usage can help to find attacks, e.g covert channels, tracker-attacks to statistical databases, anomalies such as viruses while in process. Such kinds of illegal information flow can thus be stopped in time.

As the intrusion detection subsystem is a heuristically learning component with its major part in the knowledge base and adaptive profiles, unlike the reference momitor, its formal verification is neither meaningful nor even possible. The consistency and completeness of the knowledge base might be formally controlled, e.g. the knowledge base may be formally proven to be non-contradictory, but this does not guarantee correctness. On the other hand, the intrusion detection and avoidance technique helps to protect against unknown kinds of attacks and this offers additional security, which cannot be achieved by verification techniques.

3. DANGERS TO PRIVACY AND HOW TO CONTROL THEM

Though the IDA concept might enhance system security, we are also concerned with new problems raised by this method. Intrusion detection systems may affect user's privacy rights, as they produce statistical profiles containing information about their behavior, that could be misused, e.g. for employee performance monitoring [5].

According to German law, the work council (=Betriebsrat) of a company must participate in deciding to introduce any new technique, which may be used for monitoring performance. An intrusion detection mechanism must therefore be accepted by the work council. But on the other hand, secure and safe system behavior dimishes the respective company's vulnerability.

Recent studies have shown further problems of computerized performance monitoring. For instance, the knowledge of the existence of such a system may result in an increase of productivity, stress and lower level of satisfaction [6]. This may in turn invoke anomalous user behavior, making the differentiation between normal and anomalous behavior more difficult. Consequently, an appropriate use of intrusion detection technologies should guarantee that these data are used for security purposes only.

Legal rules are needed, that restrict the profile's usage to intrusion detection only and prohibits its misuse. Prohibiting the usage of profiles, that store information typically needed for performance control, should also be taken into consideration.

Further control mechanisms should restrict access to system's knowledge base, granting access only to the inference engine and possibly to a high privileged and properly supervised security administrator. As the access to the intrusion dection system components is controlled by the reference monitor, a first step is made towards its protection. By encrypting subject IDs and subject profile pattern, that refers to certain users, and keeping the key secret, we try to reach to anonymity of the profiles. By realizing such control-mechanisms in our prototype implementation, we are trying to minimize these risks, so that the profile's misuse is too hard and too risky and it seems to be more worthwhile to do performance monitoring by other methods.

4. OPEN QUESTIONS AND CONCLUSIONS

As our research work is still going on and as a complete prototype implementation of the IDA-system has not been finished yet, there are still some open questions, as how much such a system will increase security, how it will degrade performance, how many vulnerabilities it is able to detect and prevent correctly, how many activities it will interpret falsely as intrusion and finally how it will be accepted by the users.

After all, we think, the combination with an adaptively learning intrusion detection component can still significantly enhance security of a verified security kernel. So we hope to help to arrive at safer and more secure computer architectures.

REFERENCES

1. S.Ames, M.Gasser, R.Shell, "Security Kernel Design and Implementation: An Introduction", *IEEE Computer*, 1983, Vol.16 ,No.7.

2. K.Brunnstein, S.Fischer-Hübner, "Risk Analysis of Trust *Computer Sytems*", *Proceedings IFIP-Sec'90 Conference*, Helsinki, May 1990.

3. D.Denning, "An Intrusion-Detection Model", *Proceedings of the 1986 Symposium on Security and Privacy*, IEEE Computer Society, Oakland, April 1986.

4. "DoD Trusted Computer Systems Evaluation Criteria", DoD 5200.28-STD, Washington D.C., Department of Defence, 1985

5. S.Fischer-Hübner, K.Brunnstein, "Opportunities and Risks of Intrusion Detection Expert Systems, *Proceedings of the IFIP TC-9 Conference "Opportunities and Risks of AI Systems" (ORAIS'89)*, Hamburg 1989

6. R.Irving, C.Higgins, F.Safayemi, "Computerized Performance Monitoring Systems: Use and Abuse", *CACM* Vol.29, No.8, 1986.

7. "IT-Security Criteria : Criteria for the Evaluation of Security of Information Technology", Zentralstelle für Sicherheit in der Informationstechnik, Bonn, 1989.

8. T.Lunt, R.Jagannathan, R.Lee, A.Whitehurst, "Knowledge-Based Intrusion Detection", *Proceedings of the 1989 AI Systems in Government Confrence*, March 1989.

9. T.Lunt, "Automated Audit Trail Analysis and Intrusion Detection: A Survey", *Proceedings of the 11th National Computer Security Conference*, October 1988.

10. R.Whitehurst, M.Sebring, E.Shellhouse, M.Hanna, "Expert Systems in Intrusion Detection: A Case Study", *Proceedings of the 11th National Computer Security Conference*, October 1988.

Mechanisms for Persistence and Security in BirliX

W. E. Kühnhauser, H. Härtig, O. C. Kowalski, W.Lux
German National Research Center For Computer Science (GMD)

ABSTRACT

BirliX is an operating system kernel supporting fault tolerant and secure applications in a distributed environment. Essentially it is an abstract data type management system. Its basic services are the definition of abstract data types, their instantiation, their identification, and the communication between instances. All abstract data types share a common set of type-independent attributes inherited from the kernel-defined BirliX Primary Type.

BirliX Types are persistent. Persistence of an instance depends on long term name bindings within nameservers, short term references form other instances, and internal instance activities. The kernel maintains an instance as long as there is at least one name binding, one external reference or an internal instance activity. Persistence of BirliX Types is based on persistent memory segments.

Security in BirliX is also based upon BirliX Types. Depending on their role during access, instances are classified as subjects (accessing instances) or objects (accessed instances). Access rights can be controlled from the point of view of subjects, called *subject restriction lists* (SRLs), and from the point of view of used objects, called *access control lists* (ACLs). The resulting granted access rights are the intersection of the granted rights as specified by ACLs and SRLs.

1   INTRODUCTION

The need for distributed, fault tolerant and secure application systems and the challenge of modern hardware architectures impose new requirements on operating systems. Today's conventional operating systems meet these requirements only by repeated extensions of their formerly clear structure which leads to complex, opaque systems. Therefore, extensibility is a system feature of nearly all newly developed operating systems [3, 5]. Most of them meet this goal by a small kernel which provides a flexible base by multiple threads and message passing, and a set of servers on top of that kernel which provides the more complex services. New requirements are satisfied by new servers, while the kernel itself is fairly static. The application level interface provided by most systems is that of UNIX[1], which has become a defacto standard for manufacturing independent operating systems.

In contrast to many newly designed operating systems, the BirliX kernel is not restricted to threads and message passing. It supports the paradigm of abstract data types for the implementation of high-level services. All kinds of BirliX resources are provided via instances of BirliX Types, which are similar to Eden types [1]. Thus the BirliX kernel essentially is an abstract data type management system; its basic functionality is the definition of abstract data types, their instantiation, their identification, and the communication between instances.

BirliX Types share a common set of type-independent attributes and functionality inherited from a single kernel-defined type called the *BirliX Primary Type*. Application systems

---

[1]UNIX is a trademark of AT&T Bell Laboratories

based on BirliX Types use the generic functions exported from the Primary Type for the implementation of application-dependent high-level policies. As an example, fault tolerance services like transaction management systems [4] may use the basic mechanisms of the Primary Type to create checkpoints of system resources. In the same way the security mechanisms are used to implement application level security policies.

The common type-independent properties of BirliX Types concern

- **naming**: each instance can have an application-level name in a global naming network,

- **identification**: each instance has a system-level identification (UId) which is unique in time and space,

- **distribution**: instances can be migrated to other hosts of a network,

- **fault tolerance**: instances can be checkpointed and recovered,

- **persistence**: instances live as long as there is a reference or an internal activity and

- **protection**: access to instances implies evaluation of access rights.

The system functionality is easily extented by adding new types. As the first non-trivial application system on top of the BirliX kernel, the bsd 4.3 Unix interface is emulated via a modest set of UNIX-tailored BirliX Types.

While definition and usage of BirliX Types are similar to data types in conventional programming languages, they differ in persistence and security. Persistence of an instance depends on long term name bindings within nameservers, short term references from other instances, and internal instance activities. The kernel maintains an instance as long as there is at least one name binding, one external reference or an internal instance activity. Persistence of BirliX Types is based on persistent memory segments. Using the efficient checkpointing facility of segments, the primary type provides sequential versions of instances to support fault tolerant applications.

Security is also based upon instances of abstract data types. Depending on their role during access, instances are classified as subjects (accessing instances) or objects (accessed instances). Access rights can be granted from the point of view of subjects, called *subject restriction lists* (SRLs), and from the point of view of used objects, called *access control lists* (ACLs). The resulting granted access rights are the intersection of the granted rights as specified by ACLs and subject restrictions. An ACL defines access rights of (human) users, BirliX Types, and type instances. Access rights are granted (positive access rights) or excluded explicitly (negative access rights).

2 PERSISTENCE

2.1 Teams

BirliX Types are implemented by a uniform and type-independent implementation structure called a *team*. A team provides all memory and computing resources needed by an instance during its lifetime. A team is created when a BirliX Type is instantiated and is destroyed with the final deletion of the instance. Teams may either be active or passive. Active teams have main memory resources, processor resources, and communication connections. Passive teams are persistent data representations in permanent memory. Any communication request to an instance automatically activates its team and establishes a communication connection between the calling team (client) and called team. The called team is passivated when the last client disposes its communication connection. This scheme is also used as the very basic fault tolerance mechanism; checkpointing a type instance creates a passive team from an active one, and recovering an instance creates an active team from a checkpoint. Type instantiation and the manipulation of team states are performed by a single type-independent *Team Manager* located on every BirliX host in a computer network.

A team is a collection of threads sharing an address space, segments providing memory resources, and communication bindings to other teams. Threads are the active parts of a team. Communication bindings are maintained in *access descriptors*. The data of an instance is contained in its *segments*. Figure 1 shows a set of interconnected teams consisting of threads, segments, and access descriptors. Communication connections are established via a pair of an access descriptor and an agent.

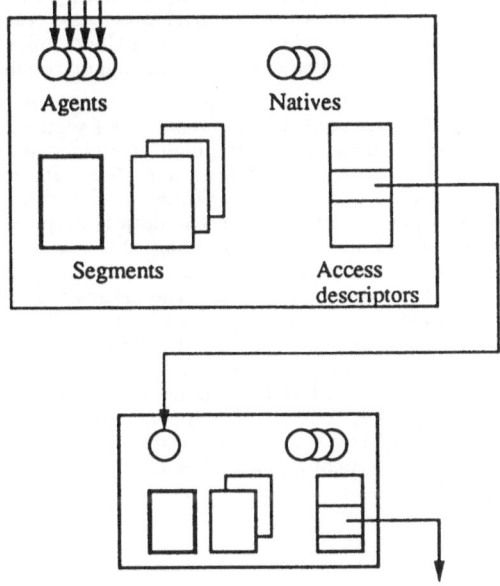

Figure 1: Teams

2.2 Threads

Threads are sequential activities running in parallel to each other. Threads are assigned to an address space, but many threads may share the same address space. Threads sharing an address space communicate by Hoare-like monitors, whereas in general message passing is used. High-level RPC is implemented based on message passing among threads. Threads are light weight processes, i.e. creating a thread does not imply creating an address space and process switching does not necessarily imply address space switching. Depending on their role within a team, threads are called *agents* or *natives*.

Within a team each client is represented by an agent. The agent authenticates its client and controls its access permissions. The agent performs the client's operations on the team, subject to granted access rights. A client calls operations on an instance by communicating with the corresponding agent. When a client closes the instance the corresponding agent releases its resources and terminates.

Natives· are asynchronous activities of the team (e.g. a local garbage collector) that run asynchronously· to agents and other natives.

2.3 Segments

Segments represent all memory resources. They are identified by UIds, too. Segments are arrays of bytes. Windows are used to *map* parts of segments into an address space so that segments are accessed using ordinary machine instructions. Segments are typed. A *physical segment* is implemented by direct use of physical memory such as the frame memory of a high resolution display. *Ordinary segments* are persistent storage resources realized by pages of a mass storage device and main memory page frames as a cache. Ordinary segments can be checkpointed, i.e. an ordinary segment stores sequential versions of segment checkpoints. Checkpointing is implemented very efficiently within the memory management by shadow pages using its copy-on-write mechanism and resource sharing in main memory and on background storage. The interface of the Checkpoint-operation does not fix shadowing, but is open for other implementations like logging techniques.

A special role is played by ordinary segments containing the data representation of passive teams. They are called *associated segments* of teams. Associated segments are identified by the UId of the containing team. An associated segment is divided into two parts: In the first part the administration information about the team (*team descriptor*) is placed, the second part contains the real data of the team. While the descriptor is copied into the assigned system table during opening the segment, the data is mapped into the teams address space to be modified by normal machine instructions. If it makes sense to separate parts of a team, additional ordinary (not associated) segments can be used. The UIds of these segments are stored in the team descriptor within the associated segment. So, the associated segment is the root of all segments belonging to a team. Two examples of our UNIX emulation show the width of usage: A team of the "small" type UNIX file only consists of one associated segment containing an inode-like descriptor for the file and the file data. There is an agent for each client, but there is no native. On the other hand a team of the "complex" type UNIX process consists of an associated segment and additional segments for the user program, the user stack, and the user data. The program is executed by one native within the team and the synchronization between parent and child processes (wait, exit) is done by agents.

2.4 Persistence Rule

Persistence of an instance is directly coupled to the state of the implementing team. When a BirliX type is instantiated, the team manager creates a team with one agent realizing a short term reference. Creating a team also means creation of an associated segment and providing an address space for the agent. Each following Open-operation creates an additional agent working within the same address space. Internal team activities executed by natives are started during initialization of the team or during type specific operations executed by agents. The state of a team is active, as long as there is at least one agent or one native within the team. While natives are deleted by the termination of the executed program, agents are deleted during the Close-operation of their client. Deletion of the last activity causes the deletion of the team and its associated segment.

To survive the termination of the last activity an instance can become persistent by establishing a name server reference to that instance. A simple example of name server reference is a directory entry within a UNIX environment. The reference is notified within the instance by execution of a primary-operation, which administrates a reference counter. The resulting persistence rule is given by:

An instance exists as long as

- there is an internal activity, or

- there is a short term reference via an agent, or

- there is a long term name server reference to the instance.

If there is a long term reference to the instance, deletion of the last activity causes the passivation of the team by the team manager. During passivation the manager puts the team descriptor and the team data to the associated segment (by unmapping the windows) and closes the associated segment. If there are additional segments, they are also closed. On the next Open-request the manager activates the team, i.e. using the UId of the instance he opens the associated segment, puts the team descriptor from the associated segment to a system table and maps the data into the address space of the team.

This scheme is also used as the very basic fault tolerance mechanism. Checkpointing an instance creates a persistent team representation from an active one. A team in state checkpointing is much more complex than one in state passive, as it contains a snapshot of all activities within the active team. To reduce the work of the team manager most parts of the activity state (user stacks, user data, ...) are contained in segments. As already mentioned segment checkpointing is done efficiently by using copy-on-write and resource sharing. During recovery of an instance the team manager terminates the activities within the team, recovers all segments and reactivates the activities from their checkpointed state.

The resulting instance state machine is shown in Figure 2.

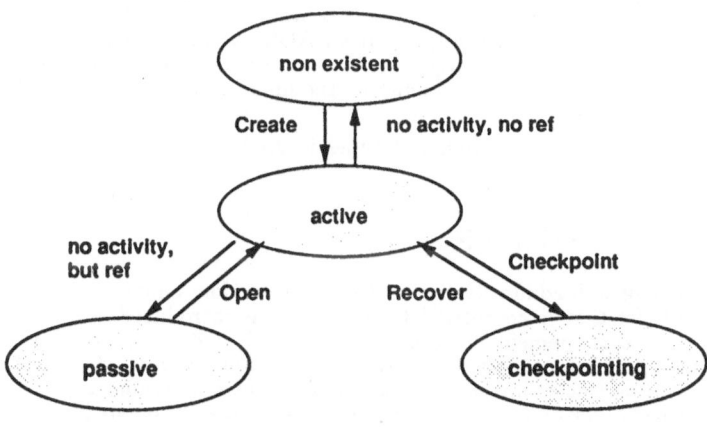

Figure 2: Team States

3   SECURITY

While the inadequacy of the security measures of many environments is agreed upon [2], there still is a lack of well understood security policies in a non military environment. To deal with that situation BirliX is designed in such a way that integrating new security policies is relatively easy.

As a basis BirliX implements the *encapsulation of instances* by guaranteeing the *autonomy* of teams and ensuring the *authenticity* of messages.

To this end access rights can be granted from the point of view of clients, called *subject restrictions*, and from the point of view of used teams, called *access control lists* (ACL). The intersection of the granted rights as specified by ACLs and the subject restrictions yield the resulting granted access rights.

3.1 Access Control Lists

An access control list defines the access rights of a using instance (called *subject*) to a used instance (called *object*).

Instances are tagged by a tuple consisting of their UId, the UId of their type description (the BirliX type) and the UId of the *human user* who created the instance. Whenever an instance is created, the new instance inherits its user tag from the creating instance. All instances contain an ACL consisting of a set of access right definitions:

- an entry defines access rights of a (human) user, a type or an instance

- access rights are granted (positive access rights) or excluded explicitly (negative access rights)

If a user is contained in an ACL the entry defines the access rights of all instances having the responsible user as part of the tag. If a type is contained in an ACL the entry defines the access rights of all instances of the type. If an ACL contains a user or a type, the protection domain may become too large. In that case access rights can be excluded explicitly. Access rights are computed by building the union of positive access rights and subtracting all negative access rights.

In the UNIX emulation, the access rights of types in ACLs are used to dispose of the setuid mechanism.

3.2 Subject Restriction Lists

Even in the presence of well administrated ACLs the protection domain may become too large. If a new subject that is considered to be suspect is introduced into a system, it may be impossible at that moment, to supplement all ACLs with the necessary negative access right. In that case subject restrictions can be used. Subject restriction lists restrict the access rights of a particular instance and all instances of a particular type. A subject restriction list consists of a global *suspect/unsuspect* mark and a list of entries. If a subject is marked as suspect, its access rights are defined by the entries. A subject restriction entry defines the subjects access rights to other instances. If a subject is marked non suspect, there are no restrictions.

If a subject is marked suspect, all instances created by the subject inherit the subject restrictions.

The primary type implements subject restrictions by suppressing calls to instances that are not covered by the list.

3.3 Base Mechanisms

The autonomy of teams is guaranteed by the team implementation. Segments containing passive data representations are accessible only by the team manager. All other segments can be accessed only by their teams. The use of teams is restricted to the communication with agents.

Since any ACL based protection policy requires safe knowledge of the caller's id, authenticity of messages is maintained with respect to a given access descriptor/agent relationship. To build up an access descriptor/agent relationship the subjects instance identification is passed encrypted to the newly created agent. Subsequently each message contains a capability securely identifying the sender. The capability is built encrypting a checksum and sequence number using a single key encryption scheme. Keys are exchanged between hosts using a public key encryption scheme.

4 CONCLUSION AND STATUS

Birlix is an operating system, which supports functional extension by the definition of new abstract data types. All system resources, cpu-like and memory-like, are accessed by type specific operations to BirliX type instances. The implementation structure team provides a wide set of mechanisms supporting fault tolerant, secure applications in a distributed environment. Persistence of teams is realized via permanent segments, which are a hardware independent abstraction of background storage. The security mechanisms of teams seem flexible enough to implement a variety of security policies.

The BirliX system is running on a network of Sun-3 systems with a 4.3BSD emulation on top of it. Most standard UNIX utilities, a Modula-2 compiler, the Emacs editor, and the X window management system have been ported to the system. In most cases porting consisted simply in relinking the utilities with our system call library. To use some special features of BirliX, like instantiation of new BirliX types, checkpointing and use of the security mechanisms, the UNIX system interface was extented by special system calls.

REFERENCES

[1] Guy T. Almes, Andrew P. Black, Edward D. Lazowska, and Jerre D. Noe. The eden system: A technical review. *Transactions On Software Engineering*, 11(1), January 1985.

[2] C.B. Hogan. Protection Imperfect: The Security of some Computing Environments. *Operating System Review*, 22(3):7–27, July 1988.

[3] S.J. Mullender, editor. *The AMOEBA Distributed Operating System — selected papers 1984–1987*. Amsterdam, Centrum voor Wiskunde en Informatica, 1987.

[4] R. Schumann, R. Kröger, M. Mock, and E. Nett. Recovery Management in the Relax Distributed Transaction Layer. In *8th Symp. on Reliable Distributed Systems, Seattle*, October 1989.

[5] A. Tevanian and R.F. Rashid. MACH - A Basis for Future Unix Development. In *EUUG Conference Proceedings*, Manchester, 1986.

Part VII

Persistence and Databases

Applications

Transactions in a Segmented Single Level Store Architecture

P. Brössler
University of Bremen, FRG

J. Rosenberg
University of Newcastle, Australia

ABSTRACT

This work describes the integration of transactions into a computer architecture with a persistent uniform virtual memory based on pages and combined with arbitrary long segments. The ultimate goal is to offer implicit synchronisation of parallel processes and recovery from a wide range of possible errors to a large number of different applications, including the operating system, without sacrificing the efficiency or the degree of parallelism. For this reason it is proposed to implement transaction management at the architectural level.

1. INTRODUCTION

The architecture of the MONADS-PC [30] has been developed mainly to fulfil software engineering and security requirements. The most important features of this architecture are

- a persistent virtual memory with very large virtual addresses

- a combination of segmentation and paging which uses capability based addressing and efficiently supports both very small and very large objects in a uniform manner [19]

- support for modules designed according to the information-hiding principle and protection of such modules using module capabilities [21]

- a process architecture based on the procedure-oriented rather than the message-oriented paradigm.

The MONADS-PC architecture has not been designed specifically with database-oriented concepts in mind. Nevertheless it offers many advantages over conventional computer architectures for these kind of applications. The architecture is still evolving and we are currently investigating areas that can greatly support efficient and reliable access to large databases on a MONADS-PC [22].

This work focuses on the integration of transactions into the MONADS-PC architecture. Transactions are a general concept for the implicit synchronisation of parallel processes and for failure recovery. The transaction concept has been developed in the context of database management systems [10, 12] but has increasingly been included in new operating systems [9, 23, 25, 27, 29, 34] and programming languages (e.g. [24]). Our approach is to place the transaction management immediately above a stable uniform virtual memory so that the transaction service is offered to all software layers, including the operating system and all kinds of application programs. The granule for concurrency control and recovery is not of fixed size as with pages but varies according to the needs of specific applications.

The paper is structured as follows. Section 2 describes those aspects of the MONADS-PC that are important for a general understanding and those that are related to transaction management. Readers familiar with the MONADS-PC architecture can skip this section. In section 3 the properties of transactions are briefly reviewed. Section 4 deals with the question of how transactions can and should be embedded in a computer architecture such as the MONADS-PC. Section 5 summarises the interface to the transaction management. The implementation of the concurrency control and the recovery mechanisms is described in detail in sections 6 and 7. The paper ends with comparison to related work and with some final remarks.

2. THE MONADS-PC ARCHITECTURE

This section briefly describes those parts of the MONADS-PC that are important for a general understanding and for the proposed transaction management.

From the user´s point of view the architecture offers support for the construction and management of objects and processes. Each object has a well defined procedural interface, which is based on the semantic properties of the object. The architecture enforces the principle of information hiding for objects by allowing access to internal data structures of objects only from within one of the interface routines or the internal routines of this object. Figure 1 shows a simple picture of such an object. Objects are persistent in the sense of persistent programming languages [3] so that no extra file management is needed.

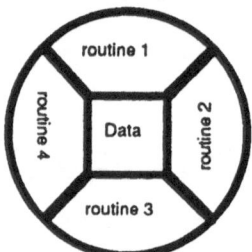

Figure 1: Information Hiding Module

This object model is used for resources and components related to hardware, the operating system, and user applications. We distinguish between three different forms of objects:

- objects with no instance data, such as libraries

- type managers for objects with instance data

- instances managed by type managers

To create a new instance of some type the **create** routine of the appropriate type manager is called. The result of each such create call is the creation of a new instance plus the returning of a module capability which enables further calls on this instance. Module capabilities can be restricted to a subset of the routines and can be passed to other users. Further copying of this capability can be allowed or forbidden. Each object has the routines **open** and **close** which have to be called before and after any other routines. The module capability has to be presented as part of the open call so that an efficient addressing and protection environment can be set up. The **delete** routine allows the deletion of any type of object (if the module capability contains the appropriate right).

The architecture efficiently supports procedure-oriented programming languages with nested scopes by a micro-coded call instruction which maintains the call linkage on the stack and also initialises bases for addressing the scopes and the instance data. The call mechanism is crucial for the security of the whole system for two reasons: it has to check the appropriate rights in the presented module capability and it has to set up a new addressing environment with each call so that no undesirable direct memory access is possible.

All objects are stored within a global, uniform virtual memory with 60 bit wide addresses. This uniform virtual memory is an abstraction of main memory, disc storage and even networks [1, 7]. The idea of placing files into virtual memory was first suggested in Multics [5]. Access to all data regardless whether it is permanent or temporary is via this virtual memory which is organised in pages of 4 KB. For management reasons the virtual memory is divided into areas called address spaces and each object is stored within a separate address space. The address space number (32 bits) is used as the unique identification of the object and is part of a module capability. This address space number is never reused after an object has been deleted. Instance address spaces are linked to the corresponding type managers by storing the address space number of the type manager within the instance address space. Instance address spaces are organised as heaps of variable length objects called segments.

From an architectural point of view an address space consists of segments. A high-level programming language hides these segments since the compiler automatically maps program variables onto these segments. The length of a segment can be anything from 1 byte to the length of the whole address space (2^{28} bytes). Typically a segment holds an array or a record but it can also be used for something as small as a character. Segments can be arbitrarily combined within pages and can cross page boundaries [19]. Access to segments is controlled by segment capabilities which consist of a full virtual address, type information, length, and access rights. Segments form the base of the protection scheme of the MONADS-PC since they protect both kinds of capabilities from being modified arbitrarily. Before a process can access a segment an appropriate segment capability has to be loaded into one of the 16 capability registers. At this moment and at the time of accessing a segment checks are carried out, such as for type and length. Each segment consists of three parts (see Figure 2). The pointer part contains abbreviated segment capabilities and can be used to create arbitrarily complex structures of segments (see Figure 3).

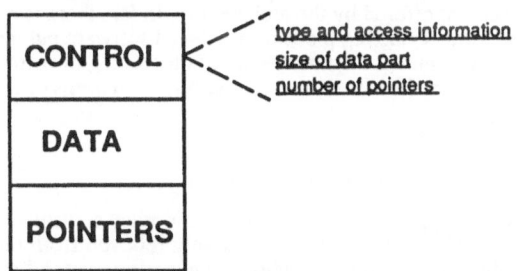

Figure 2: Structure of a segment

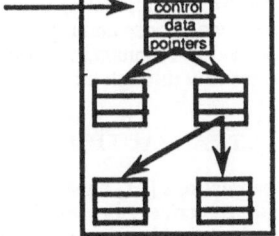

Figure 3: Heap with segments

The main data structure for a process in the MONADS-PC is its stack. Each stack is stored in a separate address space. The first consequence of this is that again the address space number can be used as a unique identification, this time for processes. Secondly the MONADS-PC allows *"persistent processes"* without any additional effort since all the process-related information is stored within the persistent uniform virtual memory (see Figure 4).

With each open of an object a retained heap is created. It holds all local and retained data generated by called routines of this object. Retained data is used for information that has to be retained from one routine call to another, such as the current line pointer when reading a sequential file. The **prepare_open_call** instruction takes a module capability and creates a so-called *module* *call segment* (MCS) which can be regarded as a kind of handle to an opened object and is presented with every routine call on behalf of that open. Closing of objects can either take place explicitly by calling the close operation or implicitly by deleting the MCS e.g. due to exiting the scope of the variable that holds the MCS.

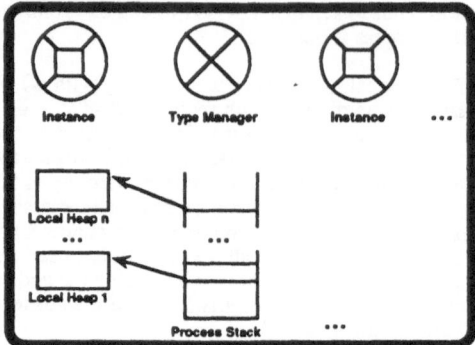

Figure 4: Uniform Virtual Memory

Each routine can have an associated exception handler[1] which is called whenever an exception occurs within this routine. If there is no such exception handler then the routine is exited and the exception is raised again within the caller of the routine. Exceptions can be caused by access violations, improper arithmetic instructions, parameter errors, etc. They can also be raised directly from within programs to signal an error to the caller of the routine. Within an exception handler the exception can be either cleared and the execution continued or the exception can be passed on to the caller of the routine.

Most of the instruction set of the MONADS-PC is micro-coded. The kernel is responsible for the virtual memory management, process management including scheduling and synchronisation, control of and access to devices, and some of the more complicated instructions. Even the hardware and kernel resources are regarded as objects and access to these is controlled via module capabilities. An operating system for the MONADS-PC is very simple because of the uniform virtual memory and the process management offered by the architecture. In fact there is no need for a traditional operating system in the form of one big piece of privileged software but the users can choose and replace objects such as the command language interpreter (CLI), directory and text file management freely. All objects can be either used within compiled programs or interactively through the CLI [16].

3. TRANSACTIONS IN THE MONADS-PC SYSTEM

Transactions [11] have proven to be a successful approach for handling concurrency control and failure recovery in an orthogonal manner [13, 42]. Programmers are largely relieved from the burden of taking care of synchronisation problems and failure situations. Integrating transactions into the MONADS-PC architecture does not only aim at supporting traditional database applications but also at providing these facilities to all kind of applications, ranging from operating system modules to all kind of user applications. Since the MONADS-PC architecture already provides all kinds of objects with uniform addressability, protection, and persistence (in the sense of persistent programming languages) it is natural to extend this to failure recovery and synchronisation.

---

[1] We are using an extended Pascal (Pascal/M) that allows for this.

Transactions can be characterised by the following four so called **ACID** properties [14]: Atomicity, Consistency, Integrity, and Durability. In our approach the mechanisms for the realisation of these properties will be placed at different levels.

Durability means that none of the updates made by a transaction should be lost once this transaction has passed the so-called commit point. Very often this is also called persistence. Two problems with current hardware technology make it necessary to look at durability. One is the volatile nature of current RAM memories and the other is the risk of damaged disc storage. Mechanisms to solve these problems heavily depend on the characteristics of the particular memory hardware and, in the case of a persistent uniform virtual memory, also on the paging strategies. In the MONADS-PC this should therefore be the sole responsibility of the virtual memory. Rosenberg et al have recently shown how the MONADS-PC virtual memory can be extended by to behave like a stable store by using a modified shadow paging algorithm [32]. For application areas with high requirements for fault-tolerance we are also looking at uninterrupted power supplies and disc mirroring.

Integrity refers to the set of all constraints that are part of application objects. The object implementations are responsible for detecting violations of these constraints. There are two important connections to transaction management. One is that constraints may be violated temporarily during the execution of transactions. However these violations must be removed before the transaction commits. The other is that if constraint violations persist until the end of a transaction then the transaction has to be aborted. In this case all updates that have been performed on behalf of the transaction have to be undone. Because a system by definition starts in a consistent state with respect to the constraints it is guaranteed that transactions always perform transformations from one consistent state to another.

Atomicity means that a transaction either finishes correctly and completely, or disappears without leaving any effects behind. The former is called commit and the latter abort. Aborts can be caused by external errors such as hardware errors or power failures, by internal errors such as division by zero or access violations, by program or user request, or by the transaction management system itself such as in the case of deadlocks. In our approach atomicity is not achieved by the same mechanism as durability. A major reason is that the stable storage operates on pages and in the case of the MONADS-PC guarantees the basic durability and consistency of the virtual memory itself. In contrast transactions operate on arbitrarily short or long objects which have no direct relationship to pages. Therefore undoing the effects of aborted transactions does not merely imply the use of old backups of modified pages.

Consistency has strong links to atomicity. The effect (state transformations and output) of transactions being executed in parallel has to be equivalent to some serial order of the successful transactions. This places two requirements on the transaction mechanism. First, no intermediate state of aborted transactions may be observed by another transaction. Without this rule programs operating on shared objects would never be able to guarantee integrity. Second, access to shared objects has to be synchronised in such a way that there is no cycle in the graph corresponding to the dependency relationship of transactions. The resulting single-transaction image relieves the programmer from dealing with concurrency explicitly and allows straightforward formal reasoning about the correctness of parallel programs. It is proposed to use the well known two-phase locking protocol for achieving consistency.

The granules of transactions in the MONADS-PC for locking and recovery are segments. Many systems (database management systems [17, 37] as well as novel operating systems with transaction support [9, 34]) use pages as the smallest base granule. Using segments in the MONADS-PC instead of pages as the base for transactions has the following advantages:

- it avoids unnecessary blocking of transactions when they update different segments that happen to be stored on the same page

- only one lock is necessary for large segments that are stored on many different pages

- the programmer (via the compiler) can control the possible degree of parallelism by placing variables into one or into several segments; with page-level locking this adjustment is much harder to achieve efficiently because placing objects in different pages leads to higher amounts of I/O)

- lock handling needs to take place only when a segment is made addressable to a process instead of with every virtual memory reference.

4. EXECUTION MODEL

What should be the relationship between transactions and the flow of execution in a general object-oriented environment? In conventional computer architectures transactions are often realised by dedicated processes for reasons of security and addressability. This can lead to severe performance problems due to the high amount of inter-process communication and due to the many necessary process switches. The MONADS-PC is strictly procedure-oriented[1]. This is possible because addressability of all objects and their protection is absolutely orthogonal to process boundaries. Therefore transactions can always be executed as part of normal processes.

Transaction management needs to be optional in a general environment such as the MONADS-PC because application level consistency (as compared to the consistency of the hardware and the kernel) does not have to be maintained for temporary or unimportant objects. The decision which operations should be executed as transactions can not be taken by the system but has to be taken by the programmer. Once a process operates in transaction mode all accesses to objects obey the transaction properties.

There are several possibilities for the relationship between transactions and operations on objects which include:

(a) No connection between transactions and routines at all; i.e. a transaction is started and finished with dedicated machine instructions.

(b) A transaction can only be started when an object is opened and ends with the corresponding close. The open call has an additional parameter to start a transaction optionally and the return from a close routine always finishes the transaction.

(c) A transaction can be be started at any time with a dedicated machine instruction but has to be finished before the close of the object in which the transaction has been started.

(d) A transaction can only be started as part of the call of a routine and and the return from this routine finishes this transaction.

(e) A transaction can be started at any time with a dedicated machine instruction but is bound to last no longer that the routine in which it has been started. This means that a transaction is finished either explicitly by a dedicated machine instruction or implicitly by returning from the routine in which the transaction has been started.

(f) Same as (e) but with the additional restriction that an explicit end of a transaction needs to be within the same routine as the start of the transaction.

The problem with approach (a) is that there would be no way of combining exception handling and abort of transactions because there is no point at which a missing commit would be detectable and therefore no automatic abort could be generated. At the other end of the spectrum the approaches (b) and (d) do allow for automatic aborts but they are not flexible enough since the programmer or the user could not freely choose to run some parts of a routine or some routine calls of a series of routine calls as transactions. Approaches (e) and (f) are preferable to (c) be-

---

[1] This is also true in a network of MONADS-PCs. All explicit communication between objects takes place via the one procedure call mechanism by using a network paging protocol [1, 7].

cause with these it is possible to define the local exception mechanism within routines such that an exception which is not handled leads to an abort of the corresponding transaction. Approach (e) could lead to very complicated transaction programs since a routine which starts a transaction and then calls another routine would have to handle a situation in which the called routine finishes normally (without an exception) even if it aborted the transaction. For these reasons we decided to use approach (f).

We consider a transaction to be local to a routine if it has been started within that routine. A transaction is global to a routine if it has previously been started by one of the routines in the dynamic call chain of the routine. A routine in execution can be either part of no transaction or of a local transaction or of a global transaction. At this stage we will not consider nested transactions [26] or layered transactions [41]. We are currenttly working on the integration of these mechanisms into our scheme.

Figure 5 shows the most simplest type of transaction in the MONADS-PC: a routine is called in which first a transaction is started, then instance and local data are accessed and then the transaction is finished. We call this a *"single transaction routine"* . It can for example be used for a routine that inserts an entry into a shared directory. A and B can refer to the same object which means that from within a routine in some object a routine of the same object can be called and is executed as a transaction.

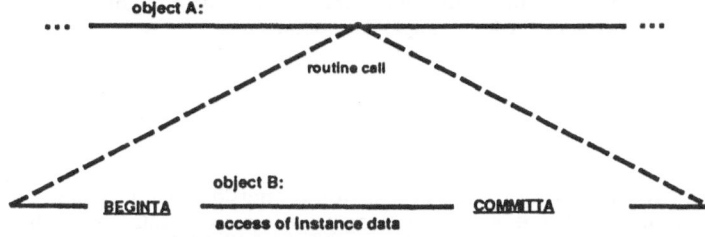

Figure 5: Single Transaction Routine

Figure 6 shows a slightly more complicated situation where a routine starts and finishes several transactions. This happens in situations where a routine performs independent parts, e.g. a "make" routine that compiles the several parts of a system.

Figure 6: Multiple Transaction Routine

The examples so far assume that the transaction control and the execution to be controlled take place within the same routine. This is not the case in another type of transaction, which is called *"conversational transaction"* in [40]. This type of transaction separates the implementation of the semantic operations from the transaction control (see Figure 7). A transaction can contain calls of operations on more than one object. These operations on different objects can either be called directly from within the transaction routine or indirectly from within called routines.

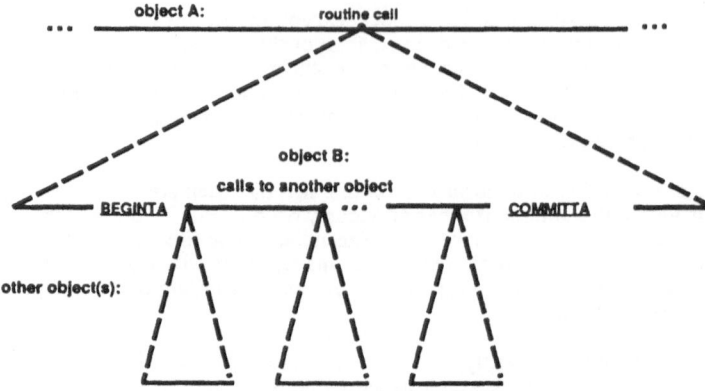

Figure 7: Conversational Transaction

Transactions can be used within compiled programs or interactively. The command language interpreter (CLI) on an MONADS-PC allows the user to call any routine of any of the existing objects. The only command the CLI understands itself is **EXIT** for leaving the CLI. All other commands are realised by calling some routine. It seems that there might be a problem with approach (E) if the user could issue for example the commands

BEGINTA
{operations}
COMMITTA

because if **BEGINTA** is implemented in some routine outside then the end of this transaction would be expected at the end of this routine (long before the user wants to finish the transaction). The solution to this problem is a routine (e.g. called TRANSACTION) which starts a transaction, then calls the CLI recursively, and then commits the transaction. After typing the command TRANSACTION the user sees a normal prompt from the newly started CLI and can then commit by exiting the CLI normally or abort by raising an exception. In fact the proposed routine TRANSACTION can have a module capability and a routine number as parameters thereby offering the ability to call any routine as a transaction without re-compiliation.

5. INTERFACE TO THE TRANSACTION MANAGEMENT

We now describe the architectural interface to the transaction management system. A new local transaction for the current routine is started by the machine instruction **BEGINTA.** If this routine is already within a transaction an exception is caused. The machine instruction **COMMITTA** finishes the current local transaction. There is no separate machine instruction for aborting a transaction since this is done automatically whenever a routine is left via an exception instead of normally. If the programmer wants to abort a transaction he simply raises an exception that is not handled by the local exception handler associated with this routine. If there has been no matching commit instruction at the time when a routine is exited via the normal return then a commit is performed implicitly.

Three machine instructions for loading a segment capability into one of the 16 registers are related to transaction management: **LOADC** for loading a segment capability for read/write access (if the appropriate rights are set in the capability), **LOADCR** for loading a segment capability for pure read access, and **CRHSEG** for creating a new segment. Once a process is in transaction mode all access to heap segments (whether these are instance, retained, or local) is guaranteed to follow the transaction properties. In fact also segments on the process stack are covered by transactions simply by collapsing stacks as part of exception handling. Because "fire walls" in the form of transaction boundaries can be set arbitrarily within complex calling structures it makes sense to restore all kind of data and not just the persistent objects.

A routine can not detect that it has been called as part of a transaction. The only differences to non-transaction mode may be that

- loading of a segment capability may be suspended for some time, but apart from reading time information this is invisible to the executing routine

- when the routine is called again after an abort (unhandled exception) then it can discover that the instance variables are in the same state as they were at the start of the aborted routine.

Because there is a limited number of capability registers in the MONADS-PC it is quite possible that a capability is loaded into some register more than once. An implementation has to be optimised for the situation in which a register is used for many accesses once it has been loaded, but in order to achieve the transaction properties it is important to detect this situation and handle it properly.

The transaction management system is responsible for making all read and write accesses to segments atomic and consistent. It does not control access to real resources such as the user´s terminal. More generally, an abort does not attempt to undo actions. This is either the responsibility of the programmer (as part of exception handlers) or it can be part of a higher level transaction mechanism based on objects and operations [8, 33].

6. CONCURRENCY CONTROL

This section presents the scheme for achieving serialisability of transactions in the MONADS-PC. We based our decission for the appropriate concurrency control on the assumption that the number of read-only transactions will not be substantially greater than the number of updating transactions. For this reason we have chosen a pessimistic concurrency control for synchronising access to segments. Read or write access to a segment is granted when the segment capability is loaded into a register. At this time an appropriate read or write lock is acquired. To enable the abort of a transaction without affecting any other active transaction locks are not released before the end of a transaction. This is exactly the strict 2-phase locking protocol which guarantees level 3 consistency [11].

The lock information is part of the segment itself. This has several advantages over a central lock table:

- there is no access of another page containing the lock table

- the amount of storage needed for lock information increases linearly with the number of segments and does not have to be arbitrarily set

- there is no need for extra global lock names

- appropriate lock information does not have to be searched for (e.g. in a linked list) because the address of a segment serves also as the address of the lock information

The load capability register instructions contain the tests whether a transaction

- already has the appropriate read or write lock for the segment (from a previous load) or

- possesses a read lock for the segment but needs to upgrade it to a write lock or

- does not have a lock for the segment yet

and the resulting actions of

- suspending the current transaction (process) or

- granting the new lock or

- upgrading an existing lock

need to be indivisible. In the MONADS-PC these instructions can be either micro-coded or implemented in the kernel. The former is obviously the more efficient solution but even the latter is still reasonably efficient since no expensive context switch is necessary for executing in kernel mode.

The structure of a lock is similar to a reader/writer semaphore [20], which is a special-purpose semaphore for regulating access from readers and writers to a shared resource. A lock additionally holds all the information about waiting readers and waiting writers. With reader/writer semaphores the programmer issues a P operation once. However since locks are automatic from the programmer's point of view, a lock could be acquired more than once due to multiple loading of a segment capability. There are two options for handling this case: either there is no special treatment but the lock is properly granted several times and released the same number of times. Alternatively the information as to which transaction (process) already holds a lock for a segment could be efficiently coded as part of the lock information. Figure 8 shows such a lock structure in a Pascal like notation.

```
type
  process  = 1 .. max_processes;
  processes = set of process;
  lock = record
    in_write_mode       : boolean;
    holding_processes   : processes;
    waiting_readers     : processes;
    waiting_writers     : processes;
    next_writer         : 0 .. max_processes;
  end;
```

Fig. 8: Structure of a lock

The algorithms for acquiring and releasing locks are shown in Figures 9 and 10. These too are given in a Pascal like notation. They implement reader priority but other priorities could easily be realised along the lines of [12]. To save the management of a FIFO queue for writers the next writer is chosen in circular order based on the process number. This prevents starvation between writers. Assuming a maximum number of parallel transactions of 32 the size of the lock structure is 3 words for an architecture with 32 bit wide words.

```
(* process_nr: process is the number of the current process held in a register *)
procedure acquire_lock(l:lock; write_access:boolean);
begin
   with l do
      if write_access then begin
         if (holding_processes - process_nr) <> () then begin
            waiting_writers:= waiting_writers + process_nr;
            if next_writer = 0 then
               next_writer:= process_nr;
            SUSPEND(process_nr)
         end else begin
            in_write_mode:= true;
            holding_processes:= holding_processes + process_nr
         end
      end else begin (* read access *)
         if in_write_mode and not (process_nr in holding_processes) then begin
            waiting_readers:= waiting_readers + process_nr;
            SUSPEND(process_nr)
         end else
            holding_processes:= holding_processes + process_nr;
      end
end;
```

Figure 9: Algorithm for acquiring locks (reader priority)

```
procedure release_lock(l:lock);
begin
   with l do begin
      holding_processes:= holding_processes - process_nr;
      if waiting_readers <> () then begin (* release all waiting readers in one go *)
         in_write_mode:= false;
         holding_processes:= waiting_readers;
         waiting_readers:= ();
         ACTIVATE(holding_processes)
      end else
         if next_writer <> 0 then begin
            in_write_mode:= true;
            holding_processes:= (next_writer);
            waiting_writers:= waiting_writers - next_writer;
            if waiting_writers = () then
               next_writer:= 0
            else begin
               repeat
                  if next_writer = max_processes then
                     next_writer:= 1
                  else
                     next_writer:= next_writer + 1
               until next_writer in waiting_writers
            end;
            ACTIVATE(holding_processes)
         end else (* no waiting processes *)
            in_write_mode:= false;
   end
end;
```

Figure 10: Algorithm for releasing locks (reader priority)

The process scheduler offers two routines for the purpose of synchronisation: **SUSPEND** immediately removes a process from the set of active processes until it is activated again and **ACTIVATE** sets a whole set of suspended processes into active state (but without immediate rescheduling). The scheduler implements these operations via private semaphores and they are commutative.

With a general locking mechanism deadlocks can not be prevented in advance but have to be detected and resolved. One simple approach would be to use a time-out mechanism. Each process could call the kernel to set a process-specific or even a routine-specific time it accepts for waiting on a lock. If the lock can not be granted within this time then the process is rescheduled with an exception. The problem with time-outs is that it is rather hard to find an appropriate time-out value, especially in a distributed environment. Nevertheless there are many advantages, namely ease of implementation and a sound base for interactive routines where the user will not accept arbitrarily delays. Thus even if a universal deadlock detection mechanism is used time-outs are still useful.

There is an algorithmic approach for reducing the probability of deadlocks. Very often a segment is first read and then modified by a routine later. If there are multiple readers on such a segment then deadlocks are very likely to occur. It would be unreasonable to have exclusive locks only since this would dramatically decrease the potential parallelism. There are two (non-contradictory) solutions to this problem. First of all the compiler could pessimistically load a segment capability for write access at the first load if a later update is intended. Secondly the locking algorithm could be modified in such a way that a new reader has to wait if there is a waiting writer that already has a read lock for this segment. This is called the *lock escalation priority*.

Despite the attempt to reduce the probability of deadlocks the kernel has to offer general deadlock detection and resolution for transactions on segments. Therefore it maintains a wait-for graph [2] of processes waiting for other processes to release locks. The interface to the deadlock handler is shown in Figure 11. The routine WAITING_FOR is set-oriented so that multiple dependencies (such as one writer waits for several readers) can be passed in one call and included into the wait-for graph. The graph can be checked for cycles either on each call or less often. A very efficient algorithm that can be used is presented in [6]. The routine NOT_WAITING_ANY_MORE removes all edges that lead to a set of processes in the wait-for graph. The modified reader-priority versions of the locking routines calling the deadlock detection can be found in Figures 12 and 13.

```
procedure WAITING_FOR(waiting, awaiting: processes);
(* when this routine detects a cycle it then reschedules one of the
    processes that take part in the cycle with an exception *)

procedure NOT_WAITING_ANY_MORE(p: processes);
```

Fig. 11: Interface to deadlock handler

```
(* process_nr: process is the number of the current process held in a register *)
procedure acquire_lock(l:lock; write_access:boolean);
begin
   with l do
      if write_access then begin
         if (holding_processes - process_nr) <> () then begin
            waiting_writers:= waiting_writers + process_nr;
            if next_writer = 0 then
               next_writer:= process_nr;
            WAITING_FOR((process_nr), holding_processes);
            SUSPEND(process_nr)
         end else begin
            in_write_mode:= true;
            holding_processes:= holding_processes + process_nr
         end
      end else begin (* read access *)
         if in_write_mode and not (process_nr in holding_processes) then begin
            waiting_readers:= waiting_readers + process_nr;
            WAITING_FOR((process_nr), holding_processes);
            SUSPEND(process_nr)
         end else begin
            if waiting_writers <> () then
               WAITING_FOR(waiting_writers, (process_nr));
            holding_processes:= holding_processes + process_nr
         end
      end
end;
```

Figure 12: Modified acquire algorithm (including calls to deadlock handler)

```
procedure release_lock(l:lock);
begin
   with l do begin
      holding_processes:= holding_processes - process_nr;
      if waiting_readers <> () then begin (* release all waiting readers in one go *)
         in_write_mode:= false;
         holding_processes:= waiting_readers;
         waiting_readers:= ();
         NOT_WAITING_ANY_MORE(holding_processes);
         if waiting_writers <> () then
            WAITING_FOR(waiting_writers, holding_processes);
         ACTIVATE(holding_processes)
      end else
         if next_writer <> 0 then begin
            in_write_mode:= true;
            holding_processes:= (next_writer);
            waiting_writers:= waiting_writers - next_writer;
            if waiting_writers = () then
               next_writer:= 0
            else begin
               repeat
                  if next_writer = max_processes then
                     next_writer:= 1
                  else
                     next_writer:= next_writer + 1
               until next_writer in waiting_writers
            end;
```

```
        NOT_WAITING_ANY_MORE(holding_processes);
        WAITING_FOR(waiting_writers, holding_processes);
        ACTIVATE(holding_processes)
    end
  end else
      in_write_mode:= false;
  end
end;
```

Figure 13: Modified release algorithm (including calls to deadlock handler

One question that still remains to be answered is how the lock structure would be maintained if sets could not be used to represent processes holding a lock and waiting processes. This could for example be the case when the number of possible processes is too large. The representation of the waiting processes is not really a problem since two counters and two pointers for linked lists of process numbers could be used instead without too much loss in efficiency. The major problem presents the field holding_processes that serves the purpose of checking quickly whether a process already has a specific lock. With a large number of processes searching in any kind of data structure could take too long. A solution that works in constant time can be achieved by making the following two changes: (1) storing the process number of the current writer within the lock structure and (2) for read access not checking whether the process already holds the lock in read mode but simply acquiring the lock regardless and releasing it at the end of the transaction as many times as it has been acquired.

The last problem to solve in order to realise the transaction-oriented concurrency control is the releasing of locks. Releasing of locks has to happen automatically on return or the exceptional exiting of a routine without any interference by the programmer or by the user. The algorithm for releasing a lock has been presented in Figures 10 and 14, but we have not described how all the locks of a transaction can be found and released. This requires an additional structure containing pointers to all the locks held by a process. This structure will be put into an extra address space called the transaction space which will be also used for recovery (see section 7). Part of each process context (which is stored at the bottom of the process stack) is a pointer to a transaction control segment (see Fig. 14). If the pointer is null or invalid then the process is not executing within a transaction. The transaction control segment contains the commit record and the root of a linked list of pointers to locks (in other address spaces). The transaction space is created at the start of a transaction if the process does not already have an associated transaction space. Commit and abort can delete the transaction space but it may be preferable to retain the space for the next transaction and to garbage collect it regularly instead. In Figure 15 the simple algorithm for commiting or aborting from the point of view of concurrency control is given. After a crash or a fast shutdown the restart procedure inspects all transaction control segments which are known via the registered processes. Note that the stable uniform virtual memory can checkpoint a state at any time, e.g. in the middle of abort processing. The states aborting and committing are used to detect the situation that aborting or committing of a transaction has to be continued. Recovery is dealt with in section 7. The procedures for acquiring and releasing locks need to be extended in order to add the pointer to acquired locks to the list in the transaction space.

```
segment_reference = record
  ptr        : ^lock; (* this must be a full virtual address! *)
  next       : ^segment_reference
end;
ta_control = record
  ta_state  : (inactive, active, committing, aborting);
  segments   : ^segment_reference;
  last      : ^segment_reference
end;
```

Fig. 14: Structure of transaction control segments

```
procedure commit(ta_c: ^ta_control);        | abort
begin
      ta_state:= committing;                 | aborting
      while segments <> nil do
         with segments do
            begin release_lock(ptr^); segments:= next end;
      ta_state:= committed;                   | aborted
end;
```

Figure 15: Algorithm for commit and abort (Concurrency Control)

At the time an address space is created it must be decided whether the lock part will be prepended to all segments that are created in this address space. Address spaces that have not been created in this way can not be opened by processes executing in transaction mode. On the other hand non-transactional processes set a lock for whole opened address spaces so that processes executing as transactions are synchronised with these.

7. RECOVERY

Recovery is the mechanism to achieve atomicity (see section 3). There are three types of recovery: Abort recovery, crash recovery, and recovery from media failure. Different recovery strategies can be classified mainly on what actions need to be taken when restarting after a crash [14, 43]. This can range from no actions at all, through redo actions only, undo actions only, to undo and redo actions.

From the point of view of recovery the transaction mechanism in the MONADS-PC is based on a 2-level scheme. A stable uniform virtual memory using shadow pages and regular checkpointing [32] forms level 0. No redo or undo is necessary but the checkpointed states are not necessarily operation-consistent or even transaction-oriented [42]. This does not matter since a checkpointed state always contains the passive objects as well as the processes in the form of their stacks and register contents.

In conventional approaches recovery and durability are treated together because what is done to make updates durable is at the same time the problem for atomicity when an abort occurs. In our approach durability is a separate issue except for the checkpointing that is necessary as part of the commit operation. Level 1 is the segments that were already discussed in the context of concurrency control. Segments are updated in place. This means that for aborting a transaction undo-processing has to be performed, but redo is never needed.

In the MONADS-PC the rebooting can continue the execution of all active processes at the time of the last checkpoint. This means that transactions can, but do not necessarily have to, be aborted at reboot. The decision mainly depends on the type of the transaction and the time the system has been down. To give programmers the chance to handle such a situation each process that is active when rebooting receives an exception called **REBOOTED**.

Before a segment is updated for the first time from within a transaction a *before-image* has to be taken. When a write lock is acquired by a transaction for the first time the original state of the segment is copied regardless of its type into the transaction space (see also section 6). The whole segment (control, data, pointers, but without the lock) is placed as the last part of a segment reference segment. For very large segments a copy on write scheme based on the hardware feature to allow read access only for a set of pages is used.

Since segments can not be dynamically resized in case of lock escalations in order to hold the before-image additionally the existing reference segment in the transaction space is removed and a new one that is large enough to hold the before-image is inserted.

At the time of commit the before-images are simply ignored and discarded. At abort they are copied back to their original place in order to restore the referenced segment. A lock can only be released after restoration of the segment has been finished.

The operations commit and abort are too complex and need too much time for large transactions which have accessed many segments to keep them indivisible since this would severely hold up scheduling of other processes with timing constraints. Fortunately this is not a problem as long as one iteration for one segment is indivisible, namely the eventual restoring, the releasing of the lock and the setting of the pointer to next referenced segment. Otherwise a lock could be released several times thereby corrupting the state of the lock. If one iteration is indivisible then abort and commit can simply be restarted by looking at the current state of the transaction control segment first. Finally commit needs to issue a checkpoint operation to guarantee durability.

Theoretically it would be sufficient to create before-images for local and retained heaps without any locking since no parallel processes access this kind of data. On the other hand the lock structure efficiently holds the information whether a before-image has been taken already and the overhead is small enough not to pursue this potential optimisation any further.

For newly created segments an empty before-image part shows that the segment can be deleted at abort. Nevertheless our first implementation will leave this to the garbage collector. A program can not delete a segment explicitly so this is not a problem for the transaction management system. The algorithms for taking a before-image, committing, and aborting are relatively straightforward extensions of those already given. For the purpose of illustration an example situation is shown in Fig. 16.

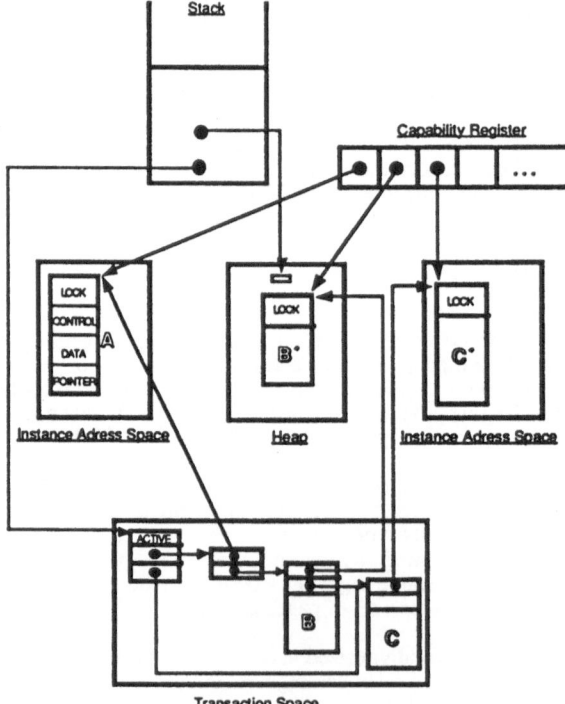

Fig. 16: An example situation of the transaction space

8. RELATED WORK

The idea of integrating transaction management into virtual memory has been discussed by several researchers as in [35, 36, 39]. Traiger points out the advantages of shadow paging compared to logging as part of virtual memory. The advantages are mainly efficiency and simplicity. He also describes the database management system System/R in which locking and logging takes place on top of the shadow paging level to achieve high concurrency. The approach presented in this paper supports these two levels directly within the architecture. No fixing of pages and no operation-consistency is necessary since in our approach the undo logs for modified segments are part of the checkpointed state. Stonebraker's observations in [36] such that the unit of locking can not be smaller than a page and that LRU can not be used as the page replacement policy are not valid in the MONADS-PC with stable uniform virtual memory and transactions on segments.

There are several other architecture-oriented approaches for the support of transactions, such as [9, 18, 38]. Thatte's persistent memory for the TI Explorer Lisp machine comes very close to our approach since it offers a uniform virtual memory abstraction with shadow paging and checkpointing and aims at supporting object-oriented databases. In contrast to transactions in the MONADS-PC there is no direct support for transactions in Thatte's approach. Instead the so called resilient objects are implemented in an external transaction management package. For example this needs to be called for locking and it has to maintain a global lock table. Transactions in the MONADS-PC acquire locks on segments automatically and these locks are stored as part of the segments. The transaction package also needs access to a disc outside virtual memory for the external redo log. Our approach uses the force-strategy [14] for commit processing and therefore no redo logs are written. In both approaches undo logs are stored within the checkpointed virtual memory, but in the MONADS-PC processes running in transaction mode can restart themselves from the last written checkpoint. Mutabor [18] is a coprocessor-based object store developed at the GMD which offers functionality for optimistic concurrency control and recovery. The architecture records dependencies between transactions operating on common objects. The virtual memory is divided up into an active space and a recovery space so that two different page directories need to be maintained. Segments in the recovery space roughly serve the purpose of checkpointed states in case of crash and of undo logs in case of aborts. The 801 store [4, 9] consists of a uniform virtual memory with 40 bit wide addresses. Segments are always multiples of 4KB pages. As with transactions in the MONADS-PC locks are implicitly acquired as a side effect of normal machine instructions. The address translation hardware supports locking of pages or 128 byte long parts of pages which is not as flexible as our approach since these units do not necessarily correspond to the logical units of information.

In a number of projects and products transactions have been integrated into operating systems (e.g. [10, 25, 27, 29, 34]). Some, such as Locus [27], can only handle transactions on Unix files. In contrast TABS [10] which is implemented on top of the Accent kernel has a transaction manager responsible for transactions on recoverable objects. Similar to our approach recovery segments are created whenever a segment is updated by a transaction for the first time. In contrast to the MONADS-PC pages that have been modified by transactions have to be pinned in main memory and unpinned only after the corresponding recovery segments has been written to disc. Also the costs for the communication between the paging software and the Transaction/Recovery Manager can become quite high. Many of these problems seem to have been removed in the successor Camelot [34]. Other projects, such as Birlix [15] or Profemo [19] concentrate on a base for recovery but do not provide full support for transactions.

9. CONCLUSION

A general transaction management facility for the unconventional computer architecture MONADS-PC which aims at security of information and support for object-oriented software engineering has been presented. The proposed transaction concept can be used for all kinds of objects and not just for traditional database objects. An important advantage in terms of efficiency is that transactions are executed in-process and that they are integrated into the virtual memory without all the disadvantages that have been described in [35, 36, 39] by using segments as variably sized locking and recovery granule instead of pages. Dedicated hardware support is not needed for the proposed transaction mechanism. Instead special reader/writer semaphores for efficient locking are proposed as part of the kernel. Persistence and low-level consistency are realised within the uniform virtual memory with shadow paging and checkpointing thereby cleanly separating the different issues.

Apart from the implementation and evaluation of the proposed transaction management there are still many open research issues. Very important is the incorporation of other resources such as devices into the transaction management system (and into the deadlock detection scheme). Also we are formulating the generalisation of the scheme to nested transactions for finer failure control and for parallel execution of subtransactions. Even higher parallelism will be achievable by taking advantage of the semantic properties of objects [8, 33] and using the concept of layered transactions [31, 41].

10. ACKNOWLEDGEMENTS

We would like to thank J. L. Keedy for the fruitful discussions on the subject of this paper and for commenting on drafts of this paper. The first author also likes to thank G. Weikum for all the inspirations he gave him on transaction management.

REFERENCES

1. Abramson, D.A. and Keedy, J.L. "Implementing a Large Virtual Memory in a Distributed Computing System". *Proc. of the 18th Hawaii International Conf. on System Sciences*, 1985.

2. Agrawal, R., Carey, M.J. and DeWitt, D. "Deadlock Detection is Cheap". *ACM SIGMOD Record*, 13, 2, 1983.

3. Atkinson, M.P. and Buneman, O.P. "Types and Persistence in Database Programming Languages". *ACM Computing Surveys*, 19, 2, 1987.

4. Attanasio, C.R. "801 Architecture Support for Database – a Case Study", Technical Report RC 12416, IBM T.J. Watson Research Centre, 1987.

5. Bensoussan, C.T., Clingen, C.T. and Daley, R.C. "The Multics Virtual Memory: Concepts and Design". *Communications of the ACM*, Vol. 15; No. 5, 1972.

6. Jiang, B. "Deadlock Detection is Really Cheap". *ACM SIGMOD Record*, 17, 2, 1988.

7. Brössler, P., Henskens, F., Keedy, J.L. and Rosenberg, J. "Addressing Objects in a Very Large Distributed System". *Proc. of the IFIP Conf. on Distributed Systems*, Amsterdam, 1987.

8. Brössler, P. and Freisleben, B. "Transactions on Persistent Objects". *Proc. of the International Workshop on Persistent Object Systems*, Newcastle, Australia,1989.

9. Chang, M. and Mergen, M. "801 Storage: Architecture and Programming". *Proc. of the 11th ACM Symposium on Operating Systems Principles*, 1987.

10. Eppinger, J.L. and Spector, A.Z. "Virtual Memory Management for Recoverable Objects in the TABS Prototype", Technical Report CMU-CS-85-163, Carnegie-Mellon Univ., 1985.

11. Eswaran, K.P., Gray, J.N., Lorie, R.A. and Traiger, I.L. "The Notion of Consistency and Predicate Locks in a Database System". *Communications of the ACM*, 19, 11, 1976.

12. Freisleben, B. and Keedy, J.L. "Priority Semaphores". *The Computer Journal*, 32, 1, 1989.

13. Gray, J.N. "The Transaction Concept: Virtues and Limitations". *Proc. of the 7th International Conf. on Very Large Databases*, 1981.

14. Härder, T. and Reuter, A. "Principles of Transaction-Oriented Database Recovery". *ACM Computing Surveys*, 15, 4, 1983.

15. Härtig H., Kühnhäuser, W.E., Lux, W., Streich, H. and Goos, G. "Recovery in the BirliX Operating System". Technical Report, GMD, Birlinghoven, 1986.

16. Hitchens, M. "The Structure of a Command Language Interpreter". *Proc. of the 4th IFIP Working Conf. on User Interfaces*, North Holland, 1989.

17. IBM Systems Journal. *Special Issue on DB2*, 23, 2, 1984.

18. Kaiser, J., Nett, E. and Kröger, R. "Mutabor – An Intelligent Memory Management Unit for an Object-Oriented Architecture supporting Error Recovery". *Proc. of the 3rd Int. GI/NTG Conf. on Fault-Tolerant Computing Systems*, 1987.

19. Keedy, J.L. "Paging and Small Segments: A Memory Management Model". *Proc. of the 8th World Computer Congress*, 1980.

20. Keedy, J.L., Rosenberg, J. and Ramamohanarao, K. "On Synchronising Readers and Writers with Semaphores". *The Computer Journal*, 25, 1, 1982.

21. Keedy, J.L. and Rosenberg J. "Support for Objects in the MONADS Architecture". *Proc. of the International Workshop on Persistent Object Systems*, Newcastle, Australia,1989.

22. Keedy, J.L. and Brössler, P. "Implementing Databases in the MONADS Virtual Memory". Technical Report, University of Bremen, 1990.

23. Kröger, R. "PROFEMO — A Transaction-Oriented Distributed System". *Proc. of the Workshop on Fault Tolerance in Parallel and Distributed Computing*, San Diego, 1987.

24. Liskov, B. "The Argus Language and System". *Distributed Systems — Methods and Tools for Specification: An Advanced Course*, Lecture Notes in Computer Science 190, Springer Verlag, 1985.

25. Marques, J.A. and Guedes, P. "Extending the Operating System to Support an Object-Oriented Environment". *Proc. of the Conf. on Object-Oriented Programming Systems Languages and Applications*, 1989.

26. Moss, J.E.B. "Nested Transactions: An Approach to Reliable Distributed Computing", *Information Systems*, 1, The MIT Press, 1985.

27. Mueller, E.T., Moore, J.D. and Popek, G.J. "A Nested Transaction Mechanism for LOCUS". *Operating Systems Review*, 17, 5, 1983.

28. Nett, E., Kröger, R. and Kaiser, J. "Providing Recoverability in a Transaction-Oriented Distributed Operating System". *Proc. of the 6th IEEE Int. Conf. on Distributed Computing Systems*, 1986.

29. Pu, C. and Noe, J.D. "Nested Transactions for General Objects: The Eden Implementation". Technical Report TR-85-12-03, Univ. of Washington, 1985.

30. Rosenberg, J. and Abramson, D.A. "MONADS-PC: A Capability Based Workstation to Support Software Engineering". *Proc. of the 18th Hawaii International Conf. on System Sciences*, 1985.

31. Rakow, T.C., Gu, J. and Neuhold, E.J. "Serializability on Object-Oriented Database Systems".Technical Report 396, GMD, Birlinghoven, 1989.

32. Rosenberg, J., Henskens, F., Brown, F., Morrison, R. and Munro, D. "Stability in a Persistent Store Based on a Large Virtual Memory". *Proc. of the Int. Workshop on Computer Architecture to Support Security and Persistence of Informations*, Bremen, FRG, 1990.

33. Schwarz, P.M. and Spector A.Z. "Synchronizing Shared Abstract Data Types". *Transactions on Computer Systems*, 2, 3, 1984.

34. Spector, A.Z. et. al. "Camelot: A Distributed Transaction Facility for Mach and the Internet - An Interim Report". Technical Report CMU-CS-87-129, Carnegie-Mellon Univ., 1987.

35. Stonebraker, M. "Operating System Support for Database Management". *Communications of the ACM*, 24, 7, 1981.

36. Stonebraker, M. "Virtual Memory Transaction Management". *Operating Systems Review*, 18, 2, 1984.

37. Stonebraker, M. "The Ingres Papers — Anatomy of a Relational Database System", Addison-Wesley, 1986.

38. Thatte, S.M. "Persistent Memory: A Storage Architecture for Object-Oriented Database Systems". *Proc. of the Int. Workshop on Object-Oriented Database Management Systems*, 1986.

39. Traiger, I.L. "Virtual Memory Management for Database Systems". *Operating Systems Review*, 16, 4, 1982.

40. Walter, B. "Nested Transactions with Multiple Commit Points: An Approach to the Structuring of Advanced Database Applications. *Proc. of the 10th International Conf. on Very Large Databases*, 1984.

41. Weikum, G. "Principles and Realisation Strategies of Multi-Level Transaction Management". Technical Report DVS1-T1, Univ. of Darmstadt, 1987.

42. Weikum, G. "Transactions in Database Systems" (in German), Addison-Wesley, 1988.

43. Weikum, G., Hasse, C., Brössler, P. and Muth, P. "Multi-Level Recovery". *Proc. of the ACM Symposium on Principles of Database Systems*, 1990.

The RelaX Transactional Object Management System

R. Kroeger, M. Mock, R. Schumann
German National Research Center for Computer Science (GMD)

ABSTRACT

RelaX (Reliable distributed applications support on UNIX) is a portable and extensible system software layer on top of UNIX-like operating system kernels supporting reliable distributed applications by a generalized transaction mechanism. The transactional object management system provides access to shared persistent objects which can be manipulated within transactions. It is complemented by a C++ language port on top. It provides fast recovery in virtual memory and efficient commit protocol processing by applying modern virtual memory management techniques of next-generation UNIX-like systems. The transactional object management system is intended, in a long range, to be merged with the object-oriented, hardware supported trusted computing base developed in the ASA project at GMD.

RelaX contributes the transaction mechanism to the ESPRIT project COMANDOS (Construction and Management of Distributed Open Systems). A prototype implementation of the transaction mechanism is running at GMD.

1. INTRODUCTION

Distributed systems offer some commonly desired advantages like the possibility for enhanced fault tolerance due to inherent redundancy, increased performance by concurrency and better resource utilization through sharing. However, mastering the problems of concurrency and error recovery becomes much more complex. A general solution to these problems is necessary in order to avoid that each programmer becomes overloaded with performing concurrency control and error recovery in every application. Such a mechanism should be provided as a system-layer supporting a broad range of distributed applications.

The transaction concept stemming from the database world also tackles the problems of error recovery and concurrency control. Each transaction guarantees that it either completes correctly according to the commonly used serializability criterion [9] and that its effects are permanent by means of a commit protocol, or it is aborted without leaving any effect in the system using an abort protocol. However, by implementing transactions at the system-level, they cannot be optimized to a specific application such as short-running transactions in the database world but have to consider a broad range of distributed applications. Especially, transactions of long duration have to be supported. To meet these various requirements, it is commonly accepted to introduce flexibility into the transaction concept [3, 11]. In the PROFEMO approach [15], which is developed further in the RelaX project [21], this flexibility is expressed by the concepts of the premature release of data objects as a basis for the optional use of uncommitted data, separating the successful completion of a transaction from its commitment, group commitment, extended nesting and multiple processes per transaction per site. These items are thoroughly treated in [14, 21] and are briefly sketched later on.

As transactions only concern the recovery and synchronization aspect of applications, they are independent of (and thus do not provide) a computational paradigm and a data paradigm for the construction of distributed applications. In this field, the object oriented paradigm is often considered to be the key for the construction of distributed systems and applications [2, 6, 7]. Emerging from programming languages like Simula and Smalltalk, object oriented principles can also be found in the design of database systems and operating systems, e.g. in [4, 13, 23]. Furthermore, providing atomic objects that are manipulated within transactions is widely advocated for constructing robust distributed systems and has been demonstrated by several prototype systems like Argus [12], Camelot [24], and Arjuna [22]. Argus and Arjuna follow a language based approach and put most of the transaction and object functionality into the run-time system of the language. Our approach is closer to the Camelot view in providing a language independent system layer with a language port on top [8], but offers a more flexible transaction functionality via the generalized transaction concept and integrates the object management into the virtual memory management instead of putting it into a client/server architecture.

Combining generalized transactions and objects into a general purpose, fault-tolerant distributed system architecture has already been the objective of the GMD project PROFEMO [15]. RelaX (Reliable Distributed Applications Support on UniX) carries on the software work of PROFEMO and provides the transaction mechanism as a portable and extensible software layer on top of modern UNIX-like kernels. Global transaction management and management of resources, which transactions can access, are clearly separated in order to enable extensibility of the RelaX layer. To do this, the transaction mechanism is isolated in a server (TM) and cooperates via a standard interface with an extensible set of resource managers (RMs) which provide different kinds of persistent, sharable data (e.g. object management systems, file systems or specialized databases). New RMs can be built using generic RelaX components to support transaction management. These modules do concurrency control based on read/write locking of fragments, recovery control and handle the interface to the TM.

The RelaX transactional object management system is a special RM which includes mechanisms for naming, locating and invoking (local and remote) objects that reside in a system wide global object space. Remote objects are either mapped to the calling site or accessed by RPC. Mapping of objects into the application's address space allows to execute the type specific operations within the application. This eliminates difficulties of passing complex data structures as parameters from the application to the operation (no restriction to value parameters) and minimizes the overhead for accessing a shared, persistent object since an object, once mapped, now can be accessed nearly like an application's private object. Mapping of objects, access to remote objects and the required operations for handling recovery points and to update committed object versions are efficiently implemented by exploiting the advanced virtual memory management facilities of next generation UNIX systems. A C++ language port and an extended C++ run-time system on top of the object management system allow to define and use the objects as instances of C++ classes.

As conventional hardware only supports virtual memory management on page boundaries, handling of small sub-page object structures has to be done in software, thus entailing impacts on protection and performance. The design of the transactional object management allows the integration of dedicated hardware to enhance conventional virtual memory management in order to support sub-page structures. It is intended, in a long range, to be merged with the object-oriented, hardware supported trusted computing base developed in the ASA project at GMD [10]. The final goal is an integrated software-hardware solution providing dependable, atomic objects of arbitrary sizes.

The generalized transaction concept of RelaX is treated in chapter 2. Chapter 3 describes the overall structure of the RelaX layer and addresses the separation of transaction management from resource management by defining the external interfaces of the transaction management. Chapter 4 outlines the general structure of a RelaX RM with special emphasis on the interfaces of the RelaX generic transaction support components. Chapter 5 presents the design of the RelaX transactional object manager with special emphasis on the integration of recovery and commitment into virtual memory management techniques. Chapter 6 contains a summary.

2. THE GENERALIZED TRANSACTION CONCEPT

In this section the generalized transaction concept of RelaX suitable for structuring reliable distributed applications is briefly described. For a detailed description the reader is referred to [14, 21].

The fault model comprises transaction faults, site faults and media faults. For media faults standard techniques for stable storage are applied and are not considered in this paper. A transaction fault implies the system-wide abort of that transaction. A site fault results in loosing any data maintained in volatile storage. On the surviving sites a site fault is mapped to a set of transaction faults of those transactions that visited the faulty site. To ensure the all-or-nothing property of transactions, all uncommitted transactions that visited the faulty site are aborted.

In conventional implementations of transactional systems, only committed data can be shared between different transactions. This restriction makes recovery and commitment easy because it keeps transactions independent from each other (so called "isolation property"). The penalty for this damage confinement strategy is paid in terms of restrictions on concurrency, communication and resource utilization. Thus, the fault-free case in running transactions is burdened in favour of a simplified recovery management [24].

In the RelaX architecture, we allow the use of uncommitted data in order to increase flexibility and efficiency of the system. This facility is especially valuable to increase concurrency between long running transactions. Concurrency control is performed by non-strictly two-phase-locking [9]. Each transaction is subdivided into a growing phase and a shrinking phase. During the first phase locks can only be aquired. After reaching its lockpoint the transaction enters the second phase. From now on no further acquiring of locks within this transaction is possible but optionally locks can be released. By using this valid but uncommitted data a transaction becomes dependent on the releasing one. As a consequence, these transactions cannot commit or abort independently in order to ensure the all-or-nothing property of transactions. Therefore, the system has to keep track of the dependencies between transactions and to consider these dependencies during commit/abort protocol execution. These dependencies are stored by the system locally at each site in a data structure called local recovery graph. All these local recovery graphs make up the recovery graph, a distributed data structure, which stores the whole set of dependencies between transactions in the distributed system [14]. Based on the recovery graph, the set of transactions affected by the commit/abort of a transaction can be computed. In order to avoid a multi-level commit/abort protocol execution including sub-coordinators, RelaX uses a redundant recovery graph, on which very efficient commit/abort protocols are based [21].

We separate the successful completion of a transaction from its commitment by introducing the additional transaction state "completed". This is mandatory in order to commit several transactions within one protocol execution (group commit). This approach reduces the number of commit protocol executions. According to reported measurements [26] the commitment of transactions causes the paramount costs in running distributed transactions. Therefore the separation of the successful completion of a transaction from its commitment can be used for efficiency reasons mainly reducing the overhead in running transactions.

Finally, nested transactions are briefly discussed. Nested transactions are especially valuable for transactions of long duration due to their independent abort from their calling transaction. Furthermore, they can be run in parallel increasing system performance. Furthermore, we allow multiple processes per site per transaction, so that concurrency within a transaction is also possible without the overhead related to concurrency control and error recovery. In order to introduce further flexibility into the transaction concept, we also allow the nesting of transactions only with respect to recovery purposes meaning that the synchronization level remains the same, i.e. the resulting subtransactions in that case get rid of the unneeded synchronization overhead [20].

3. THE RELAX ARCHITECTURE

This section discusses the implementation structure of the RelaX distributed transaction layer. The main goals are extensibility and portability. The RelaX architecture conforms to the structure of the proposed X/Open model for distributed transaction processing [27]. Fig. 1 depicts the overall architecture of the RelaX layer at a single site.

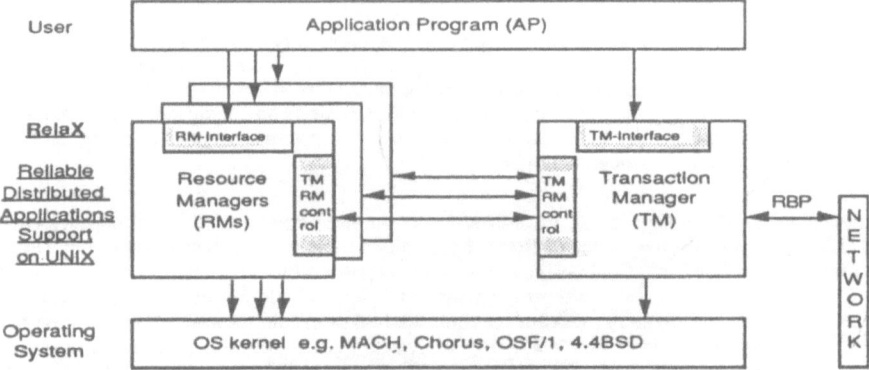

Fig. 1: The RelaX architecture.

The transaction manager at a site is responsible for transaction control at the specific site and performs, together with the TMs at the other sites, the commit/abort protocols described above. Especially, the TM manages the redundant recovery graph. The TMs communicate via an efficient Reliable Broadcast Protocol (RBP), which requires only one acknowledgement per broadcast message in the fault-free case [5, 25]. The TM requires only minimal functionality from the underlying operating system kernel. The OS-interface is isolated in a separate module in order to achieve easy portability to various operating systems.

A resource manager provides synchronized and recoverable resources via a specific resource manager interface to the application. A RM is, for example, an object management system offering operation calls to persistent, typed objects as will be described below, a transactional file system with its traditional read/write interface or a database system with its queries. There might be several RMs on a node, coordinated by a single TM. This structure reflects the clear separation of transaction management from resource management and is the basis to achieve extensibility. According to the distinction between transaction management and resource management, the commit/abort protocols are extended by a local protocol between the TM and the RMs. This local protocol is concerned with the relevant state changes of transactions (commit/complete/abort). The RM's behavior with respect these events is controlled by the standardized TM-RM control interface (*local_complete- local_abort-*, *local_prepare-*, *local_commit- transaction*). In addition to this cooperation, a RM can interact also with the TM via the TM-interface, for example, in order to abort a transaction or to record arising dependencies between transactions.

Concurrent accesses to shared resources are synchronized by the RM via non-strict two-phase read/write locking. The application progam announces its lockpoint to the TM via the TM-interface (*setlockpoint*), which propagates the fact that a transaction reaches its lockpoint to all relevant RMs (*local_setlockpoint*). Higher level concurrency control schemes like type specific locking can be integrated later on by mapping them to read/write locking of disjoint fragments of the resources. Furthermore, the RM detects arising dependencies between transactions that are caused by using uncommitted data and informs the TM (*add_dependency*).

The application program (AP) defines transaction boundaries via calls to the TM-interface (*begin-, end-, abort- transaction*) and, inside these transactions, it uses resources of one or more RMs via their specific RM-interfaces. The AP maintains transaction relevant information such as the current transaction identifier in a small run-time layer which is managed by RelaX library routines linked to the application. Calls to the TM interface are performed within these library routines. With respect to distributed computations, the RelaX architecture allows APs and RMs that reside on different sites to communicate by any protocol they like, e.g. remote procedure calls. It is only required that the involved TMs get notice of the fact that a transaction spreads out to another site. This is indicated by calling the library routine *expand_ta*.

4. GENERIC TRANSACTION SUPPORT FOR RESOURCE MANAGERS

In the following, we concentrate on the design of RMs conforming to the RelaX architecture. In order to support the construction of new RMs, RelaX provides generic software components as building blocks for any kind of RM. Fig. 2 shows the general structure of a RM and outlines which parts of a RM are covered by the generic transaction support components.

The resources provided by the RM are contained in a layered resource store: the bottom layer comprises the storage component providing the long term storage facility for the resources. In general, a conventional background storage will be associated to the storage component, but, for instance, in order to support diskless nodes, a protocol can be used instead to access a remote storage component. The layer above, the active resource component, manages the memory representations of activated resources and maps requests from the application interface for non-activated resources to the storage component.

On top of the resource store there are the generic transaction support components, which are of main interest here. They implement the local functions of synchronization and recoverability for the resources. The generic transaction support consists of three modules: the TM-RM control module implementing the interface between the RM and the TM, the (local) concurrency control module implementing non-strict two-phase read/write locking and the (local) recovery control module supporting the commit/abort of transactions, i.e. it associates with each transaction the set of recovery points needed to restore its before image in case of an abort. In case of a (group) commit, it computes the after images of the resources modified by the transactions that have to be committed. The functions of these modules are used by the RM's access component that implements the application interface of the RM.

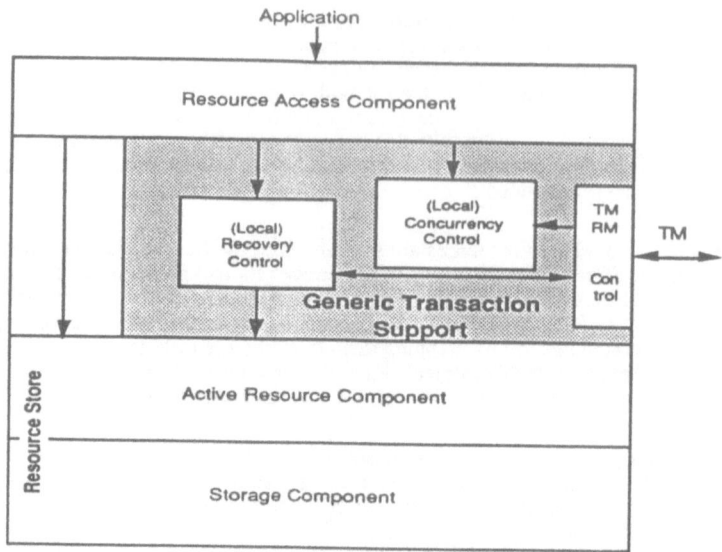

Fig. 2: General Structure of a Resource Manager.

In the following, the operations required from the resource store to support the generic components are considered. With respect to the concurrency control module no supporting operation of the resource store is required. This is due to the fact that the routines that decide on the granting of locks are independent of the storage representation of resources. Concerning the recoverability of the resources, the resource store has to support the following model of resource management: for each resource, there is a committed state that will be updated only within the commit protocol. Optionally, the previous committed state can be retained in order to provide a basic versioning support. All accesses to a resource are directed to its actual state, that initially corresponds to the committed state, and reflects all modifications of the resource. If a transaction modifies a resource, the RM establishes a recovery point for the resource. This recovery point contains enough information to restore the actual state to the before image of the transaction in case of an abort. Note that, as we allow the use of uncommitted data, there might be a set of recovery points associated with a resource, i.e. the actual state of the resource is accessible to all active transactions, each saving its individual before image in a recovery point. This before image corresponds to the after image of the preceeding transaction. Recovery points will be value based in general, but other approaches are not precluded. Their storage representation is hidden to the upper layers.

The operations required from the resource store to support the recovery control module split into a set of recovery point operations and a group of operations to support the commitment of transactions. The recovery point operations are essentially copy operations in virtual memory (*SaveResource*, *RestoreResource*). Commitment of transactions has to be supported by two-phase update operations on committed states of resources according to the well-known two-phase commit protocol. As a basis for this proceeding a data log can be used within the storage component.

The most efficient and our favourized way to implement recovery points is to maintain them as logical (i.e., complete or incremental) copies of activated resources in the active resource component. This is possible, since in RelaX, transaction faults are recovered in virtual memory, thus avoiding to store recovery information stably. Only during commitment after images have to be stored stably. This approach is more efficient than the usual database approach to store before images and after images of transactions on a log and to use this information for handling transaction faults as well as site faults. Our approach supports the following "activation cycle" for a resource: The "passive" state of a resource corresponding to its last committed state is represented in the (background) storage component. A resource becomes "active", i.e. is brought into virtual memory, when it is accessed by a transaction for the first time. All modifications are performed in virtual memory on the representation of the actual state of the resource. Once activated, a resource can be used by all active transactions, each of them copying its before image into a recovery point. The last committed state of the resource maintained by the background storage component will be updated only after a commit protocol execution. This is done by the storage component concurrently with the ongoing system activity.

5. THE RELAX TRANSACTIONAL OBJECT MANAGER

A computational model that has been widely accepted for constructing reliable distributed applications is based upon transactions operating on persistent objects. Thus, an object management system providing mechanisms for naming and locating of objects and invocation of operations on these objects seems to be the natural counterpart of the transaction mechanism. This chapter gives an overview on the design of an examplary RM, the RelaX Transactional Object Manager (TOM).

The TOM provides a system wide global object space containing shared, persistent objects which are uniformly addressed by low-level, globally unique names. High-level user oriented names are assumed to be supported by other components (e.g. name service, object database management system). Objects are typed and can be manipulated only by their type-specific operations. Objects may contain references to other objects which are represented by the corresponding low-level names. Objects are recoverable and can be manipulated within transactions. The TOM supports basic version control by allowing to maintain a sequence of versions for each object, on which a higher level version management system can be built. Objects can be clustered to increase performance. Fine-grained concurrency control and recovery of objects is based on object fragments in order to allow multiple modifying transactions at the same time.

5.1. Overall design of the Transactional Object Manager

The overall design of the TOM corresponds to the general resource manager structure and is depicted in Fig. 3. It is based on a modern operating system kernel like Chorus, Mach, or OSF/1-2 [17, 18, 19]. According to Fig. 2 the TOM consists of four components. These are the object storage system, virtual object management, transaction support and a language independent interface. The TOM is complemented by an extended C++ run-time system, supporting a C++ language port for atomic, i.e. synchronized and recoverable persistent objects. Other language ports are possible. The transaction support component is the generic one described in the previous chapter and is therefore not considered further.

The object storage system serves for two purposes: first, it is the long term repository for committed object versions, and second, it acts as a paging device for activated long objects, i.e. objects consisting of more than one page. The virtual object management maintains the activated objects and their recovery points. The object access interface is language independent and provides operations for object mapping, concurrency and recovery control. The language independent run-time system interfaces to the TOM and logically belongs to the virtual object management. The extended C++ language port integrates constructs for handling persistent objects into the C++ language (AT&T 2.0).

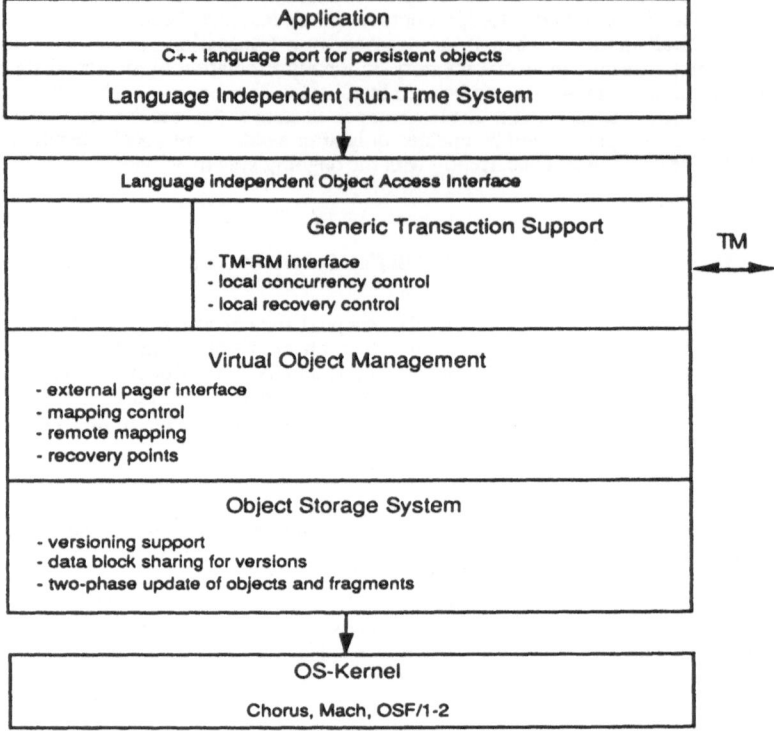

Fig. 3: The Structure of the RelaX Transactional Object Manager.

In the following, we concentrate on the architectural system aspects of the TOM, i.e. background representation of objects in the storage component, memory representation in the virtual object management, impact of transaction management on both representations, and the representation of objects in the language independent run-time. In addition, we show how small, sub-page objects are supported in the software solution and we outline a migration path to integrate an dedicated object oriented hardware base.

5.2. Object Storage System

The object storage system is the long term repository for committed object versions and serves as a paging device for activated objects. All objects are identified by unique, low-level names. The object storage system offers operations to activate and to update objects for given low-level names. Activating an object simply means to bind it to a (paged) virtual memory object maintained in the virtual object management layer. Each page of the object will only be paged in on demand when it is first accessed.

The update operation allows to address arbitrary fragments of an object. It proceeds, according to the prepare and commit phase of the commit protocol, in cooperation with an integrated data log in two phases: first, the updates are stably saved, and second, they are propagated to the objects. The following two techniques are offered to process the update: first, updates are taken from memory. In this case, the updates are forced to the data log in the first phase (only in order to read them in case of a restart) and are retained in memory. In the second phase, they are propagated from memory to the committed object versions. The second technique takes the updates from disk. In the first phase, updates are brought to (stable) storage that also holds the committed versions. This is done by flushing the dirty pages of the active object representation. Then, only a small entry that describes these updates on disk is forced to the data log. Propagating the updates results in merging the flushed pages with the unmodified pages of the last committed object version as described below. The first technique is appropriate when only small fragments of an object are involved in the update. The second technique promises performance advantages when committing large fragments or whole objects

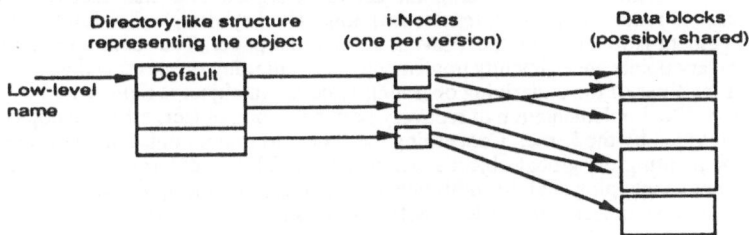

Fig. 4: Storage format for object versions.

The implementation of the object storage system is based on the structure of a 4.4BSD file system. In contrast to a conventional file system, it provides versioning by maintaining increments (see Fig. 4). Each version of an object is identified by an i-Node and consists of the data blocks reachable from this i-Node. The whole object is represented by a directory like structure that holds the i-Node numbers of the different versions. There is a distinguished default version representing the last committed state of the object. The versions of the object can share data blocks, i.e, in contrast to a conventional UNIX file system, a data block can belong to different i-Nodes. A reference count for a shared data block will be maintained based on a new interpretation of the conventional bmap-structure of the file system. Operations for adding and deleting versions (or the whole object) are provided. In order to create a new version, two or more i-Nodes have to be specified in linear order, the first of them representing the base version and the others holding the modified data blocks. The new version is created by merging the block references into one i-Node which will be incorporated into the object directory. A version is deleted by eliminating its i-Node from the object directory and by decrementing the reference counts of its data blocks. Data blocks with reference count zero will be freed.

Let us finally discuss the problem of handling media faults. They are addressed in the first version by standard techniques such as mirrored disks and by adopting ideas of the "journalled" file system [1]. A possible alternative is to integrate the object storage subsystem into a distributed network file system and to achieve stability via replication.

5.3. Virtual Object Management

Let us introduce some notions and mechanisms of virtual memory management as a common base for the following subsections. For convenience, we mainly rely on the terminology used in

Mach [18]. The basic unit of resource allocation is a *task* (process). The address space of a task is composed of several non-overlapping *regions*, each representing a consecutive range of virtual addresses of that task. The size of a region must be a multiple of the page size supported by the underlying architecture. Read/write/execute protection attributes and inheritance attributes can be specified for each region. All regions of an address space are described by an *address map*, whereby each entry of a map describes the *mapping* of a region to a *memory object*. A virtual memory object (VM object) is a pageable data repository bound to units of backing store. It is associated with a *pager* or *mapper* which is responsible for handling page faults and page-out requests. An *external pager* is a pager task that runs outside the kernel. Sharing of VM objects is supported in several ways: a VM object can be read/write shared between distinct tasks which have all mapped the object to a region. Shared VM objects can be copy-on-write protected by the use of *shadow objects*. A shadow object provides read access to the original copy-on-write protected (shadowed) object and contains the modified pages of the shadowed object.

The virtual object management maintains the activated objects and their recovery points. It provides access to remote objects by remote mapping. The key design decision for the virtual object management is to conceive the TOM as an external pager. The required operations for handling recovery points are efficiently implemented by exploiting the advanced virtual memory management facilities of the underlying operating system. An object is represented by a virtual memory object. The implementation of recovery points for long objects relies on copy-on-write techniques provided by the kernel. Concerning the access to remote objects, distributed shared memory implementing the global object space is achieved by an external pager protocol that implements remote mapping [28]. In addition to remote mapping, the application may invoke an RPC to access remote objects. Access to remote objects is not considered further in this paper.

The basic idea for implementing recoverability for an object is to bind it to a (paged) VM object and to perform modifications on shadow memory objects, keeping the shadowed object as recovery point. In contrast to the normal usage of shadows as independent copies of the shadowed object, the TOM preserves a semantic relationship between a shadow and its shadowed object. Modifications on the shadows will be reflected in the shadowed object upon two-phase commit. Fig. 5 sketches the general approach to implement recoverable objects via shadows:

Fig. 5.a) depicts the following initial situation: Transaction T1, represented by one process, did not use any object and object O has not been used by any transaction so far. Fig. 5 b) shows what happens when T1 maps O: a virtual memory object O_1 is created and mapped into T1's address space in a so called "private write" mode. This means that O_1 initially holds no pages and is filled from the committed version of O by page faults. However, page out requests are not written back to the committed version of O, but to another, newly created non-committed version within the paging store. The reason for this is twofold: first, the committed state of O must not be overwritten until T1 commits, and second, it acts as the before image of T1. Now assume that T1 releases O in an uncommitted state and that a second transaction T2 uses this state. Then the situation illustrated in Fig. 5c) will arise: another virtual memory object O_2 is created as a deferred copy (or shadow) of O_1 and will be mapped into the address space of T2. By this O_1 remains unmodified and can thus be used as recovery point of T2. Furthermore, it represents the after image of T1 with respect to O. An abort of T2 simply requires to release O_2 in order to restore the correct state of O which is O1, the after image of T1. On the other hand, if T1 commits, its after image is found in O_1. Note that pages belonging to the after image of T2 can be contained in O_2 and O_1. In order to commit T1 only the modified (dirty) pages of O_1 have to be flushed (under the assumption that the paging store is stable). Thus, both the old committed version and their incremental changes are stored stably. After successful commitment it is up to the object storage to merge them as described above in order to establish a new committed version of O.

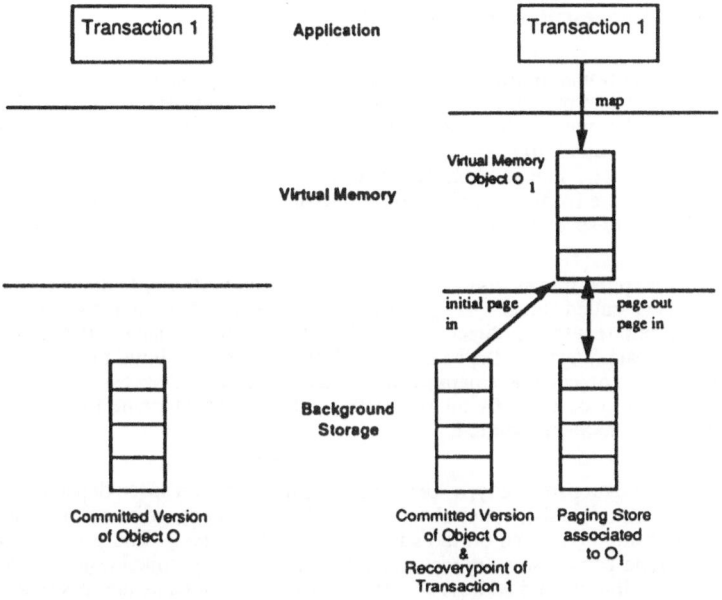

Fig. 5a) initial situation

Fig. 5b) Transaction 1 uses Object O

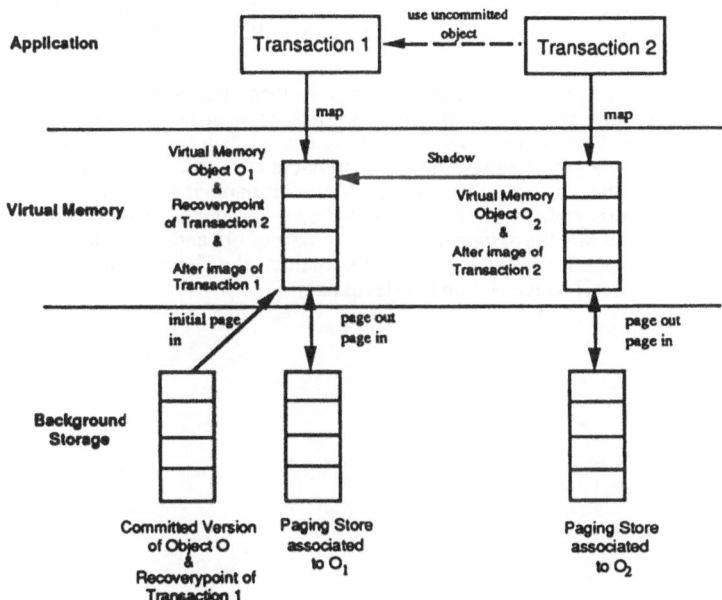

Fig. 5c) Transaction 2 uses uncommitted after image of transaction 1

Fig. 5: Example of recovery points for a VM object.

5.4. Run-Time Representation of Objects

We assume a conventional architecture that provides linear, process specific virtual address spaces with the facility of mapping shared memory. Objects and type objects (i.e. objects which contain the code of the type specific operations) are mapped into the application's address space and the type specific operations are executed inside the application. This allows the TOM interface to be language independent and eliminates difficulties of passing complex data structures as parameters from the application to the operation. Object sharing is supported by mapping the object into several applications.

For every object mapped into an address space, the run-time system maintains a private header and an associated so called "local" data part (see below). A header contains the low-level name of the object and pointers to the object's type object, to the object's shared data part, and to the object's local data part. Together, the headers of all mapped objects build the active object table of the application. An object, once mapped into an address space, is accessed through its header by a usual virtual address. This obviously speeds up the access, since no further translation of the object's low-level name is required.

The associated local data parts are type specific and contain address space dependent data for the object, which is neither persistent nor shared (e.g. I/O-descriptors, pointers to string constants, data that can be computed based on the shared part of the object). The primary usage of the associated local data parts is to store virtual addresses of other mapped objects. As the shared data can be mapped into several address spaces, it must not include any address space dependent information. Thus, object references in shared data cannot be virtual addresses but must be full references, i.e. low-level names. The local data parts make addressing by address space dependent virtual addresses applicable for objects referenced in the shared data part. A similar indirect addressing scheme can be found in the Multics [16] operating system for handling dynamic binding information. The mechanism works as follows (see Fig. 6):

When an object O1 is mapped into an address space, its local data part contains, possibly among other type specific components, placeholders (initialized with NIL) for all virtual addresses corresponding to low-level names contained in the shared data part of O1. Instead of always using the low-level name, the corresponding placeholders are used. Suppose there is a low-level name of object O2 in the shared data part of O1. When this name is evaluated for the first time, it will result in the virtual address of O2 in the address space under consideration. This virtual address is then inserted into the associated local data part of O1 and, from there on, will be used inside this address space for accessing O2. Nevertheless, the shared data part of O1 remains fully sharable, since it still contains only low-level names.

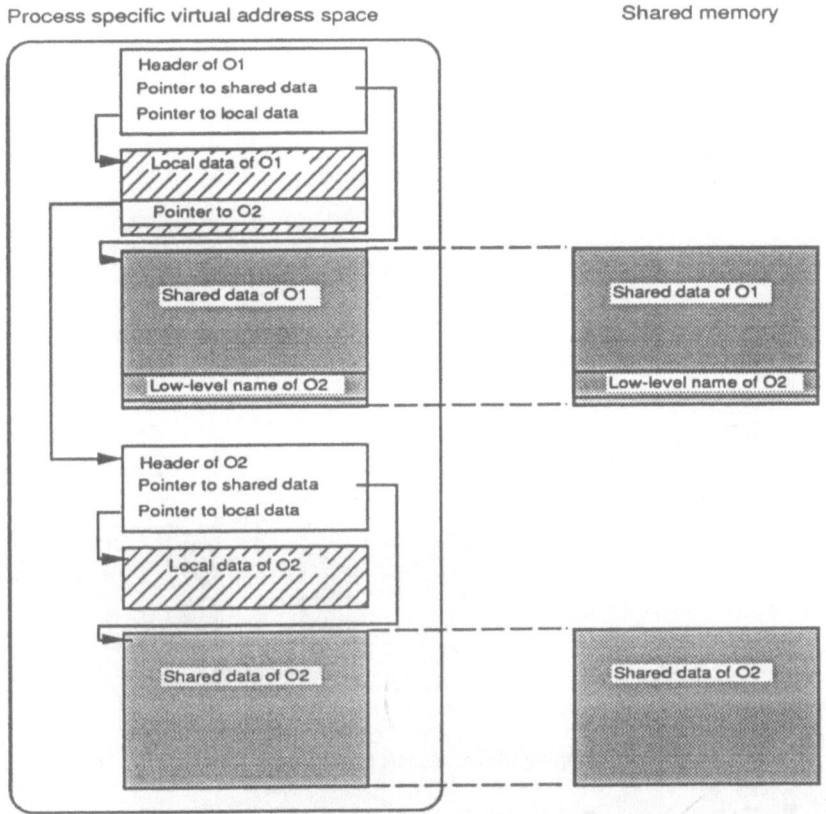

Fig. 6: Indirect addressing scheme inside of an address space.

5.5. Supporting Small Objects

Conventional architectures often refer to pages the as smallest units supported. Disk traffic is performed on a block (page) basis, virtual memory management does not apply to units smaller than a page, mapped regions of virtual memory must be multiples of pages, and access rights are defined on a page basis. However, objects usually do not fit into this page pattern. Handling of long object that consist of multiple pages can be mapped to a paged architecture easily, but manipulating small objects that (perhaps together with other objects) completely fit into a single page is not supported and must be programmed on top of the architecture.

The TOM uses a "clustering approach" to handle small objects. Groups of small objects (which are supposed to be related to each other) are stored continuously in a so-called *cluster object*. A cluster object contains small objects and a cluster header which describes the internal structure of the cluster. Mapping a small object actually results in mapping its whole cluster object into the address space. The interpretation of the cluster header is done in the run-time system that provides the illusion of accessing inidividual, independent objects to the application (Fig. 7).

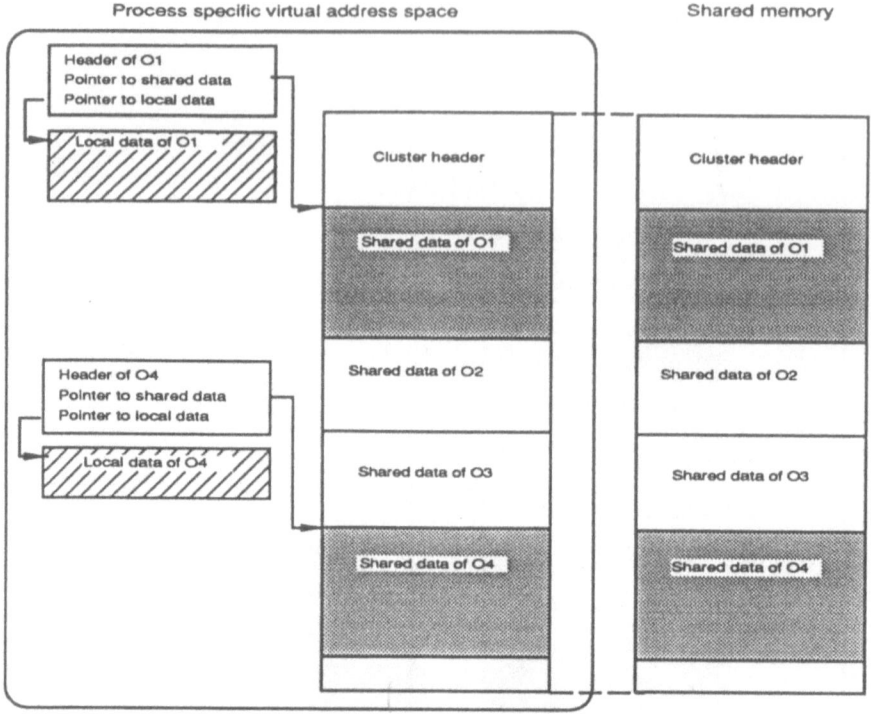

Fig. 7: Mapping of two objects from the same cluster.

The impact of clustering on the lower levels of the TOM (Virtual Object Management, Object Storage System) is very low, since the small objects contained in the cluster object correspond to the fragments of the cluster object. The distinction between a cluster object and a normal (long) object is transparent to the lower levels. They only deal with fragments of objects and do not care about their interpretation. Accessing and modifying a small object eventually results in the update of a fragment of its cluster object. The only consequence of clustering for the Object Storage System is that several low-level names (of short objects) are bound to the same (cluster) object.

The described approach is light-weight in the sense that the interpretation of sub-page structures is performed at very early stage and therefore allows for acceptable performance. Its drawback consists of putting the whole responsibility into the run-time system, which logically belongs to the TOM, but is physically subject to an application's misbehaviour. For instance, checking for access rights is done when mapping an object. In case of a small object, other objects with possibly other access rights are made physically accessible in the application's address space, even if they are not logically mapped.

Shifting the management of sub-page structures into lower levels of the TOM is possible and leads to an higher level of protection, but inevitably downgrades the performance on a conventional architecture. Consider, for instance, a software emulation of small objects inside of the operating system kernel. The virtual memory management is extended in order to support cluster objects as special kind of virtual memory objects, i.e. the knowledge of the internal structure of a cluster is integrated into the kernel. Then, regions of virtual memory in application address spaces are no longer restricted to be multiples of pages, but can have an arbitrary length. As before, mapping of a small object results in activating its entire cluster object into the shared virtual memory, but only the needed fragment is individually mapped into a region of the application address space. By this, the application address spaces are provided with objects of arbitrary length while keeping the virtual memory management inside of the kernel and disk traffic for paging on a page basis. However, because a conventional memory management unit (MMU) does not support mapping of sub-page structures, in the described solution, every access to a small object produces a miss in the MMU and involves the kernel in interpreting the layout of the application address space.

If, however, additional architectural support is given, like, e.g. the object-oriented MMU developed in ASA [10], fine-grain protection can be achieved at reasonable costs. This MMU has knowledge about the layout of the application address space on a per mapped object basis and knows about the corresponding object location in physical memory. A miss in the MMU leads as usual to a kernel request to reload the MMU and, if the corresponding page is not present, can be satisfied by a normal page-in procedure. The advantage of this scheme lies in supporting fine grain protection by a hardware interpreted layout of the application address space, while retaining the usual paging mechanism inside of the kernel.

Further enhancements of the object-oriented hardware support can be used in the TOM. For instance, the integration of a hardware supported object invocation mechanism that performs type-specific access right checks on every invoke, and the possibility to isolate the currently used objects inside an address space by adjusting the access environment of a process on every invoke. We are investigating in merging these features into the design of the TOM.

6. SUMMARY

RelaX is a portable distributed software on top of UNIX-like operating system kernels that provides system-support for the construction of reliable distributed applications in form of a generalized transaction concept. The transaction mechanism especially allows for the optional use of uncommitted data. It is isolated in a server that cooperates with an extensible set of resource managers, which provide the data transactions can access.

The transactional object management system is such a resource manager providing shared persistent objects that can be manipulated inside of transactions. The overhead to implement recoverability of the objects is minimized by heavily relying on advanced virtual memory management techniques. Recovery points are maintained in virtual memory as incremental copies achieved by copy-on-write techniques. The background storage integrates commitment and versioning of objects into the paging mechanism. Object management for objects mapped into an application's address space is performed by a language independent run-time system. Support for small objects is achieved by a (software) clustering approach. The integration of a dedicated object-oriented hardware support for fine-grain object protection has been considered in the design.

REFERENCES

1. AIX 3.0, System Manuals, IBM Corp., 1990.

2. G. Almes, A. Black, A. Lazowska, J. Noe:"The Eden System: A Technical Review". *IEEE Trans. on Software Engineering*, vol. SE-11, no 1, Jan. 1985.

3. K.P. Birman, T.A. Joseph:"Exploiting Virtual Synchrony in Distributed Systems", *Proc. of 11th SOSP*, Austin, 1987.

4. M. Carey, D. DeWitt, D. Frank, G. Graefe, J. Richardson, E. Shekita, M. Muralikrishna:"The Architecture of the Exodus Extensible DBMS", *First Int. Workshop on Object-Oriented Database Systems*, Pacific Grove, Cal., 1986.

5. J. Chang, N. Maxemchuk:"Reliable Broadcast Protocols", *ACM Transactions on Computer Systems*, Vol. 2, No. 3, Aug. 1984.

6. "COMANDOS: Object Oriented Architecture". Esprit Project 834 -Delivrable D2-T2.1, Sep. 1987.

7. P. Dasgupta, R. LeBlanc, W. Appelba:"The Clouds Distributed Operating System", *Proc. of the 8. IEEE Distributed Computing Symposium*, June 1988.

8. D. Detflefs, M. Herlihy, J. Wing:"Inheritance of Synchronization and Recovery Properties in Avalon/C++". *IEEE Computer*, Dec. 1988.

9. K. Eswaran, J. Gray, R. Lorie, I. Traiger:"On the Notions of Consistency and Predicate Locks", *CACM*, Vol. 19, No. 11, 1976.

10. J. Kaiser:"An Object-Oriented Architecture to Support System Reliability and Security", *International Workshop on Computer Architectures to Support Security and Persistence of Information*, Bremen, May 1990.

11. K.H. Kim, J. You, A. Abouelnaga:"A Scheme for Coordinated Execution of Independently Designed Recoverable Distributed Processes", *Proc. of FTCS 16*, Vienna, 1986.

12. B. Liskov, R. Scheifler:"Guardians and Actions: Linguistic Support for Robust Distributed Programs". *Proc. 9th ACM Symp. on OS Principles*, Bretton Woods, 1983.

13. D. Maier, J. Stein:"Development of an Object-Oriented DBMS", *Object-Oriented Programming Systems, Languages and Applications (OOPSLA)*, Portland, Oregon, Sep. 1986.

14. E. Nett, J. Kaiser, R. Kröger.:"Providing Recoverability in a Distributed Operating System", *Proc. 6th Int. Conf. on Distr. Comp. Systems*, Cambridge, Mass., May 1986.

15. E. Nett, K.-E. Großpietsch, A. Jungblut, J. Kaiser, R. Kröger, W. Lux, M. Speicher, H.-W. Winnebeck:"PROFEMO - Design and Implementation of a Fault-Tolerant Distributed System Architecture", GMD-Studie Nr. 100, 1985.

16. Organick:"The Multics System", MIT Press, 1972.

17. OSF:"Operating System Component (OSC) Kernel Architecture Overview, Revision 1.0", Apr. 1989.

18. R. Rashid, A. Tevanian, M. Young, D. Young, R. Baron, D. Black, W. Bolosky, J. Chew:"Machine-independent virtual memory management for paged uniprocessor and multiprocessor architectures", *IEEE Transactions on Computers*, 37(8):896-908, Aug. 1988.

19. M. Rozier, V. Abrsossimov, F. Armand, I. Boule, M. Gien, M. Guillemont, F. Herrmann, P. Léonard, S. Langlois, W. Neuhauser:"Chorus distributed operating systems", *Computing Systems*, 1(4), 1988.

20. R. Schumann:"Transaktionsverwaltung in einem verteilten, objektorientierten System", GMD-Studie Nr. 134, Jan. 1988.

21. R. Schumann, R. Kröger, M. Mock, E. Nett:"Recovery Management in the RelaX Distributed Transaction Layer", *8th Symp. on Reliable Distributed Systems*, Seattle, Oct. 1989.

22. S. Shrivastava, G. Dixon, G. Parrington:"An Overview of Arjuna: A Programming System for Reliable Distributed Computing", University of Newcastle upon Tyne, UK; to appear in *IEEE Software*.

23. A. Skarra, S. Zdonik, S. Reiss:"An Object Server for an Object-Oriented Database System". *Int. Workshop on Object-Oriented Database Systems*, Pacific Grove, Sep. 1986.

24. A. Spector:"Camelot: A Distributed Transaction Facility for Mach and the Internet - An Interim Report", TR CMU-CS-87-129, Computer Science Department, Carnegie-Mellon-University, 1987.

25. R. Vonthin:"Spezifikation des PROFEMO-Reliable Broadcast Protokolls in UNIX 4.2BSD", GMD-Studie 127, Birlinghoven, 1987.

26. M.J. Weinstein, T. Page, B. Livezey, G. Popek: "Transactions and Synchronization in a Disitributed Operating System", *10th ACM Symp. on Operating System Principles*, 1985.

27. X/Open company:"Interim Reference Model for Distributed Transaction Processing", Transaction Processing Working Group, July 1989.

28. M. Young, A. Tevanian, R. Rashid, D. Golub, J. Eppinger, J. Chew, W. Bolosky, D. Black and R. Baron,:"The duality of memory and communicatoin in the implementation of a multiprocessor operating system", in *Proc. Symp. Oper. Syst. Principles*, Nov. 1987.

Towards New Architectures for Distributed Autonomous Database Applications

Malcolm Atkinson
GIP Altaïr

Andrew England
Perihelion Software Ltd

Abstract

For large enterprises it is important to improve information flow, and hence facilitate collaboration. In such systems it is incorrect to assume dedicated involvement. Similarly we have to accept that complete data consistancy is not an achievable goal. Information systems which support collaborations have to respect these restrictions, and then use high-level knowledge about data and working-practices. This is illustrated by an example from health-informatics, and some related algorithms. Its use of application-specific knowledge to organise distribution, autonomy, stability, security and recovery raise questions about the utility of building-in such mechanisms at the memory-level.

1 INTRODUCTION

Several current proposals for object stores propose a low-level mechanism for distribution[4,5,6,3, 7]. For example, address spaces are arranged so that they include a part of the address (say 32 bits) which specifies the machine on which an object resides. Such strategies are also included in operational hardware, such as the IBM series 38 machines[2]. Underlying mechanisms can then either ship operations to the objects [10], or automatically move all or part of objects, or make copies of objects. Such algorithms clearly have a rôle in the context of closely-coupled systems, but they depend on all the components having high reliability, transactions being brief, and nearly continuous involvement of all subsystems in the cooperative provision of a single object store.

It is argued here that such systems may be viewed as one distributed computation engine, but that there is also a need for various forms of less closely-coupled collaboration between computational systems. These may best be provided by mechanisms well above the level of the store mechanism, where more knowledge about the data and processes may be exploited.

The paper reports an example of the sort of human system that may require such autonomous models of distribution. A few strategies for providing such autonomy show how knowledge about the content or logical-use of data may be exploited. Their purpose is two-fold: as an illustration of the kind of higher-level distribution mechanism that will need to be supported, and as a provisional and initial report on algorithms that are currently the topic of experiment and implementation.

It is suggested that these algorithms could exploit very large stores and address spaces, but that it is unlikely that they will benefit significantly from complex addressing, protection, transaction and distribution mechanisms in the underlying system.

2 MOTIVATION for AUTONOMY

A major use of computation and digital communication is to improve the information flow throughout some organisation. This may be considered to be of fundamental human significance — the success of humans as an animal may be attributed to their ability to cooperate on common tasks, such cooperation becomes more challenging as the common tasks become more complex. Today such cooperations spread across progressively wider domains, and perhaps the ultimate valid model is like that of the Gia model of earth, in which the totality has to be seen as one interacting system[1].

At present, however, practical support for cooperation is limited to (often extensive and overlapping) sub-organisations. Typical examples are, cooperation over the design and construction of large artefacts (buildings, ships, aircraft, etc.); cooperation over administration and management (local and national goverment, large companies, etc); operational control of a system (a utility such as electricity generation, a service such as banking, airlines, or health-care, etc). These cooperative ventures have certain common features:

1. Many different people are involved over a wide geographic area;

2. Most of them do not want to consciously use an elaborate information system (they wish to make a minimal effort to understand only that part that concerns them);

3. They are divided into different sub-groups, each with a different (but sometimes overlapping) domain of interest;

4. Each sub-group will take responsibility for some of the data but wish to use data which is either common or which belongs to other sub-groups (there is significant variation in requirements, even among sub-groups with nominally the same rôle);

5. Working-practices already exist to allow these separate sub-groups to operate together towards their common interest;

6. These practices will reduce unnecessary interference, particularly conflict over data, and establish identified responsibilities, eg for the correctness of certain data or for the decisions that data reflects;

7. Within such working-practices, sub-groups or individuals want to work for long periods without interference from others and without compliance to unnecessary constraints;

---

[1] In which case we might postulate a world-wide object store supporting all information storage and communication.

8. Sub-groups, or individuals (eg consultants, structural engineers, accountants, subcontractors, etc) may want to be participants in several cooperations simultaneously, without those cooperations becoming inter-linked;

9. Communication with the participant sub-groups may be unreliable, they own, and may disconnect, their link, and may withdraw their equipment and data from general access for a time;

10. The composition of the total group is itself dynamic, sub-groups may come and go;

11. The sub-groups may themselves have many or all of these properties.

An ineluctable consequence of these features, and of the typical working-practices, is that consistancy throughout the system is unachievable. One person will be utilising data, which another already knows needs ammendment, and perhaps has already changed, but that change has not yet propagated. Nevertheless, such systems work, and have a high tolerance to such inconsistency, provided that inconsistancy conforms to the working-practices.

Given that there are many examples of such (professional) cooperative systems, and that our society has a notable dependence on their efficient functioning, it is appropriate to consider how to build information systems that match these requirements. A priority must be to support change, since such cooperations must adapt their structures and activity in response to changing circumstances and expectations[2].

3   TECHNOLOGICAL ISSUES

The above cooperations among people are not new, and they have long been the target of computational assistance. However, most previous attempts have been limited by the performance or cost of current technology. In the last decade, there have been dramatic improvements (typically by factors of 10 or more) in the speed of computers, in the capacity of long-haul and local area digital communications, in the typical capacity of stores, in the economy of processors, memory and communications, and in the reliability of such computational components. These are the very factors which enable the serious consideration of large high-performance object-stores, the topic of many papers in these proceedings. They also enable a more complete, ambitious and integrated approach to be taken to the support for cooperation. For example, perhaps it is no longer necessary to ignore some of the attributes in the list above, relenting from requiring rigid adherence to a fixed, fully integrated structure. Possibly, with these extra technological resources, we can relax constraints, and comply with requirements such as 7, 8 and 9 above.

4   A SPECIFIC EXAMPLE

To enable the description of strategies, an example is introduced, which is a cooperative system providing the health-care of all the people living in a particular area. This application has many

---

[2]It is suspected that tolerance to inconsistency and tolerance to change are inter-related, and at least in part, depend on common mechanisms.

properties enabling autonomy, eg medical-notes and test-results are *appended* to a patient's medical record. Such properties are believed to be the *normal consequence of effective working-practices* in cooperative systems. In that health-care system and the geographic area it serves are: the potential patients; the professionals (doctors, specialists, nurses, dieticians, administrators, physiotherapists, etc.); the sub-systems (medical-practices[3], hospitals, wards, laboratories, operating-theatres, intensive-care units, kitchens, reception areas, clinics, etc.); and the groups that may interact with this system, and with others (eg government agencies, financial management, site and plant management, personnel management, social services, emergency services, etc).

Each group or individual working in this system will be provided with hardware and software that supports their activities, maintains their data, and interacts with a corporate body of data supporting the whole cooperative task.

As an example, at the reception desk, a receptionist can direct patients to their ward, or clinic, at the same time recording their arrival, and hence alerting the nursing group concerned. Automatically, a new icon, for this patient, is displayed in the expected-arrivals area of the relevant ward's screen. At each ward the system enables nurses to allocate, and keep track of, bed-usage, patient-location (eg in-theatre, on weekend-leave, etc), and to gain access to relevant medical information. In bed-bureau, staff can observe bed-occupancy and plan future admissions. In the laboratory, results are entered into the system, and they are 'immediately' available in the ward or in the GP's consulting room. In the GP's practice particulars of new patients are entered, these should not need entering again when the patients return or visit other parts of the system. Bar-stripe encoding will be used throughout the sytem to avoid data re-entry even of identification data.

Within a hospital we may expect a high-performance reliable network, and committed dedicated processors of adequate performance. In the envisaged system, each work-place is served by a workstation and local Unix processor supporting a colour X11 user interface. There may be many data repositories (RAM and Disc) around this network. Between hospitals we may well be able to arrange nearly the same reliability and performance. But the connection to a laboratory, a small practice, a district health worker, etc. cannot be assumed permanent. Furthermore, there will be considerable independence in styles of use, choice of equipment, working-practice, etc in laboratories and GP practices.

Those at the administrative interface of the health system will want to interact with this system, using (and possibly changing) information, but also interact with other systems, seen here as external. For example, the medical information officer extracts data on the performance of the health system, but then supplies it to a central government system as part of a statutory requirement. An accountant may extract data from the GP's practice records, and process that for tax and statutory records. Later that accountant may deal with another practice, but there should not be any conflation or interaction of the information from the two practices.

Each independently operable site in this system has a relational database which is intended to hold enough information to enable it to operate under local control in isolation if desired or necessary. The collection of databases are managed by software which presents a health-specific higher-level

---

[3]Doctors who work in the community, and are the first point of contact for a patient with almost any medical problem are called "General Practicioners (GPs)" in the United Kingdom. Such GPs form themselves into groups sharing facilities such as a building, medical-records, receptionists, etc. We envisage they will also share computational resources.

model, the Health Management System(HMS). All applications are written in a scripting language (Hippo) that is coupled to the design of the HMS. This language has operations for remote and local data access and manipulation, has an action semantics, and is coupled to the screen management system. The screen manager is also purpose-built, above X11, and provides an iconic interface (eg nurses may select a patient in *their* ward, by pointing at the relevant bed, on the displayed plan of the ward) and then 'send' that patient to X-ray.

Warning Although the present tense is used throughout the following sections, not all of the algorithms and details are yet implemented and tested. Furthermore, the details have been altered (mostly omitted), both to aid communication, and because the project is developing so rapidly that it is impracticable to keep the paper in-step with the project.

5 AUTONOMOUS REQUIREMENTS

In a traditional distributed database application, the aim is to maintain a completely consistent database over the whole system, for all data that results from *committed* transactions. This requires techniques such as two-phase commit, and rather than the overall database being allowed to contain any committed contradictory data, transactions will be automatically rolled-back. Such roll-back will occur rapidly if the whole system is active, and the units of transaction are small. When it occurs the loss of data will be small if the transactions are small, and that data may still be available at the initiating work-station, furthermore, the user initiating the transaction is likely to still be available.

Where it is possible that some part of the system is not currently (eg for the weekend[4]) part of the collaboration such a transaction model cannot be used. For example, those working in Accident-and-Emergency cannot have all their transactions on accident victims, or even just those that use this GP's practice, held in a pending state until the practice re-opens.

To meet this criterion, it is not possible to ensure that the whole database contains only data that is consistent[5]. For example, the GP's practice's local database will hold information about the patients of that practice, so that the GP's may work locally. The hospital at which a patient is currently being treated will also have an overlapping collection of data about that patient. Were the GP to update the information about the patient, while disconnected from the hospital, and the hospital to update that patient's data, *during the period in which the two fragments of the system are incommunicado* then the updates are **potentially** in conflict.

If both are to be allowed to proceed during the incommunicado period, then the total HMS model must be allowed to persist in a potentially inconsistent state. Note that the working-practices will ensure that this potentiallity is only actual on very rare occasions. For example, if the GP always makes medical notes during a consultation, and if the registrar at the hospital does likewise, they will not conflict because the patient can only be in one place at once.

---

[4]For example, a GP went home leaving some process specific to the practice running, or the machine disconnected.

[5]Consistent in this context means that no two update operations may have made conflicting changes - eg changed the same datum, or made an update using a value that may have depended on an out-of-date value for some other datum.

The weaker requirements for autonomous cooperation then are:

1. Allow independent local working (including updates) on local, potentially duplicate, copies of data;

2. Ensure that the fragments of the database do not diverge;

3. Examine every potential conflict as soon as possible, and detect the actual conflicts[6];

4. Process the actual conflicts, handling them according to a policy that is consistent with the current working-practices, eg allowing a particular organisation's updates to dominate, and warning the other party, or refer to a 'referee' authority, etc;

5. Verify that the conflict has eventually been dealt with.

At the same time, many of the properties of a typical distributed sytem are necessary, for example:

1. It must be possible to start the system;

2. It must be possible to recover from various local or total failures;

3. It must utilise copies of data to perform with reasonable efficiency, and access remote data to give complete logical access;

4. It must permit installation of new versions of all or suitable parts of the supporting software, protocols, and databases.

6   AUTONOMOUS MECHANISMS

Whatever strategy is used, certain subtasks need to be accomplished, and these are now identified. Not all of them will be discussed further in this paper.

6.1   Meta-Data Management

The meta-data to name, describe, and specify the logical properties of the data will be needed as usual. But four additional forms of meta-data are now required:

- The meta-data to control placement,

- The meta-data that records the current placement,

- The meta-data to direct distributed queries,

---

[6]This can be 'fail-safe' by detecting a superset, but every effort should be made to keep this set minimal, so as not to 'cry-wolf' too often.

- The meta-data to handle update conflicts.

Meta-data appropriate for each site has to be shipped to that site, and possibly combined with the meta-data parochial to that site. Mechanisms are needed to support revision of any aspect of this meta data in subsequent releases. Because, at the time of meta-data broadcast, a site may not be receptive, mechanisms to allow this to occur incrementally are necessary. Protocols must detect attempts to use incompatable meta-data at two sites trying to cooperate.

6.2   Software Distribution

Initially, after certain failures, and when new versions are issued, software has to be shipped to sites. As sites may not all be active at one time, or may not cooperate with installation instructions, this means that incremental strategies are needed, and protocols must detect attempts to communicate between sites supporting incompatible software versions.

Experience with ARPAnet suggested that a totally automatic replacement mechanism for meta-data and software would be inappropriate. This is likely to apply in these circumstances, for example, revision of the meta-data may require restructuring of the local database, a potentially lengthy process. Hence human intervention is expected, probably a minimal 'go ahead' confirmation, but this again increases the chances of delay.

6.3   Data Load

The data has to be made active throughout the cooperation. Common data may be bulk-loaded and archived at a unique site. During initial-load and total re-loads, it would then be propagated to all sites which are to hold copies according to the meta-data. Again, a site may not be ready to recieve its data, in this case, the incremental propagator should probably insist on acceptance before conducting any other dialogue with that site.

Initial-load will include intermittent data acquisition from existing operational systems (current patient administration, and payroll systems for example). This is likely to take place at different sites, corresponding to the different responsibilities of the sub-groups at those sites. At some stage this data has to be correlated and checked for mutual consistency, if it is eventually to be used together. Once again this may have to be done incrementally in arrears. In some cases, data also has to be despatched to independently run systems, eg banking, government departments, existing subsystems already supporting a sub-activity within the cooperation. We may expect that the release and despatch of such information will also be under explicit local direction.

6.4   Query Processing

The strategy needs to use the local data where possible, but to obtain data from other sites whenever this is necessary to correctly answer the query. An implementation needs to analyse each query to determine how it may be subdivided into local queries, and minimal queries against other sites[7]. In some cases the algorithm should be offered no choice, for example, when a GP arranges an appointment at a clinic for a patient, it is important the definitive record of appointments at that clinic is consulted, so patients can be given instructions before they leave. For some strategies (see Logical Strategy below) the query analysis can be largely static, whereas, in the Statistical strategies, it is of necessity dynamic. Occasionally a user may be involved in the decision as to whether a query should propagate to a remote site. For example, a GP trying to find a patient's details, believing that the patient is registered with this practice, might check the spellings of the identification-data *before* an external search is initiated.

6.5   Distributed Updates

An update must be done first at the site specified in the meta-data, the local site in many cases. This allows the local screen to show the change. It must then be propagated to other sites with a need to know, ultimately changing data on their screens if that datum is displayed, and drawing the user's attention to the remotely initiated change. If the update initiator is not able to propagate the update to the authority site, or all the need-to-know sites, then enough data must be kept to allow subsequent reconciliation, and notification.

Other update propagation strategies are possible, for example those used in federated systems. Typically, in those, the update is not *pushed* as above, but *pulled*. Another site wishing up-to-date data simply refetches. This strategy is likely to involve more redundant queries and messages. There is no reason why a mixture of both strategies shouldn't be used, separated by controls in the meta-data. The pushing version predominates in this application, since we want to make the laboratory aware a test is no longer required, or the surgeon that the result is ready — and can't rely on them to ask — mirroring the current working-practice, where a form is sent by the person with the information.

6.6   Reconciliation

This is the name given to the process peculiar to autonomous distribution. It is invoked if two sites have been executing (and locally committing) updates, which may potentially conflict, while they have been out of communication. It should be triggered on resumption of communication, and in most strategies it is then given a high or dominant priority.

The sites each send to the other information about updates that they have locally conducted. For any given update a site is chosen or specified which has responsibility for reconciliation in that case, usually determined via the meta-data on the basis of the data updated. This update data is then processed to detect the *actual* clashes, all other updates can be simply copied and acknowledged. The actual clashes are then processed to either automatically resolve the conflict, or to refer it to a resolution authority. In those cases where a resolution authority was notified, it is necessary to monitor whether the resolution has been decided. If it hasn't progressively more severe notifications are submitted to control authorities, so that the DB cannot remain indefinitely out of step[8]. After

---

[7]There is a choice of cost functions to minimise, eg volume of data transfer, number of signalling cycles, etc

[8]Unless a person takes a decision that this is sensible, eg the patient has died, or left the district.

resolution, the site that has lost is duly notified, and sent the correct data to install. The other site has its update confirmed. Usually the user will be advised (eg by a warning marker) if he/she is using data that has not yet been reconciled. Similarly the users at a site which has had its update over-ridden will recieve a warning and may need to deal with consequential changes[9].

6.7 Dumping and Logging

The requirement to recover after failures will mean that data has to be duplicated. This is usually done by dumping, but a dump that allows reasonably straightforward recovery, is usually a snapshot of the data. To get such a snapshot of the data, requires all the sites to dump synchronously, and not to update during the dump. Neither requirement is consistent with autonomy.

To move forward or backward through the states, requires logging information. This could in principle be saved at every site, but loss of a site's one disc or store would render that strategy useless, and to insist all have a reliable configuration may be in conflict with autonomy. A small subset of sites can be archive and logging servers for a subnet. This subnet can then operate autonomously, only if consistent marking in the logs allows multiple site recovery. Protocols need to propagate information from which such consistency may be established. These have yet to be developed.

6.8 Protection and Security

As the network becomes more autonomous so it becomes more vulnerable to an intruder site on the network collecting and updating data. Enforcement of the working-practices, and suspicous handling of message traffic are necessary (see section 9).

7 A STATISTICAL STRATEGY

Two strategies for arranging autonomous data use are sketched in the next two sections. They give concrete, but simplified, examples of the mechanisms introduced in the previous section.

7.1 Data Classification

The data is classified into four categories:

- essentially **static** — propagated to all sites on release of new system versions.

- **stable** — propagated to relevant sites on a scheduled basis.

- dynamic **synchronous** — held at exactly one site.

---

[9]Working-practices, which enable cooperation, already minimise these over-rides.

- **mobile** — câched at relevant, currently active sites.

To keep the examples simple, let the categories apply to whole relations[10]. Examples of the categories in the HMS context are:

- essentially **static** —Wards: mapping wards to hospitals, ward names, area, floor, abbreviations for the ward name, etc. Medical/Nursing abbreviations. Colour coding for Medical Teams. Itegrity rules enforced particular to this health district. Data in this category should be of small volume, used frequently, and altered rarely.

- **stable** — Allocation of staff to nursing and medical teams, Medical status of personnel, Layout of Wards, etc. The volume of data in this category is again relatively small. To change such data while people are active may engender the feeling of administrative instability. To avoid this, yet to keep the data timely, it is updated and distributed at agreed times, eg midnight.

- dynamic **synchronous** — Day-Diary, specifying intended admissions into the hospital — managed and located within Bed-Bureau — consulted and updated by medical teams — consulted by nursing staff. Out-Patient clinic appointments — managed and located at Out-Patients — consulted and updated by GPs and Medical Teams — consulted by nurses and receptionists. Data in this category may be quite large. It is crucial that there are transactional updates, eg to avoid double-bookings.

- **mobile** — Medical and general information about a patient. Migrates in response to activity. Câched at the ward the patient is in, prefetched to the clinic and specialist unit. Held at the GP's practice this patient frequents. A definitive copy will be held at a defined site. Very large volumes of mobile data will accumulate, but only a small proportion is active, and only a small proportion of that is required at a given site.

Some of the operations on these categories of data are further discussed below.

7.1.1 Distributed static data

The treatment of static data is straightforward. Queries are always local, updates are disallowed, hence reconciliation is not required. Such data has to be marked with a release number, so that when a new release of the system is propagated, the new data is shipped contemporaneously with the new software to each site. For efficiency, the application and display managers may then contain code derived from, or incorporating properties of, this static data.

7.1.2 Distributed stable data

This data is updated in a delayed release version at a specified authority site. When it is scheduled for release, it is simultaneously substituted as the definitive version at this site, and propagated

---

[10]It is believed to be straightforward to similarly categorise logical, disjoint horizontal partitions of the relations.

(or the changes propagated) to all the other sites that are specified as recipients of this data. Queries are usually local, and only in exceptional circumstances are they refered to the authority site. Updates are disallowed, but may be transformed to requests to the authority site to include a change in the next dissemination. Reconciliation is unnecessary.

7.1.3 Distributed synchronous data

The meta-data specifies at which site this data is held. It is never copied to other sites, and all queries and updates are refered to this site. Updates are shipped as transactions, and the shipper can expect a prompt reliable and definitive response. Such operations are typically small units of change — booking a place in a list of appointments for a clinic, for example.

7.1.4 Distributed mobile data

Data in this category are more complex to handle. It is typified by data about a patient. For most 'patients' in the system, as they are not currently ill or undergoing treatment, their data is rarely accessed. For the 10% or so, who are currently ill, they may generate bursts of activity over a period of days or weeks - eg on each visit to the GP's surgery, or each time the consultant visits them on the ward. A dynamic câching strategy is required, so that it is always known where there is a definitive, reasonably up-to-date, copy of the data, but all activities can proceed rapidly at a local site.

7.1.5 Meta-data for mobile data

The meta-data records the site which holds the definitive copy, and the rule used to identify tuples in this data, for example, the PID, Patient IDentifier in many relations of this application. That identifier is then used at the definitive site to record which sites hold copies of which tuples, ie

> relation DefSite (Rel#, Site#, IdCol#)[11]
> relation Copies (Rel#, Site#, Id#)

The definitive site will normally take the responsibility for bulk-load, archiving, re-load, restructuring, reconciliation, and update propagation. The meta-data will restrict which other sites may câche this data.

> relation PermittedCache (Rel#, Site#)

---

[11] A tuple would appear in this for relations of all categories, and extending this tuple to hold a logical expression over the values in the corresponding relation's tuples would allow the logical specification of responsibility for a subset of the relation. The update and query strategies are straightforwardly extended, except when an update has changed the subset in which a tuple resides - but an equivalent problem is discussed below.

7.1.6   Version propagation and mobile data

When a new version of the software and meta-data reaches a site, that site will be required to clear its backlog of update-propagations, reconciliations, etc., and then clear its câches. Câche reload may then be stimulated by running a re-start script which includes initial queries that have the side-effect of correctly loading the câche.

7.1.7   Initial data load for mobile data

Data-load will occur at the definitive site. All other sites would begin with their câches empty. They may provoke filling by a script similar to that associated with version propagation, e.g. the script for a ward might retrieve all the PIDs of patients currently associated with that ward, then retrieve all the general, and medical data for those persons, and their recent medical histories. At a GP's practice, a script would request similar data for everyone registered with that practice, and their family and relationship data. At a clinic, a script might be run at night to obtain such data, for the next day's appointments.

7.1.8   Query processing and câche load/unload

Internally, all queries are transformed so that, if they retrieve mobile data from another site, they retrieve full width tuples, suitable for the câche[12]. A query is analysed to see if it expects a singleton set as a result[13]. If this is the case, try the câche first, then escalate to a remote query if an empty result is obtained.

If the query involves joins, then analyse it to find sub-queries that can be treated as above. If they succeed, back substitute in the original query replacing joins with selections. Repeat until the query is irreducible. Send fragments of the remaining distributed query to the determined sites and reconstruct the results using conventional distributed DB algorithms. The automatic local attempt followed by an automatic escallation to remote can be over-ridden in the Hippo-script, eg so that a refer-back to the user occurs between the local and remote attempt.

The main motive for removing tuples from a câche is to reduce update propagation activity. This can be done as part of a script.

> **forget** *ThisPatient*

should remove from the local câche all the mobile tuples pertaining to a patient with the PID that is secretly held with *ThisPatient*. For example, the patient-discharge script that is run at a nursing-station would use this to clear out the câches of data held about the discharged patient.

---

[12]They are projected locally if necessary before being displayed.

[13]Meta-data specifies which attributes of a relation are uniquie under equality - eg the many cases where we retrieve on PID, hospital number, national insurance number, etc.

7.1.9   Update processing for mobile data

When an update to a câched tuple occurs, the local tuple is updated immediately, and an update-pending record is stored in a relation:

> **relation** UpdatesPending (Rel#, Id#, LUSeq#, Actor, Action, OldValue, NewValue)

The Local Update Sequence number, LUSeq#, is sufficient to give a local ordering on updates. Actor, and Action will determine who was doing what - information necessary for reporting a problem during reconciliation. OldValue and NewValue enable the comparisons necessary during reconciliation.

While this record exists, the data displayed for which OldValue and NewValue differ is marked (eg a thin red line through it on the screen) to warn people that it may be subject to subsequent agreement or reversal. As soon as possible this update-record is sent to the definitive site for update propagation and reconciliation. If reconciled, the change is acknowledged, and the record can be removed. After an incommunicado period the batch of outstanding update records is sent.

If a negative acknowledge is received, the local update is identified, and the over-riding action specified. An update-conflicts record is then produced, with the conflation of this data, so the update-record can be removed. An update-conflicts event is generated, which should cause the script to run which warns the user of the conflict, and eventually gets some action undertaken which removes the conflict. If the update-conflicts record is not removed within a specified time, the over-ride is applied, and an escallated-update-conflicts event triggered to warn the users concerned.

7.1.10   Reconciliation for mobile data

On receiving an update-record, the definitive site verifies that the old value matches the stored value, if it does it is considered safe to perform the update and send a positive acknowledge, and procede to propagate the update.

If it doesn't, then an attribute by attribute comparison is made. If independent updates have been made — eg one updating address and telephone number, the other updating GP — then it is assumed to be safe to merge the two. Propagation and positive acknowledge then occur.

If the reconciliation reaches this point, we have an *actual* conflict. An appropriate action is taken, depending on the data, and the altering agents (site, action, actor) and usually a negative acknowledge and update-conflicts message are returned. Update propagation will occur as soon as possible. Until a site has communicated that it has received the update, it is necessary to record the need to send it. To decide which site should receive the updates, the relation Copies is consulted.

8   LOGICAL STRATEGY

The principal disadvantage of the statistical strategy is that it requires analysis of queries during execution, this is avoided in the logical strategy, which only requires static analysis of queries.

Another possible disadvantage may be that it is difficult to arrange the categorisation of data, so that sufficient data is held locally to enable most queries to be run locally[14]. This logical strategy depends on stability in the system between releases. At each release, meta-data specifies the placement of all relations in terms of logical expressions (a restricted set of the possible query expressions). These should reflect working-practice, and the processing strategy will ensure that they are always valid assumptions when query processing. A logical subset of the data is maintained at each site.

8.1 Meta-data

The site of the definitive copy of each relation is specified by:

> **relation** DefinitiveSite (Rel#, Site#)

Such sites are chosen so that the principal updators are normally on a closely coupled network with that site, as updates are performed at the definitive site first in this strategy. Distributed copies are relative to these sites. The distribution rules are specified using suitable predicates

> **relation** CopySite (Rel#, Site#, Predicate)

The predicates should be kept simple to facilitate query and update analysis. The static and stable categories of the previous strategy are achieved by the predicate **true** being specified for every site. The synchronous category is achieved by having no entries in CopySite. The mobile data is achieved by using predicates involving joins, so that when the other relation is updated, it causes copies of tuples in this relation to be made at the appropriate site. For example, if there is a

> **relation** InWard (Ward#, PID)

then, an addition of a tuple to this assigning a person to a ward will cause the patient's data to be copied to the ward, via a series of joins with each relation that holds information pertinent to ward activities.

8.2 Version Distribution

When a new version of the system is propagated, it is necessary, at least logically, to simultaneously replace the software, the meta-data, and the distributed copies. ie

> **for each** site
> > **for each** relation
> > > Delete existing copy
> > > Copy specified subset

---

[14] Preliminary measurements suggested this, but they were not on a tuned operational system.

Autonomy requires that any site that was incommunicado must accept these new versions and values before it can engage in new interaction.

8.3 Query Processing

The major part of query decomposition and the planning of result reconstruction[1] can be done by static analysis. Three results are possible, the query can always be run locally, the query may be distributed depending on the value of some of its parameters, or the query is always distributed. Essentially, relational manipulation code is constructed for the local and distributed cases which can occur, and in the conditional case, the appropriate one is chosen at execution-time.

8.4 Update Processing

The requirement for the definitive site to also be the Primary Update Site (PUS) is not essential, but it reflects authority structure and simplifies algorithms. When an update is initiated, a similar update-record to that in the statistical strategy is despatched to the PUS. The PUS then has to:

1. Verify that the update is acceptable — the prior-state in the update-record corresponds with the current state at the PUS.

2. Perform and log the update at the PUS — it can then no longer be lost.

3. Send an acknowledge to the update initiator site — which may then perform the update locally, and continue normally.

4. Propagate *all* of the consequences of this update — discussed below.

If the PUS denies the update, then the reply gives the PUS state. The client raises a local event, which provokes a script to explain the conflict to the user, and to allow the user to develop a revised update, with the local data corresponding to the definitive state.

Traditional transaction processing attempts a more sophisticated verification, namely, it attempts to check that any data read, and hence which might have influenced the update, has not been changed. That is infeasible, and probably incorrect in these autonomous systems. It is impossible to know what information has been remembered and re-used by the person, either in their head or on their local system. The alternative, used throughout, is to draw attention to data that changes because of someone else's actions, and expect the user to use judgement as to whether that invalidates an action. Changes to significant data are rare, the main mode of operation being to add information in a way which identifies the temporal ordering if it is significant — again the effective working practices.

Where an update applies to a set of tuples, it is either reduced to a tuple-at-a-time update, or a check is made that the prior set of tuples at the update initiator and at the PUS are identical, and that the update expression evaluates to the same result at the PUS as it did at the initiator.

8.5 Update Propagation

This is performed by the PUS. It is described using a case analysis. In all cases, temporary relations are needed, to perform the calculation of the consequential changes, we name these systematically, ie R' is the *shadow* of R, with the same type. It is also assumed that a sparse sensitivity matrix will be constructed, for each type of update, so that only those predicates that may have been affected are re-evaluated - eg

relation SensitiveToInsert (<u>UpdatedRel#</u>, <u>SourceRel#</u>, <u>Site#</u>)

8.5.1 Tuple insertion

For each sensitive site that has a copy of this relation, evaluate the selection expression against the new tuple. If there is a non-empty result, send an insert instruction to the site. This is illustrated with an example:

Suppose the allocation of patients to specialists is represented as:
relation Patient (<u>PID</u>, ...)
relation Specialist (<u>PID</u>, ...)
relation CaresFor (<u>SpecialistPID</u>, <u>PatientPID</u>)

and the new allocation of a patient to a speciallist results in a tuple being inserted in CaresFor. The tuple is placed in *CaresFor'*. The predicate which sends data to the specialists' sites will be re-evaluated into *Patient'*. In the case of the site which this particular specialist uses the result in *Patient'* will be his/her new patient's record which will be sent to that site.

To avoid excessive computation, predicates depending on set differences or negation are disallowed. The predicate may produce a result which contains tuples already at the site, redundant insertion messages can be avoided at the expense of keeping track of these, and performing a set difference. Traffic can be reduced, by building a batch of consequences per site.

8.5.2 Tuple deletion

Make the old tuple value the sole member of the shadow relation. Re-evaluate the sensitive predicates, and send deletion messages where there is a non-empty result, in a similar manner to insertion. This algorithm is not adequate where the copies are determined by joins. For example, if there were two specialists in the above case sharing the same machine and the same patient, and one of them ceased to care for the selected patient, the other would still want that patient's records. This problem is avoided by the following refinement. Note only one predicate is permitted per site per relation. If a join predicate has predicted a deletion propagation, the original predicate is now re-evaluated on the main data, after the deletion has been performed, and the result subtracted from the value in the shadow. If the shadow is still non-empty, the deletion is sent.

8.5.3 Tuple update

Let the relation being updated be R, and construct its new value in R''. For each sensitive site(S) relation(T) pair do the following:

1. Calculate the subset of T to copy to S using R in $\hat{T}$.

2. Calculate the subset of T to copy to S using R'' in T'.

3. Send delete operations to S for $\hat{T} - T'$.

4. Send insert operations to S for $T' - \hat{T}$.

5. If T is R and id(tuple) $\in Id(\hat{T}) \cap Id(T')$ then send an update operation to S, where id(X) is a function that yields the identification attribute, eg PID, of a tuple, and Id(Y) projects Y onto its identification attribute.

8.5.4 Message delays

For all messages, including those propagating the consequences of updates, there will generally be delays, as some sites will have been incommunicado. These messages have to be kept, and then applied when the destination sites resume communication. At that time, there will be a burst of updates. Potentially, they could be out of context, and hence uninterpretable, but these internal update messages are each concerned with only one relation, and the identification of the tuples has been reduced to the immutable identifier, eg PID. As the despatcher for a given relation is only the PUS, and as it retains the message order, these can safely be re-run at the client. Each PUS will maintain a MessagesToSend relation of these pending messages, and tuples are only removed from it when the client confirms that the update has been done. Examination of the age of tuples in this relation will enable sites that have dropped out of the collaboration to be recognised.

8.6 Autonomy assessment

The autonomy here is less than that for the statistical model, the client here has to be in contact with, and wait for the PUS. A site may be incommunicado while reading any data it has copies of, and only updating data for which it is the PUS. It may get a burst of remotely generated updates when it resumes communication, which will have a high priority, and may result in screen changes to alert the user to data changes. As subnets having their own data with respect to updates may proceed independently, it is likely that logical disjoint subsetting of relations when specifying PUSs will be advantageous, especially if the subsets are based on static or at least rarely updated values in the tuples.

Further autonomy may be introduced, but only by increasing the awareness of users of remote clients. Users of 'central' clients are assumed to be supported by a dedicated, and continuous service - there may be more than one such centre. They will be less aware of autonomy, and have no need to explicitly exploit it. A 'remote' user may well wish to control his/her commitment and involvement and so has to be more aware. For example, a GP may have local data, local software, and operational procedures associated specifically with the practice. A mode of voluntary isolated running may therefore be required. Then, the user would not be able to commit updates with the 'DO-IT' button, since an indefinite wait would ensue. In this context, the 'DO-IT' button is replaced by a 'SAVE-IT' button. Each transaction is then saved, with enough information to reconstruct the screens that lead to it.

On resumption of cooperative working, after all the delayed updates have been received, the user can replay the **saved** updates, and any data changes in the interim will be highlighted by being surrounded by a red flashing box. The user may make any modifications and then press 'DO-IT' for each saved operation, they may also be 'CANCELLED' in the usual way. This form of autonomy depends on responsible behaviour, which is precisely the foundation on which all cooperative enterprises are built.

8.7 Mobile and variable users

The logical model depends on stable use of data per geographic location. In such applications there is a minority group of users that do not fit this assumption. Consider, as an example, the consultant, who does ward-rounds, has meetings to plan admissions, reviews medical notes in the vicinity of an operating theatre, holds clinics, and works in a nearby university. This consultant may wish to access information about any of his/her patients at any site, though normally he/she would access patient information from a consistent administrative site and in the vicinity of the patient. Similarly, a GP may act as an anæthestist in a local hospital, and wish to access data associated with the other rôle during a lull at the present site.

Such behaviour has to be accommodated by the system, but our view is that it will involve remote access, and hence slower response. 'Out-of-character' behaviour could be accomodated by constructing a relation LoggedIn, which records who logged-in, or who is still loged in. Joins with LoggedIn as predicates, would result in data migration similar to that in the statistical case.

There are also mobile subjects; patients visiting clinics, physiotherapy etc. In most cases, since they are probably moving about within the hospital, their data is not copied, and 'remote' access strategies are used. But a visit to an outpatients' clinic is a case where medical records are likely to be needed and may be at a physically remote site. They could be drawn in preparation, and held at the clinic site, pending the patient's arrival. This introduces an interesting predicate, eg one which at midnight fetches all the coming day's patient records and releases yesterday's. The predicate superficially changes its value depending on the time. It can be transformed into a join of the kind seen above, by having a relation TODAY, holding one tuple, the date today. Then a script is triggered to update TODAY soon after midnight.

9 AUTHORITY, SECURITY and ACCESS CONTROL

Since the transmissions are across public space, it is important to protect against the data being read, or against intruders on the net. This can be achieved by suitable network encryption strategies. Messages which do not decrypt to a comprehendable message are faulted and ignored. They may also cause an event, which provokes a script that may raise alarms, or keep records.

It is assumed that the network is only accessed by the software provided for the HMS application. This is weakly verified, since it is the software that encrypts and decrypts. The protection can be broken by someone who modifies the application support software. This is unlikely to be worthwhile, as the effort of altering the binary is significant. However, occasional verification that some derived properties, eg sum-checks, of this software haven't changed would be worthwhile.

The scripts which are interpreted by this support software are also vulnerable to tampering, but, if we assume the integrity of the support software, it can check the validity of the script each time it loads it. The scripts can then be assumed correct, ie as delivered at the last release.

Each site, via such scripts, only displays screens appropriate to activities at that site. These screens only permit access to objects that are displayed, and to operations for which there is a button. The user interface therefore presents the system via a limiting and tailored ADT appropriate to the current locality and context.

Initially at a site, the only facilities in that ADT are those available to everyone who may be in the vicinity of that workstation. To accommodate those with more power and the mobile users described above, an authority mechanism is provided. Each bone fide user has an identification card[15], possibly more than one if they have several rôles some of which may be delegated. Before being able to change data, or to access other data, or to use other buttons, the user must swipe their card accross the reader. The additional status times-out, but may be repeated.

Authority may be rapidly withdrawn if a card is stolen. The card identifies the user, the rôle, and some parameters. The authority is then looked up in a table to verify that the user still has authority for that rôle at this site. This verification precedes the display of the extra buttons or data corresponding to the extra facilities. A script may require the card to be re-presented, eg just before the 'DO-IT', in a particularly sensitive case.

In case archive material is stolen, all data should have the information which can form a link with individuals suitably encrypted. The encryption key includes the PID, so that the same name does not lead to the same encrypted data. This leads to problems searching on identification attributes, since decryption tuple-by-tuple is necessary. The search is shortened by a partial-match table based on hashing, which is not stored on external media. Such tactics seem to be necessary to ensure privacy.

10   LARGE STORES PLEASE

Almost all the mechanisms for protection, distribution and data identification used in this application exploit application domain knowledge, and can make little use of the low-level general purpose mechanisms for distribution and protection. Many problems may best solved with application specific methods. Carefully constructed software may provide adequate security[16]. In such cases low-level protection and distribution mechanisms may not be used.

---

[15] A bar stripe behind opaque plastic which is transparent in the IR used by the bar-stripe reader.

[16] Fine-grained security is provided by scopes, types, procedural encapsulation, and ADTs, enforced by the compiler[9], and the encryption, particularly of messages, should make this difficult to circumvent.

What would be helpful would be uniformly addressed large computational stores. In the current application we may then expect to bring the logically identified data directly into store. Furthermore, the data structures used in the algorithms could be constructed and kept in store. A good examples in this case are the sensitivity matrices (INSERTIONSENSITIVE, ...), the distribution rules (COPIES), the shadow data ($R', R'', \hat{R}$, for all R), etc. The present system uses relations on the standard DBMS for these, but this is very inefficient, as that has transaction, concurrency and stability mechanisms running. It uses them to take advantage of the bulk operations of the relational algebra, which provide succinct notations compared with explicit iterations, and avoid the HMS implementors having to manage issues arising from these structures getting too large for main memory.

The arrangements above are all concerned with collecting the relevant data, and getting it in the right place when it is active. Since only a small part of the population is ill at any one time, and only their recent medical history is relevant, the logically required data is well identified. It is likely that we could use this description to bring all the relevant active data into a store of about 1Gbyte, and build all our temporary structures in another 1Gbyte. It may be usefull to have another 2Gbytes for bringing in other logical collections that are wanted for reference.

It is a moot point whether relations would still be useful in this new environment, but some such expression language is needed to identify the logically required data. The logical subset needed to support the human activity is limited by the capacity of those humans to take on complex tasks, and can probably be kept within bounds that enable us to load and unload stores of this magnitude on a logical basis.

There seems to be a case for allowing several large logical domains to exist within a store, with strong separation, similar to that achieved by the encrypted message interface between machines.

It may be useful to distinguish between **stable** stores and **transient** stores cf Argus's **atomic** concept[8]. It would be wasteful to utilise stable store mechanisms if they are expensive on data movement for transient structures, which can be reconstructed easily from small quantities of data, such as the shadow relations in the above algorithms.

11   CONCLUSION

The Health Management System, which is currently undergoing development, provides a typical example of a general class of application systems which support human cooperation on a large scale. Such systems need forms of loosely coupled, flexible, autonomous distribution.

Some algorithms were presented, as examples, that illustrate the use of knowledge about the data and working-practices. It is possible that many problems in distribution and protection, may be best dealt with using application specific knowledge and techniques. This may be particularly the case where the scale and diversity of the human cooperation makes attempts at maintaining data consistency automatically, infeasible.

It is suggested that computers with large regular address spaces, and very large volumes of RAM, may significantly assist in the task of constructing the software for such applications. The greater the reliability that can be assumed from these stores the less the application is distracted into arranging its own recovery mechanisms. But, it is not clear whether the hardware-based protection mechanisms proposed in other papers in these proceedings, could be utilised in the construction of such an application system. They may actually be an impediment to achieving the necessary capacity for incremental change.

12   Acknowledgements

Discussions with Professor R Needham at the workshop, sharpened the first author's resolve to question the case for complex addressing structures and fine-grained hardware protection. The first author is also grateful to GIP Altaïr for support during his sabbatical, and to Dr Tim King of Perihelion Software Ltd for involving him in this project.

References

[1] S. Ceri and G. Pelagatti. *Distributed Databases: Principles and Systems*. McGraw-Hill International, 1985.

[2] R.E. French, R.W. Collins, and L.W. Loen. *System/38 machine storage management*, pages 59–62. Volume Publication no. 0-933186-00-2, General Systems Division, International Business Machines Corporation, 1978. Not checked MPA.

[3] F. Heskens, J. Rosenberg, and M. Hannaford. Stability in a network of monads-pc computers. In J. Rosenberg and L. Keedy, editors, *Proceedings of the international workshop on Computer Architectures to Support Security and Persistence of Information (Breman, Germany, May 1990)*, Springer-Verlag, May 1990.

[4] J.L. Keedy and J. Rosenberg. Support for objects in the MONADS architecture. In *Proceedings of the Workshop on Persistent Object Systems, Their Design, Implementation and Use (Newcastle, New South Wales, January 1989)*, pages 202–213, 1989.

[5] J.L. Keedy and J. Rosenberg. Uniform support for collections of objects in a persistent environment. In *Proceedings of the Twenty-Second Annual Hawaii International Conference on System Sciences, Volume II Software Track (January 1989)*, pages 26–35, January 1989.

[6] D.M. Koch and R. Rosenberg. A secure risc-based architecture supporting data persistence. In L. Keedy and R. Rosenberg, editors, *Proceedings of the international workshop on Computer Architectures to Support Security and Persistence of Information (Breman, Germany, May 1990)*, Springer-Verlag, May 1990.

[7] R. Kröger, M. Mock, and R. Schumann. The relax transactional object management system. In J. Rosenberg and L. Keddy, editors, *Proceedings of the international workshop on Computer Architectures to Support Security and Persistence of Information (Breman, Germany, May 1990)*, Springer-Verlag, May 1990. Part of COMANDOS.

[8] B. Liskov, M. Herlihy, P. Johnson, G. Leavens, R. Scheifler, and W. Weihl. *Preliminary ARGUS reference manual*. Technical Report Memo 39, Programming Methodology Group,

Massachusetts Institute of Technology, Laboratory for Computer Science, Cambridge, Massachusetts 02139, USA, October 1983.

[9] R. Morrison, A.L. Brown, R.C.H. Coonor, Q.I. Cutts, G. Kirby, A. Dearle, J. Rosenberg, and D. Stemple. Protection in persistent object systems. In L. keedy and J. Rosenberg, editors, *International Workshop on Computer Architectures to Support Security and Persistence of Information*, pages 4-1 to 4-17 in preprints, Springer-Verlag, May 1990.

[10] F. Wai. *Distributed Concurrent Persistent Programming Languages: An Experimental Design and Implementation*. PhD thesis, Department of Computing Science, University of Glasgow, April 1988.

Persistence for Arbitrary C++ Data Structures

Frances Newbery Paulisch, Stefan Manke, and Walter F. Tichy

University of Karlsruhe

ABSTRACT

This paper presents an external representation that may be automatically generated from arbitrary C++ data structures. This representation can be used to achieve persistence in various applications. We describe the existing facilities for persistence in the EDGE graph editor. A similar technique can be used to achieve persistence in general. In addition to generating code for an external representation, a menu-controlled data structure editor for arbitrary C++ classes may be generated using the same technique.

1. INTRODUCTION

The recent proliferation of high quality graphics workstations has led to increased popularity of interactive environments. When using an interactive tool, a user would like to be able to save the current state of the system and be able to restart later with exactly the same configuration. In general, what the user really wants is for the tool's data structures, which are usually held in main memory, to be saved to secondary storage in some external representation. Various terms have been used for this idea including persistence [1], passivation [2] and pickling [3].

Numerous methods for achieving persistence have been proposed. These can be categorized into solutions that save the data in an operating system and machine independent format (usually ASCII text), those that are based on virtual memory management techniques, and those that rely on an underlying persistent database. Our solution is based on *textual flattening* [4], one of the simplest of the machine-independent methods. The internal data structures are simply written to an external medium in a textual representation. Procedures are provided that convert between the internal and external representations of the data structure.

One of the best known textual external representation languages is that used by IDL [5, 6, 7]. IDL (Interface Description Language) is a language for describing structured data so that it can be exchanged safely by a set of related tools. IDL is mainly used in compiler construction for representing intermediate code transmitted between single passes in a multipass compiler. A *reader* procedure converts from an external representation to an internal representation. A *writer* procedure converts from an internal representation to an external representation. The user must provide an abstract description of the data structure in IDL and the reader and writer procedures are generated from this description. A similar approach is taken in the PGRAPHITE [8] persistent object system. Given a description of the object's data structure in a special notation, PGRAPHITE generates code for saving and retrieving objects from persistent store. Our solution differs from IDL and PGRAPHITE in that our external representation is designed for representing C++ [9] data structures only, rather than being language independent. The benefit of this specialization is that we can generate input and output routines for our representation from the C++ data structure declarations directly rather than requiring the user to provide a description of the data structures in a special notation. In addition, our solution takes advantage of the object-oriented nature of C++ when generating the input and output routines.

In the extensible database management system EXODUS [10] a persistent programming language E [11] is used to support persistence. E is an extension of the C++ language which allows the user to define, create, and manipulate persistent objects which are stored in the EXODUS storage manager. The E compiler will translate references to persistent objects into the appropriate set of calls to the storage manager to access the object, thus making persistence transparent to the user. This solution relies on the underlying EXODUS database system to provide a storage manager whereas our solution is machine and system independent.

The first part of this paper will describe how we achieved persistence in EDGE, an interactive tool for editing graphs. In EDGE, a program generating tool automatically generates code that can save or load the graph editing session; it also generates menus for editing the graph. The remainder of the paper describes how this same technique can be used to achieve a more general solution to the problem of preserving data structures.

2.   PERSISTENCE IN THE EDGE GRAPH EDITOR

Graphs can be used to represent concepts and relationships in many different application areas. A *graph editor* is a graphical user interface tool that displays information as a graph and allows the user to edit the graph and its contents. Although graph editors can provide an effective presentation of graphs to the user, many designers are hesitant to use them because of the high cost of generating the graphical interface. By using the customizable graph editor EDGE [12], the advantages of a graph editor can be available for a minimal customization effort.

EDGE provides an aesthetically pleasing layout of the graph automatically, thus freeing the user from extensive cut-and-paste work. Several different layout algorithms are available. Any subgraph may be grouped into a *subgraph abstraction*, where it may be viewed either as an icon or in its entirety. EDGE is written in C++ [9] and uses the X Window System [13]. Base classes for node, edge, and graph are provided which the user may extend for a particular application. Current applications include project management, program animation, a directory browser, and a logic simulator.

The external representation language used by EDGE is an encoding of the graph data structure as text. It is called GRL (Graph Representation Language) and is a high-level description of the format and layout of the nodes and edges of a graph. One can specify graph layout information such as the layout algorithm and spacing between nodes; one can specify the list of nodes and their attributes (e.g. title, font, borderwidth, icon, etc.) and the list of edges and their attributes (e.g. name of source and target nodes, edge thickness, arrowhead style etc.). If several graphs, nodes or edges have the same set of attributes, one can create a common type with that set of attributes and state that the objects are of that type.

GRL is powerful enough that it can be used to save an entire editing session, allowing a user to restart later with exactly the same configuration. Therefore, GRL also records the position and size of the EDGE window, the current scrolling position, and the current set of abstraction subgraphs. The complete list of graph, node, and edge attributes is given in [14].

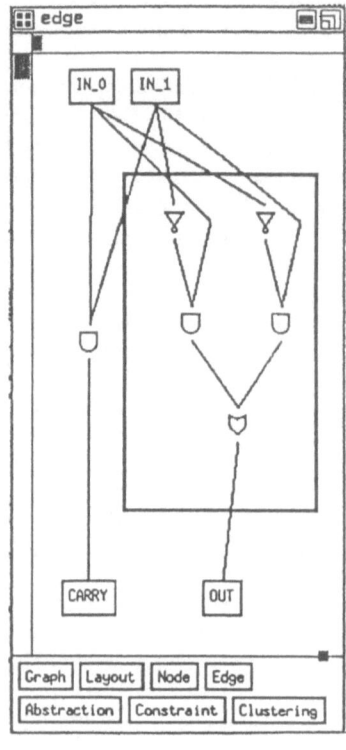

```
graph:
  and.iconfile: "../icon/and"
  or.iconfile: "../icon/or"
  not.iconfile: "../icon/not"
  edge.arrowstyle: none
  nodes:
    title: "IN_0",
    title: "IN_1",
    title: "OUT",
    title: "CARRY",
    title: "AND_2"  label: ""  typename: "and",
    graph:
      title: "X_OR"
      status: white
      nodes:
        title: "OR"     label: ""  typename: "or",
        title: "NOT_1"  label: ""  typename: "not",
        title: "NOT_0"  label: ""  typename: "not",
        title: "AND_0"  label: ""  typename: "and",
        title: "AND_1"  label: ""  typename: "and",
      endnodes:
      edges:
        source: "AND_0"  target: "OR",
        source: "AND_1"  target: "OR",
        source: "NOT_1"  target: "AND_0",
        source: "NOT_0"  target: "AND_1",
      endedges:
    endgraph:
  endnodes:
  edges:
    source: "AND_2" target: "CARRY",
    source: "IN_0"  target: "NOT_0",
    source: "IN_1"  target: "NOT_1",
    source: "IN_1"  target: "AND_1",
    source: "IN_0"  target: "AND_0",
    source: "OR"    target: "OUT",
    source: "IN_0"  target: "AND_2",
    source: "IN_1"  target: "AND_2",
  endedges:
endgraph:
```

Figure 1: A Single Bit Adder with XOR operation as an abstraction

The individual attributes are specified in the form of *<attribute name>*:*<attribute value>* pairs. The format [*<type name>*.]*<attribute name>*:*<attribute value>* is used to specify a value for the attribute of a particular type. For subgraph abstractions, the list of nodes and edges in the subgraph are bracketed by the keywords "graph:" and "endgraph:". Such an abstraction definition may appear anywhere a node may normally be specified. Edges that cross between abstractions are associated with the innermost common graph.

Figure 1 shows a graph displayed by the EDGE graph editor as well as the associated GRL input file. Three different node types "and", "or", and "not" are used in this example. For each node type, the name of a file containing a bitmap for the icon is specified. The style of arrowhead used for the edges is set to "none", so the edges appear as straight lines. There are six nodes in the outer graph, bracketed by the keywords "nodes:" and "endnodes:". The two input nodes, the output node, and the "carry" node specify only a title, which is the minimal specification for a node. AND_2 is a node of type "and", meaning that it will inherit attributes from that type (in this case the name of the icon file). The "label" specifier is used when the text displayed in the node's window is different from the unique identifier given in "title". In this example, we do not want any text to appear in the window so the label is set to the null string. The final node is the subgraph abstraction X_OR with its list of nodes and edges bracketed by the keywords "graph:" and "endgraph:". The list of nodes is followed by the list of edges. Each edge has two attributes specifying the titles of the source and the target nodes.

2.1   Automatic Generation of the GRL Parser and Menus

An application developed using EDGE can extend the base classes offered by EDGE to suit the application. We have developed a program generator tool [15] that reads the C++ class declarations used by the application and produces a set of input, output, and menu routines. These routines allow the user to specify values for application-specific attributes as well as the standard set of attributes used by the EDGE.

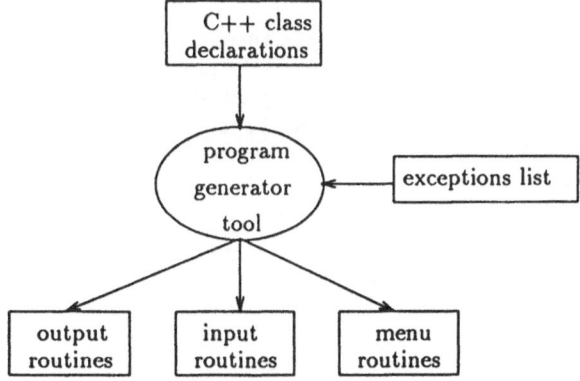

Figure 2: Program Generator Tool

The input routines include a set of rules for the Lex scanner and Yacc parser for EDGE's graph representation language GRL. Lex [16] is a program that takes a a list of regular expressions together with the associated actions to be executed when these expressions are found and generates a simple lexical analyzer. Yacc's [17] input is an LALR(1) grammar describing the structure of the input together with code to be invoked as each item is recognized. Default constructors and destructors for each class may also be generated. The output routines consist of source code for saving the graph and the editing session in the GRL format. The menu routines include a table of menu entries for each of the attributes.

The generated code is then compiled together with the rest of the EDGE and application source code. To avoid conflicts between the generated code and code specified by the application, the user can specify a list of procedure names that should not be generated in an "exceptions" file. For example, the user may want to use a node type constructor specific to the application rather than the automatically generated one. Additionally, the user can specify a list of variable names in the "exceptions" file for variables that should be ignored by the generator.

Consider, for example, an application using EDGE to display and evaluate integer expressions (Figure 3). Each of the nodes may take on an integer value. The user assigns initial values to the leaf nodes in the input file or interactively through the node's menu. When the expression is evaluated, the calculations are performed and are passed up to the root of the graph where the expression's value is kept. In order to customize EDGE for this application, the only code that the application developer has to provide is the code for evaluating the expression and a class declaration for a new node type called "evalnode" that is derived from the EDGE base node class. the "evalnode" has an additional integer variable for the value.

```
#include "node.h"             // include base class node
class evalnode: public node { // evalnode is derived from base class node
     int value;               // extra variable for node's value
public:
     evalnode(char* typename); // constructor for evalnode
};
```

"Evalnode" is an application-specific node and therefore its extra attribute "value" is not known in the default version of EDGE. We use the program generating tool to automatically extend EDGE so that the value can be specified in GRL and will be offered in the menus when an "evalnode" is selected. Figure 3 shows the appearance of the editor after the user has selected the "edit node" operation for an "evalnode". Note that the "value" variable is offered in the menu.

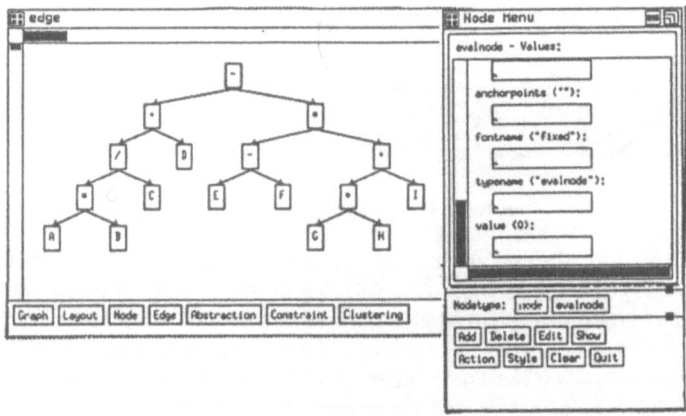

Figure 3: Expression Evaluation Application using EDGE

When the graph is saved in file, the external representation will also have the new keyword value. For example the saved file would contain the following:

```
graph:
  nodes:
    typename "evalnode" title:"A" value: 2,
    typename "evalnode" title:"B" value: 3,
    typename "evalnode" title:"times_1" label:"*" value: 6,
```

```
  ...
endnodes:
edges:
  source:"times_1" target:"A",
  source:"times_1" target:"B",
  ...
endedges:
endgraph:
```

3. A GENERAL SOLUTION FOR PERSISTENCE

In this section we present a flat, textual, external representation for C++ data structures that can be used to achieve persistence in various applications and may be automatically generated from the application's data structure declarations. Additionally we generate window based menus for each data structure which the application can use to add, edit or show the data structure values interactively. This solution works for all C++ data structures, including pointers.

Our general solution uses a generator tool similar to the EDGE generator tool shown in Figure 2. For each data type, we generate a set of procedures that may be used to store the data structure to its external representation, to load the data from an external representation back into main memory, and to produce menus for interactively adding, editing or showing the data structure's values.

For simple C++ data types (*int*, *float*, *long*, *char*, *enum* etc.) and for other named types (i.e. those defined with a typedef), we generate a set of procedures for each type. We also treat *char* *(pointer to character) as a simple data type called *string*. We generate a set of generic procedures for each *class* or *struct*[1]. For unnamed types (e.g. a pointer to an array of integers), we must rely on the user to invoke the appropriate generated procedure(s).

The generator's exception list can be used to ignore particular types or variables. As with the EDGE generator tool, Lex and Yacc must be run and the system must be compiled before the new facilities for persistence and menu generation are available.

Throughout the remainder of the paper we will use a structure containing a doubly linked list as an example. We assume that the following classes have been declared and instantiated as given in Figure 4. Furthermore we assume that the pointer my_company points at the company data structure representing the root of the data structure.

---

[1]In C++ *struct* and *class* are equivalent data types with the exception that classes may have private variables and procedures. Henceforth we refer only to classes.

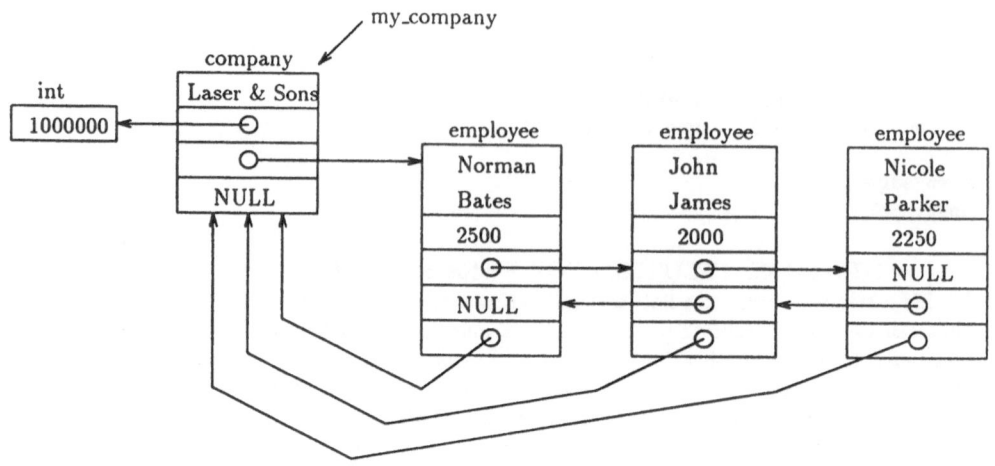

Figure 4: A simple list data structure

```
company *my_company;        /* declaration of a company pointer */

class company {                          class employee {
  char *trade_name;                        struct {
  int *sales;                                char *first_name;
  employee *employees;                       char *last_name;
  company *subsidiary_companies;           } name;
public:                                    int income;
  company();                               employee *next;
  ~company();                              employee *previous;
  write_all(ostream);                      company *employer;
  write_this(ostream);                   public:
  read_all(istream);                       employee();
  read_this(istream);                      ~employee();
  menu_add();                              write_all(ostream);
  menu_edit();                             write_this(ostream);
  menu_show();                             read_all(istream);
  ... /* public member functions */       read_this(istream);
};                                         menu_add();
                                           menu_edit();
                                           menu_show();
                                           ... /* public member functions */
                                         };
```

The following section gives a very brief overview of the relevant details of C++. Section 3.2 describes the format of our external representation. Sections 3.3 through 3.5 detail the user interface and implementation of the generated software used for output, textual input, and menu input. Finally, Section 3.6 describes the generator's exception list.

3.1   C++ Basics

C++ [9] is an object-oriented superset of C. In C++ an object is defined in a *class* declaration. The class declaration specifies the structure of the object as well as a set of functions that are associated with the class. Such functions are called *member functions* of the class. The variables in the class and the member functions may be declared *public* (accessible everywhere) or *private* (accessible only to the class) thus supporting the techniques of data abstraction and data hiding. A class may specify *constructor* member functions to create and initialize an instance of the class and *destructor* member functions to clean up when an instance is deleted.

The standard input/output mechanism in C++ is called a *stream*. The class "istream" is used for input and an "ostream" is used for output. C++ provides a standard input stream "cin", and a standard output stream "cout". To access a file, the user must open the file and then associate the file with a stream.

3.2   External Representation

This section describes the format of the external representation of data structures. It is quite similar to the flat external representation used in IDL [5].

For simple data types, a unique identifier, a typename, and a textual representation of the value is used. So the general format for simple data types look like:

```
<id> : <typename> : <value>
```

The value field can either contain a number, a character (delimited by quotes), a string (delimited by double quotes) , a keyword (for enumerated types) or a reference to the unique identifier of another entry in the external representation.

For each instance of a class, a unique identifier, a typename, and a set of name/value pairs for each variable in the class is used. So the general format looks like:

```
<id> : <typename> : {
                  <list of name:value pairs>
                  }
```

The value field will either be a textual representation of the attribute's value or a reference to the unique identifier of another entry in the external representation.

For each instance of an array, a unique identifier, a typename, and a set of index/value pairs is used. So the general format looks like:

```
<id> : <typename> : {
                  <list of index:value pairs>
                  }
```

The value field will either be a textual representation of the attribute's value or a reference to the unique identifier of another entry in the external representation. If all array entries have the same value, an abbreviated form *:<value> will be used.

For our example, the data structure shown in Figure 4 would have the external representation:

```
0: company: { trade_name: "Laser & Sons"
              sales: ^1
              employees: ^2
```

```
              subsidiary_companies: NULL
          }
1: int: 1000000
2: employee: { name: { first_name: "Norman" last_name: "Bates" }
               income: 2500
               next: ^3
               previous: NULL
               employer: ^0
          }
3: employee: { name: { first_name: "John" last_name: "James" }
               income: 2000
               next: ^4
               previous: ^2
               employer: ^0
          }
4: employee: { name: { first_name: "Nicole" last_name: "Parker" }
               income: 2250
               next: NULL
               previous: ^3
               employer: ^0
          }
```

3.3 Output

The program generator tool generates source code to save arbitrary C++ data types in an external representation.

User Interface

For writing values of simple data types and any other named data types, we offer procedures which take the general format:

```
write_<typename> (<typename> t, ostream os);
```

All generated output procedures take a variable and a C++ output stream as arguments. It is assumed that this output stream has been opened by the user and represents the file in which the external representation will be saved.

For example to write the *int* variable x on the standard output in its external representation the user may call the procedure:

```
write_int (x, cout);
```

or, assuming that array a has been defined as

```
typedef int any_array[20];
any_array a;
```

then the user may call the procedure

```
write_any_array (a, cout);
```

to write the array of integers to its external representation.

To be able to save a class to its external representation the user has to declare one or both of following procedures as member functions of the class:

```
write_all (ostream);
write_this (ostream);
```

The difference between the procedures `write_all` and `write_this` is in how they handle pointers. Calling `write_all` results in writing all values for the class instance, including all those attained by following pointers. Calling `write_this` saves the class instance without following any further pointers.

In our example the user could write the following code segment to save the entire data structure in a file. The file would then contain the external representation which we have already shown at the end of Section 3.2.

```
/* open an output stream for the file named "save_data" */
filebuf f1;
f1.open("save_data", output);
ostream my_out(&f1);
/* save the contents of the structure pointed to by my_company */
my_company->write_all(my_out);
```

Implementation

We use a simple hash table of memory addresses in which we enter addresses of each class instance we have already written out. Each output procedure tests whether it has already been called for this instance of a class. If so, the output procedure simply returns, thus preventing a data structure from being saved twice. This allows us to handle arbitrary data structures including circular lists.

3.4   Input

The program generator tool generates source code to load arbitrary C++ data types from an external representation.

User Interface

In an analogous way to output routines, we offer input routines for all simple data types or other named data types. These input routines have the general format:

```
read_<typename> (<typename> p_var, istream is);
```

The user must provide a pointer to the variable as an argument because C++ passes arguments to functions using "call by value". The user must pass an open input stream representing the data file as a parameter to the input routines.

For example the user may call

```
read_int (&i, cin);
```

to read an *int* value from its external representation into the variable i.

To be able to load a class instance from its external representation the user has to declare one or both of following procedures as member functions of the class:

```
read_all (istream);
read_this (istream);
```

As with the output procedures, the difference between the two procedures is in how they handle pointers. Procedure `read_all` reads from input stream until all unsatisfied forward references have been completed or, if reading from file, the end of file mark was reached. Procedure `read_this` reads one instance of the class it is called for. As with the simple

388

data types, it is the user's responsibility to allocate storage for the class being read. The input procedure will allocate the necessary storage for any recursively encountered classes. For our example, the user could write the following code segment to load the company data structure from a file:

```
/* open an input stream for the file named "save_data" */
   filebuf f2;
   f2.open("save_data", input);
   ostream my_in(&f2);
/* allocate storage for the company data structure */
   my_company = new company();
/* load the contents into the structure pointed to by my_company */
   my_company->read_all(my_in);
```

Implementation

As with the EDGE generator, we generate input files for the lexical analyzer generator Lex [16] and the parser generator Yacc [17]. The parser will copy the values into the internal data structures.

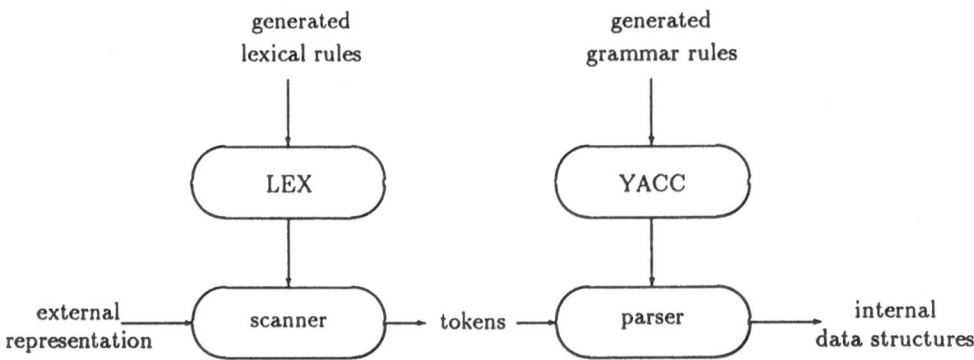

Figure 5: Parsing input using Lex-scanner and Yacc-parser

3.5 Menus

The program generator tool generate a menu-controlled data structure editor for arbitrary C++ data types, which can be used to add, edit or show variables of these data types interactively.

User Interface

The menu procedures for simple data types or data types with a given typename have the general format:

```
menu_add_<typename> (<typename>* p_var);
menu_edit_<typename> (<typename>* p_var);
menu_show_<typename> (<typename> var);
```

For example to edit an *int* value i the user may call procedure

```
menu_edit_int (&i);
```

The user has to declare one or all of following procedures as member functions of the class to be able to generate menus from the C++ class declaration:

```
menu_add ();
menu_edit ();
menu_show ();
```

Each of these procedures produces a menu containing the names and associated values of all possible entries of the class, it is called for. menu_add shows the default values of the entries whereas menu_edit or menu_show show the current values of each variable. menu_show does not allow the user to change the values.

For simple data types the menu displays a text input box which the user may edit. Enumerations are displayed as a set of button menus each representing one possible value for this enumeration type. Pointer variables are displayed as button menus which bring up additional menus for the data type they point to when selected.

In our example a call of my_company->menu_edit would bring up the menu shown on the left side of Figure 6. This menu shows a text input box for the character string trade_name and three button menus for the pointers sales, employees, and subsidiary_companies. After clicking the button menu employees, the menu shown on the right side of Figure 6 will also be shown. All text input boxes are filled in with the current values and the user may change these values by simply typing in new values and confirm or cancel these changes by clicking either button menus OK or Cancel. This menu interface for pointers could be further improved by also allowing the user to select from a (scrollable) list of all variables of that type.

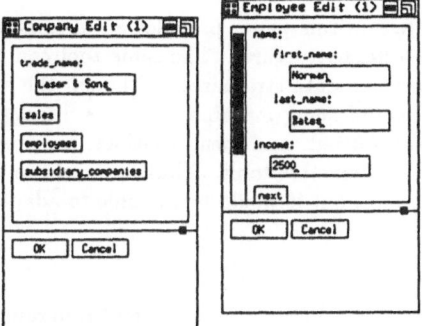

Figure 6: Generated menus for classes *company* and *employee*

Implementation

The source code which implements menus consists of three different parts:

- An automatically generated table, containing names and data types of each variable for all classes.

- Source code which uses the generated table to build up menus using the X Window System. This code is independent of the application's classes. It initializes all menus and determines what kind of input method is offered for each data type.

- Automatically generated menu procedures (`menu_add`, `menu_edit`, `menu_show`, ...) and miscellaneous other procedures for setting and changing the individual values of class variables.

We chose the X Window System because it is commonly available on most graphics workstations. The generator could easily be ported to another window system by replacing the hand-coded source code. All generated source code is independent of the window system.

3.6 The Generator's Exceptions List

The generator will produce input, output, and menu routines for all simple C++ data types, all named data types, and any classes that declare them. By default, these routines will include entries for all variables in the class. The user can specify a list of types and a list of variables for which the input/output should be suppressed. For example, if the data structure contains variables which are always set to a particular value by the application itself, then those variables should be ignored in the input, output, and menu routines. The syntax of an entry in this exceptions list is:

```
<typename>[.<variablename>]
```

Specifying only a type name forces the generator to ignore this entire data type. Particular variables of a class can be ignored by specifying the typename and the variable name. In our example an entry of

```
company.subsidiary_companies
```

in the exceptions list would result in ignoring variable `subsidiary_companies` of class `company` during generation of all procedures.

4. CONCLUSION

The generator tool described in this paper provides an automatic way of achieving persistence for arbitrary C++ data structures. The same tool can be used for generating a menu-controlled editor for C++ data structures. Although the external representation is simple, it has the advantages of being machine and system independent. By automating the generation of the input, output, and menu routines, we provide a solution that can be easily added to existing interactive tools. Thus far we have only considered C++ as our source and target language, but it would be possible to adapt the generator to handle other languages as well.

REFERENCES

[1] Malcolm Atkinson and Ronald Morrison. Persistent programming and object oriented databases. In *Proc. of the Joint University of Newcastle Upon Tyne/ International Computers Limited Seminar*, Sept. 6-9 1988.

[2] W.A. Wulf, R. Levin, and S.P. Harbison. *Hydra/C.mmp: An Experimental Computer System.* McGraw-Hill, 1981.

[3] A.D. Birrell, M.B. Jones, and E.P. Wobber. A simple and efficient implementation for small databases. Technical Report 24, Digital Systems Research Center, 1988.

[4] W.P. Cockshott. Addressing mechanisms and persistent programming. In Malcolm P. Atkinson, Peter Buneman, and Ronald Morrison, editors, *Data Types and Persistence*, chapter 15. Springer Verlag, 1988.

[5] David Alex Lamb. IDL: Sharing intermediate representations. *ACM Transactions on Programming Languages and Systems*, 9(3):297–318, July 1987.

[6] Richard Snodgrass and contributing authors. *The Interface Description Language: Definition and Use.* Computer Science Press, Rockville, MD, 1989.

[7] John R. Nestor, Joseph M. Newcomer, Paola Giannini, and Donald L. Stone. *IDL: The Language and its Implementation.* Prentice Hall, Englewood Cliffs, NJ, 1990.

[8] Jack C. Wileden, Alexander L. Wolf, Charles D. Fisher, and Peri L. Tarr. PGRAPHITE: An experiment in persistent typed object management. In Peter Henderson, editor, *Proceedings of the ACM SIGSOFT/SIGPLAN Software Engineering Symposium on Practical Software Development Environments (Software Engineering Notes Vol. 13, No. 5 or Sigplan Notices Vol. 24, No. 2)*, pages 130–142, Boston, MA, Nov. 28-30 1988. ACM.

[9] Bjarne Stroustrup. *The C++ Programming Language.* Addison Wesley, 1986.

[10] Michael J. Carey, David J. DeWitt, Goetz Graefe, David M. Haight, Joel E. Richardson, Daniel T. Schuh, Eugene J. Shekita, and Scott L. Vandenberg. The EXODUS extensible DBMS project: An overview. Technical Report 808, University of Wisconsin-Madison, Computer Sciences Department, November 1988.

[11] Joel E. Richardson and Michael J. Carey. Persistence in the E language: Issues and implementation. *Software—Practice and Experience*, 19(12):1115–1150, December 1989.

[12] Frances Newbery Paulisch and Walter F. Tichy. EDGE: An extendible graph editor. To appear in Software – Practice and Experience, Special Issue on Unix Tools ca. June, 1990.

[13] Robert W. Scheifler and Jim Gettys. The X window system. *ACM Transactions on Graphics*, 5(2), April 1986.

[14] Frances Newbery Paulisch. The design of an extendible graph editor. PhD Thesis (in preparation), University of Karlsruhe, Institute for Informatics, 1990.

[15] Stefan Manke. Generierung von Graphbearbeitungsprogrammen aus objektorientierten Spezifikationen (Generation of graph manipulation programs from object-oriented specifications). Master's thesis, University of Karlsruhe, Institute for Informatics, March 1990.

[16] M. E. Lesk and E. Schmidt. LEX - A Lexical Analyser Generator. *Bell Laboratories Computing Science Technical Report 39*, October 1975.

[17] S. C. Johnson. YACC: Yet Another Compiler Compiler. *Bell Laboratories Computing Science Technical Report 32*, July 1975.

Author Index